D0085471

CRIME CONTROL AND SOCIAL JUSTICE

CRIME CONTROL AND SOCIAL JUSTICE

THE DELICATE BALANCE

Edited by Darnell F. Hawkins, Samuel L. Myers, Jr., and Randolph N. Stone

Contributions in Criminology and Penology, Number 55

GREENWOOD PRESS
Westport, Connecticut · London

Library of Congress Cataloging-in-Publication Data

Crime control and social justice : the delicate balance / edited by Darnell F. Hawkins, Samuel L. Myers, Jr., and Randolph N. Stone.
    p. cm.—(Contributions in criminology and penology, ISSN 0732-4464 ; no. 55)
    Includes bibliographical references and index.
    ISBN 0–313–30790–3 (alk. paper)
    1. Crime prevention—United States. 2. Criminal justice, Administration of—United States. 3. Juvenile delinquency—United States—Prevention. 4. Juvenile justice, Administration of—United States. 5. Punishment in crime deterrence —United States. 6. Hate crimes—United States. 7. Racial profiling in law enforcement—United States. I. Hawkins, Darnell Felix, 1946– II. Myers, Samuel L. III. Stone, Randolph N. IV. Series.

HV7431 .C718 2003
364.4′0973—dc21   2002024479

British Library Cataloguing in Publication Data is available.

Copyright © 2003 by Darnell F. Hawkins, Samuel L. Myers, Jr., and Randolph N. Stone

All rights reserved. No portion of this book may be reproduced, by any process or technique, without the express written consent of the publisher.

Library of Congress Catalog Card Number: 2002024479
ISBN: 0–313–30790–3
ISSN: 0732–4464

First published in 2003

Greenwood Press, 88 Post Road West, Westport, CT 06881
An imprint of Greenwood Publishing Group, Inc.
www.greenwood.com

Printed in the United States of America

The paper used in this book complies with the Permanent Paper Standard issued by the National Information Standards Organization (Z39.48–1984).

10 9 8 7 6 5 4 3 2 1

Copyright Acknowledgment

The editors and publisher gratefully acknowledge permission to reprint excerpts from:

Butler, Paul, *Affirmative Action and the Criminal Law, 68 U. Colo. L. Rev.* 841 (1997). Reprinted with permission of the University of Colorado Law Review; Davis, Angela, "Race Cops and Traffic Stops." Reprinted from the *University of Miami Law Review* 51 U. MIAMI L. REV. 425 (1997), which holds copyright on this article; and Quinney, Richard, "Criminology as Moral Philosophy: Criminologist as Witness" *Contemporary Justice Review*. Vol. I: 2, 3: 347-364.

Contents

Preface

This book has been a long time in the making. Some of the chapters were initially solicited more than six years ago. Such a lengthy delay is not uncommon in the world of edited book publishing; however, it does increase the probability that contributed work will be dated when finally published. We are convinced that the passage of time has actually contributed to the salience and importance of most contributions to this volume. The themes and issues explored in the present volume are topics of perennial concern and debate. Yet, many significant and widely publicized events and developments that have occurred since the mid-1990s, when this project was conceived, have no doubt heightened scholarly and public interest in the problems examined by contributors to the volume. These include (1) several instances since 1995 of hate crime and lethal violence aimed at African Americans, Asian Americans, Jews, and Latinos; (2) repeated use of deadly force by the police against African Americans in several major American cities and resulting protests and violence; (3) continuing debate regarding the fairness of the death penalty amid a resumption of federal executions and accelerated state executions; (4) a debate on the merits of racial profiling that became a campaign issue in the 2000 presidential election and continues to affect race relations and perceptions of racial justice; and (5) a peaking of the nation's incarceration "binge" with more than 2 million persons currently being detained in the nation's prisons, jails, and juvenile facilities.

The title of the volume represents our belief that the "get tough on crime" policies enacted in the United States during the last three decades of the twentieth century pose a significant challenge to the nation's ongoing struggle for social justice and human and civil rights. It also reflects our belief that crime and criminal victimization are themselves social ills that also threaten basic human rights. Particularly in a society that continues to be characterized by much racial, ethnic, and socioeconomic inequality, the balancing of the goals of controlling crime and assuring social justice is extremely difficult and poses distinct challenges for communities of people of color. In a post–civil rights America, that task is also increasingly more complex. This volume probes various dimensions of this multifaceted set of social problems. As intended, its chapters represent a diversity of disciplinary views, including contributions from criminologists, economists, geographers, legal scholars, political scientists, and sociologists. All have provided insightful and informative reflections on the volume's overall theme—balancing crime control and social justice.

Furthermore, at the beginning of an era that may come to be known best for unprecedented global efforts to fight terrorism, they remind us of the delicate balance in protecting both our physical safety and our democratic ideals.

We thank the authors and the publisher for their patience as this project unfolded. We are grateful to Martha Jacob of the University of Illinois at Chicago for her editorial assistance in reviewing earlier and final drafts of the manuscript. We also acknowledge the clerical assistance provided the editors by Mildred McGinnis of the University of Illinois at Chicago and by Judy Leahy of the University of Minnesota.

Introduction

Samuel L. Myers, Jr.

Is it just to incarcerate disproportionate numbers of African-American males? Is it fair to deny innocent children strong, stable families by punishing drug and other nonviolent offenders with imprisonment? The United States spends large sums of money on crime control, which ultimately results in greater proportions of nonwhite than white youth being arrested, prosecuted, convicted, and imprisoned. Is this equitable, when social expenditures could focus instead on improved schooling, education, training, and employment opportunities? What is "just" about a criminal justice system that tries a 14-year-old Mexican-American youth—an unarmed accomplice to a robbery in which a store clerk was murdered—as an adult, convicts him, and sentences him to 25 years to life in a California prison while it tries a 14-year-old Anglo—who took his father's gun and murdered his mother over a dispute about cookies—in juvenile court and sentences him to a juvenile detention facility from which he will be eligible for parole before he reaches maturity?

What is just? What is fair? What is equitable? These questions occupy many of the chapters in this volume. And rightfully so, because such sentences do occur within the criminal "justice" system. It is appropriate to ask whether this system is fair or just.

But analysts often disagree over what constitutes fairness, what makes for social justice. Should a justice system be deemed fair if all persons are treated the same, as is the objective of sentencing guidelines that would extend the same prison terms to all persons convicted of identical offenses with the same level of culpability? Or, perhaps, is it fair if each person has the same opportunities to enter or avoid entry into the system—even if once in the system they are treated according to different rules or criteria? The chapters in this volume do not resolve these issues of fairness or justice. But they do offer an alternative lens through which a policy analyst might view the outcomes of crime control.

In addition to asking whether the system is fair or just, it seems reasonable also to ask whether it is efficient. Does crime control really control crime? Doesn't society ultimately pay a price for pulling large numbers of black, Hispanic, and other disadvantaged youth out of the labor force and into the prisons and jails? Do the costs of incarceration go far beyond the social goals of deterrence, incapacitation, or rehabilitation? Could sentencing reforms that seek to increase penalties for drug offenses or for repeat offenders have adverse social consequences? Could attempts to shift young violent offenders into the adult criminal justice system contribute to increased harm either to the children themselves or to society in general?

Put differently, if one had the choice between two systems that shared the same measures of fairness or justice but differed substantially in how well they worked, how efficiently they operated, how costly they were, and how many adverse social impacts arose, which would one prefer? It might be important to know whether, for example, punishment by incarceration really does what it is supposed to do. Alternative policies, such as employment policies or improved schooling, might be examined to see if they do the job just as well, perhaps even less expensively.

The variety in this volume will help the reader to appreciate the underlying tension between the goals of equity and the goals of efficiency within the criminal justice system. The chapters in Part I, "From Cradle to Grave," present this contrast most starkly. These essays deal with the political economy of criminal justice policy from diverse perspectives. Barry Krisberg's "The End of the Juvenile Court: Prospects for Our Children" and Harold Votey and Llad Phillips's "Crime, Youth, and the Labor Market: Are We Any Closer to Answers?" review prior research. William Sabol and James Lynch's innovative econometric analysis in "Assessing the Longer-run Consequences of Incarceration: Effects on Families and Employment," Nolan Jones's review of legislation in "Three Strikes and You're Out: A Symbolic Crime Policy?" and Todd Clear and Dina Rose's theoretical discourse in "Individual Sentencing Practices and Aggregate Social Problems" examine this tension between equity and efficiency in criminal justice policies, while exposing important unintended consequences of punitive criminal justice policies.

For example, Todd Clear and Dina Rose suggest that a concentration of imprisoned persons—often poor, disadvantaged, and minority—from specific census tracts or neighborhoods can contribute to the weakening of informal mechanisms of social control. That is, crime control that decimates local communities or neighborhoods is not really efficient. They cite statistics on a single block in East New York where $3 million is spent annually on processing citizens through the criminal justice system. This results in a critical form of disinvestment in the community and carries adverse consequences. They suggest that crime policies should include social investments in high crime areas, in order to return some of the money spent on crime control to a community. Implicit in this critique is the unfairness of spending huge sums of money on crime control in very well defined places—largely to pay the salaries of criminal justice workers who do not live in those places—and leaving those places no social capital to sustain themselves.

Another example of this tension between equity and efficiency can be seen in Votey and Phillips's essay. They note that while little has changed in the past thirty years since their pioneering research showed that improved employment opportunities reduce crime among youth, there are substantive differences in how these factors work for white and for nonwhite young people. Votey and Phillips, whether intentionally or not, have exposed the folly of a race-neutral employment policy as a crime-fighting tool. A policy that fails to appreciate the differences in the labor force participation rates and employment experiences of young African-American males (who are often discouraged workers when they are out of the labor market) and white males (who are often in school when they are out of the labor market) may be ineffective. But a policy that focuses specifically on African-American males who are out of the labor market at the expense of, say, African-American males who are looking for work or unemployed seems on its face to be both discriminatory and unfair. Why should the tax dollars go to those who have withdrawn from the market completely, rather than to those who keep trying to find a job? The classic analysis by Votey and Phillips, though, suggests that a dollar spent on reducing unemployment rates among young black males will have a smaller impact on crime rates than would an identical expenditure on increasing labor force participation rates. In short, asking whether a system of punishment via incarceration achieves goals of reducing crime or deterring criminals also requires that we ask whether some people are disproportionately affected by these policies.

Part II, "Gangs, Drug Law Enforcement, Racial Profiling, and Social Justice," makes more explicit the racial dimensions of the efficiency-equity trade-off. African Americans—in particular, African-American males—are disproportionately found in the criminal justice system. From arrest to release on parole, blacks are many more times likely to be entrapped in the criminal justice system than are whites. Policies such as sentencing reforms that abolished parole or created determinate sentencing have had ambivalent impacts on overall racial disproportionality. Consider parole. Reforms underway promise to improve how prisoner reentry into communities is managed. With the abolition of parole in many communities, concerns have arisen about the large numbers of ex-offenders who are being returned to their neighborhoods with little support or accountability. Will attempts to reinvent post-prison management systems reduce or increase racial disparities? How will we know? How will we measure and detect possible racial bias in managing prisoner reentry?

Most clearly indicative of the pull between the norms of social justice and the dictates of law enforcement efficiency is the broad problem of racial profiling, so brilliantly detailed in Angela Davis's "Race, Cops, and Traffic Stops." After reviewing and critiquing the constitutional issues and case law underlying racially biased methods of conducting traffic stops, Davis provides insightful documentation on the real costs associated with violation of the rights of innocents. One can paraphrase her conclusions in these stark economic terms: While police often justify their use of racial profiling (either explicit or through the use of markers that have racially disparate impacts) as efficient law enforcement, there are substantial secondary costs to victims of profiling. Innocent African Americans stopped for no reason other than that they are African Americans—or that they match markers that are highly correlated with race—often suffer indignities, embarrassment, humiliation, and psychological and emotional damage that far outweigh the putative benefits of increased apprehension of drug dealers. Thus, the issue concerns not only the fairness of racial profiling pitted against its efficiency in traffic stops, but also whether appropriate account has been taken of all relevant direct and indirect costs of profiling.

Nearly the same issues arise in racial profiling in the U.S. Customs Service, with the added nuance that probable-cause expectations need not be met, as Lee E. Ross and Simon Adetona Akindes discuss in their chapter, "In Search of Probable Cause: U.S. Customs, Racial Profiling, and the Fourth Amendment." Research in this area poses this substantive dilemma: Law enforcement personnel never know what they will find when they begin a search. The authors contend that the U.S. Customs Service often engages in a practice of "looking and searching for reasons to search further." What matters here is not so much whether searches occur at all or whether race is used to create markers for initiating searches. What matters is the extent of searches, especially in light of the special provisions that deem the standards for Fourth Amendment protections to be, in the authors' words, "somewhat relaxed in comparison with other enforcement agencies." What matters is that ultimately persons of color are far more likely than others to be subjected to the most humiliating and most intrusive of searches.

Other examples of racial profiling include efforts to target likely gang members or initiatives designed to provide tightened airport security. Stacey Leyton in "The New Blacklists: The Threat to Civil Liberties Posed by Gang Databases" reviews the explosive growth in the use of gang databases at the state and federal levels. While these computerized sources of information on alleged gang members promise to increase the speed of detection and apprehension of suspected members of criminal enterprises, they also pose significant problems of fairness. Leyton contends that information contained in these databases is often inaccurate and that the criteria for inclusion go far beyond those mandated by various state penal codes. Old information may not be purged, updates are not consistently conducted, and the standards for data entry are not consistent, according to Leyton. Other policy concerns are related to the fact that markers used in the creation of the databases—such as dress, mannerisms, symbols, or tattoos—are not restricted to members of gangs. They often are more generically related to inner-city or racial minority group membership. The effect, then, is that racial minority group members are overrepresented in gang databases, which are, in essence, blacklists.

Leyton's conclusions contrast with those of Marjorie S. Zatz and Richard P. Krecker, Jr.'s "Anti-gang Initiatives as Racialized Policy." Because the war on gangs appears to be race neutral, one must look carefully at the actors within the system to determine whether racially disparate outcomes can be attributed to particular anti-gang policies. Anti-gang initiatives can have discriminatory impacts, according to Zatz and Krecker, *if* they are implemented. How these disparate impacts come about requires an understanding of the actions, attitudes, and perceptions of many stakeholders within the criminal justice system. Zatz and Krecker interview judges, prosecutors, defense counsel, and probation officers. They point out that anti-crime policies would have a racially disparate impact on persons of color, *if they were followed*. The Zatz-Krecker interviews, however, seem to suggest that the racialized anti-gang policies, in Arizona at least, *were not followed*. The reader is left with this contrast between the Leyton and the Zatz-Krecker chapters: Gang designations disproportionally target juveniles of color for arrest and apprehension, but within the criminal justice system, gang designations are often ignored. What this suggests is that racial bias within any one part of the system can lead to racially unequal outcomes even if the outcomes are not directly tainted by racial bias.

Thus, the tension between efficiency and equity arises indirectly. If anti-gang policies have the potential for generating racially disparate outcomes, but policy makers do not act on these policies, is the outcome any more just? And, if the policy is enforced at only one point along the way—say, by police engaged in apprehension and arrests—is the policy any more or less efficient because at subsequent points the policy is ignored?

Two empirical studies in Part II highlight the conflict between findings in this area. Cassia Spohn and Jeffrey Spears, after reviewing much of the often ambiguous literature on race and sentencing, show that there is no consistent impact of race or ethnicity on drug sentences in three cities chosen for study. After controlling for seriousness of offense, type of drug, and other legally relevant factors, blacks are not more likely to be sentenced to prison or more likely to receive long prison sentences than whites. Hispanics, however, do seem to be disadvantaged. Spohn and Spears conclude that drug punishments may not necessarily be more severe and/or discriminatory for blacks than for whites once they enter the system.

Tracey Meares, in "Simple Solutions? The Complexity of Public Attitudes Related to Drug Law Enforcement," looks not at whether blacks are more likely to be sentenced or to receive longer sentences than whites but instead at attitudes that might affect sentencing policies. Meares examines attitudes toward the legalization of marijuana and toward the harshness of sentences. A "get tough on drug offenders" position is deemed one that both favors harsh sentences and opposes legalizing marijuana. The majority of African Americans, like other Americans, favor the get-tough position, according to Meares's results. However, substantially more blacks than whites hold ambivalent views of drug policies, a point that Meares suggests may result from the greater involvement of blacks in the criminal justice system.

Taken together, then, these two empirical analyses suggest that there is substantial support even among African Americans for tough drug punishments even if there may be racially disparate impacts—impacts that may well be "explained" by blacks' greater risk of exposure to drugs in their communities. The question that then evokes the efficiency-equity tension is: Can racially disparate outcomes that appear to be unfair on their face be justified by differential exposure or harm to communities? As Meares concludes, this type of conflict of values—equity versus efficiency—often leads African Americans to be ambivalent about criminal justice policies that have disparate impacts on their communities.

Part III, "Emerging and Critical Perspectives on Crime Control and Social Justice," includes chapters that force us to reflect on the "delicate balance," challenging any notion of justice or fairness based on grounds of efficiency. William Chambliss, in his introduction to "Drug War Politics: Racism, Corruption, and Alienation," brings up a familiar scenario. A young black male is arrested after an illegal search that is both demeaning and conducted with unnecessary roughness. The illegality and the punitiveness of the search reveal its unfairness. The fact that the search culminated in an arrest, presumably with sufficient evidence for conviction, suggests to the police officer that it was both efficient and justified. It is as though the end justifies the means. Chambliss provides this additional perspective:

Current law enforcement policies that concentrate on policing the ghetto not only produce widespread disrespect for the legal system, but they also reinforce the belief that ethnic cleansing is a white conspiracy. This belief is further reinforced by widespread corruption of the law enforcement system that is an inevitable offshoot of the war on drugs. (Chambliss, p. 304)

Although the war on drugs has not succeeded in reducing the production and consumption of illicit drugs, according to Chambliss it has succeeded in "legitimizing the creation of a virtual police state in the ghettos of our cities." It has also contributed to police corruption and violence, Chambliss writes. These conclusions may indicate that many additional costs are associated with racially disparate administration of drug control policies. There are fundamental costs, alluded to by Chambliss, related to the very support and legitimacy of the criminal justice system.

David Greenberg, in "'Justice' and Criminal Justice," makes the connection between efficiency and notions of justice most clearly. He points out that for some, justice *is* efficiency. He states, "[C]riminal justice sanctions are often justified on the basis of claims about the technical efficiency of these measures in preventing crime." But, he also notes that another highly prevalent concept of justice is one that "inflicts costs or pains on wrongdoers." Research summarized by Greenberg supports the notion that the level of punishment advocated by many exceeds the level of punishment necessary for optimal deterrence or law enforcement. But perceptions vary by race, with the vast majority of African Americans believing that the criminal justice system is racially biased, while the vast majority of whites disagrees with these conclusions. Greenberg contends, though, that the voluminous evidence showing that racial discrimination in the criminal justice system is not the sole cause of the overrepresentation of blacks demands a new theoretical perspective on the "justice" in criminal justice. We need a better understanding of how racially disparate outcomes may exist without specific race or class bias or, in Greenberg's words, "strong racial or class agendas." This is particularly important in the current era, when overt, explicit forms of racism seem to have diminished even though the racial disproportionality in the prisons and the entire criminal justice system seems to rise unabated. Clues can be found in Greenberg's cogent discussions of the evolution of racial profiling and related criminal justice practices that appear on their face to be race neutral but in fact have racially disparate impacts. Greenberg points to "unconscious stereotyping" and perceptions about justice to help us to better understand racialized patterns of law enforcement.

Richard Quinney, in "Criminology as Moral Philosophy, Criminologist as Witness," forces the reader to return to these unanswered questions: What is fair? What is just? Quinney surveys alternative conceptualizations of justice, from the prophetic to Marxist, capitalist, Buddhist, and socialist humanism perspectives. Pitting the idea of justice that supports and sustains the ruling class against that which supports each individual's self-interest, Quinney forces us to look at how various notions of justice compel us to accept or reject alternative forms of punishment. He offers a peace agenda that calls upon criminologists to be witnesses to the pain and suffering of the oppressed as a prelude to seeking justice.

The "witnessing" approach that Quinney advocates might be regarded by some as passive. Two penultimate chapters unabashedly offer action agendas for approaching justice in the criminal justice world. Wilson Palacios, Chinita Heard, and Dorothy Taylor, in "At a Crossroad: Affirmative Action and Criminology," modestly offer a proposal for expanded affirmative action in law enforcement and legal professions. They note that the continued underrepresentation of African Americans among lawyers and other legal professionals and, in many jurisdictions, among police and sheriff's officers implicates the system that leaves African Americans overrepresented among those arrested, convicted, and incarcerated. Paul Butler goes much further in "Affirmative Action and the Criminal Law." He calls for affirmative action to redress directly the overrepresentation of African Americans in the criminal justice system. This would entail racially representative juries' direct efforts to change punishments that disproportionately imprison blacks and other people of color. His cogent argument stems from the belief that political expediency or public opinion is not the norm for measuring whether a policy is just or fair. Thus, readers who contend that this proposal—or any other form of affirmative action—is poor public policy because of the difficulties of obtaining significant public support will find little sympathy from Professor Butler.

The final and concluding chapter in this volume is "On the Horns of a Dilemma: Criminal Wrongs, Civil Rights, and the Administration of Justice in African-American Communities," by Professor Darnell F. Hawkins. This chapter uses critical race theory and other methods to demonstrate that public perceptions and opinions about the overall state of conditions faced by African Americans influence the degree to which racial disparities in the criminal justice system are seen as evidence of racism. Within the context of the previous chapters that reveal the tension between equity and efficiency and the balancing between crime control and social justice, this chapter shows that how (and whether) we see this tension depends on how factual claims about the causes of racial disparities are processed. Are the racial disparities due to racial discrimination or racism? Or, are the radcial disparities due to other factors such as differences in underlying criminality, or social and economic conditions? Hawkins shows that the balance between admission of the role of discrimination and racism and conclusions that the disparities arise from other sources has shifted over the years.

An admission that the source of racial disparities in the criminal justice system lies in racial discrimination or racism is an admission of a social justice and equity root of the disparity. A claim that the source of racial disparities in the criminal justice system lies in the inherent criminality of African Americans or is rooted in the devastating social and economic fabric of the lives of African Americans, is a claim that the root of the disparity lies outside of criminal justice unfairness or inequity. Such a claim could easily escalate to an efficiency issue.

These chapters do not ask the reader to agree with the various notions of fairness or justice embraced herein, nor with the specific policies advocated. Rather, they force the reader to reassess the balance between the efficiency goals of criminal justice policies and their equity implications.

This volume will challenge and perhaps even provoke readers. When one thinks of the rationales often provided for racial profiling or for disparate sentences for crack cocaine and powdered cocaine, one will have to think simultaneously of the equity and the efficiency goals of criminal justice. Do we seek to use racial markers because we believe that the cost of securing justice—borne by us all—is lower when such markers are employed? Do we distinguish among different types of drugs because we believe that some drugs have greater social costs than others do? And, if we do embrace these cost-effectiveness criteria in making criminal justice decisions, do we also embrace the unintended costs, the secondary or spillover costs associated with these policies? Do we account for the costs of foregone justice and unfairness at all? Or, do we see justice and fairness—particularly as it relates to racially disparate outcomes—to be something quite different? Are justice and fairness part of our social calculus in seeking criminal "justice"?

Such is the delicate balance that the chapters in this volume seek.

Part I

From Cradle to Grave: Families, Youths, and the Political Economy of Contemporary Criminal Justice Policy

Assessing the Longer-run Consequences of Incarceration: Effects on Families and Employment

William J. Sabol and James P. Lynch

INTRODUCTION: INTENDED AND UNINTENDED EFFECTS OF INCREASES IN INCARCERATION

Between 1980 and 1995, the number of people incarcerated in U.S. state or federal prisons more than tripled, from 319,598 to 1,078,545. In 1995, more than 1.5 million offenders were housed in correctional facilities, including sentenced prisoners in local jails, as compared to about half a million so held in 1980. During the same period, the incarceration rate also tripled from 139 incarcerated per 100,000 population to 411 per 100,000 population. During the same period, violent crimes reported to the police doubled and reported property crimes increased by about 30 percent, both measured on a per-capita basis. Victimizations increased while the percentage of them reported to the police remained flat. That huge increases in incarceration were not associated with obvious decreases in crime raises questions about the effects of incarceration in fighting crime.

Despite the unprecedented growth in the use of incarceration, very little analysis has been done on the question of whether this dramatic growth in the prison population has affected the crime rate. A recent review by Daniel Nagin (1998) cited a few important articles on the deterrent effects of incarceration on crime. Their conclusions ranged from a negligible effect of incarceration on crime (Zimring and Hawkins 1995) to Levitt's (1996) estimate that an additional prisoner prevents about fifteen index crimes. The work of Spelman (1994) and Marvel and Moody (1994) generated intermediate-range effects of incarceration on serious crime. Levitt's estimates can be interpreted to indicate that index crime rates would be even higher were it not for the increase in incarceration.

However, studies have not been able to find crime-reducing benefits of incarceration for drug crimes, and a major source of growth in the prison population has been in the use of incarceration for offenders convicted of drug crimes (e.g., Tonry 1995). Between 1985 and 1996, for example, the percentage of offenders in state prisons for drug crime convictions increased from about 8 percent to about 23 percent, while the prison population itself doubled (Beck et al. 1997). Studies of the effects of incarceration in reducing drug crimes have shown that it has had little or no effect on reducing drug use or drug trafficking (Caulkins et al. 1997; Cohen and Canela-Cacho 1994). The explanations for the lack of effect prison has on drug crimes relate the economic motivation for drug crimes and the short careers of most dealers, who probably would have stopped dealing if they had not been incarcerated, but who are replaced by other young dealers (e.g., Blumstein 1995).

Thus, the current understanding of the relationship between prison and crime suggests that prison has:

- some deterrent effects, but these are limited to index crimes and to changes in sentence lengths brought about by constraints imposed on parole boards or other administrative reductions in sentences. Further, these effects probably are not generalizable to drug and other crimes such as weapons offenses that are punished by mandatory sentences; nor are they generalizable to specific sentencing reforms such as California's "three-strikes" laws. (Nagin 1998)

- some incapacitative effects but these also are limited to violent crimes, and the effect on violent crimes of increases in prison are many times smaller than the increases in the prison population; further, heterogeneity in offending complicates the methodology for estimating incapacitative effects. (Cohen and Canela-Cacho 1994)

- neither deterrent nor incapacitative effects on drug crimes, and at best incarceration leads to negligible reductions in drug crimes, but is more likely to result in more low-level dealers entering into the trade or to lead to increases in other income-generating crimes.

- no cost-effect way to address the problem of drug crimes. (Caulkins et al. 1997)

Further, as Nagin (1998) points out, there are large differences in the nondrug felony offending rates of drug dealers as compared to other offenders. Drug dealers have *lower* rates of nondrug felony offending than do offenders convicted of burglary and robbery (Cohen and Canela-Cacho 1994). Thus, increasing incarceration of drug dealers is less likely to result in additional deterrent effects on other crimes.

In addition to research on the potential crime-reducing effects of the fifteen-year buildup in incarceration, there has also been a small body of research that attempts to address the so-called "unintended consequences" of incarceration. Unintended consequences are usually considered to be negative consequences or those that go beyond the crime-reducing or punitive aspects of incarceration. These lead to things such as family disruption or changes in family structure, decreases in human capital and employability, and ultimately—through such intermediary effects—increases in crime (e.g., Sampson 1987). For example, during the 1980 to 1995 period in which incarceration increased so massively, the number of families headed by single women also increased: for whites it increased from about 3.5 million to 4.8 million families, while for blacks it increased from about 1.8 million to 2.5 million families (Bureau of the Census 1996). The relationship between incarceration and family structure is complex. Some argue that it affects family structure by making incarcerated men less attractive as marriage partners, while at the same time it lowers the supply of men; it may also alter the incentives for the remaining men to form families (Darity and Myers 1994).

Other possible unintended consequences of incarceration are in employment. For example, Grogger (1995) shows that while sanctions short of imprisonment do not reduce wages and employment of young men, incarceration does reduce their future employment and earnings. Freeman (1996) reports how the collapse of the inner-city job market and declines in wages for low-skill men coincided with the development of drug markets.

Even attitudes toward formal sanctions such as incarcerations have been shown to be affected by experience with the criminal justice system. Non-blacks, for example, who know someone who has been incarcerated report low opinions of both formal sanctions and informal social control, while non-blacks with no knowledge of someone who has been incarcerated hold different opinions of the two forms of social control (Rose and Clear 1998). To the extent that attitudes affect behaviors, a low opinion of both incarceration and informal social control can lead to crime, as the restraints offered by both systems of social control are ignored.

Thus, the overarching question about the effects of incarceration on crime is: Does incarceration lead to net reductions in crime, given possible intermediary effects on families and employability? The purpose of this chapter is to attempt to estimate the relationship between removal (prison admissions) and drug enforcement policy (fraction of all arrests for drug crimes) on female-headed families and on male employment.

HOW INCARCERATION CAN LEAD TO DISRUPTION IN COMMUNITIES

We suggest that incarceration can have such unintended consequences for communities as disrupting family structure or leading to increases in unemployment in several ways. First, the sheer scale or size of the incarcerated population may disrupt communities. When a relatively small fraction of a community's population is incarcerated and subsequently returned from prison, the community may have the resources to help the ex-offender reintegrate. As the fraction of the population that has been incarcerated increases or is returned, the capacities of the community to adapt may be strained beyond capacity. This may especially be the case in poorer communities, or in black communities, where incarceration rates average six–eight times those of whites.

Second, the clustering of incarceration can lead to disruption. During the past fifteen years, incarceration has increased and become more concentrated in specific locations and for specific groups. Increases have been greater in central cities and for blacks than for whites (Lynch and Sabol 1997). It has been estimated that more than one of every four black males will be incarcerated over a lifetime, compared to 4 percent of white males (Bonczar and Beck 1997). There is some evidence that the clustering is even more severe in geographically defined communities. Baltimore, for example, accounted for 56 percent of admissions to Maryland state prison and only 13 percent of the state population. The clustering is even more extreme at the neighborhood level. Gottfredson and Taylor (1988) found that 75 percent of Baltimore residents released from Maryland state prison came from just nine of the 244 neighborhoods in that city. This clustering of incarceration increases the chance that, for these groups and in these areas, incarceration will disrupt communities.

Third, the type of offender incarcerated also has changed, both in terms of the type of crimes committed and in terms of his connections to mainstream institutions of social integration such as families, schools, and labor markets. Sentencing reforms of the 1980s and early 1990s targeted not only violent criminals but also repeat offenders and drug offenders. In an earlier assessment of the effects of changes in incarceration policies, we found that the sentencing reforms of the 1980s and 1990s led to increases in the incarceration of violent offenders with lengthy criminal histories. But they also led to even larger increases in the number of offenders who were first-time offenders committed for nonviolent crime, including drugs (Lynch and Sabol 1997). Also, many of these offenders, especially drug offenders, had ties to the community institutions before being incarcerated. These ties included marriage, holding jobs, and having high school diplomas. Thus, removing men with ties to the community can lead to disruption in the community.

Fourth, upon return from prison, the human capital of young offenders may be reduced. Post incarceration, young men are less likely to find jobs and if they find jobs, are more likely to have reduced wages (Lott 1993; Grogger 1995). As the number who were in prison cumulates in the community so that relatively larger fractions of a community have been in prison over some period, the overall effect on the human capital of the community may be negative. If only a few men can't find jobs because of incarceration, a community should be able to adjust. However, if 10 percent of the men in a community have been through prison during a relatively short period and are consequently less able to find jobs, the effects on employment in the community can be quite large.[1]

Thus, the scale, concentration, and characteristics of incarcerated persons have changed. Combined, these factors can impact community structure. This brings us to our main hypothesis. We believe that removing large numbers of marriageable men from communities with high incarceration rates will lead to reductions in the number of families formed in those communities or to increases in the number of children born to single mothers. The reduction in family formation will occur because (1) fewer men are available, since some are incarcerated; (2) the eligible men still in the community have fewer incentives to form unions with women; (3) the "taint" of imprisonment will reduce the value of "ever-imprisoned" men in the labor market and thereby make them less attractive candidates for marriage; and (4) at the community level, severing the ties of men to labor markets reduces the community's levels of income and employment, thereby leading to greater reliance on illegitimate income such as drug dealing.

Marriage as an Institution of Less Coercive Social Control

It is widely recognized in criminology and other social and behavioral sciences that families are one, if not the, major socializing institution through which children receive the norms and values that can encourage or discourage criminal behavior (Hirschi 1969). Strong families, whether two-parent or single-parent families with sufficient resources, influence not only their own children but also the children of their neighbors. Families with sufficient material and psychic resources can engage in neighboring and voluntary associations that provide the level of interaction necessary for community life (Janowitz and Suttles 1985; Hunter 1979). In such places neighbors can collectively monitor the behavior of children and adolescents and thereby reduce crime (Sampson 1987). Places without strong families have higher crime rates. We argue that the availability of marriageable men will increase the number of strong families in communities that will, in turn, increase the ability of communities to control crime.

The Taint Factor

Time spent incarcerated can be expected to have long-term effects on both a man's employment and on his desirability as a mate. In addition to the difficulties that having a criminal record pose to finding meaningful employment (Grogger 1992, 1995; Freeman 1996), other employment concerns caused by incarceration are an interrupted history of holding a job, fewer years of job experience because of time lost while in prison, and the degradation of skills held before incarceration. Incarceration can be expected to lower desirability as a marriage partner because of negative associations of a criminal history, lowered employability, and lower earning potential.

Unemployment Levels

High levels of incarceration alone may not lead to increases in unemployment; however, when the incarceration is concentrated in certain areas and large fractions of men from communities are removed, then the cumulative effects of incarceration on employment may be large. High incarceration levels for adult males in a community can also have the unintended effect of lowering the access to jobs for youth in the community. It is through connections with working adults that young people often find their first jobs (McGahey 1986; Sullivan 1989; Granovetter 1974). To the extent that imprisonment weakens the ties of adult males to the labor force, it will also lessen the ability of those men to serve as mentors and connectors who can introduce their children to the world of work.

Other Factors Affecting Family Formation

There are factors other than imprisonment that affect family formation, and these influences must be taken into account in assessing the effects of imprisonment. Most of these factors affect the attractiveness of men as marriage partners or the marriageability of men. The sheer volume of men in a jurisdiction should affect family formation. This volume can be determined by factors other than removal through imprisonment. Given a certain volume of available men, the attractiveness of these men as marriage partners must be considered. We assume that employment or labor force participation is one determinant of attractiveness: Employed men are more desirable as partners. Income is also a factor: The higher a man's income, the more desirable he is as a partner.

ANALYTIC APPROACH: ATTEMPTING TO ESTIMATE THE EFFECTS OF INCARCERATION ON FAMILIES

To measure the impacts of incarceration on "unintended consequences" such as the number of families headed by single women or the number of men employed, we estimate aggregate elasticities for these relationships. The approach is similar to that taken by Levitt (1996) and Marvel and Moody (1994), which estimated the elasticity of crime with respect to prison populations.

One of the problems confronting this approach is that the relationship between incarceration and family structure (e.g., the number of families headed by single women) is not unidirectional. Rather, high incarceration is likely to be a result of high levels of families headed by single women, as that variable has consistently been shown to be positively related to crime (e.g., Sampson 1986). Therefore, an alternative hypothesis to incarceration leading to family disruption is that increases in the use of incarceration have occurred where there are high concentrations of families headed by single women. Therefore, high levels of families headed by single women should be expected to correlate with increases in crime, arrests, and incarcerations.

We attempt to address this problem of simultaneity between incarceration and female-headed families by using an instrumental variables technique ap-

proach to estimating the relationship. Following Levitt (1996, 1997), we identify instruments that are correlated with increases in the use of imprisonment
but that are not correlated with changes in family structure. Specifically, we use
variables that describe the sentencing structure of states that implemented
mandatory sentences for drug crimes, changed to determinate sentencing, or
implemented sentencing guidelines during the 1980s as instruments for the increase in the number of prison admissions and the growth in the prison population. Between 1980 and 1990, many states implemented sentencing reforms,
but a selected subset implemented the reforms used to instrument the growth
of prison populations. In these states, the prison admission rate (per 100,000
population) increased by almost 20 percent between 1980 and 1990; by comparison, the prison admission rates in other states that did not implement these
changes remained roughly constant.

We argue, therefore, that changes in sentencing structure will be related to
family structure (employment) only through its impact on prison admissions
or, alternatively, on returns from prison. If so, the exclusion of sentencing structure from the family structure and employment equations is valid.

The results from using the sentencing structure as an instrument show that
prison admission rates are positively associated with increases in the number of
families headed by single women—for both blacks and whites—and that rates
of return from prison are negatively associated with employment for blacks but
not for whites. Extrapolating from the estimated elasticities to the 280 counties
in 96 metropolitan areas in our sample and controlling for drug and violent arrest rates, the 50 percent increase in the level of prison admissions resulted in
an additional 7 percent of black families headed by single women.

DATA USED IN THIS STUDY

The dataset used in the study is a file of county-level data on crime, arrests,
prison admissions, prison releases, and social and economic characteristics of
counties for 1980 and 1990. The county-level unit of analysis was chosen in part
because of our belief that the processes leading to changes in family structure
operate at comparatively low levels of aggregation, such as the neighborhood or
community. State- and national-level data are at too high a level of aggregation
to detect the effects of removal on family structure, although Darity and Myers
(1994) have used state-level incarceration rates in their micro-level models that
predict the effects of incarceration on family formation through changes in the
supply of men and sex ratios.[2]

The larger data file on which this dataset is based consists of observations on
all counties for selected variables for several periods between 1980 and 1995. For
this analysis, we restricted the analysis to data for 280 counties in 96 metropolitan areas. The number of counties was restricted by the availability of prison
admission data; only 18 states reported county-level prison admissions data with

sufficient regularity and apparent reliability to be included in the sample.[3] The sample was further restricted to metropolitan areas with populations greater than 200,000 in 1990 in order to eliminate counties with very few blacks. These restrictions on the sample preclude our generalizing results to the nation as a whole and diminish our ability to generalize to all metropolitan areas. Nevertheless, the counties in our sample contain about half of the population in the United States and more than 75 percent of the population in their respective states.

In constructing our dataset, we faced two major constraints: data on prison populations at the county level over time and race-specific data at the county level on the social and economic characteristics of counties. The source for the prison population data was the Bureau of Justice Statistics' National Corrections Reporting Program (NCRP). These data contain annual files of the individual-level records of persons admitted into state prisons for felony convictions and annual data files for the persons released from state prisons. The NCRP data include information about type of crime, length of sentence, county of sentencing, and age, race, sex, and education level of defendants. The NCRP data start in 1983; at the time this paper was written, data through 1994 are available to the public. As many as 38 states participate in the NCRP; nonparticipating states tend to have smaller populations (with the exception of Arizona). Some states did not participate every year. In this chapter, we used 1983 prison data as an estimate for 1980 prison data.[4]

The data on social and economic characteristics of counties come from the Census data files; consequently, they are limited to 1990. Currently, there are no other data at the county level that measure important social and economic indicators such as family structure, education, employment, and labor-force participation by race for years beyond 1990.[5]

CHANGES IN SENTENCING STRUCTURE AND PRISON ADMISSIONS

The objective of this chapter is to estimate the relationship between incarceration and family structure using instrumental variables. The instruments that we chose reflect the sentencing structure of states. Sentencing structure is measured by indicator variables for attributes such as mandatory sentences for drug crimes, determinate sentencing, and sentencing guidelines. These structural changes in sentencing are associated with prison population growths, but they are not theoretically related to family structure or to employment.

Between 1980 and 1990, California, Minnesota, Mississippi, Missouri, Maryland, Michigan, Oregon, Pennsylvania, and Wisconsin implemented or had sentencing structures that included mandatory sentences for drug crimes, determinate sentences, or sentencing guidelines. We estimated logistic regressions of the probability that a state implemented or had such a sentencing structure as a function of the number of families headed by single women and the number admitted into prison. We estimated such models separately by race. In none of the models was the coefficient for families headed by females statistically significant.[6] In addition, the number of admissions was significant and positively associated with the probability that a state adopted such sentencing structural changes.

ESTIMATES OF THE ELASTICITIES OF FAMILY STRUCTURE WITH RESPECT TO PRISON ADMISSIONS

This section applies the instrumental variables technique to estimate the elasticities of family structure with respect to prison admissions. As we believe that the processes leading to female headship and other outcomes affect blacks and whites differently, we estimate separate models by race. Two sets of models are estimated: natural logs of the levels and differences in natural logs of the levels or percentage change. The structure of the model for the effects on the level of families headed by single women is:

$$\ln(\text{family structure})_{it} = \beta \ln(\text{number admitted into prison})_{it} + \delta \ln X_{it} + \epsilon_{it} \tag{1}$$

where the subscript i refers to counties and t identifies years. Family structure is measured as the natural log of the number of families headed by single women; prison admission is the log of the number admitted into prison. The X_{it} refers to a vector of covariates that are described hereafter. All covariates are also measured as natural logs of the variables.

Similarly, a model for percentage changes was also estimated. It assumes that percentage changes in the number of families headed by single women and percentage changes in the level of prison admission are determined by:

$$\Delta \ln(\text{family structure})_{it} = \beta \Delta \ln(\text{number admitted into prison})_{it} + \delta \ln X_{it} + \epsilon_{it} \tag{2}$$

where the subscripts are as in Eq. 1 and the X vector refers to a vector of covariates. Here again, models are estimated separately by race.

Variables in the Models and Hypothesized Relationships

The variables in the models include a range of relevant variables for each equation. Enforcement policy variables such as the prison admission rate and the prison return rate are included in most equations, as they are central to the hypotheses. The variables in the models fall into several categories: crime and enforcement policy variables, demographic variables, social-structural characteristics, economic variables, time, and state-specific effects.

Crime and Enforcement Policy Variables

The number of admissions into prison is one of the primary enforcement variables in the model. "Removal," as we call it, refers to the incarceration of a person in a state correctional facility. Prison admissions include "new court commitments" or those commitments from courts following a conviction for a new crime and also include "other commitments," such as commitments for violating parole with or without committing a new crime. Removal is hypothesized to lead to increases in the number of families headed by single women. Removal reduces the supply of men, and it lessens the chances that the remaining men will form stable relationships. For men already in stable relationships who are removed, their incarceration may lead to instability and increases in female-headed families.

The number of offenders returned from prison, "returns," is also included as a covariate in both the female headship and employment equations. According to Grogger (1995), incarceration reduces the chances of employment and lowers the earnings of youth, whereas sanctions short of incarceration appear not to have so negative an effect. Consequently, we hypothesize that "returns" should lead to lower levels of employment in a county, especially as the fraction of the population that has been through prison increases.

The arrest variables are designed to measure the criminal justice system response to crime. The fraction of arrests that are drug arrests is a policy variable that helps to indicate the prospective nature of drug enforcement. Enforcement of drug crimes, unlike crimes of violence or property crimes, is proactive rather than reactive. For violent crimes, the police respond to calls for service or complaints. For most drug crimes, the police develop strategies for arresting suspects, as few drug arrests result from calls for service, with the possible exception of some calls about crack houses or open-air drug markets. Drug dealing transactions that occur in private spheres such as homes or college dormitories are more difficult to police or enforce than those that occur in public spheres such as street corners. In short, drug enforcement may reflect more of a policing strategy than a response to actual calls. As a control for variations in enforcement policies, the fraction of all arrests for violent crimes is included.

Enforcement practices are included to control for differences in crime rates (through the response to violent crimes) and differences in police targeting (through the drug arrests). We expect the fraction of arrests for violent crime to be positively correlated with female headship. We have no expectations about the effects of the fraction of arrests for drug crimes. One reason that we are uncertain about the effect on female headship of the fraction of arrests for drug crimes is that we have recently shown (Lynch, Sabol, and Shelly 1998) that the prevalence of arrests of blacks for drug crimes has increased in suburban areas more rapidly than in central cities (or in the counties that contain central cities of metropolitan areas). For example, drug arrests of blacks in core counties increased by about 70 percent, from 103 per 10,000 to 170 per 10,000, between

1984 and 1993. During that same period, drug arrests of blacks in suburban counties more than doubled from 50 per 10,000 to 99 per 10,000.

In addition, the probability of imprisonment for blacks arrested for drug crimes also changed dramatically. By 1993, for example, blacks arrested for drug trafficking in suburban counties were almost twice as likely as blacks arrested in core counties to be admitted to prison. For blacks in core counties, the probability of an admission into prison given a drug trafficking arrest was about 16 percent; for blacks in non-core counties, it was about 22 percent. Given that drug admissions in non-core counties increased as a fraction of all prison admissions, but given that families headed by single women are concentrated in core counties, the effects of drug arrests on female headship are difficult to predict.

Demographic Variables

For all models estimated in levels, population data are included on the right-hand side. Population may be measured differently across specifications, as it may be measured as the total population or the population between the ages of fifteen and fifty-nine; male and female population may also be included in models. In addition, the racial composition of the population—the percentage of the population that is black—is used to control for heterogeneity in population. In the literature on social organization, a heterogeneous population or a population with rapid change in its composition has greater difficulty maintaining order.

Social Structural Characteristics

Variables that measure the structural characteristics of counties include number of families, the number of families with children, the number with high-school degrees, the number with college degrees, and the location of the county as a "core" or "non-core" county. Core counties are counties that contain the central city of a metropolitan area; non-core counties are the counties that surround the core but that also are within the metropolitan area.

Structural characteristics are predicted to impact female headship and employment in logical ways. For example, as education levels increase, female headship is expected to decrease. However, if there is a "Murphy Brown" effect, education levels could be negatively correlated with female headship for more highly educated populations. The core-county indicator is a proxy for the central city of a metropolitan area, as data on prison admissions were not available at the city level.

Economic Variables

Variables that measure economic aspects of counties include the number in poverty, the number of men and women employed, the size of the male and female labor force, and the number of women receiving income assistance. We expect female headship to be positively related to poverty but negatively related to the number of men employed. Poverty decreases the marketability of men as marriage partners, while employment increases it. We hypothesize that income assistance is positively related to female headship.

Results

We review briefly the descriptive statistics for the data used in the models before moving on to discuss, first, our results for the models that predict female headship, and, second, the models for the effects of incarceration on employment.

Descriptive Statistics

Table 1.1 shows the descriptive statistics for the data used in the models. Variables are shown in per capita rates rather than as logs of levels as used in the models for ease of interpretableness. Between 1980 and 1990, the number of black families headed by single women increased from about 796,000 to almost 939,000. The rate per population increased from 590 per 10,000 to 616 per 10,000. By contrast, for whites the increases were less than for blacks.

Black male employment increased from 1,546 per 10,000 black population in 1980 to 1,702 in 1990. By contrast, white male employment increased from 2,493 per 10,000 white population to 2,739 per 10,000. Black labor force participation rates increased, but the rate of employment remained at about 85 percent of the labor force participation rate.

As with other variables, there also are racial differences in the arrest and incarceration measures. While in 1980 blacks had a prison admission rate of 32 per 10,000, this was 6.5 times the rate for whites of 5 per 10,000. By 1990, the black prison admission rate had doubled, to about 69 per 10,000, and the white rate also had doubled, to 11 per 10,000. The largest increase in prison admissions rates came for black drug admissions. In 1980, the black drug prison admission rate was about 3 per 10,000; by 1990, this rate had increased eightfold, to 24 per 10,000. Meanwhile, the white drug prison admission rate, which was about one-fifth the size of the black rate at 0.6 per 10,000 in 1980, increased to 2.7 per 10,000 in 1990. By 1990, the black drug prison admission rate was now nine times the rate for whites.

Effects on the Number of Families Headed by Single Women

Table 1.2 shows the results of the instrumental variables estimates of the relationship between prison admissions and the number of single female–headed families separately for blacks and whites. In general, the models show differences between blacks and whites either in the direction of effects or in their

Table 1.1
Descriptive Statistics for Variables in Regression Models

Variable	1980 Blacks Sum	1980 Blacks Rate per 10,000 population	1980 Whites Sum	1980 Whites Rate per 10,000 population	1990 Blacks Sum	1990 Blacks Rate per 10,000 population	1990 Whites Sum	1990 Whites Rate per 10,000 population
Population	13,486,365	--	82,921,990	--	15,229,671	--	80,477,184	--
College degrees	533,629	395.7	8,643,401	1,042.4	666,593	437.7	8,318,919	1,033.7
High school graduates	1,959,232	1,452.7	16,008,540	1,930.6	2,274,811	1,493.7	16,004,269	1,988.7
Persons in poverty	3,926,116	2,911.2	6,516,868	785.9	4,054,351	2,662.1	6,257,582	777.6
Number of men 15 to 59 years old	3,889,285	2,883.9	25,898,842	3,123.3	4,219,907	2,770.8	26,786,440	3,328.5
Men employed	2,085,472	1,546.4	19,419,197	2,341.9	2,592,607	1,702.3	22,042,785	2,739.0
Men in the labor force	2,445,954	1,813.6	20,672,059	2,493.0	3,048,560	2,001.7	23,225,432	2,886.0
Female headed households with children under 18	796,217	590.4	1,234,332	148.9	938,960	616.5	1,344,702	167.1
All women with children	1,663,986	1,233.8	8,914,579	1,075.1	1,755,532	1,152.7	9,223,884	1,146.1
Unemployed women	292,032	216.5	868,424	104.7	404,495	265.6	885,738	110.1
Total arrests	1,544,552	1,145.3	3,004,988	362.4	1,675,211	1,100.0	3,042,003	378.0
Violent arrests	130,573	96.8	113,900	13.7	161,832	106.3	166,612	20.7
Drug arrests	129,235	95.8	216,776	26.1	231,599	152.1	298,071	37.0
Fraction of arrests for drug crimes	--	0.05	--	0.05	--	0.09	--	0.06
Fraction of arrests for violent crimes	--	0.07	--	0.03	--	0.07	--	0.03
Num. of men released from prison	38,345	28.4	37,093	4.5	90,096	59.2	78,096	9.7
Num. of men admitted into prison	43,733	32.4	42,071	5.1	104,879	68.9	87,922	10.9
Num. of men admitted into prison for violent offenses	18,743	13.9	13,785	1.7	30,598	20.1	21,643	2.7
Num. of men admitted into prison for drug offenses	3,850	2.9	4,984	0.6	36,216	23.8	21,818	2.7

Table 1.2
Estimated Effects of Prison Admissions on Families Headed by Single Women, Using Instrumental Variable Technique

| | Natural log of the number of families headed by single women | | | | | | | |
| | Blacks | | Whites | | Blacks | | Whites | |
Variable	Estimate	Standard error	Estimate	Standard error	Estimate	Standard error	Estimate	Standard error
Constant	-1.424	2.777	-3.146	0.242 **	0.408	2.514	-3.476	0.231 **
College degrees	-0.126	0.045 *	0.187	0.030 **	-0.126	0.046 *	0.209	0.031 **
High school graduates	-0.027	0.076	0.332	0.057 **	0.045	0.076	0.168	0.054 *
Welfare recipients	-0.264	0.192	0.083	0.022 *	-0.413	0.157 *	0.036	0.022
Persons in poverty	0.223	0.051 **	0.223	0.031 **	0.253	0.051 **	0.227	0.030 **
Unemployed women	0.137	0.035 **	0.188	0.041 **	0.163	0.035 **	0.138	0.041 **
Men employed	-4.746	1.307 **	1.050	0.514 *	-4.785	1.261 **	-1.252	0.497 *
Men in the labor force	5.195	1.313 **	-1.570	0.541 *	5.190	1.272 **	0.888	0.522
All women with children	0.589	0.060 **	0.533	0.057 **	0.569	0.060 **	0.592	0.059 **
Fraction of arrests for drug crimes	0.090	0.052	-0.018	0.014	0.086	0.051	-0.007	0.014
Fraction of arrests for violent crimes	-0.034	0.055	0.001	0.011	-0.058	0.054	0.004	0.011
Number of men admitted into prison	0.136	0.065 *	0.035	0.024	0.136	0.066 *	0.069	0.025 *
Number of men released from prison	0.182	0.061 *	-0.008	0.024	0.166	0.061 *	-0.016	0.025
Core county	-0.346	0.295	0.051	0.017 *	-0.412	0.288	0.038	0.019 *
Year	-0.013	0.023	0.019	0.002 **	-0.019	0.024	0.020	0.002 **
State controls?	Yes		Yes		No		No	
R^2 (from OLS equations)	0.806		0.986		0.788		0.981	

Note: The dependent variable is the natural log of the number of families headed by single women. All variables are in natural logs. The dataset is comprised of data for 280 counties in 96 metropolitan areas in 1980 and 1990. The number of observations is equal to 528 in all columns. In the instrumental variables specifications, an indicator corresponds to the states that enacted or had mandatory drug sentences, determinate sentencing, or guidelines between 1980 and 1990.

* $p < .05$

** $p < .001$

magnitude. The first set of models shows results with controls for state effects, while the second set shows the results without controls for state effects. (The following discussion focuses on the results for the models with the state effects.)

First, the estimated elasticities on prison admissions are in the predicted direction for both blacks and whites. The estimated elasticity for blacks is 0.136 and for whites is 0.035. However, the figures are significant for blacks but not for whites.[7] The number of black men admitted into prison in the counties in our sample more than doubled between 1980 and 1990, from 43,566 to 104,942, an increase of 140 percent, while the number of black families headed by single women increased from 795,970 to 938,724. The estimated elasticity of 0.136 for the effect of prison admissions suggests that in response to the 140 percent increase in prison admissions, 19 percent of the increase in black families headed by single women was due to the effects of increases in prison admissions.

The effects of returns from prison also are positive and significant in the black equations but negative and not significant in the white equations. The estimated elasticity of the number of black men returned from prison back into the community is 0.214, significant at the 0.05 percent level.

Other criminal justice variables do not have significant effects in these equations. The fraction of arrests for drug crimes—a measure of law enforcement discretion—for example, is negatively associated with female headship for both blacks and whites, is larger for blacks than whites, but is not significant in either equation. The same holds for the fraction of arrests for violent crimes, a measure of law enforcement's responsiveness to crimes.

Two economic variables have relatively substantial effects on families headed by single women: the number of men employed and the number of men in the labor force. For blacks, the effects of these two variables are in opposite directions. The estimated elasticity for black male employment is large, negative, and highly significant. This indicates that increases in black male employment lead to relatively large *decreases* in the number of black families headed by single women, as hypothesized. Conversely, the number of black men in the labor force leads to *increases* in the number of families headed by single women.[8] In fact, the difference between the number of black men employed and the number in the labor force is the number of unemployed black men, and the difference in the estimated elasticities for those employed and those in the labor force is 0.449, suggesting that black male unemployment has the largest estimated effect of any variable on the number of families headed by single women. Thus, a 1 percent increase in black male unemployment leads to almost a 0.5 percent increase in the number of black families headed by single women.

For whites, the effect of the number of men employed and the number of men in the labor force differs from that for blacks. Increases in white male employment lead to *increases* in white families headed by single women, while increases in the number of white men in the labor force lead to *decreases* in the number of white families headed by single women. The net effect of these two variables is −0.52, indicating that a 1 percent increase in white male unemployment leads to about a 0.5 percent *decrease* in white families headed by single women. Note, however, that the effects of white male employment and labor force participation are not robust across specifications. In the models without state effects, as compared to the models with state effects, the signs on white male employment and labor force participation switch, and the estimated elasticity for labor force in the models without state effects is not significant.

The effects of education are not significant for blacks, but for whites the high school graduation variable is significant. Increases in the number of persons in poverty are positively and significantly related to increases in families headed by single women for both blacks and whites. Welfare participation does not significantly impact the number of families headed by single women for either whites or blacks. Finally, the effects of the year dummy variables (1 if 1990) are negative but not significant for blacks and positive and significant for whites.

Effects on the Change in the Number of Families Headed by Single Women

Table 1.3 shows the results for the models that measure the percentage change in level of families headed by single women. The specifications are fairly similar to those for the models of levels, but all variables are measured as differences in the logs of the levels and represent elasticities with respect to the percentage changes. In addition, as the models are estimated for one period only (1990), the percentage changes reflect changes between counties, and the models do not include a dummy variable for "year."

The effects of removal and return—the change in the number admitted into prison and the change in the number released from prison—on changes in the number of families headed by single women are positive and significant for blacks but are not significant for whites. The estimated changes elasticities for blacks are slightly larger than the elasticities for the levels. For example, the estimated elasticity for the change in the number of men admitted into prison is 0.256, and the elasticity on the change in the number of men returned from prison is 0.214. Criminal justice enforcement variables (fraction of arrests for drugs and fraction of arrests for violent) are not significant in the change models, as was the case in the levels. However, employment is significant in the change models, as was the case in the models for levels.

Effects on Employment

We hypothesized that incarceration can affect the employability of men in communities. Removing currently employed men will reduce the number employed, while returning previously incarcerated men may reduce the overall community employment rates. We estimated the employment models in order to describe more fully the paths of the effects of incarceration on communities that we outlined earlier. We estimated models of the level of employment and

Table 1.3
Estimated Effects of Prison Admissions on the Percent Change in Female Families Headed by Single Women, Using Instrumental Variables Techniques.

| | Change in the natural log of the number of families headed by single women | | | | | | | |
| | Blacks | | Whites | | Blacks | | Whites | |
Variable	Estimate	Standard error	Estimate	Standard error	Estimate	Standard error	Estimate	Standard error
Constant	0.640	0.694	0.294	0.042 **	-0.074	0.327	0.194	0.019 **
College degrees	-0.026	0.075	0.029	0.063	-0.064	0.073	0.044	0.056
High school graduates	0.225	0.143	0.669	0.076 **	0.198	0.141	0.536	0.057 **
Welfare recipients	-0.211	1.619	0.021	0.064	0.401	1.190	0.023	0.051
Persons in poverty	0.428	0.086 **	0.342	0.055 **	0.403	0.082 **	0.390	0.047 **
Unemployed women	-0.149	0.048 *	-0.038	0.043	-0.114	0.047 *	0.027	0.038
Men employed	-6.605	2.069 *	-0.890	0.558	-6.709	1.928 **	-0.689	0.534
Men in the labor force	6.619	2.119 *	0.299	0.569	6.755	1.981 **	0.199	0.553
All women with children	0.326	0.101 *	0.906	0.073 **	0.302	0.098 *	0.891	0.072 **
Fraction of arrests for drug crimes	-0.127	0.088	-0.005	0.013	-0.127	0.085	-0.006	0.012
Fraction of arrests for violent crimes	-0.032	0.085	-0.003	0.013	-0.051	0.082	0.006	0.011
Number of men admitted into prison	0.256	0.105 *	0.002	0.020	0.224	0.101 *	0.012	0.017
Number of men released from prison	0.214	0.116 *	-0.007	0.021	0.197	0.111 *	0.009	0.018
Core county	0.100	0.427	-0.054	0.016 **	0.263	0.396	-0.053	0.015 **
State controls?	Yes		Yes		No		No	
R² (from OLS equations)	0.420		0.859		0.363		0.838	

Note: The dependent variable is the natural log of the number of families headed by single women. All variables are in natural logs. The dataset is comprised of data for 280 counties in 96 metropolitan areas in 1980 and 1990. The number of observations is equal to 528 in all columns. In the instrumental variables specifications, an indicator corresponds to the states that enacted or had mandatory drug sentences, determinate sentencing, or guidelines between 1980 and 1990.

*p < .05

**p < .001

of changes in the levels of employment as a function of prison variables, business establishments, the overall demand for labor, and measures of poverty and education levels.[9] As employment and incarceration can be correlated, we used the instrumental variables approach to estimate the effects of incarceration on employment.

Table 1.4 provides the estimates for the models of the levels of employment; Table 1.5 provides the change model estimates. Variables in both models are estimated as natural logs so that the coefficients are interpreted as elasticities.

In the employment models, we used the annual number of male prisoners released back into the county from which they were sentenced. If prison affects the employability of men, then high return rates should have negative effects on community employment rates. The sign on the estimated elasticity (Table 1.4) is negative for blacks and positive for whites. For neither race is it significant, but for blacks it approaches significance at the 10 percent level.[10] Including state effects has no effect on the estimated elasticities for blacks; but for whites, the state effects reduce the magnitude of the elasticity and move it from insignificant to significant.

Other variables in the employment models have predicted effects: The level of education is positively associated with employment for both black men and white men, while the number in poverty is negatively correlated with levels of male employment. The number of establishments has different effects on employment depending on the type of establishment and the race of men employed. For example, the number of manufacturing establishments is positively correlated with white male employment, while the number of retail establishments is negatively correlated with white male employment.[11]

INTERPRETATION AND SUMMARY

We set out to investigate whether incarceration had negative effects on family structure and employment. Specifically, we examined whether incarceration was associated with increases in the number of families headed by females and decreases in employment. Our results were mixed. The estimated elasticities of prison admissions on female headship were positive and significant for blacks but not for whites. This result held both for models in logs of the levels and in the differences of logs (percentage change). In addition, elasticity on the annual number of men returned from prison also was significant and positive for blacks but not whites. The size of the effects of removal and return were smaller than effects of social-structural variables such as poverty and welfare recipiency, but they were larger than the estimated effects of education. The largest elasticities were the effects of employment in the black equation. Future work should focus on the longer-run effects of removal by using data on prison stocks.

One striking result of these estimates is the racial differences in the effects of removal and employment on female headship. Black families are affected by

Table 1.4
Estimated Effects of Prison Admissions on the Number of Men Employed, Using Instrumental Variable Technique

	Natural log of the number of men employed							
	Blacks		Whites		Blacks		Whites	
Variable	Estimate	Standard error	Estimate	Standard error	Estimate	Standard error	Estimate	Standard error
Constant	0.049	0.083	-0.123 **	0.021	0.064	0.082	-0.095	0.022 **
High school graduates	0.006 **	0.002	0.025 **	0.002	0.007	0.002 **	0.021	0.002 **
Persons in poverty	-0.010 **	0.002	-0.029 **	0.002	-0.008	0.002 **	-0.027	0.002 **
Number of men released from prison	-0.002	0.001 +	0.002	0.001	-0.002	0.001	0.006	0.001 **
Number of construction businesses	0.004	0.011	0.000	0.002	0.027	0.010 *	0.005	0.002 *
Number of manufacturing businesses	0.011	0.010	0.007 **	0.002	-0.015	0.009	-0.001	0.002
Number of retail trade businesses	-0.018	0.012	-0.008 **	0.002	-0.023	0.012 *	-0.010	0.003 **
Number of service businesses	0.003	0.011	0.002	0.002	0.011	0.011	0.005	0.002
Core county	-0.019	0.010	0.004	0.002	-0.019	0.009 *	0.004	0.002
Year	-0.001	0.001	0.001 **	0.000	-0.002	0.001 *	0.001	0.000 *
State controls?	Yes		Yes		No		No	
R^2 (from OLS equations)	0.200		0.562		0.110		0.335	

Note: The dependent variable is the natural log of the number of families headed by single women. All variables are in natural logs. The dataset is comprised of data for 280 counties in 96 metropolitan areas in 1980 and 1990. The number of observations is equal to 528 in all columns. In the instrumental variables specifications, an indicator corresponds to the states that enacted or had mandatory drug sentences, determinate sentencing, or guidelines between 1980 and 1990.

*p < .05

**p < .001

Table 1.5
Estimated Effects of Prison Admissions on the Change in the Number of Men Employed, Using Instrumental Variable Technique

| | Change in the natural log of the number of men employed | | | | | | | |
| | Blacks | | Whites | | Blacks | | Whites | |
Variable	Estimate	Standard error	Estimate	Standard error	Estimate	Standard error	Estimate	Standard error
Constant	0.011	0.028	0.014	0.004 **	-0.002	0.014	0.012	0.002 **
High school graduates	-0.003	0.004	0.020	0.005 **	-0.002	0.004	0.010	0.005 *
Persons in poverty	-0.002	0.003	-0.003	0.006	-0.003	0.003	0.006	0.005
Number of men released from prison	-0.004	0.003	-0.001	0.002	-0.005	0.002 *	0.000	0.002
Number of construction businesses	0.007	0.026	0.005	0.003	0.004	0.024	0.006	0.003 *
Number of manufacturing businesses	-0.006	0.027	-0.003	0.003	0.003	0.022	-0.004	0.003
Number of retail trade businesses	-0.016	0.017	-0.003	0.002	0.002	0.015	-0.002	0.002
Number of service businesses	-0.004	0.014	0.000	0.002	-0.012	0.013	0.000	0.002
Core county	-0.006	0.017	-0.002	0.002	-0.008	0.015	-0.003	0.002
State controls?	Yes		Yes		No		No	
R² (from OLS equations)	0.140		0.293		0.036		0.068	

Note: The dependent variable is the natural log of the number of families headed by single women. All variables are in natural logs. The dataset is comprised of data for 280 counties in 96 metropolitan areas in 1980 and 1990. The number of observations is equal to 528 in all columns. In the instrumental variables specifications, an indicator corresponds to the states that enacted or had mandatory drug sentences, determinate sentencing, or guidelines between 1980 and 1990.

* p < .05

** p < .001

removal but white families apparently are not, as the removal variables were not significant in the white equations. Black families are affected by male employment; white families are not. The reasons for these differences may be due to differences in the scale of incarcerations in black communities, to their concentrations, or both. Prison environments can have negative effects on the socialization of men and may make them less fit for forming and maintaining stable unions. The clustering and concentration of incarcerations for blacks as opposed to whites make them more pronounced in black communities.

On the other hand, the effects of imprisonment on employment were marginal at best. While this may suggest that the hypothesized relationship was not correct, we have reason to believe that the measure of return from prison may be wrong. Rather than estimating the effects on employment by the annual number returned from prison, the effects may be cumulative over several years. Therefore, a better measure of the effects of return may be five-year cumulative probabilities of first incarceration.

Alternatively, the obvious effects of imprisonment on female headship may be occurring through more direct processes. The process may be one in which large numbers of previously marriage-eligible men become less attractive as companions and fathers in stable relationships because of the socialization effects of imprisonment. While these effects may not necessarily be criminogenic, they may nonetheless affect how men interact in interpersonal relationships.

NOTES

Extremely valuable and capable research assistance was provided by Mary K. Shelley of the Urban Institute and Michael Planty of the American University.

1. We are using National Corrections Reporting Program (NCRP) data to develop county-level estimates of the number of men who were ever incarcerated during the five- and ten-year periods 1990–95 and 1986–95. For a sample of counties in 92 of the largest metropolitan areas of the country, preliminary estimates of the five-year ever-been-incarcerated-in-state-prison rate are in the range of 5 percent to 8 percent of black men.

2. Ideally, we would want to use data at lower levels of aggregation, such as the neighborhood or community. However, data on crime and incarcerations are not readily available at these lower levels of aggregation. Alternatively, it is possible to conduct further analysis of the data after aggregating it to the metropolitan level. At that level, more recent data on characteristics of the area by race are available, and crime and incarceration data can be aggregated to the metropolitan level.

3. The eighteen states whose data were included in the study are Alabama, California, Georgia, Illinois, Kentucky, Maryland, Michigan, Minnesota, Mississippi, Missouri, Nebraska, New Jersey, New York, Ohio, Oregon, Pennsylvania, South Carolina, and West Virginia.

4. To further test the validity of that assumption, we can estimate 1980 arrests using the ratio of 1984 arrests to prison admissions times the 1980 arrests. Preliminary analysis of arrest to imprisonment ratios in the early 1980s showed very little change

over time before 1987. Also, the levels of admissions changed very little between 1983 and 1986.

5. In future versions of this paper, we could use CPS data to estimate social and economic characteristics by race for metropolitan areas. We would plan to aggregate the prison and crime data to that level and explore effects of imprisonment on family structure at the metropolitan level as well as at the county level controlling for metropolitan area effects.

6. Results are available from the authors.

7. The parameter estimates of the elasticities for the OLS models differ from the estimates in the instrumental variables specifications, and the differences differ by race. For example, the estimated elasticity for prison admissions for blacks when prison admissions is treated as exogenous is 0.122, which is smaller than the instrumental variables estimate, but for whites the OLS estimate is 0.035, which is larger than the instrumental variables estimate. A full set of these results is available from the authors upon request.

8. In an alternative specification in which black male population between fifteen and fifty-nine was used, the estimated elasticity was also large and positive. This suggests that unemployed black men and black men out of the labor force have similar types of effects on families headed by single women. These characteristics of these two groups of black men—unemployed or out of the labor force—may be very similar so that their effects are similar.

9. Wage data at the county level by race were not immediately available in the source data files. We estimated models with measure of the per-capita payroll in business establishments as a proxy for wages. These variables did not have significant effects on employment.

10. At the time we estimated the models, we had not completed the county-level estimates of the five-year and ten-year cumulative probabilities of first incarceration. As noted earlier, preliminary estimates of the five-year rates were in the range of 5 percent to 8 percent of men in the population. We suspect that for blacks the rates are higher than these averages.

11. The results for the percentage change models in Table 1.5 are very similar to those of the models in the logs of the levels and are not discussed here.

REFERENCES

Beck, Allen, et al. *Correctional Populations in the United States, 1995.* Washington, DC: Bureau of Justice Statistics, May 1997, NCJ-163916.

Blumstein, Alfred. *Youth Violence, Guns, and the Illicit Drug Industry.* Working Paper Series, H. John Heinz III School of Public Policy and Management. Pittsburgh: Carnegie Mellon University, 1995.

Bonczar, Thomas P., and Allen Beck. *Lifetime Likelihood of Going to State or Federal Prison.* Washington, DC: Bureau of Justice Statistics, 1997.

Bureau of the Census. *Statistical Abstract of the United States.* Washington, DC: U.S. Department of Commerce, Bureau of the Census, 1996.

Caulkins, Jonathan P., C. Peter Rydell, William L. Schwabe, and James Chiesa. *Mandatory Minimum Drug Sentences: Throwing Away the Key or the Taxpayers' Money?* Santa Monica, CA: RAND, 1997.

Cohen, Jacqueline, and Jose A. Canela-Cacho. "Incarceration and Violent Crime: 1965–1988." In *Understanding and Preventing Violence: Volume 4, Consequences and Control,* ed. Albert J. Reiss, Jr., and Jeffrey A. Roth. Washington, DC: National Academy Press, 1994.

Darity, William A., Jr., and Samuel L. Myers, Jr. *The Black Underclass: Critical Essays on Race and Unwantedness.* New York: Garland Press, 1994.

Freeman, Richard B. "Why Do So Many Young American Men Commit Crimes and What Might We Do about It?" *Journal of Economic Perspectives* 10(1) (1996): 25–42.

Gottfredson, Stephen D., and Ralph B. Taylor. "Community Contexts and Criminal Offenders." In *Communities and Crime Reduction,* ed. Tim Hope and Margaret Shaw. London: Home Office Research and Planning Unit, 1988.

Granovetter, Mark. *Getting a Job.* Cambridge, MA: Harvard University Press, 1974.

Grogger, Jeff. "Arrests, Persistent Youth Joblessness, and Black/White Employment Differentials." *Review of Economics and Statistics* 74 (1992): 100–116.

Grogger, Jeff. "The Effects of Arrests on the Employment and Earnings of Young Men." *Quarterly Journal of Economics* 110 (1995): 51–71.

Hirschi, Travis. *Causes of Delinquency.* Berkeley: University of California Press, 1969.

Hunter, Albert. *Symbolic Communities: The Persistence and Change of Chicago's Local Communities.* Chicago: University of Chicago Press, 1979.

Janowitz, Morris, and Gerald D. Suttles. "The Social Ecology of Citizenship." In *The Challenge of Social Control: Citizenship and Institution Building in Modern Society: Essays in Honor of Morris Janowitz,* ed. Gerald D. Suttles and Mayer N. Zald. Norwood, NJ: Ablex, 1985.

Levitt, Steven D. "The Effect of Prison Population Size on Crime Rates: Evidence from Prison Overcrowding Litigation." *Quarterly Journal of Economics* (May 1996): 319–351.

Levitt, Steven D. "Using Electoral Cycles in Police Hiring to Estimate the Effect of Police on Crime." *American Economic Review* 87 (1997): 270–290.

Lott, John. "Do We Punish High Income Criminals Too Heavily?" *Economic Inquiry* 30 (1993): 1307–1316.

Lynch, James P., and William J. Sabol. *Did Getting Tough on Crime Pay?* Crime Policy Report. Washington, DC: Urban Institute, 1997.

Lynch, James P., William J. Sabol, and Mary K. Shelley. "Spatial Patterns of Drug Enforcement Policies in Metropolitan Areas: Trends in the Prevalence and Consequences of Incarceration." Paper presented at the Annual Meeting of the American Society of Criminology, Washington, DC, 1998.

Marvel, Thomas, and Carlisle Moody. "Prison Population Growth and Crime Reduction." *Journal of Quantitative Criminology* 10 (1994): 109–140.

McGahey, Richard M. "Economic Conditions, Neighborhood Organization, and Urban Crime." In *Communities and Crime,* ed. Albert J. Reiss, Jr., and Michael Tonry, pp. 231–270. Chicago: University of Chicago Press, 1986.

Miller, Ted R., Mark A. Cohen, and Brian Wiersema. *Victim Costs and Consequences: A New Look.* Washington, DC: U.S. Department of Justice, National Institute of Justice, 1996.

Nagin, Daniel. "Criminal Deterrence Research at the Outset of the Twenty-First Century." In *Crime and Justice: A Review of Research,* ed. Michael Tonry, pp. 1–42. Chicago: University of Chicago Press, 1998.

Rose, Dina, and Todd Clear. "Unintended Consequences of Incarceration: Exposure to Prison and Attitudes toward Social Control." Paper presented to the Association for Public Policy and Management, New York, 1998.

Sampson, Robert J. "Crime in Cities: The Effects of Formal and Informal Social Control." In *Communities and Crime*, ed. Albert Reiss, Jr., and Michael Tonry. Chicago: University of Chicago Press, 1986.

Sampson, Robert J. "Urban Black Violence: The Effects of Male Joblessness and Family Disruption." *American Journal of Sociology* 93 (1987): 348–382.

Spelman, William. *Criminal Incapacitation*. New York: Plenum, 1994.

Sullivan, Mercer. *Getting Paid: Youth Crime and Work in the Inner City*. Ithaca, NY: Cornell University Press, 1989.

Tonry, Michael. *Malign Neglect: Race, Crime and Punishment in America*. New York: Oxford University Press, 1995.

Zimring, Franklin, and Gordon Hawkins. *Incapacitation: Penal Confinement and the Restraint of Crime*. New York: Oxford University Press, 1995.

2

Individual Sentencing Practices and Aggregate Social Problems

Todd R. Clear and Dina R. Rose

Incarceration policy in the United States fundamentally changed in the last quarter of the twentieth century. The use of prison as a primary means of formal social control both expanded in scope and intensified in effect. In 1973, approximately 60 percent of felons were sentenced with probation rather than imprisonment, and the median length of stay for those sentenced to prison was about twenty months (Clear 1994). Since then, a steady stream of sentencing reforms has dominated penal policy, gradually increasing the certainty and severity of incarcerative penalties for those convicted of a crime. By the end of the century, 65 percent of felons received sentences involving some form of incarceration, and the median length of stay neared thirty months (Clear and Cole 2000). The result of the increasing rate of incarceration along with longer sentences has been a persistent increase in the size of the incarcerated population over time. Before these reforms began, there were fewer than 350,000 citizens behind bars; today, that number approaches two million. When the acceleration in imprisonment started, U.S. incarceration rates had remained steady at between about 90 and 120 per 100,000 citizens for most of the century (Blumstein and Cohen 1973). By the end of the century, however, the incarceration rate exceeded 600 per 100,000, among the very highest in the world (Tonry 1999). Never before in modern history has there been such a dramatic and persistent shift in the punitive philosophy of a nation's penal system.

Scholars have debated the wisdom of this shift in penal policy. Some attribute a portion of the recent reduction in crime to this systematic growth in incarcerated populations (DiIulio 1990; Reynolds 1990). Their argument is based primarily on an incapacitative rationale: As the number of criminally active offenders removed from the streets increases, the number of crimes on the streets decreases. Other scholars (Clear 1994; Beckett 1997; Mauer 1999), unconvinced by this argument, point out that prison population increases have had less to do with crime rates than with modern electoral politics.

Evidence that changes in levels of incarceration are due more to changes in policy than to changes in crime rates is clear, because the escalation in incarceration since 1973 has remained steady throughout periods of both increasing crime (18 years) and decreasing crime (17 years) alike. While it is true that the number of offenders arrested and prosecuted has generally grown since the 1970s, studies of the expansion in incarceration confirm that this escalation is more a result of changes in sentencing policy than of growing numbers of offenders being processed by the system (Beck 1997). For the most part, these sentencing changes have been centered on drug laws that continue to impose harsher punishments on those convicted of these crimes. Thus, imprisonment rates continue to grow, even in the face of the substantial drops in crime experienced across the country during the second half of the 1990s (Mauer 1999). Even Professor John DiIulio of the University of Pennsylvania, formerly one of the most vocal proponents of imprisonment growth, has begun to call for a moratorium on the prison population increase (DiIulio 2000).

Whatever one's view of these developments, two points cannot be debated. First, crime policy in the United States targets individual offenders for removal from their communities with faith that the only impact on those communities of their removal will be positive—the prevention of crime through incapacitation and deterrence. Second, the growth in imprisonment has disproportionately affected communities of color, especially in those inner-city neighborhoods already decimated by poverty and inequality. In this chapter, we explore the implications of the first point for the second. We argue that the aggregate results of removing offenders from their communities are not solely positive for those communities, and we assess the implications for the communities of color that are so heavily affected by incarceration policy.

AGGREGATE IMPACT OF INDIVIDUAL POLICY

Crime policy in the United States targets individuals and, increasingly, has the effect of removing them from their communities. As a result, evaluations of crime policies typically focus on whether a particular individual has been prevented from committing further criminal acts, and our attention on crime as a social problem is fixed on individuals and their proclivities. Because crime policy focuses on individuals, its broader impact on communities often is overlooked. In the aggregate, however, individualistic crime policies impact community-level systems, sometimes impeding crime, other times making crime possible. Thus, overlooking the aggregate impact of crime policy as a determinant of crime leaves a gap in our understanding of the processes that contribute to community life and the social order. This chapter addresses that gap by investigating the impact of incarceration on African-American communities.

The impact of high rates of incarceration is most significant for black communities since the experience of incarceration in the United States is very much a question of race. Recent studies of lifetime probabilities of incarceration show that African Americans are eight times more likely to be sent to prison than white Americans (Bonczar and Beck 1997). In addition, black citizens are far more likely than non-blacks to have a family member, friend, or acquaintance sent to prison. While this is particularly true for poor black communities, it also is true for all black communities. As Pattillo (1998) points out, not only do black middle-class communities suffer more crime than their white middle-class counterparts, but middle-class blacks tend to know more offenders than do whites. This is because blockages to black mobility result in middle-class blacks living in closer proximity to poorer communities with higher crime rates. Thus, blacks in general have a broader range of social ties that connect upstanding members of the community to neighborhood delinquents (Pattillo 1998, 759). As a result, the unintended consequences of incarceration can reach far deeper into African-American communities than into other racial or ethnic groups.

Our argument is not that the impact of incarceration on community life is similar across all types of communities. Instead, we argue that removing offenders from socially *disorganized* areas may undermine other social control efforts there. Conversely, incarceration may reinforce social control efforts in socially *organized* areas. This occurs because social networks and ties, which are the foundation of local social control, are already weakened in disorganized areas. Incarceration weakens them further. The result of an overreliance on incarceration, then, is a reduction in human and social capital and an increase in social isolation. This has led to the proliferation of communities without the tools necessary for adequate informal social control. Literature on the urban underclass documents such a growth (see Wilson 1987, 1996; Anderson 1990).

Alternatively, incarceration may be a policy that works well in areas with low levels of social disorganization because they have low levels of incarceration overall. For them, network disruptions are rare. When they do occur, residents in these areas have sufficient supplies of human and social capital to withstand the disruption that incarceration causes to social networks and ties. Furthermore, as residents of organized communities tend to have more faith in the legitimacy of the criminal justice system (partly because of their limited access to it), removing offenders does make people feel safer. Thus, many of us, including individuals who develop crime policy, may fail to recognize the deleterious impact of incarceration on some communities because in socially organized communities, incarceration is a response to crime that may indeed shore up the local social structure.

Residents of high-crime communities often express a desire for greater law enforcement because they wish to live in safer areas, and public debate centers on the quantity and quality of formal social control. Nonetheless, in practice, heightened formal controls may undermine their effectiveness and that of their more informal counterparts. One study (Peek, Lowe, and Alston 1981) shows that people from high-crime neighborhoods trust the police and courts less; another study (Rose and Clear 1998a) shows that for people exposed to incarceration, negative attitudes towards formal control predict negative attitudes towards informal social control. Thus, people who are exposed to an increase in formal control are less likely to have a positive opinion of that control and probably less likely to submit to its authority. In addition, undermining support for one form of control inadvertently undermines support for the other. If attitudes are linked to the efficacy of control, then increasing formal control can undermine both formal and informal control.

RACE AND INCARCERATION IN AMERICA

It is important to understand the degree to which incarceration has become a core part of the African-American experience in most large urban areas. Nationwide, over 7 percent of African-American males aged twenty–forty are in prison or jail (Bureau of Justice Statistics 1995). In some inner-city areas, such as certain Washington, D.C., neighborhoods, the figure may be as high as 25 percent (Lynch and Sabol 1997). Minorities almost always heavily populate neighborhoods with these high rates of incarceration. While the lifetime probability of incarceration for African-American males is 28 percent (Bonczar and Beck 1997), it is not known what the rate is for underclass African-American males, but their rate is certainly much higher.

The concentrations of incarceration that affect African Americans in both rural and urban areas also affect other racial/ethnic groups. The lifetime probability of going to prison for Hispanic males is almost four times that of white males (Bonczar and Beck 1997). And while detailed statistics are not available for Native Americans, it is generally known that in jurisdictions with large reservations, this racial group is considerably overrepresented in the prison system. Prison is a common experience for many minority populations in the United States. But even with this pattern, prison stands out as a particularly salient experience for African-American males more than any other group.

Neighborhood-specific incarceration rates in Brooklyn, New York, illustrate this point.[1] Brooklyn is divided into 38 officially designated neighborhoods. As is the case in most urban areas, many of these neighborhoods are racially and ethnically segregated. Table 2.1 shows the rates at which residents were removed from these neighborhoods for incarceration in either prison or jail, in 1996.

The eight most heavily African-American neighborhoods and the eight most heavily Hispanic neighborhoods all have incarceration rates five–six times higher than the eight most heavily white communities. Even though the total populations of these three groups of neighborhoods are not very different, two of the

Table 2.1
Incarceration Rates for Neighborhoods in Brooklyn, NY, with the Highest Concentrations of African-Americans, Hispanics, and Whites, 1996[a]

Race/Ethnic Concentration of Neighborhood	Self Identified Race/Ethnicity			Incarceration Rate per 1,000	
	% Black	% Hispanic	% White	All Ages	Ages 18-39
African-American (N=8; pop=570,861)	.875	.101	.068	4.6	12.4
Hispanic (N=8; pop=531,190)	.365	.463	.302	5.2	14.2
White (N=8; pop=523,275)	.022	.079	.866	0.8	2.7

[a]Race/ethnicity categories are based upon census data from 1990. Only those identifying themselves as black, Hispanic, or white are counted; others are excluded from the counts; and double counting occurs for some of those identifying themselves as of Hispanic lineage.

black neighborhoods and three of the Hispanic neighborhoods each sent more residents to prison and jail in 1996 than did all eight white neighborhoods combined.

When we take the age and sex distributions into account, we get rough estimates of the annual Brooklyn neighborhood removal rates for incarceration. In the eight white neighborhoods, about one adult male in 180 was removed in 1996 for incarceration; in the black and Hispanic neighborhoods, the figure is about one in 35. In the Fort Hamilton neighborhood, which is 92 percent white, about one in 240 adult males was removed in 1996; but in the black neighborhoods of Brevoort and the Hispanic/black neighborhoods of East New York and Brownsville, the figure was nearly one in 20. Adjusted for age, the CASES researchers have estimated that in some Brooklyn Council districts, one in eight parent-age males went to prison or jail in 1998 (CASES 1999).

A single year's rates do not tell the full story. About half of those removed on criminal sentences go to Rikers Island, where they stay for a period of only a few months; the remainder go upstate to serve prison terms lasting years. This occurrence happens every year. To be fully understood, the impact of this pattern has to be added across the years of a young man's life. A black man living in Brownsville can see that, over the years, the chances of being removed for a prison term mount up as the number of people he knows who are incarcerated also mounts up over time. Equally important, those who live with him and depend upon him for personal or economic support—those who are located within his social network—are likely to experience a disruption in that relationship due to his incarceration. Ultimately, a multitude of social networks are damaged as different people are sentenced to prison year after year. This reality that exists for residents in the severely disadvantaged neighborhoods in our cities is completely foreign to the everyday U.S. citizen living outside those areas. It would be implausible to argue that such a remarkable structural force would *not* affect neighborhood life for those who remain as well as for those who go. Our point is that such high levels of residential instability and flux have effects that are damaging to the social control capacity of these places.

THREE THEORETICAL PROPOSITIONS

A substantial body of indirect evidence exists on the social impact of high incarceration rates on communities. We detailed this in an earlier paper (Rose and Clear 1998b), where we made the argument that it is necessary to move beyond the individualist paradigm that dominates contemporary thought about crime and crime policy to a more inclusive ecological model of crime control and neighborhood life. Here we continue this line of inquiry and examine three propositions about the way high levels of incarceration impede informal social control in socially disorganized areas.

- Proposition One: Incarceration reduces the human capital of imprisoned individuals and their families.
- Proposition Two: Incarceration disrupts local social ties and networks in the community and reduces the social capital available to that area.
- Proposition Three: Decreases in human and social capital lead, nonrecursively, to an increase in social isolation from mainstream society and institutions for both the individuals and their communities.

Communities and Crime: The Importance of Human and Social Capital

In a recent paper (Rose and Clear 1998b), we show how an overreliance on incarceration may disrupt the networks that lay the foundation for private and parochial control. Our argument expands on the model of community control proposed by Bursik and Grasmick (1993), which merges social disorganization and systemic theories to include a feedback loop for the effects of incarceration rates on community life. Thus, in our conceptual model we examined the effects of formal, public social controls on the functioning of informal social controls and their ability to regulate criminal behavior. We theorized that high levels of incarceration undermine social, political, and economic systems that are the foundation of informal control. In the extreme, then, not only are formal controls relied upon because of the absence of informal controls (Black 1976), but relying upon formal controls can contribute to the extinction of informal ones.

This would be the case especially when high incarceration rates are concentrated in communities already weakened by low levels of human and social capital.

The salience of human and social capital for understanding crime has received a lot of attention recently (Decker and Van Winkle 1996; Elliott et al. 1996; Hagan 1994; Hagan, Merkens, and Boehnke 1995; Taylor 1997) because it has become clear that both are needed for effective social control. Human capital, the resource individuals need to function effectively in society, and social capital, the linkages and associations communities need to function effectively, are reciprocally related. Communities rich in one resource tend to be rich in the other. In combination, human and social capital provide individuals (and groups of individuals) with the tools necessary to navigate mainstream institutions successfully. Thus, sufficient supplies of human and social capital result in communities and residents adept at securing other types of resources and well-connected to the larger society. Sampson and his colleagues (Sampson, Raudenbush, and Earls 1998) refer to this overarching community capacity as "collective efficacy," which they believe helps reduce crime.

Conversely, communities and residents deficient in human and social capital become increasingly disadvantaged and isolated from mainstream society. This is important because social isolation is at the heart of ineffective social control. For instance, Bursik and Grasmick (1993) show the importance of being connected to the larger society for local social control efforts, and Decker and Van Winkle (1996) show how social isolation contributes to the formation and maintenance of gangs.

Social isolation also is at the crux of the research on the urban underclass. This body of research draws our attention to how structural disadvantages and discrimination have led to extreme poverty for a group of people who are increasingly isolated from mainstream society because of intergenerational deficits in human and social capital. The result has been geographic concentrations of social pathologies such as unemployment, single-parent families, and crime.

Incarceration damages both human and social capital. At the individual level, incarceration reduces the ability of individuals to find employment (Grogger 1995) and increases their propensity for a range of personal problems (Glaser 1964), at the same time that it damages their social networks and community attachment. For the community, removing large numbers of individuals through incarceration disrupts many of the networks that form the basis of social control.

High rates of incarceration produce effects similar to Wilson's (1987) observations regarding the flight of the middle class from inner-city neighborhoods. This exodus, according to Wilson, left neighborhoods with insufficient financial and human resources to maintain social order. Our argument is that these neighborhoods are even less capable of sustaining order when the remaining fragile linkages are further damaged by excessive incarceration, even if the people who are being removed have committed crimes. This is true because at the same time that offenders are liabilities to their communities, many of these brothers, fathers, and cousins are assets to their social networks. Since the communities are already damaged, the total costs of the damage done to the community by offenders must be understood in light of the assets they contribute (limited though they may be), because of the diminished availability of other assets. We do not make the argument that offenders necessarily contribute to the social order directly. Rather, their removal disrupts networks to which they belong, undermining the effectiveness (or willingness) of the social control efforts of those they leave behind. This has particularly important implications for black neighborhoods, since black residents populate underclass areas overwhelmingly.

PROPOSITION ONE: INCARCERATION REDUCES THE HUMAN CAPITAL OF IMPRISONED INDIVIDUALS AND THEIR FAMILIES

Human capital refers to the human skills and resources individuals need to function effectively, such as reading, writing, and reasoning ability. It is the capital individuals acquire through education and training for productive purposes (Hagan 1994). Labor force participation, then, is both an indication of human capital and a producer of human capital. A central component of research on the urban underclass addresses the relationship of residents in extremely poor neighborhoods to work. Here, we add to this discussion consideration of how incarceration impacts the ability of individuals and their families to work.

Wilson's research on the urban underclass (1987, 1996)—pivotal in the debate on poverty—is illustrative of the changes that have occurred in poor, urban communities since the 1960s. He describes these communities as characterized by "joblessness, lawlessness, low-achieving schools" and increasing isolation from mainstream society (1987, 58). Wilson views these changes in urban life as the result of a racial division of labor in which poor blacks increasingly are disadvantaged and left without jobs. It is the impact of joblessness on social dislocations (family structure, teen pregnancy, welfare dependency, and crime), which is crucial to understanding the underclass (see also McGahey 1986).

Severely impoverished communities are hit hardest by problems associated with poverty. This occurs because, though social problems increase as neighborhood quality decreases, they do not increase at a constant rate. Rather, a jump in the extent of problems occurs when the percentage of workers holding high-status jobs drops to approximately 4 percent (Crane 1991).

Though there is some research that supports the idea that joblessness has increased (Jencks 1991), other research (Tienda and Stier 1991) provides little evidence that the type of joblessness specifically attributed to the culture of poverty, "shiftlessness," has, in fact, increased. In their study, Tienda and Stier (1991) find that unemployment is pervasive, but shiftlessness is not. To the extent that incarceration is a significant catalyst that damages the capacity of individuals to find employment, it is a factor that contributes to the continuation of an underclass.

In one of the more disturbing portraits of street criminality, Fleisher (1995) describes the lives of petty criminals and the cycles of despair experienced by persistent offenders. The men whose world he describes are shiftless in the most extreme sense, occupying a place that seems orthogonal to legitimate society. They are in and out of prison and jail, and each incarceration period is typically followed by a further spiral into the street life of substance addiction and pugnacious criminality. Fleisher does not make the following point, but his data do: Periods of imprisonment provide breaks in the bleakness of offenders' lives, but the net effect of the incarceration is further damage to their capacity to function in regular society. These men return to areas of the city where others like them also live, and they add to the numbers living in the street. Thus, at the aggregate level, incarceration serves as the key link in a chain of human decapitalization by concentrating ever-larger numbers of men of reduced capacity in already undercapitalized areas.

Many who engage in intermittent, instrumental criminality, however, are also involved in the world of work. Fagan's (1999) exhaustive review of legal and illegal work illustrates that it is simplistic to view offenders as solely illegally employed. Research shows that many, if not most, criminals also have legal employment. In local areas where a high proportion of residents engage in both legal and illegal work, Fagan notes that removing many individuals can impair the local economy. In large numbers, it removes supplies of local human capital and leaves a gap in employable residents. The result is that numerous household units suffer specific losses and the community suffers a net loss. Even families that reap the individual benefit of newly available employment (due to a vacancy created by an offender being incarcerated) suffer the costs of depleted neighborhood economic strength.

Imprisonment also affects the prisoner's level of human capital directly. Grogger (1995) demonstrated that merely being arrested has a short-term, negative impact on earnings, while Freeman (1992) has shown that suffering a conviction and imprisonment has a permanent impact on earning potential. Individuals suffering from insufficient supplies of human capital are destined to low-level jobs that not only pay poorly but also offer no vision for the future. Individuals whose jobs hold no future have less of a stake in conformity and are more likely to engage in criminal activity (Crutchfield 1997). Experience with the criminal justice system, then, contributes to the very inequality in economic means that promotes street crime in the first place (Braithwaite 1979). Thus, the criminal justice system leaves economic scars on its clients long after its formal involvement in their lives has ended. With the number of incarcerated juvenile offenders growing at a pace now similar to that of adults (Clear and Cole 2000), these deleterious effects appear ever earlier into the lives of inner-city males.

In addition, to the extent incarceration primarily removes young men from the neighborhood, it also increases the likelihood of single-parent families being headed by women. Recent research (Browne 1997) shows that long-term exposure to welfare, lack of work experience, and having never been married characterize disarticulation from mainstream society for women: a condition contributing to earning differences between black and white women. Thus, large-scale incarceration of men may influence the earning power of the women they leave behind. For example, Farkas, England, Vicknair, and Kilbourne (1997) recently found that differences in cognitive skills (human capital) explain a large part of the pay differences between ethnic groups. They conclude that these differences arise largely from social sources such as school, family, and neighborhood experiences.

These effects are limited to disorganized areas. One reason incarceration has a less deleterious (or even positive) impact on socially organized areas is that most individuals from these areas who are incarcerated have more human capital to begin with. Thus, the loss of this resource these individuals experience is insufficient to incapacitate them after their release, since individuals with an adequate supply of human capital can withstand the attack they sustain from incarceration. Indeed, there are many instances where individuals (such as some notorious white-collar criminals) return to mainstream society from prison nearly as capable of functioning in society as they were before. Some even capitalize on their experiences (for example, by writing books and becoming public speakers), turning it into more human capital.

PROPOSITION TWO: INCARCERATION DISRUPTS LOCAL SOCIAL TIES AND NETWORKS IN THE COMMUNITY AND REDUCES THE SOCIAL CAPITAL AVAILABLE TO THAT AREA

In the search to explain spatial variation in crime rates, social disorganization theorists have explored the structural characteristics associated with crime. Shaw and McKay's (1942) social disorganization theory and more recent work done by Bursik (1986, 1988), Sampson (1985, 1986a, 1986b, 1986c, 1987, 1988) and others focus on group adaptations to social processes such as urbanization and shifting patterns of economic growth, rather than concentrating on individual criminality. The essence of this theory is that some communities are unable to self-regulate effectively because of the damaging effects of certain environmental characteristics.

Disorganized communities are unable to realize the common values of their residents and are unable to solve commonly experienced problems (Kornhauser 1978) because they cannot establish or maintain consensus concerning values, norms, roles, or hierarchical arrangements among their members (Kornhauser 1978; Shaw and McKay 1942). As a control theory, social disorganization theory assumes that one common goal residents in all neighborhoods share is the desire to live in an area that is safe to inhabit (Bursik and Grasmick 1993, 15). We assume *all* residents share in this, since even offenders do not wish to be victimized.

Researchers working within this theoretical domain have focused their efforts on identifying which ecological conditions are most associated with crime. Recently, attempts have been made to explore the "black box" of disorganization. Sampson (1987) and Sampson and Groves (1989) have investigated the mediating effects of guardianship, community attachment, and informal social control. They have shown that integration and social ties are important mediators between social conditions and crime. For instance, Sampson (1988) finds that integration, a function of individuals' local friendships, attachment to the community, and participation in local activities, fosters participation that fosters deeper integration.

Whereas these scholars focus their efforts on identifying dimensions of control, Bursik and Grasmick (1993) have identified different levels of control. They merge systemic and social disorganization theories to examine the mediating role of private, parochial, and public controls. Bursik and Grasmick's extension of disorganization theory shows how ecological factors influence different levels of control. Social control, they argue, represents an effort by neighborhood residents to regulate the behavior of both locals and outsiders to achieve the goal of a safe living environment.

These efforts by Sampson (1987), Sampson and Groves (1989), and Bursik and Grasmick (1993) highlight the significance of networks in neighborhood control of antisocial behaviors. Sampson and Groves primarily focus their efforts on components of the primary and parochial levels. They recognize that the extent to which individual residents are integrated and tied to the neighborhood influences its capacity to self-regulate. Conversely, when residents' ties are attenuated, when they feel anonymous and isolated, local control is difficult to achieve. Social control becomes compromised because there is a lack of community interaction and shared obligation. As a result, the community is weakened and can no longer intervene on its own behalf (Sampson 1987). Bursik and Grasmick add to this the idea that public control plays a role in neighborhood regulation to the extent that relations between the community and the state determine the type and quality of services and resources provided. To these arguments, we (Rose and Clear 1998b) added the point that networks of interaction between the community and the state influence the community's receptivity to coercive controls and determine whether they have a largely cooperative or adversarial relationship.

Social disorganization theory is implicitly based upon the notion of social and human capital, even if the terms have not been explicitly adopted. Social capital refers to the social skills and resources needed to effect positive change in neighborhood life. It is the aspect of structured groups that increases the capacity for action oriented toward the achievement of group goals (Hagan 1994). Goals are accomplished by transforming resources gathered in one forum, for one purpose, into resources for another forum and for another purpose (Coleman 1988). Social capital is the essence of social control, for it is the very force collectives draw upon to enforce order. It is what enables groups to enforce norms and, as a result, to increase their level of informal control. Disorganized communities, then, suffer from high rates of crime and other negative conditions partly because they have insufficient supplies of social capital.

Social capital works by facilitating certain actions and constraining others. It stems from a sense of trust and obligation created through interaction among community members and serves to reinforce a set of prescriptive norms. Thus, social capital effectively unites individuals within a neighborhood, thereby initiating and enhancing a sense of collectivity (Coleman 1988). High levels of social capital augment the community's capacity to sanction transgressors. In communities with large supplies of social capital, adolescents are encouraged to complete their education, are discouraged from stealing cars, and are sanctioned appropriately in informal and intimate relationships. Sampson and Laub (1993) concluded that social investment (or social capital) in institutional relationships is a central component of the salience of informal social control at the individual level. They found that trajectories of crime and deviance could be modified by the bonds that serve as a basis for social capital: families, jobs, and neighborhood organizations. Other studies show that over the long term, factors such as marriage can be inhibiting forces that provide incentive for offenders to desist (Laub, Nagin, and Sampson 1998).

The strength of social bonds and the web of social relationships are important sources of control within the community (Kornhauser 1978, 45). Thus, social interaction is important for local social control (Bellair 1997). Other studies focusing on parochial control (for example, Elliott et al. 1996; Taylor 1997) highlight the importance of social support networks and other forms of neighborhood bonding.

It is tempting to think that removing offenders from communities would increase the conditions necessary for social capital to thrive. Social capital requires (and fosters) a common set of norms and values. Removing people who violate these norms should result in safer neighborhoods. The problem is that social capital is not simply built upon normative consensus but, more important, requires a solid framework of social networks and ties. These networks and ties are disrupted by incarceration.

In small doses, incarceration disruptions are few. In large doses, however, the impact can undermine social control because incarceration disrupts not only the network ties of offenders, but those of their families and friends too. For instance, disrupted network ties that limit access to noncash resources have been shown to be a primary determinant of whether women are working or on welfare (Edin and Lein 1997). Thus, incarcerating men who play a role in the lives of poor women debilitates those women, too. Ethnographic studies of the young, inner-city males (Decker and Van Winkle 1996; Hagedorn 1988; Sullivan 1989; Vankatesh 1997) who make up the bulk of the offending population there show that these men play substantial economic roles in their families' and associates' lives. Even gang members have been shown to have both positive and negative effects on their communities. For instance, Vankatesh (1997) reported that although many problems within the housing project he studied were gang-related, gang members were accepted there because they contributed to the well-being of the community in a variety of ways—by providing security and material assistance to residents, for example. Removing these individuals from the community, then, removes their role as neighborhood assets as well as their role as deficits.

Incarcerating a large proportion of the adult males in a community over time also decreases the human and social capital of those left behind. After a male's imprisonment, the responses of the jailed inmate's family to his incarceration include going onto welfare; moving into more cramped quarters and new school districts; family disruption, including the arrival of new male roles into the family, replacing the inmate; and reduced time for maternal parenting due to taking secondary employment. All these factors are potentially disruptive forces for the family, and each tends to disturb family cohesiveness, which studies show predicts serious delinquency (Sampson 1987). And these types of family disruptions also have been shown to reduce the capacity of informal social controls systems and increase the likelihood of crime (Horney, Osgood, and Marshall 1995).

At some point in the process of removing males from the local areas, the sheer numbers add up and begin to matter. Single mothers who seek companions and co-parents are forced to compete for someone from a shrinking pool of eligibles, perhaps most of whom offer limited human capital as a consequence of previous experiences with incarceration and life in impoverished communities. The chance of having a critical core of politically effective citizens who have sufficient time and support for political activity is reduced. A reduction in the number of men available for parenting reduces the overall capacity for supervision of children in that neighborhood. There are fewer able bodies to work on local tasks such as maintaining property and generating economic activity. The point we emphasize is that men and women who commit crimes are not islands. Every person bound for prison lives in a network of associations and interdependencies. When that person is removed, the network must replace that person's functions within it, or become weaker. When large numbers are removed in a repeated pattern, the capacity to restore the viability of the networks is severely hampered, if for no other reason than because of sheer numbers.

Our argument derives support from a study by Warner and Rountree (1997) that demonstrated the importance of local social ties in mediating between ecological conditions and crime. They found that the existence of local social ties decreased assault rates for predominantly white neighborhoods, but not for predominantly black and/or minority neighborhoods. This result shows that within the context of severe neighborhood deterioration, local social ties lose their ability to serve an informal social control function. One of the explanations is that the social ties in these disadvantaged neighborhoods are thin and fragmented, partly due to the disruption caused by severe levels of male migration to and from the prison. It may be that in socially disorganized areas there is relatively little variation in the strength of social ties because they already have been severely diminished, with incarceration being one of the reasons.

PROPOSITION THREE: DECREASES IN HUMAN AND SOCIAL CAPITAL LEAD, NONRECURSIVELY, TO AN INCREASE IN SOCIAL ISOLATION FROM MAINSTREAM SOCIETY AND INSTITUTIONS FOR BOTH INDIVIDUALS AND THEIR COMMUNITIES

One conclusion that can be drawn from the research on the urban underclass is that people are more likely to conform to mainstream norms and values when they have the skills, incentives, and opportunities to do so. This is not to say that individual proclivities for crime would be completely eradicated if offenders lived in communities rich in human and social capital. The existence of white-collar crime and random acts of violence demonstrates that offenders exist even in those communities. It is to say, however, that communities with adequate supplies of these forms of capital produce fewer offenders. What happens in disorganized communities is that residents' lives become increasingly attenuated from mainstream social institutions, with the exception of those operated by the state for purposes of social control. As the distance grows between conventional aspirations and realistic possibilities, those who live in disorganized places find themselves disconnected from the main economic and social processes of the world outside their local area.

Social isolation, then, is the link between human and social capital and crime, since isolation decreases opportunities for conventional behavior and rewards and increases incentives for alternative lifestyles and cultures. This is the point Decker and Van Winkle (1996) make in their study of gangs. Their main point is that individuals choose to join gangs as a functional way to manage threat in their lives. Decker and Van Winkle also show that the threat gangs pose to community residents increases gang members' social isolation and reduces their chances and opportunities for leaving the gang. Moreover, the parents of gang members lose their moral sway over their teenagers because of their own deficit of human and social capital. Because these parents are unable to provide the monetary, social, and intellectual resources necessary for their children to manage the threat that exists in their lives or to become successful in mainstream society, children's strategic bonds to peers strengthen and parental attempts at discipline and control eventually go unheeded. Thus, children whose parents cannot help them successfully navigate school and other social institutions (increasingly the criminal justice system) eventually drop out of the pretense of conventional lifestyles. Children whose parents cannot provide spending money turn to alternative sources of income. Children whose parents have reaped few social rewards from hard work see no point in following their parents' example. In combination, the deficit in human and social capital creates incentives for alternative lifestyle choices, at the same time that it decreases the ability of families and neighbors to function as agents of informal social control. The net result is a social environment in which youngsters turn to a social institution that, to them, seems to work: gangs.

The absence of large numbers of adult males, who are incarcerated, also feeds isolation from conventional civic life for those they leave behind and damages the families who remain. Single mothers who may work off-hour shifts in service employment may find it harder to attend teacher-parent meetings after school. Schools that experience limited parental involvement find it harder to be relevant to students' lives and interests. The absence of fathers and other male relatives who might provide supervision of adolescents is also a source of isolation of those adolescents from adult role models. Increasingly, as young black men are more and more marginalized through their declining ability to participate effectively in the labor market, they become less desirable as fathers and marital partners. A version of this argument sometimes referred to as the Darity-Myers thesis points to the growing gap between a managerial society and the readiness of inner-city black men for positions in it (Darity and Myers 1994). The result is increasing social marginalization of black men, of which incarceration is considered one factor. The impact on families is important, too. Mothers who seek adult partners are forced to compete in a declining pool of suitable prospects, and those prospects have less incentive to commit to any particular family group (see Tucker and Mitchell-Kernan 1995). Thus, social isolation leads to further deficits in human and social capital in a nonrecursive system.

If anything, damage to the parenting of affected families is even more marked when mothers are incarcerated. While the number of black mothers removed for incarceration is not nearly as large as that of black fathers, black women are still more than seven times more likely to be incarcerated than white women (Bonczar and Beck 1997), and some researchers estimate profoundly negative effects occur to children of incarcerated mothers (Baunach 1985). Even when the numbers are relatively small the effects can be significant due to the concentrations of women incarcerated from neighborhoods with high incarceration rates of men. In the New York City data presented earlier, for example, it may be that as many as one in fifty mother-aged women went to prison or jail in 1998.[2]

At the community level, a lack of human and social capital means that residents do not have the capacity to secure resources from mainstream society. In the systemic model of social control developed by Bursik and Grasmick (1993), it is the interrelationship among community institutions and between community organizations and outside agencies that draws upon and produces social capital. The density of these types of networks is differentially distributed across neighborhoods. This model explains how areas with well-developed networks are able to acquire externally based goods and services that enhance their ability to fight crime locally. Conversely, communities without such programs may not have extensive connections to the wider community or may not know how to obtain external funding and other necessary resources.

In addition, most successful neighborhood programs build upon existing networks (Bursik and Grasmick 1993), and strong networks are indicative of large supplies of social capital. For instance, community action requires a process of social learning in which residents develop the skills and knowledge necessary to engage in collective problem solving. Since much of the local action taken requires connections with outside agencies, a level of cooperative relations needs to be developed and policies and regulations learned (Bennett 1995). Therefore, communities that successfully organize are those that are able to manufacture and maintain social capital. Those that are unable to successfully organize increasingly become more isolated.

The political capacity of the community is particularly important for communities that need to increase their external resources (Bennett 1995). In other words, while communities vary in their desire and capacity to organize, whether or not a community is able to organize partly is a function of the extent to which the neighborhood has developed a network of political and social institutions (Henig 1982). Minority communities are characterized by doubts about the formal social control agencies at work within them; for instance, African Americans are far more likely to disapprove of the police, the courts, and severe penal sentences than are whites (Rose and Clear 1998a), reflecting a sense of alienation and isolation from the work of the state agencies. Since most offenders come from communities significantly isolated from most mainstream institutions, their experiences with the criminal justice system take on exaggerated importance, as there are few other institutional experiences to counterbalance this one. Therefore, to the extent these experiences are negative, incarceration increases dissatisfaction with and isolation from important social institutions, further damaging their sense of civic justice.

Exposure to prison through a loved one or acquaintance also leads to more negative attitudes toward the justice system, because when faced with a conflict between agents of the state and close associates or family, people tend to take the side of the party with whom they are more intimate. They know that person's history, and they can evaluate the person's problem—even if it is a crime problem—with some sympathy. They may also tend to view the unsympathetic, bureaucratic actions of the law in negative terms. If contact with the formal justice system—either personally or indirectly—might be expected to lead to a more negative view of that system, on the average, this is a particularly concentrated effect in high-crime neighborhoods where nearly everyone has such contact personally or through a family member or friend.

The negative view of the justice system leads to a kind of civic isolation, in which the workings of the state are seen as alien forces to be avoided rather than services to be employed. It is not easy for communities dominated by civic doubt to become effective politically. Social isolation, then, increases as residents in disadvantaged communities become more disenchanted with the state and with political processes in general. As a result, they become less adept at operating as civic citizens and more removed from the civic community, where egalitarian political relations, a social fabric of trust, and cooperation are the norm (Putnam 1993, 15). Since differences in the quality of the civic community are linked to political institutional success, disorganized communities become more disadvantaged as they become increasingly less able to shape relations between their community and broader society, as well as less effective at self-regulating through local institutions. Therefore, to the extent the experience of incarceration delegitimates social institutions in particular and political activism in general, it undermines the capacity and willingness of individuals to engage in civic citizenry. To the extent that high rates of incarceration tend to promote social isolation, they help to produce a localized ethic of isolation that makes neighborhoods less capable of sustaining quality of life.

The idea that deficits in human and social capital produce social isolation, which, in turn, produces more deficits in human and social capital, is embedded in a research tradition that has begun to move beyond simple recursive models of crime to incorporate the non-recursive or systemic features of the phenomenon. For the most part, work on non-recursive models has dealt with the causes and effects of crime. For instance, Cook (1986) describes a "feedback loop" in which individuals limit their exposure to potential victimization as a result of their assessment of the likelihood of being victimized; in doing so, they reduce the number of criminal opportunities. Skogan (1986, 1990) argues that higher levels of crime increase fear, which results in psychological and physical withdrawal from the neighborhood. This in turn weakens informal control, damages the organizational life and mobilization capacity of the community, and deteriorates business conditions, all of which leads to more crime. Our argument is that communities lacking in human and social capital become increasingly socially isolated, and in socially isolated communities, it is difficult to gain these forms of capital. Any factor that affects one aspect of the system affects other aspects too.

DISCUSSION AND CONCLUSION

Popular crime policy presents offenders as though they live in isolation from their immediate environments—disconnected from the people around them except as crime-prone deficits in their lives—and yet directly responsive to the dominant, mainstream political and social policies about crime (this logic is the essence of deterrence theory). We would, instead, urge adoption of a view of offenders as living lives encased in exactly opposite forms of relationships: deeply embedded in their immediate worlds as both resources and deficits and largely separated from the remote world of legislative and penal policy. The cumulative effects of the criminal law are felt more in the way it alters the positive and negative contributions of offenders to their immediate environments by removing them from where they live than by the way it changes how offenders act in those environments.

The nature of high-crime environments must be understood as both fragile and complex. They are fragile in that the networks on which social capital are built are typically thin and vulnerable. They are complex in that offenders serve multiple roles within them—as parents, providers, and supports as well as victimizers and exploiters. Crime policy that targets individual offenders intervenes into these fragile and complex environments.

Policy makers hope for a systemic, positive effect: By increasing incarceration in response to crime, they hope to promote a social structure that inhibits crime. By making convictions costly to offenders, they hope to discourage crime through deterrence. Little attention is paid to the way these interventions affect the structure of community life in high-crime locations, by altering the fragile relations that exist within them.

The impact incarceration has on community structure is a function of the interaction between the rate of incarceration and the level of community social organization. In highly organized communities with low crime rates, incarceration positively affects the social structure, including mechanisms that promote human and social capital and decrease social isolation. In highly disorganized communities, however, the opposite occurs.

As a direct attempt to control crime, incarceration is a weak intervention into this system of relationships. The incapacitative and deterrent effects of incarceration have been the subject of substantial research. Reliable studies estimate that incapacitative effects are quite small (Spelman 1994; Zimring and Hawkins 1995), and the effects of increasing the prison populations further promise dramatically decreasing returns (Canelo-Cacho, Blumstein, and Cohen 1997). Studies of the deterrent impacts of imprisonment are not more promising (Blumstein 1978). The reasons for the limited impact of incarceration on crime have to do with criminal replacement effects and the crime-age curve (Canelo-Cacho, Blumstein, and Cohen 1997; Reiss 1988). The reasons for weak deterrence have to do with the very limited way imprisonment changes the reward structure of inner-city street life for young males (Decker and Van Winkle 1996).

In addition, the prison experience does not produce much in the way of positive change, on the average (Myers 1980). While popular discourse about incarceration almost always includes some discussion of its positive effect on individuals through rehabilitation and on community residents through deterrence, these effects are not the norm. Most prisoners return to their communities less capable of contributing to their local society than when they left, and in areas of high rates of incarceration, community residents are hardened to the deterrence of imprisonment. In this light, it becomes clear how incarceration can positively impact human and social capital in one neighborhood while negatively impacting it in another. Furthermore, it is a commonly held belief that people who interact with a social institution frequently will become more masterful at maneuvering through it. However, this idea that frequent offenders are adept at "working the system" is not supported by some research. Decker and Van Winkle (1996) find that gang members whose interaction with the criminal justice system increases as their interaction with other social institutions decreases, are profoundly uninformed about its workings. Further association with the criminal justice system does little to increase their knowledge about it.

The weak impact of incarceration on individual criminal proclivities must be contrasted with the multiple ways in which removing large numbers of residents from socially disorganized places affects the complex and fragile social structure that exists there. When an adult is removed, the children and partners are affected, economic dependents suffer losses, and the commitment to mainstream political life is reduced for those who remain. When the incarcerated adult returns a couple of years later, he adds his own damaged human capital to an area already deficient in building blocks for social capital. When a young adult is removed, these processes begin earlier and last longer.

Our argument is that incarceration is not merely an intervention into individual lives of specific offenders. Because incarceration is such a powerful intervention—it removes people from their natural settings—it must also be seen as an intervention into the settings from which those people hail. These settings have, or lack, the resources needed to sustain a community quality of life that includes, in part, public safety. So long as the focus is only on what the offender might have done *criminally* had he not been removed, the answer can only be that public safety is enhanced by his removal. But once we consider the offender's relationship to an interplay of networks that have to do with public safety and social control, the picture becomes much more complicated. These offenders are not solely drains on the local capacity for social control, they also occupy support roles in familial, economic, and political systems that have important implications for informal social control. In particular, their removal serves to further isolate those who remain from the social control supports that might strengthen community social capital.

We recognize this is not the kind of model most people use when they think about crime policy. Americans are used to thinking in straightforward cause-effect terms: increase public confidence in criminal justice by punishing the guilty; prevent crime by locking people up. This is an individualistic view of the world, inferring that people who do bad are only and always bad. We have sufficient data from the last quarter century to question the wisdom of this model: the incarcerated population has gone from 350,000 to nearly two million, and crime rates—which are down in recent years—are still higher today than they were when the prison expansion began in the early 1970s (Mauer 1999).

Our analysis provides one reason why an historically unprecedented change in penal policy can have had so little impact on crime. Crime is changed little, because the small doses of incapacitation and deterrence that penal policy produces are counterbalanced by moderate damage to the social capital of disorganized neighborhoods, thus promoting more crime.

In effect, we see a deep conflict between two orientations in crime policy. Criminal justice orientations emphasize individual accountability for crime, with the result of increasingly harsh punishments that, operating at very high levels in high-crime communities, spread unintended negative consequences for local informal social control. This approach might be contrasted with what might be called a "community safety" ideal that would focus not on individual offenders but on the quality of community life in which crimes occur. This alternative would seek to understand individual accountability for criminal acts within a broader concern for the places and the other people who live in those places who are affected by crime and justice policies.

If our analysis is correct, even in part, it raises a profound and urgent question about contemporary penal policy: What should we be doing instead of today's emphasis on the prison? The irony, as Randall Kennedy (1998) has pointed out, is that the same inner-city communities whose members suffer the broad-scale indignities of arrest, prosecution, and incarceration at the hands of the justice system are precisely the places most in need of programs that improve public safety. There is not enough space here to develop a full model for a different form of justice, though others are writing on this topic (see Clear and Karp 1999). We can identify three themes for a more effective penal policy that our analysis suggests need to be emphasized if a more effective policy model is to be developed. Here we will summarize each.

1. *We should emphasize crime policies that produce social capital for high-crime areas.* Sampson and his colleagues (Sampson, Raudenbush, and Earls 1998) have coined the term *collective efficacy* to refer to the capacity of residents in some Chicago neighborhoods to come together in ways that promote informal social control. This overarching term refers to a collective sentiment among neighbors living in close proximity to one another that leads to collective behalf in the common good, especially as regards public order. Collective efficacy also is the ability to attain that common good. When we think about strategies that would promote public safety without the damaging effects of high levels of incarceration, we are referring to strategies that might promote "collective efficacy" among residents. How would this occur?

To begin with, it is important to note that a great deal of money is spent on today's crime policies, and most of that expenditure is concentrated in high-crime areas. An organization in New York City (CASES 1998) has estimated that in East New York alone, $50 million is spent on criminally processing the citizens there—$3 million *on a single block*. The dramatic point is that almost all of this money goes to local criminal justice officials—mostly corrections workers in state prison facilities—who live well outside the East New York community. This represents enormous disinvestment in crime problems in East New York, especially since the net effect is to remove the citizens for months at a time and then to return them as damaged human capital to be absorbed in the already weakened community.

A policy sensitive to social capital in East New York would call for spending a greater portion of the existing crime policy dollars in that neighborhood. Justice practices would be local, investing resources locally and focusing on local problems. Instead of finding new dollars to spend on the social organization of East New York, existing expenditures would be reengineered to be a part of the local economy and, by extension, local networks of informal social control.

2. *We should develop penal policies that strengthen the positive contributions of offenders to their social networks.* Removing offenders from their neighborhoods not only removes their actual contributions to informal social control networks, but removes their potential contributions as well. In contrast, we can imagine a social policy in which offenders would be required, as a part of their sentences, to help improve the infrastructure of the local areas by working on renovation projects, performing support roles in social services strapped for volunteer assistance, and providing restitution to crime victims and their families.

High-crime neighborhoods have numerous needs. There is an insufficient stock of reasonable housing, many physical structures are in need of repair, social programs for young people and the elderly lack staff, streets are littered, and recreational areas need attention. Using offenders to provide this sort of labor not only strengthens the underlying social network but also links the offenders more closely to their pro-social functions.

3. *We should concentrate crime prevention efforts on approaches that enable local networks to remain intact.* There would be an added benefit to using offenders in the fashion we have identified: they could continue to serve roles of parent and partner, providing economic and interpersonal support to children and others to whom they are intimately connected. This would be true even for offenders who are under some form of confinement locally, for they could have regular and variable contact with those in the community on whom they will rely for future community adjustment.

There would be a dual benefit to such an approach. The public visibility of the sanction would reinforce social norms. Citizens would know that lawbreaking has consequences, because those consequences would be more visible to the general community. At the same time, the ability of the offender to sustain ties to local supports would help the bonds to family and friends stay strong—and these are the bonds that will be needed to support successful return to community life.

We conclude by noting that our very unconventional line of inquiry flows from very conventional theoretical arguments. For instance, Shaw and McKay (1942) posited that residential mobility negatively impacted communities because it disrupted network ties, neighborhood stability, and the development and maintenance of consensus regarding norms and values. Of course, Shaw and McKay were witnessing voluntary mobility, when neighborhood residents moved to better communities when they were able. We have outlined similar effects from incarceration: a form of involuntary residential mobility. Hirschi's social bonding theory (1969) shows how important attachment, commitment, involvement, and belief are to preventing delinquency. We have shown that incarceration can attenuate ties and attachment to others, hinder commitment to conventional goals, and undermine belief in the mainstream social order. Finally, Merton (1939) put forth the idea that when conventional goals are accepted but conventional means are blocked, people are more likely to turn to crime. We have shown how incarceration makes conventional means more unattainable by decreasing human and social capital and by increasing social isolation. Furthermore, these outcomes affect not only the individuals who are incarcerated, but their friends and relatives, too.

NOTES

1. Data were provided by CASES, Inc., New York, NY.
2. This estimate is derived from applying the national rate of seven male inmates for each female inmate to the rates of removal of males in the aforementioned Council Districts.

REFERENCES

Anderson, Elijah. (1990). *Streetwise: Race, Class and Change in an Urban Community.* Chicago: University of Chicago Press.
Baunach, Phyllis Jo. (1985). *Mothers in Prison.* New Brunswick, NJ: Transaction.
Beck, Alan J. (1997). "Growth, Change, and Stability in the U.S. Prison Population, 1980–1995." *Corrections Management Quarterly* 1(2): 1–14.
Beckett, Kathryn. (1997). *Making Crime Pay.* New York: Oxford.
Bellair, Paul E. (1997). "A Social Interaction and Community Crime: Examining the Importance of Neighbor Networks." *Criminology* 35(4): 677–703.
Bennett, Susan F. (1995). "Community Organizations and Crime." *Annals of the American Academy of Political and Social Science* 539: 72–84.
Black, Donald. (1976). *The Behavior of Law.* New York: Academic Press.
Blumstein, Albert (ed). (1978). *Deterrence and Incapacitation: Estimating the Effects of Criminal Sanctions on Crime Rates.* Washington, DC: National Research Council.
Blumstein, Albert, and Jacqueline Cohen. (1973). "A Theory of the Stability of Punishment." *Journal of Criminal Law and Criminology* 64: 198–207.
Bonczar, Thomas P., and Allen J. Beck. (1997). "Lifetime Likelihood of Going to State or Federal Prison." Washington, DC: U.S. Department of Justice. March.
Braithwaite, John. (1979). *Inequality, Crime and Public Policy.* London: Routledge and Kegan Paul.
Browne, Irene. (1997). "The Black-White Gap in Labor Force Participation among Women." *American Sociological Review* 62(2): 236–252.
Bureau of Justice Statistics Reports. (1995). *Prisoners in 1994.* Washington, DC: U.S. Department of Justice.
Bursik, Robert J., Jr. (1988). "Social Disorganization and Theories of Crime and Delinquency: Problems and Prospects." *Criminology* 26: 519–551.
Bursik, Robert J., Jr. (1986). "Ecological Stability and the Dynamics of Delinquency," in Albert J. Reiss, Jr., and Michael Tonry (eds.), *Communities and Crime.* Chicago: University of Chicago Press.
Bursik, Robert J., Jr., and Harold G. Grasmick. (1993). *Neighborhoods and Crime: The Dimensions of Effective Community Control.* New York: Lexington Books.
Canelo-Cacho, Jose, Alfred Blumstein, and Jacqueline Cohen. (1997). "Relationship between the Offending Frequency of Imprisoned and Free Offenders." *Criminology* 35(1): 133–176.

CASES [Center for Alternative Sentencing and Employment Services]. (1999). *Demonstrating the Uses of Mapping in Corrections: A Proposal to the National Institute of Justice.* A research proposal submitted by CASES of New York City to NIJ [National Institute of Justice], November 13, 1999.

CASES. (1998). *A Proposal for Community Justice Centers.* New York: CASES, May 29.

Clear, Todd R. (1994). *Harm in American Penology: Offenders, Victims, and Their Communities.* Albany, NY: State University of New York Press.

Clear, Todd R., and George F. Cole. (2000). *American Corrections.* Belmont, CA: Wadsworth.

Clear, Todd R., and David R. Karp. (1999). *The Community Justice Ideal: Preventing Crime and Achieving Justice.* Boulder, CO: Westview Law and Society Series.

Coleman, James. (1988). "Social Capital and the Creation of Human Capital." *American Journal of Sociology* 94 (Supplement): S95–S120.

Cook, Philip J. (1986). "The Demand and Supply of Criminal Opportunities," in Michael Tonry and Norval Morris (eds.), *Crime and Justice: An Annual Review of Research*, Vol. 7. Chicago: University of Chicago Press, pp. 1–27.

Crane, Jonathan. (1991). "The Epidemic Theory of Ghettos and Neighborhood Effects on Dropping Out and Teenage Childbearing." *American Journal of Sociology* 96: 1126–1259.

Crutchfield, Robert. (1997). "Labor Markets, Employment, and Crime." *Research Preview.* Washington, DC: United States Department of Justice.

Darity, William A., Jr., and Samuel L. Myers, Jr., with Emmett D. Carson and William Sabol (eds.). (1994). *The Black Underclass: Critical Essays on Race and Unwantedness.* New York: Garland Publishing.

Decker, Scott H., and Barrik Van Winkle. (1996). *Life in the Gang: Family, Friends and Violence.* New York: Cambridge University Press.

DiIulio, John. (2000). "A Moratorium on Prison Population Growth." Research in progress presentation to the National Institute of Justice, April 19.

DiIulio, John. (1990). *Crime and Punishment in Wisconsin: A Survey of Prisoners.* Madison: Wisconsin Policy Research Institute (November).

Edin, Kathryn, and Laura Lein. (1997). "Work, Welfare and Single Mothers' Economic Survival Strategies." *American Sociological Review* 62(2): 253–266.

Elliott, Delbert S., William Julius Wilson, David Huizinga, Robert J. Sampson, Amanda Elliott, and Bruce Rankin. (1996). "The Effects of Neighborhood Disadvantage on Adolescent Development." *Journal of Research on Crime and Delinquency* 33(4): 389–426.

Fagan, Jeffrey. (1999). "Legal and Illegal Work: Crime, Work and Unemployment," in Burton Weisbrod and James Worthy (eds.), *Dealing with Urban Crises.* Evanston: Northwestern University Press.

Farkas, George, Paula England, Keven Vicknair, and Barbara Stanek Kilbourne. (1997). "Cognitive Skill, Skill Demands of Jobs, and Earnings among Young European American, African American, and Mexican American Workers." *Social Forces* 75(3): 913–940.

Fleisher, Mark S. (1995). *Beggars and Thieves: Lives of Urban Street Criminals.* Madison: University of Wisconsin Press.

Freeman, Richard B. (1992). "Crime and Unemployment of Disadvantaged Youth," in Adele Harrell and George Petson (eds.), *Drugs, Crime and Social Isolation: Barriers to Urban Opportunity.* Washington, DC: Urban Institute.

Glaser, Daniel. (1964). *The Effectiveness of a Prison and Parole System*. Indianapolis, IN: Bobbs-Merrill Co.

Grogger, Jeffrey. (1995). "The Effect of Arrests on the Employment and Earnings of Young Men." *Quarterly Journal of Economics* 110(1): 51–71.

Hagan, John. (1994). *Crime and Disrepute*. Thousand Oaks, CA: Pine Forge Press.

Hagan, John, Hans Merkens, and Klaus Boehnke. (1995). "Delinquency and Disdain: Social Capital and the Control of Right-Wing Extremism among East and West Berlin Youth." *American Journal of Sociology* 100(4): 1028–1052.

Hagedorn, John M. (1988). *People and Folks: Gangs, Crime and the Underclass in a Rust-belt City*. Chicago: Lake View Press.

Henig, Jeffrey R. (1982). *Neighborhood Mobilization: Redevelopment and Response*. New Brunswick, NJ: Rutgers University Press.

Hirschi, Travis. (1969). *The Causes of Delinquency*. Berkeley: University of California.

Horney, Julie, D. Wayne Osgood, and Ineke H. Marshall. (1995). "Criminal Careers in the Short-Term: Intra-individual Variability in Crime and Its Relation to Local Life Circumstances." *American Sociological Review* 60: 655–673.

Jencks, Christopher. (1991). "Is the American Underclass Growing?" in Christopher Jencks and Paul E. Peterson (eds.), *The Urban Underclass*. Washington, DC: Brookings Institute.

Kennedy, Randall. (1998). *Race, Crime, and the Law*. New York: Pantheon.

Kornhauser, Ruth Rosner. (1978). *Social Sources of Delinquency: An Appraisal of Analytic Models*. Chicago, IL: University of Chicago Press.

Laub, John, Daniel S. Nagin, and Robert J. Sampson (1998). "Good Marriages and Trajectories of Change in Criminal Offending." *American Sociological Review* 63: 225–238.

Lynch, James P., and William J. Sabol. (1997). *Did Getting Tougher on Crime Pay? Crime Policy Report*. Washington, DC: Urban Institute State Policy Center.

Mauer, Marc. (1999). *Race to Incarcerate*. Washington, DC: The Sentencing Project.

McGahey, Richard M. (1986). "Economic Conditions, Neighborhood Organization, and Urban Crime," in Albert J. Reiss, Jr., and Michael Tonry (eds.), *Communities and Crime*. Chicago: University of Chicago Press.

Merton, Robert. (1938). "Social Structure and Anomie." *American Sociological Review* 3: 672–682.

Myers, Samuel L., Jr. (1980). "The Rehabilitation Effect of Punishment." *Economic Inquiry* 18: 353–366.

Pattillo, Mary E. (1998). "Sweet Mothers and Gangbangers: Managing Crime in a Middle-Class Neighborhood." *Social Forces* 76(3): 747–774.

Peek, Charles W., George D. Lowe, and Jon P. Alston. (1981). "Race and Attitudes toward Local Police: Another Look." *Journal of Black Studies* 11(3): 361–374.

Putnam, Robert D. (1993). *Making Democracy Work: Civic Traditions in Modern Italy*. Princeton, NJ: Princeton University Press.

Reiss, Albert J. (1988). "Co-offending and Criminal Careers," in Michael Tonry and Norval Morris (eds.), *Crime and Justice: An Annual Review of Research*, Vol. 10. Chicago: University of Chicago Press.

Reynolds, Morgan. (1990). *Crime in Texas: NCPA Policy Report no. 102*. Dallas: National Center for Policy Analysis (February).

Rose, Dina R., and Todd R. Clear. (1998a). "Who Doesn't Know Someone in Jail?: The Impact of Exposure to Prison and Race on Attitudes of Formal and Informal Control." Paper presented to the 1998 Southern Sociological Society Annual Meeting, Atlanta, Georgia, April.

Rose, Dina R., and Todd R. Clear. (1998b). "Incarceration, Social Capital and Crime: Implications for Social Disorganization Theory." *Criminology* 36(3): 441–480.

Sampson, Robert J. (1988). "Local Friendship Ties and Community Attachment in Mass Society: A Multilevel Systemic Model." *American Sociological Review* 53: 766–779.

Sampson, Robert J. (1987). "Communities and Crime," in Michael R. Gottfredson and Travis Hirschi (eds.), *Positive Criminology*. Beverly Hills: Sage, pp. 91–114.

Sampson, Robert J. (1986a). "Crime in Cities: The Effects of Formal and Informal Social Control," in Albert J. Reiss, Jr., and Michael Tonry (eds.), *Communities and Crime*. Chicago: University of Chicago Press.

Sampson, Robert J. (1986b). "The Effects of Urbanization and Neighborhood Characteristics on Criminal Victimization," in Robert M. Figlio, Simon Hakim, and George F. Rengert (eds.), *Metropolitan Crime Patterns*. Monsey, NY: Criminal Justice Press.

Sampson, Robert J. (1986c). "Neighborhood Family Structure and Risk of Personal Victimization," in James Byrne and Robert Sampson (eds.), *The Social Ecology of Crime*. New York: Springer-Verlag, pp. 25–46.

Sampson, Robert J. (1985). "Neighborhoods and Crime: The Structural Determinants of Personal Victimization." *Journal of Research in Crime and Delinquency* 22: 7–40.

Sampson, Robert J., and W. Byron Groves. (1989). "Community Structure and Crime: Testing Social Disorganization Theory." *American Journal of Sociology* 94: 744–802.

Sampson, Robert J., and John H. Laub. (1993). *Crime in the Making: Pathways and Turning Points Through Life*. Cambridge, MA: Harvard University Press.

Sampson, Robert J., Stephen W. Raudenbush, and Felton Earls. (1998). "Neighborhood Collective Efficacy—Does It Help Reduce Violence?" National Institute of Justice Research Preview. Washington, DC: National Institute of Justice, April.

Shaw, Clifford R., and Henry D. McKay. (1942). *Juvenile Delinquency and Urban Areas*. Chicago: University of Chicago Press.

Skogan, Wesley G. (1990). *Disorder and Decline: Crime and the Spiral of Decay in American Neighborhoods*. New York: Free Press.

Skogan, Wesley G. (1986). "Fear of Crime and Neighborhood Change," in Albert J. Reiss, Jr., and Michael Tonry (eds.), *Communities and Crime*. Chicago: University of Chicago Press.

Spelman, William. (1994). *Criminal Incapacitation*. New York: Plenum.

Sullivan, Mercer L. (1989). *Getting Paid: Youth, Crime and Work in the Inner City*. Ithaca, NY: Cornell University Press.

Taylor, Ralph. (1997). "Social Order and Disorder of Street Blocks and Neighborhoods: Ecology, Microecology and the Systemic Model of Social Disorganization." *Journal of Research in Crime and Delinquency* 34(1): 113–155.

Tienda, Marta, and Haya Stier. (1991). "Joblessness and Shiftlessness: Labor Force Activity in Chicago's Inner City," in Christopher Jencks and Paul E. Peterson (eds.), *The Urban Underclass*. Washington, DC: Brookings Institute.

Tonry, Michael. (1999). "Why Are U.S. Incarceration Rates So High?" *Overcrowded Times* 10(3): 1–7.

Tucker, Belinda M., and Claudia Mitchell-Kernan (eds.). (1995). *The Decline in Marriage among African-Americans: Causes, Consequences, and Policy Implications*. New York: Russell Sage Foundation.

Vankatesh, Sudhir Alladi. (1997). "The Social Organization of Street Gang Activity in an Urban Ghetto." *American Journal of Sociology* 103(1): 82–111.

Warner, Barbara D., and Pamela Wilcox Rountree. (1997). "Local Social Ties in a Community and Crime Model: Questioning the Systemic Nature of Informal Social Control." *Social Problems* 44(4): 520–536.

Wilson, William Julius. (1996). *When Work Disappears: The World of the New Urban Poor*. New York: Knopf.

Wilson, William Julius. (1987). *The Truly Disadvantaged*. Chicago: University of Chicago Press.

Zimring, Franklin, and Gordon Hawkins. (1995). *Incapacitation: Penal Confinement and the Restraint of Crime*. New York: Oxford University Press.

Three Strikes and You're Out: A Symbolic Crime Policy?

Nolan E. Jones

Much of the making of criminal justice policy in the United States reflects a set of interactions among politicians, the citizens whom they represent, and those who administer justice. Politicians and the public often criticize the criminal justice system for not dealing effectively with crime. There is a perception that judges are too lenient and that criminals are not given maximum sentences that would prevent them from continuing to commit crimes. The public tends to have an attitude of "out of sight and out of mind" when it comes to dealing with the punishment of criminals. For politicians, this translates into a fight for longer and tougher prison sentences. Responding to criticisms of the criminal justice system for which they are deemed to be ultimately responsible, public officials tend to search for solutions that will be perceived by the public as adequately dealing with the crime problem, while helping them maintain their elective offices. Especially during the last several decades of American politics, not wanting to be labeled as being "soft on crime" has become a preoccupation for politicians who want to appear to offer effective solutions to the crime problem. On the other hand, the "toughness" shown by politicians when it comes to crime may be in the form of real public policy or may be largely rhetorical. Often it is the rhetoric of crime and punishment, even more so than the actual implementation of "tough" policies, that leads to the perception among the public that the officials are serious and plan to develop policy to address the problem.

Rhetoric plays a crucial role in the politician's development of crime fighting policy because it helps allay the public's fear of crime and gives the impression of the politician as a caring person who feels the pain of the community. Much of this rhetoric is "symbolic," and it plays a major role in political discourse of all types. Rhetorical symbols provide the images for reacting to and developing

a policy about the particular policy issue at hand. Political scientist Murray Edelman wrote about the importance of symbolic rhetoric in his book *Symbolic Uses
of Politics*. Edelman says, "Every symbol stands for something other than itself,
and it also evokes an attitude, a set of impressions, or a pattern of events associated through time, through space, through logic, or through imagination with
the symbol" (1964, 6). Crime policy is often prone to symbolic rhetoric. Common phrases, such as "you do the crime, you do the time" and "one with a gun
gets you two" can often be heard in political discourse about crime and justice
in the United States. In some instances such phrases may reflect major shifts in
public policy; in other instances they may have little impact on crime control
efforts.

"Three strikes and you're out" statutes are part of more recent sentencing
reform policies that have been advanced to address public demand for crime
control. The label used to describe these statutes evokes much of the same
rhetorical imagery as do the other two commonly used phrases. The idea is
taken, of course, from a very familiar symbol of America: baseball. On the third
criminal act, like the third strike at bat, you are out of the game (presumably
out of crime-doing or at the end of a criminal career). During the last decade,
three-strikes statutes and their enforcement have been perceived as a "tough"
and controversial response to crime control in the United States.

This chapter examines "three strikes and you're out" as a function of the public's perennial demand for crime control policy and the response of policy makers
to this demand. It does not provide a scientific assessment of the effectiveness
of three-strikes policies or prove whether or not they actually reduce crime or
the fear of crime. The emphasis is on exploring whether the outcome of the
three-strikes policy provides value of a symbolic nature in the policy process.
This should enhance understanding of the usefulness of symbols and rhetoric
in policy making. Given the great fanfare of three-strikes laws by governors,
mayors, prosecutors, and even the president of the United States, the use of the
statutes in jurisdictions that enacted them should be a good indication of their
value or usefulness. If the statutes are praised by politicians but are not put into
action very often by criminal justice officials, one could say that the value is
more symbolic than real policy.

SENTENCING REFORM

In the 1970s the public and policy makers grew disenchanted with the sentencing process. Among the issues debated was a belief that prisoners were not
serving the time they deserved. A call went out for more accountability from the
criminal justice system, especially from courts and correctional systems. A policy
answer to this call was that certain offenses began to carry mandatory sentences,
making it impossible for an offender to make parole before serving the maximum
sentence prescribed by law. This took away some of the discretion of judges and

courts. "Sentencing reform" became the battle cry, according to James Lynch and William Sabol, and was supported by three beliefs: (1) punishments for serious crimes were too lenient; (2) criminals targeted by reforms were dangerous people who must be incarcerated because lesser sanctions would not be effective; and (3) imprisonment would reduce crime by incapacitating or deterring these offenders (Urban Institute 1997). This reform in sentencing led to major increases in prison populations, with little reduction in crime. Between 1980 and 1993, the number of people incarcerated in prisons grew from approximately 330,000 to 950,000; by the end of 1996, close to 1.5 million people were in prisons and jails throughout the nation (United States Department of Justice 1997).

The National Research Council (NRC) examined sentencing reform in the 1980s, in an attempt to explore the reasons behind sentencing reform initiatives. The NRC explored the issue of whether it was possible to identify the "career criminal," an idea based on earlier work by Peter Greenwood of the RAND Corporation. Greenwood and associates had asked prison inmates about their history of criminal activities and found patterns of numerous crimes being committed prior to an inmate's being caught and sentenced for an offense (1982). It was believed that if these career criminals could be identified earlier and incarcerated for a long period, crime would be reduced. A separate study conducted by Blumstein and Cohen (1986, 15), who also were contributors to the NRC efforts, found that:

Distinguishing among the various dimensions of career criminals may also serve to enhance the crime control potential of alternative strategies by more effectively targeting various crime control efforts. Effective policy strategies may emerge from knowledge about individual offending patterns and the relationship of different attributes of offenders to the dimensions of their criminal careers.

Sentencing reforms of this period related to career criminals did not appear to have a substantial impact on the public's fear and/or perception of the crime problem, which is the driving force behind crime policy. Fear of crime is much greater than the actual crime rate warrants (DeFrances and Smith 1998). Fear has led communities to enact irrational crime policies, spend unnecessary funds to house less dangerous criminals, and develop crime prevention protocols that may not be needed. Noting this problem, Lynch and Sabol said:

Using incarceration to control crime may be an effective strategy to combat some types of crimes, particularly those involving violent offenders and offenders with long and serious criminal careers. Ironically, as imprisonment increases, its marginal crime reduction potential decreases. This is because at any point in time, offenders who commit more crimes are more likely to end up in prison than are the less serious offenders, and expanding incarceration to include these lower-rate offenders will produce smaller reduction in crime. (1997, 9)

While this is difficult for the average citizen to believe, the truth of the matter is reflected in the overall crime rate data.

THREE STRIKES AND YOU'RE OUT

Largely in response to these continuing fears, sentencing reform took on a new theme in the early 1990s. During this period the citizens in the state of Washington passed a ballot initiative that became the rallying cry of "three strikes and you're out." For these citizens, the legislature was not enacting enough tough statutes and judges were not giving enough lengthy sentences. The three-strikes laws were intended to make sure that repeat offenders were locked up for a long period of time, at least on the third criminal act. Between 1993 and 1995, some twenty-four states and the federal government enacted laws around the style of "three strikes." The governor of California signed a statute in March 1994, which made California the second state to enact a three-strikes statute. In signing the bill, then Governor Wilson made this statement: "Three strikes and you're out will finally put an end to revolving-door justice. It sends a clear message to repeat criminals: find a new line of work, because we're going to start turning career criminals into career inmates" ("Wilson Signs Three-Strikes Legislation" March 7, 1994).

In order to understand the "three-strikes" phenomenon as it relates to the crime problem, it is necessary to dissect the issues and ask a few questions. Extending the baseball analogy, we must ask: What does "you're out" really mean? Is it for the remainder of the game, and if so, how long is the game? What counts as a strike? What is the strike zone? The answers to these questions vary from state to state. For example, in Connecticut, the strike zone is defined as murder, attempted murder, assault with intent to kill, manslaughter, arson, kidnapping, aggravated sexual assault, robbery, and first-degree assault. Thus, the strike zone is the nature of the offense as defined by statute. In the case of Connecticut, any felony is strike one. After the second offense (strike two, which could be another felony), a sentence of up to forty years in prison may be given. The third offense (strike three), "you're out," means up to life in prison. In Kansas, any second felony against a person is strike two, and the count may double the term specified in the sentencing guidelines. "You're out" on the third felony against a person; the court may triple the term specified in the sentencing guidelines. Table 3.1 gives a brief summary of each of the twenty-four state statutes regarding "three strikes."

The state of California's three-strikes law presents a unique situation. Enacted a few months after Washington State enacted its statute, the California statute has many "strikeable" offenses. However, after the second "strikeable" offense, any third felony puts the offender out of the game for a mandatory indeterminate life sentence, with no parole eligibility for twenty-five years. It is defining "you're out" in the California statute that has raised questions about its efficacy. Everything, from stealing a slice of pizza to possessing a small amount of drugs, could trigger the third strike, and "you're out" for at least 25 years.

Overall, from 1994 to 1996, some twenty-four states and the federal government enacted some form of a "three-strikes" statute. Their impact and consequence have been the subject of debate and criticism. The impact on public policy will be explored in the remainder of this chapter.

Table 3.1
Summary of Three Strikes and You're Out Laws in the United States

State Year Passed	Strike Defined	Strike Count	Penalties
Arkansas (1995)	Murder, kidnapping, robbery, rape, terrorist act	Two	Not less than 40 years in prison; no parole
	First-degree battery, firing gun from vehicle, use of prohibited weapon; conspiracy to commit murder, kidnapping, robbery, rape, first degree battery, or first degree sexual abuse	Three	Range of no-parole sentences, depending on the offense
California (1994)	Any felony if one prior felony conviction from list of strikeable offenses	Two	Mandatory sentence of twice the term for the offense involved
	Any felony if two prior felony convictions from list of strikeable offenses	Three	Mandatory indeterminate life sentence with no parole eligibility for 25 years
Colorado (1994)	Any Class 1 or 2 felony or any violent Class 3 felony	Three	Mandatory life in prison with no parole eligibility for forty years
Connecticut (1994)	Murder, attempted murder, assault with intent to kill, manslaughter, arson, kidnapping, aggravated sexual assault, robbery, first degree assault	Two	Up to 40 years in prison
		Three	Up to life in prison
Florida (1995)	Any forcible felony, aggravated stalking, aggravated child abuse, lewd or indecent conduct, escape	Three	Life, if third strike involves first degree felony; 30 to 40 years if second degree felony; and 10 to 15 years if third degree felony
Georgia (1995)	Murder, armed robbery, kidnapping, rape, aggravated child molestation, aggravated sodomy, aggravated sexual battery	Two	Mandatory life without parole
	Any felony	Four	Mandatory maximum sentence for the charge
Indiana (1994)	Murder, rape, sexual battery with weapon, child molestation, arson, robbery, burglary with weapon or resulting in serious injury, drug dealing	Three	Mandatory life without possibility of parole
Kansas (1994)	Any felony against a person	Two	Court may double term specified in guidelines
	Any felony against a person	Three	Court may triple term specified in sentencing guidelines

Table 3.1 (Continued)

State	Strike Defined	Strike Count	"You're Out"
Louisiana (1995)	Murder, attempted murder, manslaughter, rape, armed robbery, kidnapping, any drug offense punishable by more than five years, any felony punishable by more than twelve years	Three	Mandatory life in prison with no parole eligibility
	Any four felony convictions if at least one was on the above list	Four	Mandatory life in prison with no parole eligibility
Maryland (1994)	Murder, rape, robbery, first- or second degree sexual offense, arson; burglary, kidnapping, carjacking; manslaughter, use of firearm in felony, assault with intent to murder, rape, rob, or commit sexual offense	Four, with separate prison terms served for first three strikes	Mandatory life in prison with no parole eligibility
Montana (1995)	Deliberate homicide, aggravated kidnapping, sexual intercourse without consent, ritual abuse of a minor	Two	Mandatory life in prison with no parole eligibility
	Mitigated deliberate homicide, aggravated assault, kidnapping, robbery	Three	Mandatory life in prison with no parole eligibility
Nevada (1995)	Murder, robbery, kidnapping, battery, abuse of child, arson, home invasion	Three	Court has option to sentence offender to one of the following: life without parole; life with parole possible after 10 years; or 25 years with parole possible after 10 years
New Jersey (1995)	Murder, robbery, carjacking	Three	Mandatory life in prison with no parole eligibility
New Mexico (1994)	Murder, shooting at or from vehicle and causing harm, kidnapping, criminal sexual penetration, armed robbery resulting in harm	Three	Mandatory life in prison with no parole eligibility
North Carolina (1994)	Forty-seven violent felonies; separate indictment is required with finding that offender is "violent habitual offender"	Three	Mandatory life in prison with no parole eligibility
North Dakota (1995)	Any Class A, B, or C felony	Two	If second strike is for Class A felony, the court may impose extended sentence of up to life in prison; if Class B felony, up to 25; or if Class C felony, up to 10 years

Table 3.1 (Continued)

State	Strike Defined	Strike Count	Penalties
Pennsylvania (1995)	Murder, voluntary manslaughter, rape, involuntary deviate sexual intercourse, arson, kidnapping, robbery, aggravated assault	Two	Enhanced sentence of up to 10 years
	Same offenses	Three	Enhanced sentence of up to 25 years
South Carolina (1995)	Murder, voluntary manslaughter, homicide by child abuse, rape, kidnapping, armed robbery, drug trafficking, embezzlement, bribery, certain accessory and attempt offenses	Two	Mandatory life in prison with no parole eligibility
Tennessee (1995)	Murder, especially aggravated kidnapping, especially aggravated robbery, aggravated rape, rape of a child, aggravated arson	Three, if separate prison terms served for first two strikes	Mandatory life in prison with no parole eligibility
Utah (1995)	Any first or second degree felony	Three	Court may sentence from 5 years up to life in prison
Vermont (1995)	Murder, manslaughter, arson causing death, assault and robbery with weapon or causing bodily injury, aggravated assault, kidnapping, maiming, aggravated sexual assault, aggravated domestic assault, lewd conduct with child	Three	Court may sentence up to life in prison
Virginia (1994)	Murder, kidnapping, robbery, carjacking, sexual assault, conspiracy to commit any of above	Three	Mandatory life in prison with no parole eligibility
Washington (1993)	Homicide, sexual offenses, robbery, felony assault	Three	Mandatory life in prison with no parole eligibility
Wisconsin (1994)	Murder, manslaughter, vehicular homicide, aggravated battery, abuse of child, robbery, sexual assault, taking hostages, kidnapping, arson, burglary	Three	Mandatory life in prison with no parole eligibility

*Adapted from *Research in Brief,* National Institute of Justice, "'Three Strikes and You're Out': A Review of State Legislation," September 1997.

POLICY GOALS AND ACCOMPLISHMENTS

At a National Workshop on Sentencing and Corrections Challenges in 1998, a state legislator said in his opening remarks: "Crime control policy is about one part public safety and two parts politician safety" (United States Department of Justice 1998). There is a great deal of truth to this statement when one examines how politicians deal with the crime control issue. They tend to search for simple solutions to complex problems, especially if these solutions convey the intended symbolic messages. The continued outcry of the public about crime control and the fear among politicians of being labeled as soft on crime add to their need to find quick and politically safe solutions to an age-old problem. In speaking about crime, the politicians use language to convince the public that they understand the problem and can and will do something about it. Choosing the right rhetoric when making pronouncements about crime policy is very important to politicians, because the public wants them to institute public policy that will lead to a solution. This rhetoric is all the more important because the average citizen often has only limited knowledge of what laws have been passed and how effectively they have been enforced. The public and the politician then share a common vision, through rhetoric, about solving the crime problem. Thus, the politician may use the phrase "one with a gun gets you two" to promote a policy of sentencing reform for gun control where a mandatory sentence of two years in prison should be given to any criminal who uses a gun to commit a crime. But the issue is in the rhetoric of this empty phrase that the public understands and can identify with.

Edelman explains: "The word is not in itself the cause; but it evokes everything about the group situation that lends emotion to its political interests, abstracting, reifying, and magnifying. That a term masquerades as description while appraising and condensing doubtless heightens its emotional impact" (1964, 116). The rhetoric surrounding the "three-strikes laws" has been a part of the symbolic language used by politicians to reassure the public that they are trying to control crime, in this instance repeated criminal offending. Both the widespread use of the term and the actual enactment of statutes across many regions of the United States attests to its popularity in the decade of the 1990s. Whether or not the three-strikes laws have effectively controlled persistent criminal involvement is another question. The evidence seems to be mixed.

The rhetoric about the effectiveness of three-strikes laws seems to center around the decline in the crime rate and the restoration of some public confidence. It is conceivable that interrupting the careers of criminals by placing them in prison for long periods should decrease the amount of crime in the communities. If such a decrease were realized, it would give concrete and practical meaning and accuracy to the public's understanding of three-strikes laws. In a 1996 article published in *Policy Review*, former California Attorney General Dan Lungren said that the statute was working and pointed out that crime statistics for 1995 showed that the overall crime rate in California fell 8.5 percent, violent crime dropped 5.5 percent, and property crime fell 10.1 percent (Lungren 1996). However, the law had only been on the books for one and a half years, and no major scientifically sound evaluation of its impact had been undertaken. In a month-to-month review of the data following the passage of the law, one observed a reduction in both serious crime rates and in petty theft. Thus, Lungren told Californians the three-strikes law was working: "What accounts for these astonishing numbers? I would suggest it is in large part due to California's passage of a 'three-strikes-and-you're-out' law, which has done more to stop revolving-door justice than any other measure in state or federal law" (1996, 34).

In 1994, before the California three-strikes statute took effect, researchers at RAND Corporation led by Peter Greenwood and his colleagues undertook an analysis of the proposed statute and its likely impact on the state. They developed analytic models predicting how populations of offenders on the street and in prison (using data on these populations) would change under the proposed three-strikes law. Their conclusion was that over the next twenty-five years after passage, the three-strikes law would "prevent on the order of 340,000 serious crimes per year in California at an additional cost of roughly $5.5 billion annually, or about $16,000 per serious crime prevented" (Greenwood et al. 1994, xi).

A more extensive study of the California three-strikes statute in the *Stanford Law and Policy Review*, which examined crime, arrests, and sentencing from 1991 to 1997, found little evidence that three-strikes sentencing reduced crime in California counties. The analysis points out that California counties have different rates of sentencing under the law. The sentencing rate ranged from 0.3 per 1,000 violent crime arrests in San Francisco, to 3.6 in both Sacramento and Los Angeles. Furthermore, this data shows that the highest sentencing counties invoked the law at rates three to twelve times higher than the lowest counties. However, those counties that strictly enforced the three-strikes law did not experience a decline in any crime category relative to more lenient counties of San Francisco and Alameda. In fact, San Francisco, where the prosecutor seldom uses the three-strikes law, saw a greater decline in violent crime, homicides, and all index crime than most of the counties with the heaviest three-strikes law enforcement. Santa Clara, one of the heaviest-sentencing counties, witnessed a rise in violent crime after implementing three-strikes (Males, Macallair, and Taqi-Eddin 1999).

Another criticism of the California three-strikes law focuses on its disproportionate impact on certain ethnic groups, mainly African American. A study by the Center of Juvenile and Criminal Justice says that African Americans are being imprisoned under the California three-strikes law at 13.3 times the rate of whites. The center found that while blacks make up 7 percent of the state's population, they make up 20 percent of felony arrests, 31 percent of state prisoners, and 43 percent of those imprisoned for a third strike. In other words, "blacks are arrested at 4.7 times the rate of whites, and imprisoned for third strikes at 13.3 times the rate of whites" (Schilraldi, Davis, and Estes 1998).

The Supreme Court of California dealt a major blow to the three-strikes statute in a unanimous ruling that said: "When the decision to prosecute has been made, the process which leads to acquittal or to sentencing is fundamentally judicial in nature. The judicial power must be independent, and a judge should never be required to pay for its exercise" (*The People v. Jesus Romero*, 53 Cal. Rptr. 2d, 789, 1996). The case arose when Jesus Romero was charged with cocaine possession, to which he originally pleaded not guilty; however, at a subsequent hearing, the court indicated its willingness not to consider his prior felony convictions, for burglary and attempted burglary, if he changed his plea to guilty. The prosecutor objected, arguing that the court had no power not to consider prior felony convictions in a three-strikes case unless the prosecutor made such a request. The court disagreed, and instead of sentencing Romero to the mandatory twenty-five years to life under the law, sentenced him to six years in prison. Prosecutors appealed, and the Court of Appeals held that the trial judge had no authority to impose the reduced sentence. On June 20, 1996, the state high court reversed, ruling that "the disposition of a charge is a judicial responsibility," and noted that the statute's silence on the subject did not eliminate a judge's discretion; any attempt to bar judicial involvement would be unconstitutional, according to the court.

Several California politicians went on record expressing their alarm about the court's decision. Governor Pete Wilson called it "potentially dangerous to public safety," and Secretary of State Bill Jones said, "This is a war, and I do not believe this is the appropriate time for a turf war—which is what I believe this is—over judicial discretion" ("Justices Deal Blow to '3 Strikes'" 1996). Conspicuously, the state legislature was indifferent and cautious. One probable reason is that they had seen the reports of the number of future prison beds needed to fulfill the statute and prevent overcrowding. Furthermore, they had been considering ways to limit the statute's impact on the state's budget.

With the exception of California, states' experiences with three-strike statutes are very limited. Prosecutors in other states point out that those who are convicted would have received similar sentences under the law prior to three-strike statutes. The former district attorney in Maryland's Montgomery County said that his state has barely used the statute because most eligible offenders are going to get the maximum time anyway ("'3 Strikes' Strike Out Except in California" 1996). Although some twenty-two states followed the example of California and Washington by passing a three-strikes law, for the most part the law has seldom been used outside of California. As of September 1996, six states—Colorado, New Jersey, New Mexico, North Carolina, Pennsylvania, and Tennessee—had no convictions under their three-strikes laws; Wisconsin had one conviction; Washington had 63; and California had more than 15,000. Several leading newspapers such as the *New York Times* (September 10, 1996) wrote that despite widespread publicity, three-strikes laws were rarely involved in courtrooms; and the *St. Louis Post-Dispatch* headlined an article, "3-Strike Laws Get Little Use" (September 10, 1996). However, the policy purpose of the three-strikes statutes may have eluded these critics.

AN ALTERNATIVE POLICY GOAL

Are three-strikes laws an ineffective method of dealing with crime, since in many states they have been seldom used? The Washington state statute was a voter initiative that passed by a three-to-one margin, and the California statute received a 72 percent vote on a referendum from the legislature (Lyons and Yee, 1995). Other states saw bills pass legislatures, and President Bill Clinton fought to make a three-strikes provision part of the 1994 crime bill that passed Congress. GOP presidential nominee Bob Dole criticized him during the 1996 election for "weak enforcement" of the law. "Three-strikes-and-you're-out has been a get-out-of-jail-free card for tens of thousands of violent criminals," a Dole spokeswoman said ("Three Strikes Laws Rarely Used" 1996).

Many articles have begun to focus on the ineffectiveness of the three-strike statutes, pointing out that they are seldom used outside California. The Campaign for Effective Crime Policy *Public Policy Report* (1996) said, "Three-strike laws are textbook examples of the complexity of affecting behavior through the use of criminal law. Although there is undoubtedly some reduction in crime, it is not at all clear that it is cost-effective or fairly accomplished." An editorial in the *Daily Camera* in Boulder, Colorado, said, "The evidence is in, and the verdict is clear. Three-strikes-and-you're-out was a good political slogan, but it's a poor excuse for crime control" ("Three Strikes Laws Don't Work" 1996).

With so much criticism, is it possible that the policy objective of the three-strikes statutes has been realized? An argument can be made that one possible policy objective was accomplished through the symbolic three-strikes rhetoric alone. It may have reduced both fear of crime among the public and anxiety among policy makers who were attempting to find solutions to a very complex crime problem with limited resources and other pressing priorities. Three-strikes statutes were enacted with much fanfare and public support; California and Washington enacted statutes with direct public support by referendum and initiative. It is easy and plausible to argue that there are better solutions to the crime problem for policy makers. But one must take into consideration the cost of implementation and the nature of a politician's responsibilities. If the public believes that the three-strikes laws work, why should politicians and policy makers try to convince them differently? They may not have the resources to implement an alternative policy; and if three-strikes laws are perceived to work, the public will not be constantly criticizing them.

One official reported to a newspaper that a three-strikes policy was almost a placebo. He said that the "public thinks something is happening that will make them feel safer, but keeps us (politicians) from looking at the real issues, such as dealing with drugs in our society" ("Three Strikes Doesn't Cut Muster" 1996). This official may or may not realize that giving the public such a placebo keeps them from demanding that politicians and policy makers attack the real problems causing crime, which are very costly to fix and may require structural and ideological changes. Using the rhetoric of three strikes enables policy makers to deal symbolically with this complex crime issue without using the resources needed to bring about a real solution.

Many proponents of the three-strikes laws view the current declining crime rate as affirmation of their policy. Opponents of the statutes have raised issues about prison and jail overcrowding, more money going to prisons than to schools, courts clogged with lengthy trials, and a criminal justice system that could grind to a halt. In California, during a debate about three strikes, it was suggested that college tuition might be increased to pay for the prison space needed to house three-strikes offenders. A three-strikes spokesman responded that a college education isn't going to do you any good if you are too scared to walk to the campus. Or, as a state governor responded after being informed that the three-strikes law had not been used in the state even though it was a statute: "Maybe it means the three-strikers have figured out New Jersey isn't the place to do it. I'll take that, if that's what it means" ("No One Jailed under Three Strikes Law" 1996). Facts and logic may not be sufficient in dealing with this type of rhetoric.

Most examinations of the three-strikes laws have focused on their effectiveness in reducing crime, an inferred assumption that the statute's impact would have measurable impact on the crime problem. Assessment of effectiveness has centered on whether the crime rate has declined in areas affected by the statute. The *Stanford Law and Policy Review* study (Males et al. 1999) offers evidence that the three-strikes law has not been effective in reducing crime in many California counties. The RAND study by Greenwood (1994) found that the statute could be effectively implemented, but at a very high cost. Likewise, prosecutors have not demonstrated much enthusiasm for the three-strikes statutes, with some saying that they prefer not to use the statutes.

In addition to evaluating the impact that three-strikes statutes may have on reducing crime rates, researchers and policy analysts should also pay attention to the contextual political rhetoric about the statutes. Most public officeholders and those seeking office used the three-strikes rhetoric to win office. The public had no idea how the statutes would work, but they responded to their fears at the polls and by lobbying legislatures to pass the statutes. This raises the question of whether the fear of crime is greater than the actual amount of crime in certain communities. If symbolic rhetoric can allay the public's fear, then there should be greater understanding of the nature and substance of the fear. This calls for a different way of looking at what it means for a crime statute to be effective—not just from a factual reduction in the crime rate, but also from the impact on how the public feels about crime and what politicians say and do.

CONCLUSION

It seems that although some twenty-four states have enacted three-strikes statutes in some form, only one state, California, has used the statute extensively. Most of the other states used the statute only rarely, with six states having no convictions under the statute as of 1996. There will always be disagreement about the three-strike statutes. Are they working? Are they fair? Are they cost-effective? These are questions that deserve definitive examinations. However, in evaluating these questions, the role of symbolic rhetoric should not be overlooked. Three-strike laws may not seem to be good public policy, but if they serve to calm the fears of the public (at least for a while), then the political and symbolic purpose of the statutes may have been accomplished. In understanding public policy, the role of symbols and rhetoric cannot be ignored.

REFERENCES
Books and Articles

Blumstein, Alfred, Jacqueline Cohen, and others (eds.). 1986. *Criminal Careers and "Career Criminal."* Washington, DC: National Academy of Science Press.

Campaign for an Effective Crime Policy. 1996. *The Impact of "Three Strikes and You're Out" Laws: What Have We Learned?* Public Policy Report. Washington, DC: author.

DeFrances, Carol J., and Steven K. Smith. April 1998. *Perceptions of Neighborhood Crime, 1995.* Washington, DC: U.S. Department of Justice, Office of Justice Programs, Bureau of Justice Statistics.

Edelman, Murray. 1964. *The Symbolic Uses of Politics.* Urbana: University of Illinois Press.

Greenwood, Peter, and associates. 1982. *Selective Incapacitation.* Santa Monica, CA: RAND Corporation.

Greenwood, Peter, C. Peter Rydell, and others. 1994. *Three Strikes and You're Out: Estimated Benefits and Costs of California's New Mandatory Sentencing Law.* Santa Monica, CA: RAND Corporation.

Lungren, Dan. 1996. Three Cheers for 3 Strikes. *Policy Review* (November/December): 34.

Lynch, James P., and William J. Sabol. 1997. Did Getting Tough on Crime Pay? *Crime Policy Report.* Washington, DC: Urban Institute, August.

Lyons, Donna, and Adelia Yee. 1995. Crime and Sentencing State Enactments 1995. *State Legislative Report* 20(16) (November).

Males, Mike, Dan Macallair, and Khaled Taqi-Eddin. 1999. Striking Out: The Failure of California's "Three Strikes and You're Out" Law. *Stanford Law and Policy Review* 11 (Winter): 65; cited online as http://www.cjcj.org/jpi/strikingout.html.

People v. Jesus Romero, 53 Cal. Rptr. 2d 789, 1996.

Schilraldi, Vincent, Christopher Davis, and Richard Estes. 1996. *Three Strikes: The New Apartheid.* San Francisco, CA: Center of Juvenile and Criminal Justice.

United States Department of Justice. 1997. *Prisoners in 1996.* Washington, DC: Bureau of Justice Statistics.

United States Department of Justice. 1998. *First National Workshop on Sentencing and Corrections Challenges.* St. Petersburg, FL: National Institute of Justice, June 8–9.

News Articles and Press Releases

"Justices Deal Blow to '3 Strikes.'" *Los Angeles Times,* June 21, 1996.

"No One Jailed under 3-Strikes Law." *Bergen Record,* September 11, 1996.

"Three Strikes Doesn't Cut Muster." Editorial in the *Yakima Herald-Republic,* September 13, 1996.

"Three Strikes Laws Don't Work." Editorial in the *Daily Camera*, September 11, 1996.

"Three Strikes Laws Rarely Used." *Tulsa World*, September 10, 1996.

"'3 Strikes' Strike Out Except in California." *San Diego Union-Tribune*, September 10, 1996.

"Wilson Signs Three-Strikes Legislation." California Governor's Office Press Release 94:244. March 7, 1994.

4

Crime, Youth, and the Labor Market: Are We Any Closer to Answers?

Harold L. Votey, Jr., and Llad Phillips

INTRODUCTION

Popular discussions over the last twenty-five years of trends in criminal offenses by criminal justice experts focus on a number of themes. One that invariably arises is the effect of demographic shifts as the proportion of young people grows and diminishes with the baby boom and subsequent echoes of the baby boom. Others include the effects of crack cocaine, the proliferation of handguns, and the decline of family values. A factor that, until recently, has been largely ignored by criminologists has been the effect of economic opportunities on crime participation by youths, especially disadvantaged youth. As economists, our investigation into crime participation, on the other hand, has focused largely on the latter effects, while simultaneously investigating some of the others. We have also taken a little time to consider the evidence of population age-distribution effects on crime. In fact, it was curiosity about those effects that inspired our interest in crime participation in the first place. This chapter chronicles our own take on these issues with an economist's focus and techniques.

This chapter, consequently, is a review of the implications of a selective line of research, much of it by the authors, commencing in 1968. It began by focusing primarily on economic factors affecting participation in crime by youth. As our work progressed, our focus expanded to develop models that were more complete. We sought to explain differences in crime participation among ethnic groups, going beyond labor-market forces. Realizing that crime generation and control were a kind of circular process, we also examined the factors leading to effective apprehension, prosecution, and adjudication of criminals and evaluated the effectiveness of alternative punishments in controlling crime rates. Being aware, from the very beginning, of the age-crime profile, we began to seek answers as to why youth get into crime and sought to learn what prompted some to get out early while others chose crime as a long-term career. At some point, we got a better sense of the dynamic that was pushing rates up from the early 1960s until the mid-1990s with an ever-increasing flow of youth into the serious-offender population.

Our ultimate purpose has always been to attempt to learn how policy might be guided to ameliorate the enduring upward trend in crime—and in youth crime in particular. Official crime rates, as reported in the Uniform Crime Reports of the FBI beginning in 1952, had risen by 135 percent by 1970 and by a further 48 percent by 1991, when they began a gradual downturn. Over most of that time, based on arrest data, youth crime rates were rising more rapidly than adult rates. In the ten years from 1987 through 1996, index crime arrests for youth under 18 rose 13.9 percent, while those for 18 and over rose by 2.0 percent. These differences are explained in part by observing that, even following the downturn in the aggregate in 1991, youth crime continued to rise for several more years. Circumstances suggest that the same economic factors revealed in our earliest study to be influential have been playing a role in the decline in crime participation that began in the mid-1990s.

Our focus on youth and crime had a curious inception. Our initial investigation into the topic was undertaken in response to our curiosity as to whether aggregate crime rates might be explained by changes in the population age distribution. This idea stemmed from an economic analysis of population trends before we were exposed to any idea in the literature that changes in crime rates might be explained. We were prompted by the observation that crime rates for youth were considerably higher than rates for older individuals and that the age distribution of the population, since World War II, had been shifting to a lower median age. It was our expectation that this could explain much of the then current rise in crime. When analysis revealed that the shift in age distribution from 1952 through 1967 could explain roughly 15 percent of the rise in rates for a typical property crime such as larceny, we looked for other explanations of the remaining 85 percent. To two economists, lack of viable legitimate earning choices seemed an obvious possibility. At the time, we noted further that crime seemed to be mostly male and mostly urban and that blacks were reportedly involved to a considerably greater extent than represented by their population proportions. We had observed that, while unemployment rates remained relatively low for older individuals, those for eighteen–nineteen years old were on an upward trend that we now know continued into the 1990s. Our conjecture was that crime rates were rising because the proportion of the population that was economically disadvantaged, namely youths, was rising. We developed a research design that would take advantage of this and other correlates of crime. It seemed logical to focus on labor market opportunities, one age group at a time, to abstract from age-distribution effects. Our discussion begins with a review of results of that earliest effort to explain youth crime on the basis of causal factors, which focused on eighteen–nineteen-year-old males for the years 1952 to 1967.[1] Much of our later research has reinforced and expanded upon its results.

That first study investigated the extent to which crime participation by youth was influenced by lack of economic opportunities as reflected by labor market status. That is, crime involvement would be a reflection of whether individuals were employed, unemployed, or not in the labor force.[2] More precisely, our modeling of the problem assumed that average youth crime rates in each of the labor force categories were fixed and that what led to crime was worsening economic conditions, leading to variation in the distribution of youth among those categories. The labor force data were tabulated separately for whites and non-whites. Our study revealed a difference in behavior between non-whites and whites. For whites, unemployed youth had higher crime rates than those employed, who in turn had higher crime rates than those not in the labor force. For non-whites, which in those years implied predominantly blacks, not in the labor force had higher crime rates than those unemployed, who in turn were more involved criminally than those employed. All the coefficients were statistically significant in separate estimations for larceny, burglary, robbery, and auto theft. Of note, the relationships did not hold for ages twenty–twenty-four and older groups and were not significant for sixteen–seventeen-year-olds.

We speculated that the reason for the difference in ordering between white and black youth was that blacks not in the labor force were less likely to be enrolled in school than white youth. They were more likely to be classed as "discouraged workers," having dropped out of the labor force because of inability to obtain employment. Enrollment in school constituted an economic opportunity reflecting an expectation of higher future income. The basic theoretical model underlying our continuing investigation was what is now referred to as the economic model of crime, in which an individual is perceived to be making a rational choice among alternatives for income, selecting the alternative with the greater expected net benefits. If a legitimate job providing a reasonable income is available, one would not be expected to choose to participate in crime. The data were limited in that we were not able to compare alternative income levels from legitimate work and crime, but we could model the likelihood of engaging in crime as it varied with labor market status. In our view, statistical results strongly supported our expectations that youth who desired work and were employable would be less likely to be involved in crime.

While the differences between blacks and whites were explained at that time only by our speculation, subsequent analysis was based on data that included whether an individual was enrolled in school or not as well as labor market status not separated by race. In the year of the most recent data of our study (1967), school enrollment rates for eighteen–nineteen-year-old white males were approximately 62 percent, while for non-whites they were 55 percent.[3] We found, for eighteen–nineteen-year-olds, that criminality coefficients for school dropouts not in the labor force were greater than for youth enrolled in school but not in the labor force. Those for dropouts unemployed were greater than for dropouts not in the labor force, which in turn, were greater than dropouts employed. There was no statistical difference in criminality coefficients among school enrollees whether employed, unemployed, or not in the labor force. Thus, there was support for our speculations. These results were limited, however, to burglary and robbery. Results were insignificant for auto theft and larceny.

Today, not much has changed regarding these correlates of crime showing youth predominating, males and blacks being charged more often, and the locale of crime being urban. Crime rates, however, rose much higher and violence increased markedly before starting a decline in the mid-1990s. What follows attempts to explain what we have learned in the thirty years since we began that first study into crime causality for youth. Based largely on those results, we attempt to explain what policies we believe might lead to an improvement in the next thirty years.

THE ECONOMIC APPROACH AND COUNTER VIEWS

As noted, our crime studies were not limited to investigating the role of causal factors. We also looked into the productivity of law enforcement in controlling crime.[4] Shortly after the study just discussed, we were able to show, for the index crimes, that law enforcement expenditures were productive of arrests and ultimately prosecution. Furthermore, a clear reason for rising crime rates was that real expenditures for law enforcement had not been keeping pace with rising crime levels.[5] Despite our early evidence and the widespread belief by those economists studying crime and justice that expenditures for law enforcement and sanctions could be effective in containing crime through deterrence effects, many criminologists showed more interest in taking criminal tendencies among individuals as a given.[6] The increasing trend among policy makers and the public was to favor imprisonment of known criminals. Many authorities were skeptical that added expenditures for law enforcement would be effective in slowing crime, as is evident if one examines growth rates for expenditures on law enforcement from the mid-1960s to recent times.[7]

In our view, a trade-off was made clear: Policy makers must choose between expenditures for crime control that will result in increased apprehensions, convictions, and imprisonments for criminals, or expenditures on social measures that will enhance the potential for legitimate employment. The latter will affect preferences that make crime and violence less appealing. Numerous studies, by then, had recognized the benefits of investment in human capital. Other studies revealed the uneven distributions of such investments among youth and ethnic groups.[8]

To be sure, all crime is not committed for economic gain, but given that property crimes greatly outnumber personal crimes and that many crimes of violence are committed in the process of committing property crimes, useful analysis can result from economic reasoning. Furthermore, lack of opportunity may lead to lack of hope and hence to violence. Social programs can lead to a reduced tendency for violence as well as to greater economic opportunity. How this may be true becomes clearer when one takes account of the arguments about how moral suasion may alter preferences, particularly with respect to crime and violence.[9] On the basis of these considerations, a meaningful trade-off exists between using resources to control crime and using them to modify causal conditions, making individuals less likely to resort to crime. The utilitarian approach to understanding behavior that underlies both classical criminology theory and the economic model of crime provides a useful framework within which to analyze the alternatives for crime control.

From an economist's perspective, the obvious objective is to minimize the sum of victim costs and control costs.[10] In the 1970s we would have recommended a balanced approach to crime control. This policy would have expenditures on the criminal justice system for crime control rising at least as rapidly as crime rates, but with concurrent efforts to remedy the lack of economic opportunities for youth. The latter would include broadly based programs to encourage investment in human capital for those individuals most likely to be tempted by the potential gains from committing crime.

Our earliest studies were conducted on an aggregate level, using state or national data. Such studies, however, were regarded as clouded by aggregation bias by many concerned with issues of human behavior. The trend in analysis since that time has been to focus on studies of individuals. Furthermore, studies that focused on alleged deterrence effects tended to be rejected as a fallout of the debate over the deterrent effect of the death penalty. This was, primarily, a consequence of the 1978 study supported by the National Academy of Science that called on the talents of the famous econometrician Franklin Fisher. He was able to show that some of the underlying assumptions of the econometric analysis in the simultaneous equation studies might not be perfectly met, thus calling into question the identification of deterrence coefficients.[11] A key issue of identification was whether enough was known to control for causal factors and thereby adequately specify the relationships that would allow one to identify control effects and thus deterrence. The issue of whether we understand the factors that cause crime remains today as a limitation to developing effective policies to reduce criminal tendencies.

With seemingly little belief in the existence of a strong deterrent effect from criminal justice activities, policy subsequent to the National Academy of Sciences study of 1978 tended to focus on incapacitation as the only sure way to reduce crime. A further compelling factor in the focus on incapacitation policy was the statistic from one research study that roughly half of all offenses were committed by as few as 6 percent of the criminal population.[12] The obvious answer thus seemed simply to assure that the element of the population committing the major share of crime was behind bars so that crime could be vastly reduced.

A problem with a policy focusing on such serious offenders relates to what is generally referred to as the age crime profile. Crime participation by individuals tends to rise in the early years, peaking, for property crimes, at age sixteen to seventeen, somewhat later for personal crimes, with the numbers participating in crime declining somewhere beyond age thirty-five.[13] Participating individuals, however, are not likely to be identified as serious criminals before they have been apprehended several times as adults and convicted to hard time for felony offenses. Thus, by the time that an individual reaches the point in his crime career at which he can reliably be identified as one of the more serious offenders, his threat to society is likely to be on the decline.[14] Consequently, long-term incapacitation at the time when these persons are identified will not prevent a major share of the offenses they will commit, despite imposing immense costs on the public for prison construction and operation. Additionally, even if the policy focusing on serious offenders could be made to work effectively, a policy is still needed to target the less criminal individuals committing an equally large proportion (the other 50 percent) of the crimes.

In spite of these flaws in emphasizing incapacitation to the neglect of policies that might affect the career decision to participate in crime, public interest has been captured by the argument of being tough on serious criminals. It is an approach the public understands. The consequence has been that sentence lengths have been increased substantially across the country and increasing numbers of individuals have been incarcerated in local jails and in state and federal prisons. This has led to a rise in imprisonment rates for the United States to 548 per 100,000 in 1993 compared to 161 reported for 1970, an increase of 340 percent.[15] This shift in policy to a primary emphasis on imprisonment resulting from public pressure on authorities and from popularly sponsored legislation is reflected in the data. While real expenditures for all criminal justice activities rose at an annual rate of 3.3 percent from 1970 to 1992, imprisonments rose at the rate of 5.1 percent.[16] By 1993, incarceration of prisoners in the United States was 6.7 times as great as for ten high-income countries reporting imprisonment rates for 1990 in the UN's *Human Development Report 1995*.

Social policy aimed at reducing criminogenic conditions is being rejected as a way to coddle individuals in society who are less responsible. An additional legitimate reason blocking implementation of such policies is that they are regarded as an unproven approach. The fact is, it has been difficult to establish, for example, that a policy to improve an individual's earning potential will have a meaningful impact on his likelihood to participate in crime. Since the benefits of investing in human capital accrue over a lifetime, often long after the effort to improve the individual's potential, it is difficult to establish cause and effect through statistical analysis.[17]

There was even a problem with establishing that there is a beneficial effect from improving economic opportunities in order to reduce the tendency for an individual to participate in criminal earning activities. There have been a number of studies attempting to relate the business cycle to crime that have found a weak or no relationship between business conditions and crime. More specifically, unemployment rates were found to have little relationship to crime levels or rates.[18] Our research does not disagree with those results, but we believe our own studies reveal that their emphasis is misplaced. The increasing lack of economic opportunities for inner-city youths would not be reflected simply in unemployment statistics, because most of these youths would have dropped out of the labor force and thus not be included among the ranks of the unemployed.

Furthermore, many studies using individual data tend to show only weak tendencies even for arrests to reduce crime participation. Some show a positive relationship between arrests and crime participation.[19] There is a broadly held perception that persons who become criminal not only will tend to reject legitimate approaches to income,[20] but also will be oblivious to the threat of arrest and incarceration.[21] Our own studies tend to confirm this latter perception.

Unfortunately, high-intensity focus on an imprisonment policy has not worked in the way that those advocating it might have hoped. In comparison with other advanced countries, property crime rates are not significantly lower and violence rates appear to be several times higher.[22] In spite of gains in the last several years in bringing down overall levels of crime and violence, these levels remain close to historic highs in this century. The associated social costs to victims and control costs are enormous. Even scholars who have been recommending incapacitation policies are now recommending a renewed focus on social or causal factors.[23]

Our position is not that incapacitation policy, per se, is bad. In fact, there is solid evidence that, for some kinds of offenses, incapacitation policy has not been used to full advantage and the press for more severe sentencing is correct.[24] At the same time, imprisonment is the most costly of treatments and is not a cost effective option in many cases. We need to consider a broader range of options.

It is a good time to reflect on a few of the things we have already observed about crime generation and control. We argue that the focus needs to be more on the factors influencing individual behavior. Our recommendation is to start by reconsidering the results of our first study and to see where that has led research in terms of the behavior of individuals.

STUDIES USING INDIVIDUAL DATA

One problem in attempting to study individual behavior, including the role of economic opportunities, is that there are almost no data on individuals that include appropriate economic data while providing adequate crime participation and arrest histories. One exception is the National Longitudinal Survey and what originally was called the New Youth Cohort (NLSY), which covered 12,686 individuals over a number of years. These data include involvement in crime for one of those years (1979) as well as retrospective data on contacts with police and other information that may lead to the reported degree of crime involvement.[25] Another exception is a study supported by the Vera Institute that followed an arrest cohort of Brooklyn men and obtained data on employment, education, and extensive criminal histories.[26] Both play a strong role in what we have learned about crime participation by youth.

A number of interesting results have been obtained using these data. One important result is in regard to specific deterrence measures. That result is supported by both data sources. From the NLSY data one can obtain the result that prior stops by police show an interesting relationship to subsequent criminal behavior and how it varies across individuals. One finds that individuals with no prior stops by police (and not being charged with a crime), other things equal, are more likely to be involved in crime than those with one or two prior stops. However, individuals with greater numbers of prior stops are unlikely to be deterred by the further threat of police action.[27] This accords with the characterization of individuals as being experimenters with crime, persisters, and desisters.[28] Among those who experiment, it was found that a portion of them (desisters) will be deterred by law enforcement activity and will not commit another offense. It is also consistent with the expectation that once some individuals become committed to active involvement in crime (persisters), further police activity is not a deterrent. This same pattern is revealed with the Vera Institute Brooklyn data, except that the measure in this case is prior arrest, rather than simply being stopped without being charged.[29] A similar result has been found in a study of drunken driving for Sweden, using data on all arrestees for drunken driving over a period of four years.[30] There, it was found that individuals with one or two previous arrests for drunken driving were less likely to commit a further offense. However, individuals who had three or more prior arrests had a much higher probability of being arrested again for the same offense. This suggests that, during a brief period in one's career, before an individual is firmly committed to flouting the law, specific deterrence measures have a beneficial impact, but for those who are not so affected, specific deterrence measures become less relevant as a control measure.

Not only do these results tend to confirm that deterrence works, they also yield insight into the dynamic process depicted by the age-crime profile. They provide a partial explanation why some youth, having experimented with crime, later desist.

What is interesting about studies of crime participation by youth, in which legitimate earning possibilities and educational attainment are taken into account, is that both have a moderating influence on crime participation.[31] To be sure, these data focus on youth, and the moderating role of legitimate income has not been shown to have much of a beneficial impact on older participants in crime. In fact, in a study in which the authors investigated the impact of providing services to newly released prisoners, assistance in obtaining employment was almost never successful in preventing an ultimate return to crime.[32] Nevertheless, it turned out to be a cost-effective means to extend the period of time before the former felon's return to crime. The fact is, career criminals are not easily influenced either by threat of punishment or help in obtaining legitimate means of support in refraining from a return to crime.

The details of these results regarding economic opportunities and deterrence measures using either the NLSY or Brooklyn data formed the basis for a number of independent studies. Our most important results are largely captured or summarized in three papers, discussed in the next section.

CRIME GENERATION AND CONTROL BASED ON INDIVIDUAL-LEVEL DATA

The culmination of over twenty years of effort, which reflects an increase in our understanding of the youth crime problem, is best represented by three published articles that have the most to offer for policy prescription. The papers are entitled "Rational Choice Models of Crime by Youth,"[33] "Employment, Age, Race, and Crime: A Labor Theoretic Investigation,"[34] and "The Influence of Police Interventions and Alternative Income Sources on the Dynamic Process of Choosing Crime as a Career."[35] These studies are based on the economic model of criminal behavior and benefit from advances in econometrics and labor economics. It is useful to review and summarize the findings in these papers in more detail, particularly in regard to the prescriptions they offer for policy. They tend to support earlier findings based on aggregate analyses.

The first paper incorporates virtually all of the aspects of crime causality that we have found to be important in earlier work and adds some new influences that needed to be considered. It is based on the largest random sample of youthful longitudinal behavior including both economic, human capital, and crime data in a single sample.[36] We consider rational choice among possibilities, including both legitimate employment and crime, not simply as mutually exclusive choices but as activities that can be combined, which the data clearly show is a likely scenario. In these results, moral compliance with the law emerges as important to the final outcome, as affected by family and religion. Schooling, an investment in human capital, is shown to be an important influence on the choice to commit crime or not. Similarly, previous work experience and the availability of legitimate opportunities play an important role. Finally, prior stops by the police are shown to influence crime participation.

The results with respect to moral compliance with the law and the role of family influences is perhaps more compelling now than at the time the results were published because of the public's increased sense of the importance of "family values." The data contained two aspects of family values for the period in which crimes were reported: first, eight responses to questions of family attitudes prevailing in the home, and second, three questions relating to the degree of religious involvement of the individual surveyed. Where the crimes were theft or simply defined as the portion of income earned illicitly, we were able to relate these variables, along with variables representing family financial help, job income, and prior stops by the police, to whether an individual was an "innocent/experimenter" with crime, a "persister," or a "desister."

The role of family attitudes reflects the dilemma that modern families face, that is, the fact that, for most families, to maintain an acceptable standard of living requires two income earners in the household. The effects of the eight attitude questions were evaluated. Among "innocents/experimenters" and among "non-persisters," the one family attitude that was positively related to participating in crime was derived almost entirely from the statement, "a working wife feels more useful." This implies that, in households in which the wife felt a need to work outside the home, youth in the household were more likely to commit crimes for income. A stronger result for "desisters/persisters" and "persisters" was related to the statement "both parents need to work to make ends meet," and was positively related to participation in crimes for income. At the same time, the variable significant in deterring participation in crime was based on the attitudinal statement, "a man should share in the household chores." The variable based on the statements "a woman's place is in the home," "a wife has no time for employment," "a working wife leads to juvenile delinquency," "traditional husband-wife relationships are best," and "a wife is happier in a traditional role" was unrelated to crime participation in most of the estimates.[37] These results suggest that, while having both parents working leads to a greater likelihood of youths in the home participating in crime, if the parents share the household chores, perhaps reflecting a more generally cooperative relationship within the household, the tendency for crime participation by youth is moderated.

The role of religion was to moderate criminal tendencies, but was found no more important in retarding an innocent from becoming an experimenter than in moderating the criminal tendencies of a desister or persister. That analysis considered three questions: whether the individual was raised in a religion, whether the individual saw himself as having a religious affiliation at the time of the interview, and an indicator of the frequency of church attendance that ranged from not at all to once a week. In different analyses this information was treated in different ways. In an analysis that focused primarily on moral influences, a weighted average of the influences of the three questions invariably was negatively related to participation in crimes for income with little difference in their influence between innocents, experimenters, persisters, and desisters. For a variable weighted most heavily and negatively on the degree of church attendance, the coefficients were positive and significant with little difference between innocents, experimenters, desisters, and persisters, indicating that church attendance also was a favorable factor in reducing the incidence of crime. From these results, one must conclude that religion plays a beneficial role in reducing potential crime incidence, but one cannot conclude that it has any effect on the either/or choice of whether to experiment in or continue to participate in crime.

In the same analyses, it was found that availability of earned legal income did not play a significant role with respect to the likelihood of participating in crime for the overall sample, or of innocents/experimenters, to do so. It was significant in reducing crime involvement for the desister/persister subset of the sample and for persisters alone, however.

The results that focus on moral compliance with the law indicate a role for family support, as well as for the role of family and religion. That is, having considered the factors relating to moral compliance, a significant finding is that supplemental income from family sources moderates participation in crime, presumably reducing the need for economic opportunities outside the family. An influence for innocents/experimenters and non-persisters not participating in crime was to have a supplemental source of income, presumably from parents, but in any event unearned. For the most part, innocents were from homes in which there was full parental support and no need to seek financial help from other sources. Such a finding is hardly reassuring in an era in which single-parent households abound and youth are on their own when it comes to providing their own financial means for even incidental expenses.

While the effect is smaller and less significant, it also exists for desisters/persisters and for persisters alone: Supplemental income exerts a negative influence on crime involvement. Still, with the NLSY data, it can be shown that, even after taking account of family income, having a father present is an important factor moderating crime participation for youth. Specifically, it can be shown that, after standardizing for family income, the probability of a youth being charged for an illegal activity is approximately 44 percent higher if no father is present.[38] This is a daunting result in view of the increasing proportion of households headed by a single parent.

After all of these factors are taken into account, area of residence, that is, the greater likelihood of urban residence in contrast to rural non-farm or rural farm residence, is positively related to crime participation.

A subsequent section of this paper presents analyses of the role of school attendance and prior work experience in affecting the decision to remain in school or take a job. These estimates strongly support that individuals are making career choices on the basis of available opportunities, which are improved by investment in human capital, that is, by education and work experience. The choice to remain in school and/or to avoid crime at early ages is shown subsequently to have an influence on being employed in a legitimate job.

Examination of aspects of career choice is revealing in a model in which the four choices are participation in only crime, only work, both crime and work, and neither. We find that educational attainment is strongly and positively related to the choice of legitimate work exclusively, and somewhat less to the choice of combining work and crime. It is negatively but only marginally significant in choosing to commit crime exclusively. Work experience is positively and significantly related to choices of work or work and crime and negatively, though not significantly, related to choosing only crime. Raised in a faith is negatively related to crime, but not significantly related to either choice that includes work. Church attendance is negatively related to either choice that includes crime. Current school enrollment is strongly negatively related to either work, crime, or combination of the two.

A most interesting result in this analysis has to do with race. Being black is strongly and negatively related to either choice that includes work, with the larger coefficient and greater significance for work by itself. It is *not* significantly related to crime. One has to interpret this to mean that, once investment in human capital and work experience are taken into account, blacks in this very large sample were no more inclined to participate in crime than whites. At the same time, the data show that, when investment in human capital and prior work experience are not taken into account, blacks in the sample, as they age, increase their participation in crime to a greater extent than whites. To us, this implies strongly that the black participation in crime largely relates to lack of employment. In view of the importance of educational attainment and school enrollment in influencing the choice for non-involvement in crime, the problem becomes one of lack of sufficient investment in human capital, or of failure to remain in school. It may also be a problem of black family structure, since more black youth are in single-parent households than whites.

The second article that captures the culmination of research efforts to explain crimes by youth raises some of the same questions within a framework of data in which crime participation is based on official police reports rather than on self-reports, as is the case with NLSY data. Because these data are based on an initial arrest, they do not include information on individuals not choosing to participate in crime; thus, the picture cannot be as complete as with the NLSY data. However, there is a longitudinal element to these data with respect to crime participation not available in the NLSY data. This is provided for a portion of the sample by follow-up interviews along with official reports of crime participation during the intervening interval. To a considerable extent the findings of the previous study tend to be confirmed by the Brooklyn data.

For a group comprised of 702 individuals for which the data are complete, it was possible to investigate a two-way choice between work and crime and crime only. The factors most important to holding a job as compared to only participating in crime were, not surprisingly, the extent of educational attainment and prior work experience, that is, the individual's investment in his own human capital. Having a problem with drugs also had a negative impact on a person holding a legitimate job. It was not possible to consider the role of prior contacts with police in connection with committing a crime or not, but it was clear that increasing contacts with police were negatively associated with the individual's likelihood of being employed. An individual who was black, after account was taken of these other effects, was more likely not to be employed.

For the group that was re-interviewed one year later, the only significant variable in predicting whether an individual was employed was the fraction of weeks worked in the previous period. Whether an individual of that group committed a crime depended very significantly on the prior arrest experience. Those who had been innocents prior to the original sample, and hence experimenters in crime, had a higher likelihood of committing a crime than individuals with a single arrest or two prior arrests. However, for those with greater numbers of prior arrests, the likelihood of participating in crime rose substantially above that of experimenters. Thus, in both studies we have found a U-shaped relationship with respect to prior influences by police affecting crime participation. Experimenters with no prior stops are more likely to be criminal than individuals with one or two stops, but after three or more stops the likelihood of crime participation rises. In short, if an individual does not become a desister after two stops or arrests, he is unlikely to with a greater number of stops or arrests. Weeks worked in the interval between arrests had a negative influence on the likelihood the individual would commit another offense. After these factors were taken into account, age continued to have a negative effect on the likelihood of being arrested again.

The original investigators of the Brooklyn data concluded that age was a factor in its own right.[39] More precisely, the investigators concluded that unemployment could not have had very much to do with crime participation because many of those in the sample had been involved in crimes before they had ever had a job. Yet, they found crime participation for the individuals in the sample to be declining as they aged, suggesting to them that youths tended to "mature out of crime." In our view, the data revealed that individuals who were unable to find jobs were more likely to commit crimes for income. We leave it to the reader to determine which is the more logical interpretation.

Greenberg argues, to explain the age-crime curve, that youth wish to participate in social activities but, because they are excluded from the labor market or limited to part-time employment, they turn to crime to support their activities.[40] As a greater variety of legitimate opportunities become available with age, they tend to reduce participation in crime. His view is supported by this research.

In fact, child labor laws make it difficult or impossible for persons younger than eighteen to hold a wide variety of jobs they would be competent to handle. This is confirmed by examining the data for males not enrolled in school in 1980. For youth sixteen and seventeen, the percentage not in the labor force plus those in the labor force not working comes to 47.8 percent. For eighteen- and nineteen-year-olds, this number drops to 27.7 percent, based on published data on unemployment and labor force participation.[41] Much of this disparity certainly has to be a consequence of constraints imposed on the labor market by well-intended legislation. At this same time, in many states, an individual is treated as a juvenile until reaching the age of eighteen, facing less severe treatment by the criminal justice system than an adult.

To attempt to focus explicitly on the transition from juvenile to adult (presuming that with respect to law enforcement the transition occurs at age eighteen), the age variable was redefined. An AGE18 dummy variable was used instead of actual age to separate those eighteen and over from those younger. Depending on what group was considered of three subsamples—whites, blacks, or all individuals age 25 and younger—the dummy variable explains 33 to 100 percent of the age effect on crime participation.

Further analysis of the Brooklyn data reveals additional insights into the transition process. For example, one can find a distinct turning point in criminality roughly between ages nineteen and twenty.[42] This is consistent with more severe treatment by the criminal justice system only beginning to have an impact at age eighteen and a reasonable lag for such effects to begin to appear in police data as criminality after eighteen leads to arrest. This becomes clearer when the data are separated by age before estimating the crime participation response to economic opportunities and to previous arrests by police. This, in effect, allows for both the magnitudes of the deterrence and economic opportunity variables to vary with age as well as the coefficients reflecting individuals' responses to deterrence forces and economic opportunities. Doing this, the deterrent effect of prior arrest is found to increase after age eighteen, while the effect of economic opportunities reducing crime becomes less. The age at which economic opportunities are most important is earlier than eighteen. The deterrent effect of law enforcement becomes relatively more important for those who might be turned around after age eighteen. But, among persisters, neither economic opportunities nor police interventions play an important role once an individual is solidly into crime as a major provider of income.

Through all of this, an effect consistent with the estimations using the NLSY data is that, when all other factors are considered, being black is not significantly related to the likelihood that an individual will participate in crime. Again, the relationship between race and crime appears to be more an employment problem than one of having a greater likelihood to be a participant in crime.

It has been gratifying to us, in comparing these two data sets, that, whether the crime data are self-report data as in the NLSY sample or are based on police reports, as are the Brooklyn data, the estimation results tell essentially the same story about virtually all of the relationships with which we have been concerned. Not only does this tend to validate the reasonableness of using the NLSY self-report data to investigate behavioral relationships affecting crime participation, it tends to generate greater confidence in the use of self-report data generally. This is an important result in view of the great difficulty and costs involved in generating longitudinal data that include information on crime participation.

Further analysis was conducted for age groups seventeen, eighteen, nineteen, and twenty and older.[43] This had the effect of allowing both the coefficients on deterrence effects and the status of prior arrest numbers to vary with age. Similarly, the coefficient on the variable representing economic opportunities, that is, weeks worked prior to arrest, can vary as well as the magnitude of the variable. When this was done, the transition by age, relating to the specific deterrence from arrest, was found to be greatest between the ages of nineteen and twenty. This should not be an unexpected finding when one considers that for specific deterrence to have an impact would require arrest and sentencing after age eighteen. While one might expect a greater general deterrence effect at reaching age eighteen, specific deterrence is unlikely to coincide with turning eighteen but rather will take place after a reasonable lag during which offenses and subsequent apprehension take place. At that point, age twenty and above, the effect of arrest likelihood has a substantially higher impact.

Similarly, the transition from a labor market in which there are institutional constraints like child labor laws to reduce employment opportunities to one of enlarged opportunities has a substantial impact. Below eighteen, the lack of opportunities has a substantially greater impact. At eighteen and over, a greater number of the individuals in the sample were employed and the lack of economic opportunities played a smaller role in affecting crime participation.

To summarize, the deterrent effect of prior arrest is found to increase after age eighteen while the effect of economic opportunities reducing crime becomes less. Economic opportunities are most important prior to age eighteen. The deterrent effect of law enforcement becomes relatively more important to those who might be turned around after age eighteen. However, among persisters, neither plays an important role once an individual is solidly into crime as a major provider of income. Such results lead logically to the third paper we wish to emphasize.

The third paper considers crime involvement as a dynamic process of individuals either remaining innocents, not involved in crime, or experimenters and subsequently either desisters or persisters for a subsequent decade or longer as serious offenders. Our dynamic model shows that this process of experimentation and either desistence or persistence leads to a stable distribution of crime participation. It is this analysis of behavior that shows that once an individual has three or more arrests, the likelihood of becoming a desister falls to insignificance. The size of the crime participating population over the pattern of the age/crime profile will depend largely on what happens before those three or more arrests. One hope is that individuals will remain innocents, and this paper has something to say about that. Beyond that there is hope that the experimenter will become a desister. Here, there is the same evidence that what will help is economic opportunities that are made greater by investment in human capital.

From these results, one may conclude that there is a narrow window in age within which economic opportunities and/or deterrence effect may influence behavior that will determine the ultimate magnitude of the subpopulation of eighteen- to thirty-plus-year-old participants in crime. If this window of opportunity is not exploited, then the only alternative is to rely on an incapacitation policy. The window for deterring crime by police intervention is largely closed down following a third arrest, which is likely to have taken place by age eighteen or soon thereafter. Furthermore, the power of alternative legitimate economic opportunities to lead to a non-criminal future is substantially diminished at about the same time. The number continuing to be offenders provides a compelling argument for focusing seriously on the dynamic process of individuals getting into the serious criminal population and making greater efforts to stem the inflow into the population rather than simply attempting to incapacitate those who enter.

INTERPRETING A PUZZLE

Having indicated our satisfaction that we obtain almost identical results from analysis of the NLSY data and the Vera Institute Brooklyn data, we still recognized a puzzle regarding the NLSY results that raised a question when our results were first presented. How could we believe the NLSY self-report data with regard to blacks where they showed similar behavior to that of whites when official report data invariably show blacks to be more criminally involved than whites? We had no satisfactory response at the time. Finding that our results were consistent between the official report data of the Brooklyn study and that of the NLSY seemed to confirm the validity of our statistical result but didn't answer the puzzle. A recent analysis supplies a logical answer.

In the NLSY User's Guide one can find the following in regard to questions of non-response or refusal to answer questions about delinquency "were higher for males, minorities, the economically disadvantaged and high school dropouts ... those expected to have higher rates of illegal activities."[44] An explanation may be that refusal to admit serious involvement with the criminal justice system is rational for those discriminated against by the system. This hypothesis finds support in a study of the probability of ever being charged with a crime as it varies with family structure and family income.[45]

In that study, a model for the probability of ever being charged for a crime was estimated using separate coefficients for black, Hispanic, and all others. There was no significant difference among the ethnic groups for the variables age, family income, the score on the Armed Forces Qualification Test, and whether the father was in the household when the youth was fourteen. The one difference was separate intercepts for blacks and separate coefficients for the variable "no man present in the household when the respondent was fourteen."

The authors concluded that there was very little difference in behavior among the three ethnic groups, that is, age, income, the measure of intelligence, and the presence of a father in the household all have the same effects on delinquency, unconditional on ethnicity. The more negative intercept for blacks than others can be interpreted as a rational reluctance to self-report participation in crime, since the criminal justice system can be perceived as discriminating against blacks.[46]

This result was used to investigate two questions: (1) what would be the probability of ever being charged for black youths if they had the same intercept, that is, reporting ratio, as the non-black, non-Hispanic group? (2) what would be the probability for black youth of being charged if they had the same average for age, family income, family structure, and so on as the non-black, non-Hispanic youths? In the sample, the average family income for blacks was 69 percent lower, and the father was present in only 54 percent of households compared to 80 percent for the other group.

Further calculations led to the conclusion that delinquency for black youths would be at least 25 percent lower if their family structure and family income were comparable to those of white youth. These calculations supported the conclusion that the effect of social and economic conditions on delinquency does not vary by ethnicity. It was stated further, "If social and economic conditions did not vary by ethnicity, then neither would delinquency. Because the criminal justice system does discriminate, researchers should be aware that self-reporting of delinquency can vary by ethnicity."

Such findings are consistent with the finding of comparable results between the studies using the NLSY self-report data and the Vera Institute data for Brooklyn that uses official reports. Such evidence provides added assurance that our perception of the dynamic process for youthful entry into criminality and the factors influencing it are correct.

THE CONSEQUENCES OF THE DYNAMIC PROCESS OF CRIME GENERATION

To gain insight into the magnitude of change resulting from the dynamic process of growing numbers of young entrants into the criminal population, it is useful to make a comparison of estimated criminal populations including both those imprisoned and those at large in the United States from 1970 to 1993. It also sheds some light on the extent to which past efforts at controlling crime by a mostly incapacitation policy have been disappointing, if we consider the aforementioned historical imprisonment and crime rates.

The approach used here has been to consider the levels of index crimes reported to the police, not including offenses for larceny, using estimates of criminality of serious offenders to approximate the criminal population at large in the United States. By taking the number of non-larceny index crime offenses reported in 1993 and using an estimated criminality coefficient (λ), based on estimates by class of offense from Cohen,[47] weighted by the proportion of those offenses in 1993, one obtains an estimate of the number of serious offenders at large in 1993. The total comes to 964,892. Adding to this the number of serious offenders in state and federal prisons, not including drug offenders, of 662,862 yields an estimate of 1,627,754 serious offenders in the United States in 1993, representing 0.63 percent of the U.S. population. Of these, 40.7 percent are in state or federal prisons. A similar calculation for 1970 yields an estimate that 0.36 percent of the population were serious offenders, of which 23.8 percent were in state or federal prisons.

Thus, we get an estimate of the force of this dynamic process of crime generation in which increasing fractions of our youth were entering the serious criminal population. We observe that, in spite of the increase in imprisonment ratios from 96.4 per 100,000 population in 1970 to 350 per 100,000 in 1993, an increase of 263.1 percent, the proportion of population who are serious offenders has risen by 72.2 percent. While this is hardly an argument for relaxing our efforts to incapacitate serious offenders, it seems to be a compelling argument for ways to stem the *inflow* of new offenders. A reduction by one of the inflow into serious crime will have the same impact on the crime level in a given period as that of incarcerating another serious offender. However, saving of one individual from a criminal career not only will lower the equilibrium level of the serious criminal population but will have other, positive benefits on society, by creating greater levels of legitimate output and supporting economic growth.

That is, successful policies to expand individuals' investment in their own human capital and greater availability of legitimate earning opportunities before age eighteen could ultimately reduce the population of active participants in crime, thus reducing the aggregate crime burden. At the same time, a greater proportion of youth in legitimate work would make a positive contribution to society, while reducing the need for incapacitation in high-cost facilities. In view of recent estimates of the aggregate cost of crime in the United States, the reduction in the sum of costs to victims and control costs could be great enough to justify substantial investments in policies that could yield a more crime-free society.[48]

Consider the dynamic process and how it works in reality. The criminal population begins with youth experimenting with crime, either getting out early, say at around age eighteen, or staying in until age thirty-five or greater. With a stable population and a rate of entrance to the criminal population that is approximately constant, a society will end up with a stable criminal population proportional to the number of new entrants per year, with an equal number getting out at the upper end of the age distribution. If we could take measures to reduce the inflow by as little as 10 percent, the equilibrium criminal population will be 10 percent smaller and, with a constant rate of criminality (λ), the crime level will be reduced to 10 percent below what it would otherwise be.

We might attempt to estimate the social saving due to this change in a number of ways. One is to use the recent estimates of the total cost of crime annually for the United States of $450 billion.[49] This implies a social saving of $45 billion annually. In other words, the saving in expenditures for criminal justice and the value of losses by victims would, on the average, sum to such a number. We could consider another estimate of saving by considering only the cost of criminal justice for local, state, and federal institutions in the United States, if it could be reduced by 10 percent by a reduction in crime. This ignores the savings associated with prevented loss of life, reduced injuries and hospitalizations, and reduction in the need for insurance and private protection, accompanying reduction of homicides by 2,453, rapes by 65,958, assaults by 113,510, burglaries by 283,480, and so on. The saving would be $9.38 billion in expenditures annually just for criminal justice services provided by government.[50]

Are we willing to risk $45 billion in what are essentially investments in human capital to achieve this sort of objective? Consider, further, that most investments in human capital have a benefit-to-cost ratio of greater than one. That is, the individual for whom the investment is made will be likely to enjoy a future income stream whose present value is increased at least by the value of the investment. Should that be true for the sorts of expenditures discussed here, the $45 billion expenditure would be costless from a social perspective. This follows because the affected individual will be earning greater income and spending more for his or her own support, as well as paying more in taxes, tending to offset the cost of such investment. In contrast, one who turns criminal will be preying on others and likely spending time as a ward of the state.

A TIME OF OPPORTUNITY

We believe that recent data on crime levels in the United States tend to reinforce the inferences from our overview of our own research. One sees substantial declines in overall crime rates over the most recent years. At first, some criminologists were suggesting that this was only a temporary phenomenon, in view of the forthcoming shift in the population age distribution toward a younger median age. What was particularly disturbing to these individuals was that, when one viewed crime participation by age, one found that crimes by youth were increasing in the face of overall levels of crime declining.[51] Clearly, the threat of incapacitation some years into the future was having little impact on present crime participation by youth.[52] A successful longer-run strategy of bringing down the high social costs of crime depends on having some impact on the dynamic process that begins with the onset of criminal behavior and either encourages non-participation of innocents or deters and encourages experimenters to desist from further crime involvement. A number of criminologists who a decade earlier were unwilling to recognize economic opportunities as having much effect on crime were now attributing much to the state of the economy.[53] Because we would all agree that the decline in unemployment rates alone is unlikely to be the explanation, this must mean that a broader explanation based on economic opportunities must be playing an important role. In all fairness, it is too soon to have been able to conduct serious empirical investigation of causes for the decline in the crime rate, but it would be hard to argue that the decline has been a result of any cohesive crime policy.

One often touted source of possible increases in aggregate crime needs to be put to rest as a matter for concern. That is the effect of the increase in proportions of youth in the population as a consequence of the "baby boom" and echoes of that boom. As we mentioned at the start of the chapter, we found that from 1952 to 1967 that effect accounted for 15 percent of the rise in the larceny aggregate arrest rate. An estimation of a more sophisticated model that took account of the changes in population proportions for the period 1964 to 1987 for "high risk populations," both youth and minorities, yielded a similar conclusion.[54] By assuming arrest rates by age and race did not change, i.e. only population subsets changing, it was possible to calculate that the age proportion change contributed to a 9.7 percent decline in aggregate crime rates. The change in racial/ethnic proportions alone would have yielded an offsetting 10.8 percent increase, and changes in age-specific arrest rates would have accounted for a 98.9 percent rise in crime rates. This implies that it wasn't the rise in the numbers of youth or in the numbers of any specific subset of youth that accounted for most of the year-by-year rise in crime. Rather, it was the proportion of youths that were lured into crime or a change in individual crime rates (λ's) that accounted for most of the huge increase in crime from the early 1960s to the end of the 1980s. Thus, while the age-distribution hypothesis is a valid logical argument, it is of little historical importance, even with the large population age-distribution shifts we have observed in the last fifty years.

Studies have shown that the gap between rich and poor in the United States has gotten worse. History tells us not to expect the current level of prosperity to continue uninterrupted. U.S. incarceration rates remain among the world's highest, keeping the total cost of crime high. If we do not make an effort to deal with the dynamic process of entry into the criminal population by youth, the overall cost of crime may still be increasing and too many disadvantaged youth will continue on the path to hard time.

The cynic will argue that, if that were really true, we would be investing in ways to come to grips with the problems of youth already. The fact is, we will only have done so if the benefits can be directly identified as being in our personal self-interest. We tend not to invest in someone else's human capital. If we could link directly the reduced risks of crime to the taxes we would pay for human capital investments for others unable to make them, then the answer might be different. Perhaps we should take another look at the investment in the G. I. Bill following World War II. This was a social experiment with a huge recognized social payoff.

It may be time to reevaluate our options. Clearly, the huge investments in criminal justice, including high levels of imprisonments at the expense of investments in education at all levels, have not produced the sort of society we all wish to attain. Taking account of the ethnic disparities in the numbers of youth who are becoming educated and entering the ranks of the economically successful, one can only predict that many minority youth are doomed to be candidates for crime or, at best, to end up in the ranks of the poor. The potential for crime reduction is only one reason for investing in youth.

RELATING TO CURRENTLY POPULAR CONCERNS

What are the factors that we have found to be important? The public, today, talks of family values. Our own research tends to illuminate the role of family attitudes in crime involvement by youth. It shows that homes in which the father is present and the mother is at home are the most nurturing environment for crime-free youth. Furthermore, as our studies show, youths having family financial support are less likely to be involved in crimes for income.

Economic realities for today make the attainment of all of this difficult, if not impossible, for many families. Society cannot simply legislate family attitudes, nor can it impose behavioral standards on a resistant society. While we may deplore the rise in the numbers of single-parent households, there are often legitimate reasons why those households lack two parents. Furthermore, there are probably many single-parent households in which the children are better off than if the parental couples had remained together. In any event, we live in a society that will not tolerate interference in a family's right to decide its own attitudes toward one another or form of organization.

So what is the fallback position? Beyond using the stick, we can provide incentives to achieve desired social outcomes or behavior. Our studies show that crime participation for youth is less likely in a household where the father is present. We cannot force this to be so, but we can modify the incentive structure to make it more likely. Perhaps we have made divorce too easy, the costs too low. We find that youth are less likely to be involved in crime when the father is a full participant in household efforts. Establishing rules in the workplace that make it easier for a father to exercise parental responsibility may impose some restrictions on firms, but they may also make for a better society. Our data show that a youth is less likely to become an experimenter in crime if he has some unearned financial support. This is easier in a two-parent household. In one that is not, we need to do more to make absent parents more financially responsible. The current record on this is abysmal. Furthermore, we need to provide positive incentives to single parents to assure that quality childcare facilities are available and to assure that children are able to continue in school to the completion of their education.

Among single-parent households, which will continue to be inevitable, we need to provide appropriate incentives as well. Incentives that will encourage women to be employed rather than on welfare must include easier access to child care.

Some policies need to be targeted directly at youth. Young members of low-income and single-parent households need unearned financial support to match more nearly support of youth from more affluent two-parent households. To achieve this, there must be the possibility of legitimate part-time employment, which also could encourage good work habits. At the same time, youths need to be encouraged to stay in school to raise their potential for future employment. Social institutions to supplement the role of parents to help to achieve these goals need to be expanded and maintained. We can, as a society, make the attainment of these things easier. These do not have to be government-operated activities, but incentive may need to be provided to encourage their increased provision.

That black youth are found to be more likely participants in crime does not mean that their problems are different, only more intense. If the incentives for remaining in school are strengthened, legitimate jobs are made more accessible, and family situations can become more stable, they will perform well in society. These are big ifs, however. We are still a long way from the level playing field and equal opportunity. In particular, a great effort will be needed to deal with the problems of the inner city, where most youths in trouble reside.

The trade-offs for crime control remain the same. To discourage the commission of crimes, we can establish penalties to incapacitate or deter as well as punish offenders, or we can try to alleviate factors that make crime involvement more likely, particularly for youths who may still be susceptible to such influences.

In our view, our own research suggests that a change in policies to reduce crimes by youth holds a promise that has been neglected too much and for too long.[55] We need to be changing, for the better, the dynamics of the growth of the criminally involved element of the population, to create a better society.

NOTES

1. L. Phillips and H.L. Votey, "Crime, Youth and the Labor Market," *Journal of Political Economy* 5(2) (1972): 463–478.

2. In data provided by the U.S. Bureau of Labor Statistics, the civilian population is often divided between the categories "Labor Force" and "Not in the Labor Force." Persons in the labor force, in turn, can be divided between "Employed" and "Unemployed." Thus, it is possible to account separately for the population subsets "Employed," "Unemployed," and "Not in the Labor Force." A part of labor economics focuses on how individuals choose to be in one or the other of these categories.

3. The relevant time series for male school enrollments by race were presented in H.L. Votey and L. Phillips, "The Control of Criminal Activity: An Economic Analysis," in D. Glaser, *Handbook of Criminology* (Chicago: Rand-McNally, 1974).

4. See H.L. Votey and L. Phillips, "Police Effectiveness and the Production Function for Law Enforcement," *Journal of Legal Studies* 1(2) (1972): 423–436; L. Phillips and H. L. Votey, "An Economic Analysis of the Deterrent Effect of Law Enforcement on Criminal Activity," *Journal of Criminal Law, Criminology and Police Science* (1972); *The Economics of Crime Control* (Beverly Hills, CA: Sage, 1981).

5. Votey and Phillips, ibid., pp. 182–184.

6. The shift in focus of research is revealed in the series by M. Tonry and N. Morris, *Crime and Justice: An Annual Review of Research*, first published in 1979. Relatively few of the articles deal with crime causality. There is a considerable focus on criminal careers, as exemplified by the voluminous research of Blumstein, Cohen, and others, cited in Jacqueline Cohen, "Incapacitation Research," in volume 5 (1983). In those studies, a common perception, supported by research, is that career criminals commit crimes at a more or less constant personal rate, referred to as their λ. This set the stage for a further round of research, including writers such as Peter W. Greenwood, "Controlling the Crime Rate through Imprisonment," in James Q. Wilson, *Crime and Public Policy* (San Francisco: ICS Press, 1983). In a major work setting the stage for future crime research, by David Farrington, Lloyd E. Ohlin, and James Q. Wilson, *Understanding and Controlling Crime* (1986), there is virtually no mention of economic factors influencing causality and no proposal to study such possible effects.

7. In Votey and Phillips, op. cit., we noted a statistically significant turning point in the trend of real expenditures on law enforcement in the period 1952–1967. Prior to 1958, they were rising at 5.3 percent annually; subsequently, they rose at only 4.5 percent. By the period 1980–1993, as reported in *Sourcebook of Criminal Justice Statistics, 1997*, there was almost no increase in per capita deployment of police in the United States. The increase was a mere 3.9 percent in thirteen years. In the same thirteen-year period, em-

ployment of state and local corrections officers per capita increased by 88.1 percent or almost twenty-three times.

8. George J. Borjas, *Labor Economics*, chapter 7, "Human Capital: Education and Earnings" (New York: McGraw-Hill, 1998), provides a detailed picture of disparity in educational attainment by race/ethnicity. For example, in 1992 in the United States, 32.2 percent of black and 47.4 percent of Hispanics had less than a high school education, compared to 19.1 percent for whites. For whites, 14.6 percent had obtained a bachelor's degree versus 8.3 percent of blacks and 6.3 percent of Hispanics.

9. An expanded presentation of the modern utilitarian approach to individual behavior including criminal activity is in Llad Phillips, "Economic Perspectives on Criminality: An Eclectic View" in Brian Forst (ed.), *The Socio-Economics of Crime and Justice* (Armonk, NY: M. E. Sharpe, 1993).

10. The social-cost-minimizing approach to crime policy is spelled out in Llad Phillips and Harold L. Votey, Jr., *The Economics of Crime Control* (Beverly Hills, CA: Sage, 1981).

11. Franklin M. Fisher and Daniel Nagin, "On the Feasibility of Identifying the Crime Function in a Simultaneous Model of Crime Rates and Sanction Levels," in Alfred Blumstein, Jacqueline Cohen, and Daniel Nagin, *Deterrence and Incapacitation: Estimating the Effects of Criminal Sanctions on Crime Rates* (Washington, DC: National Academy of Sciences, 1978).

12. This first comes from Marvin Wolfgang, Robert Figlio, and Thorsten Sellin, *Delinquency in a Birth Cohort* (Chicago: University of Chicago Press, 1972).

13. See David P. Farrington, "Age and Crime," in M. Tonry and N. Morris, op. cit., vol. 7, 1986, for a discussion of the age/crime profile and the views of criminologists as to its cause.

14. See J. Petersilia, "Crime and Punishment in California," *CPS Brief*, Berkeley, CA: California Policy Seminar Vol. 5, No. 4 (1993); Blumstein, A., Cohen, J., Roth, J. A., and Visher C., (eds.), *Criminal Careers and "Career" Criminals*, vol. 1 (Washington, DC: National Academy Press, 1986).

15. U.S. Department of Justice, *Historical Corrections Statistics in the United States, 1950–1984* and *Sourcebook of Criminal Justice Statistics, 1994* (Washington, DC: U.S. Government Printing Office).

16. Estimates based on U.S. Department of Justice, *Justice Expenditure and Employment in the U.S., 1971–1979, Justice Expenditure and Employment Extracts: 1982 and 1983*, and *Sourcebook of Criminal Justice Statistics 1994*.

17. Most studies are funded by grants of one to two years, whereas the benefits to investment in human capital accrue over periods as much as 20 years later when both investigators and funding agencies have moved on to new agendas. An exception is Peter W. Greenwood, Karyn F. Model, et al., *Diverting Children from a Life of Crime* (Santa Monica, CA: RAND Corporation, 1998), which calculates positive net benefits from just this sort of investment.

18. Richard B. Freeman, "Crime and Unemployment," in J.Q. Wilson, op. cit., analyzes a number of empirical studies on the relationship between "unemployment (and other labor market variables) and crime" and concludes that "they fail to show a well defined, clearly quantifiable linkage." He goes on to conclude that "sanctions tend to have a greater impact on criminal behavior than do market factors."

19. A basic problem confronted by anyone who has studied individual crime participation data and arrest records is that numbers of arrests will invariably be correlated with the number of offenses an individual has admitted to. It is only with careful modeling of individual behavior that plausible measures of deterrence effects can be estimated.

20. Freeman, op. cit., reviews a number of studies that find little evidence that job opportunities reduce opportunities to recidivate.

21. Joan Petersilia, "Criminal Career Research," in N. Morris and M. Tonry, op. cit., vol. 2, 1980, states "No consistent effect on the termination of criminal careers as a result of criminal justice sanctions or treatment programs has been demonstrated."

22. James Lynch, "Crime in International Perspective," in J.Q. Wilson and Joan Petersilia, *Crime* (San Francisco: ICS Press, 1995), finds property crime rates in the United States to be somewhat lower, to very nearly the same, as in other high-income countries and violent crimes such as homicide to be two to eight times as high.

23. See Joan Petersilia, op. cit., and Peter W. Greenwood, Karyn F. Model, et al., op. cit.

24. Phillips and Votey, "Crime Control Policy in California: The Decade Ahead," paper prepared for presentation at the Annual Meeting of the Western Economic Association International, San Francisco, CA, Summer 1996.

25. Center for Human Resource Research, Ohio State University, National Longitudinal Survey of Youth, 1979–1987.

26. James W. Thompson, *Relationships Between Employment and Crime: A Survey of Brooklyn Residents, 1979–1980* (Ann Arbor, MI: Inter-university Consortium for Political and Social Research); the original award for the research was made by the National Institute of Justice to the Vera Institute, New York, NY.

27. Phillips and Votey, "The Influence of Police Interventions and Alternative Income Sources on the Dynamic Process of Choosing Crime as a Career," *Journal of Quantitative Criminology* 3(3) (1987): 330–342.

28. This characterization of behavior first appears in A. Blumstein, D.P. Farrington, and S. Moitra, "Delinquency Careers: Innocents, Desisters and Persisters," in M. Tonry and N. Morris (eds.), *Crime and Justice: An Annual Review of Research*, vol. 6 (Chicago: University of Chicago Press, 1985), pp. 187–219.

29. Votey, "Employment, Age, Race and Crime: A Labor Theoretic Investigation," *Journal of Quantitative Criminology* 7(2) (1991): 123–153.

30. Perry Shapiro and Harold L. Votey, Jr., "Deterrence and Subjective Probabilities of Arrest: Modeling Individual Decisions to Drink and Drive in Sweden," *Law and Society Review* 18(4) (1984): 583–604.

31. Phillips and Votey, "Rational Choice Models of Crimes by Youth," *Review of Black Political Economy* 16(1–2) (1987): 1–90.

32. Phillips and Votey, *Recidivism Criteria and the Determination of Best Policy: Research Report to the National Institute of Justice* (Santa Barbara, CA: Community and Organization Research Institute, 1993).

33. Phillips and Votey, "Rational Choice Models."

34. Votey, op. cit.

35. Phillips and Votey, "The Influence of Police Interventions."

36. Phillips and Votey, "Rational Choice Models."

37. Of more than a dozen estimates conducted, including some not reported, one coefficient was weakly significant, positively, for desisters/persisters.

38. William S. Comanor and Llad Phillips, "The Impact of Income and Family Structure on Delinquency," working paper, Department of Economics, University of California, Santa Barbara (July 1995, Revised).

39. M. Sviridoff and J.W. Thompson, *Employment and Crime: A Summary Report* (New York: Vera Institute of Justice, 1984).

40. David F. Greenberg, "Delinquency and the Age Structure of Society," in *Criminology Review Yearbook*, S. Messinger and E. Bittner (eds.) (Beverly Hills, CA: Sage, 1979); and "Age and Crime" in *Encyclopedia of Crime and Justice*, S. H. Kadish (ed.) (New York: Free Press, 1983).

41. Votey, "Employment, Age, Race and Crime."

42. Harold L. Votey, Jr., "Youth, Maturity and Participation in Crime for Income: Isolation of Causes for the Age Effect," paper presented at the Western Economic Association International Annual Meeting, Lake Tahoe, CA, 1989.

43. Votey, ibid.

44. Center for Human Resource Research, Ohio State University, *NLSY* [National Longitudinal Survey of Youth] *79 User's Guide 1997*, pp. 98–99.

45. Comanor and Phillips, op. cit.

46. E. Drucker, "Drug Prohibition and Public Health," *Public Health Reports* 114 (January/February 1999): 14–29.

47. Jacqueline Cohen, "Incapacitation as a Strategy for Crime Control: Possibilities and Pitfalls," in Tonry and Morris (eds.), *Crime and Justice: An Annual Review of Research* (Chicago: University of Chicago Press, 1983). Based on Cohen's most conservative estimates of criminality coefficients (λ) by offense, ranging between 10.4 to 15.8 for the higher estimates and 4.5 to 8.2 for the lower set, we obtained values of 6.82 and 6.55 for 1970 and 1993 respectively. Offense and imprisonment data are from Bureau of Justice Statistics, *Sourcebook of Criminal Justice Statistics* (appropriate issues) and *Historical Corrections Statistics for the United States, 1850–1984*.

48. Mark A. Cohen, Ted R. Miller, and Brian Wiersema, *Victim Costs and Consequences: A New Look* (Washington, DC: National Institute of Justice, 1995).

49. Ibid.

50. This was the figure reported for combined local, state, and federal expenditures for criminal justice in the United States for 1993 in *Sourcebook of Criminal Justice Statistics 1994*.

51. *New York Times*, May 6, 1996, in a story on the decline in reported crime in 1995, Alfred Blumstein is quoted regarding the rise observed for larceny offenses, as saying "This is the first visible sign of the anticipated new wave of crime by the future generation of kids." James Alan Fox was quoted that the declining figures "are certainly encouraging, but no reason for celebration" because "there are two different crime trends in America, one for the young and one for adults, and they are moving in opposite directions."

52. *New York Times*, January 11, 1999. In response to the suggestion that the decline in crime could be attributed to the higher levels of incarceration that are currently in effect, Alfred Blumstein labeled this as "too simplistic," pointing out that "it ignores the fact that, throughout the 1980's, crime rates were going up when the prison population was rising just as fast as it has in the 1990's." "To gauge how much impact prison has on crime, it is important to separate older and younger criminals."

53. Asked to explain the cause of the dramatic decline in violence rates announced in September 1996, Dan Glaser, professor emeritus of sociology at the University of California, responded that, "Full employment is the major factor" (*Los Angeles Times*, September 7, 1996). On December 20, 1998, "The booming economy of the 1990's has also helped," the experts agreed. Alfred Blumstein, after mentioning the decline in the crack trade, was quoted as saying, "Fortunately, that was accompanied by good economic times so that there were legitimate jobs for the young people" entering the workforce.

54. Phillips and Votey, "Demographics and Trends in Crime: A Failed Hypothesis," paper presented at the Law and Society Association Annual Meeting, Berkeley, CA, June 4, 1990; presented, revised and expanded, to the Annual Meeting of the Western Economic Association International, Seattle, WA, July 1, 1991.

55. While our focus is narrower and more technical, we find an amazing agreement with the prescriptions of the thirty-year update of the National Commission on the Causes and Prevention of Violence, *To Establish Justice, To Insure Domestic Tranquility* (Washington, DC: Milton S. Eisenhower Foundation, December 10, 1999).

5

The End of the Juvenile Court: Prospects for Our Children

Barry A. Krisberg

With the passage of H.R. 3 in 1997 (introduced by Rep. William McCollum, R., Florida), the vast majority of members of the U.S. House of Representatives joined in the death watch for the American juvenile court.[1] That same summer, the Senate began debate on its version of federal juvenile justice legislation. The Senate bill prepared by Senators Orin Hatch (R., Utah) and Jeffrey Sessions (R., Alabama) differed only in minor ways from H.R. 3. Both bills assumed that juvenile crime was out of control and that the juvenile court was far too weak to deal with the new breed of "super predators" among our young. The proposed solution was to dismantle key elements of American jurisprudence that had guided our treatment of wayward children since the end of the nineteenth century. The new paradigm of justice emphasized prosecuting more juveniles as adult offenders, relaxing prohibitions on housing children in prisons and jails, ending the confidentiality of juvenile court hearings, and mandating punishments for even minor offenses committed by juveniles. The proposed federal juvenile crime bills also reduced the authority of juvenile court judges to decide which youths should be tried in adult courts. Congressional actions altered the federal justice system with respect to children, although very few youths are charged with violations of federal laws.[2] More important, the Congress offered substantial grants to states provided that they enact the "get tough" provisions contained in the bills.

The Clinton administration's reaction to H.R. 3 was only somewhat negative. The changes in the federal prosecution of juvenile offenders were quite similar to those proposed by the Clinton administration. Nonetheless, Attorney General Janet Reno criticized McCollum's bill for its lack of effective gun control provisions and its inadequate funding for prevention programs. The president suggested that states be given more latitude in the *methods* by which juveniles would be selected for adult prosecution, but there was no explicit rejection of the congressional policy direction that more juveniles be treated as if they were adult offenders.

These radical changes in the proposed federal legislation were met with substantial professional and media opposition. Virtually no reputable law enforcement, prosecution, judicial, or corrections organization endorsed the proposed federal juvenile justice law. Youth advocates launched a steady attack on the provisions of H.R. 3 and S. 10. A poll suggested that the vast majority of the public did not support the goals of these proposed new laws (Schiraldi and Soler 1998). A number of editorial writers for such papers as the *Washington Post*, the *Baltimore Sun*, and *USA Today* described the content of the proposed federal laws as "deranged." By the summer of 1998 it was beginning to look as if S. 10 was doomed and the entire federal package would be stalled until the next Congress. But the tragic killings of schoolmates by an 11-year-old and a 13-year-old in Jonesboro, Arkansas, stimulated public debate and gave S. 10 a new lease on life. Many of the same ideas contained in H.R. 3 and S. 10 were reintroduced in the next Congress. Once again, these later bills were stalled in a Republican and Democratic party dispute over gun control. Few congressmen opposed the basic dismantling of the juvenile court.

Unfortunately, this federal policy debate was not an isolated phenomenon. Legislative activity in the nation's capitol mirrored actions in many states. During the past five years, over forty states have passed laws lowering the age at which juveniles could be prosecuted as adults, giving more discretion to prosecutors to make these decisions, increasing penalties for offenders in the juvenile court, and eliminating the confidentiality of juvenile court proceedings (Torbet et al. 1996).

This political frenzy to reform the juvenile court came at a time when juvenile crime rates, even for violent crimes, were dropping. Politicians and the media continued to scapegoat children for America's violent crime problem, although adults commit the vast majority of serious and violent offenses (Jones and Krisberg 1994). The media dwells on a very small number of violent crimes committed by very young children—retelling these stories over and over again. Academics such as Princeton Professor John DiIulio (1995) have warned about a new wave of "super predators," but his dire forecast is based on an inaccurate reading of research and statistics on youth crime. Criminal justice officials and youth-serving agencies also have fueled public fears about growing levels of youth violence in order to attract new sources of public and private funding for their programs. Violence prevention has replaced drug prevention as the new way to claim funding for youth programming.

The juvenile court has been under siege for several years, attacked by critics from both ends of the political spectrum. Conservatives have asserted that the juvenile court is too lenient with serious juvenile offenders. Liberals have complained about the inadequate legal representation of youths, the limited due process protections of the juvenile court, and the overreach of the court into matters such as truancy and family conflicts. The juvenile court has few defenders, and the public is, at best, unaware of how the court actually operates. At worst, the citizenry doubts that the court has the will to control violent youths.

It is likely that the 1999 centennial celebration of the founding of the juvenile court will be more of a wake than an anniversary celebration. Already many states are creating new systems of dealing with adolescents under the auspices of criminal courts and adult corrections systems.

Will anything be lost by letting the juvenile court ideal go "quietly into that good night"? This is a serious and sobering question that should be answered before the juvenile court movement dies for lack of interest. What are the human consequences of embracing the new paradigm of justice for youths propounded by Rep. McCollum, Senators Hatch and Sessions, and their supporters? This question can be answered in terms of both research data and poignant individual stories of how the new paradigm of juvenile justice is a recipe for disaster.

America's most famous legal philosopher, Roscoe Pound (1965), claimed that the American juvenile court was the greatest step forward in Anglo-American law since the Magna Carta. What impressed Professor Pound was the redemptive vision of the juvenile court that focused on individual offenders and attempted to diagnose and remediate the underlying problems that contributed to the criminal behavior. Whereas the criminal law was grounded in concepts of deterrence, retribution, and social revenge, the juvenile court ideal embraced the idea of restoring young offenders to become productive citizens. The founders of the juvenile court were guided by Enlightenment and Utilitarian philosophers, who assumed the perfectibility of the human spirit. The juvenile court acted as if children were not just small adults—they needed to be protected and nurtured, even if they violated the law. Anglo-American criminal law assumes a less optimistic view of human nature, relying instead on a calculation of the impact of repressive measures to produce behavioral compliance. The juvenile court set forth a more noble ideal, albeit one that was rarely realized in practice.

A TALE OF TWO CHILDREN

There are volumes of research studies citing the strengths and weaknesses of the juvenile court. There are many excellent statistical analyses showing the questionable benefits (and potential harm) of treating children as if they were adults (see, for example, Howell 1996 and Krisberg 1997). Later in this chapter, I summarize the key findings of this research. But these scientific efforts do not begin to capture the true dangers of the current frenzy to kill the juvenile court. Moreover, the available research has been repeatedly discarded by the elected officials who are championing the "get tough" policies. Since the juvenile court was created to introduce a human dimension to the handling of troubled youngsters, the story of two such children best illustrates the folly of where our nation is headed.

In 1995 a politically ambitious California legislator, Charles Quackenbush, proposed trying children in criminal courts who were as young as fourteen years of age and who were charged with murder. Previously, children under sixteen who were charged with homicide were handled in juvenile courts and were confined in the California Youth Authority. A frightened California public, believing that there were no other practical approaches to preventing youth violence, reluctantly supported that law. It should be noted the practical effect of this legal change was far less radical than the provisions of the current federal juvenile crime bills. The California law continued the practice of holding hearings before a juvenile court judge to determine the youngster's fitness for retention in the juvenile justice system. The proposed federal legislation—and the laws of several states—shifts this decision-making process to the whims of legislators. Another increasingly popular reform gives discretion directly to prosecutors, eliminating the need for judicial hearings with youths represented by counsel. Prosecutors will no longer be required to present evidence before a specially trained judge that the child defendant is not redeemable.

The stories that follow concern the first two fourteen-year-olds who were tried under the new California statute. I have given them fictitious names to protect their confidentiality, but all the other facts of their cases are accurate to the best of my knowledge. These are tragic and compelling tales of justice gone haywire. And if such manifest injustices occur under the relatively limited California law, the possibilities of social harm under broader "get tough" schemes are far greater.

In a southern California county an Anglo youngster, Sean, took his father's gun and killed his mother. The murder occurred over a dispute about cookies. Within a few weeks of this tragedy, a fourteen-year-old Mexican American, Hector, was an accomplice to an armed robbery during which his co-defendant murdered a convenience store clerk. Hector had no weapon and fired no shots. Under the new California law, both youngsters were eligible to be tried in criminal courts, but these two cases ended up quite differently. Sean was kept in the juvenile justice system, was sent to a juvenile treatment facility, and will be eligible for parole in a few years. Hector was tried in a criminal court and is now serving a term of twenty-five years to life in a California prison. Both youths were initially sent to the Youth Authority Reception Center, where correctional professionals concluded that both Sean and Hector were amenable to the rehabilitative programs of the Youth Authority.

Sean became a subject of the national media, and his father pleaded for mercy on ABC's *Nightline* show. Hector's case received a very brief report in the Orange County edition of the *Los Angeles Times*. Sean came to be viewed by the court as a sympathetic figure in need of treatment services. Hector was described by the judge as a "cancerous growth on society."

Neither boy's family had much money. Sean was defended by a public defender, whereas Hector was represented by an assigned counsel. Juvenile law specialists have noted that the more experienced public defenders have more success in juvenile court proceedings than assigned counsels, who may have had only limited juvenile law experience. Most telling, at the fitness hearing, Sean's attorney put on a very complete case, which included the testimony of many adults who knew Sean from birth, as well as the testimony of a psychiatrist. Sean's lawyer put on a virtual capital defense to acquaint the court with all aspects of the youngster's life. Hector had no such comprehensive hearing. His attorney filed a paper petition to the court that argued that Hector should be retained in the juvenile justice system. Hector's lawyer had none of the financial resources of the County Public Defender's Office. He doubted that his request for a court-financed psychiatric exam would have been honored by the court. There were no mental health professionals called to testimony. Indeed, no one spoke up for Hector.

In court, Sean, a tall and muscular high school football tackle, acted sorrowful and contrite. Hector, a short and very slightly built youth, swaggered and grinned, showing the bravado that the fourteen-year-old had learned from his fellow gang members. Neither boy said that they could remember the details of the crimes with which they were charged. Sean's lack of memory was explained by the court-appointed psychiatrist as "post traumatic amnesia." Hector's inability to recall the crime was interpreted by the prosecutor and the court as "a lack of remorse."

Hector's previous gang involvement was viewed as an aggravating factor. Sean had used a plastic soda container as a makeshift silencer for shooting his mother. He claimed that he learned about this technique from the Internet. The court felt that Sean's behavior was naive and reinforced the view that he was too immature for the criminal court system.

Both Sean's father and Hector's mother wanted their children to be kept in the juvenile system. Sean's father was a highly respected official in the Fire Department, whereas Hector's mother was a part-time worker, raising other younger children. Hector's father was serving time in state prison. Sean had attended church regularly and appeared to have a stable home environment. Hector had been raised on the streets and had been placed in a variety of group homes during his early years. While Hector had been arrested for joyriding and other minor crimes, he had never been charged with a violent crime. Sean had no official history of delinquency. These differences in courtroom demeanor, personal histories, and family backgrounds are important, but are insufficient to justify the vast disparity in how these cases were handled by the justice system.

At the time of Sean's arrest, homicidal behavior by a white, middle-class teenager was an exceedingly rare event. It attracted national media attention and permitted his lawyers to marshal community sympathy and to receive substantial county resources to pursue Sean's defense. One wonders if the same conditions would occur today after the long string of murders by white teenagers in suburban and rural communities in Mississippi, Kentucky, Arkansas, Tennessee, Pennsylvania, Oregon, and Colorado.

Hector was not the beneficiary of community compassion and understanding. As one observer noted, "there is a sea of Hectors in southern California, and
we hardly can even distinguish them as individuals."

It would be easy to dismiss the vast disparity in the treatment of these two children as the result of blatant racism. After all, the outcome was fairly predictable:
The white youth got lenient treatment; the Hispanic youngster was punished
harshly. Set within the racially charged atmosphere of southern California, the
reactions of justice system decision makers seem sadly foreshadowed. This region
has been the center of intense racial antagonism aimed at minority youths, especially those perceived as immigrants or "illegal aliens." But this is too facile an
explanation for what transpired.

It is unlikely that professionals in the local justice system set out to conspire
against Hector or to give excessive leniency to Sean. While it is clear that two
different standards of justice were applied in these cases (punitive justice in Hector's case and redemptive justice in Sean's case), it is more plausible that unconscious racial and class biases came into play (see, for example, Charles
Lawrence 1987).

Unarticulated racial stereotypes made a range of absurd decisions, such as
trying a fourteen-year-old as if he were an adult, seem rational. The intellectual
climate for these racialized decisions has been legitimated by conservative scholars, who have warned us that a new breed of super predators is about to storm
the gates (DiIulio 1995) or that supposedly mentally inferior lower-class people
will respond only to blunt sanctions (Murray and Herrnstein 1994). Motivated
by deep-seated racist conceptions, the behavior of the attorneys, probation staff,
the media, and the general public seems even more troubling.

The stories of Sean and Hector are horrible harbingers of things to come. The
movement to treat children as if they were little adults is sweeping the nation.
Most states have already enacted laws that are far more punitive than California's juvenile laws. The potential passage of federal "get tough" juvenile crime
laws may overwhelm rational juvenile justice policies in jurisdictions in which
a moral frenzy over youth crime has yet to take hold. In my view, conscious and
unconscious racist beliefs and fears seem to be at the core of this frenzy.

RESEARCH FINDINGS

The simple truth is that waiver and transfer laws have little or no research or
theoretical foundations. Research has consistently shown that treating children
as if they were little adults is a poor strategy in terms of crime control (Krisberg 1997). Indeed, we do not even have a firm grasp on the number of youngsters who are transferred to adult courts. One of the first national studies on this
subject estimated that, in 1982, there were over 9,000 transfers through the
juvenile court; another 2,000 cases were waived through the discretion of prosecutors; and more than 1,300 children's cases were handled in adult courts,

because of statutory requirements that excluded certain offenses from the juvenile court (Hamparian et al. 1982). No estimates were given on the number of youths moved to the criminal courts because the age of criminal court jurisdiction had been lowered. More recent estimates suggest that over 176,000 youths below the age of eighteen are tried in adult courts in states that set the upper age of juvenile court jurisdiction at ages sixteen or seventeen (Snyder and Sickmund 1995). In 1992, at least 11,700 cases were waived to criminal courts via juvenile court transfer proceedings. There are no national data on the number of "direct filings" in which prosecutors decide which juvenile cases get tried in criminal courts. This occurs in states in which the legislature has given the juvenile and adult courts concurrent jurisdiction. In Florida alone there were 7,000 such direct filings in 1991 (Snyder and Sickmund 1995).

A review by the Government Accounting Office (GAO 1995) documented the increasing popularity of laws permitting transfers of juveniles to criminal courts. GAO reported that since 1978, forty-four states and the District of Columbia have passed laws affecting the process by which juveniles could be transferred. Between 1993 and 1995, there was a major push across the nation to make transfer even easier and to extend adult court jurisdiction to a much broader category of youthful offenders (Torbet et al. 1996). The GAO study noted that there were wide variations among the states in the conviction rates of juveniles in criminal courts.

In 1992, the National Correctional Reporting Program (NCRP) found that there were nearly 6,000 persons under the age of eighteen who were admitted to adult prisons in the thirty-seven states participating in the NCRP (Perkins 1995). It is important to remember that not every youth who is tried in the adult court system is sent to prison. Many of these cases are dismissed or receive lesser sentences, especially probation. Adolescents sent to prison constituted less than 1 percent of all the prison admissions in these states. These imprisoned teens almost always were males and were typically seventeen years old. About 47 percent of persons under age eighteen who entered prisons were charged with violent crimes as their most serious offense; 53 percent of the group were convicted of serious property crimes or drug offenses. African-American youngsters represent nearly two-thirds of the youngest persons sent to prison. These youthful prisoners generally come from the states with the lowest age of original juvenile court jurisdiction.

The average prison stay for those entering prison before age eighteen was slightly over two years—almost three times as long as the most serious juvenile offenders admitted to juvenile correctional facilities. Future research will need to determine if the prior offense histories or aggravating circumstances of their crimes accounts for this large disparity in average lengths of confinement. Some research suggests that the younger prisoners commit many institutional infractions, thus losing "good time" release credits and lengthening their periods of incarceration (Forst et al. 1989). This study also found that the youngest inmates of prisons were less likely to receive educational or treatment services and were more likely to be assaulted by other inmates or correctional officers than youths confined in juvenile facilities.

There is little official documentation on how transfer decisions are actually made. Howell's (1996) excellent review of the literature points out that the available data is mostly concerned with judicial transfer hearings, even though these represent no more than 10 percent of all juveniles who are tried as adults. Howell further notes that the studies of judicial waiver practices are confounded by legislative and prosecutorial factors that weigh heavily on decision making by juvenile court judges. The research tells us little about the relative merits of mandatory waiver provisions, direct file procedures, or more traditional judicial waiver hearings. In fact, there is a melange of policies and practices operating across the nation; we have not even developed an adequate typology by which to sort out these practices.

There have been numerous studies designed to assess the rationality of waiver decisions in the juvenile court. Howell (1996) found thirty-seven such studies. In the main, these decision-making studies have found that juveniles who are transferred are not necessarily the most serious offenders (Howell 1996). Some studies have suggested that racial factors strongly influence the transfer decision. For example, Eigen's (1972) study of juvenile homicides in Philadelphia found that African-American youngsters who murdered white victims are the most likely to be tried as adults. Other studies have demonstrated the racial and class disparities endemic to the administration of transfer laws (Fagan, Slaughter, and Hartstone 1987; Howell 1996). A study of New York mandatory transfer laws revealed vast differences in the use of these laws across different counties (Singer and McDowell 1988).

Data on the comparative outcomes of prosecuting juvenile offenders in criminal courts make a convincing case that such policies have little or no crime control value. Studies of the New York Juvenile Offender Law have shown no measurable deterrent impact on juvenile crime rates (Singer and McDowell 1988; Jensen and Metsger 1994). An earlier study by White (1985) compared juveniles charged with very serious crimes in the juvenile justice system with young adults charged with similar crimes in adult courts. While he found that criminal courts were slightly more likely to convict and incarcerate offenders than the juvenile courts, the young adults served considerably more time in prisons than juveniles sent to state training schools. Yet the young offenders had a recidivism rate that was much higher than the juveniles. In another study, Fagan contrasted the handling of serious and violent juvenile offenders in New York and New Jersey. He looked at almost 1,200 felony offenders, ages fifteen and sixteen, who were arrested for robberies in matched counties. Because of state laws, the New Yorkers were much more likely to be handled in the criminal justice system, whereas the New Jersey youths were primarily processed in the juvenile court system. In fact, Fagan found that the sanctions were more certain and severe for the New Jersey sample than for the New York youngsters. However, the New York youthful offenders had higher recidivism rates, committed more new offenses, and were crime-free for a shorter period of time than the New Jersey youths (Fagan 1995). While these results are intriguing, the findings are clouded because it is difficult to truly match offenders from the same jurisdiction. Also, we are unsure whether the results observed were produced by the lesser penalties of the New York system or by the adverse effects of adult correctional interventions.

A Minnesota study by Podkopacz and Feld (1995) looked at youths waived to the adult court versus those retained in the juvenile court. Transferred youths were more likely to be incarcerated and for longer periods of time than the juvenile justice comparison group. Recidivism data showed that the transferred youths had a 58 percent rearrest rate versus a 42 percent rearrest rate for the non-transferred youths during the next 24 months or more of "street time." Podkopacz and Feld suggest that this finding may be the result of the juvenile court transferring more higher-risk defendants to the adult system. But they also speculated that the differences in recidivism rates might be due to superior treatment resources that are available through the juvenile court or the failure of adult court sanctions to deter juveniles from committing more crimes.

Donna Bishop and her colleagues (1996) have produced a more compelling study of the longer-term outcomes of transfer decisions in Florida. This study compared the recidivism rates of youths who were waived to the criminal courts compared with those retained in the juvenile justice system. The authors report: "To ensure equivalence across the two groups, we sampled the non-transfer population and employed a matching procedure to control for seriousness of transfer offense, number of charges, number of prior charges, severity of prior offenses, and sociodemographic characteristics" (Bishop et al. 1996, 175).

The resulting study group in Florida consisted of 5,476 transferred and non-transferred juveniles who were at risk for reoffending during some part of the follow-up period. The transferred group had much higher rates of recidivism, committed more serious subsequent offenses, and experienced a shorter time to failure than the matched sample of non-transferred youths. Bishop and her colleagues concluded that Florida's transfer practices had little deterrent value. They note that the short-term benefits of incapacitating juveniles in the criminal justice system were negated quickly as the transferred youths returned to the community and committed many more crimes than their juvenile justice counterparts.

While the study by Bishop and associates is the best that has been conducted to date, it is far from conclusive. For example, the study fails to account for the social or psychological processes that might have produced the observed results. For example, the careful efforts to match the two offender groups on background and a few legal factors may have included individuals who experienced a diverse array of sanctions, including probation, house arrest, and incarceration in prisons or jails. We still do not know what effects these sanctions may have exerted on the recidivism results. There also may be case factors that differentiated the two groups on such matters as aggravating and mitigating circumstances. The Office of Juvenile Justice and Delinquency Prevention (OJJDP) is presently funding a more detailed study of Florida transfer policies that may answer these questions. Some previous research suggests that incarceration in the juvenile system may be longer than the terms of adult confinement in some jurisdictions (Jones and Krisberg 1994). In at least one Florida county, the practice of transferring youths to the adult system resulted in shorter stays and more treatment resources for such youths than for those sent to juvenile facilities (Rasmussen and Yu 1996).

CONCLUDING OBSERVATIONS

While the research on transfer is hardly without its flaws, it is worth noting that there is virtually no evidence that these policies actually deter youth crime or reduce recidivism. Research data played little if any role in the national political movement to expand the transfer of youths to criminal courts. Indeed, proponents of prosecuting children as adults have argued for these policies less on utilitarian grounds than for symbolic or moral purposes. They employ a series of pat phrases to defend these policies. We have all heard the popular jingo about "if you are old enough to do the crime, you are old enough to do the time." Of course, this explanation makes little real sense. For example, very young children can physically engage in adult behavior such as voting, consuming alcohol, smoking tobacco, driving a car, entering into binding legal contracts, and sexual activities, but our laws are designed to protect children, and society in general, from the adverse consequences of these behaviors. In fact, the legal system severely punishes adults who encourage these activities among youngsters. The crucial issue here is whether the individual is mature enough to understand the consequences of his or her actions.

The public has also been told that the victims of crime do not care about the age of the offenders who harmed them. The media has featured victims of violent crime who have greatly suffered as the result of juvenile crimes. However, there are many examples of crime victims who have channeled their anger and grief into gun control campaigns or efforts to reclaim high-risk juveniles. More fundamentally, the suffering of crime victims should be only one component of crime policy. Consider the experiences of people whose loved ones have died after a protracted illness. It is not uncommon in these cases for the survivors to blame themselves or the medical practitioners for the death. While there may be some cases in which treatment could have been improved, most survivors come to see that the passing of a loved one was due to the ravages of aging or a fatal disease.

These examples of "sound bite" politics applied to juvenile crime have been influential in allowing politicians to reduce complex legal issues to simplistic formulae. The citizenry never got to hear enough about Hector to decide if his harsh treatment was warranted or if Sean's sanction was appropriate. The powerful issues of race and class disparities in the use of transfer have not received adequate public discussion. Moreover, we need to consider the role of the gun industry and its lobbyists, who have deflected attention away from the easy availability to our children of powerful weapons by calling for crackdowns on youthful offenders.

In 1999, the American Juvenile Court will achieve its one-hundredth birthday. Our unique contribution to international legal practice in treating juvenile offenders has been impressive. Most industrialized nations have attempted to implement the American model of a separate children's court, and despite the loud chorus of critics, the juvenile justice system has proven its value. The big question has always been whether our nation will ever actually give the court the necessary resources to fulfill its mission.

Also obscured in the debate over harsher punishments for juveniles are the blatant failures of the criminal court system. Does anyone really believe that adult courts are at all effective at deterring serious crime? We have witnessed the ascendancy of the "get tough" mentality for adult offenders. The results have been disastrous. Money needed for education has been devoured by the binge of prison building. The growth in minority imprisonment that was vastly accelerated by the "War on Drugs" has destroyed many families and communities. The surge in imprisonment produced little or no reduction in crime. Even the very recent drops in crime rates have occurred previously (e.g., the early 1980s) without the extraordinary investments in crime control that are part of the current public policy agenda. Why ought the same policies that failed with adults work with our children?

There is a fundamental question that is illustrated by the stories of Hector and Sean and the research data that has been assembled. If our own child or grandchild had committed some horrible crime, what kind of justice system would we be seeking? Most Americans would fight to get their relatives into a treatment-oriented system that tried to understand their youngster and would provide firm, but compassionate, sanctions. Few of us would prefer a punitive, mechanical, and politically driven criminal justice system for our own children. This, of course, is the main point. We seem to tolerate a harsh response to "other people's" children. The extremes to which this sort of thinking can go is illustrated by a 1999 case in Pontiac, Michigan, in which an African-American youngster was tried as an adult for an offense committed when he was eleven years old. Recall Eigen's research in Philadelphia that was discussed earlier. Our unconscious or conscious biases allow this moral double standard to exist. However, if we allow ourselves to even consider that Hector and his gang friends are not so different from Sean and his sometimes violent peers, we may find a more reasonable path toward a safer society for all of our children.

NOTES

1. H.R. 3 was approved by a vote of 282 to 132 in 1997.
2. In 1995 there were fewer than 500 juveniles arrested and referred to federal prosecutors. In 49 percent of these cases no prosecution was filed. In all, only 122 cases resulted in a completed federal court proceeding. Only 65 juveniles in the federal system were tried as adults.

REFERENCES

Bishop, Donna, Charles Frazier, Lonn Lanza-Kaduce, and Lawrence Winner. 1996. "The Transfer of Juveniles to Criminal Court: Does It Make a Difference?" *Crime and Delinquency* 42: 171–91.

DiIulio, John. 1995. "Crime in America: It's Going to Get Worse." *Reader's Digest* (August): 55–60.

Eigen, Joel. 1972. "Punishing Youth Homicide Offenders in Philadelphia." *Journal of Criminology and Criminal Law* 72: 1072–93.

Fagan, Jeffrey. 1995. "Separating the Men from the Boys: The Comparative Advantage of Juvenile versus Criminal Court Sanctions on Recidivism among Adolescent Felony Offenders." Pp. 238–60 in *A Sourcebook: Serious, Violent, and Chronic Juvenile Offenders*, edited by J.C. Howell, B. Krisberg, J.D. Hawkins, and J.J. Wilson. Thousand Oaks, CA: Sage.

Fagan, Jeffrey, E. Slaughter, and Elliott Hartstone. 1987. "Blind Justice? The Impact of Race on the Juvenile Justice Process." *Crime and Delinquency* 33: 224–59.

Forst, Martin, Jeffrey Fagan, and T. Scott Vivona. 1989. "Youth in Prisons and State Training Schools." *Juvenile and Family Court Journal* 81: 314–47.

Government Accounting Office. 1995. *Juvenile Justice: Juveniles Processed in Criminal Court and Case Dispositions.* Washington, DC: GAO.

Hamparian, Donna, Linda Istep, Susan Muntean, Roamon Priestino, Robert Swisher, Paul Wallace, and Joseph White. 1982. *Youth in Adult Courts: Between Two Worlds.* Washington, DC: Office of Juvenile Justice and Delinquency Prevention.

Howell, James C. 1996. "Juvenile Transfer to the Criminal Justice System: State-of-the-Art." *Law and Policy* 18: 17–60.

Jensen, Eric, and Linda Metsger. 1994. "A Test of the Deterrent Effects of the New York Juvenile Offender Law." *Crime and Delinquency* 40: 96–104.

Jones, Michael, and Barry Krisberg. 1994. *Images and Reality: Juvenile Crime, Youth Violence, and Public Policy.* San Francisco: National Council on Crime and Delinquency.

Krisberg, Barry. 1997. *The Impact of the Justice System on Serious, Violent, and Chronic Juvenile Offenders.* San Francisco: National Council on Crime and Delinquency.

Lawrence, Charles R., III. 1987. "The Id, the Ego and Equal Protection: Reckoning with Unconscious Racism." *Stanford Law Review* 39: 317–88.

Murray, Charles, and Richard Herrnstein. 1994. *The Bell Curve.* New York: Simon and Schuster.

Perkins, Craig. 1994. *The National Corrections Reporting Program, 1992.* Washington, DC: Bureau of Justice Statistics.

Podkopacz, Marcy R., and Barry C. Feld. 1995. "Juvenile Waiver Policy and Practice: Persistence, Seriousness and Race." *Law and Inequality: A Journal of Theory and Practice* 14: 73–178.

Pound, Roscoe. 1965. "The Rise of Socialized Criminal Justice." In Roscoe Pound, *Criminal Justice*, edited by Sheldon Gluck. Dobbs Ferry, NY: Oceana.

Rasmussen, David, and Yiuen Yu. 1996. *An Evaluation of Juvenile Justice Innovations in Duval County, Florida.* Tallahassee, FL: Florida State University.

Schiraldi, Vincent, and Mark Soler. 1998. *The Will of the People? The Public Opinion of the Violent and Repeat Juvenile Offender Act of 1997.* Washington, DC: Youth Law Center.

Singer, Simon, and David McDowell. 1988. "Criminalizing Delinquency: The Deterrent Effects of the New York Juvenile Offender Law." *Law and Society Review* 22: 521–35.

Snyder, Howard N., and Melissa Sickmund. 1995. *Juvenile Offenders and Victims: A National Report.* Washington, DC: Office of Juvenile Justice and Delinquency Prevention.

Torbet, Patricia, Richard Gable, Hunter Hurst IV, Imogene Montgomery, Linda Szymanski, and Douglas Thomas. 1996. *State Responses to Serious and Violent Juvenile Crime.* Washington, DC: Office of Juvenile Justice and Delinquency Prevention.

White, Joseph. 1985. *The Comparative Dispositions Study.* Report to the U.S. Department of Justice, Office of Juvenile Justice and Delinquency Prevention.

Part II

Gangs, Drug Law Enforcement, Racial Profiling, and Social Justice

6
The New Blacklists: The Threat to Civil Liberties Posed by Gang Databases

Stacey Leyton

The street gang has replaced godless Communism as the most popular threat to the American way of life.[1]

It's hard to ignore the similarity to the blacklists created in the 1950s. Then, people were labeled based on who they associated with. People didn't know they were on the list. Once you got on the list you couldn't get off. Now the lists are on computers, and people are being labeled gang members instead of communists. If it wasn't just happening to young people of color, I think it would be causing a lot of outcry.[2]

In a move that demonstrates the level of resources the government is willing to devote to fighting gangs, in May 1992 the FBI transferred several hundred FBI agents, whose jobs had become less important because of the end of the Cold War, from foreign counterintelligence to gang investigations.[3] Unfortunately, some of the practices utilized by law enforcement agencies to investigate and target street gangs raise many of the same civil liberties concerns implicated by the tactics utilized to target internal dissidents during the height of the Cold War.

No one may realize how widespread the gang problem truly is, for estimates of the extent of gang activity vary. According to a 1993 estimate by the United States Department of Justice, there are almost 17,000 gangs, which include over 555,000 members who are involved in 580,000 gang-related crimes annually in the United States.[4] A 1994 report produced by the organization that runs the gang databases in California estimates that there are between 175,000 and 200,000 gang members in California alone. Moreover, this organization warns, gangs have moved out of local urban centers and into suburban and rural areas throughout the state and, in some cases, even across state lines.[5] A 1996 survey of 341 law enforcement agencies by the National Drug Intelligence Center supports such claims, documenting that 88 percent reported gang activity, including 78 percent of localities with populations of under 50,000 and 68 percent of jurisdictions with populations of under 25,000.[6]

Violence is, of course, the principal consequence of gang activity that the public fears.[7] Murders by juvenile gang members increased by 500 percent between 1980 and 1994.[8] Although violent crime has declined since 1994, public fear of gang violence remains high.[9] In a 1992 report on gangs, the Los Angeles District Attorney's Office suggested that innocent bystanders represented about 10 to 25 percent of all victims of gang violence in the county.[10]

In this context of heightened gang activity, law enforcement efforts to combat gang violence have also intensified. Increasingly common techniques include arresting gang members for minor offenses, issuing anti-gang injunctions under nuisance abatement laws, instituting sentence enhancements for gang-related crimes, conducting anti-gang police sweeps, and targeting gang leaders for police investigation and prosecution.[11] Many localities have also employed social and community-based strategies.[12] In this context, law enforcement compilation of databases of gang members is but one of the techniques currently employed to control gangs. This technique has primarily emerged in the last decade.[13] Law enforcement officials justify the use of gang databases by pointing out the utility of such databases in identifying suspects and investigating crimes.[14] Supporters of California's statewide gang database (CalGang), which has been termed "the nation's pre-eminent gang database,"[15] attribute reductions in gang-related crime in some jurisdictions and the conviction of individuals for many crimes that might otherwise go unsolved to the success of the database.[16]

In this essay, I discuss the serious threat to civil liberties, particularly to the rights of young Black, Asian, and Latino individuals, posed by the explosive growth of gang databases. Although I focus primarily on California, I also discuss the growth and development of these programs on the national level. The first section, "The Growth of Gang Databases," provides an overview of the nature and the extent of the use of gang databases throughout the country. In "Civil Liberties and Other Policy Concerns," I discuss the policy concerns raised by critics of gang databases, which include civil libertarian critiques of improper information gathering about individuals, the problems posed by inaccurate identification of individuals as gang members and the lack of protections for those mistakenly included, the over-inclusion of racial minorities in the database, and the harassment and other negative consequences faced by those who are identified as gang members. Finally, in "Legal Challenges to Gang Databases," I explore the possible legal challenges to gang databases under federal and state law, including the right of association, protection from unreasonable search and seizure, the right to privacy, the right to procedural due process, and the right of equal protection. Given the civil liberties threat posed by these databases and the practices used to assemble them, one might assume that there would be an array of strong legal challenges to raise. However, the various constitutional and statutory grounds for challenging gang databases all pose serious problems and, potentially, insurmountable barriers to success. This paper evaluates the strength of the different bases for legal challenges to gang databases and offers suggestions for overcoming the barriers to successful litigation.

THE GROWTH OF GANG DATABASES

In order to understand the manner in which law enforcement agencies assemble and utilize gang databases, it makes sense to focus on California, because most observers would agree with that state's claim that its gang database "is the most comprehensive automated gang information system in the nation."[17] CalGang (formerly called GREAT, the Gang Reporting, Evaluation, and Tracking System) is a statewide database containing the names of over 200,000 suspected gang members.[18] It is used primarily for investigative purposes, by gang units of police departments as well as other law enforcement agencies.[19]

GREAT was developed by the Law Enforcement Communications Network[20] in conjunction with the Los Angeles County Sheriff's Department and has been in use since 1987.[21] Before GREAT existed, police departments collected information on gang members in locally maintained files, which were sometimes included in local computerized databases, but could not access information that had been collected by other law enforcement agencies. Then, in 1993, GREAT offered the opportunity to centralize data and make it widely accessible.[22]

In March 1997, California Governor Pete Wilson announced plans to spend $800,000 to integrate the regional GREAT databases and transform them into a new unified statewide system called CalGang, a change that increased the ease of use and decreased the cost of access to the system.[23] In addition, over the past decade, the state government has given out over $7 million in grants to enable local law enforcement agencies to start their own databases and connect with the statewide system.[24] An advisory committee made up of law enforcement agencies from around the state called CGNAC (California Gang Node Advisory Committee) initially oversaw the functioning of GREAT and now serves in the same role for CalGang.[25]

CalGang tracks 200 data fields on gang members; these fields include personal information (such as name, address, physical description, gang moniker, social security number, and associates or acquaintances) as well as information about the gang (such as its type and racial makeup) and a record of all police encounters with the individual.[26] The system also includes photographs and can produce instantaneous photographic lineups or generate "link diagrams" of associates out to three levels, which include photographs and are color coded to show associates' gang affiliations.[27] CalGang, a Web-based intranet system, is currently fully operational and accessible by local police departments through a computer, telephone and modem, and Web browser.[28] The CalGang system is fully integrated, allowing police from all over the state to check an individual's records in "real time" rather than having to call someone who can access the database in order to check out a name for them.[29] Thus, individual officers in police departments that purchase laptop computers can access the database directly from their patrol cars.[30] It is estimated that over 550 agencies in California had access to CalGang by the end of 1999.[31]

According to GREAT materials, agencies that participate in the GREAT database must follow designated procedures for data entry. The definition of gang employed by GREAT/CalGang is much broader than that delineated in the California Penal Code.[32] CalGang officials did not make available their current criteria for data entry, but state that the criteria closely resemble the factors that have historically been employed by GREAT.[33] In fact, there is some controversy over whether GREAT/CalGang's criteria are utilized statewide by those entering records into the database.[34] Whether or not they are consistently utilized throughout the state, the following six designated conditions for identifying gang members appear in GREAT materials:

1. When an individual admits membership.

   a. An individual admits membership to law enforcement officer and such admission is recorded and dated. Examples include field identification card or interview document.

2. When a reliable informant identifies an individual as a gang member.

   a. A reliable informant is one who has demonstrated consistent veracity in previous contacts with law enforcement, or in testimony before any court.

3. When an informant of previously untested reliability identifies an individual as a member and it is corroborated by independent information.

4. When an individual frequents a particular group[']s area or activities, affects two or more of the following criteria or conditions[:] their style of dress, use of hand signs, symbols or tattoos and associates with known members.

   a. Prior documentation is required to utilize this section.

5. When an individual has been arrested several times in the company of identified gang members for offenses which are consistent with usual group activity.

6. When there is a criminal predicate and association with a known gang.

   a. The individual must have a criminal record of crimes common to a gang(s) activities. These crimes need not be identified in conjunction with a particular group.

   b. The associated individual must exhibit a repeated tendency toward association with identified gang members. The individual may affect identification attempts with one or more of the previously mentioned criteria.[35]

The GREAT guidelines also require that individuals whose records have not been updated in the past five years be purged from the system, but there has been some controversy over whether GREAT/CalGang has consistently conducted such purging.[36]

All over the country, local law enforcement agencies are increasingly employing the computer database as an important tool for tracking gang members. A recent survey of newspaper accounts reveals that statewide databases are already in operation in Florida, Minnesota, and Ohio; and databases are also used by localities such as Cincinnati, Ohio; Columbus, Ohio; Gwinnett County, Georgia; Keller, Texas; Memphis, Tennessee; Phoenix, Arizona; Providence, Rhode Island; St.

Charles County, Missouri; Suffolk, New York; and Fairfax County, Virginia.[37] Furthermore, there are plans to develop statewide databases in Illinois, South Carolina, Tennessee, Texas, and Wisconsin, as well as plans to create local gang databases or enter suspected gang members in a national database in localities such as Albuquerque, New Mexico; Buffalo, New York; Charlotte, North Carolina; Cincinnati, Ohio; Garland, Texas; Grand Prairie, Texas; Houston, Texas; Marion County, Indiana; New York, New York; Palm Beach, Florida; Portland, Maine; Tavares, Florida; Wichita, Kansas; and Wilmington, North Carolina.[38] In an interesting reminder of the similarity of the concerns raised by gang databases and anti-Communist blacklists, a controversy erupted in the late 1990s when the Chicago police department was unable to join the statewide Illinois gang database because of a consent decree, imposed in response to disclosures that Chicago's Red Squads had maintained extensive intelligence information on political dissidents and community organizations during the 1960s and 1970s, that barred the police from collecting and maintaining such intelligence information.[39]

The federal government is also actively monitoring gangs. Then President Clinton explained that the federal government stepped up its involvement through Justice Department funding of the National Gang Tracking Network, which was announced in May 1997.[40] The FBI runs its own database, the FBI Violent Gang and Terrorist Organization File, which became operational in 1995.[41] The FBI defines a gang as "an ongoing organization or association or group of three or more people with a common interest and/or activity characterized by commission of or involvement in a pattern of criminal or delinquent conduct" and includes in its database members who are at any level of gang involvement.[42] Prior to 1995, the FBI had assembled information only on individuals who had been arrested or convicted.[43] Although any local agency may enter suspected gang members, there were just 4,617 individuals from 1,668 gangs in the FBI system as of January 1998.[44] Over 80,000 agencies have access to the FBI database.[45] Individual officers can access the FBI database by contacting their dispatcher for an NCIC check or through a mobile terminal in their squad car.[46] Finally, the United States Department of Justice sponsors the Regional Informational Sharing System, which provides support and information to local law enforcement agencies that are monitoring gang membership and awards grants to states and localities for use in initiating or building gang databases.[47]

CIVIL LIBERTIES AND OTHER POLICY CONCERNS[48]

In Building a Gang Database, the Government Is Collecting Extensive Information on Thousands of Individuals without Any Underlying Criminal Predicate

Opponents of gang databases raise the concern that the government is gathering and maintaining extensive intelligence information on citizens without evidence that they are involved in illegal activity.[49] Critics point out that because gang membership itself is not illegal, it does not qualify as an underlying criminal predicate and therefore does not justify maintenance of intelligence information.[50] Moreover, the assumption that gang members inevitably engage in illegal activity may be false. As one social scientist pointed out, the most prevalent activities of gang members are not necessarily violent, but rather "the same as those of many adolescent friendship groups—partying, hanging around and getting high."[51] In fact, a 1992 GAO study of GREAT found that just under half of the suspected gang members included in the database had ever been *arrested* for a felony.[52] Government information gathering about large numbers of citizens solely on the basis of suspicion of gang involvement, when no independent criminal arrest or conviction justifies such record keeping, raises a number of civil liberties concerns.

Even more controversial is the inclusion in databases of those identified as "gang associates" who are not necessarily even gang members. GREAT formerly allowed entry of suspected associates who did not meet any of the other criteria for inclusion, as long as there were strong indications of a close relationship with a gang, a practice that raised concerns even within its own governing body.[53] In 1994, in response to a memorandum authored by California Supervising Deputy Attorney General Margaret Garnand Venturi that identified potential legal problems with the definition and use of the "gang associate" category, the Orange County GREAT node coordinator ordered the purge of all associate records from the database; however, a new, "affiliate" category was created just a few months later.[54] In other jurisdictions, the "gang associate" category still appears to be in use, and the criteria for identification of "associates" continue to be subject to criticism from civil liberties advocates.[55]

The Difficulty of Identifying Gang Members May Lead to Inaccurate Entries and Thus the Presence in the Database of Many Individuals Who Are Not Even Involved with Gangs

Some inaccuracy in the database may be attributable to the difficulty of defining what constitutes a "gang."[56] Social science researchers tend to emphasize the social and cultural aspects of gang activity, while law enforcement personnel instead emphasize the criminal activities of gang members.[57] The California statute that provides for punishment and sentence enhancements for gang-related criminal conduct defines "criminal street gang" in a very specific manner: "any ongoing organization, association, or group of three or more persons, whether formal or informal, having as one of its primary activities the commission of one or more of the criminal acts enumerated ... which has a common name or common identifying sign or symbol, whose members individually or collectively engage in or have engaged in a pattern of criminal gang activity."[58] However,

GREAT/CalGang's current standards do not limit the definition of a gang to groups organized for the purpose of criminal activity.[59]

Even if it were possible to accurately identify a gang, determining who makes up the membership of that gang would be even more difficult. Most gangs are loosely structured, and many young people may join solely for safety or acceptance reasons rather than to participate in the gang's criminal activities.[60] Levels of "membership" range from those most heavily involved in criminal activity to those who assert their gang affiliation but participate only in social gang activities.[61] The varied motivations and activities of gang members renders identification of gang members difficult and highly dependent upon the definition of the level of involvement that qualifies an individual as a gang "member."

Furthermore, the factors utilized by police to determine which of the young people who live in neighborhoods where gangs are active actually belong to or are affiliated with these gangs may exacerbate these inherent difficulties. While the criteria used to identify gang members varies according to the jurisdiction, the factors identified in CalGang/GREAT materials commonly appear in guidelines provided to individual police officers.[62] Although the establishment of such guidelines serves to rein in the discretion of individual officers, the criteria commonly used may heighten the risk of inaccuracy and arbitrariness in identifying suspected gang members, particularly when an individual qualifies for inclusion solely based on meeting one criterion.[63] Don Mace, the former chairman of CGNAC and currently Attorney General Investigator in Charge at the California Department of Justice, asserts that most individuals in the database have met multiple criteria for inclusion (he estimates four to five), but this figure has not been confirmed by any independent audit or analysis.[64]

In the summer of 1999, California's Attorney General Bill Lockyer, who took office in January 1999, publicly stated his conclusion that the CalGang database may include many inaccurate records. He described the database as "mix[ing] verified criminal history and gang affiliations with unverified intelligence and hearsay evidence, including reports on persons who have committed no crime."[65] As justification for California's failure to share the CalGang database with the FBI, he stated that, until the database entries were reviewed and reformatted, "this database cannot and should not be used, in California or elsewhere, to decide whether or not a person is dangerous or should be detained."[66] Justice Chin of the California Supreme Court has also expressed concern about the reliability of the criteria utilized for identifying gang members for purposes of naming them in anti-gang injunctions, which are the same as those that provide a basis for entry into a gang database:

Under these criteria, the City would consider a person to be a member of a Sureño gang if, for example, that person on two occasions wore baggy pants, blue clothes, or "Los Angeles Raiders" garments. The City also identifies persons who admit gang membership as gang members, regardless of the circumstances of their admission. . . . Thus, a person who merely claims membership in one of the Sureño gangs may not fully share that gang's aims.[67]

A discussion follows of some problems posed by the various criteria employed by law enforcement agencies to identify gang members for inclusion in gang databases.

Self-Admission[68]

The primary problem with the criterion of self-admission is that young people may have reasons for identifying themselves as gang members when this may not be the case. Some individuals who are not gang members will claim gang membership to the police when confronted in front of others in response to peer pressure, or will do so for personal safety reasons or in order to avoid contact with gang members from rival neighborhoods while in police custody.[69] Finally, police may misconstrue what a young person says or coerce a youth to claim gang membership.[70]

Identification by a Reliable Informant or Identification by an Unknown Informant Along with Corroboration

As a general matter, little guidance is provided to police responsible for identifying gang members as to how they should determine who is a reliable informant for purposes of entry into the database. The absence of such guidelines allows police officers unconstrained discretion in applying this criterion, and the resultant designations do not always prove accurate. In fact, many statements implicating others as gang members may be tainted by self-interest (gaining favor from police or revenge, for example). According to the National Youth Gang Suppression and Intervention Program, "[t]he most immediate of direct data source, the gang member, is unreliable. Gang members tend to conceal and exaggerate information and, in fact, may not know the scope of the gang's activities."[71] Furthermore, an informant who reliably reports facts to police officers may not be necessarily as reliable in concluding whether an individual is a gang member.[72]

The question of corroboration involves similar problems; police departments are given no guidance regarding what level of evidence or information is required or whether the supposed corroboration must bear on gang membership at all.[73] Without guidelines as to what constitutes sufficient information, innocent activity such as spending time in a gang's area or wearing gang-style clothing may serve to "corroborate" gang membership.[74]

Frequenting a Known Gang Area

This criterion is subject to criticism both because of its lack of clarity and because in operation it may be fundamentally unfair. First, guidelines usually do not define what it means to "frequent an area." Second, the fact that an individual lives in an area in which a great deal of gang activity occurs should not render that individual more susceptible to inclusion in a database designed to track gang activity of *actual* gang members, not merely neighborhood residents.[75]

Associating with Known Gang Members

Guilt by association is an inappropriate means for determining gang membership. In neighborhoods with intense gang activity, individuals may end up in a gang database merely by talking to childhood friends or relatives, especially since "association" is not clearly defined.[76] This category is particularly problematic because misidentification of one individual as a gang member can trigger a ripple effect, leading to misidentification of all of his or her friends and associates.[77]

Gang Dress, Mannerisms, Symbols, or Tattoos

Distinguishing teen fashion from gang attire is often difficult, since baggy, oversized clothing is fashionable in urban and, increasingly, in rural and suburban neighborhoods.[78] The Los Angeles District Attorney's office has acknowledged that the clothing, tattoos, and music of young African Americans are similar to those popular among gangs and may be equated with gang membership by police officers.[79] Young people offer bitter complaints that urban style is inevitably interpreted as a sign of gang affiliation by the police.[80] In unintentional corroboration of such complaints, one police chief in Orange, California, advised, "Don't dress like a gang member. It may invite trouble for you. If I had my way, everybody would wear the same thing."[81] But individuals who are not involved in gangs may nonetheless imitate gang dress; one description of the behavior of young children in Chicago's public housing projects described the imitation of gang styles of dress by children as young as four years old, who were clearly not in any way involved with gangs.[82]

While tattoos are easier to identify, an individual may have obtained a tattoo while active in a gang but now be inactive. Once obtained, tattoos are extremely difficult and expensive to remove.[83] In fact, one court, noting that the tattoo at issue had been obtained twenty years before, found a gang tattoo to constitute only weak support for a finding of gang membership.[84] Finally, in terms of mannerisms, there is no requirement that officers have particular training or experience in interpreting mannerisms such as familiarity with gang hand signification, so this criterion rests entirely on the subjective judgment of individual members of the police force.[85]

Arrests with Gang Members for Offenses Consistent with Gang Activity

Since most juvenile crimes are done in groups, use of this criterion will result in some inaccurate entries of young people who are arrested with each other despite non-involvement in gangs.[86] Furthermore, since this criterion usually refers to arrests rather than convictions, there is no way to distinguish an individual genuinely involved in criminal activities from someone who is routinely arrested for harassment purposes or for charges that are not subsequently proven. This is even more troubling because, once someone is identified as a gang member, she is at risk of being subject to increased harassment, detention, and arrests, which may or may not indicate gang membership.[87]

The Problem Is Exacerbated by the Difficulty of Controlling the Quality of Data Entry and Management by Numerous Local Law Enforcement Agencies

Even if the gang database system did employ reliable criteria for identifying gang members, there is little guarantee that system users would apply such criteria in a consistent fashion. Numerous observers, including proponents of gang databases, have suggested that such inconsistency raises additional civil liberties concerns. Local law enforcement agencies may choose not to comply with the system requirements and instead may employ their own, less restrictive criteria; the enforcement mechanism for making sure that local agencies comply with the data entry criteria is unclear and possibly nonexistent.[88] A 1994 California Bureau of Investigation audit found inconsistent procedures for data entry and warned that those entering data did not consistently comply with reasonable suspicion standards.[89] As John Crew of the ACLU points out, "the overall integrity of this database—containing records on more than 200,000 individuals, used by more than 150 agencies, and relying on entries from more than 600 different computer terminals—is dependent on the *least* careful of the agencies participating in the system."[90]

Even if the agencies do employ consistent criteria, there will be other quality-control problems. The Los Angeles District Attorney's Report identified one source of such problems: data entry by inexperienced or untrained officers.[91] The ACLU points to another: Since the basis for most data entry rests on subjective observations by individual officers in the field, there is no way to monitor the accuracy of officers' conclusions.[92] The high potential for inaccuracy is particularly problematic when funding for anti-gang initiatives creates incentives to be over- rather than under-inclusive.[93]

Defenders of CalGang object to such criticisms. Don Mace, former chairman of CGNAC and currently Attorney General Investigator in Charge at the California Department of Justice, contends that critics of gang databases exaggerate the inaccuracies and that police departments have a strong incentive for accuracy because bad records hinder or slow down an investigation.[94] Orange County GREAT coordinator Loren Duchesne states, "I personally do not know of anybody who is put into the gang system [who] does not deserve to be there. I think we do a very good job of being careful."[95] Furthermore, Mace argues that because CalGang is operated as an intelligence database and is only accessible by law enforcement, the consequences of inaccurate inclusion are minimal and should not be of much concern.[96] This, however, fails to address the concern that individuals are subjected to increased police scrutiny and contact as a result of their inclusion in the gang database.

An additional question that raises concerns about the accuracy of the records in gang databases is whether police departments are complying with the GREAT/CalGang requirement that records older than five years be purged. The importance of such purging is that, if an individual has had no law enforcement contacts for years, the underlying rationale for information gathering proves even more evasive.[97] Despite the five-year requirement, many have contended that the GREAT/CalGang system has failed to purge numerous old records that had never been accessed or updated.[98] While Mace reports that the current database software will automatically purge records that have been inactive for over five years,[99] computer problems caused the purging of records to be temporarily suspended in 1998.[100] Even if database managers were complying with purge requirements, the adequacy of the purge requirements has also been challenged. First, five years may be too long a period; the Los Angeles District Attorney's Report on Gangs notes that "many experts would say that a gang member who disappears from view for three years is no longer active."[101] Second, *any* update to a database record may trigger a new five-year period, whether or not this data entry indicates any reason for suspicion of criminal or gang activity.[102] Because of such concerns, the ACLU has recommended that individuals who have never been arrested or convicted of a crime should be purged earlier than those convicted of serious gang-related felonies, that updates to a record that do not indicate any criminal activity should not trigger a new five-year period, and that any records that were entered using invalid criteria or that can now be shown to be erroneous (for example, because an individual has left a gang) should be purged.[103]

When These Problems Result in Inaccurate Gang Identifications, Those Mistakenly Included in the Database Have No Mechanism to Contest Their Gang Membership Label

In most cases, individuals do not even realize that they have become a part of the gang database; other than in select localities that have established such policies as part of settlements of lawsuits over police gang database practices, there is no requirement that individuals be notified when their record is entered.[104] Accordingly, most individuals have no opportunity to contest their inclusion in the database. Even if individuals were to discover that they have been unjustifiably included or that inaccurate information has been entered into the database, moreover, there is no established procedure by which they can ensure that their records are removed.[105] Supporters of CalGang argue that, because the database is only accessible to law enforcement, procedural protections such as notice and the opportunity to be heard are unnecessary.[106] However, the absence of such procedural protections exacerbates the risks that inaccurate entries will be made and will remain in the database for years.

Most of the Individuals Included in Gang Databases Are Racial Minorities

"They ought to call it the blacklist. This is harassment. It's not a crackdown on gangs; it's a crackdown on blacks," commented one observer.[107]

The vagueness of the criteria employed for inclusion in the gang database along with the inconsistent use of these criteria leave the door open to relying on race as a basis for suspecting someone of gang activity. As one commentary argued, "Whether photo stops occur in Orange County or Los Angeles or San Jose, the targets have consistently been members of communities of color, thus supporting the contention that race is a primary consideration in the decision to stop, question, and photograph individuals."[108] Similarly, the ACLU accuses, "since law enforcement's definition of a gang is broad enough to encompass many groups of white persons ... these statistics clearly reflect the officers' racially-based preconceptions of gang members, rather than any objective or carefully applied criteria."[109] Most complaints by individuals who claim to have been unjustly detained and then erroneously identified as gang members for purposes of inclusion in a gang database come from minority youth.[110]

Statistics overwhelmingly demonstrate that most individuals included in gang databases are young people of color, though they do not necessarily confirm an underlying racial motive. 1997 figures from the Orange County GREAT database reveal that it is 74 percent Latino, although the county population is just 27 percent Latino, and that 93 percent of those included on the database are people of color, although non-whites make up just 50 percent of individuals in the county.[111] These Orange County statistics, along with widespread reports of "over-enforcement" directed at minority youth, caused Phil Montez, the regional director of the California Advisory Committee of the U.S. Commission on Civil Rights, to state that he had "serious questions" about the constitutionality of police practices and to call for an investigation by the United States Department of Justice.[112] Statistics from other counties prove even worse. In Los Angeles County, a 1992 report revealed that 47 percent of African-American men between twenty-one and twenty-four years of age were considered gang members by the GREAT database (as compared to 6 percent of Asian youth, 8.5 percent of Latino youth, and less than 0.5 percent of white youth).[113] In 1993, it was reported that 93 percent of Denver, Colorado's gang list was made up of African Americans and Latinos, and two out of three African-American men between the ages of twelve and twenty-four were included on the list.[114] Such concerns have spurred an investigation by the California Advisory Committee of the U.S. Civil Rights Commission, which held hearings on the issue during the summer of 1997.[115]

Database supporters, however, maintain that the disproportionate racial numbers merely reflect the racial composition of gangs.[116] One member of the Orange County Gang Strategy Steering Committee explained the numbers by stating that white gang members simply aren't a problem.[117] The Los Angeles District Attorney's report acknowledged that the statistics on identification of African-American youth as gang members merited some concern, but attributed the numbers to problems plaguing the African-American community such as high unemployment and prevalent drug dealing.[118] The report did note the possibility that police harassment would result in more frequent identification of African-American youths as gang members, but concluded that the problem was *underreporting* of other racial groups rather than *overreporting* of African-American gang members.[119] The report concluded that "it is clear that the *undercount* of young Black gang members is extremely high" and estimated that an additional 12,500 African-American youths belonged in the gang database.[120]

While there are few reliable statistics documenting the racial composition of gangs, which makes it difficult to evaluate the merit of the claim that youth of color are over-included in gang databases, the vagueness of the criteria employed, the accounts by young people of color of repeated stops and selective information gathering, and the extremely high percentage of young African-American men in certain localities who have been labeled gang members support claims that the number of racial minorities who are not gang members but are included in the database is disproportionate. Moreover, the perception by many that police target individuals as suspected gang members solely on the basis of race may carry consequences that are independent of the accuracy of this perception. Some warn that mistaken inclusion reinforces distrust of the police by young people of color and that the police harassment may actually push youth into gangs.[121] Jon Hirano, executive director of the Westminster-based Asian Pacific Leadership Council, expressed this concern: "When a child is thinking he's the proper student, the proper citizen, and then is told, 'No, you're not,' what kind of psychological effect will that have on a child? I think there's a possibility of deep psychological core problems. I think it could lead kids into doing bad."[122]

Inclusion in the Gang Database May Result in Increased Police Harassment and Other Consequences

The techniques used to gather information for gang databases are commonly implemented through widespread stops of young people without any suspicion of criminal activity. The ACLU has received complaints of such stops from localities in California such as San Francisco, Gilroy, Santa Rosa, Fountain Valley, and Redwood City.[123] While the police typically characterize such stops as consensual encounters, they are often not perceived as such by those who are detained.[124] In July 1999, a police department in Georgia utilized a new method of detaining suspected gang members, conducting a roadblock (which also looked for drunk drivers) and asking suspected gang members to leave their cars so that police could take their photographs.[125] However, supporters of gang databases maintain that police abuses such as illegal stops are caused not by maintenance of computerized records, but rather by poor training and monitoring practices in local police departments.[126]

Once listed in a database, individuals will likely encounter increased police attention and harassment.[127] Gang database systems seek to make gang identification information routinely accessible for use during traffic and other police stops.[128] Police officers have used gang databases to identify individuals to be named in anti-gang injunctions.[129] The FBI's gang database proposal acknowledged that when police find out that someone is on a gang database it "may result in a police officer being overly aggressive by taking some positive action towards the subject detainee solely as the result of the positive Gang File response."[130]

There may be consequences in other areas of the criminal justice system as well. Records in the GREAT/CalGang database are provided to probation officers and district attorneys for use in guiding discretionary decisions.[131] In 1992, Los Angeles Deputy District Attorney Michael Genelin stated that prosecutors use GREAT to identify gang members in order to select cases in which they will advocate for longer prison sentences.[132] The highly discretionary nature of decisions by prosecutors, parole or probation officers, and judges makes it extremely difficult to track the effect that suspicion of gang involvement has on bail decisions, conditions of probation and parole, and jail or prison sentences.[133]

Furthermore, there have been disturbing reports of other collateral implications of inclusion in a gang database. In 1997, a Colorado man filed an action in federal court against the city of Aurora when he was barred from visiting his three-year-old son by the landlord of the building in which his son resided because he had been included in a list of suspected gang members.[134] In Oregon, two plaintiffs claimed that police threatened to send copies of a police report that labeled them gang members to their employer.[135] In Illinois, contrary to federal law and their own guidelines, local police officers who conducted criminal record checks of individuals applying for housing with the Springfield Housing Authority were reportedly also providing Housing Authority officials with information that included the suspected gang affiliations of applicants.[136] Cooperation between police and school officials in many jurisdictions raises further concerns about possible consequences for students who are falsely identified as gang members.[137] However, despite anecdotal reports that suspicions of gang affiliation have been released, there have been no documented incidents in California in which such identifications have been shared with individuals outside of law enforcement.[138]

Moreover, although the database records themselves may not be released to the public, much of the information gathered for the database may nonetheless find its way to the public eye. For example, photographs assembled for gang databases may also be compiled in gang "mugbooks" or used in computer-generated photographic lineups, which are then shown to crime victims and witnesses.[139] Furthermore, government data files can affect one's ability to obtain a professional license, employment or security clearance, government benefits, and immigration status.[140]

LEGAL CHALLENGES TO GANG DATABASES

In light of such concerns, the ACLU has made gang databases a target for litigation and brought a number of lawsuits challenging the practices involved in compiling and utilizing gang databases. The primary ACLU lawsuit, which resulted in a favorable settlement for the plaintiffs, was initiated in Southern California and challenged the police practice of detaining young Southeast Asian individuals in order to take their photographs and enter their records as gang members in law enforcement databases, asserting causes of action based on the rights to equal protection, privacy, due process, association, freedom from unreasonable searches and seizures, and freedom from racial harassment and intimidation.[141] The following discussion reviews and evaluates the legal claims that have been or could be included in these lawsuits.

Right of Association

The right of association in furtherance of illegal activities does not enjoy constitutional protection.[142] However, gang membership is not itself illegal.[143] In fact, the United States Supreme Court has afforded some constitutional protection to membership in a gang under the First Amendment's right of association.[144] Moreover, an individual who belongs to an association that engages in illegal activities cannot be held liable unless he or she specifically intends to further the group's illegal objectives.[145] In *Sawyer v. Sandstrom*, the United States Court of Appeals for the Fifth Circuit relied upon this constitutional principle to hold that punishment of an individual for loitering with others with the knowledge that illegal drug sales were taking place punished lawful, protected activity and violated the defendant's right of association.[146]

Plaintiffs have therefore challenged inclusion in a gang database as impinging upon protected associational rights. In *Pham*, the plaintiffs argued that inclusion in a gang database inhibited them from exercising their freedom of association because they were forced to avoid several locations due to their fear of police harassment.[147] The plaintiffs in *Rivers* made a similar argument, contending that constant police harassment had caused them to stop traveling in public and visiting friends and neighbors.[148]

However, both federal and state courts are likely to reject a claim grounded in the First Amendment. First, the right of association does not encompass casual, non-expressive relationships among gang members or friends. The Supreme Court has declined to "recognize a generalized right of social association"[149] and has narrowly defined the right of association to protect only two types of association: intimate or familial association and association involving protected expression.[150] Gangs would appear to fall in neither category. While some have suggested that gangs might qualify as intimate associations that "presuppose 'deep attachments and commitments to the necessarily few other individuals with whom one shares not only a special community of thoughts, experiences, and beliefs but also distinctively personal aspects of one's life,'"[151] the Supreme Court recently concluded that a statute that punished loitering by gang members did not impair the right of association protected by the First Amendment.[152] The Court did not explain its reasoning and invalidated the statute on other grounds, but its citation of authority suggested that gangs failed to qualify as intimate associations warranting such constitutional protection.[153] Even if gangs were to qualify as intimate associations, moreover, the courts may conclude that gangs' illegal activities and purpose foreclose any associational protection.[154] In *People ex rel. Gallo v. Acuna*, the California Supreme Court noted that while a gang might "share one or two of the characteristics that define intrinsically valuable and constitutionally protected associations, ... protected rights of association in the intimate sense are those existing along a narrow band of affiliations that permit deep and enduring personal bonds to flourish, inculcating and nourishing civilization's fundamental values, against which even the state is powerless to intrude."[155] The California court concluded that, because freedom of association "does not extend to joining with others for the purpose of depriving third parties of their lawful rights," gangs and gang activities were not protected by the First Amendment.[156]

Unreasonable Search and Seizure

While the Fourth Amendment does not prohibit the practice of keeping information about suspected gang members in a computer database, it does impose some limits on the techniques that police may use in order to collect this information. This is particularly important in light of widespread complaints by minority youth that police stop them without any basis for suspicion and then take the youths' photographs for inclusion in the gang database.[157]

In order to detain someone, even briefly, the police must have reasonable articulable suspicion that the individual is engaged in some form of criminal activity.[158] Because gang membership itself is not a crime, this suspicion may not rest solely on evidence of gang affiliation.[159] However, when gang involvement is possibly connected to the crime that is under investigation, gang affiliation may be one factor in the probable cause determination.[160] The legitimacy of using gang member profiles as a justification for detaining individuals is an open question.[161] Even if a stop of an individual is justified, the detention must "last no longer than is necessary to effectuate the purpose of the stop."[162] Thus, prolonging a stop in order to take a photograph or gather additional information for inclusion in a gang database may go beyond constitutionally permissible boundaries.

Police may argue that they need not show reasonable articulable suspicion because most photographs are taken during consensual encounters, and there is no Fourth Amendment prohibition against taking photographs of individuals without their permission.[163] Courts will evaluate whether a police-citizen encounter was consensual on a case by case basis by determining whether a reasonable person would have felt free to leave.[164] However, encounters that are characterized as "consensual" often involve elements of coercion. In "consensual encounters" with suspected gang members, police practices often include direct orders, covert or overt threats, and other forms of intimidation to force young people to submit to photographs and to give the police personal information.[165]

If the use of an illegally obtained photograph or gang file results in the arrest and prosecution of an individual, the defendant may move to suppress the illegally obtained evidence. The success of this motion will likely depend on the directness of the relationship between the illegally obtained evidence and the subsequent criminal charges. In a celebrated case, a California appellate court suppressed a photograph that had been taken for gang tracking purposes. The court held that the trial court should have suppressed identification of a murder defendant in a photographic lineup because the police had taken a photograph of the defendant three days earlier solely because they suspected that he belonged to a gang.[166] The officers explained that they had taken the photograph pursuant to a police department policy of stopping suspected gang members and that they suspected the defendant because he was with a group of young men in known gang territory at a common gang-member gathering place, and at least one of them was dressed in a manner consistent with gang membership; the individuals were talking to one another and not engaged in any suspicious activity at the time of the stop.[167] The court distinguished other decisions in which courts had declined to suppress illegally obtained photographs on the ground that in this case there was a close connection between the taking of the photograph and the subsequent identification and concluded that the police were therefore exploiting the illegality in order to obtain a conviction.[168]

Nonetheless, there are four problems with relying on this suppression remedy. First, courts have admitted identifications using illegally obtained photographs as long as the illegality was sufficiently attenuated from the current crime.[169] Second, the remedy would probably not prevent police from utilizing the gang database, including illegally obtained information, to identify a suspect as long as the *witnesses* do not use illegally obtained photographs to actually identify the defendant. Third, individuals who do not become defendants in a subsequent criminal case are left without a remedy except for civil litigation, which generally provides inadequate remedies for Fourth Amendment violations.[170] And fourth, challenges under the Fourth Amendment often fail because the police claim that encounters were consensual or offer post hoc rationalizations for reasonable suspicion.[171]

Legal challenges alleging violations of the Fourth Amendment in obtaining information from suspected gang members have led some police departments to institute practices that protect the rights of young people who are stopped by the police. In the settlement of the *Pham* lawsuit, the police department agreed to take photographs only when they had a reasonable suspicion of some kind of criminal activity and had obtained written consent and to allow individuals to request removal of their photographs from police files.[172] A similar lawsuit in Reno, Nevada (as in *Pham*, filed by an honor student, this time a young Hispanic man), produced a settlement that forbade police from stopping young people based solely on a suspicion of gang membership and instead required either consent or reason to suspect actual criminal activity before any questioning or photography could take place.[173] And police in Philadelphia, in response to protests by Asian groups, agreed to take photographs only with explicit permission from the police commissioner, to destroy photographs of individuals cleared of any criminal involvement, and to notify individuals whose photographs were destroyed.[174]

Right to Privacy

The Federal Right to Be Left Alone (Informational Privacy)

Traditional conceptions of the right to privacy often encompass the right to be free from governmental information gathering. Such notions have become increasingly prevalent as the advances of modern technology have posed new threats to citizens' privacy. As early as 1890, the implications of modern technology prompted such concerns: "numerous mechanical devices threaten ... that 'what is whispered in the closet shall be proclaimed from the housetops.'"[175] However, the concept of "informational privacy" really came into being during the 1970s, as advances in the world of computers and electronic databases substantially expanded the government's power to track and monitor its citizenry.[176]

The Supreme Court confronted these concerns in the 1977 case of *Whalen v. Roe*.[177] There, the plaintiffs sought to test the constitutionality of a state law requiring doctors to report the identities of patients receiving certain prescription drugs. The Court acknowledged the validity of the heightened concern about privacy raised by technological developments: "We are not unaware of the threat to privacy implicit in the accumulation of vast amounts of personal information in computerized data banks or other massive government files."[178] Nonetheless, the Court unanimously rejected the privacy challenge.[179] In its analysis, the Court treated the privacy claim primarily as a concern about "unwarranted disclosure of accumulated private data," and concluded that the safeguards preventing improper disclosure were adequate.[180] Thus the only possible federal privacy challenge to gang databases left open by Supreme Court precedent appears to be one based on improper disclosure to entities outside of law enforcement.[181] In *Thornburgh v. American College of Obstetricians and Gynecologists*, the Court seemed to assert a stronger commitment to protection from improper disclosure of private information, citing *Whalen* for the proposition that "a certain private sphere of individual liberty will be kept largely beyond the reach of government" and striking down a state law which required that abortions be reported to the government.[182] Nonetheless, the Court's analysis did not appear to offer a basis for a privacy cause of action based on government information gathering as long as no improper *disclosure* was threatened.[183]

The final barrier to a federal privacy claim may be found in *Zurcher v. Stanford Daily*,[184] which suggests that federal privacy challenges to tactics used in a criminal investigation must be evaluated solely under a Fourth Amendment analysis.[185] However, the Supreme Court *has* recognized that disclosure of one's criminal record may violate the right to privacy.[186]

In light of such cases, it appears that as long as the government does not improperly disclose data from the gang database, federal constitutional privacy law does not offer a promising basis for legal challenges to gang databases.

The State Right to Be Left Alone (Informational Privacy)

California state privacy protections may offer a stronger basis for protection against government information gathering. When voters passed an amendment to the California constitution in 1972, establishing an explicit privacy right,[187] they were motivated in large part by a desire to protect themselves from government information gathering: "a principal aim of the constitutional provision is to limit the infringement upon personal privacy arising from the government's increasing collection and retention of data relating to all facets of an individual's life."[188] The California Supreme Court analyzed the ballot argument in favor of the constitutional amendment and concluded that the provision addressed the following four dangers: "(1) 'government snooping' and the secret gathering of personal information; (2) the overbroad collection and retention of unnecessary personal information by government and business interests; (3) the improper use of information properly obtained for a specific purpose, for example, the use of it for another purpose or the disclosure of it to some third party; and (4) the lack of a reasonable check on the accuracy of existing records."[189] The court found that this state privacy protection provided a basis for a cause of action challenging police surveillance of university students who were not known to be involved in any illegal activity.[190]

Gang databases appear to implicate a number of the interests that California voters sought to protect. First, collection of information about individuals not suspected of criminal wrongdoing does not serve any legitimate law enforcement interest; at least some of the records included in the database are therefore unnecessary.[191] Second, police and other law enforcement officials may use information regarding suspected gang affiliation for improper purposes such as to justify increased harassment or as a reason to exercise discretion unfavorably. Third, there are few safeguards to insure the accuracy of the information maintained by the government.

In *Loder v. Municipal Court*, however, the California Supreme Court rejected a legal challenge to the maintenance of arrest records that raised concerns similar to those implicated by gang databases: inaccurate or incomplete arrest records, public dissemination of arrest records, and possible denial of employment or other opportunities on the basis of one's arrest record.[192] Nonetheless, litigants could argue that the privacy interests at stake in a challenge to gang databases are stronger than those implicated by a challenge to maintenance of arrest records, for in order to arrest someone, the police need probable cause. No similar safeguard or underlying criminal predicate justifies keeping records on people not suspected of involvement in any crime.[193]

Even if it were determined that the gang databases violated the California right to privacy, opponents of this law enforcement tactic would have one more legal issue to address: whether such an invasion of privacy was justified because the use of databases is narrowly tailored to protect a compelling state interest.[194] In *Loder*, the court concluded that, even if maintaining arrest records for people never convicted of any crime infringed the right to privacy, compelling law enforcement interests nonetheless justified such a practice.[195] These government interests are less clear, however, when law enforcement officials gather information on individuals who are not necessarily suspected of any criminal activity. The use of gang databases would be more accurately compared to a police practice of keeping computerized records on every individual who they stopped for consensual questioning or on the basis of reasonable suspicion, whether or not these individuals were subsequently arrested.

Moreover, in *Loder*, the court rested its decision in part on the existence of legislative safeguards that protected an arrested individual's interests. These safeguards included a requirement that arrests not leading to convictions be listed as detentions and that the record show the final disposition of the charge, a mechanism for individuals to inspect their own criminal records and challenge inaccuracies, provisions for sealing or purging some arrest records, provisions to prevent the improper dissemination of arrest records, and prohibitions against the use of arrest records as a basis to deny employment or other professional opportunities.[196] Few of these protections are in place for those erroneously included on a gang database: there is no formal disposition of a suspicion of gang involvement that can be entered into a record; individuals do not have the right to find out whether they are listed on a gang database and challenge their own inclusion; there are weak purge provisions for gang databases but no other expungement mechanisms; and no law prohibits consideration of gang affiliation in the employment context. The only protection noted in *Loder* that does appear to apply to gang databases is that there are safeguards against improper disclosure of gang affiliation. However, despite these safeguards, there have been documented instances of such improper disclosure in other states; such disclosure, if it occurred in California, would provide the strongest basis for a privacy challenge based on the state constitution.[197]

Statutory Protection of the Right to Be Left Alone

Although the Supreme Court has not heretofore limited the ability of law enforcement to engage in information gathering as long as such information is not disclosed, federal statutes may provide an alternative source of protection. Statutes governing the confidentiality of information collected for criminal intelligence systems mandate procedures to protect the privacy of information, ensure that the information is used only for valid law enforcement purposes, and to provide for the right of individuals to review and challenge the accuracy of criminal history information about themselves.[198] These statutory provisions apply to all criminal intelligence systems that receive funding under the Omnibus Crime Control and Safe Streets Act.[199]

The regulations promulgated under this statute mandate the existence of a reasonable suspicion that an individual is involved in criminal conduct and that the information gathered is relevant to this criminal conduct as threshold requirements for entering information about an individual into a database.[200] The regulations further mandate that no unlawfully obtained information be entered into an intelligence database.[201] While many database systems may not receive federal funding, state officials in California and Colorado have expressed a desire to comply with federal regulations in order to avoid foreclosing federal funding opportunities.[202] According to Don Mace, CalGang also had decided to comply with these federal regulations because many local agencies have utilized federal funding to purchase their equipment.[203]

California state statutes also prohibit certain disclosures of personal information that have been collected by a government agency and provide for procedural protections such as notice and an opportunity to correct inaccurate records.[204] However, many of these protections do not apply to information gathered for law enforcement purposes.[205]

The Right Against Unwanted, False-Light Publicity

A final basis for a privacy challenge to gang databases could be asserted whenever police show photographs of suspected gang members to members of the public seeking to identify crime suspects.[206] This challenge would identify the privacy interest violated as the right against publicity that places an individual in a false public light, based on the assumption that individuals viewing such photographs will assume that the photographs show individuals who are engaged in criminal activity. An allegation that an individual has engaged in criminal conduct poses a greater privacy interest threat than the release of other, more benign information.[207] Some older cases have found that implying that someone is a criminal by placing his photograph in a "rogues' gallery" constitutes an invasion of the right to privacy.[208] The holdings of these cases have rested on the display of such photographs to the public. While assembly of a computer database of gang members does not necessarily involve public display, police may be using photographs collected for both purposes: for entry into the database and for photographic lineups.[209]

One modern case, however, suggests that this cause of action may prove unsuccessful, at least in California state courts. In *Sterling v. City of Oakland*, the California state appeals court held that the "rogues' gallery" line of cases was inapplicable to a challenge to the retention of photographs and fingerprint records after dismissal of criminal charges.[210] However, *Sterling* can be distinguished from cases involving gang databases in two main ways. First, the case was decided before the California voters expanded the state's privacy right in 1972. Second, the court dismissed the theory that maintenance of the arrest record would result in an increased likelihood of future arrest and the possibility of increased sentences.[211] This theory is not so easy to dismiss in the case of gang databases, in light of California statutes providing for sentence enhancements for gang-related criminal conduct; the accessibility of the gang database to patrol officers, prosecutors, and other law enforcement officials; and the reports of young people that harassment has increased after being placed on a gang database.

Disclosure of suspected gang affiliation to outside parties would present an even stronger privacy claim. Disclosure of arrest records to employers, for example, has been held to violate the right to privacy.[212] However, there does not seem to be reason to believe that such disclosure is likely to take place in California in the foreseeable future.[213]

Right to Due Process

The determination whether due process has been violated requires a two-step analysis: first, whether an individual has been deprived of life, liberty, or property; and second, whether the process afforded to the individual was adequate.

Interests Protected under Procedural Due Process

The broadest definitions of liberty encompass "those privileges long recognized ... as essential to the orderly pursuit of happiness by free men."[214] Since the early 1970s, however, the Supreme Court has employed a fairly restrictive definition of the liberty and property rights that are protected by due process. Because cases challenging gang databases would usually not involve deprivation of a property right,[215] this analysis focuses on the liberty interests that are at stake. Traditional liberty interests protected by courts include fundamental constitutional rights (such as freedom of association or the federal right to privacy) and freedom from deprivation of physical liberty (which may be violated by criminal conviction and other forms of involuntary commitment).[216] While two Supreme Court decisions in the early 1970s suggested that injury to one's reputation might implicate a protected liberty interest,[217] this prospect was foreclosed by *Paul v. Davis*, which clearly held that an injury to reputation, without more, was not a deprivation of liberty.[218] In this case, the Court held that injury to reputation caused by distribution of a list of "active shoplifters" that included plaintiff's name (although he had been arrested but never convicted of shoplifting) did not implicate a protected liberty interest.[219] Moreover, the Court rejected the plaintiff's claim that his designation as a shoplifter would inhibit his opportunities to enter stores and his future employment prospects on the grounds that allowing such a claim would allow any individuals falsely accused of a crime to claim a violation of constitutional rights.[220]

However, *Paul v. Davis* does not stand for the proposition that an individual's reputational injury is *never* actionable as a deprivation of liberty, but merely that a plaintiff must show a harm *in addition* to stigma. Novak and Rotunda explain, "If the damage to the person's reputation is so great that it will limit the individual's associational opportunities within a community or foreclose a wide range of employment to the individual, the act will constitute a deprivation of liberty."[221] For example, the Court has found deprivation of a liberty interest when discipline of a student would damage relationships with peers and other future educational and employment opportunities.[222] Furthermore, the increasingly common practice of compiling lists of suspected child abusers has been held to violate due process when inclusion damaged individuals' reputation in combination with another tangible interest such as employment or family privacy.[223]

Therefore, depending on the consequences thereof, dissemination of the information that individuals are on a gang database might violate a liberty interest under the *Paul v. Davis* test. Cases involving inclusion in a registry of suspected child abusers demonstrate that the disclosure of suspected criminal activity that causes a loss of employment or other significant opportunities is a deprivation of liberty that requires due process protection. In cases such as *Rivers*, in which suspected gang affiliation was released to employers, or in Aurora, Colorado, where an individual was prevented from visiting family members (and others may have lost their housing), it will not be difficult to assert protected liberty interests that have been deprived without affording due process protection. However, it may be more difficult to establish a liberty interest in a state such as California, where laws prevent the dissemination of the information on the gang database beyond law enforcement agencies. In cases involving sex offender registration, courts have made a very sharp distinction between *registration* as a sex offender and *disclosure* of one's status as a sex offender to the community.[224]

Paul v. Davis does leave open one other possible avenue for defining a liberty interest: When state or federal law establishes a substantive right, under certain circumstances, such a right will qualify as a liberty interest.[225] Not every state law gives rise to a constitutionally protected interest, however, and even mandatory language may not invariably create a protected right. The proper inquiry examines whether a statute creates a *substantive* individual entitlement.[226] This inquiry can be a rather difficult one, as illustrated by a conflict among New York federal courts over whether violation of a statutory right to return of a police photograph results in a constitutional injury[227] and the evolution of Supreme Court jurisprudence, which has increasingly narrowed the circumstances under which a state law gives rise to a protected liberty interest among prisoners.[228]

Given this constitutional framework, a procedural due process claim could not be asserted in every state. In California, however, plaintiffs challenging gang databases may be able to rest their claim of infringement of due process on the deprivation of an interest protected under state law: the right to privacy guaranteed by the California constitution. Litigants challenging gang databases could argue that intrusion upon the constitutional right to privacy invokes harms that are as serious as those posed by invasion of the right to family privacy, which courts have held to demonstrate deprivation of a liberty interest. The clarity of the language of and intent behind the privacy clause of the California constitution arguably establish this as a state-created liberty interest. Of course, this argument will hinge on the success of the underlying privacy claim.[229] In at least one case, a litigant challenging a sex offender registration and notification requirement succeeded in resting due process claims on state constitutional protection of privacy interests.[230]

As a final argument, inclusion in a gang database may increase the *likelihood* of police harassment and thus the deprivation of physical liberty. Thus, in cases in which this increased risk has actually played a role in causing or contributing to an actual injury, the increased risk attributable to the gang database may be actionable. In a lawsuit challenging the San Jose Police Department's use of an Asian mugbook, for example, the plaintiff—who had never before been arrested for a crime—was falsely identified as the perpetrator of a home invasion robbery by a witness perusing the mugbook. Although eventually acquitted, the plaintiff spent three months in jail awaiting trial.[231] The plaintiff argued that but for his inclusion in the mugbook he would never have spent three months in jail (which deprived him of his liberty and of property, since his business suffered during that time period).[232] The ACLU attorneys involved in this case argued that placing his photograph in the mugbook also caused stigmatic injury because it led witnesses to assume he was a criminal (and that this stigma was especially harmful in a relatively small Vietnamese community).[233]

In a similar vein, the lawyers in the *Pham* case argued that labeling individuals as gang members or associates increased the risk of adverse consequences, particularly the risk that police and others with power in the criminal justice system would exercise their discretion unfavorably in situations involving individuals identified as gang members.[234] In *Rivers*, the plaintiffs asserted a substantive due process claim based on police maltreatment during their arrest and subsequent detention, and the court refused to dismiss their request for an injunction requiring the city to expunge references to them as gang members from police files, because they claimed that the records "put them at risk of future police harassment."[235] Thus, it will be important for opponents of gang databases to establish the concrete nature of this increased risk of liberty deprivation. Given the subjective nature of many law enforcement decisions and the multitude of factors that are considered, it may be necessary to secure testimony from police officers, probation officers, prosecutors, and judges that describes the role that suspicion of gang membership plays in their decision-making process.[236]

In analyzing whether the interests threatened by gang databases merit due process protection, the historical context suggests that courts should treat the deprivation of liberty at issue in these cases with the utmost seriousness. The core purpose of the Due Process Clause is to protect individuals from "the sort of formal constraints imposed by the criminal process,"[237] and it reflects a strong constitutional commitment to protecting individuals from assignment of guilt in the criminal justice system without adequate due process. Moreover, gang databases implicate similar concerns to those that arose during other periods when individuals were placed on lists as suspected subversives and suffered adverse consequences.[238] The liberty interests that are at stake when an individual is included in a gang database—the reputational injury that results from dissemination of this label, the infringement of the state right to privacy, and the increased likelihood of deprivation of physical liberty—should therefore warrant due process protection.

Process Required

If the government has deprived an individual of protected liberty interest, it must provide that individual with adequate notice and the opportunity to be heard: "When protected interests are implicated, the right to some kind of prior hearing is paramount."[239] Yet the type of hearing and the procedural guarantees required may vary tremendously, depending on a number of factors. In determining whether procedural protections are adequate, courts employ the three-part test from *Mathews v. Eldridge*.[240] This test requires that courts weigh the importance of the private interest at stake, the risk of erroneous deprivation along with the value of additional procedural safeguards, and the government interest involved, and determine accordingly which procedures are required.[241]

The importance of the individual interest at stake in the case of gang databases will probably not rise to the level of government benefits such as the payment of welfare or Social Security benefits, which often involve questions of day-to-day survival. Nonetheless, there are potentially severe consequences of erroneous inclusion on a gang database such as increased police attention, differential treatment within the criminal justice system, and the risk of improper disclosure of one's suspected gang affiliation.[242] Given that the determination of who is a gang member relies on a set of highly subjective criteria riddled with problems, the risk of erroneous deprivation is particularly high.[243] However, there are few objective indicia to conclusively prove that a record is inaccurate.[244] Assessing the value of additional procedures, similarly, will necessarily require some speculation. At the very least, the procedure would provide an opportunity to explain facts that the police have concluded are indicia of gang involvement, which could prove extremely valuable in some circumstances. For example, an individual who obtained a gang tattoo in his teenage years but is no longer involved could explain this fact; or a person who lives in a gang area and has childhood friends who are gang members but maintains no gang involvement herself could make such an argument. The success that some suspected gang members have had in obtaining dismissal from gang injunctions demonstrates that the right to present evidence at a hearing may be useful in more accurately identifying gang members.[245]

While the government can claim a strong interest in assembling information about gang members, this interest would probably not be seriously threatened by allowing individuals to challenge their inclusion in the database. The likelihood that large numbers of gang members would contest their status is probably low; for example, very few individuals have chosen to show up to contest their inclusion in much more restrictive anti-gang injunctions.[246] Furthermore, the government interest in making sure that its records are accurate and in avoiding violations of privacy rights of law-abiding citizens would be weighed by the courts.[247]

Procedures suggested by litigants or agreed to in settlement of lawsuits provide some guidance as to the nature of the procedure that due process might require. In settlement of a lawsuit about its gang lists, the city of Portland, Oregon, agreed to notify all individuals included on gang lists and to inform them of their right to a hearing to contest their identification and to appeal this hearing's result.[248] In the *Pham* settlement, the Garden Grove police department agreed to afford individuals the right to request the purge of their pictures from police department records, appeal a negative ruling on such a request to a three-person panel, and, in the event that they are unsuccessful, receive the phone number of the ACLU.[249] In *Nguyen v. City of San Jose*, the plaintiff suggested that proper procedural safeguards would involve notice that one's photograph has been placed in the Asian mugbook and an opportunity to object to such inclusion.[250] The ACLU has advocated the following procedural safeguards: notifying individuals and/or their parents before their record is entered into the database, informing individuals of the basis for the gang label (with exceptions for information that needs to remain confidential), and offering them an opportunity to contest the accuracy of the identification as a gang member.[251]

A key question in due process cases is often whether written submissions may substitute for an actual hearing. In the case of determining whether an individual is a gang member, an actual hearing would appear necessary. The reasons that courts have found hearings less important in some cases, such as because written documentation is adequate and renders verbal discussion unnecessary, are not present in the case of gang databases.[252] Oral presentation by the accused gang member along with the police officer who has made the accusation would allow an independent body to assess credibility, the possibility of misunderstanding, and other factors. Furthermore, requiring written appeals might prove difficult for those without adequate education and training.[253] If the courts were to require a hearing, it would probably include only very minimal procedural safeguards.[254] At the very least, due process would appear to require notice of inclusion in the database along with the opportunity to discover the basis for inclusion, along with some sort of opportunity to contest gang membership and offer an alternative explanation for observations that are consistent with gang membership.

In a case involving challenges to procedures for challenging inclusion on a registry of suspected child abusers, the United States Court of Appeals for the Eighth Circuit held that allowing the subject nearly complete access to the records, destroying all records after a designated time period, affording appeals of inaccurate records through normal administrative processes, and in contested cases providing for the right to a hearing satisfied due process requirements.[255] The court also noted that the initial investigation of whether an abuse allegation was substantiated, which was required before any individual would be included in the database, was thorough and complex.[256] The standard of proof required may also be determinative of the adequacy of the procedural protections. The United States Court of Appeals for the Second Circuit struck down a system that placed the burden of proof on the subject of the abuse report (by employing a standard requiring only that there be "some credible evidence" to justify inclusion) despite the fact that the system provided otherwise extensive procedural mechanisms to contest the charge.[257] However, it will usually be even more difficult to prove gang involvement or non-involvement to a reasonable degree of certainty than it would be to establish that an individual has abused a child. Accordingly, a more lenient standard of proof, such as allowing the police to show "some credible evidence" of gang involvement and then shifting the burden of proof to the individual challenging his or her inclusion, might meet due process requirements.

Equal Protection and Racial Discrimination

A Constitutional Claim Will Likely Fail Due to the Difficulty of Proving Discriminatory Intent

Both the Fourteenth Amendment and Article I of the California constitution prohibit denial of equal protection; the applicable legal standards are essentially identical.[258] Plaintiffs challenging gang databases could allege an intent on the part of police officers or a police department to over-identify and harass members of minority groups. In Oregon, for example, the plaintiffs asserted the existence of a policy or practice of illegally detaining young African-American men, taking their photographs and labeling them gang members, and then using this label to engage in further harassment.[259]

However, establishing a violation of equal protection requires proof of discriminatory intent.[260] Statistical evidence of disparate impact can help to establish a prima facie case, but is not ultimately sufficient. Courts would be likely to apply this discriminatory intent requirement particularly stringently in the criminal justice context, where racially disparate numbers can easily indicate something other than purposeful discrimination.[261] Law enforcement agencies could assert many non-discriminatory reasons for the disproportionate numbers of minority youth included in gang databases, most obviously, that most gang members are racial minorities.[262] What might appear to be discriminatory application of the law may in fact be permissible if the class allegedly discriminated against is the group "from which the evil mainly is to be feared."[263]

An additional problem with an equal protection claim is that courts will readily find compelling interests when law enforcement goals are at issue.[264] Because of such deference to law enforcement interests, even the explicit use of race as grounds for reasonable suspicion for a police detention has been held to be permissible as long as race is not the only factor considered.[265]

Title VI Provides a Basis for a Cause of Action, but Litigants Will Need to Identify an Appropriate Comparison Pool in Order to Demonstrate Disparate Impact

Title VI of the Civil Rights Act of 1964 provides that "[n]o person in the United States shall, on the ground of race, color, or national origin, be excluded from participation in, be denied benefits of, or be subjected to discrimination under any program or activity receiving Federal Financial Assistance."[266] A plaintiff need not show that she is an "intended beneficiary" of the federally funded program that she is challenging.[267]

Regulations implementing Title VI may provide for a cause of action on the basis of adverse impact without a showing of discriminatory intent.[268] A litigant "must first demonstrate by a preponderance of the evidence that a facially neutral practice has a disproportionate adverse effect on a group protected by Title VI."[269] Once this prima facie showing is made, the burden shifts to the defendant to show that the practices causing disproportionate impact are necessary in order to achieve a "legitimate, important, and integral" goal.[270] The plaintiff may rebut the defendant's claim of necessity by proving the existence of a less discriminatory alternative.[271]

Applicability of Title VI to law enforcement practices. Plaintiffs have on occasion raised Title VI claims against police departments, usually in the course of lawsuits alleging employment discrimination by a government entity.[272] Despite the rarity of the use of Title VI to challenge law enforcement tactics, rather than employment practices, in at least three federal cases plaintiffs have maintained causes of action based on police treatment of private citizens.[273]

In order to maintain a lawsuit against gang databases under Title VI, plaintiffs would need to show that the law enforcement agency being sued receives the federal funds that make Title VI and its implementing regulations applicable to the agency's activities.[274] Police departments may receive federal money through Department of Justice grants under a variety of acts that have been passed by Congress.[275] Most receive at least some federal funding,[276] and *any* funding makes the regulations applicable to *all* of the agency's programs: Amendments to Title VI in 1988 made it clear that a plaintiff is not required to show that the federal funds went to the particular program that allegedly discriminates (in other words, there is no "nexus" requirement) as long as the agency or department itself received federal monies.[277]

Regulations implementing Title VI define the discrimination prohibited:

A recipient, in determining the type of disposition, services, financial aid, benefits, or facilities which will be provided by any such program ... may not ... utilize criteria or methods of administration which have the effect of subjecting individuals to discrimination because of their race, color, or national origin, or have the effect of defeating or substantially impairing accomplishment of the objectives of the program as respects individuals of a particular race, color, or national origin.[278]

Litigants will therefore need to specifically identify the practices that have a discriminatory impact; these practices might include the use of criteria that result in over-inclusion of youth of color (such as style of dress or frequenting areas with gang activity) as well as the use of vague criteria that allow for broad discretion by individual police officers (for example, the failure to require an underlying criminal predicate and the absence of adequate quality control measures) and are applied in a discriminatory manner.

Proving discriminatory impact: "similarly situated" analysis under Title VI. In determining whether a program or activity has a discriminatory impact, courts compare the racial composition of the affected group with the racial composition of an appropriate reference group. Most lawsuits alleging violations of Title VI involve disputes over government benefits, allocation of government services, or location of a government institution. In such cases, the reference pool is usually the pool of eligible potential beneficiaries.[279] Because the appropriate comparison pool in this case is particularly unclear, however, these other Title VI cases offer only limited guidance.[280]

There are four primary ways to approach defining the logical reference pool in the case of gang databases: first, by comparing representation in the population with representation in gang databases; second, by comparing representation on the gang database with a racial breakdown of actual gang members; third, by comparing the criminal histories and characteristics of the different racial groups that are included in the gang database; or fourth, by comparing misidentification statistics. However, all of these approaches are problematic. The first would not adequately answer the argument that certain racial groups are overrepresented in gang databases because they are overrepresented among gang members.[281] The second would be an ideal measurement standard, but because there are few reliable estimates of gang membership (and most come from the databases themselves), this would prove an extremely difficult approach. One would either need to find reliable studies, conduct a reliable study, or find a proper surrogate for gang membership (for example, rates of conviction for gang-related crimes).

The third approach appears to offer the most promise. If a more detailed racial breakdown of the criteria and characteristics of those included in gang databases were released, these statistics could be analyzed for discrimination. For example, if CalGang were to release the statistics showing a racial breakdown of the number of individuals included in the gang database who have been arrested and convicted of crimes,[282] these numbers could be analyzed to evaluate whether there is any correlation between level of criminal involvement and race: in other words, whether there is any race-based disparity in the level of criminal gang involvement that will lead to identification as a gang member. Similarly, if the criteria that provide the basis for entry of individual records were released and broken down by race, it would be possible to analyze whether a particular criterion has a disparate impact or is being used in a particularly discriminatory fashion.[283]

A fourth possible comparison pool analysis would compare *misidentification* statistics. If researchers were to study a sample group of individuals who have records in the gang database and determine how many individuals were actually gang members involved in criminal activities, how many were peripheral gang members, and how many were not gang members at all, they could then determine whether a higher proportion of minority youth were improperly included in the database.[284]

Two Title VI cases offer one final possible alternative, an analysis that has been employed when the appropriate reference pool is nearly impossible to define: the court could look *only* at the racial composition *of the affected group* to determine whether this group is predominantly made up of racial minorities. In *Coalition of Concerned Citizens v. Damian*, for example, the court determined that highway construction had an adverse impact under Title VI after noting that *most* of the individuals who would be displaced or suffer other harm were African American.[285] In *Hodges v. Public Building Commission of Chicago*, a case involving admissions practices at a magnet high school, the court similarly concluded, "disparate impact need not consist solely of an impact which affects minorities and non-minorities differently. Plaintiffs are entitled to base their disparate impact claim on statistics which establish that minorities are *primarily affected by* (and, ultimately the target of) a governmental action."[286] This method of analysis has been employed even in cases in which plaintiffs have challenged allegedly discriminatory police and prosecutorial practices, where some courts have inferred discrimination from disproportionate representation of racial minorities among the individuals prosecuted or detained by police. In *Hunter v. Underwood*, for example, the Supreme Court struck down a state law that disenfranchised individuals with moral turpitude convictions on equal protection grounds after reasoning *both* that legislators had discriminatory motives *and* that blacks were "'at least 1.7 times as likely as whites to suffer disenfranchisement ... for the commission of nonprison offenses.'"[287] Furthermore, in *United States v. Travis*, a case challenging the use of race as a criterion for making consensual stops, the court considered statistics comparing the racial composition of airline travelers with the racial makeup of those who were stopped by the police in allegedly consensual encounters,[288] noting that such statistical evidence "may ... create a strong inference that officers chose to engage in a particular consensual interview solely because of the interviewee's race."[289] If litigants challenging gang databases were able to use this standard, they could establish that gang databases are overwhelmingly composed of records of racial minorities and therefore have a disproportionately negative impact on young people of color. However, the standard suggested by these cases—that statistical documentation of overrepresentation of people of color may demonstrate discrimination even without a strong showing by plaintiffs that people of color do not commit the crimes targeted at higher rates—is seriously undermined by a 1996 Supreme Court decision on selective prosecution. In *United States v. Armstrong*, the Court held that a claimant must demonstrate that similarly situated individuals of another race were *not* prosecuted in order to establish discrimination.[290] This may indicate that a successful challenge to gang databases would require finding white gang members who were not included on such databases or white youth who met the criteria for identification as gang members but were not identified and included.[291]

Justification for practice. Even if plaintiffs could demonstrate the existence of an institutional practice that has a discriminatory impact, defendants would still have an opportunity to justify their practices. Courts have modified the Title VII "business necessity" test for the Title VI context to require the defendant to show that the challenged practice is institutionally necessary.[292] This means that the practice must be necessary to achieve a "legitimate, important and integral" goal or have a "substantial legitimate justification."[293] The importance of the purpose of gang databases—to facilitate the investigation and prosecution of gang-related crime—may make this standard fairly easy to meet, especially since courts have shown a willingness to defer to law enforcement interests in other equal protection cases.[294]

Less discriminatory alternative. However, even if a defendant can show the institutional necessity of a particular practice, the plaintiff may still succeed in striking the practice down if he can demonstrate that there are alternative practices that would have a less discriminatory impact.[295] Some of the suggestions for alternatives to current police practices include eliminating criteria found to be inherently discriminatory or consistently administered in a discriminatory fashion, offering individuals included on the database notice and an opportunity to contest their inclusion, or requiring more indicia of criminal involvement before an individual can be included in the database.[296]

CONCLUSION

The foregoing discussion demonstrates that legal challenges to gang databases are by no means guaranteed to succeed. Nonetheless, both Title VI and procedural due process jurisprudence offer sound legal arguments rooted in precedent that could force fundamental alterations in the manner in which gang databases are developed and used. In addition, Fourth Amendment challenges can limit some of the most abusive police practices associated with gang databases. And while challenges based on the right of association and right to privacy will prove difficult, especially if law enforcement has not improperly disclosed individuals' alleged gang affiliation, these arguments are important to raise in the context of lawsuits against gang databases.

While the promise offered by litigation may be limited, the civil liberties threat posed by these databases is something that all citizens have reason to fear. The use of law enforcement to gather and store information about large numbers of individuals who are not necessarily involved in any illegal activity threatens the civil liberties of all members of society, especially those from the disenfranchised populations targeted by this practice. The use of gang databases is made all the more threatening by the fact that individuals wrongfully swept up by the gang label have no opportunity to find out their status, discover the implications of their inclusion, or challenge whether they are in fact gang members. If courts prove unwilling to apply traditional legal protections and strike down the most abusive practices associated with such intelligence gathering, the implications for our society—and in particular for young people of color—are truly ominous.

NOTES

The author would like to thank John Crew and Kelli Evans of the Northern California American Civil Liberties Union and Mark Silverstein of the Colorado American Civil Liberties Union for opening up their records and sharing their knowledge and perspective on this issue. Gratitude is also owed to Michele Landis for her help in editing this work, to Robert Garcia and Paul Hoffman for encouraging this paper as part of their class on civil rights and police reform, and to Pierre Barolette for his limitless patience, interest, ideas, and encouragement. Readers should be advised that this article was completed at the end of 1999 and that subsequent developments, legal and otherwise, have not necessarily been incorporated.

1. Vanessa Place, *Cutting Off Our Arms: The Anti-Gang Statutes and the First Amendment*, 20:1 CALIFORNIA ATTORNEYS FOR CRIMINAL JUSTICE FORUM 46 (1993), *quoted in* Letter from Sue Burrell, Staff Attorney, Youth Law Center, to Rep. Don Edwards, Chairman, U.S. House of Representatives Committee on the Judiciary, Subcommittee on Civil & Constitutional Rights 10 (July 27, 1993) (on file with author).

2. Nina Siegal, *Ganging Up on Civil Liberties*, THE PROGRESSIVE, Oct. 28, 1997, at 30 (quoting John Crew, staff attorney, ACLU of Northern California). For an article that warns that "[g]angs are infiltrating the workplace," using language that is reminiscent of some of the hysteria of the anti-communist period, see L.M. Sixel, *Gangs Using Jobs to Carry Out Crime*, HOUS. CHRON., June 27, 1997, at B1. The article lists jobs that are popular targets for gang infiltration and quotes experts who offer advice on how to identify gang members (including "keep[ing] your eyes open for mysterious hand signals" and instituting background and criminal records checks on new employees). The article warns that gang members may embezzle or steal company property, recruit other employees to join the gang, and catch innocent employees "in the cross-fire when gang members decide to shoot it out in the parking lot." It ends with the admonition: "And look for gaps in employment.... When an applicant says he was working on a pig farm or staying home to care for a sick parent, he might have been doing time at the big house." The article was reprinted in newspapers across the country, including the *San Francisco Chronicle*. See L.M. Sixel, *Gangs Aren't Just on the Street, They're at Work*, S.F. SUN. EXAM. & CHRON., July 6, 1997.

3. *See* Burrell, *supra* note 1, at 10 (citing Seth Mydans, *FBI Setting Sights on Street Gangs*, N.Y. TIMES, May 24, 1992, at I-16).

4. *See* Curry & Decker, *What's in a Name?: A Gang by Any Other Name Isn't Quite the Same*, 31 VAL. U. L. REV. 501, 501 (1997). *See also* G. David Curry, Richard A. Ball & Scott H. Decker, *Estimating the National Scope of Gang Crime from Law Enforcement Data*, *in* GANGS IN AMERICA 21, 31 (2d ed. 1996) (estimating that 500,000 gang members in 16,000 gangs commit almost 600,000 crimes per year). A 1997 study by the National Institute of Justice produced the much lower estimate of 4,800 gangs with 250,000 members in the United States. *See* BUREAU OF JUSTICE ASSISTANCE, URBAN STREET GANG ENFORCEMENT 4 (1997). A 1995 study by the Department of Justice Office of Juvenile Justice and Delinquency Prevention, in contrast, reported over 23,000 gangs including over 660,000 members nationally. However, the definition of "youth gang" employed in this survey was particularly loose. *See* SHAY, OFFICE OF JUVENILE JUSTICE AND DELINQUENCY PREVENTION, U.S. DEPARTMENT OF JUSTICE, 1995 NATIONAL YOUTH GANG SURVEY xi, 6 (1997). Estimates of gang-related crime vary depending on the definitions employed. *See, e.g.*, IRA REINER, OFFICE OF THE DISTRICT ATTORNEY, COUNTY OF LOS ANGELES, GANGS, CRIME AND VIOLENCE IN LOS ANGELES 95–97 (1992) (discussing differences between definitions employed by Los Angeles and other cities, and the effect of these differences on statistics). *See also* Carey Adams, *Security Tokens Help Police Efforts Against Gangs*, ACCESS CONTROL & SECURITY SYS. INTEGRATION, Oct. 30, 1999 (reporting 1997 National Gang Youth Survey estimate that 30,500 gangs with 816,000 members operate in 4,712 cities and counties in the United States).

5. *See* Gang Reporting, Evaluation & Tracking System (GREAT), *GREAT System Overview*, The Eighth Annual Organized Crime and Criminal Intelligence Training Conference, August 23–26, 1994, publication [*hereinafter* GREAT Conference]. GREAT warns: "Gangs now spread their violence and crime to diverse areas of the state, importing their special brand of terrorism to areas that have never known gang problems." *GREAT System: General Information for Becoming a User Agency*, GREAT Conference.

6. Statement of Steven R. Wiley, Chief, Violent Crimes and Major Offenders Section, Federal Bureau of Investigation, *Hearing on Gang Activity Before the Senate Committee on the Judiciary* (Apr. 23, 1997), at 7–9. This study reported that Illinois-based gang members were active in 135 jurisdictions and 35 states, and California-based gang members in 180 jurisdictions and 42 states. *See* Ray Dussault, *GangNet: A New Tool in the War on Gangs*, Calif. Computer News, Jan. 1997 (accessible at ⟨www.ccnmag.com /Jan1997/coverstory.html⟩).

7. Concern about involvement in drug sales and trafficking is also widespread, particularly with the influx of crack cocaine into many communities. *See* Wiley, *supra* note 6, at 3.

8. *See* Peter F. Episcopo & Darrin L. Moor, *The Violent Gang and Terrorist Organizations File*, FBI Law Enforcement Bulletin, Oct. 1996, at 21.

9. Since 1994, murder rates have fallen dramatically. *See President Clinton Announces 21st Century Policing Initiative*, Associated Press Political Service, Jan. 14, 1999 (reporting 20% decline in violent and property crimes and 30% decline in homicides between 1993 and 1998). According to FBI statistics, the number of homicides in the United States decreased from 23,438 in 1990 to 16,915 in 1998. Gang-related homicides went down from 1,362 in 1993 to 1,026 in 1997. *See* Donna Leinwand, *GNS Special Report: Murder in the '90s*, Gannett News Service, Nov. 15, 1999. Between the first six months of 1998 and the first six months of 1999, murder declined by 13%. Federal Bureau of Investigation National Press Office, Uniform Crime Reports 1999 Preliminary Report, Nov. 21, 1999, found at ⟨www.fbi.gov/pressrm/pressrel/ucr0699.htm⟩ (visited Nov. 23, 1999). For newspaper articles documenting that "America continues to be preoccupied with crime" despite such statistics, see Matthew Mickle Werdegar, *Enjoining the Constitution: The Use of Public Nuisance Abatement Injunctions Against Urban Street Gangs*, 51 Stan. L. Rev. 409, 410 & nn.3–5 (1999).

10. *See* Reiner, *supra* note 4, at 107. A Chicago study of gang violence estimated that, of 956 gang-related murders between 1987 and 1994, 11 percent of victims were members of the same gang, 75 percent members of rival gangs, and 14 percent non-gang members. *See* Wiley, *supra* note 6, at 6.

11. For examples of such measures, see Federal Gang Violence Act of 1997, introduced by Senator Feinstein, incorporated into Juvenile Crime Bill, S.10, 105th Cong. (1997); Susan Burrell, *Gang Evidence: Issues for Criminal Defense*, 30 Santa Clara L. Rev. 739, 742–46 (1990). *See also* Bureau of Justice Assistance, *supra* note 4, at 86 (describing selective enforcement of laws against gang members and raising constitutional concerns about this practice); Werdegar, *supra* note 9, at 414–16 (describing California's use of public nuisance doctrine to obtain injunctions against gang members). For examples of statutes which enhance sentences for gang-related crimes, see Cal. Penal Code §186.22(b)(1) (1999), Ariz. Rev. Stat. § 13-604(T) (1999); Fla. Stat. Ann. § 874.01 et seq. (1999); Ga. Code. Ann. § 16-15-4 (1999); Ill. Comp. Stat. Ch. 730 § 85/5-5-3 et seq. (1999); Ind. Code § 35-45-9-1 et seq. (1999); Kan. Stat. Ann. § 21-4704(k) (1997); Mo.

ANN. STAT. § 578.425 (1997); LA. REV. STAT. ANN. § 15:1403 (1999); MINN. STAT. ANN. § 609.229 (1999); NEV. REV. STAT. § 193.168 (1999); N.D. CENT. CODE § 12.01-06.2-02 (1999); S.D. CODIFIED LAWS § 22-10-15 (1999).

12. *But see* CALIFORNIA DEPARTMENT OF JUSTICE, DIVISION OF LAW ENFORCEMENT BUREAU OF INVESTIGATION, GANGS 2000: A CALL TO ACTION 43 (1993) (reporting that more cities use law enforcement techniques than social or community strategies).

13. *See* REINER, *supra* note 4, at 136.

14. Telephone interview with Don Mace, Attorney General Investigator in Charge, California Department of Justice (Mar. 30, 1998). Mace is the former Chairman of CGNAC or California Gang Node Advisory Committee.

15. REINER, *supra* note 4, at 136.

16. *See* Lorenza Muñoz, *Gang Listing Questioned by Rights Groups*, L.A. TIMES, Jul. 14, 1997, at A3 (citing a drop in Orange County gang-related homicides from 70 in 1995 to 42 in 1996).

17. GREAT, WHAT IS GREAT? (fact sheet) (undated).

18. Telephone interview with Don Mace, *supra* note 14. Before the transition to Cal-Gang, the system contained information on almost 250,000 suspected gang members or associates. *See* Siegal, *supra* note 2, at 30. These numbers have been reduced somewhat through elimination of duplicates and improperly entered records. Telephone interview with Don Mace, *supra* note 14.

The number of records presents some interesting issues. Although in 1994 GREAT estimated that there were 175,000 to 200,000 gang members in the entire state, and its database included records only from part of California, 160,000 names were entered into the system. WHAT IS GREAT?, *supra* note 17. These numbers suggest the presence of large numbers of non-gang members within the database. Moreover, as the database grows, it seems that estimates of the number of gang members in the state increase proportionately. In 1992, when the GREAT database included just over 100,000 records, the GAO estimated that it included one-third of the estimated 300,000 to 350,000 gang members in the country. Harold A. Valentine, Associate Director, Administration of Justice Issues, General Government Division, GAO, *Law Enforcement: Information on the Los Angeles County Sheriff's Department Gang Reporting, Evaluation, and Tracking System, Testimony before the Subcommittee on Civil and Constitutional Rights, Committee on the Judiciary, House of Representatives* (June 26, 1992). Yet the presence of over 200,000 alleged gang members in the current database would make this 350,000 nationwide figure a gross underestimate.

Law enforcement officers may view these increasing estimates as confirming that the gang problem is more serious than they previously realized, rather than alerting them that they might be including non-gang members in the database. *See, e.g.*, REINER, *supra* note 4, at 97 ("When all the data were pulled together, it turned out that there were a great many more gang members than previously suspected. . . . GREAT did not conjure into being another 80,000 gang members [in Los Angeles], it merely counted them."). For example, the Los Angeles District Attorney's report notes that the average age of gang members in the database is higher than the average age of gang membership, and on this basis concludes that younger gang members are underrepresented rather than that the database maintains too many files on older individuals who may have already left gangs. *See id.* at 116. The report employs a similarly flawed approach in analyzing racial statistics. *See* notes 119–120 and accompanying text *infra*. One other source of the confusion over numbers may be that higher numbers provide justification for increased funding. For example, in 1997 Oakland was chosen as one of fifteen jurisdictions that would receive Department of Justice anti-gang grants, after announcing a 300 percent increase in gang membership over a three-year period (and citing this increase in their grant application). Daniel C. Tsang, *Great No More: But a New Gang Database Is Ready to Take Its Place*, OC WEEKLY, Jul. 11–17, 1997, at 10.

19. Telephone interview with Don Mace, *supra* note 14. Police officers are not the only ones who use the database. Probation or parole officers can also enter and access data, and gang units of District Attorney's offices may access the data for investigative purposes. *Id.* San Bernardino County recently used its gang database to generate a list of names of individuals who would receive a hand-delivered flier warning them of enhanced penalties for commission of crimes using guns. Tina Dirmann, *County Issues a Stern Warning to Gang Members*, PRESS-ENTERPRISE, Mar. 4, 1998, at B1.

20. The Law Enforcement Communication Network (LECN) is a private non-profit organization. *See* GREAT, WHAT IS GREAT?, *supra* note 17. The role of this private entity in law enforcement has raised an additional set of concerns about scrutiny and oversight of the gang databases. *See* Letter from Alan Parachini, Director of Public Affairs, ACLU Foundation of Southern California, and John Crew, Director, Police Practices Project, ACLU of Northern California, to Erik S. Brown, U.S. Commission on Civil Rights, Office of the General Counsel 3 (Oct. 4, 1996) (on file with author).

21. *See* Valentine, *supra* note 18, at 3.

22. *See GREAT System Overview*, GREAT CONFERENCE, *supra* note 5.

23. *See* Patrick Thibodeau, *Cops Wield Database in War on Street Gangs*, COMPUTERWORLD, Sep. 1, 1997, at 4; Dussault, *supra* note 6. Mace commented, "This system makes it easier and cheaper than we ever imagined. It is all point-and-click and pull-down menus. I can go through an entire demonstration of the system and maybe type two keys. Almost as important is the cost savings it allows. I can put 80 end users on it for what it costs me to put up one under the GREAT system, and the entire implementation has only cost $800,000." *Id.*

24. Telephone interview with Mike Van Winkle, Information Officer, California Department of Justice (Mar. 25, 1998). These grants range from $100,000 to $300,000 and are used to purchase equipment and pay for training. *Id.*

25. *See* Memorandum from John M. Crew, ACLU-NC Police Practices Project, to Stella G. Youngblood, Civil Rights Analyst, California Advisory Commission to U.S. Commission on Civil Rights 3 (May 27, 1997) (on file with author).

26. *See GREAT System: General Information for Becoming a User Agency*, GREAT CONFERENCE, *supra* note 5; Valentine, *supra* note 18, at 6, 15.

27. Telephone interview with Don Mace, *supra* note 14; Orion Scientific Systems, *GangNet/CalGANG Presentation*, available for download at ⟨www.orionsci.com/productinfo/GangPresent.html⟩. The software that allows photographs to be scanned into the database can also be used to enter fingerprints, graffiti, tattoos, and other reports. *See id.*; BUREAU OF JUSTICE ASSISTANCE, *supra* note 4, at 44. Some police departments have not purchased scanners, and most have not updated all of their records to include photographs. Telephone interview with Don Mace, *supra* note 14.

28. Dussault, *supra* note 6.

29. *See* Thibodeau, *supra* note 23, at 4.

30. Telephone interview with Don Mace, *supra* note 14; Dussault, *supra* note 6. State and federal grants are available for local police departments that are seeking to upgrade their technological capacities, including for the purchase of laptop computers for patrol

cars. *See Police Tech Efforts a Boon to Mobile Data Industry*, NEWSBYTES NEWS NETWORK, Jun. 22, 1998. *See also* note 47 *infra* (discussing receipt of grants by local police departments for purchasing laptop computers).

31. California Department of Justice "CalGang," List of Winning Agencies and Entry Descriptions, First Annual Public Service Innovation Council, ⟨www.cisco.com/warp /public/779/gov/publicsector.html⟩ (visited Nov. 19, 1999). In 1994, an estimated 125 to 150 local police departments had access to GREAT. *See GREAT System: General Information for Becoming a User Agency*, GREAT CONFERENCE, *supra* note 5; BUREAU OF JUSTICE ASSISTANCE, *supra* note 4, at 29.

In addition to California police departments, police agencies in Nevada, California, Hawaii, Missouri, Massachusetts, Texas, and even Canada can access and possibly input data into the system. *See* Valentine, *supra* note 18, at 7; Letter from Parachini, *supra* note 20, at 3 (citing tax returns of Law Enforcement Communications Network); Memorandum of ACLU, Background of GREAT (Mar. 8, 1995) (on file with author).

Local agencies may operate their own systems in addition to, or instead of, utilizing the statewide gang database. A 1994 survey by the ACLU (conducted by sending California Public Records Act requests to local police departments) found that of the Northern California law enforcement agencies that responded, approximately fourteen were members of GREAT, twelve maintained their own computer database which included gang affiliation information, and seven had no database that tracked gang membership. Of the Southern California agencies, eighteen were GREAT members or users, three maintained their own databases, and five used no database. *See* Memorandum from the ACLU, Report on Individual Law Enforcement Agencies (Mar. 8, 1995) (on file with author).

32. The GREAT definition of "gang" is less stringent than the California Penal Code in two primary ways: it includes any group whose members have been involved in a pattern of criminal activity (while the Penal Code requires that this criminal activity be a primary purpose of the group), and it allows any form of criminal activity to qualify a group for gang status (as opposed to the Penal Code, which designates 23 specific, mostly violent crimes). *See* Letter from John M. Crew, ACLU of Northern California, to Loren W. Duchesne, Chief, Bureau of Investigations, Orange County District Attorney's Office 4–5 (June 11, 1997) (on file with author); CAL. PENAL CODE § 186.22 (1999). In 1994, California Supervising Deputy Attorney General Margaret Garnard Venturi suggested that these differences were problematic and recommended that GREAT utilize the Penal Code definition to ensure compliance with the law governing intelligence databases. *See* Letter from Margaret Garnard Venturi, Supervising Deputy Attorney General, Criminal Division, Office of the California Attorney General, to Chuck Jones, Special Agent in Charge, Department of Justice, Bureau of Investigation 3 (Apr. 20, 1994).

33. Telephone interview with Don Mace, *supra* note 14.

34. *See* Letter from John M. Crew, ACLU of Northern California, to U.S. Civil Rights Commission 2 (Aug. 14, 1997) (noting that CGNAC Chair had recently informed the ACLU that they had not yet established statewide criteria, which contradicted their testimony to the Civil Rights Commission); Memorandum from Crew to Youngblood, *supra* note 25, at 2–3 & n.5 (citing conversation between Allan Parachini, ACLU of Southern California, and Bob Hagler, Fresno County Sheriff's Department, May 20, 1997) (both on file with author). The response to the ACLU's 1994 Public Records Act request also revealed variation in the criteria utilized by local law enforcement agencies belonging to GREAT as late as November 1996. *See* Letter from Crew to Duchesne, *supra* note 32, at 2.

35. GREAT, Policies and Procedures of the GREAT System: Gang Qualification Membership Criteria [*hereinafter* Gang Qualification Membership Criteria], at 2–3. A 1992 GAO study found that 70 percent of the records in GREAT did not specify the criteria that led to the identification of the individual as a gang member; however, the new software requires a person entering data to indicate which criteria justify the entry. Valentine, *supra* note 18, at 13.

36. *See* Gang Qualification Membership Criteria, *supra* note 35, at 3. For a discussion of the controversy over compliance with purging requirements, see notes 99–100 and accompanying text *infra*.

37. *See Examples Database: Solutions for Cities*, Nation's Cities Weekly, Apr. 27, 1998, at 6; Chris Conley, *City "On Alert" for Retaliation in Gang Killing*, Commercial Appeal (Memphis, TN), Nov. 12, 1999, at A1; Heron Marquez Estrada, *Experts Say Drugs Are Next for Asian Gangs*, Star-Trib. (Minneapolis-St. Paul, MN), May 15, 1999, at 1B; Chris Fiscus, *Phoenix Aims to Break Gangs' Grip*, Ariz. Repub., May 23, 1998, at A1; Dale Hopper, *Gang Task Force Stresses Many Proposals under Way*, Richmond Times-Dispatch, Dec. 7, 1998; Michael Lui, *Suffolk: Success for Gang Task Force*, Newsday, Nov. 5, 1999, at A38; Noreen Marcus et al., *Report on Gangs Finds the Familiar; But Grand Juries Lack Power to Carry Out Recommendations*, Sun-Sentinel (Ft. Lauderdale, FL), Nov. 15, 1998, at 1B; Kevin Mayhood, *Prosecutor Eyes Team to Target Gang Bosses*, Columbus Dispatch, Nov. 23, 1998, at 1B; Karen McDonald, *Canton Police Take on Local Gang Crime*, Peoria J. Star, Sep. 11, 1999, at B1; Michele Munz, *County's Anti-Gang Effort Appears to Be Working Well*, St. Charles County Post, Feb. 15, 1999, at 1; Jane Prendergast, *Group Links Gangs with Bad Housing*, Cincinnati Enquirer, Feb. 21, 1999, at C1; Jonathan D. Rockoff, *Police Defend Antigang Efforts*, Providence J., Mar. 24, 1999, at B1; Michael Weiss, *Norcross Roadblock Targets DUI, Gangs*, Atlanta J.-Atlanta Const., Jul. 19, 1999, at 2. The Florida statewide database includes photographs and allows users to communicate with one another via electronic mail. *Computer Network Will Help Tip Police*, Sarasota Herald-Trib., Dec. 5, 1997, at 1B. Nonetheless, many of these databases are in the early development stage and include a very small number of records. As of November 1998, for example, only 250 names had been entered into the Minnesota database. *See* Heron Marquez Estrada, *Gang Force Marks One Year*, Star-Trib., Nov. 16, 1998, at 1B. This is probably attributable to the newness of the database, the relatively small number of gang members in the state, and the more restrictive criteria utilized for entry into the database. *See* Jim Adams, *Officers Share Names to Battle Gangs*, Star-Trib., Feb. 24, 1998, at 1B (discussing criteria and noting that two primary cities have an estimated 30 gangs with 6,000 members). In contrast, the Illinois statewide database includes more than 68,000 suspected gang members; a 1998 survey of 129 Illinois suburbs conducted by a Chicago publication revealed that 58 percent of the 120 localities that responded maintained databases of suspected gang members. *Towns Track Gang Suspects in Databases*, Chicago Sun-Times, Sep. 6, 1998, at 4.

38. *See Anticipating Gang Violence*, Herald Rock Hill (Rock Hill, SC), Jun. 15, 1999, at 9A; *Bill Aimed at Gang Loitering*, Albuquerque J., Aug. 10, 1997, at A1; *Four Hundred Thousand Dollar Grant Targets Gangs*, Morning Star (Wilmington, NC), Mar. 3, 1998, at 2B; Rick Badie, *Tavares Police Plan to Move in on Gangs*, Orlando Sentinel, Jul. 27, 1996, at 1; Stephen Beaven, *Modest Start Matches Regional Gang Unit's Goal*, Indianapolis Star, Nov. 26, 1998, at B1; Deanna Boyd, *Police to Demonstrate Gang Unit to Gov. Bush*, Fort Worth Star-Telegram, Oct. 3, 1996, at 1; Joseph B. Cahill, *Mod Squad: City Cops Go High-Tech*, Crain's Chicago Business, Oct. 28, 1996, at 48; *Computer Network Will Help*

Tip Police, SARASOTA HERALD-TRIBUNE, Dec. 5, 1997, at B1; Judge Kent Ellis, *The Juvenile Justice System: Past and Present*, 33 HOUSTON LAWYER 24, 32 (1995); *Gang Tracking Program Reduces NYC DOC Violence*, 2:10 CORRECTIONS PROFESSIONAL, Feb. 7, 1997; Alan Johnson, *Prison Awaits Criminal Gangs Under Proposed Law*, COLUMBUS DISPATCH, Oct. 18, 1996, at C5; David Kocieniewski, *Breaking Up Youth Gangs Seen as '97 Police Priority*, N.Y. TIMES, Jan. 3, 1997, at B3; Scott Marshall, *600 in County Have Ties to Gangs*, ATLANTA J. & CONSTITUTION, Aug. 25, 1996, at J1; Hon. Gordon A. Martin, J., *Open the Doors: A Judicial Call to End Confidentiality in Delinquency Proceedings*, 21 NEW ENG. J. ON CRIM. & CIV. CONFINEMENT 393, 408 (1995); Lou Michel, *Buffalo Police Mug Shots Getting High-Tech Transformation*, BUFFALO NEWS, Sept. 18, 1997, at B5; Karin Miller, *State Will Assist Tracking of Gangs*, CHATTANOOGA FREE PRESS, Mar. 23, 1997, at A6; Charles Ornstein, *Garland Turf War*, DALLAS MORNING NEWS, Oct. 25, 1996, at J1; Mary Lou Pickel, *Sheriff's Gang Squad Doubles in Size*, PALM BEACH POST, July 15, 1996, at B1; Sarah Ragland, *Police Develop Database to Keep Tabs on Gangs*, PORTLAND PRESS HERALD, May 4, 1997, at A14; Michael Rutledge & Sarah Sturmon, *Police Look to Expand Ideas, Not Gang Unit*, CINCINNATI POST, Nov. 5, 1996; Gretchen Schuldt, *Wisconsin Proposes Databank for Gangs*, ROCKY MOUNTAIN NEWS, March 23, 1997, at A34; *Tennessee DOC Attacking Gang Problem with New Database*, 1:10 MAKING CORRECTIONS TECHNOLOGY WORK FOR YOU, Sept. 1997. The South Carolina database will be linked with nine other states' information. *See* Jennifer Holland, *Database to Monitor Gang Crime*, AUGUSTA CHRON., Jun. 5, 1999, at B2. Northern Virginia is working on building a regional database. *See* Patricia Davis, *Gathering to Address N. Va. Gang Problem*, WASH. POST, Mar. 5, 1998, at D2; Brooke A. Masters, *At Gang Summit, A Call for Answers*, WASH. POST, Apr. 21, 1998, at B8.

In other states, proposals to build databases are moving forward. In 1999, the Attorney General of Colorado proposed establishment of a statewide database. Associated Press, *Gang Database a Good Idea, Salazar Says*, THE GAZETTE, Aug. 4, 1999, at 8. The Colorado Bureau of Investigation already compiles a more limited statewide database. *See* Ovetta Sampson, *Police Defend Gang Tracking*, THE GAZETTE, Jul. 28, 1999, at 1.

39. *See Time to Loosen the Red Squad Cuffs?*, CHI. TRIB., Mar. 18, 1997, at 12; Jacquelyn Heard, *Daley Wants Fewer Limits on Police*, CHI. TRIB., Mar. 7, 1997, at 1; John Kass & Desiree Chen, *Suburbs Seek City Gang Files*, CHI. TRIB., Sept. 20, 1996, at 1; Richard Chapman, *Say Chicago Can't Share Gang Info*, CHIC. SUN-TIMES, Sept. 20, 1996, at 3. On September 30, 1999, the United States District Court for the Northern District of Illinois refused the city of Chicago's request that it overturn the consent decree to allow maintenance of files on gangs. Alliance to End Repression v. City of Chicago, 66 F.Supp.2d 899 (N.D. Ill. 1999); David Mendell, *U.S. Judge Upholds Restrictions on Police Spying*, CHI. TRIB., Oct. 2, 1999, at 5. However, Chicago police are still able to track suspected gang members with arrest records. *See Alliance to End Repression*, 66 F.Supp.2d at 911–13 (noting that decree did not prohibit investigation of gangs); *Towns Track Gang Suspects in Databases*, *supra* note 37 (reporting Illinois state police estimate that Chicago tracks 38,000 suspected gang members with arrest records).

40. *See* Letter from Parachini, *supra* note 20, at 3–4. In 1997, pilot programs funded by the National Gang Tracking Network that utilized gang databases were under way in New York, Connecticut, Rhode Island, Massachusetts, and Vermont. *See* Thibodeau, *supra* note 23, at 4.

41. FBI Website (visited March 24, 1998), ⟨http://www.fbi.gov/2000/ncicnv.htm⟩. The FBI system has been reported to be modeled after the GREAT system, Valentine, *supra* note 18, at i, and the FBI's Wanted Persons File, Wiley, *supra* note 6, at 14.

42. Telephone interview with Darrin Moor, FBI Training Instructor (Mar. 20, 1998). Moor stated that the FBI employed no set criteria for identifying gang members. *See id.*

43. *See* Letter from Edward M. Chen, Alan L. Schlosser & Mark Silverstein, ACLU, to Representative Don Edwards, Chair, Committee on the Judiciary, Subcommittee on Civil & Constitutional Rights, U.S. House of Representatives 15–16 (Aug. 6, 1993) [*hereinafter* Letter from Chen to Edwards] (on file with author).

44. Telephone interview with Darrin Moor, *supra* note 42. This does represent a large increase from figures reported in an October 1996 FBI publication: 445 groups and 180 individuals. *See* Episcopo & Moor, *supra* note 8, at 23. The FBI has encouraged state agencies to enter their data. Telephone interview with Darrin Moor, *supra* note 42. However, the state of California had declined to share its computerized criminal records with the FBI. Accordingly, the largest gang database in the country was missing from the national database. *See* Kenneth Howe, *State Lags in Giving Crime Data to FBI*, S.F. Chron., Jul. 26, 1999, at A1.

Although the FBI manages the database, state agencies are expected to comply with FBI manuals and control their own data entry. *See id.* FBI materials warn that "an agency that pronounces an individual guilty by mere association with a gang or terrorist group without concrete proof opens itself up to litigation," and reports that all records will be reviewed by auditors for accuracy and supporting documentation. *Id.* at 22. Furthermore, according to testimony by Charles W. Archer, Assistant Director of the Criminal Justice Information Services Division of the FBI, "[a]ll criminal justice agencies having access to NCIC have adopted security measures to prevent unauthorized access to the system's data and/or unauthorized use of data obtained from the system." Charles W. Archer, *Youth Violence*, before the Subcommittee on Youth Violence, Committee on the Judiciary, United States Senate (Mar. 9, 1998). More than 87,168 users have access to this database. *See id.*

45. Telephone interview with Darrin Moor, *supra* note 42. These agencies include police departments, courts, prisons, and probation officers. *See id.*

46. *See* FBI Website (visited March 24, 1998), ⟨http://www.fbi.gov/2000/ncicnv. htm⟩; Melanie Lefkowitz, *Cruiser Computers Access FBI Files Fast*, Providence J., Sep. 12, 1999, at C1.

47. *See* Bureau of Justice Assistance, *supra* note 4, at 43; Bilchik, *supra* note 4, at 3 n.6. *See also* Holland, *supra* note 38, at B2 (reporting $315,000 grant from Department of Justice to assist South Carolina in starting a gang database); Matt Kelly, *Community Policing Funds Sought*, Omaha World-Herald, Feb. 4, 1998, at 1 (reporting that $1.2 million grant in 1995 was used in part to purchase laptop computers for police cars and that other grant was used to compile database on Omaha gangs); Dan Klepal, *City Police Allocating Federal Grant*, Cincinnati Enquirer, May 22, 1999, at B1 (reporting $100,000 federal grant for database to monitor juveniles involved in violent crime and gangs); Amanda Vogt, *Cops to Use Grant to Purchase New Computers for Squad Cars*, Chi. Trib., Dec. 24, 1998, at 3 (reporting local police department's receipt of $28,000 federal grant to purchase laptop computers for squad cars, which would allow access to gang and other databases). In 1999, the Bureau of Justice Assistance awarded $8.2 million to forty-eight states "to develop or improve their computerized identification system and integrate those systems with the Federal Bureau of Investigation's national identification database." U.S. Department of Justice, 48 States Receive $8 Million to Improve Computerized Identification Systems, Oct. 16, 1999, found at ⟨www.prnewswire.com/c/s.dll/micro_s . . . /story/10-16-97/338936&EDATE =Oct+16,+1997 (visited on Nov. 23, 1999).

48. This discussion relies in large part upon the criticisms of gang databases raised by the ACLU, the primary organization that has challenged the use of gang databases. When relevant, the basis for the ACLU's statistics or information is identified. Where the ACLU is the source of a particular argument or concern, an attribution to the relevant document or materials is included.

49. The information collected about each individual is in fact very extensive; the Department of Justice lists the following data elements as commonly included in gang databases: gang name and moniker, residence address and other locations frequented, phone and pager number, social security number, race and ethnicity, physical description, photograph, identifying marks, place and date of birth, membership status, history of violent behavior, school background, associates (along with their addresses and phone numbers), criminal history, fingerprints, and family data (involvement of family members in gangs). *See* BUREAU OF JUSTICE ASSISTANCE, *supra* note 4, at 36; *GangNet/CalGANG Presentation, supra* note 27.

50. The United States Constitution bars subjecting an individual to criminal liability for gang involvement, unless it can be shown both that the gang had unlawful aims and that the individual specifically intended to further those aims: "[t]he government has the burden of establishing a knowing affiliation with an organization possessing unlawful aims and goals, and a specific intent to further those illegal aims." Healy v. James, 408 U.S. 169, 186 (1972). *See also* NAACP v. Claiborne Hardware Co, 458 U.S. 886, 920 (1982) ("Civil liability may not be imposed merely because an individual belonged to a group, some members of which committed acts of violence."); People v. Rodriguez, 21 Cal.App.4th 232, 239 (Cal. Ct. App. 1993) ("Mere membership in a street gang is not a crime."). In compliance with constitutional mandates, the California Street Terrorism Enforcement and Prevention Act (STEPA) subjects to criminal penalties only an individual "who actively participates in any criminal street gang with knowledge that its members engage in or have engaged in a pattern of criminal gang activity, and who willfully promotes, furthers, or assists in any felonious criminal conduct by members of that gang. . . . " CAL. PENAL CODE § 186.22(a) (1999). The Act also enhances the sentence of individuals who are "convicted of a felony which is committed for the benefit of, at the direction of, or in association with any criminal street gang, with the specific intent to promote, further, or assist in any criminal conduct by gang members," establishes a nuisance provision targeting buildings or places used by gang members for criminal activities and penalizes coercing gang participation. CAL. PENAL CODE §§ 186.22(b), 186.22a(a) (1999). In *Green*, the court pointed out that, "for a person to be criminally liable under section 186.22, he or she would also have to be criminally liable as an aider and abettor to any specific crime committed by a member or members of a criminal street gang." People v. Green, 227 Cal.App.3d 692, 699, 701–02, 704 (Cal. Ct. App. 1991).

Criminalizing the status of gang membership might also violate the First Amendment on vagueness or overbreadth grounds. *See* Lanzetta v. New Jersey, 306 U.S. 451, 458 (1939) (overturning on vagueness grounds a statute that criminalized being a "gangster," which was defined as having previous criminal convictions and belonging to a gang). For cases rejecting overbreadth or vagueness challenges to anti-gang state and local legislation, see State v. Baldenegro, 932 P.2d 275, 280 (Ariz. Ct. App. 1996); State v. McCoy, 928 P.2d 647, 649–50 (Ariz. Ct. App. 1996); Klein v. State, 698 N.E.2d 296, 299–300 (Ind. 1998); Jackson v. State, 634 N.E.2d 532, 535–37 (Ind. Ct. App. 1994); Helton v. State, 624 N.E.2d 499, 505–11 (Ind. Ct. App. 1993); State v. Walker, 506 N.W.2d 430, 432–33 (Iowa 1993). For two decisions striking down such ordinances, see City of Harvard v. Gaut, 660

N.E.2d 259, 262–64 (Ill. Ct. App. 1996); City of Chicago v. Morales, 687 N.E.2d 53, 60–65 (Ill. 1997), aff'd, 527 U.S. 41 (1999).

51. Moore, *Residence and Territory in Chicano Gangs*, 31 Soc. Probs. 182, 186 (1983) (quoted in Susan L. Burrell, *supra* note 11, at 748–49 (1990)). *See also* Deborah Prothrow-Smith, M.D. with Michaele Weissman, Deadly Consequences 97 (1991) (noting that principal gang activities are social in nature).

52. *See* Valentine, *supra* note 18, at 16. In Orange County, almost half of the individuals in the GREAT database had never been arrested or charged with *any* crime. *See* Siegal, *supra* note 2, at 31. These numbers may be higher than in other states and localities. Just 10 percent of those included in the Cook County, Illinois, database, for example, have never been arrested. *See Towns Track Gang Suspects in Databases, supra* note 37.

53. *See* Tsang, *supra* note 18, at 10 (citing Minutes, California GREAT Node Advisory Committee, Nov. 5, 1992) (discussing problems with employing a definition of associate that did not require suspicion of any involvement in criminal activity); Letter from Venturi to Jones, *supra* note 32, at 3.

54. *See* Letter from Venturi to Jones, *supra* note 32, at 2, 5. Venturi suggested that ACLU v. Deukmejian, 651 P.2d 822, 32 Cal.3d 440, 444 n.2, 450, 453 (Cal. 1982), raised questions about the legitimacy of collecting information on associates of criminals who were not themselves involved in any criminal activity. *See also* Tsang, *supra* note 18, at 10.

55. *See* Letter from Parachini, *supra* note 20, at 4. Nonetheless, Venturi later stated that the imposition of statewide database standards had solved this problem. *See* Tsang, *supra* note 18, at 10. In Colorado Springs, Colorado, police are authorized to enter "confirmed" gang members if they have met two of the four criteria for gang membership, and "affiliated" gang members if they have met one of the four. *See* Sampson, *supra* note 38, at 1.

56. For example, a lawsuit filed in the United States District Court in Portland, Oregon, challenged police designation of a group of artistic young men (who called themselves "Art Fiendz") as a gang and the resultant classification of the group's members as gang members. *See* Complaint, Ysasaga v. City of Portland, No. 93-1175 at 3. The Portland Police Department at this time employed a definition of "criminal gang" that stated that the group's "primary purpose" had to be "the commission of violent, street or drug-related crimes." Richard D. Walker, Bureau of Police, Portland, Oregon, General Order (subject: Gang Affiliation Designation) 1 (Mar. 25, 1990). The *Los Angeles Times* recently included a lengthy article discussing the designation of a group of young white men who called themselves "the Slick 50's" as a gang, and noting that many in the community disputed this label despite the group's history of violence. Bonnie Harris, *A Wake-Up Call for a Suburban Refuge*, L.A. Times, Apr. 18, 1999, at A1.

57. *See, e.g.*, Burrell, *supra* note 11, 748–49 (discussing divergence in definitions of gangs); Suzin Kim, *Gangs and Law Enforcement: The Necessity of Limiting the Use of Gang Profiles*, 5 B.U. Pub. Int. L.J. 265, 266–68 (1996) (same). For a study of how gang members themselves define a gang, *see* generally G. David Curry & Scott H. Decker, *supra* note 4.

58. Cal. Penal Code § 186.22(f) (1994). The enumerated crimes include assault with a deadly weapon, robbery, homicide or manslaughter, illegal drug sales, shooting at an inhabited dwelling or occupied motor vehicle, intimidation of witnesses or victims, and grand theft auto. Cal. Penal Code § 186.22(e)(1)–(8) (1999). For cases in which courts

have found insufficient evidence of a pattern of criminal activity, and therefore overturned gang enhancements, *see In re* Lincoln J., 223 Cal.App.3d 322, 331 (Cal. Ct. App.
1990); *In re* Leland D, 223 Cal.App.3d 251, 258–60 (Cal. Ct. App. 1990). For a decision
discussing the "primary activity" requirement, see In re Nathaniel C., 228 Cal.App.3d
990, 1004 (Cal. Ct. App. 1991). Other state laws providing for increased penalties for gang
members have required active participation in a gang and knowledge of or specific intent
to further the gang's criminal behavior. *See* ARIZ. REV. STAT. ANN. §§ 13-604 & 13-2308
(1999); GA. CODE ANN. §§ 16-15-4 (1999); ILL. COMP. STAT. Ch. 740 § 147/10 (1999); IND.
CODE ANN. § 35-45-9-3 (1999); IOWA CODE ANN. § 723A (1999); KAN. STAT. ANN. § 21-
4704 (1999); LA. REV. STAT. ANN. §§ 15:1403 (1999); MINN. STAT. ANN. § 609.229 (1999);
MISS. CODE ANN. § 97-44-3 (1999); MO. ANN. STAT. §§ 578.425 (1999); NEV. REV. STAT.
§ 193.168 (1999); N.D. CRIM. CODE § 12.1-06.2-02 (1999); S.D. CODIFIED LAWS §§ 22-10-
14 (1999). *But cf.* FLA. STAT. ANN. § 874.01 et seq.

59. *See* Letter from Crew to Civil Rights Commission, *supra* note 34, at 6–7 (citing
CGNAC Operational Guidelines § 1.11.1, which require only that members have individually or together "engaged in a pattern of criminal activity creating an atmosphere of
fear and intimidation within the community").

60. *See* Burrell, *supra* note 11, at 750; MARTIN SANCHEZ JANKOWSKI, ISLANDS IN THE
STREET 37–47 (1991).

61. *See* Kim, *supra* note 37, at 268–69. *See also* People v. Godinez, 2 Cal.App.4th 492,
497–98 (Cal. Ct. App. 1992) (describing individuals who are "peripheral members who
only associate with the gang for its social aspects.").

62. The state of Florida established eight criteria and allowed entry of a record if an
individual met two or more criteria. Associated Press, *Database Helps Police Track State's
Gangs*, FLA. TODAY, Dec. 1, 1997, at 6B; FLA. STAT. ANN. § 874.03(2) (1999). These criteria
include admission of gang membership; identification as a gang member by a parent or
guardian; identification by a reliable informant or an untested informant if the identification is corroborated by independent information; residence in or frequenting of a gang's
area, association with known gang members, and adoption of gang dress, signification or
tattoos; more than one arrest with gang members for offenses consistent with gang activity; more than three detentions with gang members; or identification by physical evidence such as photographs. Sarah Huntley, *Technology to Combat Gang Crime*, TAMPA
TRIB., Nov. 30, 1997, at 1; FLA. STAT. ANN. § 874.03(2) (1999). The Minnesota Gang Strike
Force requires three of the following criteria to be met before an individual can be entered into a statewide database: admission of membership; having been observed to regularly associate with gang members; gang tattoos; wearing of gang symbols; presence in
a photograph with gang members or using gang signification; presence of name on gang
document, hit list or graffiti; identification by a reliable source; having been arrested with
gang members or associates; correspondence with gang members or correspondence about
gang activities; writing about gangs on books, paper, and walls (graffiti). *See* Estrada, *supra*
note 37, at 1B. *See also* S.D. CODIFIED LAWS § 22-10-14 (1999) (listing seven criteria and
defining "street gang member" as any individual "who engages in a pattern of street gang
activity and who meets two or more of the following criteria").

63. One proponent of allowing police to stop all suspected gang members without
Fourth Amendment constraints disputes the difficulty of such identification:

> How is a criminal street gang member distinguishable from an innocent passerby? Easy.
> Members of a criminal street gang ... go out of their way to identify themselves. Visual
> presence is very much a part of the gang ambiance. Gang colors, jackets, or other distinct

articles of clothing, hair styles, and distinctive manners all provide objective positive evidence marking members of criminal street gangs. Moreover, members of criminal street gangs make no secret of the territorial haunts they purport to rule. . . . Of course, there may be social, political and emotional reasons to ape gang dress styles, without any intention to ape gang behavior. While a nervous citizen may be overly alarmed at the sight of any person not in professional dress, a streetwise cop, whose job it is to keep the peace, and who is specially trained in gang activity, would know the badge of criminal street gang membership.

Christo Lassiter, *The Stop and Frisk of Criminal Street Gang Members*, 14 NAT'L BLACK L.J. 1, 35–36 (1995) (citations omitted). Lassiter does not explain how a police officer can distinguish real gang attire from attempts to imitate gang style.

64. Telephone interview with Don Mace, *supra* note 14.

65. Bill Lockyer, *Letters to the Editor: Lockyer Responds*, S.F. CHRON., Aug. 5, 1999.

66. *Id.*

67. People ex rel. Gallo v. Acuna, 929 P.2d 596, 14 Cal.4th 1090, 1130 (Cal. 1997) (Chin, J., concurring and dissenting). Justice Chin concluded that the evidence against two defendants was insufficient to justify their inclusion in the anti-gang injunction; the only evidence against one was that she claimed gang membership and was in the gang's neighborhood wearing a black top and black jeans (which was consistent with gang attire), and the evidence against the other was his claim of gang involvement and some evidence that he had committed a crime in the gang's neighborhood. *Id.* at 1132. *See also id.* at 1133 n.1 & 1147 (Mosk, J., dissenting) (listing broad criteria used to identify gang members and noting paucity of evidence that three defendants were gang members).

68. This criterion is widely used as a basis for entry in gang databases. According to Orange County GREAT coordinator Loren Duchesne, 80 percent of those included in the Orange County database have admitted gang membership. *See* Muñoz, *supra* note 16, at A3.

69. *See Gallo*, 14 Cal.4th at 1130 (Chin, J., concurring and dissenting) ("As the declaration of Juan Pineda Hernandez indicates, people who are not gang members may assert membership for a variety of reasons, including youthful arrogance or a desire to be placed in protective custody."); *see also* Brief of Respondent Jose Saldana, The People of the State of California, *ex rel.* Richard D. Jones v. Carlos Antonio Amaya, et al., No. G015052 at 22 n.35 (Superior Court No. 713223); Burrell, *supra* note 1, at 4–5; Letter from Chen to Edwards, *supra* note 43, at 17 (citing testimony of Daniel M. Hartnett, Associate Director, Law Enforcement, Bureau of Alcohol, Tobacco and Firearms, at *Bureau of Alcohol, Tobacco and Firearms' Proposal for a Gang Information Network: Hearing Before the Subcommittee on Civil and Constitutional Rights*, 102d Cong., 2d Sess. at 50–51).

70. *See* Burrell, *supra* note 1, at 4–5; REINER, *supra* note 4, at 125. The possibility of police officer falsification is particularly troubling since individuals will never necessarily learn that a police officer has claimed that they admitted gang membership and will therefore have no opportunity to contest this statement. *See* Letter from Chen to Edwards, *supra* note 43, at 18.

71. Burrell, *supra* note 1, at 5 (quoting IRVING SPERGEL ET AL. YOUTH GANGS: PROBLEM AND RESPONSE, NATIONAL YOUTH GANG SUPPRESSION AND INTERVENTION PROGRAM, SCHOOL OF SOCIAL SERVICE ADMINISTRATION, UNIVERSITY OF CHICAGO 7) (Draft 10/91).

72. *See* Letter from Chen to Edwards, *supra* note 43, at 19.

73. *See* Burrell, *supra* note 1, at 5–6. For example, a staff paper discussing the proposed FBI database recommended requiring only corroboration of important facts pro-

vided by informant, not corroboration of gang membership. *See* Letter from Chen to Edwards, *supra* note 43, at 16 n.7.

74. *See* Kim, *supra* note 37, at 272.

75. *See* Letter from Chen to Edwards, *supra* note 43, at 20.

76. *See id*; Burrell, *supra* note 1, at 6.

77. *See* Letter from Chen to Edwards, *supra* note 43, at 20.

78. *See* Burrell, *supra* note 1, at 6. The author has not come across any reports or complaints by white teenagers who dress in gang fashion that they have been detained by police in order to enter their information into a gang database.

79. REINER, *supra* note 4, at 124–25.

80. For example, consider two comments of young black people in Los Angeles. George Bogard, an inactive gang member, asks, "What constitutes a gang member? By their criteria, you might as well consider every black man that wears a Raiders [cap] and Nikes." Teenager Nikki Jackson states, "Unless you are wearing a rayon suit, police think you are a gang member." Andrea Ford & Stephanie Chavez, *Gang Report Scorned as Unjust Stereotyping*, L.A. TIMES, May 22, 1992, at 35.

81. Doreen Carvajal, *Police Photo Policies Focus of Controversy Law Enforcement*, L.A. TIMES, May 22, 1994, at A1.

82. *See* Laurie Goering & Flynn McRoberts, *Gang Colors, Fashion Paint Good Kids as Bad*, CHI. TRIB., April 13, 1992, at C1. A police officer in Gwinnett County, Georgia, noted that "associate members" are more likely than "serious members" to dress in gang wear, use gang signals, and otherwise publicly display their gang membership, because the serious members "have more to lose if detected." *See* Michael Weiss, *Keeping Tabs on Gang Action*, ATLANTA J.-ATLANTA CONST., Jul. 19, 1998 at 1 (reporting comments by Officer Randy Holloway).

83. *See* Letter from Chen to Edwards, *supra* note 43, at 20; Burrell, *supra* note 1, at 7. Burrell points out that removal can cost $4,000 per tattoo for laser treatments. Some who seek to avoid such costs use "cut-and-sew" methods performed by clinics or friends, which often cause injury or fail to work. *See id.* at 7. *See also* In Interest of M.P., 697 N.E.2d 1153, 1158–61 (Ill. Ct. App. 1998) (overturning juvenile court judge's order of removal of gang-related tattoos and reviewing cases in which courts have discussed difficulty, pain, and expense of tattoo removal).

84. *See* People v. Maestas, 20 Cal.App.4th 1482, 1494–95 (Cal. Ct. App. 1993).

85. *See* Burrell, *supra* note 1, at 8.

86. *See id.* at 7 (citing SPERGEL, ET AL., *supra* note 71, at 12). *See also* REINER, *supra* note 4, at 57–58 ("Crimes committed by gang members are rarely gang activities. . . . The individuals (or groups, which may include non-gang members as well as homeboys) who commit such crimes do so for their own reasons and by their own rules.").

87. *See* Letter from Chen to Edwards, *supra* note 43, at 20–21.

88. *See* Letter from Crew to Civil Rights Commission, *supra* note 34, at 6. A 1993 ACLU letter stated its concern that Burbank and Westminster, for example, were using less restrictive criteria in identifying gang members. Such criteria allowed identification of a gang member if just *one* of the following criteria was satisfied: self-admission; tattoos indicating gang membership; clothing indicating gang membership; the statement of a reliable informer within the gang; or association with other gang members along with commission of gang-related crimes. *See* Letter from Chen to Edwards, *supra* note 43, at 8–9, 22 (citing declaration by Burbank officer). This problem may particularly arise when local law enforcement agencies join the GREAT/CalGang database and enter all of

the records that they have previously compiled without adherence to applicable guidelines. *See* REINER, *supra* note 4, at 137.

89. *See* Tsang, *supra* note 18, at 10 (citing 1994 Bureau of Investigation audit, memo).

90. Letter from Crew to Duchesne, *supra* note 32, at 3.

91. *See* Burrell, *supra* note 1, at 8 (citing REINER, *supra* note 4, at xxxvii).

92. *See* Letter from Chen to Edwards, *supra* note 43, at 23.

93. *See* Memorandum from Crew to Youngblood, *supra* note 25, at 8 (describing claim by city of Oakland that gang membership rose 300 percent over three years, and resultant selection of Oakland as one of fifteen jurisdictions to receive over $11 million in anti-gang funds).

94. Telephone interview with Don Mace, *supra* note 14.

95. Muñoz, *supra* note 16, at A3.

96. Telephone interview with Don Mace, *supra* note 14.

97. A 1992 GAO study of 181 records on three gangs in the GREAT database found that the average record had been created three years before and had not been modified in the past 27 months; 72 percent of the records had not been modified within the past year, and two-thirds had never been queried. The Los Angeles Sheriff's Department explained such figures by stating that the three gangs focused on by the GAO empirical study were relatively inactive. *See* Valentine, *supra* note 18, at 14–15, 18. For a story that discusses "how difficult it can be to leave one's past behind" when that past includes documented gang membership, see Armando Villafranca, *Haunted by the Life*, HOUSTON CHRON., May 30, 1999, at 1. The Villafranca article recounts the story of an individual who left his gang but continued to be targeted by the police because of the continued involvement of family members and the presence of his record in a gang database.

98. For example, a mid-1992 report claimed that the Los Angeles GREAT records had never been purged. *See* Burrell, *supra* note 1, at 8 (citing Andrea Ford, *Number of L.A. Gang Members May Have Been Overestimated*, WASH. POST, May 20, 1997, at A-2); Andrea Ford, *Doubts Cast on Data in Gang Report*, L.A. TIMES, May 29, 1992, at A1).

99. Telephone interview with Don Mace, *supra* note 14.

100. In 1999, newspapers reported that the purging of gang records, which in 1997 had resulted in the deletion of 6,657 entries in Orange County alone, had been suspended in 1998 due to programming problems. *Orange County Perspective: Progress on Gang Front*, L.A. TIMES, Jul. 18, 1999, at B6; Daniel C. Tsang, *The Computer Wore Colors*, OC WEEKLY, Jul. 16–22, 1999. In addition to the technological problems encountered, some delay in implementing purge requirements may have resulted from resistance to such purging. For example, one internal GREAT memorandum suggested maintaining purged records on floppy disks for possible future use. *See* Tsang, *supra* note 18, at 10 (citing Memorandum by Lon Erickson, Purge Criteria (Jul. 17, 1994)).

101. REINER, *supra* note 4, at 111 & n.259 (also noting a conflict between the Los Angeles Police Department and Los Angeles Sheriff's Office over how long to maintain inactive records before purging them).

102. The ACLU points out that even a change in address may trigger a new five-year period. *See* Letter from Chen to Edwards, *supra* note 43, at 21.

103. *See* Letter from John M. Crew, Police Practices Project, ACLU of Northern California, to California Advisory Committee, U.S. Commission on Civil Rights, July 3, 1997, at 3 (on file with author).

104. *See* Muñoz, *supra* note 16, at A3. Moreover, federal law requiring that individuals be afforded access to and the opportunity to amend their own files specifically exempts the FBI. *See* Burrell, *supra* note 1, at 2 (citing James W. Diehm, *Federal Expungement: A Concept in Need of a Definition*, 66 St. JOHNS L. REV. 73 (1992)). In Texas, while an individual has the right to appeal his or her erroneous inclusion in the gang database, parents have no right to discover whether their child's name is included in the database. See Polly Ross Hughes, *76th Texas Legislature*, HOUSTON CHRON., Jun. 4, 1999, at 1.

105. In a recent column in the *Los Angeles Times*, Agustin Gurza reported that, when his Latino son was recently detained by the police while skateboarding in a local park, the police completed a field interview card and entered the information about his son into a law enforcement database, while ignoring his son's two white friends. Gurza later discovered that his son's name had been mistakenly linked with two other Latino youth who had been stopped later in the day by the police; although the police "promised to 'bifurcate' the names, [they] refused to delete [his] son from the computer unless [he] sued them." *See* Agustin Gurza, *Discovering a Crackdown of a Different Color*, L.A. TIMES, Jun. 29, 1999, at B1.

106. Telephone interview with Don Mace, *supra* note 14; Telephone Interview with Sergeant Wes McBride, Vice Chair of CGNAC (Mar. 26, 1998).

107. Rev. Oscar Tillman, senior official of the Denver NAACP, *quoted in* Dirk Johnson, *2 Out of 3 Young Black Men in Denver Are on Gang Suspect List*, N.Y. TIMES, Dec. 11, 1993, at A8.

108. Jin S. Choi & Ernest Kim, *The Constitutional Status of Photo Stops: The Implications of Terry and Its Progeny*, 2 ASIAN PAC. AM. L.J. 60, 81 (1994). Choi and Kim go on to argue that police will not detain white teenagers dressed like gang members but will stop and photograph youth of color who are so attired.

109. The ACLU continues: "when officials see four young black men wearing similar attire they see a 'gang.' When they see four white men similarly attired, they see a fraternity or innocuous group of friends." Letter from Chen to Edwards, *supra* note 43, at 26.

110. For example, the files of the ACLU of Northern California document complaints from minority youth in Petaluma, Fresno, Fountain Valley, and King City, California. *See also* Russ Loar, *Officials to Study Police Photo Practices*, L.A. TIMES, Mar. 1, 1996 (reporting complaints by Asian American students at U.C. Irvine that they were stopped and photographed as gang members by police officers from Irvine and Newport Beach); De Tran & Iris Yokoi, *O.C. Asians Say Police Photos Are Harassment*, L.A. TIMES, Nov. 15, 1992, at 1 (quoting parent JoAnn Kanshige, "They're trying to say Asian is synonymous to gang. These kids are dressed as well as the hakujin [white] kids, yet the Asian kids seem to be pulled over more often."); Armando Villafranca, *Haunted By the Life*, HOUSTON CHRON., May 30, 1999, at B1 (reporting charges by Charles Rotramel, director of the Youth Advocates gang intervention program in Houston, Texas, that police "harass young Hispanics, including many not in gangs ... [and] log their names in the database"). In a recent column in the *Los Angeles Times*, a Latino father shared his anger over such police practices, reporting that when the police detained his son along with two white friends at a local park only his son's information was taken and entered into a law enforcement database. See Gurza, *supra* note 105, at B1.

111. *See* Muñoz, *supra* note 16, at A3; Siegal, *supra* note 2, at 30.

112. *See* Loretta Muñoz, *Gang Database Raises Civil Rights Concerns*, L.A. TIMES, July 14, 1997, at B1; Tony Saavedra, *Civil Rights Official Calls for Investigation of O.C. Police Practices*, ORANGE CTY. REGISTER, Apr. 8, 1999, at A12.

113. *See* REINER, *supra* note 4, at 119. The racial breakdown of the records included in the 1991 GREAT database was 57 percent Latino, 37 percent Black, 4 percent Asian, and almost 2 percent white, "stoner," and other. *Id.* at 110. The Los Angeles District Attorney's report concludes that these numbers underestimate the numbers of Asian gang members and Latino gang members; no such underreporting of white gang members is contemplated. *See id.* 44 percent of black men included in the database had *never been arrested. See* ACLU, Memorandum, The Federal Gang Violence Act of 1997: Constitutional Analysis, 9 (Feb. 18, 1997) (on file with author). The Los Angeles County District Attorney's report on gangs acknowledged the likelihood of over-inclusiveness in assigning young black men the label of gang membership: "a careful, professional examination is needed to determine whether police procedure may be systematically over-identifying black youths as gang members." REINER, *supra* note 4, at 126.

114. This was despite the fact that blacks are only 5 percent of Denver's population (but 47 percent of the gang database) and Hispanics only 12 percent (but 33 percent of the database). *See* Johnson, *supra* note 107, at A8. In response to the outcry following release of these numbers, the Denver police department purged individuals who had not had police contact within the past two years, over half of the names from its gang list; the list remained over 80 percent black and Hispanic. *See* Christopher Lopez, *City Lops 3,747 off Gang List,* DENVER POST, Jan. 20, 1994, at 1, 15. Similar statistics are not available for most other counties. However, in response to a public records request, the ACLU received racial breakdowns of the gang lists maintained by some police departments: El Dorado (19% Hispanic, 64% white, 7% black, 10% other), Modesto (37% Hispanic, 19% black, 14% Asian, 3% other, and 27% white), Hayward (17% Asian or Pacific Islander, 19% black, 55% Hispanic, 18% white, and 1% unknown), San Jose (9% black, 16.3% Asian or Pacific Islander, 70% Hispanic, and 3% white), San Leandro (62% Hispanic, 12% white, 25% Asian), Sunnyvale (26% African American, 13% white, 60% Hispanic). Source: Review of ACLU Files. Colorado Springs police reported that their database was made up of 494 black, 423 Hispanic, 240 white, and 32 other individuals. *See* Sampson, *supra* note 38, at 1. African Americans comprise 22 percent of individuals listed on the Schaumburg, Illinois, database but only 3.7 percent of its population and two-thirds of those included in the gang database of Cook County, Illinois. *See Towns Track Gang Suspects in Database, supra* note 37.

115. *See* Muñoz, *supra* note 16, at A3. In April 1999, Phil Montez, regional director of the United States Commission on Civil Rights in Los Angeles, renewed his call for investigation of police interrogation and photography of minority youth for inclusion in gang databases. *See* Saavedra, *supra* note 112, at A12.

116. *See, e.g.,* Muñoz, *supra* note 16, at A3 (citing Westminster Police Chief James Cook's argument that gangs are strongest among new immigrants and poorer areas); Siegal, *supra* note 2, at 30 (citing California Gang Node Advisory Committee Chair Robert Hagler's argument that some neighborhoods have greater gang activity); Johnson, *supra* note 107, at A8 (quoting Detective David Metzler, spokesman for Denver police department).

117. *See* Thuan Le, *Police Group Unveils Anti-Gang Strategy,* L.A. TIMES, Feb. 5, 1993, at B4.

118. *See* REINER, *supra* note 4, at 122–23.

119. *See id.* at 124.

120. *Id.* at 124–25 (emphasis added). The report also reports the uncorroborated suspicions of "one local expert in Black gangs" that "a great many young Blacks from mid-

dle class homes who are secretly involved with gangs do not show up in gang databases because they have no criminal records." *Id.* at 126 (quoting V.G. Guinses, of Say Yes).

121. *See* Burrell, *supra* note 1, at 2–5 (describing black community's reaction to report that half of young black men in L.A. on gang database).

122. Lee Romney, *Parents, Leaders Assail Police Photos of Youths*, L.A. TIMES, June 12, 1994, at B1.

123. *See* Letter from Chen to Edwards, *supra* note 43, at 5. This ACLU letter asserts that some law enforcement materials received in response to a California Public Records request encouraged the practice of taking suspected gang members' photographs without consent or probable cause. *Id.*

124. For a discussion of the legal standard that governs whether a police-citizen encounter is consensual and the problems that arise when the police and the detained individual give differing accounts of the stop, see notes 163–165 and accompanying text *infra*.

125. *See* Weiss, *supra* note 37, at 2.

126. Telephone interview with Don Mace, *supra* note 14; Telephone Interview with Wes McBride, *supra* note 106.

127. *See* Paul Hoffman, *The Feds, Lies and Videotape: The Need for an Effective Federal Role in Controlling Police Abuse in Urban America*, 66 S.CAL. L.R. 1453, 1468, 1532 n.52 (1993). In an Oregon lawsuit, two brothers alleged that their identification as gang members led to multiple stops by police without probable cause as part of a police practice of harassing young black males. *See* Rivers v. City of Portland, 1989 WL 151714 *1 (D.Or. Nov. 28, 1989).

128. Telephone interview with Don Mace, *supra* note 14 (CalGang database accessible to police units that have laptop computers). Mark Silverstein reports that he has examined the record of traffic stops of a client in Colorado, and that in each record of a stop a printout of the warning "suspected gang member" comes up on the system. Phone Interview with Mark Silverstein, Director, Colorado ACLU (Jan. 7, 1998). Thus, individual officers are made aware when they conduct a traffic stop of a suspected gang member, but receive no guidance regarding the relevance of this information and how officers should factor it into their approach to the detained individual. Letter from Mark Silverstein to Gray Buckley, Dec. 4, 1998 (on file with author). John Crew of the California ACLU reports that a young man in San Diego was arrested for carrying a seemingly legal baseball bat in his car because his suspected gang affiliation came up on officer records. Interview with John Crew, ACLU of Northern California, San Francisco (Dec. 17, 1998). Florida is also in the process of developing a computer database that will be accessible to patrol officers. *See Computer Network Will Help Tip Police*, SARASOTA HERALD-TRIBUNE, Dec. 5, 1997, at B1. *See also* BUREAU OF JUSTICE ASSISTANCE, *supra* note 4, at 46 (explaining that some patrol officers may access gang data directly); notes 30, 47 *supra* (reporting use of state and federal grants by local police departments to purchase laptop computers).

129. *See* Werdegar, *supra* note 9, at 416 (reporting general practice); Letter from Chen to Edwards, *supra* note 43, at 25 n.14 (reporting use of database to identify Blythe Street Gang members for inclusion in an anti-gang injunction).

130. Burrell, *supra* note 1, at 2 (quoting Staff Paper, Proposal for an NCIC Gang File, NCIC Advisory Policy Board, Philadelphia, PA, June 3–4, 1993, at 22).

131. *See* Kim, *supra* note 57, at 274 (citing Thuan Le, *Police Group Unveils Anti-Gang Strategy*, L.A. TIMES, Feb. 5, 1993, at B4 (Orange County Ed.).

132. *See* Leslie Berger, *Gang Statistics Compiled in Vast Database*, L.A. TIMES, May 22, 1992, at 33.

133. *See* Letter from Chen to Edwards, *supra* note 43, at 24. Probation and parole conditions often include prohibitions on associating with other gang members. See BUREAU OF JUSTICE ASSISTANCE, *supra* note 4, at 77. The ACLU has received reports that in some jurisdictions bail decisions and availability of victims' assistance funds are affected by identification as a suspected gang member. *See* Letter from Chen to Edwards, *supra* note 43, at 6.

134. *See* Siegal, *supra* note 2, at 31; Telephone Interview with Mark Silverstein, *supra* note 128; Tustin Amole, *Suit Protests Anti-Gang Policy*, ROCKY MOUNTAIN NEWS, June 13, 1997, at A48. This suit was dismissed as moot when apartment complex declined to initiate eviction proceedings against the boy's mother and the "trespass notice" that barred the father from visiting his child expired. Telephone Interview with Mark Silverstein, *supra* note 128.

135. *See* Rivers v. City of Portland, No. 88-1364-FR, 1989 WL 51032 (D. Or. April 27, 1989) at *1. Another plaintiff filed a lawsuit alleging the same practice. *See* Complaint, Ysasaga v. City of Portland, No. 93-1175 at 4. The attorney for this plaintiff also reports complaints from individuals who were denied public housing because they were labeled as gang members or associates on police lists and from teachers who have seen local gang lists supplied by police and allege that such lists contain numerous inaccuracies. *See* Memorandum from Ed Chen to Gang Task Force (Apr. 26, 1994) (on file with author).

136. *See* Lesley Rogers, *SHA Puts Tenant Requests on Hold*, STATE J.-REGISTER, Aug. 1, 1999, at 1.

137. *See, e.g.*, Letter from Chen to Edwards, *supra* note 43, at 6–7 (documenting such cooperation in San Andreas and Alameda and reporting parent concerns that labeling has led to placement at continuation schools in Antioch, Fairfield, and Gilroy).

138. Telephone interview with Mark Silverstein, *supra* note 128. The ACLU does report that Santa Rosa officials proposed publication of gang lists in order to encourage eviction of gang members. *See* Letter from Chen to Edwards, *supra* note 43, at 6. *See also* THE LOS ANGELES COUNTY SHERIFF'S DEPARTMENT: A REPORT BY SPECIAL COUNSEL JAMES G. KOLTS & STAFF 300 (1992) (reporting that deputy sheriffs photographed suspected gang members and turned over arrest records of tenants' friends and relatives).

139. *See* Letter from Chen to Edwards, *supra* note 43, at 6; BUREAU OF JUSTICE ASSISTANCE, *supra* note 4, at 90 ("Police may use photographs that they have taken of gang members for the purpose of having witnesses identify offenders and for investigative purposes."); *GangNet/CalGANG Presentation, supra* note 27. Showing photographs of suspected gang members to members of the public may increase these individuals' risk of being falsely identified as criminal offenders, as in the case of Ted Nguyen, who spent three months in jail because of a mistaken identification of his photograph in an Asian gang mugbook. *See* Kim, *supra* note 57, at 275.

140. *See* Burrell, *supra* note 1, at 2. Burrell does not document any examples of such use of information from gang databases. The FBI database reportedly allows governments to access its database for employment and licensing purposes. *See* U.S. DEPARTMENT OF JUSTICE, BUREAU OF JUSTICE STATISTICS, SURVEY OF STATE CRIMINAL HISTORY INFORMATION SYSTEMS viii (1995).

141. Civil Rights Complaint for Damages, Declaratory, and Injunctive Relief, Quyen Pham et al v. City of Garden Grove et al, No. 94-3358 21–22 (filed May 20, 1996). The suit was primarily based on two incidents, where the police detained, photographed, and

questioned three Vietnamese high school students (two were honor students) who were dressed in hip-hop style and engaging in lawful activity (spending time together in a mall or at a park). *Id.* at 11–16 (filed May 20, 1996). In the second incident, one of the girls was arrested after objecting to an illegal search of her wallet. *Id.* at 15.

142. *See* Scales v. United States, 367 U.S. 203, 229-39 (1961); *In re* Alberto R., 235 Cal.App.3d 1309, 1319 n.5 (Cal. Ct. App. 1991)). *See also* United States v. Choate, 576 F.2d 165, 181 (9th Cir. 1978) ("[T]he practice of associating with compatriots in crime is not a protected associational right").

143. *See* note 30 *supra.*

144. *See* Dawson v. Delaware, 503 U.S. 159, 163–67 (1992) (holding that informing jury of defendant's membership in white supremacist gang violated First Amendment when it was irrelevant to crime and merely informed jury of defendant's beliefs). *Cf.* Fuller v. Johnson, 114 F.3d 491, 498 (5th Cir. 1997) (upholding admission of evidence that defendant belonged to gang that had committed numerous violent crimes as evidence of future dangerousness). While some have characterized this decision as recognizing that the right of association protects gang membership, the California Supreme Court contested such a reading of *Dawson* in its decision upholding anti-gang injunctions. *See* People *ex rel.* Gallo v. Acuña, 14 Cal.4th 1090, 1111, 929 P.2d 596 (Cal. 1997).

145. *See* NAACP v. Claiborne Hardware Co., 458 U.S. 886, 919–20 (1982); Rizzo v. Goode, 423 U.S. 362, 373–87 (1976); Healy v. James, 408 U.S. 169, 186 (1972). *See also* United States v. Rubio, 727 F.2d 786, 791 (9th Cir. 1983) (motorcycle gang); The Courier Journal v. Marshall, 828 F.2D 361, 365 (6th Cir. 1987) (Ku Klux Klan).

146. *See* Sawyer v. Sandstrom, 615 F.2d 311, 316–17 (5th Cir. 1980). However, courts and legal commentators have pointed out that *Sandstrom* was decided prior to two Supreme Court decisions that appeared to limit associational rights to expressive and intimate association. *See* IDK, Inc. v. County of Clark, 836 F.2d 1185, 1192 (9th Cir. 1988); Terence R. Boga, *Turf Wars: Street Gangs, Local Governments, and the Battle for Public Space*, 29 Harv. C.R.-C.L. L. Rev. 477, 498–99 (1994).

147. Civil Rights Complaint, Quyen Pham, *supra* note 141, at 22. These locations included a popular local shopping mall.

148. Rivers v. City of Portland, 1989 WL 51032 (D.Or. April 27, 1989) at *1. The court rejected this argument and dismissed the First Amendment claim. *Rivers*, 1989 WL 51032 at *3.

149. Dallas v. Stanglin, 490 U.S. 19, 25 (1989) (internal quotation marks and citations omitted).

150. *See* Roberts v. United States Jaycees, 468 U.S. 609, 617–18 (1984) (describing the two types of protected association).

151. Board of Directors of Rotary International v. Rotary Club of Duarte, 481 U.S. 537, 545 (1987) (quoting *Roberts*, 468 U.S. at 619–20). In order to test whether an association is sufficiently intimate to warrant associational protection, the U.S. Supreme Court instructs consideration of "factors such as size, purpose, selectivity, and whether others are excluded from critical aspects of the relationship." *Id.* at 545. For example, the Court concluded that the Rotary Club did not qualify as an intimate association because its membership turned over rapidly and was inclusive rather than exclusive, and its activities were conducted "in the presence of strangers" and publicized to non-members. *Id.* at 546–47. California courts have employed these factors to find both an anti-cult network and a private social club to warrant associational protection. *See* Hart v. Cult Awareness Network, 13 Cal.App.4th 777 (Cal. Ct. App. 1993); Pacific-Union Club v. Superior Court of

San Francisco County, 232 Cal.App.3d 60 (Cal. Ct. App. 1991). In these cases, the factors pointing to intimacy included small size, selective membership at the discretion of club leaders, members-only meetings, geographic focus, the absence of ties to a national organization, deemphasis on recruitment, and inwardly focused objectives. *See Cult Awareness Network*, 13 Cal.App.4th at 788; *Pacific-Union Club*, 232 Cal.App.3d at 72–75. Some street gangs may share many of the characteristics of associations found sufficiently intimate to warrant constitutional protection: they are selective, usually relatively small in size and concentrated in particular neighborhoods, have exclusive membership policies, conduct most gang activities internally rather than for public benefit, and are often close enough to one another that they consider each other to constitute their family. For suggestions that gangs qualify as protected associations, see Brief of Respondent Jose Saldana, The People of the State of California, *ex rel.* Richard D. Jones v. Carlos Antonio Amaya, et al., No. G015052 at 28, 29 (Superior Court No. 713223). Few have suggested that gangs would qualify as expressive associations, which have the purpose of pursuing "a wide variety of political, social, economic, educational, religious and cultural ends." *Roberts*, 468 U.S. at 622. A "kernel of expression" in the activity of an organization "is not sufficient to bring the activity within the protection of the First Amendment." *Stanglin*, 490 U.S. at 25.

152. City of Chicago v. Morales, 527 U.S. 41, 53 (1999).

153. *Id.* (citing *Stanglin*, 490 U.S. at 23–25 (1989)).

154. Some of the language in the *Morales* decision supports this notion. The Court stated that it might have upheld the anti-loitering ordinance "if it only applied to loitering by persons reasonably believed to be criminal gang members." *Morales*, 527 U.S. at 62; *see also id.* at 66 (O'Connor, J., concurring).

155. People *ex rel.* Gallo v. Acuna, 929 P.2d 596, 14 Cal.4th 1090, 1112 (Cal. 1997).

156. *Id.* (quoting Madsen v. Women's Health Center, Inc., 512 U.S. 753 (1994)). Even if gangs were protected associations, a second barrier to a successful right of association challenge is that placement on a gang database may not prove to impose a significant burden on associational rights. Proponents of gang databases could argue that mere entry of a record into a computer database does nothing to limit one's right to freely associate with others. Practices that are associated with the maintenance of gang databases, such as routine stops and harassment, could arise even if no database existed.

157. The *Los Angeles Times* editorial department recognized this practice, criticizing the Orange County Police Department for "collecting photographs of young people, even without evidence or reason to believe that they have been involved in criminal activity." *Police Photo Files Foster Fuzzy Ethics*, L.A. TIMES, June 5, 1994, at B10. *See also* note 110 *supra* (discussing complaints by minority youth).

158. *See* Terry v. Ohio, 392 U.S. 1, 27, 30–31 (1968). *See also In re* Tony C., 21 Cal.3d 888, 893, 582 P.2d 957 (Cal. 1978) ("[I]n order to justify an investigative stop or detention the circumstances known or apparent to the officer must include specific and articulable facts causing him to suspect that (1) some activity relating to crime has taken place or is occurring or about to occur, and (2) the person he intends to stop or detain is involved in that activity").

159. Some elected officials would like to change this constitutional standard. In 1994, Congressmen Rob Portmand (R-OH) and Gary Condit (D-CA) introduced a bill that would designate a police officer's reasonable belief that an individual actively participates in a criminal street gang (one which engages in a pattern of criminal activity) sufficient basis for reasonable suspicion and a stop and frisk. *See* Lassiter, *supra* note 63, at 23.

160. For decisions upholding police detentions based in part on evidence of gang affiliation see, e.g., United States v. Wheeler, 800 F.2d 100, 103 (7th Cir. 1986); People v. Holguin, 213 Cal.App.3d 1308, 1315 (Cal. Ct. App. 1989); *In re* Trinidad V., 212 Cal.App.3d 1077 (Cal. Ct. App. 1989); *In re* Stephen L., 162 Cal.App.3d 257, 260–61 (Cal. Ct. App. 1984); *In re* Hector R., 152 Cal.App.3d 1146, 1150–52 (Cal. Ct. App. 1984); People v. Rodriguez, 196 Cal.App.3d 1041, 1047–48 (Cal. Ct. App. 1984). For decisions holding that stops based on suspicion of gang involvement violated the Fourth Amendment, see People v. Rodriguez, 21 Cal.App.4th 232, 240–41 (Cal. Ct. App. 1993); People v. Rahming, 795 P.2d 1338, 1341–42 (Colo. 1990); State v. Jones, 835 P.2d 863, 867 (N.M. 1992). *See also* BUREAU OF JUSTICE ASSISTANCE, *supra* note 4, at 85 ("reasonable suspicion … may be in part [based on] gang insignia or association with known gang members.").

161. The Supreme Court has upheld the use of drug courier profiles. *See* United States v. Sokolow, 490 U.S. 1, 10 (1989); Florida v. Royer, 460 U.S. 491, 506 (1983); United States v. Cortez, 449 U.S. 411, 417 (1981). Nonetheless, these profiles may not provide the sole basis for reasonable suspicion. *See* United States v. Ceballos, 654 F.2d 177, 185–86 (2d Cir. 1981). Moreover, drug courier profiles are supposed to demonstrate the likelihood that someone is involved in illegal activity. Gang member profiles do not necessarily suggest any illegal activity, since gang membership itself is legal. Thus the use of gang profiles would still not provide reasonable suspicion of specific criminal activity. Suzin Kim suggests one other difference between the profiles: while drug courier profiles typically focus on suspicious behavior, gang profiles are often based on mere physical description. *See* Kim, *supra* note 57, at 279, 281–82.

162. *Royer*, 460 U.S. at 500.

163. *See, e.g.*, United States v. McIver, 186 F.3d 1119, 1125 (9th Cir. 1999) (use of photographic equipment to gather lawfully observed evidence does not violate Fourth Amendment); Dow Chemical Co. v. United States, 476 U.S. 227 (1986) (taking aerial photographs did not constitute a "search" for Fourth Amendment purposes).

164. *See* United States v. Mendenhall, 446 U.S. 544, 554 (1980).

165. *See, e.g., Rodriguez*, 21 Cal.App.4th at 238 (police officers ordered youths to sit on ground, patted them down, interviewed them, and took photographs); Tran & Yokoi, supra note 110, at 1. One commentary has argued that examining the particular characteristics and social context of detainees produces the conclusion that young Asian Americans will rarely feel free to leave: "This is especially true in a community-wide atmosphere charged with overt hostility toward gangs that are perceived to be composed primarily of people of color." Choi & Kim, *supra* note 108, at 77. The same might be true for members of other minority groups. However, courts have focused on objective indicia of police restraint rather than social context in determining how a reasonable person would feel.

166. *Rodriguez*, 21 Cal.App.4th at 240–41. Because circumstances of the crime suggested gang member involvement, the investigating officers showed witnesses photographs in a gang book. *See id.* at 237. However, as subsequent identifications of the defendant were held to be admissible, the court's decision had no effect on the conviction. *See id.* at 241.

167. *See id.* at 237–39.

168. *See id.* at 241. Subsequent decisions have focused their inquiry on whether the purpose of the illegal arrest or detention was to obtain the photograph. *See, e.g.*, People v. Thierry, 64 Cal.App.4th 176, 183–84 & n.3 (Cal. Ct. App. 1998).

169. *See* People v. McInnis, 6 Cal.3d 821, 825–26, 494 P.2d 690 (Cal. 1972) (identification from photograph taken during illegal arrest is admissible when past arrest is not related to current charges and photograph was not purpose of arrest). A dissenting opinion strongly criticized the majority opinion's claim of attenuation by noting that the "chain of causation between identification and illegal police action" was direct and unbroken. *Id.* at 828 (Tobriner, J., dissenting).

170. Under City of Los Angeles v. Lyons, 461 U.S. 95 (1983), a plaintiff lacks standing to obtain injunctive relief unless he can show a substantial and immediate threat that he will be subject to the unconstitutional police practice in the future. In cases in which the Fourth Amendment violation results in little concrete monetary harm, compensatory damages will also be inadequate. While punitive damages may be awarded against individual police officers, *see* Smith v. Wade, 461 U.S. 30 (1983), municipalities are not liable for punitive damages for bad faith actions by police officers. *See* City of Newport v. Fact Concerts, Inc., 453 U.S. 247 (1981).

171. *See* STEPHEN A. SALTZBURG & DANIEL J. CAPRA, AMER. CRIM. P. 362 (5th ed. 1996) ("Consent cases often come down to a credibility determination between the officer's account of what happened and the defendant's account of what happened," and courts "routinely find officers to be more credible than defendants" or other witnesses). For reports that police officers lie when on the stand, *see id.* at 362–63; Joe Sexton, *New York Police Often Lie under Oath, Report Says*, N.Y. TIMES, Apr. 22, 1994, at A1.

172. *See* Siegal, *supra* note 2, at 30; *Settlement in Garden Grove Photography Case Serves All*, L.A. TIMES, Dec. 31, 1995, at B6; Davan Maharaj, *Rights Suit Involving Police Photos Is Settled*, L.A. TIMES, Dec. 12, 1995, at A1. Rather than challenging gang identification databases directly, the *Pham* plaintiffs had rested their main legal arguments on the Fourth Amendment violation. *See* Civil Rights Complaint, Quyen Pham, *supra* note 141, at 11–16. The settlement also specified that suspicion of gang membership is insufficient as a basis for taking a photograph, and that individuals whose requests for removal are denied can request review of this decision by a panel of volunteers. Garden Grove also agreed to give $85,000 to the plaintiffs.

173. *See Police Change Procedures, Medina Happy with Settlement*, DAILY J., Oct. 18, 1994.

174. *See* Doreen Carvajal, *Police Photo Policies Focus of Law Enforcement*, L.A. TIMES, May 22, 1994, at A1.

175. Warren & Brandeis, *The Right to Privacy*, 4 HARV. L. REV. 193, 195 (1890) (quoted in Gorge B. Trubow, *Protecting Informational Privacy in the Information Society*, N. ILL. U. L. REV. 521, 522 (1990)).

176. *See* Trubow, *supra* note 175, at 521.

177. 429 U.S. 589 (1977).

178. *Whalen*, 429 U.S. at 605.

179. *See id.* at 603–04.

180. *Id.* at 598–605. The Court's discussion of the privacy interest did not appear to encompass a general right to freedom from government information gathering beyond what is prohibited by the Fourth Amendment. *See id.* at 600 n.24.

181. Even the prospects of this challenge are not entirely clear from the *Whalen* opinion. While Justice Brennan's concurrence stated that such improper disclosure might violate a federal privacy right and that centralized computer storage might necessitate imposition of legal safeguards, *see id.* at 606 (Brennan, J., concurring), Justice Stewart's

concurrence disagreed and asserted that the majority opinion did not reach such a conclusion. *See id.* at 608 (Stewart, J., concurring).

182. 476 U.S. 747, 772 (1986), *overruled on other grounds,* Planned Parenthood of Southeastern Pennsylvania v. Casey, 505 U.S. 833 (1992). One treatise argues that *Thornburgh* vindicates Justice Brennan's concurrence in *Whalen. See* JOHN E. NOVAK & RONALD D. ROTUNDA, CONSTITUTIONAL LAW 857 § 14.30 (5th ed. 1995).

183. The *Thornburgh* decision struck down reporting requirements in part because the reports would be available to the public and it might be possible to discover the identity of women who had abortions, thus deterring women from exercising their right to an abortion. *See Thornburgh,* 476 U.S. at 766–67. In Planned Parenthood of Central Missouri v. Danforth, 428 U.S. 52 (1976), by contrast, the Court upheld reporting requirements that were narrowly tailored and did not pose similar risks of public disclosure. *See id.* at 81. Possibly the only part of the Court's opinion suggesting some hope for a more generalized privacy right is the Court's reliance on cases striking down requirements that individuals engaged in expressive activity identify themselves. *See id.* at 767 (citing Talley v. California, 362 U.S. 60 (1960); NAACP v. Alabama *ex rel.* Patterson, 357 U.S. 449 (1958)). However, gang databases do not implicate the same First Amendment concerns present in such cases.

184. 436 U.S. 547 (1978).

185. *See id.* at 564–68 (declining to impose additional First Amendment restrictions and instead analyzing a newspaper's claim that search violated the First Amendment under the Fourth Amendment). For one such reading of *Zurcher,* see NOVAK & ROTUNDA, *supra* note 182, at 859.

186. *See* U.S. Department of Justice v. Reporters Committee for Freedom of the Press, 489 U.S. 749 (1989). *See also* Slayton v. Willingham, 726 F.2d 631, 635 (10th Cir. 1984) (police disclosure of personal photographs may have violated right to privacy); Doe v. Poritz, 662 A.2d 367 (N.J. 1995) (sex offenders have privacy right in preventing release of inaccurate information about status to public under state law).

187. The California privacy protection reads, "All people are by nature free and independent and have inalienable rights. Among these are enjoying and defending life and liberty, acquiring, possessing, and protecting property, and pursuing and obtaining safety, happiness, and privacy." CAL. CONST., art. I, § 1.

188. White v. Davis, 533 P.2d 222, 13 Cal.3d 757, 761 (Cal. 1975).

189. *Id.* at 775 (determining these dangers by reference to the proponents' statement in the state election brochure). The ballot statement also expressed particular concern over computerization of records. *See id.* at 774.

190. *See id.* at 760, 773–76. The court also found the information gathering to infringe on First Amendment protection of expressive activity. *See id.* at 767–69.

191. The court in *White v. Davis* reasoned that the absence of illegal activity produced a "strong suspicion" that government information gathering was unnecessary. *See id.* at 776. However, one might argue that while collecting information about gangs might not implicate illegal activity in every instance, it pertains to illegal activity in a much clearer fashion than surveillance of college students engaged in political activities.

192. *See* Loder v. Municipal Court, 553 P.2d 624, 17 Cal.3d 859, 868 (Cal. 1976).

193. *See* Memorandum of ACLU, Legal Committee Write-Up 2 (Dec. 1991) (on file with author).

194. *See* Carey v. Population Services Int'l, 431 U.S. 678, 686 (1977) (right to privacy may be burdened if compelling state interest is furthered); *White,* 13 Cal.3d at 761 (ex-

plaining that the government may impinge on privacy rights only if it demonstrates a compelling state interest that "cannot be achieved by less restrictive means").

195. *See Loder*, 17 Cal.3d at 864. The court defined this interest as "protect[ing] the public from recidivist offenders" and reasoned that such records could be useful in investigating crime, making discretionary decisions such as whether to arrest someone, exercising prosecutorial discretion, and evaluating the appropriateness of pretrial release and probation. *Id.* at 864–68.

196. *See id.* at 869–75.

197. Documented instances of disclosure have taken place in Colorado (to landlords) and Oregon (to an employer). Telephone Interview with Mark Silverstein, *supra* note 128; Complaint, Ysasaga v. City of Portland, No. 93-1175 at 4 (actual disclosure to employer), Rivers v. City of Portland, 1989 WL 51032 at *1 (D.Or. April 27, 1998) (threatened disclosure to employer). In California, the ACLU has received complaints from students and their parents in San Andreas, Alameda, Antioch, Fairfield, and Gilroy reporting cooperation between police and school officials, a practice that raises the concern that suspected gang affiliation could lead to differential treatment and improper educational assignments. *See* Letter from Chen to Edwards, *supra* note 43, at 6–7.

198. *See* 42 U.S.C. § 3789g(b) (1999).

199. *See* 28 C.F.R. § 23.3(a) (1999); BUREAU OF JUSTICE ASSISTANCE, *supra* note 4, at 35.

200. 28 C.F.R. § 23.20(a), (c) (1999). In a memorandum responding to concerns about these regulations, the Department justified the reasonable suspicion standard: "the potential for national dissemination of information in intelligence information systems, coupled with the lack of access by subjects to challenge the information, justifies the reasonable suspicion standard as well as other operating principle restrictions." Department of Justice, Office of Justice Programs, Final Revision to the Office of Justice Programs, Criminal Intelligence Systems Operating Policies, effective date September 16, 1993, at 13–14.

201. 28 C.F.R. § 23.20(d) (1999). As the Venturi memorandum points out, this means that information gathered in violation of the California right to privacy would violate federal regulations. Letter from Venturi to Jones, *supra* note 32, at 6. Other regulatory requirements mandate that the information be relevant to law enforcement purposes and be purged after five years unless reviewed and validated as complying with the system's criteria, and establish other security measures designed to prevent unauthorized dissemination. 28 C.F.R. § 23.20(e) & (h) (1994).

202. *See* Letter from Venturi to Jones, *supra* note 32, at 1; Telephone interview with Mark Silverstein, *supra* note 128.

203. Telephone interview with Don Mace, *supra* note 14. He also reports that the federal government provided some startup funds for GREAT/CalGang, and that voluntary compliance with federal regulations will allow CalGang to have the option of going national in the future. *Id.*

204. *See* CAL. CIV. CODE § 1798 et seq. (1994).

205. *See* CAL. CIV. CODE § 1798.40 (1994).

206. *See* ACLU, Inc. v. Deukmejian, 651 P.2d 822, 32 Cal.3d 440, 449–50 (Cal. 1982) (right of privacy barred disclosure of personal identifiers of individuals on index of persons involved in or associated with organized crime "in view of the substantial harm that could be inflicted by a public revelation").

207. *See* CBS, Inc. v. Block, 42 Cal.3d 646, 654, 725 P.2d 470 (Cal. 1986) (distinguishing the interests implicated by disclosure of an index of organized crime in *ACLU v.*

Deukmejian from those involved in disclosure of a list of individuals who have obtained licenses to carry concealed weapons).

208. *See, e.g.,* Mavity v. Tyndall, 66 N.E.2d 755 (Ind. 1946) (characterizing the cause of action as unwanted publicity); Itzkovitch v. Whitaker, 39 So. 499 (La. 1905) (holding that government cannot intrude on the interests of individuals who have not violated the law); Downs v. Swann, 73 A. 653, 656 (Md. 1909) (indicating disapproval of display of photographs of individuals arrested but not convicted of a crime).

209. CalGang is designed for this purpose. *See GangNet/CalGang Presentation, supra* note 27.

210. 208 Cal.App.2d 1, 5–6 (Cal. Ct. App. 1962). The court dismissed some of these cases as inapplicable to modern police practices, and distinguished others as resting on the harm caused by *public* dissemination of photographs.

211. *See id.* at 7–8 ("We do not believe any weight must be given to the theory that the police would be more likely to arrest plaintiff in the future for the rather trivial offense with which she was charged because of this incident, when the case terminated so favorably to her; and we cannot place any weight at all on the proposition that a judge might be inclined to impose a heavier sentence for any other offense which plaintiff might commit.").

212. *See* Central Valley Chapter of 7th Step Foundation, Inc. v. Younger, 95 Cal.App.3d 212, 231 (Central Valley I) (Cal. Ct. App. 1979) ("Appellants' right to privacy is violated as soon as arrest records containing nonconviction data are disseminated to public employers who are prohibited by law from considering a record of an arrest which did not result in conviction.").

213. *See* Letter from Venturi to Jones, *supra* note 32, at 2 (indicating that GREAT employs procedures that restrict access to information on the gang database to agencies that use such information for gang suppression purposes).

214. Meyer v. Nebraska, 262 U.S. 390, 399 (1923).

215. Deprivation of a property right might occur in two situations: one, when an individual loses a job because her employer has discovered she is in a gang database; or two, when an individual's incarceration, caused in some fashion by her presence in the database, causes loss of employment or other harm to financial interests. *See, e.g.,* Plaintiff's Opposition to Defendants' Motion for Summary Judgment, Ted Nguyen v. City of San Jose, No. 719469 19 (Sept. 19, 1995) (attributing damage to plaintiff's business to his incarceration resulting from improper identification based on photograph in Asian mug book).

216. *See generally* NOVAK & ROTUNDA, *supra* note 182, at 518–30 § 13.4. Other protectible liberty interests include revocation of a professional license, foreclosure of a particular individual's opportunity to engage in an important area of activity (such as permission to drive or to purchase alcohol), and infliction of corporal punishment. *See id.* at 533–34 § 13.4; RONALD D. ROTUNDA & JOHN E. NOVAK, TREATISE ON CONSTITUTIONAL LAW 621–22 § 17.4 (2d ed. 1992); GERALD GUNTHER & KATHLEEN M. SULLIVAN, CONSTITUTIONAL LAW 626 (12th ed. 1997).

217. In Wisconsin v. Constantineau, 400 U.S. 433 (1971), the Court stated, "[w]here a person's good name, reputation, honor, or integrity is at stake because of what the government is doing to him, notice and an opportunity to be heard are essential." *Id.* at 437. In that case, the police had posted individuals' names and prohibited the sale of alcohol to them based on their "excessive drinking." *Id.* at 434 n.2. In Board of Regents v. Roth, 408 U.S. 564 (1972), a case that raised the question whether a public university was required to pro-

vide a hearing before terminating an employee to which it owed no contractual obligation of continued employment, the Court held that no liberty or property right was violated when the manner of firing did not impose any stigma that would foreclose other employment opportunities. *Id.* at 573–75. Termination may deprive an individual of a property interest, but only if she has a right to the job at issue. *See id.* at 577–78.

218. The *Paul v. Davis* Court characterized the *Constantineau* holding as resting on deprivation of the right to purchase alcohol in addition to the reputational harm. *See Paul v. Davis,* 424 U.S. 693, 708 (1976). *See also* Wieman v. Updegraff, 344 U.S. 183, 191 (1952) ("Yet certainly where the State attaches a 'badge of infamy' to the citizen due process comes into play.").

219. *Paul,* 424 U.S. at 701, 708–12. Some commentators have suggested that the holding of *Paul v. Davis* rested in part on the fact that the plaintiff still had a state defamation cause of action, and have argued that the absence of any other legal remedy might raise a "more serious" liberty question. NOVAK & ROTUNDA, *supra* note 182, at 534 § 13.4; ROTUNDA & NOVAK, *supra* note 216, at 624 § 17.4. *See also* Michele L. Earl-Hubbard, *The Child Sex Offender Registration Laws: The Punishment, Liberty, Deprivation, and Unintended Results Associated with the Scarlet Letter Laws of the 1990s,* 90 N.W.U. L.REV. 788, 839–40 (1996) (citing commentators who suggest that *Paul's* significance is limited to cases involving allegations of state torts).

220. *See Paul,* 424 U.S. at 697–99.

221. NOVAK & ROTUNDA, *supra* note 182, at 535 § 13.4. For other cases in which courts have held that manner of termination implicated a liberty right, see Ray v. Edwards, 557 F. Supp. 664, 670 (N.D. Ga. 1982), aff'd, 725 F.2d 655 (11th Cir. 1984) (termination violated liberty interest when defendants should have known it would result in the public perception of culpability); Zurek v. Hasten, 553 F. Supp. 745, 747 & n.5 (N.D.Ill. 1982) (accessibility of letter in personnel file to prospective employers would demonstrate public dissemination); Angrisani v. City of New York, 639 F. Supp. 1326, 1333 (E.D.N.Y. 1986) (accessibility of child abuse accusations in state registry to prospective employers sufficient to show public dissemination).

222. *See* Goss v. Lopez, 419 U.S. 565 (1975). However, *Paul v. Davis* may have limited the significance of this decision by characterizing *Goss's* holding as dependent upon the status of school attendance as a right. *Paul,* 424 U.S. at 710. *See also* Siegert v. Gilley, 500 U.S. 226, 232–34 (1991) (no due process cause of action based on sending false information to prospective employers).

223. *See, e.g.,* Valmonte v. Bane, 18 F.3d 992, 994, 1002 (2d Cir. 1994) (listing on child abuse registry that prevented future employment implicated liberty interest); Bohn v. County of Dakota, 772 F.2d 1433, 1435, 1436 & n.4 (8th Cir. 1985) (damage to reputation combined with infringement of "protectible family interest" stated due process claim); *Angrisani,* 639 F. Supp. at 1333 (liberty interest involved when individual lost job due to inclusion on child abuse registry); Sims v. State Dep't of Pub. Welfare, 438 F. Supp. 1179, 1192 (S.D. Tex. 1977), *rev'd on other grounds,* 442 U.S. 415 (1979) (placing parents' names in clearinghouse of child abuse perpetrators without judicial determination violated due process); Watso v. Colorado Dep't of Social Services, 841 P.2d 299, 303, 306–07 (Colo. 1992) (listing names in state registry of child abusers harms family and therefore infringes liberty interest). *But cf.* Hodge v. Jones, 31 F.3d 157, 164–66 (4th Cir.), *cert. denied,* 513 U.S. 1018 (1994) (concluding that inclusion in child abuse registry infringed no familial privacy or liberty interest, in part relying on the absence of a constitutional right to expunge arrest records).

224. *See, e.g.,* Artway v. Attorney General of N.J., 81 F.3d 1235, 1268 (3d Cir. 1996) (registration requirement does not infringe on any liberty interest); Cutshall v. Sundquist, 980 F. Supp. 928, 931 (M.D. Tenn. 1997) ("There is nothing inherent in the act of registering that serves to trigger the protections of procedural due process."). The U.S. Supreme Court has granted certiorari to review a decision holding that a state's publication of a sex offender registry implicated a protectible liberty interest and that a hearing on current dangerousness was therefore required. Connecticut Dep't of Safety v. John Doe, No. 01-1231 (scheduled for oral argument Nov. 13, 2002). The Second Circuit decision held the liberty interest at issue to qualify for due process protection because in addition to the stigma of publication there were other consequences of inclusion: the state's requirements of registration, notification, blood samples, and photographs. Doe v. Public Safety, 271 F. 3d 38 (2nd Cir. 2001).

225. *See* Paul v. Davis, 424 U.S. at 710–11. As examples, the Court cited state laws that authorize issuance of drivers' licenses and establish conditions of parole. *See id.* at 711.

226. *See* Watson v. City of New York, 92 F.3d 31, 37–38 (2d Cir. 1996) (citing Sandin v. Conner, 515 U.S. 472 (1995)). The court in this case held that a state statute establishing a right to arraignment within 24 hours did not give rise to a state-created liberty interest, since it was merely "a procedure that protects the true liberty interest at stake in this case—freedom from confinement." *Watson,* 92 F.3d at 38.

227. Compare Anderson v. New York, 611 F. Supp. 481, 488 (S.D.N.Y. 1985) (statute requiring return of photograph after criminal proceeding vindicates state-created liberty interest in reputation or privacy) *with* Griffin v. Kelly, 1994 WL 9670 *2–4 (S.D.N.Y. 1994) (statute did not create constitutionally protected liberty interest) *and* Grandal v. City of New York, 966 F. Supp. 197, 201–02 (S.D.N.Y. 1997) (violation of statute did not deprive individual of liberty interest). The decisions that found no protected privacy interest rested their analysis in part on the plaintiffs' failure to allege any harm to reputation, which was the interest addressed by the statute (rather than the interest in avoiding future detection or prosecution). The *Grandal* court further noted: "in order to merit constitutional protection, a procedure must protect a substantive interest to which an individual has a legitimate claim of entitlement." *Grandal,* 966 F. Supp. at 200.

228. During the 1980s, the Supreme Court twice examined the possibility that a statute created a liberty interest that was implicated when prisoners were involuntarily transferred. Compare Olim v. Wakinekona, 461 U.S. 238 (1983) (finding no liberty interest violation) *with* Hewitt v. Helms, 459 U.S. 460, 466 (1983) (finding a liberty interest and holding that one "may arise from two sources—the Due Process Clause itself and the laws of the states"). The potential for expanded recognition of liberty interests that many saw in *Hewitt* was undermined, however, by *Sandin,* which rejected *Hewitt's* approach and held that, because prison regulations were not intended to confer rights on inmates, the right to procedural due process was triggered only by a dramatic departure from basic conditions of confinement. *See Sandin,* 515 U.S. at 482–87. *See also* GUNTHER & SULLIVAN, *supra* note 216, at 625–26.

229. *See* ACLU, Legal Committee Write-Up 3 (Dec. 1991) (on file with author). Moreover, at least one court has held that the proper remedy for infringement of the California right to privacy through dissemination of arrest records would lie in state rather than federal law. *See* Hammons v. Scott, 423 F. Supp. 618, 622 n.4 (N.D.Cal. 1976). However, it may be easier to establish that the state privacy right warrants due process protection than to succeed on a freestanding claim of violation of the right to privacy. This is because, even if a court determines that legitimate law enforcement interests outweigh a

state privacy right, an individual may still have the right to due process protections. *See* Ronald K. Chen, *Constitutional Challenges to Megan's Law: A Year's Retrospective*, 6 B.U. Pub. Int. L.J. 57, 68–69 (1996) (citing Doe v. Poritz, 662 A.2d 367, 408–09, 417 (N.J. 1995) as holding that, while the state privacy right was outweighed by public safety concerns, due process protections were nonetheless triggered by its deprivation).

230. *See* E.B. v. Verniero, 119 F.3d 1077, 1104–05 & n.27 (3d Cir. 1997), *cert. denied*, 522 U.S. 1109 (1998) (state constitution established privacy interest in nondisclosure that entitles individual to due process protection). *But cf.* Cutshall v. Sundquist, 193 F.3d 466, 481–82 (6th Cir. 1999) (sex offender registration requirement did not violate state privacy right because state constitution did not establish right to nondisclosure of private facts); Russell v. Gregoire, 124 F.3d 1079, 1094 (9th Cir. 1997), *cert. denied*, 118 S.Ct. 1191 (1998) (finding no state-created right to privacy and therefore no interest protected under due process in Washington state).

231. *See* Plaintiff's Opposition, Nguyen v. City of San Jose et al., *supra* note 215, at 6–7.

232. *See id.* at 18–20. The plaintiff also argued that *Paul v. Davis* posed no obstacle to recovery because he had suffered the tangible harm of damage to his business. *See id.* at 19. ACLU attorneys also explored other ways to overcome the *Paul v. Davis* problem: claiming that the state constitutional right to privacy created a protected liberty interest; arguing that the police department's use of the plaintiff's photo led to his incarceration ("a tangible loss of liberty"); and distinguishing *Paul v. Davis* as resting on a federalism analysis (the courts' desire to avoid treating state defamation or tort claims as federal due process concerns) and arguing that state courts should therefore not rely upon the case. *See* Memorandum from Margaret Crosby et al. to ACLU Legal Committee and Board of Directors 4 (Dec. 4, 1991) (on file with author).

233. *See* Plaintiff's Opposition, Nguyen v. City of San Jose et al., *supra* note 215, at 18–20.

234. *See* Civil Rights Complaint, Quyen Pham, *supra* note 141, at 20.

235. Rivers v. City of Portland, 1989 WL 51032 **4–5 (D. Or. April 27, 1989).

236. Increased risk of harm does not establish an *actual* injury. Therefore, only individuals who have actually been unfairly arrested or prosecuted, as in the case of Ted Nguyen, and can establish that "but for" gang membership this prosecution would not have taken place, will be able to maintain a cause of action. The analysis could resemble the inquiry used in employment discrimination cases, and ask whether the suspected gang membership was a "substantial factor" in the decision to arrest (or prosecute or deny bail), or whether "but for" the suspicion of gang membership the same liberty deprivation would have taken place. *See* Mount Healthy Board of Education v. Doyle, 429 U.S. 274, 287 (1977) (plaintiff must show racial discrimination was substantial or motivating factor).

237. Board of Regents v. Roth, 408 U.S. 564, 572 (1972).

238. *See, e.g.*, Parker v. Lester, 227 F.2d 708, 710 (9th Cir. 1955) (holding that post-deprivation hearing provided to members of the Coast Guard who lost their jobs through a loyalty-security program deprived men of due process). Supreme Court cases addressing the practice of listing suspected subversives generally overturned such laws without reaching the constitutional issue. *See, e.g.*, Joint Anti-Fascist Refugee Committee v. McGrath, 341 U.S. 123, 135, 138 (1950); Peters v. Hobby, 349 U.S. 331, 342–43 (1955); Greene v. McElroy, 360 U.S. 474, 507–08 (1959). *But cf.* Cafeteria and Restaurant Workers Union Local 473 v. McElroy, 367 U.S. 886 (1961).

239. *Roth*, 408 U.S. at 569–70.

240. 424 U.S. 319 (1976).

241. *See* Mathews v. Eldridge, 424 U.S. 319, 335 (1976).

242. *See* text accompanying notes 123–140 and 231–236 *supra*.

243. *See* text accompanying notes 56–87 *supra*.

244. In order to determine how often an erroneous deprivation of liberty or property occurs, courts will sometimes consider reversal rates in existing post-termination proceedings. *See, e.g., Mathews,* 424 U.S. at 346–47; Valmonte v. Bane, 18 F.3d 992, 1004 (2d Cir. 1994). In this case, of course, there are no such statistics available because there are no established administrative processes by which a person included in a database can challenge that inclusion.

245. *See* Werdegar, *supra* note 9, at 435.

246. *See* People ex rel. Gallo v. Acuna, 929 P.2d 596, 14 Cal.4th 19, 1101 (Cal. 1997) (noting that only five of thirty-eight named defendants appeared at hearing on preliminary injunction against gang members); Werdegar, *supra* note 9, at 417 (named defendants often do not appear at these hearings).

247. *See* Goldberg v. Kelly, 397 U.S. 254, 264–65 (1970) (weighing the government's interest in providing for the poor and avoiding societal dissatisfaction).

248. *See* Ginsburg, Neal & LeSage, Press Release (April 1994) (on file with author). The city stipulated that failure to provide due process to individuals on gang lists violated the Constitution.

249. *See* Settlement Agreement, Quyen Pham v. City of Garden Grove et al., United States District Court, No. 94-3358 at 14–19 (C.D. Cal. 1994).

250. Plaintiff's Opposition, Nguyen v. City of San Jose et al., *supra* note 215, at 21.

251. Letter from John M. Crew, ACLU of Northern California, to U.S. Civil Rights Commission 2–3 (July 3, 1997) (on file with author).

252. *See, e.g.,* Mathews v. Eldridge, 424 U.S. 319, 344 (1976) (disability benefits decisions rely mostly on written medical reports).

253. *See Goldberg,* 397 U.S. at 269 (discussing such problems in the case of welfare recipients).

254. *See, e.g., id.* at 267–68.

255. *See* Bohn v. County of Dakota, 772 F.2d 1433, 1437–38 (8th Cir. 1985).

256. *See id.* at 1438.

257. *See* Valmonte v. Bane, 18 F.3d 992, 1004 (2d Cir. 1994). *See also* E.B. v. Verniero, 119 F.3d 1077, 1109 (3d Cir. 1997), *cert. denied,* 118 S.Ct. 1039 (1998) (holding that due process requires that the government bear the burden of persuasion in sex offender registration and notification proceedings).

258. *See* 8 B. Witkin, Summary of California Law § 603 at 57 (9th ed. 1988).

259. *See* Rivers v. City of Portland, 1989 WL 51032 *1 (D.Or. April 27, 1989). *See also* Farm Labor Organizing Commitee v. Ohio State Highway Patrol, _F.3d_, 2002 WL 31317699**5-9 (6th Cir. Oct. 17, 2002) (collecting cases involving allegations of discriminatory police enforcement practices); Chavez v. Illinois State Police, 251 F.3d 612, 635 (7th Cir. 2001) (showing that police "utilize impermissible racial classifications in determining who to stop, detain, and search. . . . would amount to a violation of the Equal Protection Clause").

260. *See* Washington v. Davis, 426 U.S. 229, 240 (1976); Arlington Heights v. Metropolitan Housing Corp., 429 U.S. 252, 265 (1977).

261. *See* McCleskey v. Kemp, 481 U.S. 279, 292–97 (1987) (concluding that study showing racial disparities in imposition of the death penalty was not sufficient proof of

discrimination because of the discretionary, multi-faceted and unreviewable nature of the decisions to seek and impose a death sentence).

262. *See* notes 116–120 and accompanying text *supra.*

263. Patsone v. Pennsylvania, 232 U.S. 138, 144 (1914).

264. *See, e.g.,* U.S. v. Travis, 837 F. Supp. 1386, 1392 (E.D. Ky. 1993) (compelling interest in fighting drug trafficking might justify use of race as classifier). However, the court did state that it might reach a different result if an individual brought a civil rights lawsuit rather than raising the issue in the context of a suppression motion. *Id.* at 1396.

265. *See* United States v. Brignoni-Ponce, 422 U.S. 873, 884–86 (1975); *Travis,* 62 F.3d at 174; *but cf.* United States v. Montero-Camargo, 208 F. 3d 1122, 1131-35 (9th Cir.), *cert. denied,* 531 U.S., 889 (2000).

266. 42 U.S.C. § 2000d (1994).

267. *See* Fobbs v. Holy Cross Health Corporation, 29 F.3d 1439, 1447 (9th Cir. 1994).

268. *See* Guardians Ass'n v. Civil Service Comm, 463 U.S. 582, 584 n.2, 608 n.1 (1983) (Powell, J., concurring); Alexander v. Choate, 469 U.S. 287, 292–94 (1985). However, a recent U.S. Supreme Court decision holds that there is no private right of action to enforce disparate inpact regulations promulgated under Title VI. Alexander v. Sandoval, 532 U.S. 275 (2001). Justice Stevens' dissent suggested that litigants could rely on 42 U.S.C. © 1983 to overcome this problem.

269. Elston v. Talladega County Bd. of Educ., 997 F.2d 1394, 1407 (11th Cir. 1993).

270. *Elston,* 997 F.2d at 1413; *see also* Griggs v. Duke Power Co., 401 U.S. 424, 431 (1971); Larry P. v. Riles, 793 F.2d 969, 982 (9th Cir. 1984). This test is modeled after the "business necessity" showing required in Title VII employment discrimination cases. *See Larry P.,* 793 F.2d at 982.

271. *See Elston,* 997 F.2d at 1407.

272. *See, e.g.,* Police Officers for Equal Rights v. City of Columbus, 644 F. Supp. 393, 438 (S.D. Oh. 1985) (upholding availability of Title VI cause of action because city receives federal financial assistance). For an example of a case in which plaintiffs brought a Title VI cause of action against a police department without alleging any discriminatory employment practices, see Brown v. City of Oneonta, 858 F. Supp. 340, 345 (N.D.N.Y. 1994). In *Brown,* the plaintiffs brought Title VI challenges against the police department, city government, university, and state government after the university provided local police with a list of black male students after a crime near campus involving a black suspect. Telephone interview with Scott Bassinson, attorney for plaintiffs, Whiteman, Osterman Law Firm (Mar. 25, 1998). The Title VI claims were eventually stipulated out of the case in the interest of expediting matters. *Id.*

273. *See* Chavez v. Illinois State Police, 1996 WL 66136 * 8 (N.D. Ill. 1996) (claims involving racial harassment and violations of the Fourth Amendment in stops of racial minorities); *Brown,* 858 F. Supp. at 345 (illegal police harassment and detention of African American university students after a crime near campus); Neighborhood Action Coalition v. City of Canton, 882 F.2d 1012, 1016–17 (6th Cir. 1989) (police failure to respond to calls in particular neighborhood).

274. Failure to do so will defeat a Title VI claim. *See* Association of Mexican American Educators v. State of Calif., 195 F. 3d 465, 475–81 (9th Cir. 1999), *reversed in part on other grounds on rehearing,* 231 F. 3d 572 (9th Cir. 2000) (en banc).

275. Regulations found at 28 C.F.R. § 42.201 et seq. apply to all programs that receive funding under the 1974 Juvenile Justice Delinquency and Prevention Act and the 1979 Justice System Improvement Act. Regulations at 42 C.F.R § 42.104 et seq. apply to all

programs receiving funds under the 1968 Omnibus Crime Control and Safe Streets Act. Both bar practices that have discriminatory effects. *See* 28 C.F.R. §§ 42.203(e) & 42.104(b)(2) (1999). The differences between the regulatory provisions are not relevant for the purposes of this chapter. Telephone interview with Mark Posner, U.S. Department of Justice, Civil Rights Division (Mar. 12, 1998).

276. *Id.* As one example of Department of Justice funding, since October 1994 Community Oriented Police Services (COPS) has provided grants to over 11,300 local police departments to hire additional police officers, including over 400 in California. COPS Office Announces Grants to Fund Regional Community Policing Institutes, Domestic Violence Training, Press Release, Sept. 29, 1999, found at ⟨www.usdoj.gov/cops/news_info/press_releases/default.html⟩ (visited Nov. 23, 1999); Telephone interview with Kevin Avery, Congressional Relations Office, U.S. Department of Justice, March 23, 1998. For a list of grant recipients, see ⟨www.usdoj.gov/cops/foia/foia_err.htm⟩ (visited Dec. 12, 1999).

277. *See* 42 U.S.C. § 2000d-4a(a)(A) (1994); Telephone Interview with Mark Posner, *supra* note 275.

278. 28 C.F.R. §§ 42.104(b)(2) & 42.203(e) (1999).

279. *See* Latinos Unidos de Chelsea en Accion v. Secretary of HUD, 799 F.2d 774, 790–91 (1st Cir. 1986) (pool of local businesses compared to group of businesses awarded contracts); Groves v. Alabama State Bd. of Educ., 776 F. Supp. 1518, 1526 (M.D. Ala. 1991) (comparing those who satisfy other minimum requirements with those who also have the required standardized test score); Larry P. v. Riles, 793 F.2d 969, 975, 982–83 (9th Cir. 1984) (racial composition of all students versus those identified as mentally retarded); Bryan v. Koch, 627 F.2d 612, 616–17 (2d Cir. 1980) (racial composition of all users of public hospitals compared to users of one particular hospital).

280. Title VI disparate impact analysis closely resembles that employed in Title VII cases. *See* Powell v. Ridge, 189 F.3d 387, 393–94 (3d Cir.), *cert. denied*, 528 U.S. 1046 (1999). In employment cases the appropriate comparison pool is even clearer—the similarly situated group is qualified individuals in the labor market.

281. Such an argument has proven fatal to some equal protection challenges. *See* United States v. Taylor, 956 F.2d 572, 580 n.2 (6th Cir. 1991) (Guy, J., concurring) (selecting people of color for consensual stops would not offend Constitution if police were targeting drugs from the Caribbean and found that most couriers were people of color); Ah Sin v. George W. Whittman, 198 U.S. 500 (1905) (dismissing a claim of selective enforcement against Chinese gamblers when no showing was made that there are non-Chinese offenders who have not been prosecuted). In *Armstrong*, the Supreme Court explicitly rejected the Ninth Circuit's assumption that all people commit all types of crimes as empirically false. *See* United States v. Armstrong, 517 U.S. 456, 116 S.Ct. 1480, 1488–89 (1996). *But cf.* Taylor, 956 F.2d at 581 (Damon, J., dissenting) (finding the assumption that 75 percent of the individuals smuggling drugs are black "impermissible.").

282. *See* Letter from Crew to Civil Rights Commission, *supra* note 252, at 7 (suggesting that such a breakdown should be released).

283. *See id.* at 7–8.

284. Of course, such a study would be extremely difficult to conduct. Researchers would need to find an appropriate and representative sample of individuals included in the database, and make a reliable determination of the gang involvement or membership of these individuals.

285. Coalition of Concerned Citizens v. Damian, 608 F. Supp. 110, 127 (C.D. Oh. 1984).

286. Hodges v. Public Building Commission of Chicago, 864 F. Supp. 1493, 1994 WL 506899 *1, 5 (N.D. Ill. Sep. 14, 1994) (citing Hunter v. Underwood, 471 U.S. 222, 227 (1985)).

287. *Hunter*, 471 U.S. at 227, 229 (citation omitted).

288. *See* United States v. Travis, 837 F. Supp. 1386, 1389–90 (E.D. Ky. 1993), *aff'd*, 62 F.3d 170 (1995). Nationally, airline travelers are 88% white, 5% African American, 1% Asian, and 1% Hispanic; the court adjusted for local population numbers and assumed airline travelers to be 12% African American and 9% Hispanic. Yet a police officer testified that in 1991 he stopped 38% white individuals, 49% African Americans, and 12% Hispanics, and in 1992 26% white, 56% African American, and 18% Hispanic travelers. *See id.* at 1389–90. It is significant that the court chose airline travelers as the appropriate reference group rather than looking at the racial composition of the pool of individuals engaged in drug trafficking. For a decision expressing approval of this statistical measure, see United States v. Guzman, 894 F. Supp. 642 (W.D.N.Y. 1995).

289. United States v. Travis, 62 F.3d 170, 174 (6th Cir. 1995). Although the court found that the statistics demonstrated a disparate impact, it nonetheless held that the government's practices were justified. *Travis*, 837 F. Supp. at 1386.

290. *See* United States v. Armstrong, 517 U.S. 456, 116 S.Ct. 1480, 1489 (1996). However, in *Armstrong* the plaintiffs may not have made a particularly strong showing. The plaintiffs presented the results of a study from one federal district over the course of one year and presented only anecdotal testimony of the existence of non-black individuals who the government chose not to prosecute. *See id.* at 1489.

291. For example, a plaintiff could show that white and black youths in a particular area dressed in similar clothing styles, hung out at the same location (such as a shopping mall), and engaged in similar behavior, but that police stopped only the black youth for inclusion on the gang database. Litigants might want to explore the possibility of "testers" (typically used in housing discrimination cases) for this purpose.

292. *See* Board of Education v. Harris, 444 U.S. 130, 151 (1979) (educational necessity); Jeldness v. Pearce, 30 F.3d 1220, 1229 (9th Cir. 1994) (business necessity under Title VI); Georgia State Conference of Branches of NAACP v. Georgia, 775 F.2d 1403, 1417–18 (11th Cir. 1985) (educational necessity); Larry P. v. Riles, 793 F.2d 969, 982–83 & nn.9–10 (9th Cir. 1984) (employment or educational necessity).

293. Elston v. Talladega County Bd. of Educ., 997 F.2d 1394, 1413 (11th Cir. 1993); *Association of Mexican-American Educators*, 937 F. Supp. at 1400 n.3.

294. *See* notes 264–265 and accompanying text *supra*.

295. *See Elston*, 997 F.2d at 1407.

296. This requirement of a criminal predicate could range from mandating a conviction for a gang-related crime, which would dramatically decrease the size of the database, to mere reasonable suspicion of gang-related criminal activity. A court would probably be more likely to adopt the latter alternative so as not to completely change the nature of the gang database. Others suggest narrowing the database to focus only on the most hard-core gang members, who tend to be the leaders, the most dangerous and violence prone, and the most heavily involved in criminal activity. BUREAU OF JUSTICE ASSISTANCE, *supra* note 4, at 34.

7

Anti-gang Initiatives as Racialized Policy

Marjorie S. Zatz and Richard P. Krecker, Jr.

INTRODUCTION

Youth gangs have been identified as a chronic or emerging problem in cities across the country (Spergel and Curry 1993). The Department of Justice's National Youth Gang Survey estimated that there were nearly 850,000 gang members and 31,000 active youth gangs in the United States in 1996 (Office of Juvenile Justice and Delinquency Prevention 1997). Hardly a day goes by when there is not an article in a major urban newspaper about gangs and gang violence. Politicians, the police, and the media report that people are scared and want something—anything—done to curb gang violence. The federal government and state legislatures from Alaska to Florida have passed or are contemplating comprehensive anti-gang statutes modeled after the RICO organized crime statutes, as well as local ordinances restricting the activities of alleged gang members (Belluck 1999; Rubin 1998; Villa 1999; Zatz et al. 1999). Many of these anti-gang initiatives have been supported by appellate court decisions, lending them additional weight.

The war on gangs appears on its face to be race neutral. After all, it is gang-related activity that is being targeted, not individuals. However, if gang membership is alleged primarily for youths of color and gang membership increases the severity of sanctions, then we must question this apparent neutrality.

In this chapter, we examine the anti-gang initiatives in the state of Arizona. We suggest that they may have played into racialized fears of Latinos/as and African Americans as different and scary (Fishman 2002; Hagedorn 1991; Portillos 2002; Russell 1998; Zatz 1987).[1] We take this analysis a step further by interviewing juvenile court judges, commissioners, probation officers, and defense attorneys in Maricopa County (Phoenix) regarding their views of the anti-gang policies and statutes and of the risk that they may disproportionately affect youths of color. We also consider data from juvenile probation and from a local institute that runs training programs for gang-affiliated youths referred by the court to assess the extent to which "gang member" in Arizona means "Latino youth."

The War on Gangs and Youth of Color

Like much of the rest of the country, the Arizona legislature and the governor's office pride themselves on "getting tough" on crime. "Fear of crime" in Arizona, as elsewhere, had translated into "fear of gangs," and African-American and Latino/a gangs received considerable attention in this era of repressive crime control policies.

In 1978, the Phoenix Police Department obtained $40,000 in startup funds to establish a gang squad, with another half-million dollars following over a period of three years from the federal government (Zatz 1987, 129). At that time, approximately one-quarter of the young Chicano males in the city were identified by the police as gang members (Zatz 1987, 130). In 1981, the police documented 150 street gangs in Phoenix. In that year they arrested 885 gang members for 701 offenses ranging from minor crimes to homicide. Approximately 85 percent of the gangs documented by the Phoenix Police Department in 1981 were Latino, 10 percent black, and 5 percent white (Epler 1999, 27). Thus, we see that from its inception the "gang problem" in Phoenix has been closely linked to Latino and Latina youths. According to Phoenix police sources, by 1992 "Hispanic gangs emerged as the source of most of Phoenix's gang violence and still hold that distinction today" (Epler 1999, 29). The Phoenix police also report that gang violence peaked in Phoenix in 1992. That year, the police recorded 918 gang-related violent incidents, though by 1998 the police recorded only 331 violent incidents involving street gangs (Epler 1999, 29). Yet as we will demonstrate, the state did not enact new anti-gang statutes during the peak years; rather, the new initiatives went into place in 1994 and later, when gang-related violence was already decreasing.

Phoenix is not unique in conflating youth of color with gang members. Citing 1992 estimates from the Los Angeles County District Attorney's Office, Miller reports, "Nearly half of all black men ages 21–24 living in LA county were labeled as gang members—an ominous prospect in any society" (1996, 91). Similarly, Muwakkil (1993) reports that 47 percent of all young black men in Los Angeles between the ages of twenty-one and twenty-four were on the L.A. Sheriff Department's gang database (cited in Joe and Chesney-Lind 1995).

The same picture emerges from Denver, Colorado. As of November 1993, the Denver Police Department had a list of 6,500 "suspected" gang members. Although African Americans represented only 5 percent of Denver's population, they accounted for 57 percent of those on the list. Another one-third of the "suspects" were Latino or Latina, with whites accounting for less than 7 percent of those suspected of gang membership, even though 80 percent of Denver's population was white. Moreover, the 3,691 African Americans on the police department's list constitute two-thirds of the black males aged 12–24 living in Denver (Miller 1996, 109). Similarly, in Cicero, Illinois, a town just outside of Chicago, three-quarters of the youths identified as gang members had Hispanic surnames (Belluck 1999).

Racial/ethnic minorities constituted 32 percent of the juvenile population in the United States in 1995, yet they represented 68 percent of the juvenile population in secure detention and 68 percent of those in secure institutional environments (e.g., training schools). This is a significant increase over 1983 figures of 53 percent of the detention population and 56 percent of the secure juvenile corrections population (Hsia and Hamparian 1998; Sickmund et al. 1997). In Arizona, where we conducted our research, 47 percent of the youths sentenced to juvenile corrections facilities in 1998 were Latino/a, although Latinos and Latinas made up only 32.5 percent of Arizona's youth aged eight–seventeen. Another 11 percent of the youths in locked facilities in 1998 were African American, even though African Americans constituted only 3.4 percent of the state's population aged eight–seventeen (Harker 1998, B1, B8). Thus while just under 36 percent of the state's youth were Latino/a or African American, 58 percent of the youths incarcerated in Arizona's juvenile facilities were Latino/a or African American.

To what extent, we ask, is this overrepresentation of Latino/a and African-American youths due to the war on gangs? Does the war on gangs disproportionately target members of racial/ethnic minorities? If so, what do the judicial officers charged with upholding these laws and policies think about them? Do judicial officials and probation officers agree that these initiatives are a good idea and that they reduce crime? Are they concerned about possible racial biases inherent in these policies or about racially disparate effects of the policies? To address these questions concerning the law in action, we interviewed juvenile court judges, commissioners, probation officers, and defense attorneys regarding their views of Arizona's anti-gang initiatives. We supplement these interviews with data from Juvenile Probation to more fully assess the extent to which gang membership is disproportionately ascribed to Latino/a youths. In combination, these data offer a unique view of how anti-gang statutes and policies actually operate, who they target, and what those judicial officers charged with upholding the statutes and other initiatives say about them.

We focus on three anti-gang initiatives. The first initiative we consider is a risk assessment scale developed by the Department of Juvenile Corrections in 1995. A point is added to a youth's score on the assessment scale if he or she is suspected of gang membership. With each new point, the likelihood of commitment to a secure facility and the length of the commitment become greater. While the policy was created by juvenile corrections, the juvenile court is expected to follow the scale values when sentencing youths. The second initiative we consider is a statute defining a criminal street gang as a criminal syndicate and making participation in a criminal syndicate a felony. This statute, enacted in 1994, automatically enhances offenses that might otherwise have been charged as misdemeanors to felonies if they promote or further a criminal syndicate (A.R.S. 13-2308). Since this is essentially a conspiracy law, the major problem that has arisen involves determining that the defendant is indeed a member of a criminal street gang. Criteria were defined in a related statute (A.R.S. 13-105(7) and (8)), but there is still substantial room for ambiguity. The third initiative we consider here is a judicial interpretation. In December of 1996, the Arizona Court of Appeals gave the prosecution a decided boost when it ruled that trial judges could allow police officers to serve as expert witnesses to help determine whether the defendant belonged to a gang and that juries could hear this testimony.

These three anti-gang initiatives—one an administrative policy, the second a statute enacted by the legislature, and the third a judicial interpretation—in combination have given the state new and improved weaponry in its war on gangs. The question that concerns us here is whether this war is being fought along racial and ethnic lines. If most youths who are defined as gang members are African American or Latino/a *and/or* if most African Americans and Latinos/as coming before the court are identified as gang members, then these policies may systematically increase the sentences for youths of color.

Before turning to these initiatives, we present background information on the juvenile court decisions most likely to be affected by accusations of gang membership, and we discuss our data and methods.

JUVENILE COURT DECISIONS MOST LIKELY TO BE AFFECTED BY ALLEGATIONS OF GANG MEMBERSHIP

Allegations of gang membership may surface at any point in juvenile court proceedings, but they generally are first seen in police referrals. The referral will state whether or not the youth appears on the police department's list of known or suspected gang members. Even if the youth is not on that list, police might note that they think a youth is gang-affiliated or that the offense was related to gang activity. The police may also recommend immediate detention of a youth because of known or suspected gang ties.

Next, the prosecutor may request detention during advisory hearings, based on police or probation officers' allegations. The prosecutor also may increase the charges from misdemeanors to felonies if the offense was allegedly committed for the benefit of a gang; if the youth is adjudicated delinquent (i.e., convicted), the prosecutor may request sentence enhancements for gang-related offenses. At each of the juvenile's hearings (e.g., advisory, adjudication, and disposition), the judge or commissioner has the benefit of a report written by the probation officer assigned to the case. The probation officer's recommendation includes information from the police report and any other relevant information collected from interviews with the juvenile, his or her parents and teachers, and perhaps neighbors or other interested parties. Both judicial officials and probation officers expect that the probation report will include any police allegations of gang membership, as well as admissions or denials by the youth and his or her parents. Allegations of gang membership also are noted in the risk assessment scale (discussed later) and may result in more punitive placement of youths identified as gang members. Finally, the judicial officer may consider gang membership in adjudication and sentencing (i.e., disposition). If youths are sentenced to probation, judicial officers routinely stipulate that they may not associate with gang members, and youths may have their probation revoked if they violate this condition.

Of these myriad ways in which gang membership may influence court decisions, the most critical are the risk assessment scale and the statutory enhancements, both of which were thrust upon the juvenile court in the mid-1990s. Of the two, the risk assessment scale designed by the Department of Juvenile Corrections is the more innocuous; the ramifications of the criminal street-gang statutes, while not commonly felt in juvenile court, are potentially more serious.

The Risk Assessment Scale

In 1995, the Department of Juvenile Corrections created a new risk assessment scale to be used for determining whether a youth should be placed in secure custody and for how long. One of the risk factors identified was gang membership. The other risk factors are having five or more court referrals; having five or more adjudications (of delinquency); being younger than twelve years and six months at the time of one's first referral; having two or more petitions for assaultive offenses, two or more petitions for drug offenses, three or more petitions for property offenses, one or more petitions for weapons offenses, and/or three or more petitions for felony offenses. The youth's scale score may be reduced by a point if he or she has only one or two adjudications, is enrolled in school, and/or does not use alcohol or drugs. Probation officers are expected to include the youth's scale value in their recommendations, and juvenile court judges and commissioners are supposed to make decisions consistent with this policy.[2]

One of the major problems with this scale, from the perspective of defense attorneys and judicial officers, is that it considers every offense for which the local police refer a youth to court, whether or not he or she was ultimately adjudicated guilty of that offense. Thus if the police referred the youth to court five times, he or she receives a point, even if the County Attorney's office decides not to prosecute any of the referrals or the youth was acquitted. A second, related problem is that a point is added if the youth's first referral occurred before he or she reached the age of twelve years and six months, again regardless of whether or not the referral was declined by the prosecutor's office. Third, the points based on offense type (assaultive, drug, property, weapons, felony) are awarded if the charges filed involved these offenses, regardless of whether or not a conviction was ultimately obtained. In other words, a juvenile could be charged with the number of offenses mandated for extra points to come into effect, at trial be found not guilty, and still be assessed those extra points simply because the County Attorney's office concluded that probable cause existed to proceed to that point. A fifth problem is that there is no distinction between serious gang leaders and wannabes; both receive the same additional point for alleged gang membership. Finally, although occasional use of alcohol or drugs is classified as no drug or alcohol history, there is no distinction between the regular (i.e., weekly) use of alcohol or drugs and the addict whose craving for speed or heroin leads him or her to commit crimes.

The risk assessment scale is an administrative policy, and judicial officials are not bound to follow it. Indeed, as we will demonstrate, judges and commissioners often ignore the scale, following instead their expert opinions regarding the youth and his or her case. The statutory changes that we discuss next are a different story, however, because many of them either eliminate or greatly reduce judicial discretion.

The Criminal Street Gang Statutes

In 1994, the Arizona legislature enacted statutes (Arizona Revised Statutes [A.R.S.] 13-2308 et seq.) that made participation in a criminal street gang a crime. The criminal street gang is defined as: "an ongoing formal or informal association of persons whose members or associates individually or collectively engage in the commission, attempted commission, facilitation or solicitation of any felony act and who has at least one individual who is a criminal street gang member" (A.R.S. 13-105(7)). A criminal street gang member, in turn, is an individual to whom two of the following seven criteria apply: (a) self-proclamation; (b) witness testimony or official statement; (c) written or electronic correspondence; (d) paraphernalia or photographs; (e) tattoos; (f) clothing or colors; and (g) any other indicia of street gang membership (A.R.S. 13-105(8)). Although being a gang member is not technically a crime, if the group is defined as a criminal syndicate, then participation in the syndicate is a class two felony, and assisting a criminal syndicate is a class four felony. If an offense is committed for the benefit of, at the direction of, or in association with any criminal street gang with the intent to promote, further, or assist criminal conduct by the gang, assisting the syndicate moves up to a class three felony (A.R.S. 13-2308 (D) and (E)).

Gang membership may also be an aggravating factor. For example, threatening or intimidating behavior moves from a class one misdemeanor to a class four felony if it is done "to promote, further or assist in the interests of or to cause, induce or solicit another person to participate in a criminal street gang, a criminal syndicate or a racketeering enterprise" (A.R.S. 13-1202 (A3)). Similarly, "discharging a firearm at an occupied structure in order to assist, promote or further the interests of a criminal street gang, a criminal syndicate or a racketeering enterprise" becomes a class three felony rather than a class four felony or misdemeanor (A.R.S. 13-3102 (A9)).

Finally, gang membership may result in a sentence enhancement. A.R.S. 13-604(T) stipulates:

> A person convicted of committing any felony offense with the intent to promote, further or assist any criminal conduct by a criminal street gang shall not be eligible for suspension of sentence, probation, pardon or release from confinement on any basis except as authorized by section 31-233, subsection A or B until the sentence imposed by the court has been served, the person is eligible for release pursuant to section 41-1604.07 or the sentence is commuted. *The presumptive, minimum and maximum sentence for the offense shall be increased by three years. The additional sentence imposed pursuant to this subsection is in addition to any enhanced sentence that may be applicable* (emphasis added).

While these laws are directed at adults, they affect juveniles by virtue of the fact that no independent body of law regarding acts of juvenile delinquency exists, at least not in Arizona. Juveniles are prosecuted for the same transgressions against community mores for which adults are prosecuted. The difference is that, in the case of juveniles, the offenses are referred to as acts of delinquency rather than as crimes.

These statutes affect juveniles in two ways. First, an offense such as threatening and intimidating, which is normally a misdemeanor, is enhanced to a felony if it is committed as part of a gang activity. This felony enhancement means an additional point on the juvenile's risk assessment score, in addition to the point for gang membership. Adding two points in this way could easily shift affected youths into the category where recommendations of incarceration are likely.

The second way in which this statute can affect juveniles is in the decision to request a transfer to the adult court (see generally Fagan and Zimring 2000). While transfers continue to be extremely unusual for juveniles charged with misdemeanors, in November of 1996, Arizona voters ratified a referendum proposed by the governor that provides for *automatic* transfer of juveniles 15 years or older who commit certain felonies. When a juvenile is charged with an offense that has been enhanced to a felony because of alleged gang involvement, a transfer request becomes even more likely. As a set, then, these laws increase the penalties for offenses committed by individuals who have been identified as gang members, *solely because of that identification.*

DATA AND METHODS

In 1996, we interviewed four defense attorneys who had worked for several years with juveniles, asking their views about the effects of gang membership on juvenile court processing and sanctioning decisions. Three of the attorneys interviewed are white males, the fourth is a Latino male who grew up in a part of Phoenix known for multigenerational neighborhood gangs. The interviews with defense attorneys were all conducted by the second author, who is himself a juvenile defense attorney. The semistructured interviews were tape recorded and later transcribed and ranged from thirty minutes to just over one hour (see further Krecker 1996).

Also in 1996 and 1997, we interviewed nine Maricopa County (Phoenix) juvenile court judges or commissioners and eight juvenile probation officers. Of the nine judicial officers interviewed, three were juvenile court judges and six were juvenile court commissioners. In this court, commissioners handle most of the same cases as judges, but there are three important distinctions between judges and commissioners. First, only judges and commissioners who have been assigned as pro tem judges have the authority to rule on transfers to criminal (i.e., adult) court. Second, judges are appointed by the governor and retain their jobs for life unless they are impeached by the legislature or draw less than 50 percent of the vote in an unopposed retention election held every six years. No judge has lost such a retention election in recent decades. Commissioners, in contrast, are appointed by the presiding judge and serve at his or her pleasure. Third, judges tend to rotate through various courts (e.g., criminal, juvenile, domestic relations, probate) every few years, while commissioners tend to remain in juvenile court for longer periods. Nevertheless, two of the commissioners interviewed have since been assigned to different divisions. We included them in the sample because we felt that their lengthy experience, in combination with their new distance from the juvenile court, might offer unique perspectives.

All three judges interviewed, including the then-presiding judge, are white males. Of the commissioners, three are white, two are Latina, and one is black. Three of the commissioners are male and three are female. These nine judges and commissioners represented approximately half of the seventeen judicial officers in the Maricopa County Juvenile Court. The judges and commissioners selected for interviews all had considerable experience in juvenile court, represent a range of juridical perspectives, and reflect the diversity among judicial officials in terms of race, ethnicity, and gender.

Four of the probation officers interviewed are female and four are male. One is Latino, one black, and the remaining six are white. They are highly experienced officers, having worked in juvenile probation for a minimum of five and a maximum of twenty years and having rotated through several departments (e.g., detention, transfer, field) over the years.

Semistructured interviews with judges, commissioners, and probation officers were conducted by the first author. All interviews took place in the court building, either in respondents' offices or in the cafeteria or courtyard. There are two juvenile court facilities in the county, and judicial officers and probation officers from each facility were included. Interviews were tape recorded and later transcribed. They lasted from one to three hours, averaging two hours.

In addition to the formal interviews, we draw on the second author's experience working in this court over a period of six years and on informal discussions held with judges, defense attorneys, and probation officers regarding the effects of gang membership, and allegations of gang membership, on court processing and sanctioning decisions.

After completion of the interviews, we realized that while we had soft data from judicial officials attesting to perceptions that most of the youth appearing before them who had been identified as gang members were Latino, these were impressionistic. Recognizing the need for more systematic information, the juvenile court allowed us to collect data from probation officers' current case files. The Office of Juvenile Probation provided us with a list of all probation officers (POs) who had caseloads in zip codes with at least ten Hispanic probationers. We conducted telephone interviews with these POs in September and October of 1999. Our telephone survey yielded a sample of thirty-eight probation officers, for a response rate of 67 percent with no call-backs.[3] As we discuss later, we asked POs to look through their current files and determine what percentage of the Latinos and Latinas in their caseloads had been identified as gang-affiliated by the police or some other social control agent. We also asked POs with extensive experience additional questions about the relationship between ethnicity and gang membership, and we supplemented these data with information from the National Curriculum Training Institute, which conducts specialized courses for gang-identified youths referred by the juvenile court. This institute provided us with a racial/ethnic distribution of its caseload in 1999, which, as we shall demonstrate, is very similar to the data provided by the most experienced probation officers.

In the sections that follow, we first examine the probation department and National Curriculum Training Institute data to ascertain whether, in fact, allegations of gang membership in the Phoenix metropolitan area disproportionately target Latino and Latina youths. Then, we turn to the interview data regarding allegations of gang membership and the risk that these allegations may be systematically linked to race/ethnicity. We also asked judges, commissioners, probation officers, and defense attorneys about the anti-gang initiatives, including whether they thought that the initiatives might have racially disparate impacts and if such disparities were reasonable in their opinion.

THE OVERREPRESENTATION OF LATINOS AND LATINAS IN GANG STATISTICS

On their face, the gang policies and statutes are race neutral. If they are invoked primarily for youths of color or if they systematically contribute to the overrepresentation of minority youths, however, then we must question this neutrality. Given the racial disparities in Arizona's juvenile justice system (Bortner et al. 1993; Harker 1999), it would be surprising if the effects of these policies were not felt disproportionately by youths of color. If most of the youths who are alleged to be members of gangs are Latino/a or African American, then these policies and statutes will necessarily fall most harshly on youths of color. That is, if belonging to a gang results in a harsher sentence and if most youths identified as gang members are Latino or black, then youths of color will, in part *because* they are Latino or black, receive harsher sentences.

The National Curriculum Training Institute offers a specialized course for gang-identified youths referred by the juvenile court. Of the 613 gang-identified youths in the institute's files in October 1999, 76.35 percent, or fully three-quarters of the youths, were Latino/a. Another 5.71 percent were African American, 1.63 percent were American Indian, 13.38 percent were white, 0.49 percent were coded "other," and 1.8 percent were coded "don't know."

To more fully assess the relationship between Latino ethnicity and allegations of gang membership, we asked the probation officers: *What percentage of the Hispanic males on your current caseload have been identified as gang members or affiliates?* Responses ranged from a low of zero to a high of 100 percent, with a mean of 51.78 percent, standard deviation of 30.62, and a median of 55 percent. We next asked: *What percentage of the Hispanic females on your current caseload have been identified as gang members or affiliates?* Again the responses ranged from a low of zero to a high of 100 percent, with a mean of 43.31 percent, standard deviation of 38.54, and a median of 50 percent. The percentages for females, it should be noted, were typically based on small numbers since the probation caseloads are heavily male. For example, a probation officer might have a caseload of 20 youths, only three of whom are female. Throughout we see that while the means and medians were not far apart, the standard deviations are very large, indicating substantial variation in responses. Overall the highest numbers were in intensive probation caseloads, which ranged from 80 percent to 100 percent gang-affiliated for both Hispanic males and females.

Finally, we asked juvenile probation officers with five or more years experience to think beyond their current caseloads, departments, or geographic areas and give us their overall impressions. Specifically, we asked the nineteen experienced probation officers: *Imagine a room full of youths, all of whom had been identified as gang members or affiliates. What percentage of those youths are Latino or Latina, and what percentage are African American?* The responses are quite instructive. Recalling that our respondents for this question were all experienced probation officers, their estimates ranged from a low of 45 percent Latino/a to a high of 90 percent Latino/a, with a mean of 65.7 percent, standard deviation of 13.72, and a median of 60 percent. Considering the percentage of gang identified youths who were Latino/a *or* African American, the responses ranged from a *low* of 75 percent to a high of 100 percent, with a mean of 89.55 percent, standard deviation of 7.21, and median of 90 percent. One of the most compelling points we note about these estimates is how much smaller the variation has become. The general agreement, thus, is that for the most part when we talk about youths who have been identified as gang affiliated in the Phoenix area, we are talking almost totally about youths of color, and the vast majority are Latino or Latina.

Stark as these numbers are, we must add that several probation officers warned us during the telephone interviews that the figures they were giving us were conservative estimates. Also, as one PO reminded us, "the serious cases and older kids aren't in our caseloads—they've already gone up to adult court."

It is important to note the high percentages of gang involvement for the girls in the probation data. Approximately half of the Latinos *and Latinas* who appear in juvenile court are thought to be gang affiliated. While some research has explored the lives of girls who are involved with gangs (see Curry 1998 for an overview), most scholarship on gangs addresses particular constructions of masculinity, not femininity. The growing recognition on the part of police, prosecutors, the media, and criminologists that female gang members are not just accomplices or sexual partners of male gang members suggests that girls and young women are now far more likely to receive harsher court sanctions than ever before. And like their male counterparts, we see that the females who are subject to the anti-gang initiatives are primarily Latina and African American (see also Chesney-Lind and Hagedorn 1999).

WHAT DO JUDICIAL OFFICERS, PROBATION OFFICERS, AND DEFENSE ATTORNEYS SAY ABOUT THE ANTI-GANG INITIATIVES?

Since all later actions come into play only after a youth has been identified as a "known or suspected gang member," we begin our analysis of the interview data by examining perceptions of the process by which gang members are identified, and particularly the court's willingness to accept police allegations. We turn next to perceptions of the risk assessment scale, which adds a point for gang membership, and of the statutes criminalizing participation in street gangs and enhancing sentences for gang-related offenses. Finally, we will address concerns raised by a few judges regarding the December 1996 Court of Appeals decision, which allows police officers to testify as expert witnesses about defendants' alleged gang affiliations. We focus particular attention on the perceptions held by judges and commissioners since they are the ultimate decision makers, noting any instances where POs or defense attorneys espouse differing opinions.

Identifying Gang Members

Defense attorneys who represent delinquent youths feel that allegations of gang membership are made fortuitously, and they are concerned about the ramifications of these accusations. These lawyers are often doubtful of the seriousness of the juvenile's gang affiliation (see also Krecker 1996). One lawyer who grew up in an inner-city neighborhood saw gang members as:

Poor lost souls. A bunch of kids hanging on to each other. This is a personal thing that comes to my mind. After a ship goes down and there is a piece of driftwood over here and there is a group of people that all come to that driftwood, they're all hugging for dear life, and that's the way I look at gangs—lost souls in the same geographical area clinging to each other because they are all afraid to let go.

When asked if allegations by the police or prosecutor are sufficient to conclude that the boy or girl truly is involved with gangs, one judicial officer replied:

For me to come to the conclusion that it is? *No*, but that is the initial information we receive. And sometimes that's right, and sometimes that's wrong. Sometimes there is no way to determine if it is right or wrong. Kids are identified as members of gangs by their dress, by their associations, and that, in my opinion, is not always totally correct. Kids, I would find, got involved in gangs for a lot of different reasons. Some kids were, more importantly, *identified* with gangs for a lot of different reasons. Kids would tend to dress like others, style their hair like others, act like others. These other people might have been identified as gang members, and admitted that they were gang members, and because these other children were seen with them, they were then stamped also as gang members.

Over and over, the judicial officers repeated to us that allegations of gang membership in the police reports are simply "not sufficient—it is an allegation, it is not proven." The key problem they identify with police allegations of gang membership is, "it's classic hearsay." Almost every judicial officer told us that they would not accept the police report as definitive because the information in it was obtained second- or thirdhand.

Several judicial officers and POs noted that if they had grown up in neighborhoods where gangs were prevalent, they too would have joined, whether for protection or because "you wouldn't have any friends otherwise; there isn't anyone else to play with." For these judges, commissioners, and POs, gang membership itself is not that important. Their concern is with the child's *behavior*, not his or her style of dress or with whom she or he hangs out. Some of the judicial officers' comments are instructive: "I don't give much credence to a reference to gang involvement. I wouldn't give much weight to gang involvement." And:

Gang activity doesn't enhance my sentences. I don't consider it a factor unless you can prove that he's a gang leader, and he's ordered some drive-bys or he's actually been caught selling drugs as part of a gang. You've got to show me that there's some inherent activity in that gang that's delinquent or anti-social, because I don't think just because a kid is a member of a gang it makes him a bad kid.

Another judicial officer, who has since rotated to another court, said:

I have to tell you, for me personally, whether they were or were not members of a gang did not necessarily influence my decision as to what should happen. Now I understand the law is changing a little bit, and identification as a gang member is going to enhance some of the penalties. But I tried to treat each child, each person as an individual ... and it wasn't really that important to me whether a child was identified as a gang member or not identified as a gang member. What was important to me was behavior.

These data suggest three key elements that influence how the judicial officers think about allegations that the youth is a gang member. The first issue is the veracity of the allegations: Is the youth truly a member of a gang? The second issue is the extent to which he or she is seriously involved with gangs and committing offenses because of that involvement. As several judges and commissioners pointed out, they see themselves as focusing on the youths' behaviors, not on labels that the police might attach and probation reports reify. Third, the judges and commissioners look at the context of the youths' lives. They recognize that in some neighborhoods most youths identify with a particular gang, and so simply identifying with a neighborhood gang may not influence their judgment greatly.

Until recently, judges and commissioners had relatively unlimited discretion in juvenile court. If allegations of gang membership were made in the absence of evidence that the youth was heavily involved in gangs and committing serious, violent offenses as a result, they did not have to sentence the youth more harshly. Indeed, research conducted in the early 1980s on this same court found that gang allegations had little effect on judicial officers' decisions (see Zatz 1985, 1987). This changed in the mid-1990s, however, with introduction of the risk assessment scale, the statutory enhancements for gang membership, and appellate court decisions affirming both these enhancements and the introduction of police officers as expert witnesses regarding gangs.

Perceptions of the Risk Assessment Scale

While the risk assessment scale developed by the Department of Juvenile Corrections is supposed to guide the judicial officer in sentencing the youth, the reality, we discovered, is quite different. Every probation officer we spoke with dutifully completed the forms, but they tend not to take it very seriously, commenting "gang member's just a piece of information we're giving in court." Even those probation officers who accept the scale values as reasonable were lukewarm in their praise. The following quote from a probation officer with twelve years experience is fairly typical of this perspective: "Well, I think that it is legitimate. I mean, as long as you are pretty sure that they are gang members and you're not just guessing. Some people think every kid that wears baggy pants is a gang member, and that's not true."

In contrast, another probation officer with over fifteen years experience said of the risk assessment scale:

It's really not something that I'm going to base my recommendation on. And I don't think it should be. I think it's just information. I've got to base it on my experience, the nature of the offense, what his previous history is like, whether or not he is amenable to treatment in the system, his age. All those things are factors. You can always look at, some people may look at "gang" and say that he is entrenched in a gang, and say there is no hope. And I think that's a real dangerous way to proceed on evaluating anything. . . . I know I don't do that. I know the people I work with do not do that.

The judges and commissioners were far more openly critical. They almost uniformly disdained the scale. One judicial officer called it "pathetic." A second described it as "deeply flawed . . . I don't know of a judge in the State of Arizona that thinks it's worth the paper it's written on." A third judicial officer said it was "fraught with problems." Yet another noted that the scale was developed by the Department of Juvenile Corrections and "supposedly validated based on recidivism, but it's not being used as a recidivism tool. It's being used to determine how long a child should stay in custody in a custody-treatment facility. These are two different things."[4]

Several judicial officers dismissed the scale as invalid. They had seen instances where juveniles had committed serious offenses, such as drive-by shootings or high-speed chases with stolen cars, and had received risk assessment scores of zero "because they don't smoke and they go to school. I mean, that's crazy!" A judicial officer recounted the case of a child charged with two offenses—stealing his father's gun and giving it to a youth in the neighborhood who was heavily involved with gangs, and possessing marijuana for sale in a high school. The boy received a "one" on the scale. Judicial officers also noted cases that cut the other way, where youths had accumulated four or five points on the scale but, when they looked at all of the information available and talked with the youths, they did not think the cases warranted commitment to a secure facility.

Nevertheless, a few judicial officers thought inclusion of gang membership in the risk assessment scale was appropriate. For example, we were told:

Well, it's a risk factor. They are at higher risk of re-offending. It's just one of the risk factors that you consider, just like you consider living in a single parent family or if the parent's an alcoholic or a drug addict, is the kid a dropout, is there a lack of education in the family, is there poverty, is there risk of abuse in the family, previous molestations. It's just one of the factors you are going to consider putting the kid at risk of re-offense or vulnerable in the society. . . . That's pretty well documented, you can identify high risk kids based on certain situations. I think it's *completely* appropriate.

Another said, "When I see it there it is a red flag, I'll ask questions. I take it into consideration, but you weigh and you balance the situation."

Some judicial officers questioned the scale's effectiveness, regardless of whether or not it is a valid measure. For example, a judicial officer commented:

It is supposed to be a deterrent, a deterrent to gang activity.

(Do you think it works that way?)

No, I do not believe it. I don't believe that sentence enhancements of that kind are a deterrent to gang activity any more than I believe that capital punishment is a deterrent to murder. And again I go back to my initial thoughts to you, that I believe that the effort to control gang activity is misdirected.

Overall, the judicial officers were in agreement that some of the behaviors thought to be correlated with gang involvement—namely, drugs and violence—were serious problems. That youths choose to belong to a particular group, however, does not bother most of them. In expressing her own views, one of the judicial officers nicely summarized what most of her colleagues had told us as well:

Just because it says it in a police report or because so-and-so says it, doesn't mean it's true. I can wear whatever color I want to wear, and I should be able to. And I can put tattoos on my body if I want to. And I should be able to, too. What I *can't* do is get together with someone else and sell some crack, or whatever. So you have to tie that to something illegal, and I think it's the responsibility of the court to be asking these questions.

It is the illegal behavior, in other words, and not the friendships, that court officials stress should be the focus of their attention. Having established their views about the scale, we turn next to their views about whether inclusion of gang membership in the risk assessment scale discriminates against youths of color.

Defense attorneys, probation officers, judges, and commissioners uniformly agreed that Latino/a youths, and to a lesser extent African-American youths, were disproportionately likely to be identified as gang members. As one commissioner noted, "95 percent of the youths identified as gang members in this court are Hispanic." Yet judicial officers disagree about what to do with this information. For some, it simply reaffirms their sense that poor youth of color are committing disproportionate numbers of serious offenses, and so it seems reasonable that they appear in court and in juvenile correctional facilities in disproportionate numbers. Others take this a step further, stating both that there is a disproportionate amount of crime occurring in poor communities of color *and* that government officials and community leaders need to do more to reduce the many social and economic difficulties facing the youths and their families (see similarly Zatz and Portillos 2000). For example:

The fact that they may be black or Latino is not an issue. I want this problem dealt with. I want money thrown at it. I want us to be serious about it. These problems in the minority communities go on and on, with no solutions forever. ... The answer is to eliminate the need for the problem by eliminating the problems people face in the minority communities that make them do this type of thing.

Another judicial officer stated:

Gang policies don't account for the disproportionality, violent crimes do. I think what you'll find is there are more black and Hispanic kids in the system, but I think there's a lot more violent offenses being committed by them. Not to say the white kids don't commit violent offenses too, but I don't see as much of it.

Yet another judicial officer said:

There are a lot of minority kids and adults throughout the criminal justice system. Why are they there? They're there because they've been caught committing a crime and been found guilty. . . . It's not like they're being picked on and thrown in jail because they're black or Mexican or something like that. It's because they're committing these crimes.

And finally:

I would be surprised if gang involvement was a significant accelerating factor in the overrepresentation of minorities. The truth is, any rational system used to evaluate juveniles committing serious crime will end up overrepresenting minorities. We've got to deal with overrepresentation by prevention, and by culturally appropriate intervention and treatment.

This judicial officer, like many others, kept coming back to what he wished they could do: improve the schools in inner-city neighborhoods, provide after-school sports and other organized activities for youths, offer older youths and their parents more job opportunities, and provide more support for distressed families. He concluded, "If you took these kids and gave them more of what a kid ought to have; they wouldn't be in gangs, and they wouldn't be in crimes."

In contrast, several judges and commissioners were very concerned that the anti-gang initiatives might further racial disparities. For example, "Sure it's biased. It overrepresents minorities, if you look at minorities as a percentage of the juvenile population. But that doesn't tell you a whole lot. The truth is there *are* more minority kids in gangs. The question is, what kinds of gangs, and what does it mean?" Another judicial officer reiterated, "Sure I'm concerned about that. . . . I think this goes back to what I was saying before, that the judges have to look at this very critically. That [gang membership] is a big accusation, and you'd better be able to prove it."

One of the key concerns raised by judges and commissioners who were worried about racial disparities was the possibility of biases arising in the prosecutor's office. How the prosecutor chooses to charge a case is very important, and questions of bias at this stage are quite serious. One judicial officer offered an example of a situation that bothered him greatly:

There's been a case recently where I had an Anglo, a 16-year-old, in a car accident, kill someone. It was a transfer request. The charge initially was vehicular manslaughter. Both the probation officer and the psychologist recommended against transfer. There was another, a Chicano youth, two years younger, two people were killed. He's charged with first-degree murder. The transfer report from the probation department and the psychologist's report recommended for transfer. That definitely impacted my decision *not* to transfer. I mean, it just jumped out at you. We've had at least one other judge raise this concern with the County Attorney's office a few years ago, that he feels that they have a discriminatory charging policy. I think it definitely is.

Thus, everyone we interviewed acknowledged that youths of color appear in court and are sentenced to incarceration in secure facilities in disproportionate numbers and also that allegations of gang membership are ascribed disproportionately to Latino and Latina youths. Yet while some judicial officials and probation officers accepted these disparities as reasonable, offering only mild criticisms of the failure of government officials to address the many problems facing residents of poor communities, others are deeply concerned about overly zealous policing and prosecutorial biases resulting in racially disparate practices.

Whatever factors they focus on—the amount of crime committed by minority youths, community problems, or racial biases in the criminal and juvenile justice system—the judges and commissioners still retain discretion regarding how they will use the risk assessment scores. The statutory sentence enhancements that began in criminal court and eventually found their way down to juvenile court are, however, a different matter.

Perceptions of the Criminal Street Gang Statutes

A probation officer with fifteen years experience talked about the anti-gang statutes in the following terms:

I think it's an underlying racially discriminatory policy. . . . I think it's so subtle that if you don't recognize it, it's coming back to haunt us now. As far as I'm concerned, this initiative is not about juvenile crime; it's about who is committing the juvenile crime. And I think it's racially motivated.

The big problem with this statute, in the eyes of the court, is that it is really a conspiracy law, but prosecutors try to use it without supplying evidence that a criminal conspiracy exists. While youth gangs might operate in some cities as serious drug distribution networks (Jankowski 1991; Padilla 1993), in Phoenix the Latino/a gangs are not that well organized. There is considerable concern on the part of some that it may someday reach this stage, but most if not all of the Phoenix gangs are "turf" gangs rather than businesses.[5] And if the purpose of the gang is not criminal, then it is not a criminal conspiracy. As one judicial officer noted: "How are you going to prove that the object of the gang is criminal, and not getting high, hanging out, meeting girls—or boys? A police officer comes in and says X, Y, and Z are gang members. Then you start listening to testimony. There are three people in this gang and they're all twelve!"

Conspiracy law, the judges and commissioners stressed, is quite complex. Successfully prosecuting a conspiracy case typically requires "all kinds of deals with informants, a lot of surveillance. That's not happening with this gang stuff. There's no surveillance, there's no videotaped meetings, there are no insiders coming in to testify." Another judicial officer commented on the political context within which the gang statutes were developed: "It has political meaning far beyond its practical meaning. I don't see it as something that particularly helps or particularly hurts in dealing with gangs. Like a lot of crime legislation, it makes people feel better and so they support it in the mistaken belief it'll help." Similarly, a judicial officer stated, "I get the feeling this whole gang law came into effect because of *our* fear of black groups, Hispanic groups of young men." African-American and Latino/a youths who hang out in parks because they do not have other, less visible, places to congregate (e.g., suburban malls, movie theaters, skating rinks) are likely to be identified as gang members. While some white youths have been identified as gang members, for the most part their activities are seen as innocuous, if they are even noticed at all.

Several judges and commissioners referred to gangs as the "soup du jour" or "crime du jour" of the criminal justice system. It is, they said, the crime of the year. The governor and state legislature are intent on being "tough" on crime, and the emphasis on gangs is one way of demonstrating that they are "tough." Nevertheless, at the time of our interviews the criminal gang statutes were not being invoked very often. A judicial officer commented, "I think I've seen the criminal gang charge once." Another said, "My impression is, it's rarely used." From conversations with juvenile court officials since then, it seems that use of these statutes has not increased markedly, probably because direct-file transfers to adult court became automatic for many offenses in 1996, removing those youths from the juvenile court's jurisdiction.

The Appellate Court Decisions

Throughout our discussions regarding the risk assessment scale and the anti-gang statutes, the judicial officers consistently raised the juridical question of *proof*. From their perspective, the key problem with these initiatives, and particularly the adult statute since it is an explicit sentence enhancement, is that they require proof of conspiracy, and generally the only evidence available is hearsay reported by the police. How, they ask, are you going to prove that the youths formed this group to conspire to commit a crime?

In *State of Arizona v. Baldenegro*, the prosecution sought to do so by having a police officer testify as an expert witness that Carson 13 was a gang, and that Miguel Baldenegro was a member. The officer "based his opinions on personal observations and experience, the observations of other officers in the department, police reports, and conversations with other gang members. He also identified several photographs of Carson 13 members, including Baldenegro, 'throwing gang signs' and otherwise displaying their affiliation with Carson 13" (*State of Arizona v. Baldenegro* 1996, 61). The defense appealed, contending that the statutes defining criminal street gangs and gang members are vague and overly broad and that the trial court abused its discretion when it admitted the police officer's so-called expert testimony as evidence. The Court of Appeals found that the evidence was admissible, noting that the trial court has broad discretion in ruling on evidentiary matters. The difficulty, as one judicial officer warned us, is:

It's new stuff, and no one knows what to make of it. And it's very individualized—each hearing officer really has discretion, and then again you have to have an objection. If there's no objection made (by the defense to having a police officer testify as an expert witness), the jury can hear it.

This was a serious concern to some of the judges. As the judicial officer who initially brought this case to our attention said:

I'm not happy with the Court of Appeals decision. I think it opens it up to hearsay that's not really subject to challenge. I don't think we should make it easier to prove these things, I think we should in fact make it more difficult. . . . It's just a matter of proof. It requires more work. Prosecutors should say to police agencies, 'No, go back and get me an insider who will tell me, when did this gang start? How are they initiated?' I want that testimony, I don't just want a police officer coming up six weeks later and testifying that it's a gang.

He felt quite strongly, as did other judicial officers, that the prosecution needed evidence that a criminal conspiracy existed that was independent of a police officer's hearsay. He viewed this as a particularly dangerous precedent because police agencies may have vested interests in the outcomes: "I don't know what the funding of police agencies is, but I suspect most of these gang squads are getting extra funding because they have gangs. . . . So I've got a so-called expert coming in that has an interest in perpetuating his expertise or her expertise."

Since the *Baldenegro* decision in 1996, others have also tried to challenge the anti-gang statutes on constitutional grounds. *State of Arizona v. Ochoa* and *State of Arizona v. Torres Mercado*, both decided in 1997, contended that the statutes defining criminal street gangs and gang members are vague and overly broad; that they infringe on freedom of expression and rights of assembly; that the trial courts abused their discretion when they admitted expert testimony of police officers, since their testimony allows for hearsay rather than direct evidence that a criminal conspiracy exists; and that receiving a sentence for assisting a criminal street gang and a sentence enhancement for a gang-related offense amount to double punishment. The appellate courts have rejected each of these appeals, reaffirming that the trial judge may decide whether or not to admit the expert testimony and that jurors could always ignore the testimony and base their decisions on other evidence.

In sum, the defense attorneys, judicial officers, and probation officers we interviewed expressed concerns about the standards of proof used by police to identify gang members and by prosecutors in presenting evidence that the gangs are criminal syndicates that exist for the purpose of committing crimes. Nor do they think much of the risk assessment scale developed by the Department of Juvenile Corrections. A few judges and commissioners agonized over the possibility of racial biases in the prosecutor's office. Yet as a whole they were not particularly concerned that their decisions may contribute to systematic racial biases, seeing themselves as acting on the basis of the information brought forward in each individual case.

CONCLUSIONS

Is the war on gangs racialized policy? Approximately half of the Latino boys and Latina girls appearing on the probation officers' caseloads have been identified by the police or some other social control agent as gang affiliated. When experienced probation officers are asked the racial/ethnic distribution of alleged gang members, they say that at least two-thirds are Latino or Latina and about 90 percent are Latino/a or black. These figures are reaffirmed by the National Curriculum Training Institute casefiles, which demonstrate that 76 percent of the youths referred to the program are Latino/a. Thus in Arizona, "gang member" is almost synonymous with "Latino/a."

If ascriptions of gang membership did not carry penalties, defining gang membership in racialized ways might be innocuous. That is, if gang members commit crime, they get punished for the crime, the same as anyone else. But allegations of gang membership do carry added penalties, at least in Arizona. As we have seen, they add a point to the risk assessment scale, and statutory charge and sentence enhancements are attached to gang membership. Thus we have a situation where Latino boys and girls are likely to be identified as gang members, gang membership in turn is assumed to be a Latino phenomenon, and being identified as a gang member increases the severity of sanctions. We must ask how this differs, in effect even if not in intent, from saying that the severity of sanctions is increased for Latinos?

A comparison to the war on drugs may be instructive. The war on drugs, and especially the starkly disparate sentences for crack versus powder cocaine, has been widely criticized as racialized policy (Diaz-Cotto 1996; Donziger 1996; Lusane 1991; Mauer 1995; Miller 1996; Tonry 1995). Even the United States Sentencing Commission and several judges have argued that the war on drugs has played out in a racially biased manner (e.g., U.S. Sentencing Commission 1995; *U.S. v. Clary* 1994). Whether or not the ramifications of this war for poor black communities were recognized in advance, they certainly *could* have been. As Tonry (1995, 4) argues in his scathing critique of U.S. drug policy:

The rising levels of black incarceration did not just happen; they were the foreseeable effects of deliberate policies spearheaded by the Reagan and Bush administrations and implemented by many states. Anyone with knowledge of drug-trafficking patterns and of police arrest policies and incentives could have foreseen that the enemy troops in the War on Drugs would consist largely of young, inner-city minority males. . . . Although damaging the lives of countless young blacks was probably not their primary aim, the architects of the War on Drugs no doubt foresaw the result. Any conventional ethical analysis would hold them accountable for the consequences of their policies.

What makes Tonry's argument unique is that he presents it as an ethical dilemma: If you know that your policy will result in systematic racial disparities and you have other options besides that policy, is your policy immoral? Again quoting Tonry: *"The text may be crime. The subtext is race"* (1995, 6).

We suggest that a similar pattern of racialized effects of supposedly race-neutral policies has resulted from the anti-gang initiatives. At least in Arizona, we have seen that the war on gangs disproportionately affects Latino and Latina youths. Given the way in which gang membership is identified in Arizona, we conclude that the anti-gang policies and statutes discussed in this chapter would most definitely contribute to racial disparities in sentencing—if they were followed.

Anti-crime initiatives must always be understood in their social and political contexts. The measures discussed in this chapter arose in the midst of a conflict between the governor and the courts, and especially the juvenile court. This governor, who was later convicted of federal bank fraud, wanted to be seen as tough on crime. Perhaps because the juvenile court has had battles with the governor, the legislature, and the Department of Juvenile Corrections over these and other repressive crime control policies, all of which would reduce the juvenile judge's discretion, we find that as a group the judicial officers ignore these measures, which they perceive to be invalid, unreliable, and ineffective.

We found that judicial officers are extremely leery of the gang designation as applied to particular youths by the police. The judges and commissioners are reluctant to automatically apply the additional sanctions that the anti-gang initiatives call for. Instead, they try to look at each youth and his or her situation on a case-by-case basis and to adjudicate them as they would in the absence of the guidelines.

Our findings are consistent with research in this same court in the late 1970s and early 1980s, when Chicano gangs were first depicted as a serious problem. At that time, Zatz (1985, 1987) found that allegations of gang membership did not affect juvenile court sentencing of Chicano youths, with the exception of police requests for immediate detention of gang members. Certainly, the gang situation in Phoenix has changed since that earlier study, with the violence becoming more serious (Epler 1999; Zatz and Portillos 2000), but nonetheless we continue to see that juvenile judges in this jurisdiction do not attribute great weight to gang membership in and of itself.

What happens to cases transferred to adult court is, however, unknown. There is far less flexibility in adult court for considering what is best for the child. Moreover, our sense from comments we have heard from defense attorneys and probation officers in adult jurisdictions is that the anti-gang statutes are used much more frequently there by prosecutors seeking sentence enhancements. Whether or not judges in criminal court are more willing than their colleagues in juvenile court to accept the veracity of police allegations of gang membership and to sentence young people charged with gang offenses more severely remains, however, a topic for future study.

NOTES

We wish to thank the judges, commissioners, probation officers, and defense attorneys who gave so willingly of their time. We also thank the Maricopa County Office of Juvenile Probation (Phoenix, Arizona) for making available to us data on the relationship between ethnicity and allegations of gang membership.

1. We use the terms Latino/a and Latinos/as to include both males (Latino, Latinos) and females (Latina, Latinas).

2. The following items comprise the risk assessment scale:
   R1. Number of Referrals (1 to 4 = 0, 5+ = 1)
   R2. Number of Adjudications (1 or 2 = -1, 3 or 4 = 0, 5+ = 1)
   R3. Age at first referral (under 12 years 6 months = 1)
   R4. Petition offense history
      A. Assaultive offenses (2+ = 1)
      B. Drug offenses (2+ = 2)
      C. Property offenses (3+ = 1)
      D. Weapons offenses (1+ = 1)
   R5. Petitions for felony offenses (3+ = 1)
   R6. Gang affiliation (Y = 1, N = 0)
   R7. Enrolled in school (Y = -1, N = 0)
   R8. Use of alcohol/drugs (Y = 0, N = -1)

3. The 67 percent response rate is conservative, since some of the probation officers who did not call us back shared caseloads. To avoid duplication, we only took data from one officer if they shared caseloads, making 75 or 80 percent a more realistic response rate. Our response rate is quite high for one-shot telephone surveys, probably because the chief juvenile probation officer informed the officers that we might be calling and asking them to help us in our data collection efforts.

4. Perhaps because the Department of Juvenile Corrections (DOJC) had been under a federal court order to reduce overcrowding, some of the judicial officers were unsure how the scale actually affected length of stay. One judicial officer thought the DOJC used it to release children sooner, noting that the DOJC wanted "to keep the amount of kids down because they just don't have room." Another suggested that the DOJC devised the scale to keep juveniles incarcerated for a longer time.

5. Some probation officers and youth service providers have expressed concerns that Phoenix gangs, and particularly the Bloods and Crips, are becoming better organized as drug-dealing businesses, but there is general agreement among judicial officials and community residents that most Latino gangs in Phoenix are groups of youths who live in the same neighborhood and hang out together (see Zatz and Portillos 2000). We by no means dismiss the criminal activities they engage in as a group—the burglaries, car thefts, beer runs, assaults, and even drive-by shootings. Our point is simply that there is no evidence that they organized *for the purpose* of committing criminal acts.

REFERENCES

Belluck, Pam (1999). "Illinois town hopes to exile its gang members to Anywhere Else, U.S.A." *New York Times*, April 27, p. A16.

Bortner, M.A., Carol Burgess, Anne L. Schneider, and Andy Hall (1993). *Equitable Treatment of Minority Youth: A Report on the Over Representation of Minority Youth in Arizona's Juvenile Justice System*. Phoenix: Governor's Office for Children.

Chesney-Lind, and John Hagedorn, eds. (1999). *Female Gangs in America: Essays on Girls, Gangs, and Gender*. Chicago: Lakeview Press.

Curry, G. David (1998). "Female gang involvement." *Journal of Research in Crime and Delinquency* 35: 100–118.

Diaz-Cotto, Juanita (1996). *Gender, Ethnicity and the State: Latina and Latino Prison Politics.* Albany: State University of New York Press.

Donziger, Steven R., ed. (1996). *The Real War on Crime: The Report of the National Criminal Justice Commission.* New York: HarperCollins.

Epler, Patti (1999). "Gang influence runs deep in Phoenix's roots." *Phoenix New Times* September 16–22, pp. 27, 29.

Fagan, Jeffrey, and Franklin Zimring, eds. (2000). *The Changing Borders of Juvenile Justice: Transfer of Adolescents to the Criminal Court.* Chicago: University of Chicago Press.

Fishman, Laura T. (2002). "Images of crime and punishment: The black bogeyman and white self-righteousness." Pp. 177–191 in Coramae Richey Mann and Marjorie S. Zatz (eds.), *Images of Color, Images of Crime* (2nd ed.). Los Angeles: Roxbury Publishing Co.

Hagedorn, John M. (1991). "Gangs, neighborhoods, and public policy." *Social Problems* 38(4): 529–542.

Harker, Victoria (1999). "Minorities overload juvenile system." *Arizona Republic,* October 5, pp. B1, 8.

Hsia, Heidi M., and Donna Hamparian (1998). "Disproportionate minority confinement: 1997 update." *Juvenile Justice Bulletin.* Washington, DC: Office of Juvenile Justice and Delinquency Prevention, Department of Justice.

Jankowski, Martin Sanchez (1991). *Islands in the Street: Gangs and American Urban Society.* Berkeley: University of California Press.

Joe, Karen, and Meda Chesney-Lind (1995). "'Just every mother's angel': An analysis of gender and ethnic variations in youth gang membership." *Gender and Society* 9(4): 408–431.

Krecker, Richard P. (1996). "Perceptions of gang membership." Unpublished manuscript. Arizona State University.

Lusane, Charles (1991). *Pipe Dream Blues: Racism and the War on Drugs.* Boston: South End Press.

Mauer, Marc (1995). *Young Black Americans and the Criminal Justice System: Five Years Later.* Washington, DC: The Sentencing Project.

Miller, Jerome G. (1996). *Search and Destroy: African-American Males in the Criminal Justice System.* New York: Cambridge University Press.

Muwakkil, Salim (1993). "Ganging together." *In These Times,* April 5.

Office of Juvenile Justice and Delinquency Prevention (1997). *National Youth Gang Survey, 1996.* Washington, DC: Department of Justice.

Padilla, Felix (1993). *The Gang as an American Enterprise.* New Brunswick, NJ: Rutgers University Press.

Portillos, Edwardo L. (2002). "Images of crime and punishment: Latinos, gangs, and drugs." Pp. 192–200 in Coramae Richey Mann and Marjorie S. Zatz (eds.), *Images of Color, Images of Crime* (2nd ed.). Los Angeles: Roxbury Publishing Co.

Rubin, Bart H. (1998). "Hail, hail, the gangs are all here: Why New York should adopt a comprehensive anti-gang statute." *Fordham Law Review* 66 (April): 2033.

Russell, Katheryn (1998). *The Color of Crime: Racial Hoaxes, White Fear, Black Protectionism, Police Harassment, and Other Macroaggressions.* New York: New York University Press.

Sickmund, Melissa, Howard N. Snyder, and Eileen Poe-Yamagata (1997). *Juvenile Offenders and Victims: 1997 Update on Violence*. Washington, DC: Office of Juvenile Justice and Delinquency Prevention, Department of Justice.

Spergel, Irving A., and G. David Curry (1993). "The National Youth Gang Survey: A research and development process." Pp. 359–392 in A.P. Goldstein and C.R. Huff (eds.), *The Gang Intervention Handbook*. Champaign, IL: Research Press.

Tonry, Michael (1995). *Malign Neglect: Race, Crime, and Punishment in America*. New York: Oxford University Press.

United States Sentencing Commission (1995). *Materials Concerning Sentencing for Crack Cocaine Offenses* 57 CRL 2127, May 31.

Villa, Judi (1999). "Bad seeds or victims? Gang on trial, police hope to restrict it." *Arizona Republic*, December 23, pp. A1, A13.

Zatz, Marjorie S. (1985). "Los cholos: Legal processing of Chicano gang members." *Social Problems* 33(1): 13–30.

Zatz, Marjorie S. (1987). "Chicano youth gangs and crime: The creation of a moral panic." *Contemporary Crises* 11: 129–158.

Zatz, Marjorie S., and Edwardo L. Portillos (2000). "Voices from the barrio: Chicano/a gangs, families, and communities." *Criminology* 38(2): 369–401.

Zatz, Marjorie S., Donald Tibbs, and DeAnza Valencia (1999). "Anti-gang statutes and racial politics." Paper presented at the annual meeting of the American Society of Criminology, November.

CASES CITED

The State of Arizona v. Miguel Angel Baldenegro 188 Ariz. 10, 229 Arizona Advance Reports: 59–62, 932 P.2d 275 (1996).

The State of Arizona v. Rafael Torres Mercado 191 Ariz. 279, 955 P.2d 35 (1997).

The State of Arizona v. Manuel Ochoa 189 Ariz. 279, 943 P.2d 814 (1997).

U.S. v. Clary, 846 F. Supp. 768 (E.D. Mo. 1994), Rvd, 34 F.3d 709 (8th Cir. 1994), Cert. Denied, 115 S. C. 1172 (1995).

8

Sentencing of Drug Offenders in Three Cities: Does Race/Ethnicity Make a Difference?

Cassia C. Spohn and Jeffrey W. Spears

In *Malign Neglect*, Michael Tonry (1995, 105) argues that "Urban black Americans have borne the brunt of the War on Drugs." More specifically, he charges that "the recent blackening of America's prison population is the product of malign neglect of the war's effects on black Americans" (Tonry 1995, 115). Miller (1996, 83) similarly asserts that "The racial discrimination endemic to the drug war wound its way through every stage of the processing—arrest, jailing, conviction, and sentencing." These allegations suggest not only that racial minorities have been arrested for drug offenses at a disproportionately high rate, but also that black and Hispanic drug offenders have been sentenced more harshly than white drug offenders.

There is ample evidence in support of assertions that the War on Drugs has been fought primarily in minority communities. Between 1976 and 1996 the number of persons arrested for drug offenses more than doubled. The number of whites arrested for drug offenses increased by 85 percent, while the number of blacks arrested for these offenses increased fourfold.[1] The proportion of all drug arrestees who are black also increased, from 22 percent in 1976 to 39 percent in 1996 (Maguire and Pastore 1998). These racial differentials in arrest rates are reflected in statistics on prosecution, adjudication, and sentencing. In 1994, for example, over three-quarters of all felony defendants charged with drug offenses in the seventy-five largest cities in the United States were black (46 percent) or Hispanic (32 percent) (Bureau of Justice Statistics 1998a). Among offenders convicted of drug offenses in state courts, 50 percent of the blacks but only 33 percent of the whites were sentenced to prison; the mean sentence imposed on blacks also was nine months longer than the average sentence imposed on whites (Bureau of Justice Statistics 1998b). Similar disproportions are found at the federal level. In 1998, 41 percent of the offenders sentenced in U.S. district courts for drug offenses were Hispanic, 32.7 percent were black, and 24.2 percent were white (USSC 1999).

The disparities found at the federal level are compounded by the fact that federal sentencing guidelines for drug offenses differentiate between crack and powder cocaine. In fact, the guidelines treat crack cocaine as being one hundred times worse than powder cocaine: Possession of 500 grams of powder cocaine, but only five grams of crack, triggers a mandatory minimum sentence of five years. Critics charge that this policy, while racially neutral on its face, discriminates against black drug users and sellers. As Tonry (1995, 188) notes, "The problem with distinguishing between crack and powder cocaine in this way is that crack tends to be used and sold by blacks and powder by whites, which means that the harshest penalties are mostly experienced by blacks." Statistics compiled by the United States Sentencing Commission bear this out (USSC 1999). Among offenders sentenced for offenses involving crack cocaine, 84.8 percent were black, 8.7 percent were Hispanic, and 5.7 percent were white; moreover, the average sentence imposed on offenders convicted of offenses involving crack cocaine (122.4 months) was substantially longer than the average sentence imposed on offenders convicted of offenses involving powder cocaine (79.3 months).[2] Defenders of the powder-crack distinction, while not condoning its disparate effect on blacks, suggest that it should be viewed, not as a racist attempt to incarcerate increasing proportions of young black men, but as a sensible response "to the desires of law-abiding people—including the great mass of black communities—for protection against criminals preying on them" (Kennedy 1994, 1997).

The continuing controversy concerning the War on Drugs and its effect on racial minorities attests to the importance of empirical research examining the relationship between race/ethnicity and the sentences imposed on drug offenders. In this chapter, we use data on offenders convicted of drug offenses in Miami, Chicago, and Kansas City to test the hypothesis that blacks and Hispanics are sentenced more harshly than whites. We examine both the decision to incarcerate or not and the length of the prison sentence, and we test for interactive as well as additive race effects.

PREVIOUS RESEARCH

Research investigating the relationship between the defendant's race and sentence severity has not consistently supported the conflict perspective's contention that racial minorities will be sentenced more harshly than whites. Although a number of studies have uncovered such a link (Albonetti 1997; Holmes et al. 1996; Kramer and Ulmer 1996; Petersilia 1983; Steffensmeier et al. 1998; Zatz 1984), others have found either that there are no significant racial differences

(Klein et al. 1990) or that blacks are sentenced more leniently than whites (Bernstein et al. 1977; Gibson 1978; Levin 1972). The failure of research to produce uniform findings of racial discrimination in sentencing has led to conflicting conclusions. Some researchers (Hagan 1974; Kleck 1981; Pruitt and Wilson 1983) assert that racial discrimination in sentencing has declined over time and contend that the predictive power of race, once relevant legal factors are taken into account, is quite low. Hagan (1974) and Kleck (1981), for example, have suggested that the direct effect of race on sentence severity would disappear in models that adequately controlled for the offender's prior criminal record. A recent review of thirty-eight studies published since 1975, however, challenges this prediction. Chiricos and Crawford (1995) reported that many of the studies concluded that race had a direct effect on the decision to incarcerate or not and that this effect remained even after controlling for prior record and crime seriousness. Spohn's (2000) review of studies analyzing post-1980 sentencing decisions in state and federal courts reached a similar conclusion.

Other researchers (Klepper et al. 1983; Zatz 1987) claim that discrimination has not declined or disappeared but simply has become more subtle and difficult to detect. While not discounting the possibility of a direct racial effect, these researchers argue that race influences sentence severity *indirectly* through its effect on variables such as bail status (LaFree 1985b; Lizotte 1978), type of attorney (Spohn et al. 1981–1982) or type of disposition (LaFree 1985a; Spohn 1992; Uhlman and Walker 1980), or that race *interacts* with other variables and affects sentence severity only in some types of cases (Barnett 1985; Spohn and Cederblom 1991), in some types of settings (Chiricos and Crawford 1995; Hawkins 1987; Kleck 1981; Myers and Talarico 1986), or for some types of defendants (Chiricos and Bales 1991; LaFree 1989; Peterson and Hagan 1984; Spohn and Holleran 2000; Steffensmeier et al. 1998; Walsh 1987).

A number of scholars argue that the inconsistent findings of research on race and sentencing reflect both specification error and an overly simplistic view of conflict theory. These scholars have called for research designed to delineate more precisely the conditions under which defendant race influences judges' sentencing decisions. Zatz (1987, 83), for example, contends that models of the relationship between race and sentencing that exclude indirect or interactive effects are misspecified. She asserts that "research that tests only for main effects (i.e., overt bias) and does not investigate all of the possible manifestations of discrimination may erroneously conclude that discrimination does not exist when, in fact, it does."

Miethe and Moore (1986) also argue that an interactive model is more appropriate than an additive model in assessing racial discrimination in criminal justice decision making. They suggest that use of an additive model, which "presumes that no systematic variation exists within racial groups *and* that between-race differences are constant across levels of other social, case, and legal attributes" (Miethe and Moore 1986, 230), minimizes racial differences in case processing, while use of an interactive (or race-specific) model allows the researcher to discern differential treatment within and between racial groups.

Hawkins (1987, 721) presents an analogous but somewhat different argument. He argues that many of the so-called anomalies or inconsistencies in sentencing research reflect "oversimplification" of conflict theory. He contends that the work of early conflict theorists such as Quinney (1970) and Chambliss and Seidman (1971) does not support the proposition that "blacks or other nonwhites will receive more severe punishment than whites for all crimes, under all conditions, and at similar levels of disproportion over time" (Hawkins 1987, 724). Hawkins proposes a revision of the conflict perspective on race and sentencing to account for the possibility of interaction between defendant race and other predictors of sentence severity, and especially between defendant race, victim race, and the type of crime committed by the offender.

Researchers also have questioned the validity of studies that focus exclusively on sentencing decisions and ignore presentence charging and plea-bargaining decisions (Miethe and Moore 1986; Petersilia 1983; Thomson and Zingraff 1981). These researchers argue that sentence severity is significantly affected by charge reductions and sentence concessions and that failure to consider interactions between race, plea-bargaining decisions, and sentencing decisions will lead to misleading conclusions concerning the impact of race on sentencing. As Thomson and Zingraff (1981, 871) note,

If, as the research indicates, discrimination is concentrated in the earlier decision-making stages, research which does not account for the processual nature of decision making or which analyzes populations at just the later decision points will tend to produce findings of no discrimination.

This recommendation seems particularly important given the sentencing reforms promulgated during the past three decades. As states abandoned indeterminate sentencing in favor of determinate sentencing and sentencing guidelines, discretion shifted from the more visible sentencing process to the less visible and less regulated charging and plea bargaining process. If prosecutors take race/ethnicity into account in determining the type and severity of charges to file, a finding that the sentences imposed on whites, blacks, and Hispanics are similar once crime seriousness is taken into consideration would not necessarily be indicative of a racially neutral sentencing process.

Researchers have begun to heed these recommendations for theoretical and methodological improvements in sentencing research. There is a growing body of literature demonstrating that the relationship between race and sentencing is nonlinear and nonadditive. Researchers have shown, for instance, that the offender's race interacts with the offender's prior criminal record (Spohn and Cederblom 1991; Spohn et al. 1998; Kramer and Ulmer 1996) and employment status (Chiricos and Bales 1991; Nobiling et al. 1998; Spohn and Holleran 2000). Researchers also have shown that the racial composition of the offender/victim pair may be a better predictor of sentence severity than the race of the offender. A substantial body of research demonstrates that blacks who murder whites are much more likely to be sentenced to death than blacks who murder blacks or than whites who murder blacks or whites (Arkin 1980; Baldus et al. 1983, 1985; Bowers and Pierce 1980; Gross and Mauro 1989; Keil and Vito 1989; Paternoster 1984; Radelet 1981). Similarly, there is evidence that blacks who sexually assault whites are treated more harshly than are other defendants (LaFree 1989; Spohn 1994; Spohn and Spears 1996; Walsh 1987).

In addition, researchers have shown that racial minorities are treated more harshly than whites at early stages in the criminal justice process and have demonstrated that these early decisions lead to more punitive treatment at sentencing (Albonetti 1997; Maxfield and Kramer 1998; Spohn and DeLone 2000; Walker et al. 1999). Spohn and DeLone (2000), for example, found that in Chicago and Miami the probability of pretrial detention was substantially higher for blacks and Hispanics than for whites; more important, pretrial detention was a strong predictor of the likelihood of post-conviction imprisonment. In these two cities, then, black and Hispanic defendants were more likely than whites to suffer both the pains of imprisonment prior to trial and the consequences of pretrial detention at sentencing. Maxfield and Kramer's (1998) analysis of plea bargaining under the federal sentencing guidelines produced similar evidence of cumulative disadvantage for racial minorities. They found that blacks and Hispanics were less likely than whites to receive a downward departure for providing "substantial assistance" in another case; among offenders who did receive a departure, whites received a larger sentence reduction than either blacks or Hispanics.

Race and Sentencing of Drug Offenders

Although there are dozens of studies examining the relationship between race and sentencing, few of these studies focus explicitly on sentencing of drug offenders. Among those that do, the results are somewhat inconsistent. Some researchers find that black and Hispanic drug offenders are sentenced more harshly than white drug offenders (Albonetti 1997; Chiricos and Bales 1991; Crawford et al. 1998; Kramer and Steffensmeier 1993; Myers 1989; Unnever 1982). Other researchers conclude that there are few if any racial/ethnic differences or that racial minorities convicted of certain types of drug offenses are sentenced more leniently than their white counterparts (Peterson and Hagan 1984).

Two studies (Unnever 1982; Unnever and Hembroff 1988) compared the sentences imposed on white, black, and Hispanic offenders convicted of drug offenses in Miami during 1971. After controlling for relevant legal variables, Unnever (1982) found that black offenders were over two-and-a-half times more likely than white offenders to be sentenced to prison. There were, on the other hand, no significant differences in the sentences imposed on Hispanic and white drug offenders once controls for type of bail and whether the defendant was released prior to trial were added to the model. In a later study,

Unnever and Hembroff (1988) tested Hembroff's (1982) status characteristics theory. The authors argued that "the likelihood that racial/ethnic sentencing differentials will occur is influenced by whether or not the case-related attributes locate the case in an obvious dispositional category" (Unnever and Hembroff 1988, 63). To test this, they created ten hypothetical drug cases with varying levels of consistency in case and offender characteristics. Consistent with their prediction, they found that race/ethnicity was least likely to affect sentence severity when the case attributes clearly indicated that the appropriate sentence was either probation or prison. However, when the characteristics of the case did not consistently point toward a probation or prison sentence, racial/ethnic disparities were more likely to occur. Thus, according to the authors, the effect of the defendant's race/ethnicity on sentencing was conditioned by other case-related characteristics.

Peterson and Hagan (1984) make an analogous, but slightly different, argument. They point out that previous research has tended to treat the meaning of race as a constant and its effect on sentencing as if it were static. As a result, findings of more lenient treatment of racial minorities often are characterized as "anomalies." Peterson and Hagan (1984) challenge this conclusion. They assert that "the role of race is more variable and more complicated than previously acknowledged" and that "both differential severity and leniency are possible" (Peterson and Hagan 1984, 67–69). They note, for example, that blacks who victimize whites might be sentenced more harshly, but that blacks who victimize other blacks might be sentenced more leniently.

Peterson and Hagan contend that race-related perceptions of victims and offenders might similarly affect the sentences imposed on individuals convicted of *victimless* crimes. More to the point, they suggest that minority drug users, at least during some time periods, might be typed or characterized as victims rather than as villains, and that this distinction might result in more lenient sentences for minorities. If judges view minority youth as innocent targets of big-time dealers or professional traffickers, in other words, they might be reluctant to impose severe sentences on minority drug users. The authors also assert that leniency would be reserved for minority drug *users*; they suggest that "on those rare occasions when nonwhites do rise to the position of big dealers, the predicted leniency should ... disappear" (Peterson and Hagan 1984, 66).

To test these predictions, Peterson and Hagan examined the sentences imposed on drug offenders convicted in the Southern Federal District Court of New York from 1963 through 1976. They found that nonwhite drug users were sentenced more leniently than white drug users, but that nonwhite drug dealers received substantially longer prison sentences than white dealers. Nonwhite drug users were significantly less likely than white users to be sentenced to prison; moreover, those nonwhites who were sentenced to prison received sentences that averaged about six and one-half months shorter than the sentences received by whites. In contrast, the average sentence imposed on nonwhite big dealers was nineteen months longer than the mean sentence imposed on white dealers.

According to the authors, these results suggest that it is overly simplistic to expect all racial minorities to be sentenced more harshly than all whites. Rather, "there are patterns of advantage and disadvantage that only contextualized analyses can reveal" (Peterson and Hagan 1984, 69).

Myers (1989) examined the effect of race on sentences imposed on offenders convicted of three types of drug offenses—use, sales/distribution, and trafficking—in Georgia from 1977 to 1985. In 1980, Georgia criminalized drug trafficking and increased the penalties for repeat drug offenders. The new drug trafficking statutes also restricted judicial discretion, which, according to the author, should have minimized sentencing disparities between blacks and whites. Myers argued that this uniformity in sentencing would be most prevalent during the height of legislative activity (1980–1982), but would decrease thereafter as judges reverted to previous sentencing practices.

Myers' analysis revealed that black offenders were more likely than white offenders to be incarcerated, particularly for the more serious drug offenses. There was a 25 percentage point difference in the probabilities of incarceration between black offenders and white offenders for drug trafficking, compared to a 19 percentage point difference for drug distribution and a 12 percentage point difference for drug use. Contrary to her hypothesis that reducing judicial discretion would produce racially neutral sentence outcomes, Myers found that the racial differential was consistent and significant throughout the time period examined and actually was most pronounced in the midst of the reform effort. As she concluded (Myers 1989, 312), "The symbolic crusade against trafficking led to punitiveness that was selectively directed toward black traffickers convicted at the height of the crusade."

Two studies compare the sentences imposed on black, Hispanic, and white offenders convicted of drug offenses in federal district courts and sentenced under the federal sentencing guidelines.[3] Albonetti (1997) used 1991–1992 data to test a number of hypotheses concerning the relationship between the offender's race/ethnicity, the prosecutor's charging and plea bargaining decisions, and sentence severity. She hypothesized, first, that black and Hispanic drug offenders would be sentenced more harshly than similarly situated white offenders. She also hypothesized that black and Hispanic offenders would "receive less benefit" from pleading guilty and from guideline departures than would white offenders (Albonetti 1997, 780). White offenders, in other words, would receive greater sentence reductions than either black or Hispanic offenders if they pled guilty or if the judge accepted the prosecutor's motion for a departure from the guidelines.

In support of her first hypothesis, Albonetti found that racial minorities faced higher odds of incarceration and longer prison terms than whites. She also found that white offenders received a larger sentence reduction than black or Hispanic offenders as a result of being convicted for possession of drugs rather than drug trafficking. Regarding her second research question, Albonetti found that pleading guilty produced a similar reduction in sentence severity for all three groups of offenders. The effect of a guideline departure, on the other hand, varied among the three groups, with whites receiving a significantly greater benefit than either blacks or Hispanics. Among white defendants, a guideline departure produced a 23 percent reduction in the probability of incarceration; the comparable figures for blacks and Hispanics were 13 percent and 14 percent, respectively. According to the author, "These findings strongly suggest that the mechanism by which the federal guidelines permit the exercise of discretion operates to the disadvantage of minority defendants" (Albonetti 1997, 818).

McDonald and Carlson (1993) analyzed the sentences imposed on offenders convicted of two types of drug offenses—those involving powder cocaine and those involving crack cocaine—in federal district courts in 1989–1990. They found that although race/ethnicity did not affect the likelihood of incarceration for either type of offense, racial minorities did receive longer sentences than whites. Blacks and Hispanics convicted of offenses involving powder cocaine were sentenced to prison for longer terms than whites; blacks convicted of offenses involving crack cocaine also received longer sentences than their white counterparts.

A number of additional studies, while not focusing exclusively on sentencing of drug offenders, did examine race and sentencing of these offenders as one part of a larger study. Chiricos and Bales (1991) explored the relationship between race, unemployment, and punishment in two Florida counties in 1982. When they estimated separate models for several different types of crimes, they found that race did not directly affect the likelihood of incarceration for drug offenses. Race did, however, interact with the offender's employment status in an unexpected way. Unemployed black drug offenders were 3.7 times more likely to be held in jail prior to trial than employed white drug offenders, while employed black drug offenders were 5.9 times more likely than employed whites to be sentenced to prison. Chiricos and Bales (1991, 718–719) suggest that a possible explanation for this "surprising outcome" is that "employed blacks who are involved with drugs are seen by judges as violating a more fragile trust with employers, who are generally more inclined to hire whites than blacks."

Kramer and Steffensmeier (1993) compared the sentences imposed on black and white offenders convicted of felonies and misdemeanors in Pennsylvania during the mid-1980s. They found that race had very little effect on sentence severity overall. Although the incarceration (jail or prison) rate for blacks was 8 percentage points higher than the rate for whites, there was only a 2-percentage-point difference in the likelihood of imprisonment for blacks and whites. Race also played "a very small role in decisions about sentence length" (Kramer and Steffensmeier 1993, 368). The average sentence for blacks was only twenty-one days longer than the average sentence for whites. However, when the authors analyzed drug offenses separately, they found a more substantial race effect. Black drug offenders were nearly one-and-a-half times more likely than white drug offenders to be incarcerated; they also received sentences that averaged two months longer than the sentences imposed on similarly situated white drug offenders.

Crawford and associates' (1998) examination of the effect of offender race on the likelihood of being sentenced as a habitual offender also included a separate analysis of drug offenders. The authors of this study, who suggest that the more punitive sentences imposed on racial minorities may be linked to "mainstream America's" notions of "racial threat," ask whether blacks are more likely to be habitualized for crimes, such as drugs and violence, "often described as central to the criminal threat posed by black males" (Crawford et al. 1998, 484). The results of their analysis revealed that although defendants charged with a drug offense were less likely than defendants charged with other offenses to be habitualized, *blacks* charged with drug offenses were 3.6 times more likely than whites charged with drug offenses to be sentenced as habitual offenders. In fact, 94 percent of the 449 drug offenders habitualized in Florida during fiscal year 1992–1993 were black. As the authors note (p. 496), "the combination of being black and being charged with a drug offense substantially increases the odds of being sentenced as a habitual."

Studies of incarceration rates provide additional, albeit indirect, evidence regarding the relationship between race and sentences imposed for drug offenses. The most often cited of these studies are Blumstein's (1982, 1993) analyses of state prison populations in 1979 and 1990. Blumstein, who assumed that arrest rates do not reflect racial discrimination, calculated the portion of the black prison population left unexplained by the disproportionate representation of blacks in arrest rates. Using 1979 data, he concluded that 80 percent of the racial disparity in incarceration rates was due to the overrepresentation of blacks in arrest statistics (Blumstein 1982). There were, however, crime-specific differences in the degree to which the racial disparity in incarceration rates could be attributed to racial differences in arrest rates. There was less unexplained disparity for the more serious crimes, more unexplained disparity for the less serious crimes. In fact, only about half of the racial disparity in incarceration rates for drug offenses could be attributed to the overrepresentation of blacks at arrest.

Considered together, the results of these studies provide evidence in support of assertions that racial minorities "have borne the brunt of the War on Drugs" (Tonry 1995, 105). Black and Hispanic drug offenders, and particularly those who engage in drug trafficking, face greater odds of incarceration and longer sentences than their white counterparts.

OBJECTIVES AND HYPOTHESES

The purpose of this chapter is to examine the sentences imposed on drug offenders for evidence of racial discrimination. Building on previous research, we hypothesize that black and Hispanic drug offenders will be sentenced more harshly than white drug offenders. Because we believe that it is overly simplistic to assume that racial minorities will receive harsher sentences than whites regardless of the nature of the offense or the characteristics, other than race, of the offender, we also predict that the effect of race/ethnicity will be conditioned by the seriousness of the offense, the offender's prior criminal record, and the offender's employment status. We test the following hypotheses:

Offender race/ethnicity will have a direct effect on sentence severity. Black and Hispanic drug offenders will be more likely than white drug offenders to be incarcerated, and the prison sentences imposed on blacks and Hispanics will be longer than the sentences imposed on whites.

Offender race/ethnicity will interact with the seriousness of the offense. Blacks and Hispanics convicted of drug offenses classified as less serious (i.e., in Missouri, Class C or Class D) will be sentenced more harshly than whites convicted of these crimes; there will be no differences in the sentences imposed on offenders convicted of drug offenses classified as more serious (i.e., in Missouri, Class A or Class B).

Offender race/ethnicity will interact with the offender's prior criminal record. Among offenders without a prior felony conviction, black and Hispanic drug offenders will be sentenced more harshly than white drug offenders. There will be no racial differences in the sentences imposed on offenders with a prior felony conviction.

Offender race/ethnicity will interact with the offender's employment status. Unemployed black and Hispanic drug offenders will be sentenced more harshly than unemployed white drug offenders. There will be no racial differences in the sentences imposed on drug offenders who are employed.

THE CONTEXT OF SENTENCING

The three jurisdictions included in this study are Cook County (Chicago), Illinois; Dade County (Miami), Florida; and Jackson County (Kansas City), Missouri. These jurisdictions differ on a number of important dimensions. There are jurisdictional differences in the statutory sentencing provisions and in the formal and informal policies and procedures used to process drug offenders.

Statutory Sentencing Provisions

Illinois

Judges in Illinois impose determinate sentences. Drug offenses are classified as either Class X, Class 1, Class 2, Class 3, or Class 4 felonies. Offenders convicted of Class X felonies cannot be sentenced to probation or to any other alternative to incarceration. For these offenses, the judge is required to impose at least the minimum prison sentence. The minimum and maximum terms of imprisonment for the five categories of felonies are:

Class X   6–30 years
Class 1   4–15 years
Class 2   3–7 years
Class 3   2–5 years
Class 4   1–3 years

The judge cannot impose a sentence that exceeds the maximum term of imprisonment unless he/she finds that at least one of the aggravating factors specified in the statute (e.g., the defendant received compensation for committing the crime or committed a crime against a person 60 years of age or older) was present.

Missouri

Missouri also has a determinate sentencing structure. Felonies are classified into four categories: Class A, Class B, Class C, or Class D. The terms of imprisonment associated with each category are:

Class A   10–30 years or life
Class B   5–15 years
Class C   a maximum of 7 years
Class D   a maximum of 5 years

For C and D felonies, the court can sentence the offender to one year or less in the county jail. The maximum terms for each category are increased if the offender is proved to be either a persistent offender or a dangerous offender.[4] In this case, for example, the maximum term for Class B felonies is 30 years, the maximum term for Class C felonies is 20 years, and the maximum term for Class D felonies is 10 years.

If the offender is tried and found guilty by a jury, the jury determines the sentence unless the defendant requests in writing prior to *voir dire* that the court assess the punishment or the state pleads and proves the defendant as a prior offender, persistent offender, or dangerous offender. If the jury sentences the offender to prison, the judge cannot impose a harsher sentence (unless the term of years is less than the authorized lowest term for the offense); the judge can, on the other hand, impose a shorter sentence.

In 1990, Jackson County voters approved a half-cent increase in the sales tax, with the money generated by the tax to be used in the war on drugs. The drug tax produces about $14 million in revenue each year. Half of the money is allocated to law enforcement agencies, including the Kansas City Police Department, the Jackson County Drug Task Force, and the Jackson County Prosecutor. The other half is distributed by the county legislature; agencies receiving funds include the Jackson County jail, the Jackson County Circuit Court, the juvenile court system, and various community-based treatment programs. The funds allocated to the Jackson County Circuit Court are primarily used to pay the fees of private attorneys who are appointed to represent indigent drug offenders; these types of cases are no longer assigned to public defenders.

Florida

The state of Florida has had sentencing guidelines since 1983.[5] The purpose of the guidelines is "to establish a uniform set of standards to guide the sentencing judge" and "to eliminate unwarranted variation in the sentencing process by reducing the subjectivity in interpreting specific offense-related and offender-related criteria."[6] To meet these objectives, each offender is assigned a "sentence score" based on the seriousness of the offense(s) and his/her prior criminal record.[7] This score determines the recommended sentence.

Judges retain some discretion under the guidelines. For example, if the total sentence points for a particular offender are less than 40, the presumptive sentence is a non-state prison sentence. In this situation, the judge has discretion to sentence the offender to county jail for a maximum term of 364 days or to impose probation or some other alternative to incarceration; the judge also has discretion to withhold adjudication. If the total points are greater than 40 but less than or equal to 52, the judge has discretion to sentence the offender to state prison or not. If the points total more than 52, the sentence must be a prison sentence, with the months in state prison calculated by subtracting 28 from the total sentence points; the judge can, however, increase or decrease the sentence length by 25 percent (without providing a written statement delineating the reasons for the departure) or more (with a written statement of the reasons for the departure).

Drug Offenses and Drug Courts

Each of the three jurisdictions included in our study has a drug court, or a number of drug courts, that handle only felony drug offenses. Cook County was the first jurisdiction in the United States to establish a night drug court designed to manage the burgeoning drug caseload and to alleviate stress on the felony court system (Inciardi et al. 1996). Cook County has ten night drug courts staffed by circuit court judges; judges assigned to these courts hear motions, hold pretrial conferences, take pleas, hold bench trials, and sentence offenders.

Dade County also has a drug court, but it differs in a number of important ways from the night drug courts in Cook County. The Miami court, which was established in 1989, is designed to divert first-time drug offenders into treatment. To be eligible for the court's diversion and treatment program, the defendant must have no prior felony convictions, must be charged with possession (not sale) of drugs, and must acknowledge his/her drug problem and need for treatment.[8] Defendants who refuse to admit their drug problem or to request treatment for it are prosecuted in one of the regular circuit courts. If the defendant successfully completes the treatment program designed by the drug court judge, the prosecutor dismisses the case and the defendant may request that his/her record be sealed and expunged.

The Jackson County drug court was established in 1993. The judge assigned to this court handles felony drug cases as well as the Drug Court Diversion Program. Those who qualify for the diversion program are first-time offenders who are charged with nonviolent, drug-related crimes. The minimum time for completion of the diversion program is one year. Defendants who enter the program sign a contract outlining the terms of the program; it may require frequent urinalysis to test for drug use, counseling, community service, or completion of education or job training. If the defendant successfully completes the program, the prosecutor dismisses the charges and the defendant's record is expunged. A defendant who fails the program is returned to jail to await trial before the drug court judge on the original charges.

RESEARCH DESIGN AND METHODS

Data Collection Procedures

The data used in this study are a subset of the data collected for a multi-site study of sentencing decisions. For that project, we collected data on over 7,000 offenders convicted of felonies in 1993 and 1994 in Chicago, Miami, and Kansas City. For this study, we selected all offenders (N = 3,164) for whom the most serious conviction charge was a drug offense. This includes 1,554 offenders in Chicago, 1,184 offenders in Miami, and 426 offenders in Kansas City.

The data collection procedures for the original study varied somewhat for each jurisdiction. In Chicago, we selected a random sample of all offenders convicted of felonies in 1993 from a list prepared by the clerk of the Cook County Circuit Court. Data collectors read through the court file for each case included in the sample and recorded information about the offender and the case on an optical-scan form designed for the project. In Miami, we selected a random sample of all offenders convicted of felonies in 1993 and 1994; information concerning the case and the offender was provided by the Administrative Office of the Courts. In Kansas City, we obtained data on all offenders convicted of felonies in 1993. The Department of Computer Services provided a printout listing the charges filed, the disposition of each charge, and other information about the case; information concerning the offender's background and prior criminal record was obtained from court files.

Dependent and Independent Variables

The dependent and independent variables, their codes, and their frequencies are displayed in Table 8.1. We present separate data for each of the three juris-

Table 8.1
Dependent and Independent Variables: Codes and Frequencies for Drug Offenders in Chicago, Miami, and Kansas City

Variable	Code	Chicago (N = 1554) N	%	Miami (N = 1184) N	%	Kansas City N = 426 N	%
Dependent Variables[a]							
Sentenced to jail or prison	1 = yes			846	71.5		
	0 = no			338	28.5		
Sentenced to prison	1 = yes	833	53.5	193	16.3	125	29.3
	0 = no	722	46.5	991	74.7	301	70.7
Prison sentence (months)	Mean	39.28		50.69		70.12	
Independent Variables							
Offender's Race[b]							
Black		1333	85.8	801	67.7	302	70.2
Hispanic		124	8.0	221	18.7	NA	NA
White		97	6.2	162	13.7	128	29.8
Offender's Gender	1 = male	1400	90.1	1037	87.6	356	82.8
	0 = female	154	9.9	147	12.4	74	17.2
Offender's Age	Mean	26.55		32.65		29.34	
Type of Drug Offense							
Marijuana		54	3.5	167	14.1	70	16.3
Cocaine		1181	76.0	951	80.3	301	70.0
Heroin		258	16.6	11	0.9	44	0.5
Other drug		61	3.9	55	4.6	57	13.2
Class of Most Serious Charge							
Chicago–Class X		88	5.7				
Class 1		304	19.6				
Class 2		428	27.5				
Class 3		40	2.6				
Class 4		694	44.7				
Miami–1st degree				100	8.4		
2nd degree				351	29.6		
3rd degree				733	61.9		
Kansas City–Class A						14	3.3
Class B						302	70.2
Class C						105	24.4
Class D						9	2.1
No. of Felony Convictions	Mean	1.09		1.31		1.53	
Offender on Probation at Time of Offense	1 = yes	166	10.7	143	12.1	54	12.9
	0 = no	1388	89.3	1041	87.9	366	87.1
No. of Prior Felony Convictions	Mean	1.00		3.5201.02			

Table 8.1 (Continued)

Variable	Code	Chicago N	Chicago %	Miami N	Miami %	Kansas City N	Kansas City %
Prior Drug Conviction	1 = yes	587	37.8	847	71.5	54	12.7
	0 = no	965	62.2	337	28.5	370	87.3
Private Attorney	1 = yes	136	8.9	348	29.4	175	40.9
	0 = no	1397	91.1	836	70.6	253	59.1
Offender Released Prior to Trial	1 = yes	746	48.0	574	48.5	226	52.6
	0 = no	808	52.0	610	51.5	204	47.4
Offender Pled Guilty	1 = yes	1414	91.0	1173	99.1	417	97.0
	0 = no	140	9.1	11	0.9	13	3.0
Offender Unemployed	1 = yes	1029	75.6	NA		302	77.2
	0 = no	333	24.4			89	20.7

[a]In Miami we analyze the decision to incarcerate (in jail or prison) as well as the decision to incarcerate (in prison) because of the large number of offenders who were sentenced to the Dade County Jail.
[b]There were no Hispanic drug offenders in Kansas City; we therefore compare only black offenders and white offenders.

dictions. We include two dependent variables measuring sentence severity. The first variable measures whether the offender was sentenced to prison or not. The second measures the length of sentence (in months) imposed on offenders sentenced to prison.

For Miami, we analyze the decision to incarcerate (in jail or prison) as well as the decision to sentence the offender to prison or not. We include both measures of incarceration because of the obvious difference between a state prison sentence and a jail sentence and because of the large number of drug offenders (N = 653) who were sentenced to the Dade County Jail.[9] Under the Florida sentencing guidelines in effect in 1993 and 1994, many offenders convicted of drug offenses did not qualify for a state prison sentence; instead, such offenders were sentenced to the Dade County Jail for a maximum term of 364 days.

The independent variables included in the analysis are offender and case characteristics that have been shown to affect judges' sentencing decisions. We control for the offender's race, gender, age, and prior criminal record. In Chicago and Miami, offender race is measured by three dummy variables—black, Hispanic, and white. Because there were no Hispanic offenders convicted of drug offenses in Kansas City, in this jurisdiction we compare only black offenders and white offenders. White offenders are the reference category in all of the multi-variate analyses. In Chicago and Kansas City, we also control for the offender's employment status.[10]

The data file for this study included a number of measures of prior criminal record: number of prior arrests, number of prior felony arrests, number of prior felony convictions, number of prior prison terms of more than one year, whether the offender previously had been convicted of a drug offense, and whether the offender previously had been convicted of a violent offense. Some of these measures were highly correlated with one another; they also differed in terms of their relationship to sentence severity. The two variables we use—the number of prior felony convictions and whether the offender had previously been convicted of a drug offense—were not highly correlated.[11] Both also had strong and statistically significant relationships with the two dependent variables.

We control for three measures of offense seriousness—the type of drug offense, the class of the most serious conviction charge, and the number of current felony convictions.[12] The type of drug offense is a categorical variable that differentiates among marijuana, cocaine, heroin, and other drug offenses in Chicago and, because of the small number of heroin offenders, among marijuana, cocaine, and other drug offenses in Miami and Kansas City; cocaine is the reference category.[13] Because the classification of offenses differed in each jurisdiction, the variables measuring the class of the most serious conviction charge also differ. In Chicago, we differentiate among Class X, Class 1, Class 2, Class 3, and Class 4 felonies; Class X is the reference category. In Miami, we distinguish between first-degree felonies, second-degree felonies, and third-degree felonies; first-degree felony is the omitted category. Because of the small number of drug offenders in Kansas City who were convicted of either Class A (N = 14) or Class D (N = 9) offenses, we distinguish between Class A or Class B and Class C or Class D felonies; Class A/Class B is the reference category.

We also control for characteristics of the offender's case that might influence the severity of the sentence imposed by the judge. We take into account whether the offender was on probation at the time of arrest for the current offense, whether the offender was represented by a private attorney or a public defender, and whether the offender was released or detained pending trial. Because most offenders pled guilty (this was especially true in Miami and Kansas City), we do not control for the type of disposition in the case.

Analytic Procedures

We analyze the data using both ordinary least squares (OLS) regression and logistic regression. Two different analytic procedures are required because of differences in the nature of the dependent variables. We use OLS regression to analyze the length of the prison sentence, which is an interval-level variable.

Because OLS regression is considered to be inappropriate for the analysis of dichotomous dependent variables, we use logistic regression to analyze the two incarceration decisions.

In analyzing the length of the sentence, we include a correction for sample selection bias (Berk 1983; Berk and Ray 1982). This type of bias results when some observations are systematically excluded from the sample being analyzed. Here offenders who were not sentenced to prison are excluded from the sentence-length sample. Incarcerated offenders, in other words, are a selected population from the population of all convicted offenders; they were sentenced to prison because they exceeded some threshold of "case seriousness." Thus, the length of the sentence is "a function not just of the usual linear combination of regressors (which suffices in the original population), but [of] a hazard rate capturing the impact of the selection equation" (Berk and Ray 1982, 369).

We use the procedures outlined by Heckman (1974) and Berk (1983) to correct for this problem. We use logistic regression to estimate the likelihood that the offender would be sentenced to prison. For each case the logistic regression model produced its predicted probability of exclusion from the sentence-length sample—the hazard rate. We then include the hazard rate as a control in the regression equation for sentence length.

We perform separate analyses on the data for each jurisdiction, and we use a two-stage analytic procedure to explore the relationship between race and sentencing. We first estimate the additive effects of the offender's race on sentencing outcomes, controlling for offender and case characteristics. We then test the remaining hypotheses, all of which focus on the possibility of interaction between the offender's race, other predictors of sentence severity (the seriousness of the offense, the offender's prior criminal record, and the offender's employment status), and the harshness of the sentence. In testing our hypothesis that race will interact with the offender's prior criminal record, for example, we perform a separate multivariate analysis on offenders with and without a prior felony conviction.

FINDINGS

Case and Offender Characteristics

The outcomes of cases and the characteristics of offenders in the three jurisdictions are displayed in Table 8.1. Drug offenders were most likely to be sentenced to prison in Chicago, least likely to be sentenced to prison in Miami. As noted, the low imprisonment rate in Miami can be attributed in part to the fact that a significant proportion of the Dade County drug offenders were sentenced to county jail rather than state prison. The overall incarceration rate in Miami (71.5%) is substantially higher than the imprisonment rate in Chicago (53.5%) and is over twice as large as the imprisonment rate in Kansas City (29.3%). In contrast, the mean prison sentence in Kansas City is considerably longer than the mean sentence for Miami or Chicago.

The frequency distributions displayed in Table 8.1 indicate that there are a number of similarities in offenders and their cases in these three jurisdictions. The typical drug offender in each jurisdiction was a black male in his late twenties or early thirties, who was convicted of a cocaine offense, was not on probation at the time of his arrest for the current offense, was in custody when his case was disposed, and entered a plea of guilty. About three-quarters of the offenders in Chicago and Kansas City were unemployed at the time of their arrest.

There are some differences in offender and case characteristics. Offenders in Miami were more likely than offenders in the two other jurisdictions to have more than one prior felony conviction and to have a prior drug conviction. Although the majority of defendants in each jurisdiction were represented by public defenders rather than private attorneys, over 40 percent of the defendants in Kansas City had private attorneys; as noted, the money generated by the Jackson County drug tax is used to provide private attorneys for indigent defendants.

Results of the Additive Analysis

We found very limited support for our hypothesis that offender race/ethnicity would have a direct effect on sentence severity for drug offenders. As shown in Table 8.2, which presents the results of our analyses of the decision to sentence the offender to prison or not, race/ethnicity had no effect on the likelihood of incarceration in Chicago or Kansas City and only affected the likelihood of incarceration for Hispanics in Miami. Further analysis (not shown) of the decision to sentence the offender to jail or prison in Miami revealed that neither blacks nor Hispanics were more likely than whites to be incarcerated. Moreover, when we analyzed the length of the prison sentence (see Table 8.3), we found that neither blacks nor Hispanics received longer sentences than whites in Chicago or Miami. In Kansas City, on the other hand, black drug offenders received significantly longer prison sentences than white drug offenders; net of the other variables included in the model, blacks received almost fifteen months longer than whites.

The results presented in Tables 8.2 and 8.3 also reveal that both sentencing decisions were affected by the class of the conviction charge and the offender's prior criminal record—factors of explicit legal relevance to the sentence. In all three jurisdictions, the odds of incarceration were significantly higher for offenders convicted of more serious drug offenses, offenders with prior felony convictions, and offenders on probation when arrested for the current offense. The length of the prison sentence was strongly influenced by the class of the conviction charge in all three jurisdictions and by the number of current conviction charges in Chicago and Kansas City.

Table 8.2
The Effect of Race/Ethnicity on the Decision to Sentence the Offender to Prison for Drug Offenses

	Chicago			Miami			Kansas City		
	b	SE	Odds[a]	b	SE	Odds[a]	b	SE	Odds[a]
Offender's Race[b]									
Black	.44	.34		.67	.34		.13	.36	
Hispanic	.40	.41		.97*	.37	2.64	- - - -	.- -	
Offender's Gender (Male = 1)	.91*	.27	2.50	.10	.28		1.04*	.41	2.82
Offender's Age	-.01	.01		-.01	.01		-.01	.02	
Type of Drug Offense[c]									
Cocaine (reference)									
Marijuana	-.46	.47		-1.27*	.43	0.28	-1.02	.53	
Heroin	.87	.21		- - - -	- - -		- - - -	- - -	
Other Drug	.60	.40		.72*	.33	2.05	-.19	.41	
Class of Most Serious Charge[d]									
Chicago (Class X is reference)									
Class 1	-.73*	.38	0.48						
Class 2	-1.09*	.38	0.32						
Class 3	-1.70*	.60	0.18						
Class 4	-1.58*	.38	0.21						
Miami (1st degree is reference)									
2nd degree				-1.87*	.29	0.15			
3rd degree				-2.48*	.29	0.08			
Kansas City (Class A/Class B is reference)									
Class C or Class D							-.41	.32	
No. of Convictions	.89*	.26	2.44	-.16	.14		.24	.13	
Offender on Probation	.60*	.26	1.81	.94*	.23	2.57	.96*	.35	2.62
No. of Prior Felony Convictions	1.18*	.12	3.24	.36*	.07	1.43	.41*	.10	1.51
Prior Conviction–Drug Offense	.35	.20		-.81*	.25	0.44	.33	.37	
Private Attorney	.31	.28		-.12	.20		-.25	.32	
Offender Released Prior to Trial	-2.24*	.15	0.11	-.33	.19		-.64*	.28	0.53
Constant	-.70	.68		-.18	.60		-2.05*	.73	

[a]Odds ratios are presented only for independent variables that have a statistically significant effect (P ≤ .05) on the dependent variable.

[b]Because of the small number of Hispanics in Kansas City, we eliminated Hispanics from the data file and compared the sentences imposed on black offenders and white offenders. In Chicago and Miami, white offenders are the reference category.

[c]The type of drug offenses is a categorical variable. Cocaine is the reference category. Because of the small number of offenders convicted of heroin offenses in Miami and Kansas City, we combined heroin offenses and other drug offenses into an "other drug" category.

[d]Because there were only 14 offenders convicted of Class A felonies and 9 offenders convicted of Class B felonies in Kansas City, we combined Class A and Class B. We also combined Class C and Class D.

Table 8.3
The Effect of Race/Ethnicity on the Length of the Prison Sentence[a] for Drug Offenders

	Chicago			Miami			Kansas City		
	b	Beta	T	b	Beta	T	b	Beta	T
Offender's Race									
Black	-2.74	-.04	0.83	-10.89	-.10	0.79	14.99	.21	2.43*
Hispanic	5.68	.06	1.42	3.93	.03	0.27	- - - - -	- - -	- - -
Offender's Gender (Male = 1)	5.20	.04	1.56	23.05	.14	2.27*	-4.36	-.05	0.55
Offender's Age	.08	.06	1.00	-.39	.07	1.01	-.37	-.12	1.22
Type of Drug Offense									
Cocaine (reference)									
Marijuana	5.52	.03	1.14	-4.98	-.02	0.28	-12.87	-.10	1.26
Heroin	1.10	.02	0.66	- - - -	- - -	- - - -	- - - -	- - -	- - -
Other Drug	-.15	-.01	0.44	29.19	.18	2.63*	-5.63	-.07	0.89
Class of Most Serious Charge									
Chicago (Class X is reference)									
Class 1	-24.58	-.43	9.31*						
Class 2	-41.22	-.26	11.92*						
Class 3	-31.40	-.61	8.42*						
Class 4	-53.09	-.70	19.91*						
Miami (1st degree is reference)									
2nd degree				-66.73	-.57	5.56*			
3rd degree				-66.53	-.60	5.46*			
Kansas City (Class A/Class B is reference)									
Class C or Class D							-33.96	-.51	6.12*
No. of Convictions	3.47	.05	1.97*	3.65	.05	0.74	6.75	.24	2.81*
Offender on Probation	-3.31	-.05	1.88	-4.18	-.03	0.74	-7.18	-.11	1.33
No. of Prior Felony Convictions	.47	.03	0.94	3.11	.12	1.25	3.95	.22	2.50*
Prior Conviction–Drug Offense	-.65	-.01	0.44	-4.76	-.04	0.47	13.18	.20	2.31*
Private Attorney	.06	.00	0.02	8.11	.07	1.07	.54	.01	0.11
Offender Released Prior to Trial	-1.50	-.03	0.64	6.25	.05	0.85	-9.94	-.17	2.19*
Hazard Rate[b]	.83	.01	0.16	- - - -	- - -	- - - -	- - - -	- - -	- - - -
R^2		.46			.42			.44	

[a]The sentence imposed on offenders who were sentenced to prison. The sentence is measured in months.

[b]In Miami and Kansas City the hazard rate was strongly correlated with the class of the conviction charge and with the offender's prior criminal record. When the hazard rate was included in the model, the variance inflation factors (VIFs) for the dummy variables measuring the class of the conviction charge and the VIFs for prior record and the hazard rate all exceeded 5.0. We therefore eliminated the hazard rate from the models for these two jurisdictions.

*$P \leq .05$

Two extralegal variables, in addition to race/ethnicity, were related to sentence outcomes for drug offenses. Male offenders faced significantly greater odds of incarceration than female offenders in Chicago and Kansas City; males also received substantially longer sentences than females in Miami. In Chicago and Kansas City offenders who were able to obtain pretrial release were much less likely to be incarcerated than those who were in custody at the time of trial; in Kansas City those who were released also received significantly shorter sentences than those who were in custody.

The results discussed thus far suggest that sentencing outcomes for drug offenders in these three jurisdictions are determined primarily, although not exclusively, by legally relevant considerations such as the seriousness of the offense and the offender's prior criminal record. Gender has a fairly substantial effect, but the effect of race/ethnicity, at least in the additive models tested thus far, is limited. This is confirmed by the probabilities of incarceration and the adjusted sentence means presented in Table 8.4.

We used the logit coefficients presented in Table 8.2 to calculate the estimated probability of imprisonment for a "typical drug offender" in each racial group (Hanushek and Jackson 1977; Lichter 1989). We calculated these probabilities for offenders with the following characteristics:

- male
- thirty years old
- convicted of one count of a cocaine offense
- convicted of a class 2 (Chicago), second-degree (Miami), or Class A/Class B (Kansas City) drug offense
- not on probation at time of arrest
- one prior felony conviction
- no prior drug conviction
- represented by a public defender
- in custody prior to trial

The formula used to calculate the probabilities was:

$$P_1 = \exp(Z_1)/1 + \exp(Z_1), \quad \text{where}$$
$$Z_{1_k} = \Sigma\, B_k X_{ik}$$

As an illustration, the probability of incarceration for a black offender in Chicago is computed as

$$
\begin{aligned}
\text{Prob}_{\text{black}} &= \exp(-.70 + .44 + .91 + (30)(-.009) - 1.09 + .89 + 1.18)/1 \\
&\quad + \exp(-.70 + .44 + .91 + (30)(-.009) - 1.09 + .89 + 1.18) \\
&= \exp(1.36)/1 + \exp(1.36) \\
&= .796
\end{aligned}
$$

We used the results of the OLS regression to calculate adjusted sentences for offenders in each racial group. These adjusted figures, which take all of the other independent variables included in the analysis into account, were calculated using the following formulas:

$$b^1 = -1[(b^2)(prop^2) + (b^3)(prop^3)]$$
$$adjmean^1 = M + b^1$$
$$adjmean^2 = adjmean^1 + b^2$$
$$adjmean^3 = adjmean^1 + b^3$$

where

b^1 is the adjusted unstandardized regression coefficient for the omitted category (white offenders);

b^2, b^3 are the unstandardized regression coefficients for the included categories (blacks and Hispanics);

$prop^2$, $prop^3$ are the mean of the dummy variables for black and Hispanic offenders (or the proportions of black and Hispanic offenders);

M is the mean of the dependent variable (sentence length); and

$adjmean^1$, $adjmean^2$, and $adjmean^3$ are the adjusted sentence lengths for white, black, and Hispanic offenders.

The estimated probabilities, presented in Table 8.4, reveal substantial inter-jurisdictional variation in the imposition of *prison* sentences for convicted drug offenders. They also confirm that offender race/ethnicity affected the probability of a prison sentence only in Miami. The typical drug offender faced much higher odds of imprisonment in Chicago than in Kansas City or Miami. Three of every four offenders, regardless of race, were sentenced to prison in Chicago, compared to only one of every three, again regardless of race, in Kansas City. In Miami, in contrast, the odds of a prison sentence were much lower, particularly for white drug offenders. In this jurisdiction, the typical Hispanic drug offender was twice as likely as the typical white offender to be sentenced to prison.

As explained earlier, the low rate of imprisonment in Miami reflects the fact that those convicted of less serious drug offenses normally did not accumulate enough points to qualify for a state prison sentence, but instead were sentenced to the Dade County Jail for a maximum term of 364 days. In fact, as Table 8.4 indicates, in Miami the odds of incarceration (in either jail or prison) were very similar to the odds of imprisonment in Chicago. When incarceration (rather than imprisonment) is considered, the predicted probabilities for white, black, and Hispanic offenders are very similar. In Miami, then, judges appear to take the offender's ethnicity into account in deciding between prison and either jail or probation, but not in deciding between some form of incarceration and probation.

The data presented in Table 8.4 also reveal that judges in Kansas City imposed much longer sentences on black than on white drug offenders; the mean sentence for black offenders was 73.11 months, compared to only 58.12 months for

Table 8.4
Predicted Probabilities of Incarceration and Adjusted Sentences for White, Black, and Hispanic Drug Offenders

	Chicago	Miami	Kansas City
Probability of a Prison Sentence			
White Offenders	.765	.111	.341
Black Offenders	.796	.177	.370
Hispanic Offenders	.789	.227	NA
Probability of a Jail or Prison Sentence–Miami			
White Offenders		.774	
Black Offenders		.812	
Hispanic Offenders		.804	
Adjusted Mean Prison Sentence (months)			
White Offenders	41.35	56.51	58.12
Black Offenders	38.61	46.73	73.11
Hispanic Offenders	47.03	58.49	NA

white offenders. In this jurisdiction, then, prison is used sparingly for drug offenders of either race, but among those for whom the appropriate sentence is deemed to be prison, blacks get substantially longer terms than whites.

The adjusted figures presented in Table 8.4 further suggest that in Chicago and Miami the mean prison sentences imposed on whites were very similar to those imposed on blacks or Hispanics. There were, however, more substantial differences between Hispanic offenders and black offenders; in each of these two jurisdictions blacks received the most lenient sentences, while Hispanics received the harshest sentences. The model of sentence length tested (see Table 8.3) compared the sentences imposed on whites to those imposed on blacks and Hispanics, based on our prediction that racial minorities would receive the harshest sentences. The adjusted sentences presented in Table 8.4 suggest that while the differences between whites and racial minorities are not statistically significant, the differences between blacks and Hispanics may be.

To test for this possibility, we re-ran the analysis of sentence length in Chicago and Miami, with blacks, rather than whites, as the omitted category. We found that the sentences imposed on Hispanic drug offenders were significantly longer than those imposed on black drug offenders in each jurisdiction. Hispanics received almost fifteen months longer in Miami ($b = 14.82$; Beta $= .12$; $T = 1.98$) and over eight months longer in Chicago ($b = 8.42$; Beta $= .09$; $T = 3.25$). In these two jurisdictions, then, Hispanic drug offenders were sentenced more harshly than black drug offenders. We discuss the implications of this finding in the conclusion.

Results of the Interactive Analyses

The fact that we found no direct race effects on the in/out decision in Chicago and Kansas City does not mean that the decision-making process is racially neutral in these two jurisdictions. Similarly, the fact that we found that Hispanics were more likely than whites to be sentenced to prison in Miami and that blacks received longer sentences than whites in Kansas City does not mean that race/ethnicity will affect the decision-making process for all types of offenders or all types of cases. We noted above that Hawkins (1987) and Zatz (1987) have called on researchers to abandon overly simplistic additive models of the relationship between race and sentencing. Asserting that conflict theory does not necessarily predict that racial minorities will be sentenced more harshly than whites for all crimes and under all types of circumstances, they have called for research designed to identify the conditions under which race/ethnicity influences sentencing decisions. As Chiricos and Crawford (1995, 301) note, "We are past the point of simply asking whether race makes a difference."

Building on past research, we hypothesized that offender race/ethnicity would interact with the seriousness of the conviction charge, the offender's prior criminal record, and the offender's employment status. To test these hypotheses, we ran separate analyses of offenders convicted of offenses classified by statute as more or less serious, on offenders with and without prior criminal records, and (for Chicago and Kansas City) on employed and unemployed offenders. We tested for interaction effects in the decision to incarcerate or not using data from all three jurisdictions. We also tested for interaction effects using sentence length as the dependent variable in Chicago; because our earlier analysis revealed that Hispanics were sentenced more harshly than blacks, we ran the analyses twice, once with whites as the reference category and once with blacks as the reference category. Because of the small number of offenders sentenced to prison in Miami ($N = 193$) and Kansas City ($N = 125$), in these two jurisdictions we were not able to test for interaction effects using the length of the prison sentence as the dependent variable.[14]

The results of our analysis of the in/out decision (see Table 8.5) confirm that racial minorities were not more likely than whites to be sentenced to prison in either Chicago or Kansas City. In these two jurisdictions there were no statistically significant race effects in *any* of the types of cases examined. In Miami, on the other hand, we found that black drug offenders faced greater odds of incarceration than white drug offenders under some circumstances. Blacks convicted

Table 8.5
Effect of Race/Ethnicity on the Decision to Sentence Drug Offenders to Prison in Various Types of Cases[a]

| | Chicago | | | | Miami | | | | Kansas City | |
| | Black | | Hispanic | | Black | | Hispanic | | Black | |
	b	SE	b	SE	b	SE	b	SE	b	SE
Class of Conviction Charge										
Chicago										
Class X or Class 1 Felony	-.62	.64	.12	.77						
Class 2 Felony	1.16	.76	1.10	.87						
Class 3 or Class 4 Felony	.91	.56	.56	.68						
Miami										
1st Degree Felony					-.69	.93	.10	.97		
2nd Degree Felony					.98	.78	1.45	.83		
3rd Degree Felony					1.32*	.56	.71	.64		
Kansas City										
Class A or Class B Felony									.20	.47
Class C or Class D Felony									.07	.68
Prior Criminal Record										
Prior Felony Conviction	.61	.50	.65	.61	.82*	.40	.79	.44	.57	.45
No Prior Felony Conviction	.38	.50	.43	.58	-2.60	1.60	-2.15	1.88	-.27	.61
Employment Status										
Employed or Student	.98	.69	1.11	.84	NA				-.09	.86
Unemployed	.76	.55	.66	.61					.52	.46

[a]We ran separate analyses on each type of case, controlling for offender race and for the other independent variables listed in Table 8.1. White offenders were the reference category in all of the analyses.

Table 8.6
Effect of Race/Ethnicity on the Length of the Prison Sentence in Various Types of Cases[a] in Chicago

| | Whites Omitted From Model | | | | Blacks Omitted from Model | | | |
| | Blacks | | Hispanics | | Whites | | Hispanics | |
	b	Beta	b	Beta	b	Beta	b	Beta
Class of Conviction Charge								
Class X or Class 1 Felony	-9.87	-.14	12.92	.15	9.97	.07	16.17	.19*
Class 2 Felony	-3.53	-.06	5.04	.07	3.53	.04	8.57	.12
Class 3 or Class 4 Felony	4.91	.10	6.68	.12	-4.74	-.06	1.78	.03
Prior Criminal Record								
Prior Felony Conviction	-3.16	-.04	7.84	.08	3.36	.03	10.97	.15*
No Prior Felony Conviction	-1.89	-.03	-6.99	-.08	1.86	.02	-5.46	-.06
Employment Status								
Employed or Student	-4.77	-.07	2.84	.03	4.77	.05	7.61	.09
Unemployed	-2.98	-.04	9.16	.11	2.98	.02	12.14	.15*

[a]We ran separate analyses on each type of case, controlling for offender race and for the other independent variables listed in Table 8.1.
$^*P \leq .05$

of third-degree felonies were more likely than whites convicted of third-degree felonies to be incarcerated; blacks with a prior felony conviction also were more likely than whites with a prior felony conviction to be sentenced to prison.

Our findings concerning the length of the prison sentence (in Chicago) are presented in Table 8.6. We found no significant differences between racial minorities and whites for any of the types of cases examined. We did, however, find a number of significant differences between black offenders and Hispanic offenders. Hispanics convicted of the most serious drug offenses received sixteen months longer than blacks convicted of these offenses. Hispanics with at least one prior felony conviction received almost eleven months longer than their black counterparts, and unemployed Hispanics received twelve months longer than unemployed blacks.

Some, but not all, of these interaction effects are consistent with our hypotheses. With respect to the in/out decision, race/ethnicity interacted as expected with the class of the conviction charge (significant effect found only for the least serious type of offense) but not with the offender's prior record (significant effect found only for offenders with a prior record). There were similarly inconsistent results for the length of the prison sentence. We found the expected results for employment status (significant effect only for those who were unemployed), but results contrary to our hypotheses for the class of the conviction charge and the offender's prior criminal record. Moreover, these effects were found only when we compared the sentences imposed on black offenders and Hispanic offenders.

DISCUSSION

The results of this study provide very limited support for assertions that black and Hispanic drug offenders are sentenced more harshly than white drug offenders. We found that Hispanics, but not blacks, faced greater odds of incarceration than whites in Miami, but that racial minorities and whites were sentenced to prison at about the same rate in Chicago and Kansas City. Similarly, we found that blacks received longer sentences than whites in Kansas City, but that the sentences imposed on racial minorities and whites were very similar in Chicago and Miami. We also found very little support for our hypothesis that race/ethnicity would interact with the seriousness of the offense, the offender's prior record, and the offender's employment status. In fact, the only significant interaction effects were in Miami, where blacks faced greater odds of incarceration than whites under some circumstances.

We did, on the other hand, discover that race/ethnicity affected sentencing for drug offenses in an unexpected manner. In both Chicago and Miami, the sentences imposed on Hispanic drug offenders were significantly longer than the sentences imposed on black drug offenders. In these two jurisdictions, then, judges differentiated not between racial minorities and whites, but between blacks and Hispanics. Further analysis of the sentences imposed in Chicago revealed that only certain types of Hispanic offenders—those convicted of the most serious drug offenses, those with a prior felony conviction, and those who were unemployed at the time of arrest—received longer sentences than black offenders.

Considered together, these results suggest that race and ethnicity do not affect sentencing for drug offenders in the predicted manner. Although the findings of previous studies are somewhat inconsistent, most found that racial minorities convicted of drug offenses were sentenced more harshly than whites convicted of these offenses. Moreover, consistent with Chiricos and Crawford's (1995) review of recent race and sentencing research, most of these studies found that race had more consistent effects on the decision to incarcerate or not than on the length of the sentence. Previous research also showed that the effect of offender race was confined to cases involving less serious crimes or offenders without criminal records. The findings of our study clearly are inconsistent with these conclusions.

The fact that we found relatively small racial differences in sentence severity may reflect our focus on drug offenses. Hawkins (1987, 730) argues for the "existence of a race/crime-specific perception of the appropriateness of criminal behavior that affects racial differentials in criminal sentencing." Specifically, Hawkins suggests that differences in punishment will be greatest for crimes that are seen as racially inappropriate, smallest for crimes perceived as racially appropriate. If, in other words, white-collar crimes are viewed as "white crimes" while street crimes are perceived as "nonwhite crimes," the "black-white punishment differential will be greater for white-collar offenses than for street crimes against property" (Hawkins 1987, 730). Since one component of the definition of "racially appropriate" is the level of involvement in the particular type of crime and since blacks and Hispanics are arrested for drug offenses at disproportionately high rates, our findings generally are consistent with this prediction.

It also is possible that our findings are masking racial bias at earlier stages in the criminal justice process. Each of the three jurisdictions included in this study has constrained the discretion of judges at sentencing: Illinois and Missouri through determinate sentencing and Florida through sentencing guidelines. Given this, it is possible that discretion has shifted somewhat from the judge at sentencing to the prosecutor at charging. If prosecutors charge blacks and Hispanics with more serious crimes than whites or offer whites more substantial charge reductions than blacks or Hispanics during the plea-bargaining process, it would be misleading to conclude that a finding of relatively small racial differentials at sentencing is indicative of racial neutrality in the processing of defendants. Our results, in other words, do not rule out the possibility that black and Hispanic offenders are sentenced more harshly than whites who commit identical crimes.

In terms of methodology, our results highlight the importance of testing for the effect of ethnicity as well as race; they also confirm the importance of *not* combining blacks and Hispanics into a general "non-white" category. Had we simply compared the sentences imposed on blacks and whites, we would have concluded that judges in these three jurisdictions, with one exception (longer sentences for blacks in Kansas City), did not impose harsher sentences on racial minorities than on whites. This conclusion, while accurate, would have been misleading, given our finding that Hispanics were significantly more likely than whites to be sentenced to prison in Miami. Similarly, had we simply compared the sentences imposed on non-whites and whites, we would have overlooked the fact that Hispanics received longer sentences than blacks in both Miami and Chicago.

We are somewhat puzzled by our finding that Hispanic drug offenders were singled out for harsher treatment in both Chicago and Miami. We expected, based in part on recent theoretical discussions of the "moral panic" surrounding drug use and the War on Drugs (Chambliss 1995; Tonry 1995), that both black and Hispanic drug offenders would be sentenced more harshly than white drug offenders. Moral panic theorists (Jenkins 1994) argue that society is characterized by a variety of commonsense perceptions about crime and drugs that result in community intolerance of such behaviors and increased pressure for punitive actions. Many theorists (see Chiricos and DeLone 1992 for a review) argue that this moral panic can become ingrained in the judicial ideology of sentencing judges, resulting in more severe sentences for those believed to be responsible for such problems as crime and drugs. We reasoned that both blacks and Hispanics would be associated with drug use, drug distribution, and the crimes that accompany a drug-involved lifestyle; consequently, we predicted that both groups would be sentenced more severely than whites. The fact that harsher treatment was reserved for Hispanics in *Miami*, while unexpected, is not particularly surprising; arguably, the most enduring perception about drug importation and distribution in Miami is that these activities are dominated by Hispanics of various nationalities. This explanation, however, is less convincing with regard to our finding that Hispanics received longer sentences than blacks in Chicago.

The fact that only *certain types* of Hispanic offenders were singled out for harsher treatment in Chicago suggests that judges there may be imposing more severe sentences on offenders characterized as particularly problematic. We found discriminatory treatment of Hispanics (vis-à-vis blacks) among offenders convicted of the most serious offenses, among offenders with at least one prior felony conviction, and among offenders who were unemployed at the time of their arrest for the current offense. This suggests that Chicago judges use ethnicity, offense seriousness, prior record, and employment status to define what might be called a "dangerous class" (Adler 1994) of drug offenders. The Hispanic drug offender who manufactures or sells large quantities of drugs, who is a repeat offender, or who has no legitimate means of financial support may be perceived as particularly dangerous, particularly likely to recidivate.

The results of this multi-jurisdictional study of sentencing for drug offenses offer "clues to the contextual character of possible race effects" (Chiricos and Crawford 1995, 284). Future research should continue to probe for differences in the treatment of black and Hispanic drug offenders and for the circumstances under which racial minorities are sentenced more harshly than whites for drug offenses.

NOTES

1. There were 475,209 persons arrested for drug offenses in 1976, compared to 1,127,114 in 1996. The number of whites arrested for drug offenses increased from 366,081 to 681,008; the number of blacks increased from 103,615 to 433,352. See Tonry (1995, Table 3-3) and Maguire and Pastore (eds.), *Sourcebook of Criminal Justice Statistics 1997* (Washington, DC: U.S. Department of Justice, 1998), Table 4.10.

2. In 1996 the U.S. Supreme Court ruled 8-1 that blacks who allege that they have been singled out for prosecution under the crack cocaine rule must first show that whites

in similar circumstances were not prosecuted [*U.S. v. Armstrong*, 116 S.Ct. 1480 (1996)]. The case was brought by five African-American defendants from Los Angeles, who claimed that prosecutors were systematically steering crack cocaine cases involving African Americans to federal court, where the 100-to-1 rule applied, but steering cases involving whites to state court, where lesser penalties applied. The Court stated that a defendant who claimed he or she was a victim of selective prosecution "must demonstrate that the federal prosecutorial policy had a discriminatory effect and that it was motivated by a discriminatory purpose."

3. There also are two studies that examined the effect of race/ethnicity on the likelihood of (and the magnitude of) a departure from the sentencing guidelines for providing "substantial assistance" in the prosecution of other offenders (Maxfield and Kramer 1998; United States Sentencing Commission 1995). Both studies found that black and Hispanic drug offenders were less likely than whites to receive a downward departure for substantial assistance. Maxfield and Kramer (1998) also found that the magnitude of the departure was greater for whites than for blacks or Hispanics.

4. A prior offender is an offender who has pleaded guilty to or has been found guilty of one felony. A persistent offender is one who has pleaded guilty to or has been found guilty of two or more felonies committed at different times. A dangerous offender is an offender who is being sentenced for a felony in which he murdered or endangered or threatened the life of another or in which he knowingly inflicted or attempted to inflict serious injury and who has been convicted previously of a Class A or Class B felony or a dangerous felony.

5. The sentencing guidelines, which were developed by the Sentencing Guidelines Commission, went into effect on October 1, 1983. There have been several revisions to the guidelines in the intervening years.

6. See Fla. Stat. §921.001 (4).

7. A guidelines score sheet is prepared by the Office of the State Attorney for each defendant. The score for each defendant is calculated by adding the total offense score, the total prior record score, and any enhancements for use of a weapon, habitual criminal status, and drug trafficking. The total offense score is calculated by adding the score for the primary offense, the score for additional offenses, and the score for victim injury.

8. In a 1994 interview with one of the authors, the Chief Judge of the Dade County Circuit Court stated that drug diversion and treatment was being offered to defendants "who didn't belong there." He noted that it was sometimes offered to defendants with prior felony convictions and to those charged with more serious drug offenses involving sales rather than possession.

9. Jail sentences were not common in the other two jurisdictions. Only thirty-three drug offenders were sentenced to jail in Chicago; no offender was sentenced to jail in Kansas City.

10. In Chicago and Kansas City we have data on the offender's employment status; we were not able to obtain this information for offenders in Miami. Because we believe it is important to use the same controls in each jurisdiction, we first model the sentencing decisions without this variable; we then add a variable measuring whether the offender was unemployed (coded 1) or not (coded 0) to the models for Chicago and Kansas City. We also test our hypothesis concerning interaction between the offender's race and the offender's employment status in these two jurisdictions only.

11. The correlations between prior felony conviction and prior drug conviction were .49 (Chicago), .53 (Miami), and .33 (Kansas City).

12. We controlled for both the type of drug offense and the class of the conviction charge because of the fact that each type of drug offense includes various classes of felonies. For example, in Florida possession of cocaine with intent to deliver is a second-degree felony, while possession of cocaine with intent to deliver within 1,000 feet of a school is a first-degree felony. Including both variables as controls provides a more accurate and reliable measure of offense seriousness.

13. We were not able to differentiate between powder cocaine and crack cocaine.

14. Very few offenders were sentenced to prison in some of the "categories" used to test for interaction. In Kansas City, for example, only 23 employed offenders were sentenced to prison. In Miami, only 43 offenders convicted of third-degree felonies were sentenced to prison. The SE's for many of the independent variables included in the models were very large, and the F statistics for the models were not significant.

REFERENCES

Adler, Jeffrey S. 1994. "The Dynamite, Wreckage, and Scum in Our Cities: The Social Construction of Deviance in Industrial America." *Justice Quarterly* 11: 33–49.

Albonetti, Celesta. 1997. "Sentencing under the Federal Sentencing Guidelines: Effects of Defendant Characteristics, Guilty Pleas, and Departures on Sentence Outcomes for Drug Offenses, 1991–1992." *Law and Society Review* 31: 789–822.

Arkin, Steven D. 1980. "Discrimination and Arbitrariness in Capital Punishment: An Analysis of Post-*Furman* Murder Cases in Dade County, Florida, 1973-1976." *Stanford Law Review* 33: 75–101.

Baldus, David C., George Woodworth, and Charles Pulaski. 1985. "Monitoring and Evaluating Contemporary Death Sentencing Systems: Lessons from Georgia." *U.C. Davis Law Review* 18: 1375–1407.

Baldus, David C., Charles Pulaski, and George Woodworth. 1983. "Comparative Review of Death Sentences: An Empirical Study of the Georgia Experience." *The Journal of Criminal Law and Criminology* 74: 661–753.

Barnett, Arnold. 1985. "Some Distribution Patterns for the Georgia Death Sentence." *U.C. Davis Law Review* 18: 1327–1374.

Berk, Richard A. 1983. "An Introduction to Sample Selection Bias in Sociological Data." *American Sociological Review* 48: 386–398.

Berk, Richard A., and Subhash C. Ray. 1982. "Selection Biases in Sociological Data." *Social Science Research* 11: 352–398.

Bernstein, Ilene Nagel, William R. Kelly, and Patricia A. Doyle. 1977. "Societal Reaction to Deviants: The Case of Criminal Defendants." *American Sociological Review* 42: 743–795.

Blumstein, Alfred. 1982. "On the Disproportionality of United States' Prison Populations." *The Journal of Criminal Law and Criminology* 73: 1259–1281.

Blumstein, Alfred. 1993. "Racial Disproportionality in U.S. Prisons Revisited." *University of Colorado Law Review* 64: 743–760.

Bowers, William J., and Glenn L. Pierce. 1980. "Arbitrariness and Discrimination under Post-*Furman* Capital Statutes." *Crime and Delinquency* 74: 1067–1100.

Bureau of Justice Statistics. 1998a. *Felony Defendants in Large Urban Counties, 1994.* Washington, DC: U.S. Department of Justice.

Bureau of Justice Statistics. 1998b. *State Court Sentencing of Convicted Felons, 1994.* Washington, DC: U.S. Department of Justice.

Chambliss, William J. 1995. "Crime Control and Ethnic Minorities: Legitimizing Racial Oppression by Causing Moral Panics." In Darnell F. Hawkins (ed.), *Ethnicity, Race and Crime.* Albany, NY: State University of New York Press.

Chambliss, William J., and Robert B. Seidman. 1971. *Law, Order and Power.* Reading, MA: Addison-Wesley.

Chiricos, Theodore G., and William D. Bales. 1991. "Unemployment and Punishment: An Empirical Assessment." *Criminology* 29: 701–724.

Chiricos, Theodore G., and Charles Crawford. 1995. "Race and Imprisonment: A Contextual Assessment of the Evidence." In Darnell F. Hawkins (ed.), *Ethnicity, Race and Crime.* Albany, NY: State University of New York Press.

Chiricos, Theodore G., and Miriam DeLone. 1992. "Labor Surplus and Punishment: A Review and Assessment of Theory and Evidence." *Social Problems* 39: 421–446.

Crawford, Charles, Ted Chiricos, and Gary Kleck. 1998. "Race, Racial Threat, and Sentencing of Habitual Offenders." *Criminology* 36: 481–511.

Gibson, James L. 1978. "Race as a Determinant of Criminal Sentences: A Methodological Critique and a Case Study." *Law and Society Review* 12: 455–478.

Gross, Samuel R., and Robert Mauro. 1989. *Death and Discrimination: Racial Disparities in Capital Sentencing.* Boston: Northeastern University Press.

Hagan, John. 1974. "Extra-Legal Attributes and Criminal Sentencing: An Assessment of a Sociological Viewpoint." *Law & Society Review* 8: 357–383.

Hanushek, Eric A., and John E. Jackson. 1977. *Statistical Methods for Social Scientists.* New York: Academic Press.

Hawkins, Darnell F. 1987. "Beyond Anomalies: Rethinking the Conflict Perspective on Race and Criminal Punishment." *Social Forces* 65: 719–745.

Heckman, James J. 1974. "Shadow Prices, Market Wages, and Labor Supply." *Econometrics* 42: 679–694.

Hembroff, Larry A. 1982. "Resolving Status Inconsistency: An Expectation States Theory and Test." *Social Forces* 61: 183–205.

Holmes, Malcolm D., Harmon M. Hosch, Howard C. Daudistel, Dolores A. Perez, and Joseph B. Graves. 1996. "Ethnicity, Legal Resources, and Felony Dispositions in Two Southwestern Jurisdictions." *Justice Quarterly* 13: 11–30.

Inciardi, James A., Duane C. McBride, and James E. Rivers. 1996. *Drug Control and the Courts.* Thousand Oaks, CA: Sage.

Jenkins, Phillip. 1994. "'The Ice Age': The Social Construction of a Drug Panic." *Justice Quarterly* 11: 7–31.

Keil, Thomas J., and Gennaro F. Vito. 1989. "Race, Homicide Severity, and Application of the Death Penalty: A Consideration of the Barnett Scale." *Criminology* 27: 511–531.

Kennedy, Randall. 1994. "Changing Images of the State: Criminal Law and Racial Discrimination: A Comment." *Harvard Law Review* 107: 1255, 1278.

Kennedy, Randall. 1997. *Race, Crime, and the Law.* New York: Vintage.

Kleck, Gary C. 1981. "Racial Discrimination in Sentencing: A Critical Evaluation of the Evidence with Additional Evidence on the Death Penalty." *American Sociological Review* 43: 783–805.

Klein, Stephen, Joan Petersilia, and Susan Turner. 1990. "Race and Imprisonment Decisions in California." *Science* 247: 812–816.

Klepper, Steven, Daniel Nagin, and Luke-Jon Tierney. 1983. "Discrimination in the Criminal Justice System: A Critical Appraisal of the Literature." In Alfred Blumstein, Jacqueline Cohen, Susan E. Martin, and Michael H. Tonry (eds.), *Research on Sentencing: A Search for Reform*, vol. 2, pp. 55–128.

Kramer, John H., and Darrell Steffensmeier. 1993. "Race and Imprisonment Decisions." *Sociological Quarterly* 34: 357–376.

Kramer, John H., and Jeffery T. Ulmer. 1996. "Sentencing Disparity and Departures from Guidelines." *Justice Quarterly* 13: 81–106.

LaFree, Gary D. 1985a. "Adversarial and Nonadversarial Justice: A Comparison of Guilty Pleas and Trials." *Criminology* 23: 289–312.

LaFree, Gary D. 1985b. "Official Reactions to Hispanic Defendants in the Southwest." *Journal of Research in Crime and Delinquency* 22: 213–237.

LaFree, Gary D. 1989. *Rape and Criminal Justice: The Social Construction of Sexual Assault*. Belmont, CA: Wadsworth.

Levin, Martin A. 1972. "Urban Politics and Policy Outcomes: The Criminal Courts." In George F. Cole (ed.), *Criminal Justice: Law and Politics*. Belmont, CA: Wadsworth.

Lichter, Daniel T. 1989. "Race, Employment Hardship, and Inequality in the American Nonmetropolitan South." *American Sociological Review* 54: 436–446.

Lizotte, Alan J. 1978. "Extra-legal Factors in Chicago's Criminal Courts: Testing the Conflict Model of Criminal Justice." *Social Problems* 25: 564–580.

Maguire, Kathleen, and Ann L. Pastore (eds.). 1998. *Sourcebook of Criminal Justice Statistics 1997*. Washington, DC: U.S. Department of Justice.

Maxfield, Linda Drazha, and John H. Kramer. 1998. *Substantial Assistance: An Empirical Yardstick Gauging Equity in Current Federal Policy and Practice*. Washington, DC: U.S. Sentencing Commission.

McDonald, Douglas G., and Kenneth E. Carlson. 1993. *Sentencing in the Federal Courts: Does Race Matter?* Washington, DC: U.S. Department of Justice, Office of Justice Programs.

Miethe, Terance D., and Charles A. Moore. 1986. "Racial Differences in Criminal Processing: The Consequences of Model Selection on Conclusions about Differential Treatment." *The Sociological Quarterly* 27: 217–237.

Miller, Jerome G. 1996. *Search and Destroy: African-American Males in the Criminal Justice System*. Cambridge: Cambridge University Press.

Myers, Martha A. 1989. "Symbolic Policy and the Sentencing of Drug Offenders." *Law and Society Review* 23: 295–315.

Myers, Martha A., and Susette Talarico. 1986. "The Social Contexts of Racial Discrimination in Sentencing." *Social Problems* 33: 236–251.

Nobiling, Tracy, Cassia Spohn, and Miriam DeLone. 1998. "A Tale of Two Counties: Unemployment and Sentence Severity." *Justice Quarterly* 15: 401–427.

Paternoster, Raymond. 1984. "Prosecutorial Discretion in Requesting the Death Penalty: A Case of Victim-Based Discrimination." *Law and Society Review* 18: 437–478.

Petersilia, Joan. 1983. *Racial Disparities in the Criminal Justice System*. Santa Monica, CA: Rand.

Peterson, Ruth, and John Hagan. 1984. "Changing Conceptions of Race: Toward an Account of Anomalous Findings in Sentencing Research." *American Sociological Review* 49: 56–70.

Pruitt, Charles R., and James Q. Wilson. 1983. "A Longitudinal Study of the Effect of Race on Sentencing." *Law and Society Review* 7: 613–635.

Quinney, Richard. 1970. *The Social Reality of Crime*. Boston: Little, Brown.

Radelet, Michael L. 1981. "Racial Characteristics and the Imposition of the Death Penalty." *American Sociological Review* 46: 918–927.

Spohn, Cassia. 1992. "An Analysis of the 'Jury Trial Penalty' and Its Effect on Black and White Offenders." *The Justice Professional*: 93–112.

Spohn, Cassia. 1994. "Crime and the Social Control of Blacks: The Effect of Offender/Victim Race on Sentences for Violent Felonies." In George Bridges and Martha Myers (eds.), *Inequality, Crime and Social Control*. Boulder, CO: Westview Press.

Spohn, Cassia. 2000. "Thirty Years of Sentencing Reform: The Quest for a Racially Neutral Sentencing Process." NIJ Criminal Justice 2000, vol. 3. Washington, DC: U.S. Department of Justice, National Institute of Justice.

Spohn, Cassia, and Jerry Cederblom. 1991. "Race and Disparities in Sentencing: A Test of the Liberation Hypothesis." *Justice Quarterly* 8: 305–327.

Spohn, Cassia, and Miriam DeLone. 2000. "When Does Race Matter? An Analysis of the Conditions under Which Race Affects Sentence Severity." *Sociology of Crime, Law, and Deviance* 2: 3–37.

Spohn, Cassia, Miriam DeLone, and Jeffrey Spears. 1998. "Race/Ethnicity, Gender and Sentence Severity in Dade County: An Examination of the Decision to Withhold Adjudication." *Journal of Crime and Justice* 21: 111–138.

Spohn, Cassia, John Gruhl, and Susan Welch. 1981–1982. "The Effect of Race on Sentencing: A Re-Examination of an Unsettled Question." *Law and Society Review* 16: 72–88.

Spohn, Cassia, and David Holleran. 2000. "The Imprisonment Penalty Paid by Young Unemployed Black and Hispanic Males." *Criminology* 38: 281–306.

Spohn, Cassia, and Jeffrey Spears. 1996. "The Effect of Offender and Victim Characteristics on Sexual Assault Case Processing Decisions." *Justice Quarterly* 13: 401–431.

Steffensmeier, Darrell, Jeffery Ulmer, and John Kramer. 1998. "The Interaction of Race, Gender, and Age in Criminal Sentencing: The Punishment Cost of Being Young, Black, and Male." *Criminology* 36: 763–797.

Thomson, R., and Matthew Zingraff. 1981. "Detecting Sentencing Disparity: Some Problems and Evidence." *American Journal of Sociology* 86: 869–880.

Tonry, Michael. 1995. *Malign Neglect: Race, Crime, and Punishment in America*. New York: Oxford University Press.

Uhlman, Thomas M., and N. Darlene Walker. 1980. "'He Takes Some of My Time, I Take Some of His': An Analysis of Judicial Sentencing Patterns in Jury Cases." *Law and Society Review* 14: 323–341.

United States Sentencing Commission. 1995. *Substantial Assistance Departures in the United States Courts*. Draft Final Report.

United States Sentencing Commission. 1999. *1998 Sourcebook of Federal Sentencing Statistics*. Washington, DC: United States Sentencing Commission.

Unnever, James D. 1982. "Direct and Organizational Discrimination in the Sentencing of Drug Offenders." *Social Problems* 30: 212–225.

Unnever, James D., and Larry A. Hembroff. 1987. "The Prediction of Racial/Ethnic Sentencing Disparities: An Expectation States Approach." *Journal of Research in Crime and Delinquency* 25: 53–82.

Walker, Samuel, Cassia Spohn, and Miriam DeLone. 1999. *The Color of Justice: Race, Ethnicity, and Crime in America.* 2d ed. Belmont, CA: Wadsworth.

Walsh, Anthony. 1987. "The Sexual Stratification Hypothesis and Sexual Assault in Light of the Changing Conceptions of Race." *Criminology* 25: 153–173.

Zatz, Marjorie S. 1984. "Race, Ethnicity, and Determinate Sentencing: A New Dimension to an Old Controversy." *Criminology* 22: 147–171.

Zatz, Marjorie S. 1987. "The Changing Forms of Racial/Ethnic Biases in Sentencing." *Journal of Research in Crime and Delinquency* 24: 69–92.

9

Race, Cops, and Traffic Stops

Angela J. Davis

When Wade Henderson, director of the Leadership Conference on Civil Rights, rented a car to drive to the University of Richmond Law School to give a lecture, he chose a bland family car rather than a flashy sports model.[1] Journalist and academic Salim Muwakkil not only rents drab, nondescript cars when he travels on the highway, but he also leaves his favorite black beret at home.[2] Neither man has a passion for dull-looking cars, and both can probably afford the fancier models. However, they make these decisions because they know from experience that the flashy sports car or the jaunty beret would increase their chances of being stopped by the police.

Wade Henderson and Salim Muwakkil are African-American men. That fact makes them more likely to be stopped and detained by the police than their white counterparts.[3] Flashy cars and distinctive hats attract the attention of the police even more. Neither the advancing age nor the graying hair of these men offsets the problem—a presumptive social offense that Mr. Muwakkil cogently describes as "Driving While Black."[4]

Although most police officers would deny relying on race as a reason to initiate traffic stops,[5] the practice of stopping motorists for a minor traffic infraction for the real purpose of searching or investigating them for other offenses is a common practice that the United States Supreme Court recently upheld.[6] In *Whren v. United States*,[7] the petitioners claimed that these "pretextual stops"[8] violate the Fourth Amendment to the Constitution and are racially discriminatory. The Supreme Court rejected the claim, upholding the constitutionality of pretextual stops based on probable cause and noting that claims of racial discrimination must be challenged under the equal protection clause.[9] The Court effectively sidestepped the subtextual issue of race in pretextual traffic stops,[10] despite the mounting evidence that such stops are often racially motivated.[11]

The *Whren* Court left African Americans and Latinos without an effective remedy for discriminatory pretextual traffic stops when it suggested the equal protection clause as the appropriate constitutional basis for challenging these stops. The motorist who is arrested after a pretextual stop, as well as the motorist who is eventually allowed to go his way, must overcome substantial hurdles to mount a successful challenge to discriminatory police practices under the equal protection clause. These problems may prove insurmountable for the arrested motorist and may ultimately discourage other aggrieved motorists. In this chapter, I discuss the Supreme Court's failure to provide a clear and effective remedy for discriminatory pretextual traffic stops. First, I discuss the discretionary nature of pretextual stops and their discriminatory effect on African Americans and Latinos. I then examine the *Whren* decision and the ineffectiveness of the Court's proposed remedy for both criminal defendants and motorists who are not arrested. In conclusion, I stress the need for creative legal and policy-based solutions.

THE DISCRIMINATORY NATURE OF PRETEXTUAL TRAFFIC STOPS

Police officers exercise a tremendous amount of discretion in the exercise of their official law enforcement duties.[12] The decisions to stop,[13] detain or arrest[14] an individual are all left to the discretion of police officers.[15] No scenario better exemplifies both the benefits and drawbacks of this discretionary arrest power than the traffic stop. Because most jurisdictions enact hundreds of traffic regulations,[16] it would be impossible for a police officer to issue a citation or make an arrest for every traffic violation he observed,[17] nor would motorists desire such a result. It is doubtful that motorists would support legislation requiring mandatory citations or arrests for all traffic violations. Even if motorists wanted such legislation, the administrative costs of implementing a system of mandatory citations or arrests for all traffic offenses would be staggering. These practical considerations justify the exercise of discretion, and police officers are arguably best situated to make the necessary judgments based on factors such as the seriousness of the offense and the actual or potential harm in a particular case. The obvious drawback of police discretion is that it inherently involves treating similarly situated motorists differently. A police officer may stop and ticket only one driver, even when he observes several motorists exceed the speed limit. This accepted exercise of police discretion may seem unfair to some motorists, but it is both unavoidable and legal. The more serious disadvantage of discretionary police power lies in its potential for abuse. Pretextual traffic stops exemplify this abuse when race—either consciously or unconsciously[18]—infuses the decision to stop a motorist.

The legal standard governing a police officer's decision to stop a suspect has become so flexible and loosely defined that it is difficult to know whether, and to what extent, race influences the decision. In *Terry v. Ohio*,[19] the Supreme Court adopted reasonable suspicion as the standard governing a police officer's decision to stop and possibly frisk a suspect.[20] The *Terry* Court held that the officer must have "specific and articulable facts ... taken together with rational inferences from those facts"[21] before stopping an individual. The Court held that mere suspicion and inarticulable hunches would not suffice.[22] However, in cases decided after *Terry*, the Court has exhibited increasing deference to the judgments of police officers in its interpretation of the reasonable suspicion standard.[23]

In *United States v. Cortez*,[24] the Court held that reasonable suspicion should be based on the "totality of the circumstances"[25] and that "[b]ased upon the whole picture the detaining officers must have a particularized and objective basis for suspecting the particular person stopped."[26] The Court held that the particularized suspicion must be based on all the circumstances, including inferences and deductions by a trained officer.[27] Given this flexible standard that not only acknowledges but credits the mental inferences of the police officer, it would be difficult to discern whether, and to what extent, racial considerations may be camouflaged in the midst of limitless inferences and deductions.

Police officers need not always conceal the fact that race has influenced their decision to detain a suspect, because some courts have ruled that race may be used as a detention factor in certain circumstances.[28] The Supreme Court has twice upheld the use of race in immigration detention decisions.[29] Courts that have upheld the consideration of race have held that race alone is not a sufficient basis for detention but may be one of a number of factors in the detention calculus.[30] Drug courier profiles also permit the infusion of race in the detention decision.[31] A law enforcement agent compiles a lot of characteristics that have been found through experience to be common characteristics of those engaged in a certain type of criminal activity in order to form a criminal profile.[32] Drug courier profiles have included a broad range of behaviors which often contradict.[33] For example, some drug courier profiles list individuals travelling alone by plane who exit last while others target those who leave first.[34] Travellers who carry certain types of luggage appear on some profiles while individuals who travel without luggage are on others.[35] Most if not all of the conduct and characteristics listed in the profile constitute innocent, noncriminal behavior. But in *United States v. Sokolow*,[36] the Supreme Court held that the fact that individual behaviors and characteristics were consistent with innocent behavior did not exclude them from consideration in the overall determination of whether the totality of the circumstances constituted reasonable suspicion or probable cause.[37] Race and ethnicity are two of the "innocent" characteristics specifically included in some drug courier profiles.[38]

The use of drug courier profiles may be discriminatory even when they do not list race as a characteristic because officers do not stop whites who exhibit the other innocent behaviors or characteristics as frequently as African Americans.[39] A white man dressed in a business suit who buys a round-trip plane ticket with a quick turnaround time, travels with no luggage, and deplanes last may not be detained. But a young black man or woman casually dressed who acts and travels the same way may raise the suspicions of law enforcement agents. If a police officer who uses a profile treats similarly situated blacks and whites differently, then race becomes the defining factor that elevates a suspicion or hunch to reasonable suspicion or even probable cause.[40]

Police who do not use drug courier profiles may believe that black men and women are more likely to engage in certain types of criminal behavior than whites because of statistical studies that purport to prove disproportionate criminality among African Americans.[41] Police officers who harbor these beliefs may either consciously or unconsciously consider an African American's race as a factor in the nebulous reasonable suspicion calculus. The idea that one's race may be used in the detention decision in any way other than as an identifying factor[42] troubles some scholars and jurists.[43] But even if one accepts the argument that race may be used in some circumstances as one of many factors, it would be virtually impossible to determine precisely what role race played in a particular detention decision. Did it play a minimal role or was it in fact the officer's primary or even sole reason for stopping a suspect?

Empirical evidence suggests that race is frequently the defining factor in pretextual traffic stops. Statistics gathered in connection with lawsuits filed by black motorists in New Jersey and Maryland reveal that 71 percent of the 437 motorists stopped and searched along a northeastern stretch of Interstate 95 in the first nine months of 1995 were black.[44] One hundred and forty-eight hours of videotaped traffic stops in Florida revealed that 70 percent of the 1,048 motorists stopped along Interstate 95 were black or Hispanic,[45] even though Blacks and Hispanics made up only 5 percent of the drivers on that stretch of the highway.[46] Less than 1 percent of the drivers received traffic citations and only 5 percent of the stops resulted in an arrest.[47]

In 1993, an African-American man in the city of Reynoldsburg, Ohio, sued the city after an informal group of police officers who called themselves the "Special Nigger Arrest Team" targeted him for arrest.[48] Several officers confirmed the existence of the group and admitted that its members singled out African Americans for traffic stops and arrests.[49] The city eventually settled the lawsuit.[50] Since police departments across the country have varying policies on the collection and release of information about the race of motorists who are stopped, detained, or searched, national statistics are not available.[51]

WHREN V. UNITED STATES

The Supreme Court was presented with the opportunity to remedy discriminatory pretextual traffic stops in the case of *Whren v. United States*. Despite the evidence that police officers used these stops to discriminate against people of color,[52] the Court dismissed the issue in a single sentence, noting that the

Equal Protection Clause was the appropriate constitutional basis for a claim of racial discrimination.[53] This cryptic reference to the equal protection clause constituted the Court's entire response to the petitioners' argument that pretextual stops discriminate against blacks and Latinos.

The facts of the *Whren* case reveal that the traffic stop was pretextual. Two young African-American men were sitting in a Nissan Pathfinder at a stop sign when they were first spotted by two plainclothes police officers. The officers asserted that they were suspicious because the occupants were youthful, the driver appeared to be looking into the lap of the passenger, and the car had temporary license plates.[54] In addition, the young men were driving in a "high drug area" of Washington, D.C., and the car remained at the stop sign for about twenty seconds, which the officers considered to be an unusually long period of time.[55] According to the officers, as the officers made a U-turn and drove toward the Pathfinder, its driver made a sharp right turn without signalling and sped off at a high rate of speed.[56] The police officers followed the Pathfinder until it stopped at a traffic light.[57] One of the officers got out of the unmarked car and approached the driver's side of the window.[58] The passenger was holding plastic bags containing what appeared to be crack cocaine.[59] The officers placed the two young men under arrest and charged them with various narcotics offenses.[60]

The defendants moved to suppress the drugs, alleging that the stop was illegal because the officers had neither probable cause nor reasonable suspicion to believe the defendants had drugs.[61] The defendants further claimed that the traffic stop was pretextual. The trial court denied the motion and the Court of Appeals affirmed, holding that "regardless of whether a police officer subjectively believes that the occupants of an automobile may be engaging in some other illegal behavior, a traffic stop is permissible as long as a reasonable officer in the same circumstances could have stopped the car for the suspected traffic violation."[62] The Supreme Court granted certiorari.[63]

Although the Court had not previously ruled on the constitutionality of pretextual traffic stops, it had addressed pretextual behavior in previous cases and seemed to express a general disapproval of the practice.[64] The Court acknowledged its discussion of pretextual stops and searches in previous cases[65] but noted, "not only have we never held, outside the context of inventory search or administrative inspection ... that an officer's motive invalidates objectively justifiable behavior under the Fourth Amendment; but we have repeatedly held and asserted the contrary."[66]

The Supreme Court affirmed the Court of Appeals, finding the stop legal because the police officers had probable cause to believe that the driver had committed several traffic violations.[67] The Court declined to question the motivations of the police officers and rejected the notion that the constitutional reasonableness of traffic stops depended on the actual motivations of the individual officers involved.[68] The Court noted that "the fact that the officer does not have the state of mind which is hypothecated by the reasons which provide the legal justification for the officer's action does not invalidate the action taken as long as the circumstances, viewed objectively, justify that action."[69]

The Court rejected the petitioners' argument that the standard for traffic stops should be "whether a police officer, acting reasonably, would have made the stop for the reason given."[70] The petitioners urged this standard because they claimed that a police officer could easily use a traffic stop as a pretext for investigating a motorist for some other crime for which he had neither probable cause nor reasonable suspicion.[71] The petitioners further claimed that police officers might use these traffic stops to detain motorists based on impermissible factors such as race.[72] The Court noted that the constitutional basis for challenging racially discriminatory enforcement of the law is the Equal Protection Clause, not the Fourth Amendment.[73] According to the Court, any legal challenge that requires questioning the subjective motivations of a police officer is not suitable for Fourth Amendment analysis.[74]

The Arrested Motorist

The *Whren* Court did not provide a clear, meaningful remedy for the criminal defendant who is arrested based on drugs or other contraband found during a race-based pretextual traffic stop. Although criminal defendants alleging a violation of their Fourth Amendment rights traditionally seek suppression of the illegally seized evidence under the exclusionary rule,[75] the *Whren* Court identified the Equal Protection Clause rather than the Fourth Amendment as the appropriate constitutional basis for claims based on race discrimination. However, the Court did not address the appropriate forum for raising such claims nor the appropriate remedy if the defendant prevails.

A criminal defendant could file a civil rights action under 42 U.S.C. § 1983[76] alleging that the police officer had denied him equal protection of the laws. If he prevailed, he would be entitled to damages or injunctive relief.[77] But would these remedies really compensate an incarcerated criminal defendant? Given the social hostility to citizens convicted of criminal offenses, would an individual found guilty of a criminal offense have any meaningful chance of securing a settlement or recouping monetary damages from a jury?[78] What type of injunctive relief would a court order? A judgment requiring police officers to refrain from searching a defendant or his car without probable cause to believe that criminal activity other than the traffic violation has occurred would not compensate the defendant who has already suffered harm.

Criminal defendants typically raise equal protection claims in their criminal cases based on alleged racially discriminatory behavior by prosecutors. In *United States v. Armstrong*,[79] the defendants alleged race-based selective prosecution and sought dismissal of the indictment as the appropriate remedy.[80] In *Batson v. Kentucky*,[81] the defendant alleged discriminatory use of peremptory strikes during jury selection, and at the trial stage, sought dismissal of the selected jury.[82] Although criminal defendants traditionally have not sought exclusion of evidence as a remedy for an equal protection violation,[83] exclusion would seem the most appropriate remedy for unconstitutional police behavior since it precisely meets the force of the violation. Likewise, criminal defendants typically have not sought dismissal of the indictment as a remedy for unconstitutional police behavior. However, since defendants would allege race-based selective enforcement of the law as the constitutional error, the violation is closely analogous to selective prosecution, and dismissal of the indictment might be the more appropriate remedy. The *Whren* Court provides no guidance on these issues.

Whether the criminal defendant raises the equal protection claim in the criminal or civil context, traditional equal protection analysis requires that the defendant prove that a police officer intentionally discriminated against him based on his race.[84] Specifically, the defendant must show that the law enforcement policy had a discriminatory effect[85] and that it was motivated by a discriminatory purpose.[86] A number of scholars have criticized the traditional equal protection standard as being an inadequate remedy for race discrimination because of the difficulty of proving invidious intent on the part of the state actor.[87] Motorists challenging pretextual stops would certainly face this obstacle. It would be quite difficult for a black motorist to prove that a police officer stopped or detained him because of his race. Even if the officer relied on a drug courier profile that included race as a factor, short of an admission by the police officer or similarly incriminating physical evidence, a motorist could not prove that race served as the only reason or the primary reason for the stop.[88]

The Supreme Court's recent decision in *United States v. Armstrong*[89] illustrates the obstacles a criminal defendant must overcome when he alleges a denial of equal protection. In *Armstrong*, the Court established the standard for discovery in criminal cases in which the defendant alleges race-based selective prosecution.[90] The Court held that in order to obtain discovery, the defendant would have to present some evidence that similarly situated defendants of another race could have been prosecuted, but were not.[91] The standard for prevailing on the merits is almost identical. The Court reaffirmed that a defendant attempting to prove selective prosecution based on race in violation of the equal protection clause must prove that similarly situated defendants of another race could have been prosecuted, but were not.[92] Presumably, more proof would be required to prevail on the merits than to obtain discovery, but the *Armstrong* Court does not provide much guidance on this issue.

An African-American motorist alleging that a police officer's use of a pretextual traffic stop constituted a denial of equal protection would need to show that similarly situated white motorists could have been stopped, detained, or arrested but were not. *Armstrong* suggests that they would need to provide *some* evidence of such failures to stop to obtain discovery and presumably *more* of such evidence to prevail on the merits. How could a motorist obtain such evidence? Even if he did not have to cross the *Armstrong* hurdle to get discovery, such information would not be readily available.[93] Police officers do not keep records of instances in which they could have stopped a motorist for a traffic violation but did not.

The Motorist Who Is Not Arrested

Pretextual traffic stops may have a discriminatory effect on an individual whether or not the police discover evidence of criminal activity. When the police detain and search a motorist, they intrude on his privacy and possessory rights, his right to be left alone. While one might be tempted to conclude that when the police detain an individual and ultimately release him, he suffers little or no harm, when the detention is based on race, the harm is felt long past the duration of the stop.

One would surmise that the motorist who is not arrested and therefore does not carry the stigma or bear the practical difficulties of an incarcerated criminal defendant should be able to challenge a racially discriminatory pretextual traffic stop successfully. The case of *Robert Wilkins v. Maryland State Troopers* illustrates that the *Whren* Court's proposed remedy for these stops may fail even in the best-case scenario.[94]

Mr. Wilkins does not come close to fitting a drug courier profile. With the exception of his African heritage, he displays none of the characteristics or behavior listed in the typical drug courier profile. Mr. Wilkins is 33 years old, married, and drives a 1989 Nissan Sentra. He wears horn-rimmed glasses and dresses conservatively. A graduate of the Harvard Law School and a staff attorney at the Public Defender Service for the District of Columbia, Mr. Wilkins is an active member of the Union Temple Baptist church, where he serves as a trustee and mentor in the Rites of Passage Manhood program, a mentoring program for young men eleven to seventeen years old. Despite his quiet and modest manner, Mr. Wilkins' physical appearance is almost regal, primarily because of his carriage—proud, upright, and most dignified. His speech is precise, clear, always proper, and never profane. Its content reveals his intelligence and thoughtfulness.

On May 8, 1992, Mr. Wilkins was driving from Chicago to Washington, D.C., with his aunt, uncle, and cousin. They had attended the funeral of Mr. Wilkins' grandfather, Rev. G. R. Wilkins, Sr. The family was driving a Cadillac they had rented for the trip. They had decided to drive all night so that Mr. Wilkins could arrive on time for a client's 9:30 A.M. court appearance.

At about 5:55 A.M., Maryland state police officer V. W. Hughes stopped the car on I-68 in Cumberland, Maryland. Mr. Wilkins' cousin, Scott El-Amin, was driving at the time. Officer Hughes stated that Mr. El-Amin had been driving sixty miles per hour in a forty-mile-per-hour zone. Before issuing either a ticket or a warning, Hughes produced a form requesting consent to search the car. The family declined consent and refused to sign the form. Hughes stated that the searches were routine and further stated, "if you have nothing to hide, then what is the problem?" Mr. Wilkins' uncle stated that he would not consent to the officer searching through all of their belongings on the highway in the rain. Mr. Wilkins asked Hughes why he wanted to search the car. Hughes refused to provide an explanation and merely repeated his request. He then mumbled something about "problems with rental cars coming up and down the highway with drugs." Mr. Wilkins then informed Hughes that they were returning from his grandfather's funeral in Chicago and offered to show him a copy of the obituary. Hughes declined the offer and informed the family that if they did not consent to the search, they would have to wait while he called for a narcotics dog to come and sniff the car.

Mr. Wilkins, drawing on his experience as a criminal defense appellate and trial lawyer, informed Hughes that there was a Supreme Court case entitled *United States v. Sharpe*[95] that prevented him from detaining them without a reasonable, articulable suspicion that they were carrying drugs.[96] Mr. Wilkins further noted that the officer had no such reasonable suspicion. No doubt irritated rather than enlightened by Mr. Wilkins' impromptu lesson in criminal procedure, the officer told Mr. Wilkins and his family that they would just have to wait.

At approximately 6:25, Sergeant Brown arrived with a narcotics dog and ordered them out of the car. The family asked if they could remain in the car during the dog sniff so they could stay out of the rain and away from the dog. The police officers refused their request and insisted that they stand in the rain. The German shepherd sniffed slowly and thoroughly around the car while curious motorists passed on the highway. The dog detected nothing. Hughes issued a $105 speeding ticket and at about 6:35, the Wilkins family continued on their way. Mr. Wilkins was late for his court appearance.

Mr. Wilkins and his family felt humiliated and angry. Unlike most motorists who endure this experience, Mr. Wilkins decided to pursue legal action. He wrote to the local office of the American Civil Liberties Union (ACLU). After meeting with Mr. Wilkins, the ACLU lawyers decided to represent him. Lawyers from the firm of Hogan and Hartson agreed to join as counsel. They filed a lawsuit against the Maryland State Police, alleging that Mr. Wilkins and his family had been falsely imprisoned and intentionally treated differently on account of their race in violation of the Fourth and Fourteenth Amendments to the United States Constitution, Maryland common law, Title VI of the Civil Rights Act of 1964, and 42 U.S.C. Sec. 1983.[97] In addition to violations of their Fourth Amendment right to be free from unreasonable searches and seizures, the plaintiffs claimed deprivation of "their right to equal protection of the laws as enjoyed by similarly situated Caucasian citizens of the United States secured to them by the Fourteenth Amendment."[98]

On June 5, 1995, the Maryland State Police agreed to a settlement involving monetary damages and injunctive relief.[99] The Maryland State Police consented to adopt a policy prohibiting the use of race-based drug courier profiles as a law enforcement tool.[100] They further agreed that the policy would direct all Maryland State Police not to use a race-based profile as a cause for stopping, detaining, or searching motorists traveling on Maryland roadways.[101] The policy would be enforced through appropriate investigation and disciplinary action.[102] Additional terms of the agreement included the implementation of a mandatory training program incorporating the policy and a requirement that computer records of all stops involving consent to search or dog sniffs be maintained.[103] Such records would document the date, time, and location of the consent, search, or dog sniff, the name of the officer, the race of the person(s) stopped, detained or searched, the year, make, and model of the car and the grounds for requesting the search or dog sniff.[104]

The agreement also provided that after July 1, 1995, if the plaintiffs made a reasonable showing that a pattern and practice of race-based stops existed, plaintiffs might seek to require the defendants to provide additional identifying information in the computer records and the Court's jurisdiction would be extended to June 30, 1998.[105] The information received thus far indicates a continued pattern and practice of stopping African Americans.[106] The plaintiffs have filed pleadings requesting that the defendants be held in contempt of court.[107]

In one sense, Robert Wilkins' story is a hopeful one. Despite continuing litigation, the outcome of his case was successful. He secured a settlement agreement that compels the Maryland State Police to refrain from considering race as a factor in the decision to stop, detain, and search motorists on Maryland highways. His family received monetary compensation for the harm they experienced.

On the other hand, Mr. Wilkins' case engenders pessimism about the interaction of police forces with African-American citizens on streets and highways. Despite the settlement agreement, preliminary findings indicate a continued pattern of discriminatory stops and searches by the Maryland state police. As a result, Mr. Wilkins' lawyers continue to seek judicial relief. Moreover, the ramifications of this case for most other African-American motorists are, at best, uncertain. Unfortunately, Mr. Wilkins' case cannot be used as an example of what every similarly aggrieved African American can achieve. First, Mr. Wilkins is far better educated than most motorists—black or white—particularly in the area of Fourth Amendment law, and was able confidently to assert his rights. Second, he was not arrested and charged with a criminal offense and thus had access to more legal options. Third, Mr. Wilkins' persona—intelligent, articulate, well-educated, church-going, and charismatic—had much to do with the ACLU's decision to handle his case.[108] No doubt, these factors also influenced the decision of the Maryland State Police to settle the case.[109] Finally, his case has no legal precedential value for other aggrieved motorists.

CONCLUSION

The race-based pretextual traffic stop tears a hole in the fabric of our constitution by allowing discriminatory behavior to invade the criminal justice system. Faced with the opportunity to repair the hole, the Supreme Court chose to ignore it, leaving African Americans and other people of color without a clear and effective remedy for this discriminatory treatment. In a certain sense, discriminatory police stops are the first in a chain of racially lopsided decisions by officials in the criminal justice process.[110] With the exception of its decision in *Batson v. Kentucky*,[111] the Supreme Court has consistently dodged the resolution of these issues,[112] leaving people of color without relief.

When people of color experience injustices that are tolerated and even sanctioned by courts and other criminal justice officials, they develop distrust and disrespect for the justice system. That lack of faith translates into hopelessness, frustration, and even violence. The 1992 Los Angeles riots following the acquittal of the police officers charged with the beating of Rodney King[113] and the 1996 riots in St. Petersburg occasioned by the shooting of a black motorist by a police officer[114] offer examples of what may happen when that frustration is ignored. "Discrimination on the basis of race, odious in all aspects, is especially pernicious in the administration of justice."[115] "Disparate enforcement of criminal sanctions 'destroys the appearance of justice and thereby casts doubt on the integrity of the judicial process.'"[116] Nondiscriminatory law enforcement policies and effective legal remedies accessible to all aggrieved citizens must be developed to restore the integrity of the legal process and the trust of all citizens.

NOTES

The author would like to thank Professor Kim Taylor-Thompson and Dean Jamin Raskin for their helpful comments and suggestions and Angela Collier and Marcos Roberts for their research assistance.

1. *See* Michael A. Fletcher, *Driven to Extremes Black Men Take Steps to Avoid Police Stops*, WASH. POST, Mar. 29, 1996, at A1.

2. *See id.*

3. *See generally* David A. Harris, *Factors for Reasonable Suspicion: When Stopped and Frisked Means Black and Poor*, 69 IND. L.J. 659 (1994); Sheri Lynn Johnson, *Race and the Decision to Detain a Suspect*, 93 YALE L.J. 214 (1983).

4. Fletcher, *supra* note 1, at A1.

5. *But see* testimony of defense witness Kathless Bell in trial of O.J. Simpson who stated that former Los Angeles police officer Mark Fuhrman told her "of his hatred for interracial couples and suggested he would often stop them for no reason—just to harass them." *Simpson's Lawyers Shift Gears*, CHI. TRIB., Sept. 2, 1995, at 3.

6. If a police officer has probable cause to believe that the motorist has committed a traffic violation, he may forcibly detain him in order to issue a citation or even arrest him. See United States v. Robinson, 414 U.S. 218, 234–35 (1973). If the police officer decides to place the motorist under arrest, he then has the legal authority to conduct a full-blown search incident to the arrest of the motorist and the area around him. *See* Chimel v. California, 395 U.S. 752, 762–63 (1969). Any evidence or contraband found on the motorist may be used as the basis for probable cause to arrest him for other crimes. *See* Whren v. United States, 116 S. Ct. 1769, 1774 (1996); *Robinson*, 414 U.S. at 266. Aside from the opportunity to ticket or arrest a motorist, the pretextual traffic stop gives a po-

lice officer the opportunity to request permission to search his car. The police officer may legally request such permission to search, whether or not he decides to issue a traffic ticket. Although the officer must have reasonable suspicion or probable cause to stop or arrest a motorist, once the reason for the stop or arrest is completed, the officer has the right to continue to speak with him. Even if a police officer does not have probable cause or reasonable suspicion to believe that a crime has been or is about to be committed, he nonetheless has the right to approach an individual and speak with him. *See* Florida v. Bostick, 501 U.S. 429, 434 (1991). The Supreme Court has held that if the individual does not want to talk to the officer, he has the right to decline and walk away, and the exercise of those rights may not be used as the sole basis for probable cause or even reasonable suspicion. *See* Florida v. Royer, 460 U.S. 491, 497–98 (1983). (citing United States v. Mendenhall, 446 U.S. 544, 556 (1980)). Although many people do not realize they may refuse an officer's request to speak with them or search their car, *see* Bailey v. United States, 389 F.2d 305, 364 (D.C. Cir. 1967) (stating "people generally do not know and usually do not care whether they have a lawful right to walk away without regard for the presence of the policeman"); *cf.* Richard Cordray, *Drivers Must Yield a Few Rights to Police in War Against Crime, Court Decides*, COLUMBUS DISPATCH, July 1, 1996, at 7A (arguing that a motorist may permit a search due to fear that refusal would cause harsher sanctions for an alleged violation), the Supreme Court has held that police are not constitutionally required to inform individuals of this right. *See* Ohio v. Robinette, 65 U.S.L.W. 4013 (U.S. Nov. 18, 1996) (No. 95-891).

7. 116 S. Ct. 1769 (1996).

8. Although pretextual stops may be defined as any stop in which a police officer pretends to stop an individual for one reason so that he may investigate them for another, this chapter will only address pretextual stops in the traffic context.

9. *See* 116 S. Ct. 1769, 1774 (1996).

10. *See id.* at 1774. The Court only briefly mentions the race issue in its reference to the equal protection clause as the proper constitutional basis for challenging selective enforcement of the law based on race.

11. *See* Brief for Petitioners at 21–29, Whren v. United States, 116 S. Ct. 1769 (1996) (No. 95-5841).

12. *See generally* United States v. Robinson, 414 U.S. 218 (1973).

13. A police officer may stop and frisk suspects without probable cause if they have reasonable and articulable suspicion that "criminal activity may be afoot and that the persons with whom he is dealing may be armed and dangerous." Terry v. Ohio, 392 U.S. 1, 30 (1968). The Court has defined reasonable suspicion as "specific and articulable facts which, taken together with rational inferences from those facts, reasonably warrant that intrusion." *Id.* at 21.

14. A police officer may arrest a suspect without a warrant for a felony or misdemeanor committed in his presence or for a felony not committed in his presence if there are reasonable grounds for making the arrest. *See* United States v. Watson, 423 U.S. 411, 418 (1976) (citations omitted). Probable cause is defined as "a fair probability that contraband or evidence of a crime will be found." Illinois v. Gates, 462 U.S. 213, 238 (1983).

15. The police conduct investigations of criminal activities and make arrests. Practically speaking, a decision not to stop, detain, or arrest is unreviewable. *See* STEPHEN A. SALTZBURG & DANIEL J. CAPRA, AMERICAN CRIMINAL PROCEDURE 681 (5th ed. 1996).

16. Barbara C. Salken, *The General Warrant of the Twentieth Century? A Fourth Amendment Solution to Unchecked Discretion to Arrest for Traffic Offenses*, 62 TEMP.

L. Rev. 221, 223 (1989) (stating "[t]he innumerable rules and regulations governing vehicular travel make it difficult not to violate one of them at one time or another.").

17. Driving over the speed limit, crossing the divider line, and changing lanes without signalling are all examples of traffic violations that are committed with such frequency that their volume prohibits the enforcement of the law in every case. It is probably fair to say that every single driver in America has committed a traffic violation at some point in their lives, and most probably commit them on a daily basis.

18. See Charles R. Lawrence III, *The Id, the Ego, and Equal Protection: Reckoning with Unconscious Racism*, 39 Stan. L. Rev. 317 (1987). Professor Lawrence defines unconscious racism as the ideas, attitudes, and beliefs developed in American historical and cultural heritage that cause Americans unconsciously to attach significance to an individual's race and that induce negative feelings and opinions about nonwhites. *See id.* at 322. He argues that although America's historical experience has made racism an integral part of our culture, because racism is rejected as immoral, most people exclude it from their conscious minds. *See id.* at 322–23; *see also* Sheri Lynn Johnson, *Unconscious Racism and the Criminal Law*, 73 Cornell L. Rev. 1016 (1988) (discussing unconscious racism in criminal law and procedure).

19. 392 U.S. 1 (1968).

20. In *Terry v. Ohio*, 392 U.S. 1 (1968), the Supreme Court first held that a police officer may stop and search an individual on less than probable cause. The Court established that the decisions to stop and frisk a suspect are two distinct determinations. A police officer may stop an individual if he has reasonable suspicion to believe that crime is afoot, but he may frisk the suspect only if he has reasonable suspicion to believe the suspect is armed and dangerous. *See id.* at 30.

21. *Terry*, 392 U.S. at 21.

22. 392 U.S. at 22.

23. *See* David A. Harris, *Factors for Reasonable Suspicion: When Black and Poor Means Stopped and Frisked*, 69 Ind. L.J. 659, 660–69 (1994) (suggesting that the Court has relaxed the *Terry* standard in deference to law enforcement concerns).

24. 449 U.S. 411 (1981).

25. *Cortez*, 449 U.S. at 417–18.

26. *Id.*

27. *See* 449 U.S. at 418.

28. *See* United States v. Weaver, 966 F.2d 391, 394–96 (8th Cir. 1992) (finding race coupled with other factors is a basis for reasonable, articulable suspicion justifying detention of young black male in airport); State v. Dean, 543 P.2d 425, 427 (Ariz. 1975) (deciding ethnic background of defendant properly considered where person appears out of place in neighborhood); State v. Ruiz, 504 P.2d 1307, 1307–09 (Ariz. Ct. App. 1967) (holding that police properly considered race of defendant when they stopped a Mexican in an all-black area). *But see* State v. Barber, 823 P.2d 1068, 1074–75 (Wash. 1992) (holding that a person of a specific race being allegedly "out of place" in a particular geographic area can never constitute finding of reasonable suspicion of criminal behavior); City of St. Paul v. Uber, 450 N.W.2d 623, 628–29 (Minn. Ct. App. 1990) (holding that presence of white person from suburban town in mixed, high-crime neighborhood does not constitute basis for detention).

29. *See* United States v. Martinez-Fuerte, 428 U.S. 543, 563–64 (1976) (holding that there was no constitutional violation when border patrol detained motorists even if such referrals were made largely on basis of apparent Mexican ancestry); United States v.

Brignoni-Ponce, 422 U.S. 873, 885–87 (1975) (holding that border patrol officers may consider race of suspect as a factor in decision to stop).

30. *See* United States v. Weaver, 966 F.2d 391, 394–96 (8th Cir. 1992). For a detailed discussion on race and detention, see Sheri Lynn Johnson, *Race and the Decision to Detain a Suspect*, 93 YALE L.J. 214 (1983).

31. *See* United States v. Harvey, 16 F.3d 109, 113 (6th Cir. 1994) (Keith, J., dissenting) (police officer involved in pretextual traffic stop testified that the defendants fit a drug courier profile because they were "three young black male occupants in an old vehicle").

32. *See* STEPHEN A. SALTZBURG & DANIEL J. CAPRA, AMERICAN CRIMINAL PROCEDURE 200 (5th ed. 1996).

33. *See* United States v. Sokolow, 490 U.S. 1, 13–14 (1989) (Marshall, J., dissenting) (citing examples of drug courier profiles which contradict each other).

34. *Compare* United States v. Mendenhall, 446 U.S. 544, 564 (1980) (explaining suspect last to deplane), *with* United States v. Moore, 675 F.2d 802, 803 (6th Cir. 1982) (explaining suspect first to deplane).

35. *Compare* United States v. Craemer, 555 F.2d 594, 595 (6th Cir. 1977) (suspect without luggage), *with* United States v. Sullivan, 625 F.2d 9, 12 (4th Cir. 1980) (suspect with new suitcases), *and* United States v. Sanford, 658 F.2d 342, 343 (5th Cir. 1981) (suspect carrying gym bag).

36. 490 U.S. 1 (1989).

37. 490 U.S. at 10 ("[I]nnocent behavior will frequently provide the basis for a showing of probable cause," and "[i]n making a determination of probable cause the relevant inquiry is not whether particular conduct is 'innocent' or 'guilty,' but the degree of suspicion that attaches to particular types of noncriminal acts. That principle applies equally well to the reasonable suspicion inquiry.") (citing Illinois v. Gates, 462 U.S. 213, 243–44 n.13 (1983)).

38. *See* United States v. Rosales, 60 F.3d 835 (9th Cir. 1994) (unpublished opinion) (Hispanic men driving American-made luxury or performance automobiles); United States v. Weaver, 966 F.2d 391, 392–93 (8th Cir. 1992) (young black male, roughly dressed, walking rapidly towards taxi stand, deplaned in Kansas City from L.A.).

39. For a discussion of the use of race in drug courier profiles *see* Johnson, *supra* note 30, at 233–34.

40. *See generally* Johnson, *supra* note 30.

41. *See* MICHAEL TONRY, MALIGN NEGLECT: RACE, CRIME, AND PUNISHMENT IN AMERICA 56–68 (1995) (analyzing studies which compare arrests and victim reports with incarceration rates and concluding that blacks disproportionately commit certain types of crimes). *But see* Angela J. Davis, *Benign Neglect of Racism in the Criminal Justice System*, 94 MICH. L. REV. 1660, 1681 (1996) (criticizing Tonry's analysis and arguing that the use of arrest statistics as a measure of criminal behavior is inherently flawed due to the discretionary and often discriminatory detention and arrest decisions of police officers. Davis also argues that despite the problems inherent in relying on arrest statistics, Tonry's analysis indicates the existence of substantial racial bias in the criminal process).

42. Witnesses of crime may include the race of the suspect in their descriptions. *See* United States v. Collins, 532 F.2d 79, 83 (8th Cir. 1976) (holding stop of African American driving brown Cadillac within miles of bank proper where description of bank robbery suspects indicated three black men escaped in brown Cadillac).

43. *See* United States v. Collins, 532 F.2d 79, 85 (8th Cir. 1976) (Heaney, J., dissenting) (arguing factor of race eliminates persons of another race from suspicion, but police should not suspect persons of identified race, especially in our society where "race is often an integral part of police suspicion") (citing PRESIDENT'S COMM'N ON LAW ENFORCEMENT AND THE ADMIN. OF JUSTICE, TASK FORCE REPORT: POLICE 184 (1967)); Johnson, *supra* note 30.

44. *See* Michael A. Fletcher, *Driven to Extremes*, WASH. POST, MAR. 29, 1996, at A1.

45. *See* Jeff Brazil & Steve Berry, *Color of Driver Is Key to Stops in I-95 Videos*, ORLANDO SENTINEL, Aug. 23, 1992, at A1.

46. *See* Henry Pierson Curtis, *Statistics Show Pattern of Discrimination*, ORLANDO SENTINEL, Aug. 23, 1992, at A11.

47. *See* Brazil and Berry, *supra* note 45.

48. *See* Fletcher, *supra* note 44.

49. *See id.*

50. *See id.*

51. *See id.* In examining the extent to which police officers use pretextual stops in a racially discriminatory way, one must examine the extent to which police officers fail to stop, search and/or arrest whites who commit traffic violations. When police officers stop whites for traffic violations, do they ask them for permission to search their cars as much as they ask similarly situated African Americans? Do they arrest whites for traffic violations with the same frequency as African Americans? For a discussion of the discriminatory nature of discretionary police stops, see Angela J. Davis, *Benign Neglect of Racism in the Criminal Justice System*, 94 MICH. L. REV. 1660 (1996). Since police officers do not routinely keep records of the instances in which they either decline to stop individuals or stop them without issuing a citation or making an arrest, it is difficult to document whether police officers treat white motorists more favorably than blacks. *But see infra* note 106 and accompanying text for discussion of how such practices were documented and collected as evidence in lawsuit brought against Maryland state troopers.

52. *See* Brief for the Petitioners at 21-29, Whren v. United States, 116 S. Ct. 1769 (1996) (No. 95-5841).

53. *See* Whren v. United States, 116 S. Ct. 1769, 1774 (1996).

54. *See id.* at 1772.

55. *Id.*

56. *See id.*

57. *See id.*

58. *See id.*

59. *See id.*

60. *See id.*

61. The petitioners concede that the officers had probable cause to believe that they had violated various traffic regulations (failing to give full time and attention to the operation of their vehicle, turning without signalling, and speeding). *See Whren*, 116 S. Ct. 1769 at 1772–73.

62. United States v. Whren, 53 F.3d 371, 374–75 (D.C. Cir. 1995), *cert. granted*, 116 S. Ct. 690 (1996).

63. Whren v. United States, 116 S. Ct. 690 (1996).

64. *See* Florida v. Wells, 495 U.S. 1, 4 (1990) (stating use of inventory search as front for general search for incriminating evidence improper); New York v. Burger, 482 U.S.

691, 716-17 n.27 (1987) (noting proper administrative inspection valid and not illegal); Colorado v. Bertine, 479 U.S. 367, 372 (1987) (approving inventory search where there was no showing police acted in bad faith or for sole purpose of investigation); Colorado v. Bannister, 449 U.S. 1 (1980) (per curium) (noting officer's issuance of traffic citation not pretext for confirming unrelated suspicions). *But see* United States v. Villamonte-Marquez, 462 U.S. 579, 584 n.3 (1983) (holding customs officials with valid legal justification may board vessel regardless of alleged ulterior motive); Scott v. United States, 436 U.S. 128, 138 (1978) (deciding subjective intent of agents' wiretapping not relevant to legality of conduct); Gustafson v. Florida, 414 U.S. 260, 265–66 (1973) (following *Robinson*, Court upheld full search of person incident to arrest regardless of officers' subjective fear that suspect might be armed); United States v. Robinson, 414 U.S. 218, 221 n.1, 236 (1973) (rejecting petitioner's argument that search was invalid because traffic violation based arrest was pretext for drug search).

65. *Whren*, 116 S. Ct. at 1773–74.

66. *Id.* at 1774.

67. *See id.* at 1777.

68. *See id.* at 1774.

69. *Id.* at 1774 (quoting Scott v. United States, 436 U.S. 128, 138 (1978)).

70. *Id.* at 1773.

71. *See id.* at 1772–74.

72. *See id.* at 1772–73.

73. *See id.* at 1774.

74. *See id.* Although the Court eschews questioning the motivations of police officers under the Fourth Amendment, it *requires* proof of such motivations in Equal Protection analysis. *See generally* Washington v. Davis, 426 U.S. 229 (1976); *see also* McCleskey v. Kemp, 481 U.S. 279 (1987) (defendant alleging discrimination in the administration of Georgia's death penalty statute in violation of the equal protection clause must prove that decision makers in his case acted with discriminatory purpose).

75. Courts exclude evidence from the Government's case-in-chief on the merits of guilt or innocence where the court determines that the evidence was the product of an unconstitutional search or seizure. The Court first introduced the doctrine in federal courts in *Weeks v. United States*, 232 U.S. 383 (1914), and subsequently applied the rule to the states in *Mapp v. Ohio*, 367 U.S. 643 (1961). The Court has explicitly stated that the "exclusionary rule was a judicially created means of effectuating the rights secured by the Fourth Amendment." Stone v. Powell, 428 U.S. 465, 482–93 (1976) (emphasis added).

76. 42 U.S.C. § 1983 (1994) provides:

> Every person, who, under color of any statute, ordinance, regulation, custom, or usage, or any State or Territory, subjects, or causes to be subjected, any citizen of the United States or other person within the jurisdiction thereof to the deprivation of any rights, privileges, or immunities secured by the Constitution and laws, shall be liable to the party injured in an action at law, suit in equity, or other proper proceeding for redress.

77. *See* 42 U.S.C. § 1983.

78. Criminal defendants experience difficulty securing legal representation for these claims. *See infra* note 108.

79. 116 S. Ct. 1480 (1996).

80. *See id.* at 1483; *see also infra* notes 89–93 and accompanying text.

81. 476 U.S. 79 (1986).

82. *Id.* at 83.

83. *But see* State v. Pedro Soto, Superior Court of New Jersey (unpublished opinion, March 4, 1996) (suppressing evidence seized as result of discriminatory enforcement of the traffic laws by the New Jersey State Police under the equal protection and due process clauses of the Fourteenth Amendment and citing State v. Kennedy, 588 A.2d 834 (N.J. Super. Ct. App. Div. 1991)).

84. *See* Washington v. Davis, 426 U.S. 229, 239 (1976).

85. A plaintiff can establish a prima facie case of an equal protection violation by showing that the application of the statute or regulation at issue has had a discriminatory effect. *See id.* at 241.

86. *See id.* at 239.

87. *See generally* Charles R. Lawrence III, *The Id, the Ego, and Equal Protection: Reckoning with Unconscious Racism,* 39 STAN. L. REV. 317, 319–23 (1987) (arguing that most behavior that produces racial discrimination results from "unconscious racial motivation"); Paul Brest, *In Defense of the Antidiscrimination Principle,* 90 HARV. L. REV. 1, 4–5 (1976) (setting forth a disproportionate impact doctrine as an alternative to the *Washington v. Davis* discriminatory purpose standard, arguing that the *Davis* standard ignores the fact that "race-dependent decisions are so often concealed").

88. *See supra* notes 24–51 and accompanying text.

89. 116 S. Ct. 1480 (1996).

90. *Id.* at 1487.

91. *See id.* at 1488–89.

92. *See id.* at 1487. The Court does not explain the difference between the discovery standard and the standard for prevailing on the merits. Presumably more proof would be necessary to prevail on the merits.

93. *See infra* note 106 for discussion of how such information was compiled in a pending lawsuit.

94. Although Mr. Wilkins' case was brought and resolved one year before the *Whren* decision, his claim alleged a violation of his right to equal protection of the laws under the Fourteenth Amendment to the United States Constitution, as well as violations of the Fourth Amendment, Maryland common law, Title VI of the Civil Rights Act of 1964, and 42 U.S.C. Sec. 1983 (1994).

95. 470 U.S. 675 (1985).

96. *See id.* at 683; *id.* at 689 (Marshall, J., concurring).

97. *See* Robert L. Wilkins v. Maryland State Police, Complaint filed in U.S. District Court for the District of Maryland, p. 3.

98. *Id.* at p. 12.

99. *See* Settlement Agreement, United States District Court for the District of Maryland, Civil Action No. MJG-93-468.

100. *See id.* at p. 3.

101. *See id.*

102. *See id.* at p. 4.

103. *See id.*

104. *See id.* at p. 5.

105. *See id.*

106. In preparation for further litigation, the plaintiffs and their lawyers commissioned testers to compile additional evidence. These testers drove on a stretch of I-95

between Baltimore and Delaware at exactly 55 mph (the speed limit for this portion of the highway) and documented the number of drivers who drove over the speed limit and committed other obvious traffic violations. Preliminary test results indicate that 17 percent of drivers on this part of the highway were black and that 17 percent of black drivers committed traffic violations. Ninety-three percent of all drivers committed some traffic violation. Thus, African Americans were not found to violate traffic regulations more than members of other racial groups. In fact, the statistics indicate the opposite conclusion. Interview with Robert Wilkins, October 27, 1996.

107. *See* Paul W. Valentine, *Maryland State Police Still Target Black Motorists, ACLU Says*, WASH. POST, Nov. 15, 1996, at A1. Seventy-three percent of the cars stopped and searched by troopers on I-95 between Baltimore and Delaware since January 1995 were driven by African Americans. The police found nothing in 70 percent of the drug searches. *See id.*

108. The motorist who decides to seek legal assistance must find a lawyer or organization to accept his case. Most lawyers, aware of the difficult legal standards, will only take the case if the facts and circumstances suggest a winning case. The ACLU gets hundreds of telephone calls and letters from African Americans alleging illegal and/or unconstitutional behavior by police officers. They decline the vast majority of the cases for a variety of reasons, including the unavailability of resources. One factor they consider is whether the potential plaintiff will appeal to a jury if a lawsuit is brought. Individuals with criminal records are not considered attractive plaintiffs. Telephone Interview with Debbie Jeon, attorney for the Maryland Eastern Shore branch of the ACLU (Nov. 8, 1996).

109. Because the case was settled, one can only speculate as to the difficulties Mr. Wilkins and his family may have faced in establishing invidious intent on the part of the police officer as required by *Washington v. Davis*, 426 U.S. 229, 239 (1976). *See supra* notes 84–87 and accompanying text.

110. *See generally* Angela J. Davis, *Benign Neglect of Racism in the Criminal Justice System*, 94 MICH. L. REV. 1660 (1996).

111. 476 U.S. 79 (1986).

112. *See e.g.*, Whren v. United States, 116 S. Ct. 1769 (1996); United States v. Armstrong, 116 S. Ct. 1480 (1996); McCleskey v. Kemp, 481 U.S. 279 (1987).

113. *See* Stephen J. Sansweet, *LAPD Officers Are Acquitted in King Beating, Mayor Declares Emergency Amid Rise in Violence: National Guard Is Called*, WALL ST. J., Apr. 30, 1992, at A14.

114. *See St. Petersburg's Message*, CHR. SCI. MONITOR, Nov. 18, 1996, at 20 (discussing reasons underlying riot and comparing to riots after acquittal of officers in Rodney King beating in 1992).

115. McCleskey v. Kemp, 481 U.S. 279, 346 (Brennan, J., dissenting) (citing Rose v. Mitchell, 443 U.S. 545, 555 (1979)).

116. *Id.*

10

In Search of Probable Cause: U.S. Customs, Racial Profiling, and the Fourth Amendment

Lee E. Ross and Simon Adetona Akindes

INTRODUCTION

The suspect, a Nigerian citizen, arrived at St. Louis International Airport from London and was referred (for further inspection) because of her small amount of luggage, her planned short stay in the United States, and her arrival from a source country and because her ticket was paid for in cash. The suspect's answers to questions gave the inspectors further suspicion of internal concealment. Subsequently, a pat down and a strip search revealed nothing. An officer told the suspect that she was suspected of internal drug concealment and that if she wanted, an X-ray search would confirm or dispel the suspicion. After being taken to the hospital and being given medical warnings by the hospital staff, the suspect signed a consent form for an X-ray search. Thanks to the X-ray, packets of heroin were ultimately found in her rectal cavity, and [suspect] was arrested. The United States Court of Appeals for the Eighth Circuit ruled that the fact that a hospital performed an X-ray search for a suspected internal drug smuggler was valid because the examining officers had reasonable suspicion of internal concealment. (*United States v. Oyekan*).[1] Would the decision to search have been the same if the suspect were not an "alien" from Nigeria? Would it have been the same if the suspect were a European or American white middle- or upper-class male or female?

"Search and seizure" is undoubtedly one of the most difficult tasks for all of law enforcement agents. Statutes and rules cover only a minute portion of the field, and court decisions are frequently confusing, or even contradictory. Often, the U.S. Supreme Court has not ruled on important questions of legal procedures, and officers have to look to the law of the various circuits or even the districts for guidance. To compound matters further, decisions to search are made on the spur of the moment, without the benefit of book manuals or even assistance from more seasoned supervisors. Although typically discussed in connection with local police practices, rules of search and seizure apply to all levels of law enforcement, especially federal law enforcement.

In the absence of clear rulings, the act of searching itself is subjected to innumerable factors that find their roots in the most commonly accepted representations and images individual agents have formed about professional, ethnic, and racial groups different from their own. Such images, for the most part totalizing and essentializing, cannot easily be detached from the subjects involved—law-enforcement agents and defendants. Neither can they be removed from the act of searching itself. As a consequence, they do have an impact on how the Fourth Amendment is applied in practice. The Fourth Amendment states that

The right of the people to be secure in their persons, houses, papers, and effects, against unreasonable searches and seizures, shall not be violated, and no warrants shall issue, but upon probable cause, supported by oath or affirmation, and particularly describing the place to be searched, and the persons or things to be seized.

This chapter particularly focuses on the United States Customs Service (Customs hereinafter), a federal agency where evidentiary requirements of the Fourth Amendment are somewhat relaxed in comparison with other enforcement agencies. Our purpose is threefold: first, to examine the unique authority of Customs officers to conduct warrantless searches; second, to explore and deconstruct examples of searches and seizures that fail to meet even bare minimum requirements of reasonable suspicion; and third, to examine some legal and social consequences resulting from such unlawful searches and seizures. The discussion focuses primarily on ethnic or racial profiling[2]—selecting passengers based on race or ethnicity—of alleged drug suspects at U.S. international airports and calls into question the legality and fairness of the detentions, searches, and seizures that result. It also links the latter to the history and economic forces of the society as a whole, as they shape ethnic and racial perceptions. In other words, searches and seizures are entirely situated in societal relations of power.

The "War on Drugs" Alibi

Despite the fact that more than fifty major federal law enforcement agencies are in charge of enforcing federal criminal laws, political pundits and social activists continually claim that the effort to stamp out the trade use of illicit drugs and narcotics has yielded few positive results in the past and shows even fewer indications of succeeding in the future. Among modest estimates, less than 10 percent of illicit drugs (mainly marijuana, heroin, and cocaine) smuggled into the United States are detected by federal law enforcement. The other 90 percent infiltrate our borders (usually via containerized cargo) without detection from lead agencies (Nadelmann 1989; Riley 1996). Among the agencies involved in the War on Drugs are the Federal Bureau of Investigation, the U.S. Coast Guard, the Drug Enforcement Administration, the Immigration and Naturalization Service, the Internal Revenue Service, the Bureau of Alcohol, Tobacco, and Firearms, the Secret Service, and the Customs Service, among others. Whether we refer to Richard Nixon's "war on heroin," Ronald Reagan's "War on Drugs," or Bill Clinton's continuation of criminal repression through the Violent Crime Control and Law Enforcement Act of 1994 and his foreign trade policies, Customs has assumed an active role in carrying out the mission and political agenda of the White House. In the process, it has worked closely, albeit not smoothly, with the U.S. Attorney General and the Secretary of the Treasury.

During the past fifteen years, Customs has participated and competed with other prominent federal agencies to lead in the so-called War on Drugs, which, in addition to its international dimension, as Parenti (1999, 48) pointed out, indirectly "served the purposes of class and racial containment by building up the state's repressive infrastructure and invoking the legitimizing spectacle of a grave narcotics threat." While the changing politics of such a "war" are often obscured in the murky waters of bureaucratic rhetoric, intense competition remains among federal agencies to establish themselves as leaders in the War on Drugs. The historical rivalry and bitterness among federal agencies concerning the authority for narcotic interdiction dates back to the mid-1930s. There, the Federal Bureau of Narcotics (a predecessor to the Bureau of Narcotics and Dangerous Drugs), and the Bureau of Customs earned a reputation as jealous and combative siblings jockeying within the Treasury Department for authority to control the importation and distribution of illicit drugs. Consequently, in 1973, former President Nixon sent a proposal to Congress to "reorganize" the way federal narcotic law enforcement agencies performed their functions. Specifically, the plan was designed to consolidate federal narcotics enforcement activities into one lead agency, the Drug Enforcement Administration (DEA).

Despite vehement protests and political lobbying to save its agency, Customs emerged from the reorganization proceedings in a disheveled, demoralized, and threatened state. Moreover, it lost about 700 of its elite narcotic agents and support personnel to the elite Drug Enforcement Administration. In response to this reorganization, Customs maneuvered its resources to remain involved in narcotic enforcement. When the ink had dried, the reorganization plan reserved to Customs the right to maintain a border presence. In the process, Customs retained the authority to search for and seize illicit drugs and to apprehend and detain individuals attempting to smuggle narcotics into the country at regular inspection ports of entry or anywhere along the land or water of the United States (Rachal 1982, 115). However, more and more joint policing operations will be created involving the military. Gradually, and especially after the 1878 Posse Comitatus Act was amended to permit the involvement of the military in policing in 1981, the idea of using military techniques has gained ground. In 1991, the military were allowed to train civilian police in the anti-drug operations; and in 1995, Joint Task Force 6, under the Defense Secretary, was created to police drug activities and immigration.[3]

Yet, through the years, Customs has remained active in narcotic interdiction. For example, in fiscal year 1994, Customs agents and inspectors led the way in drug seizures among federal law enforcement officers. Inspectors seized nearly 2,000 pounds of heroin from commercial air passengers. Cocaine seizures from this group more than doubled after 1993 to 4,478 pounds from the previous year's figure of 2,026 pounds.[4] The vast majority of these drug seizures resulted from excellent law enforcement efforts and practices. Many, however, resulted from questionable law enforcement techniques and procedures. Because of stiff competition between officers and the desire for occupational prestige, some Customs officers go to great lengths (whether legal or illegal) to make a drug seizure. Consequently, some officers are often characterized as overzealous to win the War on Drugs by aggressively interrogating suspected drug law violators. As with other areas of law enforcement, however, Customs officers are bound to uphold the Fourth Amendment.

Looking for Probable Cause to Search Further

Concerns for the constitutional rights of suspected drug traffickers often receive very low priority in the War on Drugs. For Customs officers in particular, the pressures to compete with more renowned agencies in the War on Drugs are very real. For instance, while interrogating and examining certain commercial air passengers who fit a "smuggler" profile, some officers stop at nothing to confirm their suspicions of passengers trafficking in narcotics. Sometimes, their suspicions are correct. More often than not, however, their suspicions are incorrect, if not baseless. In both instances, passengers and, in rare instances, even priests and diplomats[5] are subjected to derogatory interrogation tactics that are not only offensive but potentially abusive. Such tactics are part of the normal interrogation procedure, designed in part to intimidate and detect drug couriers and smugglers who, otherwise, appear as law-abiding citizens.

Officers engaged in such practices quickly realize they have nothing to lose and everything to gain. For example, occupational prestige is associated with making drug seizures. A "good seizure" (somewhat similar to a "good pinch") translates into respect from one's peers and professional recognition from management. It is a sure-fire way of moving up the ladder of promotion while earning financial rewards and "good assignments" along the way. Clearly, the incentive is there. When officers are effective in making drug seizures, the systems of rewards are quite attractive. Thus, the reward system actually encourages a proactive and aggressive interrogation of suspected drug traffickers—even terrorists— and, in the process, encourages officers to follow their hunches and suspicions regarding certain passengers. Simply stated, when officers are correct in their suspicions (that people are concealing illicit narcotics either on their person or in their effects), they look like experts. When incorrect, however, they politely apologize to offended passengers and bid them a fond farewell.[6] Offended passengers, usually foreigners with no or little ability to express themselves in English or to sue the offender, cannot defend their rights. Moreover, they may be entirely unaware of their constitutional rights or of their rights as governed by the United Nations Universal Declaration of Human Rights. Even when they are, their unfamiliarity with legal procedures in the United States and their inability (financial or other) to command the law to defend their integrity may deter them from initiating any legal action. Other factors related to the historical traditions of racial/ethnic and class profiling that have characterized law enforcement over the centuries—with little recourse for victims—complicate conditions for offended passengers of non-white ethnic, racial, and/or national origin. When viewed in this context, it is easy to anticipate that Customs officers could freely engage in unlawful searches with relative impunity.

Customs' search and seizure practices, albeit well-intended, epitomize the complexity and uncertainty of policing around the Fourth Amendment vis-à-vis unlawful searches and seizures. Ironically, at times these practices portray Customs officers as *looking and searching for reasons to search further*. Moreover, their approach resembles one in which the end justifies the means. While the practice of literally searching until you find something depicts the inherent nature of Customs interrogations in particular, it appears headed toward other levels of law enforcement as well.[7] Such practices raise a fundamental question constantly confronting police, namely, "When and to what extent does the morally good end warrant or justify an unethical, prejudicial, and unlawful means for its achievement?" Should sound law enforcement rest on the historical foundation of probable cause or should it rest on some lesser evidentiary standard?

Probable Cause

When does probable cause exist to search a passenger suspected of smuggling narcotics? In examining the issue and existence of probable cause, Ferdico (1996, 345) provides a useful definition:

Probable cause exists when the facts and circumstances within a person's knowledge and of which he or she has reasonably trustworthy information are sufficient in themselves to justify a person of reasonable caution and prudence in believing that something is true. It means something less than certainty, but more than suspicion, speculation, or possibility.

At this point it is important to understand the unique authority of Customs officers to conduct warrantless searches and to seize merchandise as part of their routine duties. Because of this, we quickly realize that the evidentiary standards (i.e., probable cause) are lower for Customs officers than for other law enforcement officers in general. Theoretically, the very nature of the Customs officer's position provides an exception to the probable cause requirement to conduct an *initial search*. Therefore, in some situations, a search may be reasonable and therefore valid under the Fourth Amendment, although there is no probable cause to search, there is no warrant, and there are no exigent circumstances or mobile conveyances. Furthermore, aside from the usual warrantless searches (i.e., plain view or exigent circumstances, among others), Customs agents benefit from other exceptions as well, including (a) administrative/regulatory searches and (b) border searches. The logic of these so-called exceptions to probable cause requirements are illustrated in Figure 10.1. Based on this "logic," *all* searches are reasonable—even where probable cause does not exist. At this point, issues of reasonableness and legality appear to be at odds. Yet, even among these exceptional circumstances, two overriding principles remain in effect: (1) the search must be reasonable and (2) the more intrusive the search, the greater is the requirement for probable cause. At this juncture, there is a tremendously thin line between that which is reasonable and that which is legal. Moreover, given the relaxed standards of law enforcement enjoyed by U.S. Customs, the ground is fertile for many unsavory law enforcement practices, especially racial profiling.

In determining probable cause, courts have considered a host of factors, which include objective facts and the experience and expertise of the officer. Customs officers, in particular, often become familiar with the methods used in particular types of criminal activity. Therefore, probable cause for a Customs officer is determined from the standpoint of a reasonable, properly trained Customs officer. When interviewing passengers, for example, officers have been known to consider the totality of circumstances that include prior criminal activity, association with other persons, gestures, answers to questions, and use of one's senses. Sometimes, however, Customs officers (and other law enforcement officers, in general) are simply wrong in their suspicion. When this happens, the consequences of a mistake can be tragic for innocent individuals or bystanders. Perhaps worse, when targeting and interrogating non-whites, Customs officers, more often than not, are perceived as discriminatory—if not racially biased—in their enforcement practices.[8]

However, such mistakes should be also examined in their relationship with the current social and economic climate, which may or may not give them more legitimacy and render them tolerable. For instance, as Parenti (1999) observed, a renewed immigration enforcement, given impetus by the Illegal Immigration Reform and Immigrant Responsibility Act (IIRIRA) and the Anti-Terrorism and Effective Death Penalty Act (AEDPA) both passed in 1996, initially restricted to the southern borders only, has now moved to the interior with increased and concerted participation of other law-enforcement agencies—local police, FBI, DEA—and even the military. This has led to the deportation of innocent individuals. For example, following a five-day "round-up" campaign characterized by house-to-house searches, warrantless searches, and public interrogations of drivers and pedestrians that started in Chandler, Arizona, on July 27, 1997, 432

Search and seizure "logic"

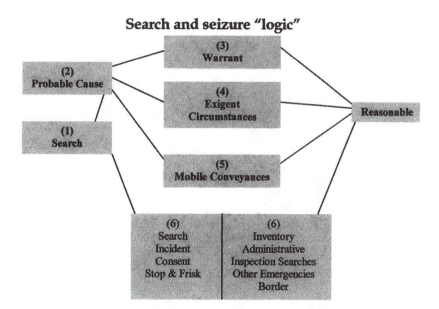

1. **Is there a "SEARCH"?**
    If not, then there is no Fourth Amendment violation.
    If so, go to 2.

2. **Is there PROBABLE CAUSE to SEARCH?**
    If so, go to 3.
    If not, go to 6.

3. **Is the search to be conducted under a valid WARRANT?**
    If so, the search is lawful.
    If not, go to 4.

4. **Are there exigent CIRCUMSTANCES?**
    If so, the search is lawful.
    If not, go to 5.

5. **Is it a MOBILE CONVEYANCE?**
    If so, the search is lawful.
    If not, go to 6.

6. **Is there an EXCEPTION to the PROBABLE CAUSE and WARRANT requirements?**
    If so, the search is lawful.
    If not, the Search is unlawful.

Figure 10.1 Search and Seizure "Logic."

undocumented migrants and two U.S. citizens were deported. After eighteen Latinos filed a class-action lawsuit against the police and the INS about violations of their Fourth Amendment rights, the attorney-general condemned the campaign

finding that searches were in fact conducted without warrants. Transcripts of police and Border Patrol radio communications reveal that officers from both agencies had cavalierly dispensed with the usual fig leaf of probable cause. . . . It seemed that the only criterion at work was skin color. (Parenti 1999, 140).

Such misconduct, not uncommon in the history of law enforcement in the United States, may not be explained solely by the absence of legal checks, lack of accountability, or individual bias or prejudice. It should be tied into the particular histories of certain locations, legal precedence, traditional practices, and equally important, into dominant political discourses that create a favorable climate for them to occur. Parenti (1999, 142) explains that "Politically, the repressive anti-immigrant impulse is both an organic expression of nativist hostility and a very useful, rational system of elite-inspired class control." Customs officers, when targeting and interrogating persons not classified as Caucasians, are exhibiting behavior and tendencies found in other spaces and walks of life and are responding to forces external to their own little professional group.

Some or Mere Suspicion

Some or mere suspicion is the lowest level of suspicion. It need not be based on any objective articulable fact and can be as little as a hunch. Articulable facts are those that one knows, can sense (i.e., see, hear, feel, or smell), and can talk about in court.

Some or mere suspicion is a *subjective* suspicion by an officer, such as suspicion of the mind. Subjective impressions are problematical to say the least. By training and experience, Customs officers, as well as officers in other agencies, are by nature suspicious of most people they encounter, especially persons arriving from narcotic source countries (e.g., Colombia, Laos, or Thailand, among many others). Part of the problem, for the purposes of this chapter, is that mere suspicion is not based on objective and articulable facts. Consequently, all passengers arriving from a foreign country are potential subjects of a search that does not require probable cause and, on occasion, can be quite arbitrary and capricious. After all, only 2 percent of all passengers are searched (in the form of a pat down).[9] Nonetheless, when confronted with threats of terrorism by foreign nationals (a frequent occurrence during the height of the Persian Gulf War and after the recent events of September 11, 2001), it might be quite reasonable for Customs officers to be suspicious of anyone entering the United States from the countries in question. Being a U.S. citizen or appearing white should not be a guarantee against interrogation or harassment, as looks may become the primary criterion for targeting.

Reasonable Suspicion

The standards of *reasonable suspicion* are easy to distinguish from that of "mere suspicion." Moreover, reasonable suspicion is based on facts that, when taken with what you can infer from those facts, would lead a reasonable officer to a suspicion that a person might be engaged or has been engaged in criminal activity. Despite the clarity of this principle, it is important to note that Customs officers are entitled to draw professional inferences based upon profiles[10] to help meet the reasonable suspicion standard. Law enforcement profiles are learned in basic or specialized training and are constantly modified by the experience of both the individual officer and that of his fellow officers. As Customs searches proceed beyond routine inspections, such as strip and body cavity searches, any further detention of the person must be supported by reasonable suspicion. Reasonable suspicion of a heroin swallower, for example, must be supported by a clear indication or plain suggestion that there might be some kind of concealment of illegal substances in an internal body cavity. Perhaps at this juncture it is useful to question the legality of whether "race" or "ethnic origin" can be taken into account when making determinations of suspicion. Moreover, by using "race" or "ethnic origin" as a sole criterion of suspicion, why not permit Customs officers to openly engage in racial discrimination routinely? Better yet, what if it were shown that race or ethnic origin, beyond correlating with certain drug trafficking offenses, was also predictive of drug trafficking? Surprisingly, away from the border, "most courts that have confronted [this] issue *have* allowed police to use race in making decisions to question, stop, or detain persons so long as doing so is reasonably related to efficient law enforcement and not deployed for purposes of racial harassment" (Kennedy 1997, 141). Nonetheless, most law enforcement agencies are too savvy to use race or ethnic origin as a "sole" factor in profiling. Properly understood, then, racial or ethnic profiling probably occurs [more than we realize] when police routinely use race as a signal that, along with an accumulation of other signals, causes an officer to react with suspicion (Kennedy 1999).

The Extent of a Search

What should happen if the initial interrogation and search of the suspect's luggage (based on some or mere suspicion) reveal nothing and yet the officer remains suspicious? Should officers be allowed to search further to confirm their suspicions? Moreover, should officers be allowed to search until they find probable cause to (presumably) search further? According to U.S. Codes, detaining suspects and searching further is perfectly reasonable. Moreover, 19 U.S.C. 1582 authorizes the detention of persons coming into the United States from foreign countries. The detentions are seizures, but are reasonable *even without suspicion* during a routine Customs inspection. They are neither a stop nor an arrest.[11] Given this unique authority to search without probable cause, Customs officers have often used their authority to search passengers at will. For a former Customs officer, authority was granted to search in each of the following scenarios where travelers (a) claimed not to have visited a certain narcotic source country, yet the passport has an immigration stamp of that country or the ticket reflected a visit to that country; (b) refused to comply with requests to open baggage, truck, or the like; or (c) eyed the officer with hostility or apprehension while waiting for inspection. Although it is debatable whether any of these scenarios constitutes a good reason to suspiciously search, searches generally resulted.

Because of this unique authority to search without probable cause, Customs officers have often used their authority to search passengers not only based on their intuition and experience but also based on their prejudices, their racial and class bias, and their desire to gain professional promotion. People of an ancestry other than the Caucasian racial group perceive such searches as acts of discrimination and harassment. Such perceptions are not often baseless, as the past and present experiences of non-whites are replete with such examples. For instance, Russell (1998), in her attempt to understand the continued police harassment of young black men today, pointed out that "Black distrust of the justice system is not new. It is historically rooted in the role police played in enforcing slave codes, Black codes, Jim Crow segregation, and the ultimate form of vigilante justice, lynching" (p. 35). In this respect, Marx (1998), by comparing the role of race in the process of nation-building in South Africa, Brazil, and the United States, some of the most violent societies of the end of the second millennium, showed how race was used especially in South Africa and the United States, as a social instrument to unify whites and to shift to the background or dilute ethnic and social conflicts that existed among them. Though the North and the South disagreed on slavery as an institution, they did not really disagree on segregation and the place of black people and Native Americans in society. Furthermore, it was not until internal strife among the whites was resolved that the Blacks could obtain the end of legal discrimination. This scenario, though different today, helps us understand the uses of race in law enforcement and politics and its role in exciting nationalist feelings and maintaining a certain form of social stability.

Exceptions to Probable Cause Requirements

As shown in Appendix A, border searches and inspection searches are well-recognized and long-established exceptions to the probable cause requirements of the Fourth Amendment. For example, Customs officers were empowered to conduct border searches to protect the revenue of the United States (i.e., to collect duties and taxes on imported goods). Even today, many returning residents and visitors fail to realize that the U.S. government retains the right to possess imported merchandise until the duties are assessed. When contrasted with the fact that most searches by law enforcement (away from the border) are searches for property *not belonging* to the government, the rationale behind a border search becomes clearer, yet merits distinction. The basic distinction is that in a border search, the government searches for property it has a right to possess until duty (i.e., tax) is paid. Furthermore, there is a reduced expectation of privacy at the border, as individuals traveling from one country to another country know they may be subjected to a search upon arrival. Indeed, this reduces the expectation of privacy in our persons and in the objects we may bring into the country. In the course of a border search, Customs officers are authorized to seize any instrumentalities or evidence of crimes they discover. Even so, the conduct of these searches, as with any search, must be *reasonable*. For instance, a Customs officer with a hunch about a person arriving from a foreign country might wish to conduct an X-ray search based on the presence of paraphernalia and related evidence of an internal concealment (i.e., bowel suppressants and suppositories, among other items).

The Exclusionary Rule

When drug seizures and arrests result from an unlawful search and seizure, what happens to the evidence? Generally, such evidence is excluded from the criminal trial (if it was obtained illegally). History tells us, however, this generality has not always held true. Before 1914, the admissibility of evidence in the United States courts was not affected by the illegality of the means by which it was obtained. In 1914, however, the Supreme Court of the United States held that evidence obtained through an unreasonable search or seizure by federal officers was inadmissible in a prosecution in federal courts against persons whose constitutional rights had been violated. A natural component of the Exclusionary Rule frequently encountered in cases involving Fourth Amendment problems is the "fruit of the poisonous tree doctrine." Simply stated, this doctrine holds that illegally seized evidence cannot be used to obtain still more evidence.[12] Within Customs, few cases involving drug seizures are rejected for violation of the Exclusionary Rule. This is especially true among cases involving nonresidents, who are limited in their knowledge of their legal rights and further limited by certain language barriers. These persons are usually arrested on simple possession charges and are prosecuted in either federal or state courts.[13]

Legal Consequences

Without question, many drug seizures and arrests of drug smugglers result from sound law enforcement practices where probable cause or at least reasonable suspicion requirements are met. Still, common sense tells us that the opposite is true as well. Moreover, persons are commonly arrested and drugs are seized even without reasonable suspicion. These "cold hits" (defined as routine border/inspections that uncover illicit narcotics), coupled with advance intelligence supplied by Customs special agents, account for nearly all of Custom's narcotic *discoveries*. As of this writing, no federal agency keeps track of sentencing outcomes for Customs-related drug arrests. The United States Sentencing Commission, an independent agency charged with developing and monitoring sentencing policies and practices for the federal courts, provides aggregate data on federal drug offenses, but it does not breakdown the data by agency type. Nonetheless, as discussed earlier, Customs officers and agents have led the way in drug seizures among federal law enforcement officers. It is reasonable to conclude that a sizeable proportion of cases involving federal drug violators resulted from Customs-related arrests and seizures.

Recent data suggest that in 1996 drug law violators accounted for approximately 22 percent of jail inmates, rising from 9 percent in 1983. In addition, drug offenders represented 23 percent of state prison population and 59.9 percent of the federal prison population.[14] On September 30, 1998, 107,912 offenders were serving a prison sentence in federal prison; 58 percent were incarcerated for a drug offense (U.S. Department of Justice 1999). The U.S. Sentencing Commission has predicted that in fifteen years the federal prison population will swell to 150,000 inmates, half of whom will be incarcerated in drug law violations (Nadelmann 1989). Furthermore, drug prosecutions have comprised an increasing portion of the federal criminal caseload—from 21 percent of defendants in 1982 to 35 percent in 1998 (U.S. Department of Justice 1999). Domestic law-enforcement efforts have proven increasingly successful in apprehending and imprisoning rapidly growing numbers of illicit drug merchants, ranging from the most sophisticated international traffickers to the most common street-level dealers. However, should the increasing number be regarded as a sign of success in the fight against drugs or as a sign of failure? Is the effect of correction not reducing the number of offenders?

Drug offenders make up a large part of the recent dramatic increase in the federal prison population. In 1980, for example, about 18 percent of the 24,000 federal prisoners were drug law offenders. In 1996, about 60 percent of nearly 77,000 sentenced inmates were confined for drug law violations.[15] Many of these reflect "low-level drug offenses." In the words of Steven Wisotsky,[16] the crackdown on certain drug offenders has led to an unexpected and ironic development. He adds:

The intensive pursuit of drug offenders has generated an enormous population of convicts held in prison for very long mandatory periods of time; so much that violent criminals (murderers, robbers, and rapists) often serve less time than do drug offenders.

Furthermore, with the enactment of the Sentencing Reform Act of 1984, we witnessed the adoption of sentencing guidelines and the abolition of federal parole. The sentencing guidelines, with federal minimum sentences, have resulted in longer prison sentences for offenders who violate federal drug laws. According to the Bureau of Justice Statistics, from 1980 to 1989, the average sentence of federal drug offenders increased by 59 percent. In 1980, drug traffickers received an average sentence of 48.1 months; in 1985, 60.8 months; in 1988, 71.3

months; and in 1990, 84 months. Furthermore, without parole, federal prisoners now serve almost their entire sentences—a noticeable difference when contrasted with state prison sentences.[17] In 1990, for instance, the average length of prison sentences imposed on persons convicted of drug-trafficking offenses in the federal courts was 83.1 months. More recent statistics show a slight decrease to 78 months as average time served in federal prison for drug-related violations.[18] In state courts, however, drug-trafficking offenders received an average sentence of 52.0 months. Today, the federal sentencing system is the most determinate in the country; it is the only jurisdiction where inmates really do serve 85 percent of their terms.[19] In the cases involving career offenders, their average length of sentencing for drug trafficking is 196.4 months![20]

The War on Drugs has led to an unprecedented explosion of racially skewed incarceration. With painstaking irony,[21] some even point out that despite the fact that most drug users are white, most of those arrested and imprisoned are people of color (Glasser 1999; Miller 1997). For some, it might explain why, in recent years, the incarceration rate among African Americans has exponentially surpassed the rate among whites (see Kennedy 1997). For others, the War on Drugs has established a pretext for racial profiling on our highways, in our airports, at our Customs checkpoints, and on our streets that is based not on evidence but on skin color (Glasser 1999; Miller 1997). Commenting on the War on Drugs and its impact on African-American communities, Miller (1997, 80) asserts:

The drug war was a disaster-in-waiting for African-Americans from the day of its conception. Despite the fact that drug usage among various racial and ethnic groups in the 1970's and 1980's remained roughly equivalent to their representation in the society, from the first shots fired in the drug war African-Americans were targeted, arrested, and imprisoned in wildly disproportionate numbers.

Beyond high incarceration rates among African Americans, vestiges of the War on Drugs continually manifest themselves in our inner cities through increased violence in the form of human bloodshed. Consequently, human life—black life in particular—has become devalued on all scales of social justice. Darker skin (even in a new millennium) still invites the usual degree of suspicion, however undeserved, which, in the eyes of some law enforcement officials, justifies closer scrutiny, increased surveillance, and lesser protection. Familiar refrains of "another one bites the dust" and "unequal protection under the law" fall on deaf ears in a time where criminal justice is, for some, synonymous with injustice. Therefore, it is most regrettable that among a free-traveling public, persons of color do not enjoy the equal freedom of movement—either domestically or internationally—that others seem to take for granted. Imagine yourself as a U.S. citizen traveling in first class from London to New York. Now, imagine being treated like a second-class citizen once you hit U.S. soil, being subjected to racial profiling by government officials—for no apparent reason other than the color of your skin. Clearly, in this scenario, equal protection under the law is but another dream deferred.

DISCUSSION AND CONCLUSION

This chapter characterizes the search and seizure practices of the U.S. Customs Service in areas of airport passenger processing. Given the uniqueness of their authority, Customs officers are entitled to search passengers without probable cause. Consequently, many, if not all Customs officers (assigned to international airports) engage in suspected unlawful searches under the guise of "protecting the revenue" and also in the name of the federal initiative, the "War on Drugs." Some commercial air passengers, mainly non-whites, irrespective of their citizenship, and the poor, are more likely to be searched without reasonable suspicion than others are. If someone is caught smuggling an illicit narcotic into the country, Customs has every right to arrest that person and seize the narcotics. Very few people would argue otherwise when circumstances warrant a search and seizure. An argument can be made, however, that many searches are highly selective, arbitrary, and sometimes ethnically or racially motivated.[22]

The reasons generally range from mere suspicion to probable cause (to search). Either way, current law-enforcement practices within the Customs amount to giving officers unlimited authority to look and search for reasons to search further. They do so without risk of reprimand because they operate on the principle that the end justifies the means. As a result, they have no scruples targeting and singling out suspects on the basis of their own prejudices, perceptions, and ideology. Such (mis)behavior does not necessarily pertain to individuals per se; it is no different from practices that prevail in other law-enforcement agencies, and it should unequivocally be linked to the role the police and other agencies have played over the centuries in enforcing the various codes and laws that have put down and demonized non-white groups in the United States. Additionally, it is a derivative and unavoidable consequence of the "normalized" view that the best way to solve the crime problem is to keep punishing, to keep fixing, and to be tougher.

Each year, the U.S. Customs Service processes more than 71 million international air travelers, and decisions are often made as to who should be searched. Because these decisions are highly discretionary, the potential for abuse and constitutional violations is always present. Practices that target certain persons, while neglecting scores of others equally disposed to criminality, provide a clear-cut example of bias and racism in the criminal justice system. These practices are particularly objectionable because more than 90 percent of all Customs examinations are conducted in the open view of on-looking passengers (who must feel privileged to find that they were not targeted and interrogated in the same way). More critically is that discriminatory practices help to define for onlookers what a suspected drug smuggler looks like and sends a clear signal to other potential smugglers of different items (e.g., expensive jewelry, paintings, sculpture), that it is safe to do so.

Regardless of an officer's motivation to search, many innocent persons run the risk of suffering from violations of civil liberties. Ethnic, racial, and class profiling has the negative consequence of making it more complicated to reduce crime and drug offenses, which have generally been on the increase in the past fifteen years. Furthermore, the business of waging an all-out "War on Drugs" has developed its own internal logic that is blind to other possible and less expensive solutions to the problem: prevention at early age, social commitment to face issues of economic inequality head on, and shifting the priorities of the criminal justice system from punishment to rehabilitation and community-based policing tactics (Currie 1998).

In conclusion, this chapter is not written to suggest that drug smugglers go free because of the lack of reasonable suspicion and/or probable cause. Rather, the purpose is to shed light on practices of search and seizure used by the Customs Service that are clearly at variance with the majority of law enforcement. These same practices are at times highly arbitrary and inherently discriminatory. Questions surrounding the legality and professionalism of a federal agency that selectively focuses on one type of suspect while neglecting scores of other potential suspects are raised. For many innocent victims, these practices reflect a certain class bias that invariably leads to charges of racism and discrimination from groups targeted by such practices. Law enforcement officers should not be allowed to simply look for probable cause to search further. Either probable cause exists —irrespective of race or ethnic background—or it does not.

NOTES

1. 786 F. 2d 832 (8th Cir. 1996).

2. For purposes of this chapter, racial profiling is operationalized to describe discriminatory practices by Customs officers of treating blackness/brownness or non-whiteness as an indication of possible criminal activity.

3. For more information on the gradual militarization of the War on Drugs, see http://www.csdp.org/factbook/military.htm.

4. *The United States Customs Service: The Year in Review, 1994*, Commissioners Forward.

5. Certain diplomats, family members in their immediate household who are not U.S. citizens, and certain administrative and technical staffs are immune from searches. Diplomatic bags are also immune, but can be detained. As a rule of thumb, and from personal experience, any officer who searches a diplomat had better have a good reason.

6. In a recent case, for instance, an African-American woman was returning from Jamaica to Fort Lauderdale, Florida, and was pulled out of the airline passenger arrival line by U.S. Customs. She was taken to a Miami hospital, handcuffed to a bed, and not allowed to call her mother. Agents, suspecting her of swallowing packets of illegal drugs, a common practice of smugglers, forced her to take a cup of laxative. A day later, with no evidence of drugs in her bowel movements, she was let go. Eight days later, after bouts with diarrhea and bleeding, she underwent an emergency Caesarian. Her son was born, weighing 3 pounds and 4 ounces. See "Two Allege Racial Bias by Customs," *Washington Post*, May 7, 1999, p. A29.

7. For example, in a recent U.S. Supreme Court decision, the court ruled that it is legal for police officers to search a vehicle, incidental to a stop for some municipal violation. In other words, if your vehicle registration has expired or if a taillight is missing,

police may rely on this to establish probable cause to search the vehicle. Arguably, searches incidental to a traffic violation are lacking in probable cause.

8. For further details of alleged racial discrimination by the United States Customs Service, see "Customs Service Appoints Panel to Probe Complaints of Racial Bias," *Chicago Tribune*, April 9, 1999, Section 1.

9. Customs officials recently report 50,892 of the 71.5 million international air travelers who passed through Customs in 1998 were subjected to some level of body search, most of them simple pat downs. For further detail, see "Customs Service Appoints Panel to Probe Complaints of Racial Bias," *Chicago Tribune*, April 9, 1999, Section 1.

10. The courts have upheld the "smuggling profile" used by the Customs Service. See for example, *United States v. Asbury-Bruce*, 586 F2d 793 (2nd Cir. 1978).

11. This area of law enforcement clearly distinguishes a Customs detention from other law enforcement detentions. In the past, the Supreme Court observed that it must be recognized that whenever a police officer accosts an individual and restrains his freedom to walk away, he has seized that person. *Terry v. Ohio* 392 U.S. 1, S. Ct. 1868 (1968). The court later amplified this observation by stating that a seizure occurs only when the restraint of freedom is such that a reasonable person, in view of all the circumstances, would believe he is not free to leave. *United States v. Mendenhall*, 466 U.S. 100, S. Ct. 1870 (1980). Contrary to popular beliefs, all persons detained by U.S. Customs, as part of a routine investigation, are effectively seized for purposes of the Fourth Amendment.

See *Law Course for Customs Officers* (training manual), Office of the Chief Counsel, United States Customs Academy, 1987. Based on circumstances, persons arrested for smuggling narcotics are usually charged with any of the following: (1) simple possession, 21 U.S.C. 844; (2) possession with the intent to distribute, 21 U.S.C. 8451(a)(1); (3) distribution, 21 U.S.C. 841(a)(1); and (4) importation, 21 U.S.C. 952.

12. See *Law Course for Customs Officers*.

13. Based on circumstances, persons arrested for smuggling narcotics are usually charged with any of the following: (1) simple possession, 21 U.S.C. 844; (2) possession with the intent to distribute, 21 U.S.C. 8451(a)(1); (3) distribution, 21 U.S.C. 841(a)(1); and (4) importation, 21 U.S.C. 952.

14. See http://www.csdp.org/factbook/prison.htm and http://www.ojp.usdoj.gov/bjs/dcf/correct.htm.

15. See Dennise E. Curtis, "The Effect of Federalization on the Defense Function," *Annals of the American Academy of Political and Social Science* 543 (January 1996): 85–96.

16. See Steven Wisotsky, "A Society of Suspects: The War on Drugs and Civil Liberties," reprinted in *Annual Editions: Drugs, Society and Behavior*, H.T. Wilson (ed.) (Guilford, CT: Dushkin Publishing, 1996), pp. 155–160.

17. See Gregory D. Lee, "U.S. Sentencing Guidelines: Their Impact on Federal Drug Offenders," *FBI Law Enforcement Bulletin* (May 1995), pp. 17–21.

18. See http://www.csdp.org/factbook/prison.htm.

19. See Franklin E. Zimring and Gordon Hawkins, "Toward a Principled Basis for Federal Criminal Legislation," *Annals of the American Academy of Political and Social Science* 543 (January 1996): 15–26.

20. U.S. Sentencing Commission, 1995 Annual Report, p. 63.

21. Racial profiling is based on the premise that most drug offenses are committed by minorities. The premise is untrue. According to the Sentencing Project, while African Americans constitute 13 percent of all monthly users, they represent 35 percent of ar-

rests for drug possession, 55 percent of convictions, and 74 percent of prison sentences. See "Young Black Americans and the Criminal Justice System: Five Years Later," Sentencing Project, October 1995. Sadly, the use of racial profiling makes the false premise of minorities as the usual drug offender a self-fulfilling prophecy.

22. If not racially motivated, such practices have certainly had a racially disparate impact. In fiscal year 1995, there were 15,168 federal drug cases. Hispanics accounted for 36.1 percent of all defendants. Specifically, they were defendants in 51.2 percent of all heroin cases and 50.8 percent of all marijuana cases. African Americans were also overrepresented, accounting for 35 percent of all defendants. Moreover, 88.4 percent of all federal crack cocaine cases involved African-American defendants. While Caucasians accounted for only 4.5 percent of crack cocaine defendants, they represented 27 percent of all cases involving federal drug defendants. Moreover, they were defendants in 72.3 percent of all methamphetamine cases and in 90.2 percent of all LSD cases. Although the U.S. Sentencing Commission does not desegregate the data by federal agency, it is reasonable to infer that many of these cases originated from U.S. Customs arrests based on the sheer volume of drug seizures (discussed earlier).

REFERENCES

Currie, E. (1998). *Crime and Punishment in America*. New York: Metropolitan Books, Henry Holt and Company.

Curtis, D. E. (1996). "The Effect of Federalization on the Defense Function." *Annals of the American Academy of Political and Social Science* 543: 85–96.

Ferdico, J. (1992). *Ferdico's Criminal Law and Criminal Justice Dictionary*. New York: West Publishing.

Glasser, I. (1999). "Criminal Justice, Drug Policy and Human Resources." Testimony before the U.S. House of Representatives. See http://www.uwp.edu/academic/criminal.justice/crmjacc.htm. (June 16).

Kennedy, R. (1997). *Race, Crime, and the Law*. New York: Random House.

Kennedy, R. (1998). "Race, the Police, and Reasonable Suspicion." In *Perspectives on Crime and Justice: 1997–1998 Lecture Series*. November, vol. 2. Washington, DC: U.S. Department of Justice, pp. 29–37.

Kennedy, R. (1999). "Suspect Policy." *The New Republic*. September 13 and 20, pp. 30–35.

Law Course for Customs Officers (training manual). (1987). Office of the Chief Counsel, United States Customs Academy.

Lee, G. D. (1995). "U.S. Sentencing Guidelines: Their Impact on Federal Drug Offenders." *FBI Law Enforcement Bulletin*, pp. 17–21.

Marx, A. (1998). *Making Race and Nation: A Comparison of the United States, South Africa, and Brazil*. Cambridge: Cambridge University Press.

Miller, J. G. (1997). *Search and Destroy: African-American Males in the Criminal Justice System*. New York: Cambridge University Press.

Nadelmann, E. (1989). "Drug Prohibition in the United States: Costs, Consequences, and Alternatives." *Science* 245: 930–47.

Parenti, C. (1999). *Lockdown America: Police in the Age of Crisis*. London, New York: Verso.

Rachal, P. (1982). *Federal Narcotics Enforcement: Reorganization and Reform*. Boston, MA: Auburn House.

Riley, J. K. (1996). *Snow Job: The War against International Cocaine Trafficking*. New Brunswick, NJ: Transactional Publishing.

Russell, K. (1998). *The Color of Crime: Racial Hoaxes, White Fear, Black Protectionism, Police Harassment, and Other Macroaggressions*. New York and London: New York University Press.

U.S. Department of Justice. (1999). "Prisoners in 1998." *Bureau of Justice Statistics Bulletin*, NCJ 175687. Office of Justice Programs. August.

Wisotsky, S. (1996). "A Society of Suspects: The War on Drugs and Civil Liberties." Reprinted in *Annual Editions: Drugs, Society and Behavior*, H. T. Wilson (ed.) Guilford, CT: Dushkin Publishing, pp. 155–160.

Zimring, F. E., and Hawkins, G. (1996). "Toward a Principled Basis for Federal Criminal Legislation." *Annals of the American Academy of Political and Social Science* 543: 15–26.

11

Simple Solutions?: The Complexity of Public Attitudes Relevant to Drug Law Enforcement Policy

Tracey L. Meares

The number of individuals incarcerated in the United States has increased massively since the 1980s.[1] Between 1975 and 1989, the total annual prison population of the United States nearly tripled, growing from 240,593 to 679,623 inmates in custody, an increase of 182 percent.[2] This upward trend continued uninterrupted through 1996, when the prison population rose to 1,138,984.[3] Put another way, the incarceration rate rose from about 145 per 100,000 population in 1980 to 445 per 100,000 in 1997.[4] Moreover, while the average probability of a person in the United States being committed to prison has increased dramatically during the last twenty years, the average sentence length once an individual is committed has also increased.

The growth in American imprisonment is, in a word, impressive, but the involvement of African Americans is staggering.[5] The growth in incarceration, by population especially, but also by rates, has been far greater for African Americans than any other ethnic or racial group.[6] A few statistics illustrate: While the number of African Americans incarcerated in state correctional facilities has long been disproportionate to the percentage of African Americans in the population, African Americans now comprise about *half* the state prison population.[7] From 1980 to 1996, the number of African-American inmates in state and federal prisons rose from 145,300 to 524,800, an increase of 261 percent. The incarceration rate for African Americans rose from 554 per 100,000 persons in 1980 to 1,574 per 100,000 in 1996, an increase of 184 percent.[8] The Sentencing Project, a nonprofit organization supporting alternatives to prison, studied the demographics of criminal justice control and recently estimated that nearly one-third of young African-American men between the ages of 20 and 29 were under the supervision of the criminal justice system—in prison or jail, or on probation or parole.[9]

Additional studies indicate that these numbers were as high as 40 percent of young African-American men in the cities of Baltimore and Washington, D.C.[10] The number of such supervised males exceeded the number who were legally working.[11]

Without question, these high rates of African-American involvement with the criminal justice system clearly are tied to drug law enforcement. Data show that in 1993 drug offenders accounted for about one-quarter of all prison and jail incarcerations, compared to 8.8 percent one decade earlier, and African Americans have borne the brunt of law enforcement efforts targeted at illegal drug use and trafficking.[12] Examination of the Bureau of Justice Statistics Surveys of Inmates of State Correctional Facilities for 1979, 1986, and 1991 reveals that the number of African-American prisoners incarcerated for drug offenses jumped from 13,974 in 1986 to 73,932 in 1991, an increase of 429 percent.[13] From 1980 to 1996, incarceration rates for African Americans for drug offenses increased an average of 20.3 percent annually, compared to 12 percent for whites and 16.0 percent for Hispanics.[14] And as the numbers of those incarcerated for drug offenses have grown over time, the racial gap in the demographics of prisoners has widened. Analysis of Bureau of Justice Statistics data indicate that incarceration for drug offending of African Americans with less than a high school education has increased from 60 in 100,000 in 1979 to 800 in 100,000 in 1991. The same rates for whites with a high school education increased from 6 in 100,000 in 1979 to 20 in 100,000 in 1991.[15] Thus, drug law enforcement in the United States is a distinctly "raced" phenomenon. It is "classed" as well.

Those who support tough sentences for drug offenders argued when those policies were enacted (and continue to argue today) that harsh punishment for drug offenders is good crime-control policy. In particular, advocates of policies subjecting even low-level drug offenders to long prison sentences argued that such policies benefited the people who were most likely to be exposed to the consequences of the activity—the residents of disadvantaged inner-city neighborhoods. In that vein, writers expressed support for or even applauded policies distinguishing between drugs typically sold and consumed in devastated inner-city communities, such as crack cocaine, and drugs more typically sold and consumed in well-off suburbs, such as powder cocaine.[16] The federal sentencing policy for cocaine offenses is an example. According to federal statute, a given amount of cocaine base or "crack" cocaine triggers the same mandatory penalties as 100 times as much powder cocaine.[17] The "get tough" approach to drug law enforcement is not universally praised, however. Those who reject tough sentencing policies counter that they are draconian and ineffective.[18] Empirical evidence appears to support this position, as there is little data to suggest that the United States' War on Drugs has made a noticeable dent in drug offending.[19]

This chapter provides a window on the current debate over drug law enforcement by looking to opinion data relevant to drug law enforcement at the time the harsh drug sentencing policies were enacted. These data do not speak to the effectiveness of the policies. Instead, they offer an opportunity to reflect on the history of our current policy by suggesting who supported the policies we have today.

To provide the illustration, this chapter compares the attitudes of African Americans and white Americans.[20] Experience shapes attitudes,[21] and the experience of African Americans with both drugs and drug-law enforcement undeniably differs from that of white Americans, or other non–African Americans. Thus, African Americans are likely to hold views about drug-law enforcement policy that are distinct from the views of non–African Americans on this topic because so many in the African-American community uniquely experience problems associated with both drugs and drug-law enforcement. With this in mind, this chapter offers data pertinent to two questions: (1) to what extent did Americans support a very tough drug-law enforcement policy at the time the harsh federal policy was adopted? and (2) how different were African-American views on drug-law enforcement from those of whites at the time?

To answer these questions, this chapter evaluates the views of African-American and white American public opinion survey respondents along four analytically distinct drug-law enforcement positions. The four positions are combinations of the two measures from the 1987 General Social Survey ("GSS"), an ongoing project of the National Opinion Research Center at the University of Chicago,[22] that are most pertinent to attitudes toward drug-law enforcement. The first measure addresses attitudes concerning the legalization of marijuana,[23] and the second measure addresses attitudes concerning whether local courts should be more harsh on criminal offenders generally.[24] Each of these measures is dichotomous, so four positions are possible. The position that combines views in opposition to legalization of marijuana and views in support of harsher courts for criminal offenders reflects a "get tough on drug offenders" outlook. A more "libertarian" view is captured by the combination of views in support of legalization of marijuana and views in support of more harsh local courts for criminal offenders. The views of those who strongly experience the "dual frustration" referred to earlier are probably best reflected by the combination of views in opposition to legalization of marijuana and views in opposition to harsher courts for criminal offenders. Finally, a fourth position combines views in support of legalization of marijuana and views in opposition to harsher courts for criminal offenders and reflects the attitudes of those who hold "anti–law enforcement" views.

Figure 11.1 illustrates the four drug-law enforcement positions.

ATTITUDES TOWARD LEGALIZATION AND LAW ENFORCEMENT

The analysis in this section focuses on GSS data collected in 1987. Data from the 1987 survey are useful to analyze because of the survey's close proximity to the passage of the Anti-Drug Abuse Act of 1988,[25] a major piece of federal legislation providing enhanced penalties for drug trafficking and focusing on

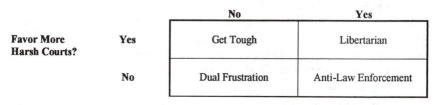

Favor Legalization?

		No	Yes
Favor More Harsh Courts?	Yes	Get Tough	Libertarian
	No	Dual Frustration	Anti-Law Enforcement

Figure 11.1   Drug-law Enforcement Positions.

Table 11.1
Drug-Law Enforcement Positions, by Race and Class, in Frequency (%) of Response

Group Surveyed	Get Tough	Libertarian	Dual Frustration	Anti-law enforcement	N
All	77.6	14.3	5.4	2.8	1702
African Americans	71.3	14.0	11.7	3.1	228
Whites	78.5	14.7	4.0	2.8	1475
	**t=6.529	t=0.136	***t=23.53	t=0.044	
< H.S.	81.7	9.0	7.5	1.8	453
>H.S.	76.1	16.1	4.6	3.1	1311
	***t=7.820	***t=12.03	*t=3.959	t=1.730	

Notes: The level of significance is calculated using a t-test; * (significant at .05 level or better); ** (significant at .01 level or better); *** (significant at .001 level or better).

particularly harsh sentences for crack cocaine trafficking.[26] Assessing opinions collected in 1987 offers a glimpse of the national level of support for "get tough" drug-law enforcement policy immediately prior to the passage of the law.[27]

Table 11.1 is a summary of drug-law enforcement positions along relevant race and class dimensions.

Table 11.1 indicates that a majority of GSS respondents favored the "get tough" drug-law enforcement position in 1987. GSS data also indicate that a majority of African-American and white survey respondents supported the "get tough" position. However, the data show that compared to whites, a lower percentage of African Americans supported the "get tough" position in 1987. The difference is statistically significant at the 1 percent level.[28] Table 11.1 reveals some additional interesting differences among groups surveyed in 1987.

Perhaps the most interesting difference between the African Americans and whites surveyed concerns responses falling into the "dual frustration" category.

Only 4 percent of whites sampled simultaneously opposed legalization of marijuana and more harsh sentences for criminal offenders, but almost *three times* as many African Americans did so. The probability that a difference this large would occur by chance is less than 1 in 10,000.

Table 11.1 also lists interesting differences in opinion between individuals with less than a high school education and those with more than a high school education. First, Table 11.1 indicates that survey respondents with less than a high school education in 1987 were more likely to subscribe to the "get tough" position than were those with more education.[29] Second, respondents with a high school education and those without differed most significantly in their respective support for the "libertarian" position. In 1987, individuals with less than a high school education were much less likely to favor both legalization of marijuana *and* harsher sentences for criminal offenders than individuals with more education. Third, the data indicate that when less educated individuals departed from the "get tough" position, they departed in favor of less harsh sentences for criminal offenders, that is, the "dual frustration" position.

In summary, a preliminary look at the data with simple statistics reveals support among a majority of Americans for a drug-law enforcement position in 1987 that reflects a "get tough" stance toward drug offenders. These preliminary results also point to some important differences among subgroups of Americans. However, it is likely that the precise nature of the differences in views about drug-law enforcement among subgroups of Americans surveyed are obscured by the summary nature of the procedures employed in Table 11.1. Undoubtedly, the experiences of African Americans with drugs and drug-law enforcement are not homogeneous. Similarly, the drug and drug-law enforcement related experiences of those with less than a high school education are undoubtedly diverse. The heterogeneity of experiences is due, in part, to the complexity of the interaction between race and class.

For example, consider the impact of drug-law enforcement by race and education level. Figure 11.2[30] demonstrates that the least educated African Americans have experienced the highest incarceration rates for drug offenses in each year that the data underlying the chart were collected.[31] While the least educated white Americans certainly experienced much higher incarceration rates in both 1979 and 1986 than more educated white Americans, in no survey year did the incarceration rate of the least educated white Americans exceed that for either group of African Americans.

Also consider the diverse experiences with drug use and marketing of African Americans and whites from varied socioeconomic groups described in sociological research and in journalistic accounts. William Julius Wilson relies on data from a 1993 survey of two high-jobless neighborhoods on Chicago's south side to document experiences of individuals who face daily a high prevalence of drug activity in their neighborhoods. One respondent surveyed said, "More people are dying and being killed. ... There are many drugs sold here every day. It's unsafe and you can't even go out of your house because of being afraid of being

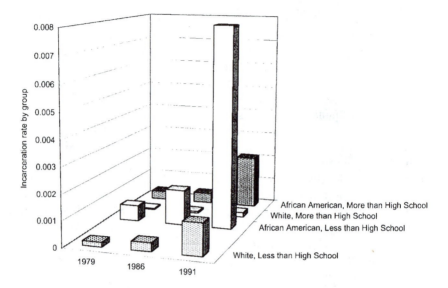

Figure 11.2   Incarceration Rates for Drug Offenses in 1979, 1986, and 1991.

shot."[32] Another stated, "I stay home a lot. Streets are dangerous. Killings are terrible. Drugs make people crazy."[33] Yet another stated that some poor residents in his neighborhood "get depressed, drink, snort, break in other people's houses. Borrow, get on aid, whore—that means prostitute."[34] Though Wilson's work captures relatively recent experiences of poor African Americans, work by others indicates that the prevalence of drug activity and the violence associated with it has been a problem in Chicago for quite some time. For example, Alex Kotlowitz's journalistic account of the ways in which drug trafficking by gangs in a public housing project in Chicago detrimentally affected the lives of two young African-American boys growing up there indicates that the drug-related problems of poor, minority communities Wilson documents have persisted since 1987.[35]

Residents of communities outside poor, inner-city neighborhoods also experience problems associated with drug use, but the picture that journalistic accounts produce of these experiences is very different from the interview excerpts that Wilson provides. The story of the Mannatt family in Atlanta, Georgia, is a good example.[36] In 1976, after their thirteen-year-old daughter's birthday party, the Mannatts discovered empty bottles of Mad Dog (a fortified wine beverage) along with marijuana "roaches" (butts of marijuana cigarettes) in their backyard. The Mannatts and several other parents formed the Nosy Parents Association in an attempt to stem teen drug use. One goal of the group was to seek and promote stiffer drug laws and increased drug-law enforcement.

Both residents of middle-class communities, such as the Mannatts, and residents of the jobless ghettoes may be very likely to support "get tough" policies. However, it should be very obvious that the impetus for their support is very different. On the margins, their different experiences could produce different ideas about the appropriate level of severity of punishment for drug offenders, the prevalence of drug-law enforcement, and who among offenders should be targeted.

Table 11.1 reveals some group differences in attitudes that may reflect different experiences, but it does not reveal the full complexity of these differences. For example, we cannot discern from the data presented in Table 11.1 the differences in attitudes between the least educated African Americans on the one hand, a population that is very likely to experience very deeply problems associated with drugs and drug-law enforcement, and better-educated non–African Americans on the other.

A more sophisticated statistical model (see Technical Appendix) better reveals the complexity of opinions about drug law enforcement along several dimensions such as urbanization, race, educational attainment, gender, and age.[37] The constant for the model indicates that most Americans did not favor the legalization of marijuana in 1987.[38] Important variations from this view are tied to the explanatory variables in Table 11.2. For example, Americans who lived in one of the 100 largest metropolitan areas were more likely to favor the legalization of marijuana than were Americans who lived in smaller locales.[39] Additionally, survey respondents without a high school diploma were less likely to favor the legalization of marijuana than were more educated Americans.[40] Thus, the model shows that Americans likely to be in the lowest socioeconomic class were less likely to favor legalization than Americans in higher classes.

By looking to combinations of these estimates, we can see how opinion varies among different subgroups of the American population. For example, starting from a baseline of men over thirty who lived in one of the largest 100 metropolitan areas in 1987, we can compute how the tendency to favor legalization varies by race and level of education. Whites with more than a high school education were 1.23 times more likely to favor legalization than African Americans with more than a high school education. More educated, city-dwelling whites were 1.6 times more likely to favor legalization of marijuana than the least educated, city-dwelling African Americans. We can also add the estimates for sex and age to the equations. These estimates indicate that women tended to oppose legalization of marijuana in 1987, while younger Americans tended to support it. Thus, the least educated African-American women were the least likely of all city-dwelling Americans to support legalization of marijuana in 1987.

Attitudes toward legalization of marijuana provide important information about what survey respondents think about drug-law enforcement generally, but the data do not provide a complete picture. Analysis of attitudes about the propriety of harsher local courts for criminal offenders provides additional and

Table 11.2
Logit of Positive Response to Legalization of Marijuana

Variable	Support for legalization	Comment
Large Metropolitan Area	.24 (2.7)	City dwellers are more likely to favor legalizing marijuana.
African American	-.21 (-1.9)	When compared to white Americans, African Americans are less likely to favor legalizing marijuana.
Less than high school degree	-.26 (-2.7)	Poorly educated Americans are less likely to favor legalizing marijuana.
Men	.26 (3.5)	Men are more likely to favor legalizing marijuana than women.
Young Americans	.38 (4.6)	Americans who are less than thirty years of age are more likely to favor legalizing marijuana.
Constant	-1.3 (-10.2)	Most Americans do not support legalizing marijuana.

Model Fit

Chi Square	Degrees of Freedom	p
Pearson = 73.4	78	.63
Likelihood Ratio = 75.1	78	.58

Note: The fit of the model is very good. The Pearson and Likelihood Ratio Chi Squares are close in their values. Moreover, the probability of committing a Type I error is high if this model is rejected.

important information about the level of support among groups, including African Americans, for stiff penalties for drug offenders. Table 11.3 is a model of attitudes towards court punitiveness.

Table 11.3 indicates that the most significant differences among the individuals who were questioned in 1987 about the harshness of local courts on criminal offenders occurred along sex and race categories. Both men and African Americans were more likely to think that courts should be less harsh on criminal of-

Table 11.3
Logit of Positive Response to Legalization of Marijuana

Variable	Support for less harsh courts	Comment
Large Metropolitan Area	-.08 (-1.0)	The association between living in a city and punitiveness is insignificant.
African American	.19 (1.8)	Compared to white Americans, African Americans tend to be non punitive.
Less than high school degree	.01 (.12)	The association between educational attainment and punitiveness is insignificant.
Men	.15 (2.1)	Women are more punitive than men.
Young Americans	.01 (.06)	The association between age and punitiveness is insignificant.
Constant	-1.2 (-8.8)	Most Americans are punitive.

Model Fit

Chi Square	Degrees of Freedom	p
Pearson = 73.4	78	.63
Likelihood Ratio = 75.1	78	.58

Note: The fit of the model is very good. The Pearson and Likelihood Ratio Chi Squares are close in their values. Moreover, the probability of committing a Type I error is high if this model is rejected.

fenders than women and white Americans. The parameter for race in the model indicates that the odds of African Americans in 1987 favoring less harsh local courts for criminal offenders were about 1.21 times the odds of white Americans doing so.[41] Likewise, male support for less harsh courts for criminal offenders in 1987 outweighed female support for less harsh courts. Again, it is likely that these variations importantly reflect the survey respondent's social context. Note that the estimates indicate that African-American men were the most likely of all groups to favor less harsh local courts for criminal offenders. No doubt these estimates reflect the unique experience of African-American men with an institution that looms large in their lives—the criminal justice system.

INTERPRETING THE RESULTS

The empirical analysis in this chapter confirms that a majority of Americans, African-American and white, supported a "get tough" position on drug-law enforcement in 1987, the year before the 1988 Anti-Drug Abuse Act was passed. But even though the data indicate that a majority of African Americans supported a "get tough" position, the data also show that they did so at a much lower rate than whites did in 1987. This result is especially intriguing in light of the relative levels of support for the "get tough" position among respondents with and without a high school education.

From the simple statistics in Table 11.1, we learn that in 1987, individuals with less than a high school education selected the "get tough" position at a higher rate than individuals with more education. Individuals without a high school education are more likely than individuals with a high school degree to occupy a low socioeconomic status and be poor.[42] Poor individuals are more likely than wealthier ones to be victimized by crime,[43] so it is likely that poor individuals are more likely than wealthier ones to experience crime and other problems associated with drugs. Thus, we should not be surprised to learn that the GSS data show that respondents without high school degrees support tougher measures for drug offenders at a *higher* rate than more educated individuals in 1987.

Now consider African Americans. In 1986, approximately one out of three African-American families lived in poverty—a rate three times the poverty rate for white families that year.[44] Moreover, the 1987 GSS data indicate that proportionately fewer African Americans had high school degrees than whites.[45] Because poverty is more prevalent among African Americans than it is among whites, we can hypothesize that African Americans as a group should experience more pervasive problems related to drugs such as open-air drug-selling and violence related to illegal drug markets than do whites as a group. And as noted, some have used similar reasoning to argue that African Americans would benefit from higher levels of support for "get tough" positions on drug-law enforcement.[46] These arguments are based on a simple proposition: Groups that experience higher levels of criminal victimization should be more likely than groups that experience lower levels of victimization to support "get tough" approaches to crime. However, the data presented here are inconsistent with this proposition as applied to African-American support for "get tough" approaches to drug-law enforcement. The data in Table 11.1 and the statistical model confirm that African Americans as a group were much *less* likely than whites to support a "get tough" position in 1987.

One possible explanation for the fact that African Americans supported the "get tough" position at lower rates than did whites is the fact that African Americans clearly experienced a high rate of drug-law imprisonment relative to whites in 1986, as Figure 11.2 clearly indicates. Indeed, African Americans experienced a high rate of imprisonment for drug offenses in absolute terms in 1986, and Figure 11.2 clearly reveals the acceleration of the imprisonment rate of African

Americans for drug offenses between 1986 and 1991. Because of this phenomenon, we might expect that to the extent that African Americans registered *less* support than whites for the "get tough" position in 1987, they registered *more* support for the "anti-law enforcement" view. Interestingly, the public opinion data do not conform to this hypothesis either. Table 11.1 indicates that in 1987, African Americans as a group favored the "anti-law enforcement" position at a rate that is statistically indistinguishable from the rate at which whites favored the position. Moreover, the statistical model highlights even more differences. It demonstrates that African-American men were the least likely respondents to support harsher local courts for criminal offenders generally. This result is consistent with the hypothesis explained earlier. On the other hand, the statistical model also indicates that African-American men were *less* likely than white men to favor legalization of marijuana. This result, of course, is inconsistent with the "anti-law enforcement" view.

The data show that African-American men were ambivalent about drug-law enforcement in 1987. In fact, the data show that as a general matter, African Americans were more ambivalent than whites in 1987 about drug-law enforcement. Most Americans surveyed in 1987 who believed that the courts should be less punitive also believed that marijuana should be legalized. Alternatively, Americans who believed that marijuana should not be legalized also believed that the courts should be more harsh. I characterize both sets of views as "noncomplex." Thus, noncomplex views are represented by the "get tough" and "anti-law enforcement" positions. Compared to white Americans, however, the data show that African Americans tended to believe either that courts should be less harsh on criminal offenders and that marijuana should not be legalized, or they tended to believe that the courts should be more harsh on criminal offenders and that marijuana should be legalized.[47] I characterize these views as "complex." Complex views are captured by the "libertarian" and "dual frustration" positions. I believe the prevalence of complex views among African Americans concerning drug-law enforcement reflects the deeper experiences of African Americans with both drugs and drug-law enforcement in their communities.

In addition to pointing out that African Americans tend to support drug-law enforcement views that reflect the difficulties of negotiating the problems associated with both drugs and drug-law enforcement, the statistical analysis also helps to predict the demographic characteristics of the African Americans who tend to hold complex views. The signs on the estimates of the statistical model tell us quite a bit about the Americans who were the most deeply ambivalent about drug-law enforcement in the 1987 survey. The "dual frustration" position is represented by estimates that are negative for legalization and positive for nonpunitiveness. A review of those estimates indicates that respondents who selected the "dual frustration" position tended to be older, less educated, African-American women. Examination of the group of African Americans who posted views consistent with the "dual frustration" position[48] indicates that 64 percent of them were women; 34 percent of them had less than a high school education,

33 percent had incomes below the poverty line and 74 percent of them were older than thirty when surveyed. The "libertarian" position is represented by estimates that are positive for legalization and negative for nonpunitiveness. A review of those estimates reveals that "libertarian" respondents tended to be young, educated men. Examination of the African Americans who supported this view in 1987[49] indicates that a majority of them were men; 81 percent had more than a high school education, and only about a quarter had incomes below the poverty line—the lowest percentage of any of the groups.[50]

Economist Glenn Loury points to a potential source of ambivalent feelings about these issues, explaining that "[t]he young black men wreaking havoc in the ghetto are still 'our youngsters' in the eyes of many of the decent poor and working-class black people who are sometimes their victims."[51] That so many of the African Americans in the "dual frustration" category are women helps to flesh out Loury's statement concerning "our youngsters." There are only a few statistics to work from here, but the information concerning race, class, and sex provides a foundation for informed speculation. African-American women in poor neighborhoods are torn. They worry about their young sons getting involved in gang activity. They worry about their sons possibly selling or using drugs. They worry about their children getting caught in the crossfire of warring gangs. In short, they worry about the very high levels of often drug-related crime in their neighborhoods. These mothers want better crime control and law enforcement. Yet, they understand that increased levels of law enforcement potentially saddle their children with a felony conviction—a mark that can insure economic and social marginalization.[52] Their ambivalence about these issues emerges in their simultaneous support for a criminal penalty for marijuana use, a level of support that surely underestimates their support for criminalization of other, harder drugs, and for *less severe* penalties for criminal offenders generally, a level of support that probably underestimates their support for less harsh penalties when nonviolent crimes are at issue.

Individuals in the "libertarian" group are ambivalent in a different way. These respondents supported tougher sanctions on criminal offenders; however, unlike "get tough" supporters, "libertarian" supporters favored legalization of marijuana. These survey respondents were younger, more educated, and more likely to be male than those in either the "get tough" or "dual frustration" category. African Americans in the "libertarian" group were the least likely out of the four groups of African Americans surveyed to be poor. These African Americans likely had greater residential mobility than the other poorer groups; thus, the "libertarians" probably were the least likely of all African-American respondents to live in very poor communities marked by high unemployment, crime, and open-air drug-selling. Residents of such neighborhoods might register opposition to legalization to make it as difficult as possible for their children to have access to drugs. Wealthier, educated individuals might be more confident in their ability to control their children's access to harmful drugs without resorting to the criminal law.[53]

Although a majority of African Americans supported the "get tough" position in 1986—a position that is congenial to the most prevalent approach to drug-law enforcement today—policy makers must understand that the ambivalence in the African-American community about the appropriateness of using harsh law enforcement to remedy the problems this community experiences relating to illegal drugs must be addressed if drug-law enforcement policy is to be efficacious. It is important to keep in mind the large percentage of African Americans who supported the "dual frustration" view, as well as those who supported a "get tough" approach. I believe that the heterogeneity of African-American attitudes toward drug-law enforcement reported here is a reflection of the social organization of the communities in which African Americans live. Paying greater attention to the social organization of poor, inner-city communities is essential to improving drug-law enforcement policy.

The important feature of the social organization approach to crime reduction is its recognition of the fact that community structures mediate individual-level factors such as low socioeconomic status and criminal or delinquent behavior.[54] There are two major dimensions of neighborhood social organization: (1) the prevalence, strength, and interdependence of social networks and (2) the extent of collective supervision exercised by residents and the personal responsibility they assume in addressing neighborhood problems.[55] Structures of social organization such as friendship networks, supervision of teenage peer groups, and participation in formal organization act to mediate individual-level predictors of crime such as low economic status, ethnic heterogeneity, residential mobility, urbanization, and family disruption. Efficacious policies reinforce, rather than weaken, community social organization.

Elsewhere I have evaluated current "get tough" drug-law enforcement policy through the lens of community social organization theory, concluding that this policy has the potential to undermine rather than promote the healing of weakened and impoverished neighborhoods because the current approach tends to exacerbate the precursors to social organization disruption such as low economic status, family disruption, and unemployment.[56] Because the "get tough" approach can reduce crime only by exacerbating community social *disorganization*, the "get tough" approach is destined to confound its own ends. We need instead a law enforcement policy that responds to the effects of concentrated poverty in inner-city communities.

The social organization approach to drug-law enforcement holds a few lessons for federal criminal law. The approach suggests that the federal government's role in drug-law enforcement should be more limited than it is now. A community-level focus argues against uniform, national-level strategies. A community-level approach suggests that law-enforcement strategies must vary to accommodate different community needs. A community-level approach implies devolution from the federal government. One should not interpret this statement as an argument against federal involvement in drug-law enforcement altogether. Neither should my statement be taken as a call for federal withdrawal from the problems generally associated with drugs. The federal government can play a useful role by paying greater attention to macro-level inputs that improve community social organization, such as education, housing, and jobs. Moreover, instead of focusing resources on a federal drug-law enforcement effort, the federal government should concentrate on supplying localities with more resources to deal with drug-related crime problems at the community level.

Additionally, and importantly, a focus on community social organization suggests that resources should be shifted from reactive strategies to preventive ones. Scholars who discuss social organization theory often focus on the potential for attention to "root causes" to repair damaged communities.[57] The macro-level inputs mentioned in the previous paragraph are examples of strategies that address so-called root causes of crime. They are preventive approaches. Law enforcement, too, can be preventive and thus can lead to social organization improvement. Governmental entities, including law enforcement agencies, are uniquely situated to provide resources and direction for affirmative organizational efforts. In fact, participation by residents in formal community policing programs is an example of precisely the type of activity that predicts social organization improvement, as participation in formal organization is an aspect of local community solidarity.[58] Moreover, participation in a neighborhood-based group in support of community policing is likely to lead *directly* to law-abiding behavior. When citizens participate in these programs, they are engaged directly in the business of constructing and transmitting law-abiding norms. Unfortunately, the strategies we focus on now are reactive instead of preventive. They are therefore more likely to be harmful to embattled communities than helpful.

CONCLUSION

The project reported in this chapter was designed to probe the level of support among African Americans for law enforcement policies that treat drug offenders very harshly. To test this support, African-American attitudes about legalization of marijuana and the harshness of courts were evaluated along with other factors that were likely to reflect an individual's experience with the problems associated with illegal drugs and drug-law enforcement and compared to the attitudes of non–African Americans. Most Americans, including African Americans, did not favor legalization of marijuana in 1987. At the same time, most Americans, including African Americans, favored harsher courts for criminal offenders. Even though these results suggest that a majority of both African Americans and white Americans held a position congenial to punitive law enforcement policies directed at drug offenders, the results reveal important differences between African Americans and white Americans. African Americans as a group were less likely to conform to the "get tough" position than whites, and African Americans surveyed were much more likely to exhibit much more ambivalence in their views on drug-law enforcement than whites.

Policy makers can learn from the results presented here. First, policy makers can learn about the opinions, attitudes, and ideas of disadvantaged African Americans—the segment of the population that bears the brunt of both the drug wars waged by gangs and the government's war on drugs. Attention to these findings is especially important in light of the fact that current drug policy is unlikely to reflect the views of disadvantaged African Americans.[59] Second, policy makers should understand that the complex views of African Americans on drug-law enforcement are likely to reflect the often low levels of social organization in communities with drug problems and that drug-law enforcement has the potential to improve community social organization by alleviating problems associated with drugs. These policy makers should also understand that drug-law enforcement should take care to avoid exacerbating precursors to social disorganization even as it attempts to improve social organization. The current federal drug-law enforcement policy and local policies that mimic it are more likely to rip apart community fabric than to strengthen it. Such policies are dangerously misguided.

NOTES

1. *See* Jacqueline Cohen and Jose Canela-Cacho, *Incarceration and Violent Crime,* in UNDERSTANDING AND PREVENTING VIOLENCE (Albert J. Reiss, Jr., and Jeffrey A. Roth, eds.) 296 (1994); Alfred Blumstein and Allen J. Beck, *Population Growth in U.S. Prisons, 1980–1996,* PRISONS (Michael Tonry and Joan Petersilia, eds.) 17 (1999); Steven Levitt, "The Effect of Prison Population Size on Crime Rates: Evidence from Prison Overcrowding Litigation," CXI QUARTERLY JOURNAL OF ECONOMICS: 319 (1996).

2. *See* Bureau of Justice Statistics, Correctional Populations in the United States, NCJ-170013 (1999).

3. *See* Blumstein and Beck, *supra* note 1, at 22 (Table 1), citing data from the Bureau of Justice Statistics, id., and the Bureau of the Census (various years).

4. *See id.* at 18. This includes both state and federal prisoners, but excludes persons in county jails.

5. Robert J. Sampson and Janet Lauritsen, *Racial and Ethnic Disparities in Crime and Criminal Justice in the United States,* in ETHNICITY, CRIME AND IMMIGRATION: COMPARATIVE AND CROSS-NATIONAL PERSPECTIVES (Michael Tonry, ed.) (1997).

6. *See* Blumstein and Beck, *supra* note 1, at 18; MICHAEL TONRY, MALIGN NEGLECT: RACE, CRIME AND PUNISHMENT IN AMERICA (1995); DAVID COLE, NO EQUAL JUSTICE (1998); MARK MAUER, RACE TO INCARCERATE (1998).

7. For a historical look at racial differences in incarceration *see* Samuel L. Myers & William J. Sabol, *Unemployment and Racial Differences in Imprisonment,* in THE ECONOMICS OF RACE AND CRIME 189, 194 (Table 1) (M. C. Simms and S. L. Myers, eds., 1988) (demonstrating average incarceration rates, by decade, of whites and blacks from 1850 to 1980). In 1993 blacks represented 49.7% of the state prison population and 33.7% of the federal population, while whites represented 45.6% and 63.1% respectively. *See* BUREAU OF JUSTICE STATISTICS, SOURCEBOOK OF CRIMINAL JUSTICE STATISTICS 1994, 546 (1994).

8. *See* Blumstein and Beck, *supra* note 1, at 22. By comparison, the increase in Hispanic sentenced prisoners was far greater, at 554 percent, but their incarceration rate in

1996 was 690 per 100,000 residents, less than half the rate for African Americans. The number of white prisoners rose by 185 percent during this period, and the white incarceration rate rose by 164 percent, but at 193 per 100,000 residents was less than one-eighth the white rate.

9. *See* Marc Mauer & Tracy Huling, The Sentencing Project, Young Black Americans and the Criminal Justice System: Five Years Later, 3 (October 1995).

10. Mauer, Race to Incarcerate, *supra* note 5.

11. *See id.*

12. *See* Marc Mauer & Tracy Huling, The Sentencing Project, Young Black Americans and the Criminal Justice System: Five Years Later, 11 Table 5 (October 1995).

13. *See id.,* at Table 7.

14. *See* Blumstein and Beck, *supra* note 1, at 24–5.

15. *See* Chart 1, *infra* at note 31.

16. *See, e.g.,* Randall Kennedy, *The State, Criminal Law, and Racial Discrimination: A Comment,* 107 Harv. L. Rev. 1255, 1278 (1994) ("disparities ... may be the mark, not of a white-dominated state apparatus 'discriminating' against blacks, but instead, of a state responding sensibly to the desires of law-abiding people—including the great mass of black communities—for protection against criminals preying upon them"). Others have advanced similar views. *See Keep Tough Penalty Boost Sentence for Powder Cocaine,* Montgomery Advertiser, Nov. 6, 1995, at 8A; Joseph Brown, *Break the Code of Silence on Black Crime: Defending Those Who Terrorize Black Communities Is Taking the Concept of Black Unity Just a Little Too Far,* Tampa Trib., Dec. 15, 1994, at 19; John J. DiIulio, Jr., *The Question of Black Crime,* Pub. Int., Sept. 22, 1994, at 3; Tom Morganthau, *The New Frontier for Civil Rights,* Newsweek, Nov. 29, 1993, at 65; Susan Estrich, *Cries of Racism Miss Point on Prison Rates,* USA Today, Feb. 15, 1996, at 12A; Bill Johnson, *Reducing Crack Sentences Hurts Blacks,* Detroit News, Oct. 27, 1995 (opinion); Richard Matthews, *The Problem Is Crime; Missing Point about Young Blacks in Prison,* Atlanta J. & Const., Oct. 12, 1995, at 10A (editorial).

17. *See* 21 U.S.C. § 841(b)(1)(A) and (B) (1994).

18. *See, e.g.,* David Cole, *The Paradox of Race and Crime: A Comment on Randall Kennedy's Politics of Distinction,* 83 Geo. L.J. 2547 (1995) (criticizing federal crack cocaine sentencing disparities). *See also United States Sentencing Commission, Cocaine and Federal Sentencing Policy* 207–12 (1995) (noting that federal public defenders and community defenders, the Probation Officers' Advisory Group, the Criminal Justice Policy Foundation, Families Against Mandatory Minimums, the National Association of Criminal Defense Lawyers, Citizens for the Rehabilitation of Errants, the Drug Policy Foundation, the American Bar Foundation, the American Civil Liberties Union, the Practitioner's Advisory Group, the National Rainbow Coalition, two federal judges, an Assistant United States Attorney, and 1,900 private citizens expressed concern about the 100-to-1 sentencing ratio or called for its discontinuation); Congressional Black Caucus, *Letter to the President* (Oct. 24, 1995) (urging President Clinton to veto a bill to overrule the Sentencing Commission's decision to scrap federal crack cocaine sentencing disparities).

19. *See* Jeffrey Fagan and Tracey Meares, "Punishment, deterrence and social control: The paradox of punishment in minority communities." *Public Law and Legal Theory Working Paper Program, Legal Scholarship Network,* <http://papers.ssrn. com/paper.taf ?abstract;_id=223148> for an account.

20. Other groups of non–African Americans are not included in this analysis.

21. "There are three basic elements in the opinion-forming process: the person, his environment, and the interaction between the two." HARWOOD L. CHILDS, PUBLIC OPINION: NATURE, FORMATION, AND ROLE 110 (1965). Chapter Six of Professor Childs' book discusses formation of public opinion. *See id.* at 110–37.

22. The General Social Surveys have been conducted almost every year since 1972. No surveys were conducted in 1979, 1980, or 1992. Each survey is an independently drawn sample of English-speaking persons, 18 years of age or over, living in non-institutional arrangements in the continental United States. *See* JAMES ALLAN DAVIS & TOM W. SMITH, GENERAL SOCIAL SURVEYS, 1972–1994: CUMULATIVE CODEBOOK 1 (1994). The analysis presented here utilizes the 1987 General Social Survey because in that year the National Science Foundation funded an oversample of blacks. *See id.* at 788. The number of blacks in the sample is an important factor in determining statistically significant differences in opinion between groups. *See* HOWARD SCHUMAN, ET AL., RACIAL ATTITUDES IN AMERICA: TRENDS AND INTERPRETATIONS 140 (2d ed. 1988) (noting that small samples of blacks in national samples of 1,500 to 2,000 yields only 150 to 200 blacks and leads to problems in sampling reliability). The 1987 oversample yielded an additional 353 black respondents to the 191 already present in the regular cross-section. The total number of unweighted cases in the 1987 sample was 1,819. In this analysis the oversampled blacks are weighted so that the combined oversample and regular cross-section data are representative of the population. *See* DAVIS & SMITH, *supra*, at 791.

23. Respondents were asked, "Do you think the use of marijuana should be made legal or not?"

24. Respondents were asked, "In general, do you think the courts in this area deal too harshly or not harshly enough with criminals?"

25. Anti-Drug Abuse Act of 1988 Pub. L. 100-690, 102 Stat. 4181.

26. It is important to note here that this analysis seeks to test levels of public support for tough drug-law enforcement measures such as the Anti-Drug Abuse Act of 1988 with GSS measures that do not refer directly to such laws. The most pertinent measures in the GSS address legalization of marijuana and harsher local courts for criminal offenders generally. Thus, there are undoubtedly biases in these measures. For a more complete description of these biases, *see* Technical Appendix, *infra.*

27. The relationship between public opinion and public policy is, of course, complex. Opinion influences policy, and policy influences opinion. For more on this process see CHILDS, *supra* note 7, at 309–319; William J. Chambliss, *Crime Control and Ethnic Minorities: Legitimizing Racial Oppression by Creating Moral Panics, in* ETHNICITY, RACE, AND CRIME 235–58 (D.F. Hawkins, ed., 1995).

28. The probability that a difference this large would occur through sampling variation alone is less than one in a hundred.

29. The difference in levels of support for this position between the two groups is statistically significant at .006.

30. The drug offense incarceration rates in the table include the data underlying Figure 11.2:

| | Less than High School | | More than High School | |
	White	African American	White	African American
1979	0.000182	0.000619	0.000049966	0.000354
1986	0.000339	0.001394	0.000067221	0.000413
1991	0.001231	0.007925	0.00017518	0.002099

31. *See* the Technical Appendix *infra* for a description of the data underlying Figure 11.2 and an explanation of the construction of the incarceration rates displayed in Figure 11.2.

32. WILSON, *supra* note 24, at 59–60.

33. *Id.* at 60.

34. *Id.* at 58.

35. *See* ALEX KOTLOWITZ, THERE ARE NO CHILDREN HERE (1992).

36. *See* Eric Schlosser, *Reefer Madness*, ATLANTIC MONTHLY, Aug. 1994, at 49–52.

37. For a detailed explanation of the model employed in this analysis, *see* Technical Appendix, *infra*.

38. $\beta = -1.3, z = -10.2$.

39. $\beta = .24, z = 2.7$.

40. $\beta = -.26, z = -2.7$.

41. $\beta = 0.19, z = 1.8$.

42. In this analysis educational attainment serves as an indicator of socioeconomic class. Social science research indicates that educational attainment is a very good proxy for socioeconomic class. See SIDNEY VERBA ET AL., VOICE AND EQUALITY: CIVIC VOLUNTARISM IN AMERICAN POLITICS 282–83 (1995). Whether or not the respondent has a high school degree (those with G.E.D.s are collapsed with those without high school degrees) is a categorical indicator of whether the respondent falls into the lowest socioeconomic class. Although educational attainment clearly is continuous, the attainment of a high school degree often marks a significant change in socioeconomic status. For an excellent description of the difference between a gradational and a categorical conception of class, see Deborah C. Malamud, *Class-Based Affirmative Action: Lessons and Caveats*, 74 TEX. L. REV. 1847, 1863–66 (1996).

43. *See* Sourcebook of Criminal Justice Statistics Table 3.9 at 234 (Kathleen Maguire & Ann Pastore, eds., 1994) (showing that individuals with the lowest income suffer the highest rate of personal crime victimization).

44. *See* U.S. Department of Commerce, Statistical Abstract of the United States Table 730 at 472 (1996).

45. About 67 percent of the African Americans in the sample analyzed had less than a high school education compared to about 77 percent of whites. Poorly educated African Americans are more likely than poorly educated whites to be poor. About 34 percent of African Americans with less than a high school degree in the sample had incomes at or below the poverty line compared to about 23 percent of whites.

46. *See* note 18, *supra*.

47. The statistical model used in this analysis quantifies this ambivalence. The model explained in the Technical Appendix controls for the association between views on legalization and views on court harshness. The log of the odds ratio of these views indicates that they are highly associated. The model also provides estimates for the effect of race, education, sex, and so on on the association between attitudes toward legalization and attitudes about the harshness of courts. Only the race effect is significant among the explanatory variables in the model ($\beta = -.43, z = 2.0$). This race estimate represents the likelihood that respondent's views do not conform to the noncomplex drug-law enforcement viewpoints—the "get tough" and "anti-law enforcement" positions. The fact that the estimate is negative means that African Americans are more likely than whites to have views in off-diagonal cells. Thus the views of African Americans are more "complex." The z-score indicates that this estimate is significant.

48. Fourteen percent of African Americans surveyed held this view.

49. Approximately 12 percent of African Americans supported this position.

50. Twenty-seven percent of African Americans who supported the "get tough" position had incomes below the poverty line in 1987, while 37 percent of those supporting the "anti-law enforcement" position did so. I should emphasize here, however, that there were only seven African American responses in the "anti-law enforcement" category.

51. Glenn Loury, *Listen to the Black Community*, Pub. Interest, Sept. 22, 1994, at 35 (commenting on article by John DiIulio, *supra* note 16).

52. Professor Randolph Stone has said that a felony conviction for an African-American youth is an "economic life sentence." *See* Randolph Stone, *Juvenile Justice: A Dream Deferred*, Criminal Justice, Winter 1994, at 50.

53. Many in the "libertarian" group are young African-American men who may not live with wives, partners, or children.

54. *See* Tracey L. Meares, *Social Organization and Drug Law Enforcement*, 35 Am. Crim. L. Rev. 191 (1998).

55. *See* Robert J. Sampson & W. Byron Groves, *Community Structure and Crime: Testing Social Disorganization Theory*, 94 Am. J. Soc. 774, 777–82 (1989).

56. *See* Meares, *supra*, note 56.

57. *See* Robert J. Sampson & William Julius Wilson, *Toward a Theory of Race, Crime, and Urban Inequality*, in Crime and Inequality 37–54 (J. Hagan and R. Peterson, eds., 1995) (advocating policies promoting housing and employment).

58. *See* Sampson & Groves, *supra*, note 57, at 779.

59. *See* Robert A. Jackson, *Clarifying the Relationship Between Education and Turnout*, 23 Am. Pol. Q. 279 (1995) (elaborating on the well-established positive relationship between education and political participation).

TECHNICAL APPENDIX

A. Data Sets

1. GSS

To evaluate opinions about drugs and law enforcement prior to the passage of the Anti-Drug Abuse Act of 1988, this analysis relies on two data sets. The first data set is the 1987 GSS. The GSS provides important information about respondents such as gender, race, educational attainment, work history, aspects of residence, and the like. This study utilizes two measures relevant to attitudes toward drug-law enforcement as dependent variables: attitudes toward legalization of marijuana and attitudes about whether courts in the respondent's area should be more harsh on criminal offenders generally. For analysis of support for tough sentences for drug offenders, each of these measures, if considered alone, is less than ideal. However, combinations of the measures along the dimensions described earlier represent interesting and distinct views about drug-law enforcement that can be assessed along different dimensions such as race, class, and urbanization to provide useful insight into attitudes toward tough drug laws. It is important to note that even if a perfect study were undertaken today, data regarding past opinions would not be captured. In light of this problem it is necessary to use the best available data.

One reason opinions either favoring or opposing legalization of marijuana are less than ideal measures of attitudes about drug-law enforcement is that many people believe that marijuana is less dangerous than other drugs. A recent Gallup Poll provides some empirical support for the idea that many people hold very different opinions about different types of drugs. Fifty-four percent of respondents listed crack cocaine as the drug they personally felt was the biggest problem in the country today, compared to 6 percent of respondents listing marijuana.[1] Thus, those who hold very conservative views about marijuana use are likely to hold even more conservative views about the propriety of legalizing drugs they believe are more dangerous than marijuana. It is therefore likely that the legalization measure used in this analysis underestimates opposition to legalization generally among more conservative respondents.

A second reason that the legalization measure is less than ideal is that the information it conveys about a respondent's attitudes about drug-law enforcement is somewhat fuzzy. To be sure, we should be able to interpret responses in *support* of legalization as responses in opposition to law enforcement with respect to marijuana usage. However, the fact that a respondent opposes legalization of a drug does not reveal more specific information about the type of drug-law enforcement the respondent believes is appropriate. We know only that the respondent believes *some* law enforcement response is appropriate.

To provide more information about the quality of law enforcement policies respondents favored, this study also analyzed attitudes about the propriety of harsher local courts for criminal offenders. In the GSS data used in this analysis, attitudes toward legalization are highly associated with attitudes pertaining to whether courts in the respondent's area should be more harsh on criminal offenders generally ($\lambda = 0.54$, $z = 6.3$).[2] The strong association between attitudes toward legalization and the harshness of courts toward criminal offenders is an important indicator of the extent to which attitudes toward legalization in the GSS capture law enforcement views.

Like the legalization measure, the court harshness measure, if considered alone, is a less than ideal measure of support for tough drug-law sentences. The survey question does not pertain directly to stiffer penalties for drug offenders; instead, it asks whether the respondent is willing to support harsher courts for criminal offenders *generally*. Obviously, the question covers drug offenders in addition to other types of offenders.

Given the general nature of the measure, an issue of concern is the direction of bias. It is not clear which way these data are biased for purposes of the analysis here. That is, it is not clear that respondents would be either more or less likely to favor harsher courts for drug offenders compared to their willingness to favor harsher courts for criminal offenders generally. However, I expect that respondents who are more likely than not to know or be acquainted with someone who is imprisoned for any type of crime also are more likely to oppose harsher courts for criminal offenders. Moreover, I expect this effect to be strongest when the crime at issue is a nonviolent one, like most drug offenses.

Because it is likely that attitudes about drug-law enforcement are influenced in part by increasingly high levels of incarceration for drug offending, a second data set, the Bureau of Justice Statistics' *Survey of Inmates of State Correctional Facilities* ("Survey of Prison Inmates") was analyzed in order to provide information about the level of drug-law enforcement among different groups of Americans.

2. Survey of Prison Inmates

The Surveys of Prison Inmates for 1979, 1986, and 1991 provide information about changes in drug-law enforcement over time, which was used to construct drug-law enforcement rates for race and class groups. These data provide context for the opinion survey analysis. Though only attitudes of survey respondents from 1987 were analyzed, I include the 1991 imprisonment rates in order to capture the dynamic aspect of incarceration for drug offenses. Based on the 1991 rates, it is very likely that when respondents in 1987 were tested, incarcerations for drug offending were on an upward trajectory.

Once every five years the Bureau of Justice Statistics conducts a national survey of thousands of inmates in state correctional facilities. Data are collected on individual characteristics of inmates, their current offenses and sentences, and family background, among other things. This study utilizes the surveys for 1979 (N = 11,397), 1986 (N = 14,649), and 1991 (N = 13,986).

To construct rates, the self-reported offense data first were recoded into the Federal Bureau of Investigation's Index Offenses (homicide, forcible rape, robbery, aggravated assault, burglary, larceny, and car theft) along with two groups of drug offenses—drug trafficking and other drug offenses. Next, these categories were grouped by race and class. The class variable was created by recoding education. As the occupation and income data in the prison survey are very poor, a proxy for socioeconomic class was necessary. Education is a widely-accepted proxy for socioeconomic class.[3] Using education as a socioeconomic class proxy also allowed comparisons to be made between drug imprisonment rates among different groups and GSS survey data, which could easily be broken into race and educational attainment groupings. The relevant educational groupings are: less than high school (including those who obtained general equivalency degrees), high school degree, and some college education. Drug imprisonment rates for each race and class group were computed by using data from the Survey of Prison Inmates as numerators and computing weighted race and educational attainment subgroupings of the United States population from the Current Population Surveys of 1979, 1986, and 1991 for the denominators.

B. Recoding of GSS Data

The model employed in this analysis requires two dichotomous variables. The responses to the legalization question were "closed." Respondents were offered two responses, "should" and "should not" when asked, "Do you think use of marijuana should be made legal or not?" In response to the court harshness question, however, some respondents volunteered answers that were not offered. Respondents were asked, "In general, do you think the courts in this area deal too harshly or not harshly enough with criminals?" Individuals were allowed to respond in five different ways: too harshly, not harshly enough, about right, don't know, and no answer. Therefore, the responses were not dichotomous. It was necessary to recode some of the values in the court harshness variable.

The recoded values used in this analysis distinguish between two kinds of individuals—those who favor more harsh courts for criminal offenders generally and those who do not. In colloquial terms, the recoded values distinguish between individuals some would describe as punitive and individuals some would describe as nonpunitive. For example, the most punitive individuals think that the courts are "not harsh enough" on criminals. Nonpunitive individuals think the courts are "too harsh." A loglinear model was used to determine whether the respondents who volunteered answers such as "about right," "don't know," or who gave a response coded "no answer" when asked about the harshness of local courts on criminal offenders were more like punitive individuals or nonpunitive individuals. The scores from the loglinear model of the courts variable determined that the most punitive individuals surveyed responded "not harsh enough," and the second most punitive individuals responded "about right." The individuals who responded either "don't know" or "no answer" were the least punitive individuals surveyed.

Although, the punitive/nonpunitive distinction clouds some of the differences between the responses, this analysis coded as "punitive" responses that characterized courts as either "not harsh enough" or "just right." All other responses were coded "nonpunitive." The following table displays values of the court harshness variable by levels of responses to the legalization question before recoding:

		not harsh enough	too harsh	about right	don't know/ no answer
Legalize?	No	1170	33	149	53
	Yes	206	22	43	26

Since there are only two values for the legalization variable, the model is saturated; therefore, issues of relative model fit cannot be discussed.

In an analysis of similar data, a group of researchers simply contrasted punitive views with nonpunitive views by grouping "about right" answers with nonpunitive views. *See* Steven F. Cohn et al., *Punitive Attitudes Toward Criminals: Racial Consensus or Racial Conflict*, 38 Soc. Probs. 287, 289–90 (1991). The method of collapsing categories employed here is more refined. For a detailed explanation of the procedures used here *see* Leo Goodman, *New Methods for Analyzing the Intrinsic Character of Qualitative Variables Using Cross-*

Classified Data, 93 Am. J. Soc. 529 (1987); Leo Goodman, The Analysis of Cross-Classified Data Having Ordered Categories (1984).

C. Statistical Model

The model used in this analysis is more sophisticated than the typical logit loglinear model. The dependent variable estimated in this loglinear model is a *composite* of two dichotomous variables: the legalization measure and the measure for attitudes toward court harshness. The model isolates the effect of different predictors of the likelihood that an individual will either favor legalization of marijuana or not favor it, and it also isolates the effect of different predictors of the likelihood that an individual will either favor or not favor more harsh courts for criminal offenders generally. At the same time, the model controls for the association between attitudes toward legalization and attitudes toward the harshness of courts.

This technique is useful for two reasons. First, it is likely that attitudes toward the harshness of law enforcement affects whether a person supports legalization of marijuana. The model employed here confirms that the association between legalization and support for local courts that are more harsh on criminal offenders is strong ($\lambda = 0.54$, $z = 6.3$). This association means that respondents who oppose legalization of marijuana are likely to support harsher courts, while respondents who support legalization are likely to oppose harsher courts. Note that these associations reflect the analytical guideposts I have selected for analysis. Entering attitudes toward court harshness as an independent factor in a logit model of legalization masks the effect of other variables on legalization. However, using the technique described hereafter, I am able to obtain estimates for factors on legalization that are independent of their effects on punitiveness. Second, isolation of the effect of other variables on attitudes toward court harshness reveals important information that is theoretically useful, as I explain in the first two sections of this chapter. The model employed in this analysis has the following form.

The dependent variable estimated in the loglinear model is a composite of two variables: whether or not an individual favors less harsh courts (nonpunitive) and whether or not an individual favors the legalization of marijuana.

Let y represent the composite variable such that

$$y = 2^* \text{(nonpunitive} - 1) + \text{legalization,}$$

where 2 is a positive response on either variable and 1 is a negative response. Consider this contrast below:

1	1	1	1
-0.5	-0.5	0.5	0.5
-0.5	0.5	-0.5	0.5
0.25	-0.25	-0.25	0.25

The composite variable has four levels, which allows effects for three independent contrasts to be estimated. There is a contrast for favoring legalization versus not favoring legalization of marijuana. There is a contrast for favoring less harsh courts for criminal offenders versus not favoring less harsh courts. And there is a contrast for the association between punitiveness and support for legalization. That is, there is a contrast between the likelihood that a respondent will favor the "get tough" or "anti-law enforcement" positions as opposed to the drug-law enforcement positions in the off-diagonals, which are the "libertarian" and the "dual frustration" views.

The saturated loglinear model for y, a composite of two dichotomous variables, can be written as:

$$\ln(F_{ij}^{AB}) = \lambda + (0.5)\lambda_i^A + (0.5)\lambda_j^B + (0.25)\lambda_{ij}^{AB};$$

where

$$\lambda_2^A = -\lambda_1^A; \lambda_2^B = -1_1^B; \lambda_{21}^{AB} = -\lambda_{12}^{AB}; \lambda_{22}^{AB} = -\lambda_{11}^{AB}.$$

Then, λ_i^A represents the log-odds of taking category 1 versus 2 of variable A, controlling for variable B; λ_j^B represents the log-odds of taking category 1 versus category 2 of variable B, controlling for variable A; and λ_{ij}^{AB} represents the log-odds ratio between variables A and B.

For another example of the model used here, see Patrick E. Shrout & Denise B. Kandel, *Analyzing Properties of Dyads: Determinants of Similarity of Marijuana Use in Adolescent Friendship Dyads* 9 Soc. METHODS & RES. 363 (1981).

NOTES TO APPENDIX

1. *See* THE GALLUP ORGANIZATION, THE OFFICE OF NATIONAL DRUG CONTROL POLICY, CONSULT WITH AMERICA: A LOOK AT HOW AMERICANS VIEW THE COUNTRY'S DRUG POLICY 28 (Mar. 1996). However, this poll is far from dispositive. Only 4 percent of these respondents listed heroin as a serious problem, and 21 percent listed all drugs (crack cocaine, powder cocaine, marijuana, heroin and other opiates, inappropriate use of prescription drugs, and LSD and other hallucinogens). *Id.* Responses obviously are dependent upon social contexts in which the seriousness of the problem depends not only upon the perceived seriousness of the drug but also upon the prevalence of the drug's use.

2. For a detailed explanation of the statistical model used to estimate this association, *see* section C.

3. *See* Michael C. Dawson, *Behind the Mule: Race and Class in American Politics* (1994).

Part III

Emerging and Critical Perspectives on Crime Control and Social Justice

12

Drug War Politics: Racism, Corruption, and Alienation

William J. Chambliss

In theory, crime control is an institutionalized means of enhancing social justice. The criminal law contributes to social justice when it is applied impartially without regard to race, class, gender, religion, sexual orientation, or any personal characteristics. When the law systematically discriminates against a group of people, it does not enhance social justice; rather, it perpetuates injustice. The systemic bias in the enforcement of the criminal law in the "war on drugs" is seriously undermining the basic principles of social justice in the United States.

THE IMPRISONMENT BINGE

As a consequence of the "war on drugs," the prisons and jails of the country are overflowing. Between 1980 and 2000 the prison population in the United States quadrupled (Pastore and Maguire 2000), which makes the United States the most incarcerating country in the world (See Figures 12.1 and 12.2).

The rapid growth in the number of people in prison in the United States has taken place at a time when the crime rate for what are generally believed to be the most serious offenses (violent and property crimes) has been declining, according to the results of the National Criminal Victim Surveys (see Figure 12.3).

Incarceration for drug offenses is a major contributor to the rapid increase in the number of people in prison in the United States. Thirty-five percent of the convicted felony defendants in 1999 were drug offenders (Uniform Crime Reports 2001). In 1997, over 60 percent of the inmates in federal prisons and over 35 percent of state prisoners were sentenced for drug offenses (Beck and Mumola 1998). Approximately one-third of the convicted drug offenders are sen-

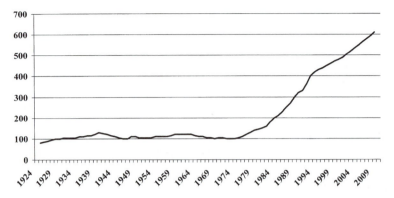

Figure 12.1   State and Federal Prison Population Growth, United States, 1925–2009.

tenced for marijuana and two-thirds for heroin and cocaine: official reports make no distinction between heroin and cocaine, but it is likely that the vast bulk of these cases involve cocaine. Drug sentences accounted for the entire increase in new court commitments to state prisons between 1977 and 1995; indeed, incarceration rates for property and violent crimes declined during this period while incarceration rates for drugs nearly tripled (see Figure 12.4).

Arrest data show an even more dramatic discrepancy in types of offenses in recent years. In 1999 there were over one million arrests for drug abuse violations (Pastore and Maguire 2000). There were more arrests for drug abuse violations than for any other single category: larceny and theft ranked second in total arrests (792,386). Three-fourths (75%) of the drug arrests every year are for possession and one-fourth (25%) for the sale or manufacture of drugs. Marijuana arrests account for over 40 percent of the total arrests each year, heroin and cocaine for about 40 percent, and synthetic or "other dangerous drugs" for the rest (Pastore and Maguire 2000).

Contrary to popular mythology, most drug offenders are not members of some violent criminal gang that preys on young people as victims. Most of the arrests are for possession, not for sale or manufacture. Furthermore, even among those convicted and sentenced to prison a large proportion are first-time offenders. According to a study conducted by the U.S. Attorney General's office, over 36 percent of all prisoners sentenced for drug offenses are "low level drug offenders with no current or prior violent offenses on their records, no involvement in sophisticated criminal activity, and no previous prison time" (U.S. Attorney General 1994, 2–3). Despite the low level of involvement in serious crime, they are sentenced to an average of 81.5 months (Pastore and Maguire 2000). These facts support the conclusion of Austin and Irwin that over 50 percent of the prisoners in state and federal prisons are in for offenses that opinion surveys show the general public think are "not very serious crimes" (Austin and Irwin 1989).

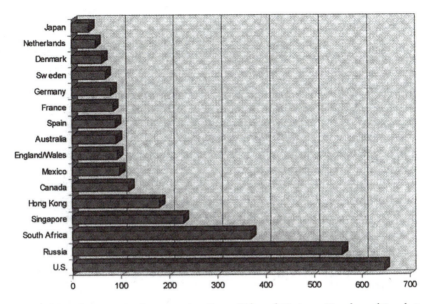

Figure 12.2   Comparative Incarceration Rates, Selected Nations: Number of People in Jails or Prisons per 100,000 Population.
Source: Nils Christie, *Crime Control as Industry*, 1993; Kathleen Maguire and Ann L. Pastore, *Sourcebook of Criminal Justice Statistics, 1996.*

Data for the United States are for 1995. For other countries, the latest available data are for 1993.

THE RACIAL CONSEQUENCES OF THE WAR ON DRUGS

The war on drugs is a classic example of how law enforcement efforts inevitably focus on the powerless, particularly the poor and minorities, while ignoring the same crimes being committed by middle- and upper-class whites (Chambliss 2001). Annual self-report surveys of illegal drug use among high school students (eighth, tenth, and twelfth graders) find that white students report using all illicit drugs at a much higher rate than blacks (Johnston, O'Malley, and Bachman 2001, 106–8; see Table 12.1). The differences in other rates of usage are even greater. Among twelfth-grade students, whites are eight times more likely than blacks to use cocaine, crack, LSD, and tranquilizers and four times more likely to use heroin, amphetamines, and barbiturates. The trends in usage among white and black adult populations show similar results (Johnston, O'Malley, and Bachman 2000; National Household Survey of Drug Abuse 1999). Since these are the age groups most likely to be arrested and incarcerated on drug charges, the comparative frequency of usage is of great significance when we look at the likelihood of arrest, conviction, and prison sentences for drugs by race.

White Americans make up 74 percent of the population, and African Americans less than 13 percent. But 40 percent of the arrests for drug offenses occur among the Black population and only 60 percent among the white population.

Year	Violent Crime	Homicides	Property Crime
1973	47.6	9.3	515.9
1974	47.9	9.7	551.5
1975	48.3	9.6	553.6
1976	47.9	8.8	544.2
1977	50.3	8.8	544.1
1978	50.5	9.0	532.6
1979	51.6	9.7	531.8
1980	49.3	10.2	496.1
1981	52.2	9.8	497.2
1982	50.6	9.1	468.3
1983	46.4	8.3	428.4
1984	46.3	7.9	399.2
1985	45.1	7.9	385.4
1986	41.9	8.6	372.7
1987	43.9	8.3	379.6
1988	44.0	8.4	378.4
1989	43.2	8.7	373.4
1990	44.0	9.4	348.9
1991	48.7	9.8	353.7
1992	47.8	9.3	325.3
1993	49.0	9.5	318.9
1994	51.1	9.0	310.2
1995	46.0	8.2	290.5
1996	41.5	7.4	266.3
1997	38.7	6.8	248.3
1998	35.9	6.3	217.4
1999	32.8	5.7	198.0
2000	27.9	NA	178.1

Figure 12.3   Violent, Homicide, and Property Crime Rates, 1973–2000.
Source: Bureau of Justice Statistics, *Criminal Victimization 2000* (Washington, DC: U.S. Department of Justice, 2001); Federal Bureau of Investigation, *Uniform Crime Reports, 1973–2001* (Washington, DC: U.S. Department of Justice).

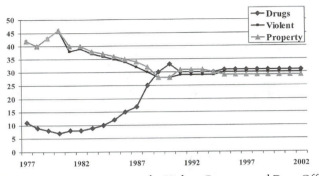

Figure 12.4   New Court Commitments for Violent, Property, and Drug Offenses.
Source: Bureau of Justice Statistics, State Court Sentencing of Convicted Felons, 1990, 1992, 1994, 1996, 1998, 2000.

When it comes to being sent to prison, the contradiction between social justice and crime control is even more dramatic: 60 percent of the new court commitments for drugs are Black offenders and only 40 percent are white. As Figure 12.5 shows, although whites have a higher rate of illicit drug use, they are much less likely to be sentenced to prison (see Figure 12.5).

African-American women and juveniles are particularly hard-hit by the systematic racism inherent in the enforcement of drug laws. Sixty-three percent of the women in state and federal prisons in 1995 were minority women, and 75 percent were mothers (Maguire and Pastore 1996). Between 1980 and 1994 the number of women in state and federal prisons increased from approximately 12,000 to over 60,000, a five-fold increase in the imprisonment of women in fifteen years. Seventy percent of the Black women in federal prisons are in for drug offenses. The pattern of discrimination in sentencing for Black juveniles is even more extreme than for the Black population as a whole. Between 1985 and 2000 the number of white juveniles in locked detention actually declined, whereas the number of non-white juveniles (mostly Black) in locked detention increased dramatically, with detention for drugs increasing by 120 percent.

It is no exaggeration to say that the lives and futures of young men and women in the poor Black and Latino communities in the United States are being systematically destroyed and the population of young males permanently alienated by the enforcement of anti-drug laws. Among young Black men between the ages of fifteen and thirty-five, 25 percent are, at any given moment, in prison or jail, on probation or parole, or facing a warrant for their arrest (Mauer 1990). In cities with large Black populations such as Washington, D.C., and Baltimore, that figure increases to nearly 50 percent. At the current rate of incarceration, 63 percent of all African-American men between the ages of eighteen and thirty-five will be in prison or jail by the year 2020 (see Figure 12.6).

Table 12.1
Illicit Drug Use Among Twelfth Graders by Race and Ethnicity

	Any Illicit Drug Other than Marijuana	Marijuana	Cocaine	Crack	Hallucinogens
Lifetime					
White	31.8	49.4	9.9	4.4	14.9
Black	10.7	45.7	1.9	0.8	2.1
Hispanic	32.1	55.0	13.3	6.3	15.3
Annual					
White	22.7	38.2	6.2	3.4	9.9
Black	6.4	30.0	1.0	0.5	1.6
Hispanic	21.2	40.5	7.6	3.4	4.6
30-Day					
White	11.3	22.7	2.5	1.0	3.2
Black	3.2	19.0	0.8	0.3	0.9
Hispanic	10.9	24.6	3.6	2.1	3.8

Source: Lloyd D. Johnston, Patrick M. O'Malley, and Jerald G. Bachman, *Monitoring the Future: National Survey Results on Drug Use, 1975–2000* (Washington, DC: National Institute on Drug Abuse, 2001).

   The fact of wholesale discrimination in the criminal justice system is widely recognized in Black and Latino ghettos, where the war on drugs has produced another war as well: a war between the police and the residents. You need only listen to the words of "gangsta rap" music to get a sense of the hostility, the war-mentality, that permeates the ghetto. Young Black and Latino men living in America's ghettos and barrios are under siege from, and at war with, the police. The process is graphically illustrated by the following field note from observations of police-community interactions conducted over several years by my students and me while riding with the Rapid Deployment Unit (RDU) of the Washington, D.C., Metropolitan Police Force (Chambliss 2001, 69). The RDU was

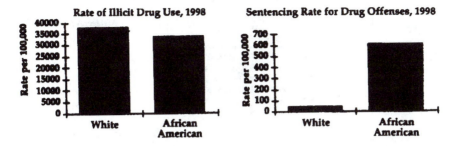

Figure 12.5   Racial Disparity in Prison Sentences for Drug Offenses.
Source: U.S. Department of Health and Human Services, *National Household Survey on Drug Abuse* (U.S. Department of Justice Statistics, 1999).
Note: "Use" is defined as whether the individual has *ever used* an illicit drug.

established as a special unit of the police following the race riots of the late 1960s. Over the years their assignment has changed from riot control to drug control. They accomplish this by patrolling the Black ghetto where the poorest 40 percent of the Black population lives. To enforce the drug laws, the RDU sets up buys with undercover agents, stops vehicles with young Black men in them, and searches apartments and homes for drugs. Violence, racist slurs, and disrespect are standard procedure in the typical arrest of minority suspects. The following field notes are illustrative of the process (Chambliss 2001, 69).

Field Notes. RIPS: CASE #2.

It is about 10:25 at night when an undercover agent purchases $50.00 of crack cocaine from a young Black male. The agent calls us and tells us that the suspect has just entered a building and gone into an apartment. We go immediately to the apartment; the police enter without warning with their guns drawn. Small children begin to scream and cry. The adults in the apartment are thrown to the floor, the police are shouting, the three women in the apartment are swearing and shouting, "You can't just barge in here like this ... where is your warrant?" The suspect is caught and brought outside. The identification is made and the suspect is arrested. The suspect is sixteen years old. While the suspect is being questioned one policeman says:

"I should kick your little Black ass right here for dealing that shit. You are a worthless little scumbag, do you realize that?"

Another officer asks:

"What is your mother's name, son? My mistake ... she is probably a whore and you are just a ghetto bastard. Am I right?"

The suspect is cooperative and soft-spoken. He does not appear to be menacing or a threat. He offers no resistance to the police. It seems that the suspect's demeanor is causing the

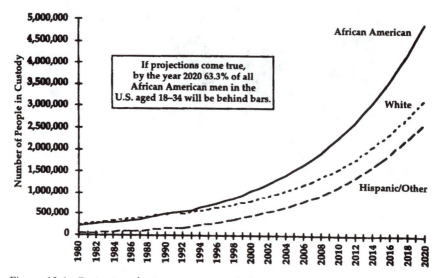

Figure 12.6   Projections for Persons in Custody by Race/Ethnicity.
Source: Projected from data in Kathleen Maguire and Ann G. Pastore, *Sourcebook of Criminal Justice Statistics* (Washington, DC: U.S. Department of Justice, Bureau of Justice Statistics, 1999).

police officers to become more abusive verbally. The suspect is handled very roughly. Handcuffs are cinched tightly and he is shoved against the patrol car. His head hits the doorframe of the car as he is pushed into the back seat of the patrol car. One of the officers comments that it is nice to make "a clean arrest."

When asked whether or not it is legal to enter a home without a warrant, the arresting officer replies:

"This is Southeast [Washington] and the Supreme Court has little regard for little shit like busting in on someone who just committed a crime involving drugs. . . . Who will argue for the juvenile in this case? No one can and no one will."

The Impact on the Black Community

These observations are only suggestive of the oppressive and racist law enforcement practices that prevail throughout the country. Left out of these observations are the many instances of Black and Latino men brutalized and killed by overzealous policing. One of the consequences is that the African-American and Latino communities view the police with suspicion and often disdain.

Because arrests take place in crowded areas, children as well as adults bear witness to the racism and violence of the police as often as they witness the violence of drug dealers. No wonder many in the Black community view the police as an alien occupying army rather than protectors of citizens' rights. No wonder the gangs that occupy the streets often are seen as more in tune with the needs of the community than the police officers who ride through in their patrol cars harassing every young Black male in sight (Jankowski 1991). No wonder the police cannot find witnesses to come forth. The police blame this on fear, which no doubt is a factor in some cases. But in many others it is a lack of faith in the justice system itself.

When laws are blatantly racist, as is the case when possession of a small amount (5 grams) of crack-cocaine, the drug of choice of people in poor Black communities, carries a mandatory five-year prison sentence without the possibility of parole but possession of 100 times that amount of cocaine powder (the drug of choice of the white middle class) has no mandatory sentence, any illusion of an impartial judicial system is permanently shattered (Doob 1993).

Even the Black middle class and upper class understand the racism inherent in the system. Because of the tendency of police to stop cars driven by African Americans, "driving while black" (DWB) has become a catchword for institutionalized racism in the criminal justice system.

The police assigned to the ghetto recognize their reason for being there as well as do the residents; they see their job as "keeping a lid on so this place won't blow up." The institutional memory of the riots of the 1960s and 1970s is clear and present in the lives of the ghetto police. Those who doubt it are reminded how tenuous is the control by such occurrences as the Los Angeles riots of 1992 and the day-to-day instances of hostility and resistance to policing. For example, on patrol one night the police pursued a speeding vehicle into a cul-de-sac. People were sitting on their porches and observed the arrest of a young Black man. As the police approached his car, the residents left their porches and began throwing rocks, boards, and debris at the police. It was a scene out of East Jerusalem, but it was Northeast Washington. Passersby who tried to divert the arrest surrounded the police attempting an arrest of a man in the afternoon. Someone from a building nearby shot an automatic weapon into the air, apparently not wanting to hit anyone but trying to distract the police from the arrest. These were ordinary citizens expressing their distrust and disbelief in the legitimacy of the police right to arrest African Americans.

Current law enforcement policies that concentrate on policing the ghetto not only produce widespread disrespect for the legal system, but they also reinforce the belief that ethnic cleansing is a white conspiracy. This belief is further reinforced by widespread corruption of the law enforcement system that is an inevitable offshoot of the war on drugs.

CORRUPTION

The *San Jose Mercury News* ran a series of articles by reporter Gary Webb that detailed a working relationship between the CIA and an informant who was a major cocaine dealer responsible for organizing the sale and distribution of cocaine to the Black ghetto in Los Angeles. This story spread through the Black community nationwide. It lent support to a widely held belief in the African-American community that there was a government plan to suppress the Black population by inundating it with cocaine. The national press and media disdainfully dismissed the report without mentioning that the CIA has in fact been complicitous in drug trafficking for at least the past forty years.

The CIA cooperated with the Medellin drug cartel to ship one ton of cocaine into the United States in 1993 (Weiner 1993). The CIA claimed that this was done to infiltrate the cartel. Despite the fact that a former head of the Drug Enforcement Agency publicly accused the CIA of criminal activities in this case, it was never investigated; the $20 million (wholesale price in Latin America) the cartel paid the CIA agents for the cocaine has never been accounted for. Rather, the whole affair was quietly swept under the rug; one of the two agents who negotiated the sale retired immediately afterward, the other was transferred. Nor was this the first time the CIA was implicated in international narcotics smuggling. There is overwhelming evidence of cooperation between the CIA and opium smugglers in Laos during the Vietnam War and of complicity with cocaine smugglers in Latin America during the attempt to overthrow the Sandinistas in Nicaragua (McCoy 1991, 1973; Chambliss 1989; Sharkey 1988; Cockburn 1987; Kwitny 1987).

John Stockwell, a former high-ranking CIA official, claims that drug smuggling and the CIA were essential components in the private campaign in support of the Contras in Nicaragua (Stockwell 1986). Stockwell's assertions recently were supported by an investigation by the Inspector General of the CIA, who reported to the House Intelligence Committee that the CIA "was aware" that people and companies it supported in Latin America were connected to drug trafficking (Pincus 1998). George Morales, one of the largest drug traffickers in South America, testified that the CIA approached him in 1984 to fly weapons to Nicaragua. Morales claimed that the CIA opened up an airstrip in Costa Rica and provided his pilot with information on how to avoid radar traps. According to Morales, he flew twenty weapons shipments into Costa Rica in 1984 and 1985. In return, the CIA helped him smuggle thousands of kilograms of cocaine into the United States. Morales' pilot Gary Betzner testified that he flew 4,000 pounds of arms into Costa Rica and 500 kg of cocaine to Lakeland, Florida (Pincus 1998).

Drug enforcement police, whether federal, state, or local, are particularly vulnerable to bribes and corruption, which is not surprising given the immense amount of money involved. The Drug Enforcement Agency (DEA) agent who arrested Manuel Noreiga in Panama was undercover, working to launder money prior to Noreiga's arrest. He admitted diverting $700,000 into his own bank account in Switzerland, which he was supposed to turn over to the government (*Washington Post* 1994). U.S. police departments are riddled with corruption fueled by the extraordinary profits in drugs (Chambliss 1988; Daley 1978). Robert Daley's rendering of corruption throughout the police department in New York and my own study of Seattle, Washington, supports the conclusion that "you could write this story in any city, any town in the country. It used to be a story in eastern urban centers. But now it's true throughout the U.S." (Daley 1978). In a repeat of Daley's expose, in 1993 the Mollen Commission in New York sat stone-faced as police officers told how they had accepted bribes from drug dealers, engaged in drug trafficking, and stole drugs to sell (*Washington Post* 1993). Fourteen New York police officers were charged and eleven others were disciplined. One can scarcely keep up with the corruption of police officers in the United States. Between 1994 and 1996, over 500 police officers were indicted for accepting bribes and payoffs. In Cleveland, fifty-five officers were arrested in an FBI sting operation (U.S. Department of Justice 1998). In Washington, D.C., seventy-seven police officers faced criminal charges connected with selling drugs or accepting payoffs from drug dealers. Only weeks before the arrest of the police officers, twelve corrections officers were arrested on charges of taking drugs into Lorton, the D.C. prison, and selling them to inmates. Former police chiefs in Rochester, New York, and Detroit were convicted of drug-related offenses; and police officers in Philadelphia, Miami, Los Angeles, and Cleveland have been convicted of accepting bribes, theft, and complicity in drug trafficking in recent years (Gladwell 1994).

A Los Angeles police officer, Rafael Perez, was caught stealing six pounds of cocaine from a police storage unit. In a plea bargain deal, Perez agreed to testify about widespread criminal offenses committed by the "ramparts" division of the L.A. Police. In over 2,000 pages of testimony, Perez detailed how police planted evidence, used excessive force (including murder and rape), and took bribes from drug dealers. Practically all of the offenses committed by the police were against Latinos and blacks.

One of the more telling cases underscoring the impact of drug money on the criminal justice system occurred in Louisiana, where for the first time in the 200-year history of the federal judiciary a federal district judge was convicted of taking a $100,000 bribe from a drug smuggler (*Los Angeles Times* 1992).

A search of newspaper articles (which represent only a fraction of the total cases) recorded on Nexus revealed the following list of cases in recent years. Some of these cases reflect the fact that in order to be an effective undercover agent the police officer must become a drug user. People selling drugs are not going to provide drugs on a regular basis to an agent who is never seen consuming the drugs. The government is in effect forcing agents to become drug users in order to do their job. Some of these agents then steal drugs to support their habit. Others accept bribes and steal drugs simply for profit. To wit:

- Joel Audain was a special operations inspector for the INS in Miami. In 1998 Audain was arrested by FBI agents and charged with smuggling over thirty-three tons of cocaine into the United States over a ten-year period.
- On December 30, 1996, Allen Wilson of the Philadelphia Police Department pled guilty to stealing more than $46,000 from drug dealers and splitting another $43,000 with High-

way Patrolman Michael Stieber, money they had stolen from drug dealers. Eleven other former and current Philadelphia police officers have been charged with similar crimes.

- Since 1983, at least fifteen DEA agents have been convicted of federal felonies.
- May 1989: Two veteran DEA agents, Drew Bunnel and Al Iglesias, were charged with taking bribes from a drug dealer.
- April 1989: DEA agent Jorge Villar was indicted for selling confidential information and names of drug informants to drug dealers. When arrested he was carrying a briefcase with $350,000 in bank certificates of deposit.
- July 1990: A sheriff's deputy in Clark County, Washington, Herbert Pacheco, was convicted of conspiracy to commit murder, conspiracy to deliver cocaine, and attempted cocaine delivery.
- March 1988: Four New York City police officers were convicted of beating and torturing a drug dealer.
- October 1988: Tommy Pruitt, head of a Georgia drug task force, was sentenced to fifteen years in prison for selling at least $10,000 worth of drugs to a drug dealer.
- July 1990: Carlos Simon, a Hialeah, Florida, police officer, was sentenced to thirty years for the murder of an alleged drug dealer and his girl friend.
- March 1993: Edward K. O'Brien, a former DEA agent, was sentenced to six years in prison for cocaine smuggling and embezzlement of $140,000 in drug money.
- October 1990: Eddie Hill, DEA supervisor, was put on trial for embezzling drug money and filing false vouchers.
- June 1990: The police chief of Brockton, Massachusetts, received a seven–ten-year sentence for stealing cocaine from the police department's evidence room. Three hundred seventy-five cases had to be dismissed because of the missing evidence.
- January 1990: Four Philadelphia police officers who were members of a special antidrug unit were sentenced to prison for stealing money and drugs from the drug dealers they arrested.

The list could be expanded indefinitely. Suffice it to say that the corruption of police involving drug profits is ubiquitous at all levels of policing in the United States (Woodiwiss 1988).

In other, less obvious, ways the legal system is corrupted by the overzealous enforcement of drug laws in the United States. Cocaine trafficker Javier Cruz negotiated a plea bargain for the murder of Mark Garrett in which he worked as an informant for the DEA. In return he was sentenced to only sixteen months in prison, for murder. He was not sentenced on drug charges that carry a mandatory life sentence.

The question raised by such cases is not just whether "justice" in some abstract sense is accomplished; the more telling issue is whether the information and testimony of someone paid off with a short prison sentence instead of life behind bars can be relied upon to put other people in prison. The trial and conviction of Manuel Noreiga is a case in point. To obtain Noreiga's conviction, government lawyers relied almost entirely on the testimony of convicted drug dealers who were bribed by the government to testify against Noreiga (*Newsweek* 1992). The bribes the government paid included cash payments of hundreds of thousands of dollars as well as reduced prison sentences and promises of a lifetime of support and protection under the witness protection program (*Washington Post* 1991).

Carlos Lehder, a major figure in an international drug trafficking cartel who in 1988 had been sentenced to life plus 135 years in prison for drug trafficking, was released from prison and with his family given a lifetime income and put into the witness protection program.

Charges against Luis del Cid could have sent him to prison for seventy years. In return for his testimony against Noreiga, prosecutors recommended a ten-year maximum sentence (he will be eligible for parole after three and a half years), dropping deportation procedures, and release of $94,000 in his pension account, which the government had confiscated.

Accused of organizing transportation of drugs through Panama, Max Mermelstein was facing a prison sentence of life plus ninety years. For his testimony he was released after two years and twenty-one days, paid a $700,000 reward, and put into the witness protection program with yearly payments for living expenses.

Floyd Carlton, a pilot who was charged with smuggling 880 pounds of cocaine into the United States, gave testimony that was rewarded with a nine-year suspended prison sentence and three years probation.

The bribing of witnesses to testify in court makes a mockery of criminal justice. The heavy emphasis on gaining convictions encourages government agents to lie, distort, and make up evidence. The necessity for relying on informants and undercover agents leads government agencies to protect people whose crimes often are more heinous than the drug dealing for which they were arrested.

The combination of pressure to make arrests and the fact that drug enforcement agents often think they "know who is a dealer" incites agents to plant drugs on suspects. For example, Robert Sobel, of the Los Angeles Sheriff's narcotics unit, testified against seven sheriff's narcotics agents in March 1993 for planting cocaine in the bag of a suspected dealer. In Oakland, California, drug agents were found guilty of planting drugs, beating suspects, and sexually assaulting them. A Los Angeles County Sheriff's Department officer planted heroin on a woman to whom he owed money. Again, these are but a smattering of the cases; the practice of illegally planting drugs on suspects or in their homes is rampant and for the most part goes undetected.

Finally, lately the incentive has dramatically increased for law enforcement officials to plant evidence and gain convictions through distortions and lies and by bribing witnesses, with passage of laws that reward law enforcement agencies with a percentage of the property seized in drug arrests. Houses, cars, boats, airplanes, and other personal property can be seized and sold if the owner is found guilty of possessing drugs. When the property is sold, the agency making the arrest keeps a percentage of the value, ordinarily 50 or 60 percent. The abuse of these laws is rampant. In Louisiana, according to a report on "Dateline," police officers began seizing the property of motorists who were stopped and arrested even where there was no evidence of drugs in their possession.

The Impact of Decriminalization

Were the Surgeon General's recommendation followed and a study conducted, the findings most certainly would suggest the necessity for a major shift in policy. The Netherlands has been a leader in the search for alternatives to policing as a solution to social problems associated with the use of drugs. Their solution has been (1) to decriminalize the use and sale of marijuana and (2) to decriminalize de facto the possession and sale of small amounts of other drugs. Marijuana and hashish can be purchased in over 2,000 coffee shops, which even advertise the availability of the drug by displaying a drawing of a marijuana plant on their signs. Other forms of advertising are prohibited. Almost every kind of drug is readily available on the streets of major cities in the Netherlands (Grapendaal, Leuw, and Nelen 1992). The operating rules that govern police enforcement of anti-drug laws specify that the police are to serve as a bridge between drug addicts and treatment services. The net result is that there are few arrests and even fewer trials and convictions for possession and sale of drugs.

What has the effect of these policies been? Substantial research has been conducted to evaluate the impact of the Dutch policies, all of which come to the conclusion that the decriminalization of the use, possession, and sale of small amounts of drugs (1) has not led to any increase in usage and (2) has decreased the amount of crime associated with drug use and dealing (Grapendaal, Leuw, and Nelen 1992; Wijngaart 1990; Vliet 1990; Eisner 1994). Research conducted by the Public Health and National Police in the Netherlands found that there was no change in the frequency of the use of heroin, cocaine, amphetamines, marijuana, or any other drugs and that crimes associated with drug use such as those motivated by attempts to support a drug habit declined after decriminalization between 1987 and 1990 (Ministry of Welfare, Health and Cultural Affairs and the Ministry of Justice 1992). Furthermore, the use of cannabis, cocaine, and heroin among secondary-school students is lower in the Netherlands than in the United States (see Table 12.2). Drug use by people aged twelve–seventy shows the same pattern: A higher percentage of people report using drugs in the United States than in the Netherlands (see Table 12.3).

Other countries have experimented with alternatives to police enforced prohibition. The cities of Zurich and Geneva in Switzerland periodically have permitted "needle parks" to be established, where addicts could openly purchase drugs. The government has provided sterile needles and medical help for addicts in these places. These policies have been sporadic and must be evaluated in the context of an overall "repressive environment" (Eisner 1994). The positive results of these experiments are that there is a significant decline in the spread of AIDS and hepatitis among addicts (Hornung, Grob, and Fuchs 1989).

Negatively, during periods when there were open drug markets in parks, non-residents to the cities came in large numbers with an attendant increase in mugging and robberies. That this increase can be attributed to the open drug markets, however, is questionable in view of the fact that the increase in robberies (but not mugging) continued even after the markets were closed and police repressed the distribution of drugs. As Eisner points out, the fact that there is a slight increase in mugging and robberies in areas where open drug markets existed

should not be read as evidence against liberal policies towards legalized drugs. Rather they are evidence of the fact that the local toleration of open drug scenes within a repressive environment generates spatial mobility patterns into those places which accordingly accelerates processes of marginalization. (Eisner 1974)

The negative effects of open drug scenes have led to a change in Swiss policy, which has established a three-year experiment with "drug vans" that visit parks where drug users congregate and distribute sterile needles. The head of a medical team that examined the impact of the open drug scene on addicts and the community concluded that

two major lessons should be learned from the needle park experiment: on the side of the social and medical institutions, the need to work side by side with the communities, the drug users in the street, etc. Secondly, the law and its executive arms, the courts and the police, should realize that their influence is limited and potentially harmful but that their role in balancing the interests of drug users and those of the population is essential in helping to create a climate in which drug users can be taken care of not only by in-house specialists but by the whole society. (Grob 1994)

Spain followed the Netherlands and de facto decriminalized drug possession or sale of small amounts. Reports from Spanish police and academics are based on less carefully conducted research than the Dutch and Swiss studies but the results are similar: neither usage nor crimes associated with drug dealing rise appreciably, and diseases associated with drug use decline.

Ironically, the Surgeon General need not go to the Netherlands for data on the impact of decriminalization: eleven American states (Ohio, North Carolina, California, New York, Mississippi, Alaska, Minnesota, Colorado, Maine, Utah, and Oregon) have decriminalized the possession of small amounts of marijuana (Galliher 1992; DiChiara and Galliher 1994). Surveys of high school and college students' use of marijuana from 1975 to 1980 (after decriminalization) shows no difference in the frequency of use among students in states that have decriminalized marijuana compared to that of students in those that have not. Comparison of prevalence of use shows "convincing evidence that there is no systematic gain or loss" in marijuana usage (Johnston, O'Malley, and Bachman 1981).

There is other evidence that de facto decriminalization reduces crimes associated with drugs, especially murder and violence. In Seattle, Washington, where I conducted a ten-year study of organized crime, I found that when the police

Table 12.2
Cannabis, Cocaine, and Heroin Use among Students in Secondary Schools (Age 13–18 Years) in the Netherlands and the United States

	13-14 Years		15-16 Years		17-18 Years	
LIFETIME	USA	NL	USA	NL	USA	NL
Cannabis	14.6%	2.6%	35.0%	10.8%	43.7%	17.7%
Cocaine	3.6%	0.6%	7.7%	1.2%	10.3%	1.6%
Heroin	NA	NA	NA	NA	1.3%	0.5%
PAST MONTH	USA	NL	USA	NL	USA	NL
Cannabis	5.4%	1.3%	14.9%	5.2%	16.7%	4.6%
Cocaine	1.6%	1.2%	2.7%	0.5%	2.8%	0,2%
Heroin	NA	NA	NA	NA	0.3%	0.3%

Source: Michael Eisner, *The Sociology of Reefer Madness: The Criminalization of Marijuana in the USA.* Unpublished Ph.D. dissertation, American University, 1994.

were taking bribes and protecting drug dealers, murder and assaults associated with drug dealing were low, but when the police enforced anti-drug laws these offenses increased appreciably (Chambliss 1988). The reason is quite simple: When the police cooperate with drug dealers, they essentially give them an informal "license" to traffic and trade in certain areas of the city. Competitors are "discouraged" by being arrested. Lacking competition, the licensed dealers do not need to resort to violence to protect their territory; they need only call their partners on the police force and have their competitors arrested. Decriminalization has positive effects that go well beyond the reduction in the amount of violence and crime associated with drug dealing. The spread of AIDS, hepatitis, and other diseases through the use of shared needles and the human suffering and deaths caused by impure drugs are commonplace, well known to users, and

Table 12.3
Illicit Drug Use in the United States and the Netherlands among 12–70-Year-Olds

	Lifetime Use		Past Year		Past Month	
	NL	USA	NL	USA	NL	USA
Cannabis	24%	32%	10%	12%	6%	6%
Cocaine	5%	11%	1%	4%	0.4%	1%
Heroin	1%	0.8%	0.1%	0.3%	NA	NA

ineffective as a deterrent, or the rates of drug use would have declined with the onset of AIDS and the knowledge that the risks of intravenous injection had gone up.

THE CONSEQUENCES

The international market in opium, heroin, cocaine, and marijuana now constitutes at least a $200 billion-dollar-a-year business. The growing, manufacture, and distribution of illegal drugs have become one of the largest industries in the world. Whole nation-states—Turkey, Pakistan, Colombia, Peru, Puerto Rico, Bolivia, Malaysia, Thailand, Mexico, and Laos—depend upon opium, coca, and hemp production for their agricultural base and on the manufacture of heroin, cocaine, and marijuana as a significant productive sector of the economy (Salamat 1993; *The Economist* 1987, 1988, 1989; Grimond 1993; Lintner 1991). The export of cocaine provides Bolivia with more income than all other export products combined (*The Economist* 1988). The economies of other nations, including the United States, are so deeply enmeshed in the production and distribution of illegal drugs that they would be severely damaged were the international market in drugs to dry up. It is estimated, for example, that the growing of marijuana is the second largest agricultural product in the United States (Galliher 1992).

Faced with evidence that our "war on drugs" is a failure and that we should examine alternatives, government officials respond with knee-jerk irrationality.

When William Bradford Reynolds was assistant attorney general under George Bush, he issued a memo to the "Heads of Department Components" in the Department of Justice: "Overall, we should send the message that there are two ways to approach drugs: the soft, easy way that emphasizes drug treatment and rehabilitation versus the hard, tough approach that emphasizes strong law enforcement measures and drug testing. Naturally, we favor the latter."

Why should the Justice Department "naturally favor" strong law enforcement measures and drug testing over treatment and rehabilitation unless it could be shown that "strong law enforcement measures" are more likely to reduce consumption than treatment? Because they think it will work better? Because there is evidence of its beneficial consequences? Hardly. Favoring the "hard, tough approach" is an ideology; it is part of the law enforcement definition of reality; it is the same kind of ignorant response to social problems that led to burning witches and public executions. It helps maintain a huge, expensive bureaucracy: it is organizationally useful, but it is counterproductive social policy that undermines the very fabric of social justice in the United States.

Since drug use was criminalized in the United States (mainly between 1914 and 1937), there has been a steady and constant increase in the availability of drugs and the number of drug users. Marijuana and cocaine are readily available on every college campus and in every office building, not to mention the streets of every city. Since 1975 the Institute for Social Research at the University of Michigan has been conducting anonymous surveys of high school and college students' use of illegal drugs. Every year, from 1975 to 1991, between 45 and 60 percent of students admit to using an illegal drug. Between 18 and 30 percent admit to using some illegal drugs at least once during the preceding thirty days. According to surveys by the National Institute of Drug Abuse, every year some 8.2 million people between 18 and 25 years of age use cocaine (National Institute on Drug Abuse 1994). Two and a half million of the respondents admitted using it within the preceding month, and 250,000 use it weekly. The argument that decriminalizing drugs would increase their availability flies in the face of the fact that criminalizing them has in no way decreased their availability. Almost 90 percent of the respondents said marijuana and over 50 percent said cocaine would be "fairly easy" or "very easy" for them to get (Johnston, O'Malley, and Bachman 2000). Indeed, it is arguable that decriminalizing drugs but restricting access, accompanied by warnings and increasing awareness of their potential hazards, would lead to a reduction in usage.

Most people who use cocaine and marijuana are occasional users. Most users have no trouble stopping if they decide to. Only 3 percent of the people who tried cocaine reported problems giving it up. With marijuana the number of people who use the drug is much higher but the proportion of those who report difficulty in giving up the drug, even after a long period of heavy usage, is negligible. The most highly addictive of these illegal drugs are the opiates and their derivatives (particularly heroin). We do not have good data on the addiction rate among opium users, but we do know that when opium was legally and easily available to addicts through medical doctors, as it was in Great Britain until the 1970s, the illegal drug market and the number of new addicts was minuscule compared to the United States case.

A comparison of the addictive qualities of illegal drugs with tobacco and alcohol is informative. A survey of high school seniors asked those who admitted to using marijuana, cocaine, and cigarettes if they had ever had difficulty stopping. Less than 4 percent reported difficulty stopping cocaine; 7 percent had trouble with marijuana and 18 percent with cigarette smoking (Johnston, O'Malley, and Bachman 1981).

Education programs and self-help community groups substantially reduce cigarette smoking and alcohol consumption. Alcohol and nicotine addicts benefit substantially from self-help groups. Community groups such as Alcoholics Anonymous are certainly more effective in changing addictive behavior than prisons or jails. If the drugs were legal and the stigma of criminality was not attached to the user, problem drug users would seek the help they need. Addicts would not have to pay outlandishly for drugs ($4,000 worth of cocaine in Colombia sells in Miami for $20,000 wholesale, $70,000 on the streets), share dirty needles, and risk illness and even death from impure drugs. Decriminalization would also facilitate the accurate dissemination of knowledge about the drugs. Everyone knows the difference between the effects of beer, wine, and whiskey. Possessing this knowledge enables all of us to choose rationally which to drink under what circumstances. The law enforcement propaganda, which lumps all illegal drugs together as equally dangerous, makes sensible policies and rational personal decisions impossible. It reinforces the belief on the part of potential users that everything they hear about drugs is the big lie. Every twelve-year-old in the ghetto knows that marijuana is very different from cocaine, but they are not told exactly how and why. When they are choosing between cocaine, crack, and heroin, they do not have the necessary information even to consider the difference between the drugs. All they know is that their experiences contradict the lies and propaganda of the government.

Government Policy

The U.S. Surgeon General Jocelyn Elders spoke the unspeakable at a press conference on December 8, 1995. She courageously suggested that the government look at the experience of countries that had decriminalized drugs. She said it was her understanding that in other countries the crime rate and the incidence of drug abuse had actually declined with decriminalization. The White House was apoplectic and dismissed the idea out of hand. One would think the Surgeon General had proposed legalizing rape. The administration's denials came faster than planes flying cocaine from Venezuela to Miami: Under no circumstances would there be such an inquiry.

The response of the administration was particularly unfortunate since the Surgeon General's proposal was not to legalize drugs, as the American press erroneously reported. She proposed only that we look at the facts to see if the experience of other countries might provide a clue to a better approach than the "War on Drugs," which almost everyone, including Attorney General Janet Reno, acknowledges has been an utter failure. The ineffectiveness and absurdity of putting so many people in prison for drug offenses has led police chiefs, prison wardens, some big-city mayors, the governor of New Mexico, and even some conservative politicians and pundits including William Buckley, Former Secretary of State George Schultz, and Nobel economist Milton Friedman, to speak out in favor of decriminalization. Judges, under legal proscription to sentence drug offenders to long-term mandatory sentences, recognize the injustice and folly of the system and often refuse to impose the sentences (Thompson 1991). On the other hand, drug offenders are sentenced without the possibility of parole, which means they spend more time in prison than most violent offenders. Had the Clinton administration been willing to open its eyes and look objectively at the facts, as the Surgeon General suggested, it would not have found a utopian solution in the policies of other countries. No one in the Netherlands, Switzerland, Spain, or the twelve states that have decriminalized marijuana believes that they have found the perfect solution to problems associated with drugs. The fact is that an ideal solution does not exist. Drugs have been part of people's lives in every culture forever. What is needed is an exploration of the best way to deal with the reality, not a blind adherence to failed policies.

The Crime Control Industry

What the noted Norwegian criminologist Nils Christie calls "the Crime Control Industry" is an all-powerful lobby in the United States (Christie 1993). In California the Correctional Officers Association is the second largest contributor to political campaigns in the state. The Department of Justice is the only source of nationwide statistics on crime, which enables them to selectively inform the media and the public to serve their own interests. When the Uniform Crime Reports published by the FBI released data to the media showing that the murder rate increased between 1988 and 1992, it was front-page news and helped to justify the Senate passing a bill to spend $22 billion on more police officers and prisons. What the report failed to mention, however, is that between 1980 and 1988 the homicide rate actually declined, a fact conveniently left out of the report (see Figure 12.3). Today we are witnessing just the opposite propaganda blitz from law enforcement agencies claiming that the increased expenditures and getting tough on crime has worked as evidenced by declining crime rates. Once the air clears from this tactic it is quite predictable that we will discover that the alleged changes in crime rates are due either to the manipulation of data by law enforcement agencies or to periodic fluctuations of little significance.

The crime control industry's interests, like those of any other industry, are in expanding resources. Millions of arrests combined with a constant stream of misinformation serve their interests well. It takes a strong and principled politician to fly in the face of such well-organized propaganda. Unfortunately, principled politicians are in short supply in today's world. And the people who need principled politicians most—African Americans, Latinos, and American Indians—are being systematically disenfranchised as they become ineligible to vote while in prison and, in many states, for years after they are released.

CONCLUSION

The war on drugs is a failure by any objective measure. It has not reduced drug consumption, the prevalence of drug-selling gangs, the production of new products for consumers, or the volume of drugs flowing into the United States. It has been successful, however, in legitimizing the creation of a virtual police state in the ghettoes of our cities. The war on drugs has created a chasm between the white and Black populations in their perception of social justice and the workings of the criminal justice system. It has defined a segment of the population (young Black men) as inherently criminal and led to the incarceration of a substantial percentage of their population.

The war on drugs also has led to widespread police corruption and the misuse of police violence. Not since the early days of the Civil Rights Movement has there been such a gap between the views of minority and white communities on the legitimacy of the criminal law. We face a crisis unprecedented in our history with the creation of a crime control industry and a criminal justice system that is out of control. Reconciling the contradiction between social justice and crime control will require a massive effort, one that is certain to be resisted by those with a vested interest in the status quo.

REFERENCES

Austin, James, and John Irwin. 1989. *Who Goes to Prison?* San Francisco: National Council on Crime and Delinquency.

Beck, Alan J., and Christopher J. Mumola. 1999. *Prisoners in 1998.* Bureau of Justice Statistics Bulletin. Washington, DC: U.S. Department of Justice, August.

Chambliss, William J. 2001. *Power, Politics, and Crime.* Boulder, CO: Westview Press.

Chambliss, William J. 1994. "Policing the Ghetto Underclass: The Politics of Law Enforcement." *Social Problems* 41(2) (May): 177–194.

Chambliss, William. 1989. "State Organized Crime." *Criminology* 27(2): 215–230.

Chambliss, William J. 1988. *On the Take: From Petty Crooks to Presidents.* Bloomington: Indiana University Press.

Christie, Nils. 1993. *Crime Control as Industry.* London: Routledge.

Cockburn, Leslie. 1987. *Out of Control.* New York: Atlantic Monthly Press.

Colett, M. 1988. "Cocaine Capitalism." *New Statesman and Society*, August 12, pp. 14–17.

Daley, R. 1978. *Prince of the City: The True Story of a Cop Who Knew Too Much*. Boston: Little, Brown.

DiChiara, A., and J. Galliher. 1994. "Dissonance and Contradictions in the Origins of Marihuana Decriminalization." *Law and Society Review* 28(1).

Doob, A. 1993. "The United States Sentencing Commission Guidelines: If You Don't Know Where You Are Going, You Might Not Get There." Paper presented at the Colston International Sentencing Symposium, University of Bristol, April.

Drug Policy Foundation. 1993. *The Drug Policy Newsletter*. Washington, DC.

The Economist. 1989. "The General and the Cocaleros," v. 313 (December 9): 40–1.

The Economist. 1989. "Sex, Drugs and Radicals," v. 311 (April 8): 54 ff.

The Economist. 1988. "The Cocaine Economies: Latin Americas Killing Fields," v. 309 (October 8): 21 ff.

The Economist. 1987. "Fighting Drugs," v. 328 (August 7): 39–40.

Eisner, Manuel. 1994. "Policies Towards Open Drug Scenes and Street Crime: The Case of the City of Zurich." *European Journal on Criminal Policy and Research* 1(2): 61–75.

Galliher, John F. 1992. "Illegal Drugs: Where We Stand and What We Can Do." In H. H. Traver and M. S. Gaylord, *Drugs, Law and the State*. Hong Kong: Hong Kong University Press, pp. 153–165.

Gladwell, Malcolm. 1994. "In Drug War, Crime Sometimes Wears a Badge." *Washington Post*, May 19, pp. A1, 16.

Grapendaal, M., E. Leuw, and H. Nelen. 1992. "Drugs and Crime in an Accommodating Social Context: The Situation in Amsterdam." *Contemporary Drug Problems* 19 (summer): 303–326.

Grimond, J. 1993. "The Other Obstacles to Change." *The Economist* 329 (November 13): 25–27.

Grimond, J. 1989. "Under the Influence." *The Economist* 312 (September 30): 38.

Grob, Peter J. 1994. "The Needle Park in Zurich: The Story and the Lessons to Be Learned." *European Journal on Criminal Policy and Research* 1(2): 59–60.

Gugliotta, A. 1991. "The Sleaze Connection." *Washington Post*, September 22, p.C1.

Harrison, K. 1993. "12 on D.C. Force Arrested in Corruption Probe." *Washington Post*, December 15, p. A1.

Hornung, R., P. Grob, W. Fuchs, et al. 1989. "Zurcher Aids-Intervention-Pilotprojekt fur Drogengefahrdete und Drogenbhangige (ZIPP-AIDS): Ergebnisse,m Eindrucke und Erfahungen. *Drigenbulletin*, no. 1: 2–13.

Jankowski, Martin Sanchez. 1991. *Islands in the Streets*. Berkeley: University of California Press.

Johnston, L., P. O'Malley, and J. Bachman. 2001. *Monitoring the Future: National Survey Results on Drug Use, 1975–2000: Volume 1: Secondary School Students (2001)*. Washington, DC: National Institute on Drug Abuse.

Johnston, Lloyd D., Patrick M. O'Malley, and Jerald G. Bachman. 1999. *National Survey Results on Drug Use from the Monitoring the Future Study: Secondary School Students, 1975–1998, vol. I*. Washington, DC: National Institute on Drug Abuse, pp. 86–88.

Johnston, Lloyd, Patrick M. O'Malley, and Jerald G. Bachman. 1981. "Marijuana Decriminalization: The Impact on Youth, 1975–1980." Monitoring the Future Occasional Paper 13. Ann Arbor: Institute for Social Research, University of Michigan, p. 18.

Johnston, L., P. O'Malley, and J. Bachman. 1981. *Monitoring the Future: Occasional Paper #9*. Ann Arbor: Institute for Social Research, University of Michigan.

Kwitny, Jonathan. 1987. *The Crimes of Patriots*. New York: W.W. Norton and Co.

Lintner, B. 1991. "Poisons and Politics." *Far Eastern Economic Review* 154 (November 14): 52–54.

Los Angeles Times. 1992. "Judge Is First Federal Jurist Convicted of Taking Bribe." June 30, p. A4.

Maguire, Kathleen, and Ann L. Pastore. 1996. *Sourcebook of Criminal Justice Statistics, 1996*. Washington, DC: Bureau of Justice Statistics.

Mauer, Marc. 1990. *Young Black Men and the Criminal Justice System: A Growing National Problem*. Washington, DC: The Sentencing Project, p. 3.

McCoy, Alfred. 1991. *The Politics of Heroin: CIA Complicity in the Global Drug Trade*. New York: Lawrence Hill.

McCoy, Alfred. 1973. *The Politics of Heroin in Southeast Asia*. New York: HarperCollins.

Miller, Jerome G. 1992. *Hobbling a Generation: Young African American Males in Washington, DC's Criminal Justice System*. Alexandria, VA: National Center on Institutions and Alternatives, April.

Ministry of Welfare, Health and Cultural Affairs and the Ministry of Justice. 1992. *The Drug Policy in the Netherlands*. The Netherlands, December.

Newsweek. 1992. "Noreiga: How the Feds Got Their Man." April 20, p. 37G.

Pastore, Ann L., and Kathleen Maguire, eds. 2000. *Sourcebook of Criminal Justice Statistics*. Washington, DC: U.S. Department of Justice, Bureau of Justice Statistics.

Pincus, Walter. 1998. "Inspector: CIA Kept Ties with Alleged Traffickers." *Washington Post*, March 15.

Salamat, A. 1993. "Opiate of the Frontier: Pakistani Tribes Find It Hard to Give Up Poppy Crop." *Far Eastern Economic Review* 156 (May 27): 18.

Sharkey, Jacqueline. 1988. "The Contra-Drug Trade-off." *Common Cause*, September–October, pp. 23–33.

Stockwell, John. 1986. "The CIA, Drugs and the Contras." *The Guardian*, May.

Thompson, T. 1991. "Mandatory Terms: Routinely Evaded But Still Popular." *Washington Post*, September 24, p. A21.

U.S. Department of Justice. 1994. "An Analysis of Non-Violent Drug Offenders with Minimal Criminal Histories" (unpublished report). Washington, DC: U.S. Department of Justice, pp. 2–3.

Vliet, H. 1990. "Separation of Drug Markets and the Normalization of Drug Problems in the Netherlands: An Example for Other Countries?" *Journal of Drug Issues* 20 (summer): 463–471.

Weiner, T. 1993. "Anti-Drug Unit of CIA Sent Ton of Cocaine to U.S. in 1990." *New York Times*, November 20, p. A1.

Wijngaart, G. 1990. "The Dutch Approach: Normalization of Drug Problems." *Journal of Drug Issues* 20 (fall): 667–678.

Woodiwiss, Michael. 1988. *Crime, Crusades, and Corruption: Prohibitions in the U.S., 1900–1987*. Totowa, Canada: Barnes and Noble Imports.

13

"Justice" and Criminal Justice

David F. Greenberg

JUSTICE IN CRIMINAL LAW AND CRIMINAL JUSTICE ADMINISTRATION

According to standard philosophical definitions, justice consists of giving to each what he or she is due (Audi 1999, 456–57). This applies to the distribution of both goods—those things that people consider desirable—and bads, or undesirables. In any society, people hold beliefs that certain distributions of goods and bads are right because they allocate to people what they deserve. Other distributions are wrong, that is, undeserved and unjust.

Because the criminal law designates certain distributions and procedures for changing them as legitimate and others as illegitimate, it inevitably involves issues of justice. Thefts, for example, are appropriations that the law defines as illegitimate; they deprive their victims of goods wrongly. Assaultive crimes inflict unjustified pain and injury (bads) on their victims. The criminal justice system imposes sanctions on those convicted of crime that are generally considered bads (e.g., fines, imprisonment, death), but it defines these sanctions as legitimate and just. Though criminal justice sanctions are often justified on the basis of claims about the technical efficiency of these measures in preventing crime, claims are also made that it is right and just to inflict costs or pains on wrongdoers (von Hirsch 1976). Members of the public form their own judgments of whether criminal activities and criminal justice policies and decisions are just or unjust.[1] Where these assessments differ, social conflicts over them may ensue.

The Importance of Perceptions of Justice

Criminologists have paid relatively little attention to perceptions of justice held by the public or by law enforcement officials, notwithstanding their centrality to important criminal justice issues. In this chapter, I attempt to demonstrate the value of examining these perceptions for understanding how contemporary criminal justice systems operate. Then I will suggest ways that perceptions of justice might help us to understand the relationship between race and criminal justice outcomes.

JUSTICE AND THE CRIMINAL JUSTICE SYSTEM

Justice and the Evaluation of Penalties

Do people assess the criminal justice system by evaluating outcomes in light of standards of justice? Two small-scale studies of assessments of punishments suggest that they might (Sunstein, Schkade, and Kahneman 2000). In the first, subjects were presented with hypothetical court cases and were asked to assess punitive damages. In the second, law students were asked about penalties in hypothetical cases. Large majorities of the subjects in both studies rejected policies that would be optimal from the point of view of maximizing deterrence. Presumably they were constrained by beliefs that extremely severe penalties for lesser wrongs are unjust.

Qualitative evidence suggests that in real cases, people think about penalties in these terms, at least to a degree. Thus, last year, when a seventeen-year-old was sentenced to life in prison for shooting his parents and two high school students to death and injuring almost two dozen others, the mother of one of the wounded children expressed her satisfaction at the sentence by telling the youth, "For you to be tortured and troubled as we are is to me the final justice" (Verhovek 1999). She did not express relief that imprisoning the killer would deter others from killing or prevent him from killing again. She said that it was *just* for someone who had caused so much suffering to suffer himself.

These examples suggest that the principles by which many contemporary Americans evaluate criminal penalties may not be utilitarian principles of maximizing crime reduction irrespective of normative considerations specifying what a "just" penalty would be. To be sure, this does not mean that people disregard crime prevention and considerations of efficiency altogether. Hogarth's (1971) study of Canadian judges suggests that utilitarian considerations, such as rehabilitation and deterrence, do influence the sentences judges impose in criminal cases. It would seem odd were laypeople not also to take them into account. However, utilitarian considerations may not be as important as many policy analysts suppose.

Public Opinion and Crime Policy

As early as 1870, when the National Congress on Penitentiary and Reformatory Discipline, meeting in Cincinnati, adopted its "Declaration of Principles"

declaring that "the supreme aim of prison discipline is the reformation of criminals, not the infliction of vindictive suffering" (Wines 1871), penologists have
sought to reorient criminal justice goals in directions they consider more humane and effective. Usually this has meant a greater emphasis on rehabilitation.
Criminologists in recent decades have attempted to draw on their research to
support similar goals. For decades, those same penologists and criminologists
have been frustrated by the resistance of politicians and the public to these same
proposals—proposals that the criminologists maintain will improve public
safety.

A few years ago, although research indicated that prison inmates who earned
college degrees while in prison were less likely to return to crime after release,
Massachusetts Governor William Weld announced the cancellation of the Massachusetts program permitting prison inmates to earn college degrees (private
communication from James Gilligan). He argued that if law-abiding citizens
were not given free college tuition, it would be unjust to give it to convicted
felons.

If public sentiment strongly opposes the adoption of penalties considered
optimal on the basis of cost-effectiveness and efficiency considerations, this
opposition will be an obstacle both to the imposition of penalties considered
excessive and also to those that offer "undue" leniency, even if introduced for
the purposes of effective rehabilitation and crime prevention. To constituen-
cies who think that justice requires the courts to repay serious wrongdoing
with major sanctions, it will be beside the point to note that probation or college courses reduce recidivism.

By their nature, the studies carried out by Sunstein, Schkade, and Kahneman
could not show what actions people typically take when they consider a sentence unjust or what impact their actions might have. Indeed, the largest gap in
our knowledge of criminal justice may be in the relationship between public
opinion and policy outcomes. Research has shown that in the short run, public
opinion is highly volatile and strongly influenced by political oratory as disseminated by the mass media (Beckett 1994, 1997; Chambliss 1994, 1995, 1999).
These findings have led to suggestions that public opinion is a consequence of
political stands rather than a cause of them. However, this short-term influence
does not preclude a more gradual, long-term influence of public opinion on criminal justice policy through the electoral process. Studies of government policy
formation show that politicians seeking to be elected or reelected attend to constituents' public opinion when they vote on legislation in a number of policy
areas (Wright, Erikson, and McIver 1987, 1993; Burstein 1998). Public opinion
may also create expectations that prosecutors and judges attempt to meet.

Some social scientists have argued that rises in crime rates beginning in the
1960s gave rise to harsher public attitudes on criminal justice issues. Politicians
then responded to their constituents by proposing more punitive policy measures (Wilson 1975; Greenberg and West 2001; Garland 2001). In this way,
beliefs shared by significant numbers of individuals could have aggregate

consequences for criminal justice policy. Yet the extent of this influence is largely unknown.

I suggest that attention to justice appraisals may help us to understand cross-national differences in criminal justice policies as well as trends within nations. It may also aid in the understanding of face-to-face interactions between civilians and criminal justice officials such as police.

Justice and Variation in National Policies

Cross-national research shows that countries with comparable levels of crime deal with it in quite different ways (Downes 1988; Savelsberg 1994, 1999; Greenberg 1999). A nation can deal with crime by redistributing income, social status, and power or by opening up free day-care centers, providing tutoring for students, and funding methadone clinics. It can also build prisons. A basis for any and all of these responses can be found in criminological theory and research. A crackdown on crime can target drug sellers or consumer fraud. These policy options are not mutually exclusive, but when resources are limited, choices are inevitable. Conceptions of justice may help to explain why a nation emphasizes some policy options over others.

Among the more affluent nations, prison populations are strongly correlated with income inequality (Greenberg 1999). The relationship persists when crime rates are controlled statistically. It is due to the greater reluctance of nations that reduce income inequality through progressive taxation and welfare payments to put people in prison when they break the law. Income policy and penal policy both reflect deep underlying notions of what society owes its members, that is, what they deserve. States that are comparatively generous in welfare payments regard their members as deserving minimum levels of well-being irrespective of their returns in the labor market. They also see them as undeserving of harsh treatment when they commit crimes. In societies that are stingy with their welfare payments it is just the reverse: They are punitive with criminals, and they have higher levels of wealth and income inequality.

The philosophy that dominated American discussions of penal policy in the United States in the 1950s and 1960s gave heavy emphasis to prevention and rehabilitation. It saw criminals primarily as victims of discrimination and restricted opportunity. Welfare policy advocates assumed that if people could not support themselves with jobs, it was largely for reasons outside their own control—physical or mental disability, the death of a breadwinner, or a downturn in the economy. Criminals and the unemployed both deserved help, and it was appropriate for the state to give it to them.

In the past few decades, the emphasis in the United States has shifted in relation to both punishment and welfare. Crime-preventive strategies involving social reform, the creation of legitimate opportunities, and rehabilitation are being given less emphasis; punishment (imprisonment and execution) and surveillance are receiving more. Welfare payments have fallen and are being cut further, and inequalities of wealth and income have been rising.

This trend reflects a shift in conceptions of responsibility and applicable principles of justice. The new conception is based on individual responsibility unrelated to concrete social circumstances that might make it harder for some individuals to conform to the law. These circumstances might be a stressful environment, provocation, and limited resources for coping. It follows that social and economic change is at best irrelevant to crime prevention and at worst pernicious (Reinarman and Levine, 1997b). Those who hold these views insist on punishing those who sell or possess illegal drugs, irrespective of their prospects for earning a decent living in conformity with the law.

President Ronald Reagan invoked these principles when he addressed the subject of crime causation by posing a contrast between two alternatives (which most criminologists would not see as mutually exclusive): "Choosing a career in crime is not the result of poverty or of an unhappy childhood or of a misunderstood adolescence; it is the result of a conscious, willful choice" (quoted in Beckett and Sasson 2000, 61). Welfare, Reagan insisted, undermined incentives to work and ate away at the moral fiber of the country, leading to increased drug use, the deterioration of neighborhoods and schools, and welfare dependency (Beckett and Sasson 2000, 62).

The elevation of formal principles of equality in the form of neo-retributivism and sentencing guidelines during Reagan's administration came at a time when the most influential political doctrines had called for cutting back on paternalistic regulation of the economy, curtailment of welfare payments, and reduced governmental regulation of the economy. All these developments reflect the consistent application of the same logic, and they were introduced as part of a counterrevolution to the left-liberal social and legal developments of the 1960s.

A libertarian version of this individualistic philosophy might have cut back on punitiveness by decriminalizing victimless crimes like the possession and sale of drugs. But such a proposal would have been unacceptable to much of the population, particularly to the conservative religious organizations that provided Reagan with strong backing. Reagan's moralistic individualism and that of subsequent administrations shifted the allocation of resources in the direction of more punishment rather than prevention or treatment. Spending on welfare fell between 1973 and 1994; spending on criminal justice rose (Beckett and Sasson 2000, 63).

Reflecting these trends, the criminal justice system has become more punitive in recent years (Irwin and Austin 1994; Tonry 1995; Currie 1998; Haney 1998). Sentencing legislation has led to mandatory minimums and to life sentences without parole for repeat felons. Prison populations have mushroomed; the death penalty has been restored and in some states is being applied regularly. Juvenile offenders are increasingly being tried as adults (Bradsher 1999).

It has been argued that increases in punitive attitudes on the part of the public and tougher crime control policies cannot be due to increased crime because there have been no increases in violent or property offences of sufficient magnitude to account for such toughening since the early 1970s. Though the punitiveness of the 1970s, 1980s, and 1990s may not be attributable to increases in crime during those decades, it could be a delayed reaction to the large increases in rates of violent crime and property crime that took place during the 1960s and that persisted in the 1970s and 1980s (Greenberg 1999, 2001; Garland 2001).

Yet, states have responded to increased crime in various ways. Though all have become more punitive, the trend has been stronger in some states than in others. If other factors that influence imprisonment rates (such as crime rates) are controlled, the more generous a state's welfare policies, the lower its imprisonment rates and the rate of growth in those rates (Greenberg and West 2001; Beckett and Western 2001). These differences reflect a different emphasis on principles of need regardless of fault and of responsibility for wrongdoing based on individual fault.

States in which a high percentage of the population are religious fundamentalists also have higher-than-average prison populations. American Protestant fundamentalist teachings emphasize a strict notion of morality based on individual responsibility. This morality appears to have had a strong impact on states' penal policy (Greenberg and West 2001).

Justice in Police-Civilian Interaction

Notions of justice and desert are also implicated in police use of illegal violence against civilians. A suspect who talks insolently to an officer may, in the eyes of the police, deserve to be punched, whether or not mere talk provides legally valid grounds for violence. Thus, Westley (1953) reports that when a police officer was asked about the circumstances in which it would be legitimate for him to use violence, he answered:

For example, when you stop a fellow for a routine questioning, say a wise guy, and he starts talking back to you and telling you that you are no good and that sort of thing. You know you can take a man in on a disorderly conduct charge, but you can practically never make it stick. So what you do in a case like this is to egg the guy on until he makes a remark where you can justifiably slap him, and then if he fights back, you can call it resisting arrest.

American law does not consider making a remark to be justifiable grounds for a police officer to slap someone. The officer makes a distinction here between substantive guilt and legal guilt and acts on the basis of the former (Skolnick 1966, 197–99).

Klockars (1986) suggests that this principle is widely held by police:

Any act which openly defies police authority, insults a police officer or causes a police officer to lose face merits "street justice" to even up the score and teach the offending party a lesson. . . . For example, running away from a policeman and making him give chase through back yards, over fences and down back alleys is an offense that warrants the "little street justice" of at least one or two good punches when the offender is finally caught. By extension, police morality also holds that the more serious the offense against police authority, the more severe the street justice that is warranted. Assaulting a police officer justifies street justice severe enough to require a trip to the hospital. Shooting or shooting at a police officer justifies street justice severe enough to require a trip to the morgue.

The officer's occupationally based conception of justice enables him to kill without considering himself a murderer.

RACE, JUSTICE, AND THE ADMINISTRATION OF JUSTICE

A consideration of perceptions of justice may help us to understand the racial dimension of criminal justice administration. Reflecting the limitations of the research on which I will draw, my discussion will be limited to black/white comparisons, largely ignoring other races and ethnic groups. Because some of the research needed to support elements of my argument has not yet been done, the argument will at times be speculative.

Four features of contemporary American criminal justice administration are relevant to my discussion. First, African Americans and some other minorities (Latinos, Native Americans) are very disproportionately represented among those arrested, tried, convicted, and imprisoned in relation to their numbers in the U.S. population. In 1994, for example, nearly 7 percent of all black male adults were in jail or prison, compared to less than 1 percent of white male adults (*New York Times* 1995). In California, almost 40 percent of black men in their twenties are in prison or on probation or parole (Butterfield 1996). If current rates of imprisonment persist, the lifetime chances of a newborn African-American male going to prison at some time in his life are better than 1 in 4; for Latino males, 1 in 6, and for white males, 1 in 23 (Bonczar and Beck 1997). With imprisonment rates rising—more rapidly for blacks than for whites (Duster 1997; Mauer 1999)—these figures can be expected to rise over time, more strongly for blacks than for whites.

Blacks are also disproportionately given death sentences and executed. Though a majority of those executed between 1977 and 1996 were white, the rate for blacks is almost five times as high as for whites (Snell 1997). In addition, blacks are three times more likely than whites to be shot to death by police (Walker 1993, 26, 31; Schwartz 1996). Criminologists are not in full agreement about the precise reasons for these racial disproportionalities.

Second, a truly remarkable volume of research has been undertaken to identify and explain racial and ethnic differences in American criminal justice outcomes. On the basis of many published studies, it has become the conventional wisdom that the overrepresentation of blacks and other minorities in the criminal justice system is not *primarily* due to discrimination in law enforcement, but rather to high levels of minority involvement in those crimes that the criminal justice system regularly prosecutes (Harris 1983). One argument deployed in support of this conclusion is that the racial disproportionality in admissions to prison or in prison populations is of comparable magnitude to the racial disproportionality in arrests (Blumstein 1982, 1993; Langan 1985, 1991; Willbanks 1987), suggesting that in the aggregate, the amount of discrimination originating in the courts cannot be large.

On the other hand, several studies show that when this analysis is carried out for individual states, rather than for the nation as a whole, racial disparities in some states and for some offences may be appreciable (Hawkins and Hardy 1989; Crutchfield, Bridges, and Pitchford 1994; Austin and Allen 2000).

Numerous research studies have concluded that some racial differences in criminal justice outcomes arise within the criminal justice system itself, and not from racial differences in criminality. Usually the differences disadvantage black suspects or defendants, but not invariably (Hagan 1974; Chiricos and Waldo 1975; Bernstein, Kelly, and Doyle 1977; Cohen and Kluegel 1978; Gibson 1978; Lizotte 1978; Kleck 1981; Radelet 1981; Spohn, Gruhl, and Welch 1982; Unnever 1982; Blumstein, Cohen, Martin, and Tonry 1983; Hagan and Bumiller 1983; Petersilia 1983, 1985; Peterson and Hagan 1984; Gross 1985; Radelet and Pierce 1985; Hawkins 1987; Myers and Talarico 1987; Wilbanks 1987; Zatz 1987; Developments in the Law 1988; Pommershein and Wise 1989; Unnever and Hembroff 1988; Klein, Petersilia, and Turner 1990; Nelson 1992, 1995; Mann 1993, 166–99; Chiricos and Crawford 1995; Myers 1995; Walker, Spohn, and DeLone 1996; Sampson and Lauritsen 1997; Mustard 1999; Lerner n.d.; Steffensmeier and Demuth 2000). Though in some times and places, and for some offences, black defendants are sentenced more harshly than whites for the same offence, in other times and places, and for other offences, either there is no significant difference in outcomes or the difference disadvantages whites.

Capital sentences imposed for homicide have been given particularly close study. Sentences imposed following conviction on homicide charges appear to depend much more strongly on the race of the victim than on the race of the perpetrator (Bowers and Pierce 1980; Dike 1981; Radelet 1981; Jacoby and Paternoster 1982; Paternoster 1983; Baldus, Pulaski, and Woodworth 1983; Radelet and Pierce 1985; Kennedy 1988).

Subject to some qualifications to be discussed later, this voluminous body of research sustains Harris's (1983) generalization: A substantial amount of racial disproportionality reflects underlying patterns of criminal law violation, but the criminal justice system may contribute to it in degrees that vary with time and place.

Third, allegations of racial discrimination in the criminal justice system are ubiquitous. Even though research findings point to a complicated picture of the role of race in determining outcomes, textbooks and popular discussions of criminal justice issues regularly take the pervasiveness and severity of racial discrimination for granted. So does the public. In a Gallup Poll taken in 1995, approximately two-thirds of the black respondents said that the criminal justice system was biased against them; a third of the white respondents agreed (Gallup, Jr. 1995).

Fourth, a number of multivariate statistical studies have found a relationship between the racial composition of a city or state and the resources it devotes to law enforcement. Police-force size and spending on police are higher where there are more blacks (Jacobs 1979; Jackson and Carroll 1981; Liska, Lawrence, and Benson 1981; Greenberg, Kessler, and Loftin 1985; Jackson 1989). Prison populations are positively related to the proportion of African Americans in the state's population (Bridges, Crutchfield, and Simpson 1987; McCarthy 1990; Michalowski and Pearson 1990; Greenberg and West 2001; Beckett and Western 2001). This is not because crime rates are higher in cities and states that have more blacks. Though index crime rates are higher in states where more blacks reside, police forces and prison populations are larger where there are more blacks even when crime rates are controlled statistically.

How might the facts just summarized—that blacks are punished at much higher rates than whites, that this is not primarily due to differential treatment of the races in the courts, that much of the populace believes that criminal justice officials discriminate against blacks, and that criminal justice sanctions are imposed more extensively and harshly in those parts of the country where more blacks live—be explained?

Some writers see the large number of poor, black, and Latino men in prison as a direct, intended result of a policy to attack or control poor people of color (Blauner 1972, 97; Livingston, 1992, 37–43; Barfoot 1993, 28; Miller 1996; Olson 1996). In this view, as African-American electoral strength has grown, as courts have recognized black claims to equal rights, and as African Americans have made gains in education and in the workplace, the criminal justice system is being deployed to reverse the gains. Crime control simply provides the rhetoric to legitimate a strategy for preserving white supremacy.

In addition to its effects on the crime rate, which are uncertain, imprisonment deprives felons of voting rights, disproportionately weakening black political strength (Uggen and Manza 2000). It disrupts families and impairs job prospects. When a high percentage of prisoners are members of minority groups, imprisonment also reproduces stereotypes of minority group members, damaging the life chances of all minority group members, including those who are not incarcerated. These consequences are consistent with a conflict interpretation. Highly publicized episodes of egregious police abuse of black suspects certainly lend themselves to this interpretation.

Nevertheless, there are difficulties with this position. For one thing, blacks are not only disproportionately arrested and imprisoned for crime, they are also very disproportionately victimized by it. In 1996, slightly more than half of all victims of personal violence were black (Maguire and Pastore 1998, 179). Heavy policing of black neighborhoods and severe sentences for black defendants, it might be argued, help to protect blacks (Hawkins 1999). Presumably that is why black citizens have been only slightly less supportive of prison expansion than whites. In a 1993 Gallup Poll, almost as many blacks (41%) as whites (43%) "strongly favored" putting "more police on the streets"; only 14 percent of whites and 15 percent of blacks opposed doing so (Walker, Spohn, and DeLone 1996, 91). Federal legislation requiring stiffer penalties for the possession of crack cocaine than the powdered form has drawn criticism because it has led to much longer sentences for black drug-law violators than for whites (Jones 1995). Yet this legislation was supported by leading African-American congressmen who were concerned about what they believed to be the extremely damaging effects of crack use on black communities (Kennedy 1995). Moreover, the research findings on racial discrimination in the criminal justice system are not so strong or consistent as one would expect if an anti-black campaign were taking place.

The relationship between race and resources devoted to law enforcement can be explained without assuming the existence of a conspiracy. As the size of a region's black population grows, some whites may feel more threatened by crime on the basis of a perceived correlation that has an empirical basis and whose magnitude they exaggerate,[2] leading them to favor larger police forces and prison populations. If this threat is widely felt, politicians may feel that they have to respond to it. Indeed, they themselves may share it.

This explanation suggests the desirability of developing theoretical perspectives that will allow for the emergence of complex racialized policy *outcomes* in the absence of strong racial and class *agendas*. The ideas of Evgeny Pashukanis, a Russian jurist of the 1920s, when supplemented by recent developments in cognitive psychology, may be helpful to our enterprise. We begin with Pashukanis. More than other Marxist theorists of law, he emphasized that conceptions of justice are critical elements of legal ideology.

Justice, Equality, and Race

Pashukanis (1980) argued that with the gradual spread of commodity exchange throughout society, law increasingly comes to embody principles of formal equality among individuals. Where commodity exchange dominates, market exchanges—those involving the purchase and sale of commodities, including labor power—will be understood as entailing the exchange of equal values, obscuring the exploitation that is built into the capitalist mode of production. Legal discourse in this setting will construct individuals as instances of "abstract" man, stripped of such particularities as class, sex, race, and ethnicity.

Pashukanis suggested that in modern times, when "all concrete forms of social wealth had to be reduced to the simplest and most abstract form—to human labour time" (1980, 120), this logic extends to punishments: for each crime there will be a numerical equivalent in length of prison sentence, representing the cost of "purchasing" the monetary or psychic rewards associated with committing the crime.

Pashukanis's analysis was sketchy, and it can be faulted along many lines (Greenberg and Anderson 1981, 1983). Nevertheless, he deserves credit for theorizing the existence of a relationship between market economies and a legal culture based on formal equality and individualism—a relationship also recognized by theorists with quite different allegiances (Fuller 1964; Hayek 1973; Weber 1978, 1394–95).

Because individuals' embeddedness in economic exchange relations varies, one might expect on the basis of Pashukanis's reasoning to find corresponding variation in adherence to the logic and principles of market exchanges. There is some limited evidence in support of this deduction. In experimental games testing adherence to principles of reciprocal fairness, the Machiguenga, an indigenous people of the Peruvian Amazon who until recently lived in a household-based subsistence economy with very limited exchange of products outside the household (Henrich 1997), were found to be far less devoted to principles of formal equality in the distribution of goods than people living in capitalistic societies (Bowles et al. 1997).

If Pashukanis was at least partly right about the long-term cultural consequences of commodity exchange, one would expect that over time, legal reliance on socially defined classifications of individuals such as race, sex, and age would diminish. With minor qualifications related to affirmative action, this is exactly what the trend in American law has been. For more than half a century, American law has been abandoning formal legal restrictions on racial minorities and women by eliminating mandatory segregation and by declaring most state-sponsored, and much privately sponsored, invidious discrimination to be illegal. More controversially, the legal system has instituted processes and procedures for reducing racially unequal outcomes (e.g., affirmative action and minority "set-asides").

Pashukanis's ideas are also consistent with a number of developments in American criminal law and criminal justice administration in recent decades. These developments include the expansion of rights to suspects and defendants in criminal procedure (e.g., Miranda warnings); though facially neutral as to race, they were intended primarily to prevent abuses of African-American citizens at the hands of white police officers and court officials (Kahan and Meares 1998). They also include the introduction of sentencing guidelines to reduce the arbitrariness associated with judicial discretion in sentencing and the appointment of African-American prosecutors, defense attorneys, and judges.[3]

Those studies concluding that in the aggregate, race has at best modest effects on judicial decisions to incarcerate or on length of sentence are consistent with Pashukanis's ideas about how the courts in a capitalist society should operate. Where sentencing patterns continue to disadvantage black defendants, they might be seen as survivals of a pattern that is on its way out, but that has not yet fully disappeared. Nevertheless, the persistence of race as a determinant of outcomes in some stages of criminal justice administration in a society in which commodity exchange is pervasive deserves further analysis.

As we undertake this analysis, it should be kept in mind that disparate outcomes, including those that disadvantage blacks, need not necessarily be due to prejudice on the part of criminal justice officials. Black defendants are less likely than whites to be able to afford bail and to pay private investigators, psychologists, psychiatrists, and attorneys. They may be disadvantaged in arranging private alternatives to incarceration, such as boarding schools or treatment (Emerson 1969, 98–99). Blacks convicted of misdemeanors may be more likely than whites to serve jail sentences because of inability to pay fines. These class-related disadvantages, rather than prejudice, may explain some racial differences in criminal justice outcomes (Nelson 1995; Mann 1993).

Where there is bias, it may not be on the part of the decision maker. Prosecutors may feel greater pressure to prosecute or to prosecute vigorously when a crime is particularly upsetting to the majority of a community or to its most vocal and influential members, who most often will be white. In deciding whether to prosecute a case, a prosecutor may try to anticipate a jury's reaction—and may believe (rightly or wrongly) that it will be more likely to convict when a victim is white or a defendant black (Gross and Mauro 1984). In the *voir dire*, prosecutors seeking convictions may use peremptory challenges to eliminate African Americans from a jury when the defendant is black, not because they themselves object to black jurors, but because they think that doing so will enhance their chances of gaining a conviction. Yet these possibilities do not preclude the possibility that prejudice on the part of the decision maker may nevertheless be important in some times and places.

The Psychology of Racism and Law Enforcement

Until quite recently, racism was commonly understood to be a consciously held set of beliefs that associate undesirable personal traits with a race and advocacy of the subordination or extermination of one race by another. Survey research showing that racism has been declining in recent decades is based on this conceptualization of racism (Condron 1979; Schuman, Steeh, and Bobo 1985; Firebaugh and Davis 1988; DiMaggio, Evans, and Bryson 1996; Quillian 1996).

A large number of psychological studies of prejudice conducted in the past quarter-century (Sigall and Page 1971; Donnerstein, Donnerstein, Simon, and Ditrichs 1972; Donnerstein and Donnerstein 1973; Crosby 1980; Pettigrew 1985; Gaertner and Dovidio 1886; Katz, Wackenhut, and Hass 1986; McConahay 1986; Johnson 1988) have complicated our understanding of the concept of racism in ways that may help us understand how it could be that race plays a limited and inconsistent role in determining sentencing outcomes and yet could be quite important in other phases of criminal justice administration. This body of research concludes that some stereotyping can go on without the stereotyper's being aware of it. Psychologists refer to this process as "automatic stereotyping" or, when the stereotypes are racial and invidious, to "unconscious racism."[4]

Because unconscious thoughts are, by definition, unknown to the one who thinks them, social scientists have sometimes been skeptical about explanations that invoke them. However, research has persuasively demonstrated the existence of unconscious mental processes (Claparède 1911; Cowey 1991), including unconscious racism (Crosby, Bromley, and Saxe 1980; Greenwald and Banaji 1995; Fazio et al. 1995; Paul 1998). Unconscious racist thought has been localized to a particular region of the brain (Phelps et al. 2000).

Some of this research links unconscious stereotypes to ambivalent attitudes and aggressive behavior. Studies of helping and aggressive behavior, conducted in both laboratory and natural settings, show that individuals who reject derogatory racial stereotypes, segregation, and subordination may be ambivalent about race. Their ambivalence stems from a contradiction: On the one hand, at a young age they learned to feel antipathy for blacks. This learning may have continued in adulthood through face-to-face interaction, unfavorable media portrayals, and personal experience. When confronted with someone who is black in certain circumstances, such individuals may engage in automatic invidious stereotyping and may act on the basis of these stereotypes.

On the other hand, these same individuals believe in formal equality. By contrast with the public discourse in earlier periods of American history, virtually all mainstream discussions of race now repudiate imputations of inferiority and invidious discrimination and are predicated, at least nominally, on the acceptance of legal equality. The public discourses to which all children—white and black—are exposed as they grow up, then, are largely non-racist or anti-racist. They thus grow up believing that prejudice is wrong and that all Americans should enjoy equal rights and opportunities.

Many white Americans may experience such ambivalence. Under certain circumstances, ambivalence can give rise to aggression toward the source of the ambivalence. In laboratory experiments, white subjects who held stereotypes of blacks as aggressive were more likely to administer electric shocks to black persons (Donnerstein and Donnerstein 1976). Importantly, the aggression in these studies did not originate in the subjects' conscious desires to harm blacks, but rather stemmed from a displacement of the punitive feelings aroused by the tension between the unconsciously held stereotype and the belief that it is wrong to think stereotypically.

Because it is not recognized and compensated for, unconscious racism may have greater effects on decision-making processes than consciously held stereotypes. Unconscious racism could lead four white policemen who, by conventional standards would not be considered racist, to mistake a wallet for a gun and, fearful for their lives, shoot the black man holding it forty-one times, whereas they would not do so in comparable circumstances involving a white man.[5]

Unconscious racism can lead to aggression toward blacks in some situations but not others. In some circumstances, whites who are ambivalent or who hold unconscious prejudices will treat blacks equitably or even more favorably than whites in order to avoid being considered prejudiced by others. Experiments suggest that where expectations are clear, where decisions are subject to review, and where those who make them are held accountable for their decisions, ambivalence and unconscious prejudice will not lead to worse treatment. On the other hand, when conditions arouse anger, assure anonymity, fail to provide well-defined norms, provide immunity from retaliation, and guarantee that subjects will not be held responsible for their actions, whites will act more aggressively to blacks than to whites (Crosby, Bromley, and Saxe 1980; Blanchard, Lilly, and Vaughn 1991; Duckitt 1993). These findings suggest that in some criminal justice settings unconscious racism might play a large role in shaping behaviors and decisions and in other settings play little or no role.

Contexts of Criminal Justice Decision Making

Because some prosecutorial and most judicial decisions are public, highly discriminatory decision-making patterns could expose a decision maker to public criticism. It is reasonable to assume that most judges now on the bench want to avoid being called racist by others and do not want to consider themselves racist. In these circumstances, blatant acts of discrimination such as characterized the segregationist South will be reduced or eliminated as white prosecutors and judges self-consciously try to process cases in ways that do not discriminate against black defendants. Even judges who believe blacks to be violence-prone and untrustworthy may make an effort to ignore these beliefs when they sentence defendants.

At the same time, some white prosecutors and judges may hold unconscious racial stereotypes. Unconscious beliefs that blacks do not tell the truth may lead some judges to discount the testimony of black witnesses. Stereotypes linking blacks with violence may lead individual judges to treat blacks more harshly than whites when setting bail, assessing guilt, and setting a sentence.

Because every court case is in some ways unique, exact equality of treatment may not always be possible. With a mandate to take into account such vaguely defined standards as the safety of the public, the seriousness of the offence, and the rehabilitative needs of the defendant, some individualization in criminal justice administration is inevitable. The wide discretion accorded prosecutors and judges permits much latitude as to how these nebulous objectives are to be met (American Friends Service Committee Working Party 1971, 124–44; Gottfredson and Gottfredson 1988; Hawkins 1992; Ohlin and Remington 1993), thus providing an opening for unconscious stereotypes to influence decisions about whether to drop a charge or proceed with prosecution, to lower a charge in return for a guilty plea, to incarcerate and for how long, and to execute. Parole board decisions regarding releases are equally open to unconscious influences.

Though one might expect to find such unconscious beliefs most often among whites, who may be threatened by differences in skin color and style of hair and clothing, there is no reason to think that black decision makers, who may be separated from black defendants by education, class background, and lifestyle, will be entirely free from them.

The circumstances of police-civilian interaction are rather different from those of prosecutors and judges. Police typically work alone or in small groups and are weakly supervised by superiors. Though many of the decisions they make—to stop and question, to frisk, and to arrest for minor violations—take place in public, there are often few witnesses to a police-civilian encounter. Abuse that takes place in police stations is shielded from the view of the larger public. Differential treatment of white and black civilians will normally go unnoticed and unrecorded. The standards police are to use in making important decisions, such as stopping and questioning pedestrians or drivers on the road, or frisking someone, or searching a car, are ill-defined. Uncooperative, insolent, or aggressive civilians may anger officers. Many reports indicate that the peer culture of largely white police departments is explicitly racist and accepting of the use of illegal force against civilians (Reiss 1968; Davis 1997). On-the-job experience with black suspects and criminals may generate or reinforce preexisting stereotypes (Skolnick 1966, 81).

The working conditions of the police do not discourage expression of racist attitudes, as they tend to do for judges. The likelihood of a police officer being called to account for differential treatment of civilians based on their race or ethnicity or for rude or violent behavior is extremely small, and police officers know that. Police protect one another against higher-ups or outsiders investigating misconduct; victims of police conduct often lack credibility; civilian review boards lack the powers needed to investigate complaints; supervising officers fail to discipline the handful of officers found guilty of abuse; the courts have been unwilling to throw out arrests or sanction police officers except in the most extreme cases; and mayors and governors have been unwilling to intervene (Chevigny 1969, 238; Orfield 1987, 1992; Rudovsky 1992; Patton 1993; Skolnick and Fyfe 1993; Magee 1994; Chin and Wells 1998; Cloud 1996; Yale 1997; Berlow 1999; Green 1999).

These are the conditions that laboratory experiments suggest ought to lead to higher levels of white aggression against blacks. Though persons of all walks of life can and have been the targets of police abuse—quite recently, when New York police officers shot to death a mentally disturbed Hasidic Jew, many observers at the scene considered the shooting unwarranted (Kifner 1999)—a high proportion involve white officers and nonwhite victims (Locke 1996).

This pattern could arise in various ways. It could be that nonwhites are more often the targets of police violence because they are disproportionately criminal, or disproportionately resist arrest. Geller and Karales (1981; see also Locke 1996) found that in Chicago between 1974 and 1978, blacks were much more likely than whites to be shot by police, but the rates were quite similar once felony arrests were controlled. The authors took felony arrests to be a measure of the circumstances in which an officer might have an occasion to shoot.

A few studies of police-civilian interaction have concluded that police decisions to arrest are not influenced by the race of a suspect, but are instead based on interactional cues such as lack of respect or evasiveness, the seriousness of the offence, and the wishes of a complainant (e.g., Piliavin and Briar 1964; Terry 1967; Wiener and Willie 1971; Bell and Lang 1985; Riksheim and Chernak 1993). Other studies, however, have concluded that in comparable circumstances, black suspects are more likely than whites to be arrested, especially when the victim is white (McEachern and Bauzer 1967; Black and Reiss 1970; Wilson 1970; Wolfgang, Figlio, and Sellin 1972, 220–21; Thornberry 1973; Sykes, Fox, and Clark 1976; Hepburn 1978; Liska and Taussig 1979; Smith and Visher 1981; Smith, Visher, and Davidson 1984; Petersilia 1983, 21–26; Developments in the Law 1988). Given the vagaries of individual police departments' hiring practices, policing styles, management strategies and the varying contexts of policing in different cities, as well as differences across studies in the data available for statistical analysis, these differences are no more surprising here than they are in studies of sentencing.

The focus on arrest in many studies overlooks an important dimension of police work: the decision to stop, question, and frisk or search a pedestrian or motorist. Massive numbers of citizens are stopped because police officers decide they are "suspicious." Or they may be arrested for violation of a statute that is as vague as the concept of "suspiciousness." For example, in Chicago between 1992 and 1995, almost 42,000 people were arrested for violating an anti-gang loitering statute that the Supreme Court later voided on grounds that it was unconstitutionally vague.[6]

In many instances, a determination that someone is suspicious is made in the absence of any specific, articulable behavior offering reasonable grounds for linking the suspect with a law violation. To legitimate the stops, police officers may, however, cite a traffic violation or some other trivial behavior as the basis (pretext) for their actions. In court, police officers routinely commit perjury by testifying falsely about the grounds for the stop (Comment 1987; Cloud 1994, 1996; Dripps 1996; Slobogin 1996; Chin and Wells 1998).

Although police suspicion has long been racialized in the United States (Alschuler and Schulhofer 1998; Maclin 1998a), in the past few years it has received a great deal of scrutiny. Racialized police suspicion often takes the form of "racial profiling." This is an administrative determination that it is suspect to be black or Latino—or to be black or Latino in the "wrong" place—or in combination with other circumstances, such as driving an expensive new car.[7] The profiles are distributed to law enforcement officers (police, customs officials) as guides for use in stopping civilians (Brown 1981, 166; Johnson 1983; Orfield 1987; Wycliff 1988; Maclin 1991, 1998b; Skolnick and Fyfe 1993; Chambliss 1994; Conley 1994; Harris 1994a, 1994b; Suskind 1994; Johnson 1995; Walker, Spohn, and DeLone 1996, 101–2; Davis 1996, 1997; Schwartz 1996; Kadish 1997; Kennedy 1997; Larrabee 1997; Salaam 1997; Sklansky 1997; Kelling 1999, 13–14; Thompson 1999). Where there are no formal profiles, police may still take race into account in deciding whether to stop and search someone. Here, unconscious racism may play an important role.

Stopping civilians on the basis of suspicion is not an aberrant practice. National statistics are unavailable, but in jurisdictions where they are available, the practice is widespread. A study conducted by the Columbia University Center for Violence Research and Prevention and released as a report by the New York State Attorney General found that in New York, almost 175,000 citizens were stopped by police during a fifteen-month period (Roane, 1999). These numbers are based on police records and seriously underestimate the number of stops. Speaking on radio station WNYC in April 1999, New York State Attorney General Eliot Spitzer remarked: "I've spoken to many officers who say that they do not fill out the required forms for every stop-and-frisk. They may fill out one in five or one in ten" (Hentoff 1999; see also Fyfe 1998).

According to police records, blacks were stopped six times more often than whites, and Hispanics four times more often during that same fifteen-month period. Much of this difference had to do with the neighborhoods where the stops were conducted. In the affluent, predominantly white Upper East Side of Manhattan, five out of 1,000 residents were stopped and frisked; in the low-income, predominantly black and Hispanic Mott Haven neighborhood of the South Bronx, the rate was seventy-eight per 1,000. Within each neighborhood, blacks and Hispanics were more likely than whites to be stopped (Smith 1999). These differences could not be explained by racial and ethnic differences in criminality. Less than a third of the stops occurred because someone looked like the description of a perpetrator provided by a victim. The black and Hispanic rates were still substantially different when the arrest rates of the different racial and ethnic groups were controlled statistically (Flynn 1999; Roane 1999).

As a result of this selectivity, a high percentage of nonwhites are stopped. In street interviews conducted by *Daily News* reporters with 100 black and Hispanic males between the ages of fourteen and thirty-five, 81 percent said they had been stopped, frisked, and questioned, without being arrested[8] (Casimir, Fenner, and O'Shaughnessy 1999). No precisely comparable figures for white males were provided, but white people living in New York know from their own experience that the percentage is far smaller.[9]

A court case dealing with racial profiling in New Jersey provides further information about the practice. In that state, 46 percent of the motorists who were stopped on the turnpike during a forty-month period were black, even though just 15 percent of the motorists charged with violating traffic laws during that time period were black. Over most of the last decade, at least 80 percent of the automobile searches conducted by New Jersey state troopers were on vehicles driven by blacks and Hispanics (Kocieniewski and Hanley 2000; Kocieniewski 2000). In Maryland, 44.9 percent of the motorists stopped were black (68.4 percent if Hispanics are included) although only 17.5 percent of the traffic-law violators and 17 percent of the drivers were black. In one Florida county, only about 5 percent of the drivers on a stretch of I-95 were black or Hispanic, but more than 70 percent of the drivers stopped were (Harris 1997). Research on highway traffic violations shows that almost all motorists violate some traffic laws, and blacks and whites do so at similar rates. It is not because of exceptionally poor driving habits that black motorists are stopped so much more often than whites (American Civil Liberties Union 1999; Thompson 1999).

Studies of the characteristics of illegal drug users find that blacks are—depending on the drug—only slightly to moderately more likely to use drugs than whites;[10] thus, differences in usage cannot account for the large racial disproportionality in arrests for drugs. They appear to reflect policing practices that permit officers to stop and search civilians on the basis of flimsy or nonexistent evidence, the location of open-air drug markets vulnerable to surveillance in low-income, predominantly minority urban neighborhoods, and drug sweeps in these neighborhoods that subject large numbers of residents to searches simply because they happen to be on the street when the sweep is taking place (Blumstein 1993; Tonry 1994).

Figures on stops based on inchoate suspicion have not been used in calculations to determine whether the criminal justice system discriminates on the basis of race. Research arguing that racial and ethnic discrimination in policing cannot be large because victims' reports of the race of the perpetrator correlate highly with arrest statistics (Hindelang 1978, 1982; Hindelang, Hirschi, and Weis 1979) cannot be applied to these cases because the stops are intended largely to identify individuals who can be charged with possession of narcotics or unlicensed weapons, and for these offences there are no complainants or direct, immediate victims.

A naive response to cases in which someone is stopped and frisked for no clear reason and is found to be carrying an unlicensed gun, or drugs, might be to say that police officers learn in the course of their work what behaviors are likely to be associated with criminality. Even when they cannot articulate the criteria that arouse their suspicion, their experience-based intuition might nevertheless be reliable. The fact that the suspect stopped and frisked was in fact carrying an illegal gun or weapon would seem to confirm the accuracy of the officer's intuition.

This reasoning is fallacious because it does not take into account the large numbers of individuals who are mistakenly stopped. That some of the parties police stop on suspicion are guilty of a crime is not very impressive. Stop enough people, and simply by chance some will have drugs or weapons in their possession. Were the police to stop and search white Wall Street stockbrokers at random, who knows how many might be found with cocaine in their pockets?

Exactly how many mistaken stops are made is uncertain because the efficiency of field interrogations and frisks has never been assessed, but their number appears to be large. The New York Police Department's Street Crime Unit stopped and frisked more than 20,000 innocent men in 1998. Fewer than 25 percent of those stopped were arrested, and almost 40 percent of the arrests were later thrown out of court because the arrests were unconstitutional. Because the police don't keep records on all those they stop and frisk, it is possible that the New York police stop and frisk at least a hundred thousand innocent people a year (Hentoff 1999). When these unrecorded stops are taken into account, the racial disproportionality found in police records could well be much larger than police records show.

What is true of stops in general is true of racial profiling in particular. It cannot be justified on the grounds that African Americans are more likely to be engaging in activities that reasonably warrant suspicion because the data that would be needed to support such a justification have never been produced. Law enforcement agencies say that their racial profiles are based on information given to them by law enforcement personnel, but the profiles tend to be contradictory and have never been validated empirically (Conley 1981; Becton 1987; Larrabee 1997; Kocieniewski 2000). However, in several cities the proportion of unfounded stops is higher for minority group members than for whites (Donziger 1996, 109; Flynn 1999). The New York police arrested just one white person for 7.9 stops on suspicion of involvement in a violent crime. For every arrest of a Hispanic, 14.5 Hispanics were stopped; and for every arrest of a black person, 16.3 people were stopped. These disparities suggest that something other than actuarially based policing (Feeley and Simon 1992) is at work.

New Jersey Attorney General John J. Farmer, Jr., has defended the highway searches of automobiles on the grounds that they led to the arrests of thousands of drug carriers (Kocieniewski and Hanley 2000). Random stops in high-crime neighborhoods have also been justified on the grounds that they stop crime. According to this argument, once it becomes known that people may be stopped at random and searched, they will stop carrying concealed weapons and the homicide rate will fall (Fyfe 1998). This may be true, but the research needed to prove this speculation has not been conducted (Fagan, Zimring, and Kim 1998). Researchers familiar with high-crime neighborhoods suggest that aggressive policing antagonizes neighborhood residents to the point where some consider the police to be "like just another gang" (Brooks 2000) and are reluctant to assist them.

Considered normatively and legally, it may be irrelevant whether the profiles are statistically well-founded or that police stops cut crime. American culture and law impose constraints on law enforcement agencies that preclude some policies even if they are cost-effective. One of the fundamental elements in the American conception of ordered liberty is that one is entitled to go about one's business unmolested by government agents except for good reason. When the government intervenes, the intervention should be based on one's own individual actions, not on the behavior of others.[11] Police stops based on group membership may be considered objectionable even if they "work" (i.e., reduce crime), because they violate these political principles.

From the point of view of the police it may not matter that many stops fail to lead to an arrest. A retired Detroit police officer's observation, "I would estimate—and this I have heard in the station also—that if you stop and search 50 Negroes and you get one good arrest out of it, that's a good percentage; it's a good day's work" (Maclin, 1998b), suggests that unproductive stops are virtually costless to the police. (If these stops reduce civilian cooperation with the police, the agency is unlikely to suffer as a result.)

Because civil asset forfeiture laws give police departments financial incentives to make drug arrests (Benson, Rasmussen, and Sollars 1995; Benson and Rasmussen 1996; Blumenson and Nilsen 1997), organizational pressure to conduct many such searches may be high. The civilians stopped may feel annoyed, resentful, or humiliated, but to the police this has relevance only in the exceptional case when a civilian resists the stop or sues. The great majority won't. Were the same police practices to be directed against respectable whites, there would be much more opposition.

Because some of the profiles are distributed to agents by the agencies that employ them, their use by a particular agent need not imply that the agent who uses them is operating on the basis of personally held stereotypes, conscious or unconscious. Their use, however, increases the likelihood that a black or Latino person carrying narcotics or an unlicensed gun will be arrested. Stops based on individually held stereotypes in the absence of a formal profile will have the same effect. In either case, the stereotype on which the stop is based becomes a self-fulfilling process and undoubtedly contributes to the disproportional number of blacks charged and imprisoned for narcotics and weapons offences (Blumstein 1993). The prevalence of such police practices as stopping black civilians unjustifiably and questioning and searching them for racial reasons, along with historically based memories of discrimination in the courts and occasional, highly publicized episodes of physical maltreatment, may be responsible for the widespread belief that the criminal justice system discriminates against blacks (Brooks 2000).

The Administration of Justice and Desert

When one considers that no data exist to justify singling out minority group members for indiscriminate field interrogations and searches, an explanation must be sought along other lines. For some individual officers, stopping individuals for questioning can be a form of harassment, a way to relieve boredom, or an assertion of superiority. Administrative pressures to generate arrests, combined with the relative powerlessness of minority-group members, may yield disproportionate stops and searches of black and Hispanic civilians. Yet an officer's conception of desert may also be implicated in decisions to select some individuals and not others for searches. If minority group members are, by virtue of their group membership, considered suspects or worthy of degrading treatment, there is an implicit ascription of desert to those suspected.

Ex-police officer James Fyfe (1998) has suggested that police officers and chiefs tend to believe that suspects found with illegal drugs or weapons have no right to complain of police misconduct because they are, after all, guilty, while those who are "clean" should be regarded not as innocent, "but simply not caught this time." To some officers, suspects who are black or Hispanic belong to groups that are collectively responsible for high levels of crime, warranting the distress occasioned by stopping them.[12] Members of the group deserve it. Undoubtedly they've done something that ought to be punished. The principle that someone's guilt can originate not just in his or her own words or actions but also in the misdeeds of the group with which one is associated extends beyond violations of the criminal law. These misdeeds for which someone may be considered responsible can extend to other failings, such as poverty, welfare dependency, and refusal to accept a subordinate social status.

I suggest that the limited public response to police abuse—searches, beatings, shootings, perjured testimony—can be explained only in part by factors usually mentioned: skepticism about accusations, confidence in the police, and desire not to interfere with an agency that provides protection from crime. Another part of the explanation lies in the belief that victims of police aggression usually deserve what they get. Again, this desert need not reflect legal standards for the use of violence; in some cases it may be based on an extended notion of collective guilt for a generalized failure to live up to social expectation. By the same principles, the police can be substantively innocent even though legally guilty of assaulting or killing a civilian. Someone who holds this broad notion of guilt might well see Rodney King's beating at the hands of Los Angeles police in 1991 as having been just, and the police who inflicted it as innocent. This broader notion of guilt and desert may also have helped to provide public support for massive growth in imprisonment over the past thirty years. It isn't just crime that the public has wanted punished as it demands longer sentences from the courts; it is also all the other faults that whites attribute to blacks—who, as we have already seen, are very disproportionately subjected to imprisonment.

The spatial variation of imprisonment is consistent with this analysis. As noted earlier, states with a high percentage of the population that is black tend to have larger prison populations and more rapid rates of prison growth, even when crime rates are controlled. The presence in a state of large numbers of black residents may generate anxieties and fears of crime, based on a partly accurate but exaggerated stereotype linking blacks with illegality.

This anxiety may lead residents to push for or acquiesce in prison construction and stiff penalty provisions. We cannot be certain of this because state-level variation in the public's demand for punishment has never been studied. The limited opposition to high levels of imprisonment suggests that large numbers of people consider this response to law violators to be just. That the punishment response occurs more prominently where the percentage of blacks in the population is especially high points to the existence of a collective racialized attribution of blameworthiness and guilt.

CONCLUSION

Explanatory social science models of the criminal justice system in the past few decades have been derived largely from theories of rational choice (Pyle 1983) and group conflict (Sheley 1991). This chapter suggests that these models might usefully be supplemented by two additional concepts. One is the notion of unconscious thought processes. Unconscious processes can influence individual decisions of law enforcement officers, including police, prosecutors, judges, and parole board members. They can influence levels of fear of crime.

The second notion has to do with conceptions of justice. Pashukanis's writings suggest that a culture's logic of justice is rooted in political economy. While his argument suggests that conceptions of justice should make race increasingly irrelevant to justice assessments, this ideal has not yet been achieved. Racial divisions remain large in contemporary American society, and they influence assessments of justice.

Taken together, these ideas—those involving unconscious stereotyping and those involving justice perceptions—make it possible to explain racialized patterns of law enforcement more fully than without them. These ideas are not intended to offer a complete explanation of criminal justice policy and outcomes or to displace existing paradigms such as rational choice or group conflict. I suggest only that they may need to be supplemented with the ideas proposed here. The emphasis given to unconscious racism in my discussion is not meant to imply the total absence of conscious racism. In some criminal justice contexts it may be very important. I suggest only that the processes outlined here may also be important. Criminologists, then, should give serious attention to the measurement of unconscious racism and to justice perceptions and to the analysis of the role that they play in determining criminal justice outcomes.

In principle, the ideas outlined here are potentially applicable to other patterns of criminological interest, such as those that involve gender, sexuality, and age. Although my discussion of unconscious stereotyping and justice has emphasized the cognitive dimension to both phenomena, stereotypical attributions about appraisals of justice and injustice commonly carry strong affective or emotional loadings. Thus there is room for further criminological theorizing to incorporate emotions in the theory. Chancer and Donovan (1996) and Berry (1999) have initiated efforts to draw on the social psychology of emotions and unconscious thought processes in understanding public responses to crime issues; these theoretical efforts need to be built on.

Efforts to eliminate racism from law enforcement practice will also need to be reconsidered in light of this discussion. Screening and preventing efforts based on the assumption that racism is always conscious may fail to exclude those who engage unconsciously in racial stereotyping and those whose unconscious racism develops on the job. The possibility that unconscious racism can be changed is suggested by research showing that automatic stereotyping does not occur when white subjects are presented with the faces of blacks who are familiar to them (Phelps et al. 2000). Possibly extensive racial integration of major social institutions (e.g., school, workplace, institutions of religion) will, over the long run, create greater familiarity and reduce or eliminate automatic stereotyping. Monitoring strategies might be examined for their potential to prevent prejudice (conscious or unconscious) from manifesting itself behaviorally. The rapid reduction in the ratio of blacks to whites shot to death by police after police departments began to regulate the police use of lethal violence (Walker 1993, 26, 31; Schwartz 1996) offers some ground for optimism. Though structurally determined (as suggested by Pashukanis), justice logics can be learned. Unfortunately, little is known about how they change in individuals. However, the institutional policies that embody them are potentially subject to political contest and change.

NOTES

An earlier version of this chapter was presented to the Eastern Sociological Society meeting, March 1996. I am grateful to Joseph DeAngelis, Nitsan Chorev, Darnell Hawkins, and Martha Jacob for helpful comments on the earlier version.

1. How independent people are in forming these judgments no doubt varies from one individual to another. Some may tend to assume that whatever penalty the state imposes on someone must be deserved, essentially abdicating any independence of judgment. Others maintain a critical stance and fault criminal justice authorities for penalties they consider undeservedly harsh or lenient.

2. Survey research shows that people are more fearful of crime when they have been victimized; controlling for personal victimization experience, residential proximity to blacks increases fear, suggesting an irrational overlay to a rationally based fear (Stinchcombe et al. 1980: 54–7).

3. Nationally, the numbers are still small. According to one study, just 3.8 percent of state trial court judges are African American (Graham 1990; Ifill 1997), but in states where many blacks live the percentage is probably higher.

4. As used here, the term "unconscious" is detached from its Freudian origins and refers to any cognitive or emotional processes that are unknown to the person experiencing them.

5. This is what transpired in the case of Amadou Diallo, shot to death by members of New York Police Department's Street Crime Unit on February 4, 1999. While it is impossible to state with certainty that these officers would not be considered racist by conventional criteria, no evidence to the contrary has come to light so far. One of the four is married to an African-American woman, consistent with my suggestion that they would not be considered racist. Evidence in support of my interpretation is found in Fyfe's (1983) study of fatal police shootings in Memphis. During the years 1969–1976, thirteen of the twenty-six blacks killed were non-assaultive and unarmed, compared to just one of the eight whites killed.

6. *Chicago v. Morales*, 119 S. Ct. 1949, 67 U.S. L.W. 4415 (1998) (Alschuler and Schulhofer 1998).

7. The police may also stop whites in black neighborhoods, suspecting that they are there to purchase drugs (Gonzalez 1999; Dirienzo III 2000).

8. The newspaper story said nothing about how the 100 subjects were selected.

9. A 1994 study by Browning and associates, summarized by Schwartz (1996), found 9.6 percent of whites and 46.6 percent of blacks surveyed reported having been "personally hassled by the police."

10. In 1996, 38.4 percent of the 1,127,114 arrests made in the United States for drug violations were of blacks (Maguire and Pastore 1998, 338). The 1996 National Household Survey on Drug Use, conducted by the U.S. Department of Health and Human Services, found the percentages of respondents who acknowledged the use of an illegal drug in the past month to be: blacks 7.5 percent, whites 6.1 percent, and Hispanics 5.2 percent. Among youths the rates were about the same in the three groups. The analogous figures for cocaine use were: blacks 1.0 percent, whites 0.8 percent, Hispanics 1.1 percent (www.samhsa.gov/oas/nhsda/pe1996/rtst1008.htm). The percentages of felony sentences for drug offences involving imprisonment for drug possession are 27 percent for whites, 45 percent for blacks; for trafficking, 38 percent for whites, 52 percent for blacks (Maguire and Pastore 1998, 426)—appreciable disproportionalities.

11. American law is not entirely consistent in its individualism. Some jurisdictions permit parents to be punished for offences committed by their children (Applebome 1996). Laws authorize the forfeiture of someone's real property and permit eviction from public housing when it has been used in a narcotics offence, even when the owner or tenant did not commit the offence and did not know of it (Comment 1990; Bryson and Yousmans 1990; Yoskowitz 1992; Levy 1996). The U.S. Supreme Court has upheld police stops based solely on Mexican appearance at fixed checkpoints (*United States v. Martinez-Fuere*, 428 U.S. 543 at 563–64.

12. This argument assumes that the police officers who engage in these practices know that those stopped and searched dislike being subjected to these procedures. The possibility must be conceded that they are not aware of this, but believe instead that the disruption, intrusion, and invasion of privacy are so minimal that no one would find them objectionable. Victims of these procedures assert otherwise, and I find it difficult to believe that police officers are unaware of this.

REFERENCES

Alschuler, Albert W., and Stephen J. Schulhofer (1998). "Antiquated Procedures or Bedrock Rights? A Response to Professors Meares and Kahan." *University of Chicago Legal Forum* (1998): 215–23.

American Civil Liberties Union (1999). *Driving While Black: Racial Profiling on Our Nation's Highways*. Special Report. ⟨http://www.aclu.org/profiling/report/index.html⟩.

Applebome, Peter (1996). "Parents Face Consequences As Children's Misdeeds Rise." *New York Times* (April 10): A1, B8.

Audi, Robert (ed.) (1999). *The Cambridge Dictionary of Philosophy*, 2nd edition. New York: Cambridge University Press.

Austin, Roy L., and Mark D. Allen (2000). "Racial Disparity in Arrest Rates as an Explanation of Racial Disparity in Commitment to Pennsylvania's Prisons." *Journal of Research in Crime and Delinquency* 37 (May): 200–220.

Baldus, David C., Charles Pulaski, and George Woodworth (1983). "Comparative Review of Death Sentences: An Empirical Study of the Georgia Experience." *Journal of Criminal Law and Criminology* 74: 661–753.

Barfoot, Mary (1993). *The Coming of Black Genocide and Other Essays*. New York: Vagabond Press.

Beckett, Katherine (1994). "Setting the Public Agenda: 'Street Crime' and Drug Use in American Politics." *Social Problems* 41: 425–47.

———— (1997). *Making Crime Pay: Law and Order in Contemporary American Politics*. New York: Oxford University Press.

————, and Theodore Sasson (2000). *The Politics of Injustice: Crime and Punishment in America*. Thousand Oaks, CA: Pine Forge Press.

————, and Bruce Western (2001). "Governing Social Marginality: Welfare, Incarceration, and the Transformation of Social Policy." *Punishment and Society* 3: 43–59.

Becton, Charles L. (1987). "The Drug Courier Profile: 'All Seems Infected to th' Infected Spy, As All Looks Yellow to the Jaundiced Eye." *North Carolina Law Review* 65: 417–80.

Bell, D., Jr., and K. Lang (1985). "The Intake Dispositions of Juvenile Offenders." *Journal of Research in Crime and Delinquency* 22: 309–328.

Benson, Bruce L., David W. Rasmussen, and David L. Sollars (1995). "Police Bureaucracies, Their Incentives, and the War on Drugs." *Public Choice* 83: 21–45.

Benson, Bruce L., and David W. Rasmussen (1996). "Predatory Public Finance and the Origins of the War on Drugs 1984–1989." *The Independent Review* 1: 163–89.

Berlow, Alan (1999). "The Wrong Man." *Atlantic Monthly* (Nov.): 66–91.

Bernstein, Ilene Nagel, William B. Kelly, and Patricia A. Doyle (1977). "Societal Reaction to Deviants: The Case of Criminal Defendants." *American Sociological Review* 42: 743–55.

Berry, Bonnie (1999). *Social Rage: Emotion and Cultural Conflict*. New York: Garland.

Black, Donald, and Albert J. Reiss, Jr. (1970). "Police Control of Juveniles." *American Sociological Review* 35: 63–77.

Blanchard, F. A., T. Lilly, and L. A. Vaughn (1999). "Reducing the Expression of Racial Prejudice." *Psychological Science* 2: 101–105.

Blauner, Robert (1972). *Racial Oppression in America*. New York: Harper and Row.

Blumenson, E., and E. Nilsen (1997). "Policing for Profit: The Drug War's Hidden Economic Agenda." *University of Chicago Law Review* 65: 35–114.

Blumstein, Alfred (1982). "On the Racial Disproportionality of United States' Prison Populations." *Journal of Criminal Law and Criminology* 73: 1259–81.

———— (1993). "Racial Disproportionality of U.S. Prison Populations Revisited." *University of Colorado Law Review* 64: 743–60.

Bonczar, Thomas P., and Allen J. Beck (1994). *Lifetime Likelihood of Going to State or Federal Prison*. Washington, DC: Bureau of Justice Statistics, U.S. Department of Justice.

Bowers, William J., and Glenn F. Pierce (1980). "Arbitrariness and Discrimination under Post-Furman Capital Statutes." *Crime and Delinquency* 26: 563–635.

Bowles, Samuel, Robert Boyd, Ernst Feht, and Herbert Gintis (1997). "*Homo recipro-cans*: A Research Initiative on the Origins, Dimensions, and Policy Implications of Reciprocal Fairness." Unpublished paper.

Bradsher, Keith (1999). "Fear of Crime Trumps the Fear of Lost Youth." *New York Times* (Nov. 21): WK3.

Bridges, George S., Robert D. Crutchfield, and Edith E. Simpson (1987). "Crime, Social Structure and Criminal Punishment: White and Nonwhite Rates of Imprisonment." *Social Problems* 34: 345–61.

Brooks, Richard R. W. (2000). "Fear and Fairness in the City: Criminal Enforcement and Perceptions of Fairness in Minority Communities." *University of California Law Review* 73: 1219–73.

Brown, Michael K. (1981). *Working the Street: Police Discretion and the Dilemmas of Reform.* New York: Wiley.

Bryson, David B., and Roberta L. Yousmans (1990). "Crime, Drugs, and Subsidized Housing." *Clearinghouse Review* 24: 435–47.

Burstein, Paul (1998). "Bringing the Public Back In: Should Sociologists Consider the Impact of Public Opinion on Public Policy?" *Social Forces* 77: 27–62.

Butterfield, Fox (1996). "Study Examines Race and Justice in California." *New York Times* (Feb. 14): A12.

Casimir, Leslie, Austin Fenner, and Patrice O'Shaughnessy (1999). "Minority Men: We Are Frisk Targets." *Daily News* (March 26): 34–35.

Chambliss, William J. (1994). "Policing the Ghetto Underclass: The Politics of Law and Law Enforcement." *Social Problems* 41: 177–94.

——— (1995). "Crime Control and Ethnic Minorities: Legitimizing Racial Oppression by Creating Moral Panics." Pp. 235–58 in Darnell F. Hawkins (ed.), *Ethnicity, Race, and Crime: Perspectives Across Time and Place.* Albany: State University of New York Press.

——— (1999). *Power, Politics and Crime.* Boulder, CO: Westview Press.

Chancer, Lynn, and Pamela Donovan (1996). "A Mass Psychology of Punishment: Crime and the Futility of Rationally Based Approaches." *Social Justice* 21: 50–71.

Chevigny, Paul (1969). *Police Power.* New York: Vintage.

Chin, Gabriel J., and Scott C. Wells (1998). "The 'Blue Wall of Silence' as Evidence of Bias and Motive to Lie: A New Approach to Police Perjury." *University of Pittsburgh Law Review* 59: 233–300.

Chiricos, Theodore G., and Charles Crawford (1995). "Race and Imprisonment: A Contextual Assessment of the Evidence." Pp. 281–309 in Darnell F. Hawkins (ed.), *Ethnicity, Race, and Crime: Perspectives Across Time and Place.* Albany: State University of New York Press.

Chiricos, Theodore G., and Gordon Waldo (1975). "Socioeconomic Status and Criminal Sentencing: An Empirical Assessment of a Conflict Proposition." *American Sociological Review* 40: 753–73.

Claparède, Eduard (1911). "Recognition et moiieté." *Archives de Psychologie* 11: 79–90.

Cloud, Morgan (1994). "The Dirty Little Secret." *Emory Law Journal* 43: 1311–49.

——— (1996). "Judges, 'Testilying' and the Constitution." *Southern California Law Review* 69: 1341–87.

Cohen, Lawrence E., and James R. Kluegel (1978). "Determinants of Juvenile Court Dispositions: Ascriptive and Achieved Factors in Two Metropolitan Courts." *American Sociological Review* 43: 162–76.

Comment (1987). "The Exclusionary Rule and Deterrence: An Empirical Study of Chicago Narcotics Officers." *University of Chicago Law Review* 54: 1016–69.

Comment (1990). "Congress Steps Up War on Drugs in Public Housing—Has It Gone One Step Too Far?" *Loyola Law Review* 36: 137–57.

Condron, John G. (1979). "Changes in White Attitudes Toward Blacks: 1963–1977." *Public Opinion Quarterly* 43: 463–76.

Conley, Darlene J. (1994). "Adding Color to a Black and White Picture: Using Qualitative Data to Explain Racial Disproportionality in the Juvenile Justice Data." *Journal of Research in Crime and Delinquency* 31: 35–48.

Conley, William V. (1981). "*Mendenhall* and *Reid*: The Drug Courier Profile and Investigative Stops." *University of Pittsburgh Law Review* 42: 835–67.

Cowey, Alan (1991). "Grasping the Essentials." *Nature* 349: 102.

Crosby, Faye, Stephanie Bromley, and Leonard Saxe (1980). "Recent Unobtrusive Studies of Black and White Discrimination and Prejudice: A Literature Review." *Psychological Bulletin* 87: 546–63.

Crutchfield, Robert D., George S. Bridges, and Susan R. Pitchford (1994). "Analytical and Aggregation Biases in Analyses of Imprisonment: Reconciling Discrepancies in Studies of Racial Disparity." *Journal of Research in Crime and Delinquency* 31: 166–82.

Currie, Elliot (1998). *Crime and Punishment in America*. New York: Henry Holt.

Davis, Angela J. (1996). "Benign Neglect of Racism in the Criminal Justice System." *University of Michigan Law Review* 94: 1660–86.

——— (1997). "Race, Cops, and Traffic Stops." *University of Miami Law Review* 51: 425–443.

Developments in the Law (1988). "Race and the Criminal Process." *Harvard Law Review* 101: 1472–1641.

Dike, Sarah T. (1981). "Capital Punishment in the United States, Part II: Empirical Evidence." *Criminal Justice Abstracts* 13: 426–47.

DiMaggio, Paul, John Evans, and Bethany Bryson (1996). "Have Americans' Social Attitudes Become More Polarized?" *American Journal of Sociology* 102: 690–755.

Dirienzo III, Anthony (2000). "Racial Profiling Under the Microscope." *New York Post* (Nov. 3): 32.

Donnerstein, E., and M. Donnerstein (1973). "Variables in Interracial Aggression: Potential Ingroup Censure." *Journal of Personality and Social Psychology* 27: 143–50.

——— (1976). "Research in the Control of Interracial Aggression." Pp. 133–68 in R.G. Green and E.C. O'Neal (eds.), *Perspectives on Aggression*. New York: Academic Press.

Donnerstein, E., M. Donnerstein, S. Simon, and R. Ditrichs (1972). "Variables in Interracial Aggression: Anonymity, Expected Retaliation, and Riot." *Journal of Personality and Social Psychology* 22: 36–45.

Donziger, Steven R. (ed.) (1996). *The Real War on Crime*. New York: Harper.

Downes, David (1988). *Contrasts in Tolerance: Post-War Penal Policy in the Netherlands and England and Wales*. Oxford: Clarendon.

Dripps, Donald A. (1996). "Police, Plus Perjury, Equals Polygraphy." *Journal of Criminal Law and Criminology* 86: 693–716.

Duckitt, J. (1993). "Prejudice and Behavior: A Review." *Current Psychology: Research and Reviews* 11: 291–307.

Duster, Troy (1997). "Pattern, Purpose, and Race in the Drug War: The Crisis of Credibility in Criminal Justice." Pp. 260–287 in Craig Reinarman and Harry G. Levine (eds.), *Crack in America: Demon Drugs and Social Justice*. Berkeley: University of California Press.

Emerson, Robert M. (1969). *Judging Delinquents: Context and Process in Juvenile Court*. Chicago: Aldine.

Fagan, J., F. E. Zimring, and J. Kim (1998). "Declining Homicide in New York City: A Tale of Two Trends." *Journal of Criminal Law and Criminology* 88: 1277–1324.

Farnworth, Margaret, Katherine Bennett, and Vincent M. West (1996). "Mail vs. Telephone Surveys of Criminal Justice Attitudes: A Comparative Analysis." *Journal of Quantitative Criminology* 12: 113–33.

Fazio, Russell H., Joni R. Jackson, Bridget C. Dunton, and Carol J. Williams (1995). "Variability in Automatic Activation as an Unobtrusive Measure of Racial Attitudes: A Bona Fide Pipeline?" *Journal of Personality and Social Psychology* 69: 1013–27.

Feeley, Malcolm M., and Jonathan Simon (1992). "The New Penology: Notes on the Emerging Strategy of Corrections and Its Implications." *Criminology* 30: 449–74.

Firebaugh, Glenn, and Kenneth E. Davis (1988). "Trends in Anti-Black Prejudice, 1972–1984; Region and Cohort Effects." *American Journal of Sociology* 94: 251–72.

Flynn, Kevin (1999). "Racial Bias Shown in Police Searches, State Report Asserts." *New York Times* (Dec. 1): A1, B5.

Fuller, Lon L. (1964). *The Morality of Law*. New Haven, CT: Yale University Press.

Fyfe, James J. (1993). "Blind Justice: Police Shootings in Memphis." *Journal of Criminal Law and Criminology* 73: 707–22.

——— (1998). "Terry: A[n Ex-] Cop's View." *St. John's Law Review* 72: 1231–48.

Gaertner, Samuel L., and John F. Dovidio (1986). "The Aversive Form of Racism." Pp. 61–89 in John F. Dovidio and Samuel L. Gaertner (eds.), *Prejudice, Discrimination, and Racism*. New York: Academic Press.

Gallup, George, Jr. (1995). *Gallup Poll Monthly* (Oct.): 3–4.

Garland, David (2001). *The Culture of Control: Crime and Social Order in Late Modernity*. Chicago: University of Chicago Press.

Geller, William A., and Kevin J. Karales (1981). "Shootings of and by Chicago Police: Uncommon Crises Part I: Shootings by Chicago Police." *Journal of Criminal Law and Criminology* 72: 1813–66.

Gibson, James L. (1978). "Race as a Determinant of Criminal Sentences: A Methodological Critique and a Case Study." *Law and Society Review* 12: 455–78.

Gonzalez, David (1999). "2d Thoughts After a Brush With the Law." *New York Times* (March 24): B1.

Gottfredson, Michael R., and Don M. Gottfredson (1988). *Decision Making in Criminal Justice: Toward the Rational Exercise of Discretion*. New York: Plenum.

Graham, Barbara Wick (1990). "Judicial Recruitment and Racial Diversity in State Courts: An Overview." *Judicature* 74: 28–34.

Green, Mark (1999). *Investigation of the New York City Police Department's Response to Civilian Complaints of Police Misconduct*. Interim Report. New York: Office of the New York City Public Advocate.

Greenberg, David F. (1999). "Punishment, Division of Labor, and Social Solidarity." Pp. 283–361 in William S. Laufer and Freda Adler (eds.), *The Criminology of Criminal Law*. Advances in Criminological Theory, vol. 8. New Brunswick, NJ: Transaction.

—— (2001). "The Time Series Analysis of Crime Rates." *Journal of Quantitative Criminology* 17: 291–327.

Greenberg, David F., and Nancy E. Anderson (1981). "Recent Marxisant Work on Law: A Review Essay." *Contemporary Crises: Crime, Law and Social Policy* 5: 293–322.

Greenberg, David F., and Nancy E. Anderson (1983). "The Legal Theories of Pashukanis and Edelman." *Socialtext: Theory, Culture, Ideology* 7: 69–84.

Greenberg, David F., Ronald C. Kessler, and Colin Loftin (1985). "Social Inequality and Crime Control." *Journal of Criminal Law and Criminology* 76: 684–704.

Greenberg, David F., and Valerie West (2001). "State Prison Populations and Their Growth, 1971–1991." *Criminology* 39: 615–654.

Greenwald, Anthony G., and Mahzarin R. Banaji (1995). "Implicit Social Cognition: Attitudes, Self-Esteem and Stereotypes." *Psychological Review* 102: 4–27.

Gross, Samuel R. (1985). "Race and Death: The Judicial Evaluation of Discrimination in Capital Sentencing." *University of California-Davis Law Review* 18: 1275–1325.

——, and Robert Mauro (1984). "Patterns of Death: An Analysis of Racial Disparities in Capital Sentencing and Homicide." *Stanford Law Review* 37: 27–153.

Hagan, John (1974). "Extra-Legal Attributes and Criminal Sentencing: An Assessment of a Sociological Viewpoint." *Law and Society* 8: 357–84.

——, and Kristin Bumiller (1983). "Making Sense of Sentencing: A Review and Critique of Sentencing Research." Pp. 1–54 in Alfred Blumstein et al. (eds.), *Research on Sentencing: The Search for Reform.* Washington, DC: National Academy Press.

Haney, Craig (1998). "Riding the Punishment Wave: On the Origins of Our Devolving Standards of Decency." *Hastings Women's Law Journal* 9: 27–78.

Harris, Anthony R. (1991). "Race, Class and Crime." Pp. 95–119 in Joseph F. Sheley (ed.), *Criminology: A Contemporary Handbook.* Belmont, CA: Wadsworth.

Harris, David A. (1994a). "Frisking Every Suspect: The Withering of *Terry*." *U. C. Davis Law Review* 28: 1–52.

—— (1994b). "Factors for Reasonable Suspicion: When Black and Poor Means Stopped and Frisked." *Indiana Law Journal* 69: 659–88.

—— (1997). "Driving While Black and All Other Traffic Offenses: The Supreme Court and Pretextual Traffic Stops." *Journal of Criminal Law and Criminology* 87: 544–54.

Hawkins, Darnell F. (1987). "Beyond Anomalies: Rethinking the Conflict Perspective on Racial Criminal Punishment." *Social Forces* 65: 719–45.

—— (1999). "On the Horns of a Dilemma: Social Class Divisions and High Rates of Criminal Victimization among African Americans." Paper presented to the American Society of Criminology.

——, and Kenneth A. Hardy (1989). "Black-White Imprisonment Rates: A State-by-State Analysis." *Social Justice* 16.4: 75–94.

Hawkins, Keith (ed.) (1992). *The Uses of Discretion.* New York: Oxford University Press.

Hayek, Friedrich Alexander (1973). *Law, Legislation and Liberty: A New Statement of the Liberal Principles of Justice and Political Economy.* Chicago: University of Chicago Press.

Henrich, Joseph (1997). "Market Incorporation, Agricultural Change and Sustainability among the Machiguenga Indians of the Peruvian Amazon." *Human Ecology* 25: 319–51.

Hentoff, Nat (1999). "Lawless Arrests Under Giuliani: Howard Safir—I Am the Law." *Village Voice* (Nov. 2): 33.

Hepburn, John R. (1978). "Race and the Decision to Arrest: An Analysis of Warrants Issued." *Journal of Research in Crime and Delinquency* 15: 54–73.

Hindelang, Michael J. (1978). "Race and Involvement in Common-Law Personal Crimes." *American Sociological Review* 43: 93–109.

———— (1982). "Race and Crime." Pp. 168–84 in Leonard D. Savitz and Norman Johnston (eds.), *Contemporary Criminology*. New York: Wiley.

————, Travis Hirschi, and Joseph Weis (1979). "Correlates of Delinquency: The Illusion of Discrepancy between Self-Report and Official Measures." *American Sociological Review* 44: 995–1014.

Hogarth, John (1971). *Sentencing as a Human Process*. Toronto: University of Toronto Press.

Ifill, Sherrilyn A. (1997). "Judging the Judges: Racial Diversity, Impartiality and Representation on State Trial Courts." *Boston College Law Review* 39: 95–149.

Irwin, John, and James Austin (1994). *It's About Time: America's Imprisonment Binge*. Belmont, CA: Wadsworth.

Jackson, Pamela Irving (1989). *Minority Group Threat, Crime, and Policing*. New York: Praeger.

————, and Leo Carroll (1981). "Race and the War on Crime: The Sociopolitical Determinants of Municipal Police Expenditures in 90 Nonsouthern U.S. Cities." *American Sociological Review* 46: 29–305.

Jacobs, David (1979). "Inequality and Police Strength: Conflict Theory and Coercive Control in Metropolitan Areas." *American Sociological Review* 44: 913–25.

Jacoby, Joseph, and Raymond Paternoster (1982). "Sentencing Disparity and Jury Packing: Further Challenges to the Death Penalty." *Journal of Criminal Law and Criminology* 73: 379–87.

Johnson, Erika L. (1995). "'A Menace to Society': The Use of Criminal Profiles and Its Effects on Black Males." *Howard Law Journal* 38: 629–64.

Johnson, Sherri Lynn (1983). "Race and the Decision to Detain a Suspect." *Yale Law Journal* 93: 214–38.

———— (1988). "Unconscious Racism and the Law." *Cornell Law Review* 73: 1016–37.

Jones, Charisse (1995). "Crack and Punishment: Is Race the Issue?" *New York Times* (Oct. 28): 1, 10.

Kadish, Mark J. (1997). "The Drug Courier Profile: In Planes, Trains, and Automobiles; and Now in the Jury Box." *American University Law Review* 46: 747–91.

Kahan, Dan M., and Tracey L. Meares (1998). "The Coming Crisis of Criminal Procedure." *Georgetown Law Journal* 86: 1153–84.

Katz, Irwin, Joyce Wackenhut, and R. Glen Hass (1986). "Racial Ambivalence, Value Duality, and Behavior." Pp. 35–59 in John F. Davidio and Samuel L. Gaertner (eds.), *Prejudice, Discrimination, and Racism*. New York: Academic Press.

Kelling, George L. (1999). *"Broken Windows" and Police Discretion*. National Institute of Justice Research Report. Washington, DC: National Institute of Justice.

Kennedy, Randall (1988). "*McCleskey v. Kemp*: Race, Capital Punishment, and the Supreme Court." *Harvard Law Review* 101: 1388–1443.

———— (1995). "A Response to Professor Cole's 'Paradox of Race and Crime.'" *Georgetown Law Journal* 83: 2573–78.

———— (1997). *Race, Crime, and the Law*. New York: Pantheon.

Kifner, John (1995). "Belief to Blood: The Making of Rabin's Killer." *New York Times* (Nov. 19): 1, 12–13.

————— (1999). "No Charges Against Officers in Fatal Brooklyn Shooting." *New York Times* (Nov. 2): B1, B4.

Kleck, Gary (1981). "Racial Discrimination in Criminal Sentencing: A Critical Evaluation of the Evidence with Additional Evidence on the Death Penalty." *American Sociological Review* 46: 783–805.

Klein, Stephen, Joan Petersilia, and Susan Turner (1990). "Race and Imprisonment Decisions in California." *Science* (Feb. 16).

Klockars, Carl B. (1986). "Street Justice: Some Micro-Moral Reservations—Comment on Sykes." *Justice Quarterly* 3: 513–16.

Kocieniewski, David (2000). "New Jersey Argues That the U.S. Wrote the Book on Race Profiling." *New York Times* (Nov. 29).

—————, and Robert Hanley (2000). "Racial Profiling Was the Routine, New Jersey Finds." *New York Times* (Nov. 28): A1, B5.

Langan, Patrick A. (1985). "Racism on Trial: New Evidence to Explain the Racial Composition of Prisons in the United States." *Journal of Criminal Law and Criminology* 76: 666–83.

————— (1991). "America's Soaring Prison Population." *Science* 251: 1568–73.

Larrabee, Jennifer A. (1997). "'DWB (Driving While Black)' and Equal Protection—the Realities of an Unequal Police Practice." *Journal of Law and Policy* 6: 291–328.

Lerner, Robert (n.d.). "Acquittal Rates by Race for State Felonies." Pp. 85–93 in Gerald A. Reynolds (ed.), *Race and the Criminal Justice System: How Race Affects Jury Trials*. Washington, DC: Center for Equal Opportunity.

Levy, Leonard W. (1996). *A License to Steal: The Forfeiture of Property*. Chapel Hill: University of North Carolina Press.

Liska, Allen E., Joseph J. Lawrence, and Michael Benson (1981). "Perspectives on the Legal Order: The Capacity for Social Control." *American Journal of Sociology* 87: 413–25.

Liska, Allen E., and Mark Taussig (1979). "Theoretical Interpretations of Social Class and Racial Differentials in Legal Decision-Making for Juveniles." *Sociological Quarterly* 20: 197–207.

Livingston, Jay (1992). *Crime and Criminology*. Englewood Cliffs, NJ: Prentice-Hall.

Lizotte, Alan J. (1978). "Extra-Legal Factors in Chicago's Criminal Courts: Testing the Conflict Model of Criminal Justice." *Social Problems* 25: 564–80.

Locke, Hubert G. (1996). "The Color of Law and the Issue of Color: Race and the Abuse of Power." Pp. 129–49 in William A. Geller and Hans Toch (eds.), *Police Violence: Understanding and Controlling Police Abuse*. New Haven, CT: Yale University Press.

Maclin, Tracey (1991). "'Black and Blue Encounters'—Some Preliminary Thoughts about Fourth Amendment Seizures: Should Race Matter?" *Valparaiso Law Review* 26: 243–79.

————— (1998a). "Race and the Fourth Amendment." *Vanderbilt Law Review* 51: 333–93.

————— (1998b). "*Terry v. Ohio's* Fourth Amendment Legacy: Black Man and Police Discretion." *St. John's Law Review* 72: 1271–1321.

Magee, Robin K. (1994). "The Myth of the Good Cop and the Inadequacy of Fourth Amendment Remedies for Black Men: Contrasting Presumptions of Innocence and Guilt." *Capital Law Review* 23: 151.

Maguire, Kathleen, and Ann L. Pastore (eds.) (1998). *Sourcebook of Criminal Justice Statistics 1997*. U.S. Department of Justice, Bureau of Justice Statistics. Washington, DC: U.S. Government Printing Office.

Mann, Coramae Richey (1993). *Unequal Justice: A Question of Color*. Bloomington: Indiana University Press.

Mauer, Marc (1999). *Race to Incarcerate*. New York: New Press.

McCarthy, Belinda (1990). "A Micro-Level Analysis of Social Structure and Social Control: Intrastate Use of Jail and Prison Confinement." *Justice Quarterly* 7: 325–40.

McEachern, Alexander W., and Riva Bauzer (1967). "Factors Related to Disposition in Juvenile Police Contacts." Pp. 148–60 in Malcolm Klein and Barbara Meyerhoff (eds.), *Juvenile Gangs in Context: Theory, Research and Action*. Englewood Cliffs, NJ: Prentice-Hall.

Michalowski, Raymond J., and Michael A. Pearson (1990). "Punishment and Social Structure at the State Level: A Cross-Sectional Comparison of 1970 and 1980." *Journal of Research in Crime and Delinquency* 20: 73–85.

Miller, Jerome G. (1996). *Search and Destroy: African-American Males in the Criminal Justice System*. New York: Cambridge University Press.

Mustard, David B. (1999). "Racial, Ethnic and Gender Disparities in Sentencing: Evidence from the U.S. Federal Courts." Paper presented to the American Society of Criminology.

Myers, Martha A. (1995). "The Courts, Prosecution and Sentencing." Pp. 407–427 in Joseph F. Sheley (ed.), *Criminology: A Contemporary Handbook*. Belmont, CA: Wadsworth.

———, and Susette Talarico (1987). *The Social Contexts of Criminal Sentencing*. New York: Springer-Verlag.

Nelson, James F. (1991). *The Incarceration of Minority Defendants: An Identification of Disparity in New York State, 1985–1986*. Albany: New York State Division of Criminal Justice Services.

——— (1992). "Hidden Disparities in Case Processing: New York State, 1985–1986." *Journal of Criminal Justice* 20: 181–200.

——— (1995). *Disparities in Processing Felony Arrests in New York State, 1990–1992*. Albany: New York State Division of Criminal Justice Services.

New York Times (1995). "Nearly 7% of Adult Black Men Were Inmates in '94, Study Says." December 4, p. A15.

Ohlin, Lloyd E., and Frank J. Remington (1993). *Discretion in Criminal Justice: The Tension Between Individualization and Uniformity*. Albany: State University of New York Press.

Olson, Joel (1996). "Gardens of the Law: The Role of Prisons in Capitalist Society." Pp. 40–46 in Elihu Rosenblatt (ed.), *Criminal Injustice: Confronting the Prison Crisis*. Boston, MA: South End Press.

Orfield, Myron W., Jr. (1987). "The Exclusionary Rule and Deterrence: An Empirical Study of Chicago Narcotics Officers." *University of Chicago Law Review* 1016–69.

——— (1992). "Deterrence, Perjury and the Heater Factor: An Exclusionary Rule in the Chicago Criminal Courts." *University of Colorado Law Review* 75: 108–114.

Pashukanis, Evgeny B. (1980). *Selected Writings on Marxism and Law*. Translated by Peter B. Maggs and John N. Hazard, edited by Piers Beirne and Robert Sharlet. New York: Academic Press.

Paternoster, Raymond (1983). "Race of Victim and Location of Crime: The Decision to Seek the Death Penalty in South Carolina." *Journal of Criminal Law and Criminology* 74: 754–85.

Patton, Alison L. (1993). "The Endless Cycle of Abuse: Why 42 USC 1983 Is Ineffective in Deterring Police Brutality." *Hastings Law Journal* 44: 753–808.

Paul, Annie Murphy (1998). "Where Bias Begins: The Truth about Stereotypes." *Psychology Today* (May/June).

Petersilia, Joan (1983). *Racial Disparities in the Criminal Justice System*. Santa Monica, CA: Rand.

——— (1985). "Racial Disparities in the Criminal Justice System: A Summary." *Crime and Delinquency* 31: 15–34.

Peterson, Ruth D., and John Hagan (1984). "Changing Conceptions of Race: Towards an Account of Anomalous Findings of Sentencing Research." *American Sociological Review* 49: 56–70.

Pettigrew, Thomas F. (1985). "New Patterns of Racism: The Different Worlds of 1984 and 1964." *Rutgers University Press* 37: 673–706.

Phelps, Elizabeth A., Kevin J. O'Connor, William A. Cunningham, E. Sumie Funayama, J. Christopher Gatenby, John C. Gore, and Mahzavin R. Banaji (2000). "Performance on Indirect Measures of Race Evaluation Predicts Amygdala Activity." *Journal of Cognitive Neuroscience* 12: 729–38.

Piliavin, Irving, and S. Briar (1964). "Police Encounters and Delinquency: Which Causes Which?" *Criminology* 17: 194–207.

Pommershein, F., and S. Wise (1989). "Disparate Sentencing in South Dakota." *Criminal Justice and Behavior* 16: 155–65.

Pyle, David J. (1983). *The Economics of Crime and Law Enforcement*. New York: St. Martin's Press.

Quillian, Lincoln (1996). "Group Threat and Regional Change in Attitudes toward African-Americans." *American Journal of Sociology* 102: 816–60.

Radelet, Michael L. (1981). "Racial Characteristics and the Death Penalty." *American Sociological Review* 46: 918–27.

———, and Glenn F. Pierce (1985). "Race and Prosecutorial Discretion in Homicide Cases." *Law and Society Review* 19: 587–621.

Reinarman, Craig, and Harry G. Levine (1997a). "The Crack Attack: Politics and Media in the Crack Scare." Pp. 18–51 in Craig Reinarman and Harry G. Levine (eds.), *Crack in America: Demon Drugs and Social Justice*. Berkeley: University of California Press.

Reinarman, Craig, and Harry G. Levine (1997b). "Crack in Context: America's Latest Demon Drug." Pp. 1–17 in Craig Reinarman and Harry G. Levine (eds.), *Crack in America: Demon Drugs and Social Justice*. Berkeley: University of California Press.

Reiss, Albert J., Jr. (1968). "Police Brutality: Answers to Key Questions." *Transaction* (July–August): 10–19.

Riksheim, E., and S. Chernak (1993). "Causes of Police Behavior Revisited." *Journal of Criminal Justice* 21: 353–82.

Roane, Kit R. (1999). "Safir Attacks State Finding of Racial Inequity in Searches." *New York Times* (Dec. 2): B3.

Rudovsky, David (1992). "Police Abuse: Can the Violence Be Contained?" *Harvard Civil Rights Civil Liberties Law Review* 27: 486.

Salaam, Omar (1997). "The Age of Unreason: The Impact of Unreasonableness, Increased Police Force, and Colorblindness on *Terry* 'Stop and Frisk.'" *Oklahoma Law Review* 50: 451–93.

Sampson, Robert J., and Janet L. Lauritsen (1997). "Racial and Ethnic Disparities in Crime and Criminal Justice in the United States." Pp. 311–74 in Michael Tonry (ed.), *Ethnicity, Crime, and Immigration: Comparative and Cross-National Perspectives*. Chicago, IL: University of Chicago Press.

Savelsberg, Joachim (1994). "Knowledge, Domination, and Criminal Punishment." *American Journal of Sociology* 99: 911–43.

——— (1999). "Culture, Institutions, and Criminal Punishment: Lessons from International Comparison." Paper presented to the American Society of Criminology.

Schuman, Howard, Charlotte Steeh, and Lawrence Bobo (1985). *Racial Attitudes in America: Trends and Interpretations*. Cambridge, MA: Harvard University Press.

Schwartz, Adina (1996). "'Just Take Away Their Guns': The Hidden Racism of *Terry v. Ohio*." *Fordham Urban Law Journal* 23: 317–75.

Sheley, Joseph F. (1991). "Conflict and Criminal Law." Pp. 21–39 in Joseph F. Sheley (ed.), *Criminology: A Contemporary Handbook*. Belmont, CA: Wadsworth.

Sigall, Harold E., and Richard Page (1971). "Current Stereotypes: A Little Fading, a Little Faking." *Journal of Personality and Social Psychology* 18: 247–55.

Sklansky, David A. (1997). "Traffic Stops, Minority Motorists, and the Future of the Fourth Amendment." *Supreme Court Review* (1997): 271–329.

Skolnick, Jerome H. (1966). *Justice Without Trial: Law Enforcement in Democratic Society*. New York: Wiley.

———, and James J. Fyfe (1993). *Above the Law: Police and the Excessive Use of Force*. New York: Free Press.

Slobogin, Christopher (1996). "Testilying: Police Perjury and What to Do About It?" *University of Colorado Law Review* 67: 1037–60.

Smith, Douglas A., and Christy Visher (1981). "Street-Level Justice: Situational Determinants of Police Arrest Decisions." *Social Problems* 29: 167–77.

Smith, Douglas A., Christy Visher, and Laura A. Davidson (1984). "Equity and Discretionary Justice: The Influence of Race on Police Arrest Decisions." *Journal of Criminal Law and Criminology* 75: 234–49.

Smith, Greg B. (1999). "Report Details Imbalance in Stop-&-Frisks." *Daily News* (Dec. 2): 5.

Snell, Tracy L. (1997). *Capital Punishment 1996*. Bureau of Justice Statistics Bulletin (Dec.). Washington, DC: U.S. Department of Justice.

Spohn, C., J. Gruhl, and S. Welch (1982). "The Effect of Race on Sentencing: A Reexamination of an Unsettled Question." *Law and Society Review* 16: 71–88.

Steffensmeier, Darrell, and Stephen Demuth (2000). "Ethnicity and Sentencing Outcomes in U.S. Federal Courts: Who Is Punished More Harshly?" *American Sociological Review* 65: 705–729.

Stinchcombe, Arthur L., Rebecca Adams, Carol A. Heimer, Kim Lane Scheppele, Tom W. Smith, and D. Garth Taylor. (1980). *Crime and Punishment: Changing Attitudes in America*. San Francisco: Jossey-Bass.

Sunstein, Cass R., David Schkade, and Daniel Kahneman (2000). "Do People Want Optimal Deterrence?" *Journal of Legal Studies* 29P: 237–53.

Suskind, Randall S. (1994). "Note, Race, Reasonable Articulable Suspicion, and Seizure." *American Criminal Law Review* 31: 327–49.

Sykes, Richard E., James C. Fox, and John P. Clark (1976). "A Socio-Legal Theory of Police Discretion." Pp. 171–83 in Arthur Niederhoffer and Abraham S. Blumberg (eds.), *The Ambivalent Force: Perspectives on the Police*, 2nd ed. Hinsdale, IL: Dryden.

Terry, Robert M. (1967). "Discrimination in the Handling of Juvenile Offenders by So-
    cial Control Agencies." *Journal of Research in Crime and Delinquency* 4:
    218–30.
Thompson, Anthony C. (1999). "Stopping the Usual Suspects: Race and the Fourth
    Amendment." *New York University Law Review* 74: 956–1013.
Thornberry, Terence P. (1973). "Race, Socioeconomic Status and Sentencing in the Juve-
    nile Justice System." *Journal of Criminal Law and Criminology* 64: 90–98.
Tonry, Michael (1994). "Race and the War on Drugs." *University of Chicago Legal Forum*
    1994: 25–81.
——— (1995). *Malign Neglect: Race, Crime, and Punishment in America*. New York:
    Oxford University Press.
Uggen, Christopher, and Jeff Manza (2000). "Political Consequences of Felon Disenfran-
    chisement in the United States." Paper presented to the American Sociological
    Association meeting, Washington, DC.
Unnever, James D. (1982). "Direct and Organizational Discrimination in the Sentencing
    of Drug Offenders." *Social Problems* 30: 212–25.
———, and Larry A. Hembroff (1988). "The Prediction of Racial/Ethnic Sentencing Dis-
    positions: An Expectation States Approach." *Journal of Research in Crime and
    Delinquency* 25: 53–82.
Verhovek, Sam Howe (1999). "Teenager to Spend Life in Prison for Shootings." *New
    York Times* (Nov. 11): A14.
von Hirsch, Andrew (1976). *Doing Justice: The Choice of Punishments*. New York: Hill
    and Wang.
Walker, Samuel (1993). *Taming the System: The Control of Discretion in Criminal Jus-
    tice, 1950–1990*. New York: Oxford University Press.
———, Cassia Spohn, and Miriam DeLone (1996). *The Color of Justice*. Belmont, CA:
    Wadsworth.
Weber, Max (1978). *Economy and Society: An Outline of Interpretive Sociology*, ed. by
    Guenther Roth and Claus Wittich. Berkeley, CA: University of California Press.
Westley, William A. (1953). "Violence and the Police." *American Journal of Sociology*
    59: 34–41.
Wiener, Norman L., and Charles V. Willie (1971). "Decisions of Juvenile Officers." *Amer-
    ican Journal of Sociology* 77: 199–210.
Wilbanks, William (1987). *The Myth of a Racist Criminal Justice System*. Monterey, CA:
    Brooks/Cole.
Wilson, James Q. (1970). "The Police and the Delinquent in Two Cities." Pp. 105–127 in
    Peter G. Garabedian and Don C. Gibbons (eds.), *Becoming Delinquent: Young Of-
    fenders and the Correctional Process*. Chicago: Aldine.
——— (1975). *Thinking About Crime*. New York: Basic.
Wines, Enoch C. (1871). *Transactions of the National Congress on Penitentiary and Re-
    formatory Discipline*. Albany, NY: Weed, Parsons and Company.
Wolfgang, Marvin E., Robert M. Figlio, and Thorsten Sellin (1972). *Delinquency in a
    Birth Cohort*. Chicago: University of Chicago Press.
Wright, Gerald C., Robert S. Erikson, and John P. McIver (1987). "Public Opinion and
    Policy Liberalism in the American States." *American Journal of Political Science*
    31: 980–1001.
——— (1993). *Statehouse Democracy: Public Opinion and Policy in the American
    States*. New York: Cambridge University Press.

Wycliff, Don (1988). "Black and Blue Encounters." *Criminal Justice Ethics* 7(2) (Summer/Fall): 2, 84.

Yale, Rob (1997). "Searching for the Consequences of Police Brutality." *Southern California Law Review* 70: 1841–59.

Yoskowitz, Jack (1992). "The War on the Poor: Civil Forfeiture of Public Housing." *Columbia Journal of Law and Social Problems* 25: 567–600.

Zatz, Marjorie (1987). "The Changing Form of Racial/Ethnic Biases in Sentencing." *Journal of Research in Crime and Delinquency* 24: 69–92.

14

Criminology as Moral Philosophy, Criminologist as Witness

Richard Quinney

I had decided to take the night train from Chicago to Albany. Riding the Lake Shore Limited, I would have time for needed silence and reflection. Leisurely thoughts, a few photographic shots on black-and-white film, and a couple hours of sleep along the way. The train slipped out of Union Station as the sun was setting and made its way along the shores of Lake Michigan, then over the Sandusky bridge and around the southern shore of Lake Erie to Buffalo, and by early morning we were riding through the Mohawk Valley. A day early, I would walk the once-familiar streets of Albany and prepare for a conference on "Justice without Violence." The next day I would be part of a gathering of peacemaking criminologists and church-related workers on restorative justice.

For two and a half days, usually in formal sessions, we heard and talked about the subject of our life's work. As seems to be happening more of late, I listened, took notes in my journal, but did not speak. For years we have been witnesses to the sufferings of others. We have sought ways, both structural and personal, to relieve some of the suffering associated with crime and criminal justice. And after such labors of mind and body, we too share the suffering. Being for others, as Dietrich Bonhoeffer termed it, we know that we share the common human condition of our time and place, and we suffer together (Bonhoeffer 1971). Our gathering in Albany was first about suffering—the suffering of all of us. And this time I was to be a silent witness to the suffering. But a witness nevertheless.

A realization had been developing for some time, and the conference I was attending confirmed it: Whatever else we do as criminologists, we are engaged in a moral enterprise. Simply stated, our underlying questions are these: How are we human beings to live? Who are we, and of what are we capable? And how could things be different? The criminologist, although not likely educated as a moral philosopher, operates with an implicit moral philosophy and is engaged in the construction of a moral philosophy.

The many varied issues surrounding crime and criminal justice are ultimately about how we humans might live. At the same time, what we criminologists are doing—in addition to the other things we think we are doing—is *witnessing* to all that is associated with crime and criminal justice. We are witnesses to the contemporary suffering brought about by poverty, exploitation, racism, violence in its many forms, hate and greed, brutality, prejudice, and inequality. We are also witnesses—and as witnesses also promoters—of those things that finally alleviate suffering: compassion and loving-kindness. As witnesses, we are part of the process of changing the world. Witnessing is an active vocation, one that is grounded in a particular moral stance toward human existence.

There is, of course, more to consider. As Willie Nelson sings in his song cycle *Phases and Stages*, "Let me tell you some more."

CRIMINOLOGY AS MORAL PHILOSOPHY

Let us note the varieties of moral philosophy that inform contemporary criminology. We cannot delineate forms of moral philosophy that are exhaustive and mutually exclusive. There are many dimensions to the phenomena of our attention, and there are many ways that the diverse phenomena overlap. Keep in mind, always, that in the grand reality everything happens at once. Only the human mind separates the world into discrete phenomena. Remembering this, I will go on to describe the moral philosophies I have known in the course of a career in criminology.

Conservative Moral Philosophy and the Established Order

Any criminology that favors the collective over the well-being of the individual (whether the individual is defined as criminal or not) is a conservative criminology, a criminology that is based on and fosters a conservative moral philosophy. It is a criminology that values social order and seeks to preserve the existing order. Policies and programs are aimed at control and deterrence for the benefit of the established order. Rather than changing the existing social and economic arrangements, solutions to criminal behavior are sought in controlling the individual.

I am not the criminologist to give a fair and sympathetic treatment to a conservatively grounded criminology or to analyze the merits of the moral philosophy embodied in such a criminology. But this is a moral philosophy and a criminology of consequence, affecting the lives of whole populations. Conservative criminology has guided much of criminological thought and criminal justice over the last thirty years.

When it comes to moral philosophy, one cannot be impartial or relativistic. There are choices to be made, and these choices are translated into a particular criminology. In other words, we begin our inquiries with an implicit moral philosophy, and we advance a particular understanding of crime. This is what makes criminology a vital and relevant field of inquiry and practice.

Social Construction of Reality

The social constructionist perspective assumes that reality—our perception of reality—is a mental construction rather than a direct apprehension of the world. The social constructionist is interested not in the correspondence between "objective reality" and observation, but in the utility of observations in understanding our own multiple, subjective realities.

The constructs of the social scientist are thus founded upon the world created by social actors. Alfred Schutz conceptualized the problem: "The constructs of the social sciences are, so to speak, constructs of the second degree, that is constructs of constructs made by the actors on the social scene, whose behavior the social scientist has to observe and explain in accordance with the procedural rules of his science" (Schutz 1963, 242). The world that is important to the social constructionist is the one created by human beings in interaction and communication with others. The *social reality* involves the social meanings and the products of the subjective world of everyday life (Berger and Luckmann 1966).

The social constructive mode of inquiry is a major advance over positivist thought in the crucial area of reflexivity. The social constructionist questions the process by which we know, instead of taking it for granted. The observer reflects upon the act of observation, using to advantage the social and personal character of observation.

It is often necessary to revise or reject the world as some social actors conceive it. Social constructionists give us the beginnings for examining multiple versions of reality, allowing us to transcend the official reality and, ultimately, our current existence. But they do not provide a yardstick for determining whether one reality is better than another.

The social constructionist perspective, however, has given new vitality to the study of crime. Departing significantly from positivist studies, social constructionists have exposed the problematic nature of legal order. Crime and other stigmatized behaviors are examined as categories created and imposed upon some persons by others (Becker 1963). Crime exists because the society constructs and applies the label of *crime*. Criminal law, too, is not separate from society, but is itself a construction, created by those who are in power. The administration of justice is a human social activity that is constructed as various legal agents interpret and impose their order on those they select for processing. The social reality of crime is thus a process whereby conceptions of crime are constructed, criminal laws are established and administered, and behaviors are developed in relation to these definitions of crime (Quinney 1970).

Judeo-Christian Theology and Prophetic Criticism

The roots of our contemporary world, in spite of secularity, are firmly anchored in the Judeo-Christian understanding of human existence and fulfillment. We have an image of our essential nature and the possibilities for our human existence. This essence, however, has become separated from the conditions of this world, contradicted by human existence. The separation between reality and essence can be overcome only by human action through the creative power of redemption. The modern historical consciousness, in other words, is derived from the historical thinking of the Judeo-Christian prophetic tradition (Quinney 1980b, 102–15).

Deeply rooted in the prophetic religious tradition is the urge toward justice in human affairs. This urge is seen as the will of divine origin operating in history, providing the source of inspiration to all prophets and revolutionaries. The identification of religion with political economy can be seen in the Hebrew prophets, who looked on all history as the divine law in human life. The highly ethical religion of the Old Testament prophets and the New Testament Jesus sees human society from the perspective of a holy and just God who forgives human beings, but also judges them. The prophetic soul is hopeful and optimistic in the "confidence that God will form a better society out of the ashes of the present world" (Dombrowski 1936, 26). The future in this world is built on the prophetic impulse that transcends this world.

Our prophetic heritage perceives the driving force of history as being the struggle between justice and injustice. We the people—in a covenant with God—are responsible for the character of our lives and our society, for the pursuit of righteousness, justice, and mercy. The social and moral order is consequently rooted in the divine commandments; morality rests on divine command and concern.

Prophecy thus proclaims the divine concern for justice. The idea and belief that "God is justice" means the divine support and guidance for such human matters as the critique of conventional wisdom, the humanization of work, the democratization and socialization of the economy, and the elimination of all forms of oppression (Soelle 1976). Material issues are conceived in terms of the transcendent, adding the necessary element that is missing in a strictly materialist (including Marxist) analysis. Prophetic justice is both sociological and theological. In fact, the dialectic of the theological and the sociological gives the prophetic its power as a critique and an understanding of human society.

To the prophets of the Old Testament, injustice (whether in the form of crime and corruption or in the wretched condition of the poor) is not merely an injury to the welfare of the people but a threat to existence. Moral comprehension, in other words, is rooted in the depth of the divine. This sense of justice, which goes far beyond our modern liberal and legal notions of justice, is founded on the understanding that oppression on earth is an affront to God. Righteousness is not simply a value for the prophet; it is, as Abraham J. Heschel observes, "God's part of human life, God's stake in human history" (1962, vol. 1, 198). The relation between human life and the divine is at stake when injustice occurs. Justice is more than a normative idea; it is charged with transcendent power of the infinite and the eternal, with the essence of divine revelation.

For the prophets, justice is a mighty stream, not merely a category or mechanical process. "The moralists discuss, suggest, counsel; the prophets proclaim, demand, insist" (Heschel, vol. 1, 215). Prophetic justice is charged with the urgency of the divine presence in the world.

Let justice roll down like waters,

And righteousness like a mighty stream. (Amos 5:24)

In Heschel's phrase, "What ought to be, shall be!" Prophetic justice has a sense of urgency and depth.

According to the prophetic view, justice—or the lack of it—is a condition of the whole people. An individual's act expresses the moral state of the many.

Above all, the prophets remind us of the moral state of a people: Few are guilty, but all are responsible. If we admit that the individual is in some measure conditioned or affected by the spirit of society, an individual's crime discloses society's corruption. In a community not indifferent to suffering, uncompromisingly impatient with cruelty and falsehood, continually concerned for God and every man, crime would be infrequent rather than common (Heschel, vol. 1, 16).

Prophecy is directed to the whole world as well as to the inner spirit of the individual. And the purpose of prophecy—and of prophetic justice—is to revolutionize history.

We live in an era that tends to reject the claims of a religion-based prophetic theology. Heschel notes that "owing to a bias against any experience that eludes scientific inquiry, the claim of the prophets to divine inspiration was, as we have seen, a priori rejected" (vol. 2, 192). A scientific rationality based entirely on empirical observation of this world excludes the prophetic critique of our existential estrangement from essence. History and its concrete conditions, accordingly, are bound solely by time; there is little that would guide us beyond the mortality of our earthly selves. Which also means that an evaluation and judgment of our current situation are bound by the particular historical consciousness that comprehends nothing beyond itself. Not only have we silenced God, we have silenced ourselves before our own history.

The prophetic meaning of justice is in sharp contrast to the capitalist notion of justice. Distinct from capitalist justice, with its emphasis on human manipulation and control, prophetic justice is a form of address that calls human beings to an awareness of their historical responsibility and challenges them to act in ways that will change the existing human condition. Human fulfillment is found in the exercise of moral will in the struggle for historical future. The pessimistic character of a deterministic and predictive materialism is overcome in the prophetic hope for a humane and spiritually filled existence.

The prophetic tradition, present also in the prophetic voice of Marxism (although in secular terms), can transform the world and open the future. Marxism and theology confront each other in ways that allow us to understand our existence and consider our essential nature. The human situation, no longer completely bound by time, is "elevated into the eternal and the eternal becomes effective in the realm of time" (Tillich 1971, 91).

Marxist Analysis and Social Justice

The classic dichotomy about the meaning of justice dominates the discourse of contemporary social science and ethics (Quinney 1980a, 1–37). The dichotomy is found in the debate between Socrates and Thrasymachus chronicled by Plato in the first book of the *Republic*. When the question "What is justice?" is posed, Thrasymachus responds that "justice is the interest of the stronger," elaborating that what is regarded as just in a society is determined by the ruling elite acting in its own interest (Pitkin 1972, 169–192). Later Socrates gives his formulation of justice as "everyone having and doing what is appropriate to him," that is, people trying to do the right thing.

Thrasymachus and Socrates are talking about two different problems. Whereas Thrasymachus is giving us a factual description of how justice actually operates, Socrates is telling us about what people think they are doing when they attend to that which is called "justice." There is justice as an ideal of goodness and justice in practice in everyday life. Justice as officially practiced in contemporary society is the justice of the capitalist state, and capitalist justice partakes of both the ideal and the practical. The question for us, then, given a Marxist understanding of the class and state character of capitalist justice, is, "How do we attend to correct action and the creation of a better life?"

The general concept of justice serves the larger purpose of providing a standard by which we judge concrete actions. We reflect critically upon the actions of the capitalist state, including the administration of criminal justice, because we have an idea of how things could be. Critical thought and its consequent actions are made possible because we transcend the conventional ideology of capitalism. Because we have a notion of something else, we refuse to accept capitalist justice either in theory or in practice. Critical thought, as Hannah Arendt (1971) has noted, allows us to interrupt all ordinary activity, entering into a different existence: "Thinking, the quest for meaning—rather than the scientist's thirst for knowledge for its own sake—can be felt to be 'unnatural,' as though men, when they begin to think, engage in some activity contrary to the human condition" (424). In talking and thinking about how things *could be*, we engage in thoughts and actions directed to the realization of a different life. Arendt adds that only with the desiring love of wisdom, beauty, and the like are we prepared with a kind of life that promotes a moral existence. Only when we are filled with what Socrates called *eros*, a love that desires what is not, do we attempt to find what is good. Thinking and acting critically is thus political. In a collective effort, we change our form of life and alter the mode of social existence.

If any body of thought has a notion of truth and beauty, of how things could be, it is that of Marxism. In fact, Marxism is the philosophy of our time that takes as its primary focus the oppression inherent in capitalist society. Marxist analysis is historically specific and locates contemporary problems in the existing political economy. Marxist theory provides, most important, a form of thought that allows us to transcend, in theory and in practice, the oppression of the capitalist order.

Marx avoided the use of a justice terminology (McBride 1975; Wood 1972), steering away from justice-talk because he regarded it as "ideological twaddle," detracting from a critical analysis of the capitalist system as a whole. Both Marx and Engels were in fact highly critical of the use of the justice notion as a means of mystifying the actual operation of capitalism. At the same time, they found a way to understand capitalism critically that carried with it a condemnation that goes beyond any legalistic notion of justice. Thus, Marxist analysis provides us with an understanding of the capitalist system, a vision of a different world, and a political life in struggling for that society.

According to Marx and Engels, the problem with the concept of justice, as it is used in capitalist society, is that it is fundamentally a *juridical* or legal concept. As such, the concept is restricted to rational standards by which laws, social institutions, and human actions are judged. This restricted analysis fails to grasp the material conditions of society. For Marx, society is to be understood in terms of productive forces and relations, with the state as an expression of the prevailing mode of production (Marx 1970, 19–23). To focus on the juridical nature of social reality is to misunderstand the material basis of reality. An analysis limited to legalistic questions of justice systematically excludes the important questions about capitalist society.

The critique of capitalism for Marx is provided in the very form of the capitalist system. Capitalism rests on the appropriation of labor power from the working class. Capital is accumulated by the capitalist class in the course of underpaying the workers for products made by their labor. The capitalist mode of production depends on "surplus value," on unpaid labor. Capitalism itself is a system of exploitation. The servitude of the wage laborer to capital is essential to the capitalist mode of production. Marx's condemnation of capitalism and the need for revolutionary action is based on the innate character of capitalism, on an understanding of capitalism as a whole and on its position in human history.

We have thus moved out of the classical dichotomy between value and fact. In a Marxist analysis, value and fact are integrated into a comprehensive scheme. Values are always attached to what we take to be facts, and facts cannot exist apart from values. In a Marxist analysis, the description of social reality is at the same time an evaluation. Nothing is "morally neutral" in such an understanding. The description contains within itself its own condemnation and, moreover, a call to do something about the condition. The critique is at once a description of the condition and the possibility for transforming it. All things exist in relation to one another—are one with the other.

The critical sense of justice will not disappear from philosophical and everyday discourse. That the terms "justice" and "social justice" continue to move us is an expression of their innate ability to join our present condition with an ultimate future.

Buddhism and the Way of Awareness

There is a mode of inquiry that assumes the critical mode but ultimately goes beyond it. This is the way of awareness (Quinney 1988, 1991). The way of awareness is essentially critical in that it sees things as they actually are, yet it goes beyond the critical mode of thought in its meditative character, requiring a quieting of the mind and an opening of the heart. Correct thought and action come out of such awareness. The way of awareness is the appropriate mode for the developing peace and social justice perspective in criminology.

Critical thought, especially as manifested in the way of awareness, seeks to avoid the personal and social consequences of what modern science labels as "objective" and "rational." For, as one humanistic philosopher has noted (Skolimowski 1986), the mind trained in such science "over a number of years becomes cold, dry, uncaring, always atomized, cutting, analyzing. This kind of mind has lost the capacity for empathy, compassion, love" (306). The "objective" mode of thinking affects the way people live and in the meantime prevents them from getting any closer to understanding. The way of awareness seeks a mind that, instead of producing conflict and violence, heals—a compassionate mind rather than an objective mind.

We humans—and this is what especially makes us human—have constructed webs of significance within which we have suspended ourselves. The *Dhammapada* (1936), the ancient text of Buddhism, thus states, "All that we are is a result of what we have thought" (p. 3). It is our human nature not only to be suspended in webs of significance but to try to understand them, to search for their meaning. We attempt to remove ourselves from the world of everyday life in order to understand it in a new light. The human mind is a busy and insatiable creation, craving always what is not.

Thus we come to the realization that rational thought alone cannot answer the important existential questions of being human, of being human in relation to the whole world. Cultivation of the vital energy of the universe, rather than mere intellectual speculation, is the way to self-realization and to an understanding of our shared existence. The way is simple, perhaps too simple and accessible for the rational, complex academic mind to comprehend readily.

Without awareness—without mindfulness—we are unknowingly attached to our thoughts, taking these productions to be reality itself. Many of our concepts are so deeply ingrained in our minds, in our culture, and in our education that we forget that they completely condition our perceptions of reality. In unconscious attachment to these mental productions, we are chained in the cave, observing merely the shadows of appearance on the walls before us. Awareness is a breaking of the chains of conditioned thought and a viewing of reality beyond the shadows. With awareness, we use concepts without being a slave to them, knowing that they convey a conventional reality.

We begin by being aware of the ways in which suffering is manifested. Our responsibility is to do what we can to alleviate the concrete conditions of human suffering. "We work to provide food for the hungry, shelter for the homeless, health care for the sick and feeble, protection for the threatened and vulnerable, schooling for the uneducated, freedom for the oppressed" (Dass and Gorman 1985, 87). When we acknowledge *what is* and act as witnesses in this shared reality, without attachment and judgment, we open ourselves to all suffering. Acting out of compassion, without thinking of ourselves as doers, we are witnesses to what must be done.

As long as there is suffering in the world, each of us suffers. We cannot end our suffering without ending the suffering of all others. In being witnesses to the concrete reality and in attempting to heal the separation between ourselves and true being (the ground of all existence), we necessarily suffer with all others. But now we are fully aware of the suffering and realize how it can be eliminated. With awareness and compassion, we are ready to act.

Awareness places us in the proper position to know the world, to pursue *a criminology with awareness*. Ultimately, only through awareness—beyond conditioned thought—can we understand reality as it truly is. We then begin to live in a way that takes us beyond the problems of contemporary existence, beyond the problem of crime. We would not leave society, not withdraw from fellowship with others; rather, we would renounce the appearances of reality in order to live a life of love and compassion and union with all beings. We would be part of the process of creating a world without crime.

Socialist Humanism and Peacemaking Criminology

Social action comes out of the informed heart, out of the clear and enlightened mind. We act with an understanding of our own suffering and the suffering of others. If human actions are not rooted in compassion, these actions will not contribute to a compassionate and peaceful world. "If we cannot move beyond inner discord, how can we help find a way to social harmony? If we ourselves cannot know peace, be peaceful, how will our acts disarm hatred and violence?" (Dass and Gorman 1985, 185). The means cannot be different from the ends; peace can come only out of peace. "There is no way to peace," said A. J. Muste (1942). "Peace is the way."

As in Mahatma Gandhi's *satyagraha*, the truth is revealed in the course of action. In turn, it is truth as presently conceived that guides our action. Gandhi's Hindu- and Jainist-based concept of *satyagraha* was derived from the Sanskrit word *Sat* for "it is" or "what is," things as they are. *Graha* is "to grasp," to be firm. "Truth force" is the common translation of *satyagraha*. Gandhi often spoke of his inner voice, a still small voice that would be revealed in the preparedness of silence (Erikson 1969, 410–23).

Truthful action, for Gandhi, was guided by the idea of *ahisma*, the refusal to do harm. Oppression of all kinds is to be actively resisted, but without causing harm to others. In *An Autobiography: The Story of My Experiments with Truth* (1957), Gandhi describes ahisma as the refusal to do harm (p. 349). Moreover, compassion and self-restraint grow in the effort not to harm.

Gandhi's insistence upon the truth is firmly within the tradition of socialist humanism. As Kevin Anderson (1991) has shown in his essay on Gandhian and Marxist humanism, both are radical rejections of Western capitalist civilization (pp. 14–29). Both posit a future society free of alienation, and both share a confidence that human liberation is on the immediate historical agenda. In reconstructing criminology, we are informed by a socialist humanism (Quinney 1995).

In his 1965 collection of essays, *Socialist Humanism*, Erich Fromm included an essay on Gandhi by the Gandhian scholar and former secretary to Gandhi, N. K. Bose. In this essay, titled "Gandhi: Humanist and Socialist," Bose (1965) describes the *satyagrahi*, the one who practices *satyagraha*, as a person who lives "according to his own lights," one who opposes (does not cooperate with) what seems wrong, but also one who "attempts to accept whatever may be right and just" in the view of the opponent. Bose continues: "There is neither victory nor defeat, but an agreement to which both parties willingly subscribe, while institutions or practices proven wrong are destroyed during the conflict" (p. 99). A humane society is created in the course of individual and collective struggle.

To be remembered, all the while, is the single objective of peace. Whatever the technique, whatever the philosophy or theory, the movement toward peace is the only true test of any thought or action. Erich Fromm spent a lifetime working in the movements for peace. He was a cofounder of SANE, an organization that sought to end the nuclear race and the war in Vietnam. Late in his life, Fromm worked on behalf of the 1968 presidential nomination campaign of Senator Eugene McCarthy. During the campaign, Fromm (1994) wrote: "America stands today at the crossroads: It can go in the direction of continued war and violence, and further bureaucratization and automatization of man, or it can go in the direction of life, peace, and political and spiritual renewal." His call was to "walk the way toward life" (p. 96).

Our response to all that is human is for life, not death. What would a Gandhian philosophy of existence offer a criminologist, or any member of society, in reaction to crime? To work for the creation of a new society, certainly. But, immediately, the reaction would be neither one of hate for the offender nor a cry for punishment and death. Punishment is not the way of peace. In a reading of Gandhi and a commentary on punishment, Erik Erikson writes the following:

Gandhi reminds us that, since we can not possibly know the absolute truth, we are "therefore not competent to punish"—a most essential reminder, since man when tempted to violence always parades as another's policeman, convincing himself that whatever he is doing to another, that other "has it coming to him." Whoever acts on such righteousness, however, implicates himself in a mixture of pride and guilt which undermines his position psychologically and ethically. Against this typical cycle, Gandhi claimed that only the voluntary acceptance of self-suffering can reveal the truth latent in a conflict—and in the opponent. (1969, 412–13)

Responses to crime that are fueled by hate rather than generated by love are necessarily punitive. Such responses are a form of violence that can beget further violence. Much of what is called "criminal justice" is a violent reaction to or anticipation of crime. The criminal justice system, with all of its procedures, is a form of *negative peace*, its purpose being to deter or process acts of crime through the threat and application of force.

Positive peace, on the other hand, is something other than the deterrence or punishment of crime. Positive peace is more than merely the absence of crime and violence—and of war. "It refers to a condition of society in which exploitation is minimized or eliminated altogether, and in which there is neither overt violence nor the more subtle phenomenon of structural violence" (Barash 1991, 8). Positive peace demands that attention be given to all those things, most of them structured in the society, that cause crime, that happen before crime occurs. Positive peace exists when the sources of crime—including poverty, inequality, racism, and alienation—are not present. There can be no peace—no positive peace—without social justice. Without social justice and without peace (personal and social), there is crime. And there is as well the violence of criminal justice.

The negative peacemaking of criminal justice keeps things as they are. Social policies and programs that are positive in nature—that focus on positive peacemaking—create something new. They eliminate the structural sources of violence and crime. A critical, peacemaking criminology is a form of positive peace.

Socialist humanism gives attention to everyday existence, to love and compassion, and to social justice. Its efforts are exerted not so much out of resistance, as in an affirmation of what we know about human existence. The way is simply that of peace in everyday life.

CRIMINOLOGIST AS WITNESS

Upon reviewing the preceding account, I am struck by the apocalyptic vision embodied in much of Western moral philosophy—the notion that there is an ultimate destiny, that history is moving in the direction of fulfillment, and that the better world, the new kingdom, will come with the catastrophic collapse of the old order. Such a notion provides an imperative to make a better world, but at the same time promotes a judgment that impedes the humane living of daily life.

In contrast, Eastern thought, Buddhism particularly, identifies historical change with increasing individual awareness. As individuals transform their limited selves into an identification with the larger world, a more compassionate and humane existence is created. In our own Western version of this mode of thought, existentialism, the focus is on the living of everyday life. If attention is given to everyday life, the result cannot be other than the creation of a better world. Criminology, as moral philosophy, cannot help but be a part of the major thoughts and trends of the age.

But now I need to return to my thesis that criminology is, in addition to anything else, a stance for the witnessing of contemporary history. Being witnesses, we criminologists occupy an important place in this history. What is more, witnessing is an active endeavor, not a passive observation. The criminologist is witness to the important events of the time—the atrocities, the injustices, the many forms of violence, and the sufferings of many people. The idea—the reality—that the witness is an engaged participant apparently needs to be elaborated. Our current sensibility posits action in a limited and materialistic way. I make the case that bearing witness is active participation in the ultimate sense.

Criminologists, for instruction on the bearing of witness, can become familiar with the many kinds of witnessing that are evident in a host of sources. Journalists, photographers, artists, social scientists, and many other writers report the sufferings throughout the world. For example, there are recent books on bearing witness to the Holocaust (Feingold 1995), to sexual abuse (Morris 1994), to AIDS (Kayal 1993), and to the atrocities that took place in the course of Yugoslavia's disintegration (Rohde 1997). There are the many books by photographers who have documented various aspects of the human condition (Blom 1984; Godlin 1996; Modotti 1995; Richards 1994; Salgado 1993; Vishiac 1993; Yamahata 1995).

Begin now to read the books by social scientists in the light of being a witness. Your list will rapidly develop, and you will appreciate both new and older works in a new way. Then begin to see your own work—written or otherwise—as the work of bearing witness. You may even begin to consider anew what is to be done as a witness in our times—a witness to our sufferings and to our joys.

The witness, obviously, is not a neutral observer, as the rigid materialist dichotomy of active agent and passive observer might suggest. The witness first has to be where the suffering is taking place. Once there, the witness is moved by conscience to observe and to make the report. An Armenian poet (Siamanto 1996) writes of the German woman who witnessed a mass killing nearly a century ago:

This thing I'm telling you about,
I saw with my own eyes.
From my window of hell
I clenched my teeth
and watched the town of Bardez turn
into a heap of ashes. (Siamanto 1996, 41)

Even in the quiet of the monastery, witness is being borne. Alexander Pushkin, in his story "Boris Godunov," written in verse form and completed in 1825, has the monk Primen speak of his witnessing the history of Czarist Russia. Writing by lamplight (as can be seen in Mussorgsky's opera), Primen makes a final entry (Pushkin 1918):

One more, the final record, and my annals
Are ended, and fulfilled the duty laid
By God on me a sinner. Not in vain
Hath God appointed me for many years
A witness, teaching me the art of letters;
A day will come when some laborious monk
Will bring to light my zealous, nameless toil,
Kindle, as I, his lamp, and from the parchment
Shaking the dust of ages will transcribe
My true narrations. (p. 14)

As the last lines portend, someday the report will be found, and perhaps it will be valued and of use. But even in witnessing, one cannot hope for anything beyond the act of witnessing. As the ancient Vedic text instructs in the *Bhagavad Gita* (1985, 334–36), do not to the results be attached. We are to get on with what is to be done, following the conscience of the witness.

All of this is to illustrate, and to argue, that witnessing is itself an act. The witness is appropriately placed—makes certain to be in the right place at the right time—and actively observes and (oftentimes) records and reports what is being witnessed. If other actions more physical in nature follow, they follow because first there has been the witnessing. Without prior witnessing, there will be no subsequent action that is wise and appropriate. Witnesses act with clarity and purpose because they have the awareness and conscience of a witness. Ready and with open mind, the witness truly sees what is happening and knows that further action is to be taken. Without witnessing, any action is unfocused, confused, and little more than a chasing of the wind.

There is plenty for the criminologist to witness. Make your own list of what we as criminologists should be witnessing. My own current witnessing is to the kinds of suffering and violence that are a systematic and structured part of contemporary existence. In fact, the largest portion of violence is structured and is generated by or committed by governments, corporations, the military, and agents of the law.

The war at home is against the poor. It is a war waged to maintain inequality so that the rich can maintain their position. Whole populations are being held hostage in poverty, sickness, addiction, and brutality against one another, and they remain unemployed (and underemployed) and uneducated. Prisons are overflowing, and prison construction and operation are growing industries. The rich not only create the war to secure their position but also profit from the war. In our own nonviolent actions and protests, founded on witnessing, we take our stand. Which side you are on is still the relevant question.

Directly associated with the war on the poor, the war to keep a minority of the population rich, is capital punishment. The death penalty—state-sponsored murder—is the final resort of a violent and greedy minority. That so many, the majority of the population when polled, support the practice of capital punishment is all the more reason that witnesses (criminologists) are needed to expose, to analyze, to protest, to bear witness. Someday, I am certain, historians will note that the United States was one of the last nations to continue to violate the most basic of human rights, the right to life. It was one of the last nations to systematically violate the rights of its own citizens.

In a critical essay titled "Reflections on the Guillotine," Albert Camus (1960) presented and discussed the many reasons offered for capital punishment and provided rationale for abolishing it. Capital punishment is useless and harmful, he noted, and besmirches the society that uses it. He wrote, "It is a penalty, to be sure, a frightful torture, both physical and moral, but it provides no sure example except a demoralizing one. It punishes, but it forestalls nothing; indeed, it may even arouse the impulse to murder" (p. 197). It is time to realize that there is no longer any defense for the death penalty. What is needed to achieve the abolition of capital punishment is a change in heart and mind, a spiritual and mental change.

I am certain capital punishment will eventually be abolished, but only when those who seemingly benefit from capital punishment, the minority known simply as the rich and the powerful, have lost their authority, have lost at least their authority to deny the basic human right of life.

As criminologists for the abolition of the death penalty, we are witnesses to life itself and are a part of the movement to abolish capital punishment. For years, many criminologists have been arguing for the abolition of the death penalty (Bohm 1991; Radelet 1989; Zimring and Hawkins 1986). We will continue to be witnesses to capital punishment until it is abolished. We cannot do otherwise.

To conclude my essay: Everything we do as criminologists is grounded in a moral philosophy. Whatever we think and do, our criminology is the advancement of one moral philosophy or another. And each moral philosophy generates its own kind of witnessing—in the events to be witnessed and in the form of the witnessing. The work in criminology that is historically important is the work that is informed by a moral philosophy. As witnesses, we are on the side of life. A reverence for all life. Such is the way of peace.

NOTE

This chapter is a revision of an article published in *Contemporary Justice Review* 1: 2, 3 (1998): 347–364.

REFERENCES

Anderson, Kevin. "Radical Criminology and the Overcoming of Alienation: Perspectives from Marxian and Gandhian Humanism." In Harold E. Pepinsky and Richard Quinney (eds.), *Criminology as Peacemaking*. Bloomington: Indiana University Press, 1991, pp. 14–29.

Arendt, Hannah. "Thinking and Moral Considerations." *Social Research* 38 (Autumn 1971): 417–446.

Barash, David P. *Introduction to Peace Studies*. Belmont, CA: Wadsworth, 1991.

Becker, Howard. *Outsiders: Studies in the Sociology of Deviance*. New York: Free Press, 1963.

Berger, Peter L., and Thomas Luckmann. *The Social Construction of Reality*. Garden City, NY: Doubleday, 1966.

The Bhagavad Gita. Translated by Eknath Easwaran. Petaluma: Nilgiri Press, 1985.

Blom, Gertrude. *Gertrude Blom—Bearing Witness*, ed. by Alex Harris and Margaret Sartor. Chapel Hill: University of North Carolina Press, 1984.

Bohm, Robert M., ed. *The Death Penalty in America: Current Research*. Cincinnati: Anderson, 1991.

Bonhoeffer, Dietrich. *Letters and Papers from Prison*, ed. by Eberhard Bethage. New York: Macmillan, 1971.

Bose, Nirmal Kuman. "Gandhi: Humanist and Socialist." In Erich Fromm (ed.), *Socialist Humanism*. Garden City, NY: Doubleday, 1965, pp. 98–106.

Camus, Albert. "Reflections on the Guillotine." *Resistance, Rebellion, and Death*, translated by Justin O'Brien. New York: Random House, 1960, pp. 175–234.

Dass, Ram, and Paul Gorman. *How Can I Help? Stories and Reflections on Service*. New York: Alfred A. Knopf, 1985.

The Dhammapada. Translated by Irving Babbitt. New York: New Directions, 1936.

Dombrowski, James. *The Early Days of Christian Socialism in America*. New York: Columbia University Press, 1936.

Erikson, Erik H. *Gandhi's Truth: On the Origins of Militant Nonviolence*. New York: W.W. Norton, 1969.

Feingold, Henry L. *Bearing Witness: How America and Its Jews Responded to the Holocaust*. Syracuse: Syracuse University Press, 1995.

Fromm, Erich. *On Being Human*. New York: Continuum, 1994.

Gandhi, Mohandas K. *An Autobiography: The Story of My Experiments with Truth.* Translated by Mahedeu Desai. Boston: Beacon Press, 1957.

Goldin, Nan. *I'll Be Your Mirror.* Zurick: Scalo Verlag, 1996.

Heschel, Abraham J. *The Prophets,* vols. 1 and 2. New York: Harper and Row, 1962.

Kayal, Philip M. *Bearing Witness: Gay Men's Health Crisis and the Politics of AIDS.* Boulder, CO: Westview, 1993.

McBride, William Leon. "The Concept of Justice in Marx, Engels, and Others." *Ethics* 85 (April 1975): 204–218.

Marx, Karl. *A Contribution to the Critique of Political Economy,* ed. by Maurice Dobb. New York: International Publishers, 1970.

Modotti, Tina. *Tina Modotti: Photographs,* ed. by Sarah M. Lowe. New York: Harry N. Abrams, 1995.

Morris, Celia. *Bearing Witness: Sexual Harassment and Beyond—Every Woman's Story.* Boston: Little, Brown, 1994.

Muste, A. J. *The World Task of Pacifism.* Wallingford, PA: Pendle Hill, 1942.

Pitkin, Hanna F. *Wittgenstein and Justice.* Berkeley: University of California Press, 1972.

Pushkin, Alexander. *Boris Godunov,* translated by Alfred Hayes. New York: Dutton, 1918.

Quinney, Richard. *The Social Reality of Crime.* Boston: Little, Brown, 1970.

———. *Class, State, and Crime,* 2d ed. New York: Longman, 1980.

———. *Providence: The Reconstruction of Social and Moral Order.* New York: Longman, 1980.

———. "Beyond the Interpretive: The Way of Awareness." *Sociological Inquiry* 58 (Winter 1988): 101–116.

———. "The Way of Peace: On Crime, Suffering and Service." In Harold E. Pepinsky and Richard Quinney (eds.), *Criminology as Peacemaking.* Bloomington: Indiana University Press, 1991, pp. 3–13.

———. "Socialist Humanism and the Problem of Crime: Thinking about Erich Fromm in the Development of Critical/Peacemaking Criminology." *Crime, Law and Social Change* 23 (November 2, 1995): 147–156.

Radelet, Michael L., ed. *Facing the Death Penalty: Essays on a Cruel and Unusual Punishment.* Philadelphia: Temple University Press, 1989.

Richards, Eugene. *Cocaine True, Cocaine Blue.* New York: Aperature, 1994.

Rohde, David. *Endgame: The Betrayal and Fall of Srebrenica: Europe's Worst Massacre Since World War II.* New York: Farrar, Strauss and Giroux, 1997.

Salgado, Sebastiao. *Workers.* New York: Aperature, 1993.

Schutz, Alfred. "Concept and Theory Formations in the Social Sciences." In Maurice Nathanson (ed.), *Philosophy of the Social Sciences.* New York: Random House, 1963, pp. 231–249.

Siamanto. *Bloody News from My Friend,* translated by Peter Balakian and Nevart Yaghlian. Detroit: Wayne State University, 1996.

Skolimowski, Henry. "Life, Entropy and Education." *American Theosophist* 74 (October 1986): 304–310.

Soelle, Dorothee. "Review of *Marx and the Bible* by Jose Miranda," *Union Seminary Quarterly Review* 32 (Fall 1976): 49–53.

Tillich, Paul. *Political Expectation.* New York: Harper and Row, 1971.

Vishiac, Roman. *To Give Them Light: The Legacy of Roman Vishiac,* ed. by Marion Wiesel. New York: Simon and Schuster, 1993.

Wood, Allen W. "The Marxian Critique of Justice." *Philosophy and Public Affairs* 1 (Spring 1972): 244–282.

Yamahata, Yosuke. *Nagasaki Journey: The Photographs of Yosuke Yamahata*, ed. by Rupurt Jenkins. San Francisco: Pomegranate, 1995.

Zimring, Franklin, and Gordon Hawkins. *Capital Punishment and the American Agenda.* Cambridge: Cambridge University Press, 1986.

15

Affirmative Action and the Criminal Law

Paul Butler

No one understands that surviving the impossible is sposed to accentuate
the positive aspects of a people.

Ntozake Shange[1]

When one black man graduates from college for every 100 who go to jail,
we still need affirmative action.

Colin Powell[2]

INTRODUCTION

Why are more than half of the men in state and federal prisons African American?[3] Why are almost half of the women in state prisons African American?[4]
Why are more than one in three young African-American men under criminal
supervision?[5]

Perhaps the problem is related to others:

Why is African-American academic performance worse than that of whites?[6]

Why can't many minorities get promoted to senior management positions or
win government contracts?[7]

Why aren't there more minorities in Congress?[8]

If these problems are related, perhaps the legal and public policy responses to
them should be coordinated.

Affirmative action has been one response to several of the aforementioned
problems.[9] It is a remedy that has enjoyed reasonable success.[10] However, in addressing the problems of African Americans, affirmative action largely has been
limited to the contexts of education, employment, and voting. Affirmative action has ignored one of the most troubling disparities between the white majority and the black minority in the United States. The purpose of this chapter
is to make the case for affirmative action in criminal law.[11]

In the criminal justice system, as in civil law, there is tension between the ideal
of formal equality and the reality of white supremacy, historic and present. In

civil law, one response has been to give preferences to victims of white supremacy in the distribution of benefits like education and employment. The legality and morality of race preferences rests on the assumption that white supremacy is the direct or indirect cause of substandard minority achievement. I agree and, in this chapter, I extend that assumption to crime and punishment. I argue that but for the fruits of slavery and entrenched racism, African Americans would not find themselves disproportionately represented in the criminal justice system. It is important for the law to recognize that there are so many African Americans in prison because white people have driven them there. Justice requires thoughtfulness about how race matters in the punishment of black people in the United States.

I recommend six proposals for affirmative action in criminal law, which I discuss at the end of this chapter. I suggest that retribution shall not justify punishment of African-American criminals, and that rehabilitation must be the primary justification for their punishment. I recommend that black criminal defendants have majority black juries that are authorized to sentence them. I propose that black people not be sentenced to death for interracial homicide. I recommend that African Americans be arrested, tried, and sentenced for drug crimes only in proportion to their actual commission of those crimes. Finally, I urge, as a goal for the year 2000, a prison population that more accurately reflects the racial diversity of America.

Affirmative action in criminal law is not as radical a proposition as it may initially seem. Within the criminal justice system, some criminal procedures are race conscious; some criminal procedures, moreover, reflect non-racial fairness preferences even when such preferences defeat formal notions of equality. Using affirmative action to correct race-based injuries suffered by African Americans would be consistent with the policies that underlie these procedures.

Legal and popular rhetoric against affirmative action embraces color blindness, apparently at all costs. The liberal response to critics of affirmative action is summed up in Justice Blackmun's famous aphorism: "[I]n order to get beyond racism we must first take account of race. There is no other way. To treat some persons equally, we must treat them differently."[12] People who oppose affirmative action in civil law are not likely to embrace it in criminal law. Thus, my argument will engage mainly those who lean toward affirmative action. But it may be that this reader's reaction to the extension of the policy to criminal law reveals the truth of another aphorism: a conservative is a liberal who has been mugged. I hope to demonstrate that there is no logical argument for limiting racial preferences to some victims of white supremacy, while excluding the most dangerous and pathetic victims: black criminals.[13]

Some well-meaning people think about affirmative action the way they think about abortion: allowing it may be good public policy, but the mechanics of the process are discomforting. In arguing for the extension of affirmative action to criminal law, I hope to force people to rethink the general policies that motivate racial preferences.[14] I believe this concept of justice for the oppressed can survive close scrutiny and indeed will emerge stronger.

The second part of this chapter defines affirmative action and describes its legal and moral justifications in civil law. The next part questions whether those justifications apply to criminal law and concludes that they do. The following part explores two aspects of criminal justice that pave the way for race-based affirmative action: first, lawful considerations of race in the administration of justice and, second, fairness preferences for some non-racial groups, including rape victims and death-sentenced persons. Next, the chapter makes a constitutional argument for affirmative action in criminal law, and the last part proposes six race-conscious remedies that would improve criminal justice.

WHAT IS AFFIRMATIVE ACTION?

Affirmative action extends systemic racial preferences to minorities in the allocation of government and private resources like education and employment.[15] It is official prejudice based on one's membership in a racial minority group. Proponents of affirmative action sometimes try to obscure the truth that affirmative action is race bias; they argue instead that it is a method of choosing between qualified competitors. Even under that view, however, affirmative action favors membership in a particular racial group; minority status becomes a precondition for a benefit.[16]

Perhaps some advocates of affirmative action run away from this "raced" truth because it seems "un-American" to them.[17] "Color blindness" seems to be the American ideal, even though this concept made its first appearance in constitutional analysis barely 100 years ago, in Justice Harlan's dissent in *Plessy v. Ferguson*.[18] Tension exists, however, between this ideal and the ideal that there be no racial castes in America. In fact, Justice Harlan's dissent implicitly demonstrates this tension; Harlan made the case for color blindness by appealing to the ideology of white supremacy. Justice Harlan wrote:

The white race deems itself to be the dominant race in this country. And so it is, in prestige, in achievements, in education, in wealth, and in power. So, I doubt not, it will continue to be for all time, if it remains true to its great heritage, and holds fast to principles of constitutional liberty. . . . There is no caste here. Our constitution is color-blind, and neither knows nor tolerates classes among citizens.[19]

This historical understanding that color blindness will perpetuate the dominance of the white race is a powerful argument for affirmative action.[20] Unlike color blindness, race preferences offer people of color a path toward their advancement.

The three most common moral justifications for affirmative action are first, that it is a necessary compensation for past discrimination;[21] second, that it corrects present discrimination;[22] and third, that it achieves diversity.[23] In the following section, I explain each of these rationales' moral and legal justifications.

Affirmative Action to Remedy Past Discrimination

The "past discrimination" rationale views affirmative action as reparations for slavery and racial segregation.[24] Race preferences for African Americans are the twentieth century model of the forty acres and mule, which Thaddeus Stevens recommended for freed slaves.[25] The case for reparations draws on principles of tort law. When an intentional wrong cannot be undone, it is fair to compensate the victim for her injury and sometimes it is fair to punish the wrongdoer.[26]

The difference, however, between tort remedies and past discrimination affirmative action is that "the people who will benefit from [affirmative action] are not the people who were discriminated against, but their successors or descendants. For them the relief is a windfall."[27] The adverse effect that past discrimination has on its victims' descendants serves as the moral justification for this "windfall." Virtually all of American public discourse on the unfortunate plight of African Americans, relative to whites, assumes that the explanation begins with slavery, even if it does not necessarily end there.[28] Advocates of past discrimination affirmative action insist that race preferences are necessary because, in Justice Thurgood Marshall's words, "a whole people were marked as inferior by the law. And that mark has endured. The dream of America as the great melting pot has not been realized for the Negro; because of his skin color he never even made it into the pot."[29] They claim further that the argument that past discrimination has no present effect on blacks and other minorities is wishful thinking because the United States is not "anywhere close to eradicating racial discrimination or its vestiges."[30]

Because American history has been marred by countless examples of racial discrimination, particularly toward African Americans,[31] the scope of compensation for this discrimination is potentially limitless. In *Regents of the University of California v. Bakke*,[32] Justice Powell wrote that remedying the effects of "societal discrimination" cannot be a constitutional justification of affirmative action because it is "an amorphous concept of injury that may be ageless in its reach into the past."[33] Powell noted, however, that a state "certainly has a legitimate and substantial interest in ameliorating, or eliminating where feasible, the disabling effects of identified discrimination."[34]

In a series of post-*Bakke* cases culminating in *Adarand Constructors, Inc. v. Pena*,[35] the Supreme Court narrowed the classes of people who may benefit from affirmative action to remedy the effects of past discrimination.[36] However, these cases have produced multiple opinions[37] without any majority on significant issues;[38] accordingly, it is difficult to discern the exact legal status of the past discrimination rationale for affirmative action. Judge Posner recently summed up the confusion and, perhaps, the law when he stated that "[a] majority of the Court [is] in favor of permitting some reverse discrimination. ... How much reverse discrimination is permitted is unclear. All that is clear is that discrimination in favor of a minority is sometimes permissible to rectify past discrimination against that minority by the discriminating institution."[39]

In addition to requiring that a government entity that employs race preferences must itself have discriminated, the Supreme Court has held that racial preferences must be narrowly tailored to remedy the problems caused by the discrimination. As Judge Posner observed, the entity must prove that it "had to do something and had no alternative to what [it] did."[40] As we will see, this requirement will be the most troublesome for affirmative action in criminal law.[41]

Affirmative Action to Remedy Present Discrimination

The "present discrimination" or "equal opportunity" rationale for affirmative action treats racial preferences as a fortified antidiscrimination remedy.[42] Proponents of the present discrimination rationale claim that to the extent that the Civil War Amendments[43] and Civil Rights Acts[44] mandate non-discrimination as opposed to race preferences, they cannot ensure equal opportunity for minorities. Without affirmative action, elite decisionmakers tend to prefer people who look like themselves, in other words, white men. This race preference reinforces the status quo and stymies minority progress.[45] In order for people of color simply to get their foot in the door, white decisionmakers actively must prefer them. Paul Brest and Miranda Oshige have observed that affirmative action prevents current discrimination by "placing minority professionals in visible positions of competence and power."[46]

The legal status of present discrimination affirmative action is similar to that of past discrimination affirmative action in that the Supreme Court occasionally concludes that it is constitutional.[47] The standard of review for present discrimination affirmative action is strict scrutiny, the same standard that courts apply to past discrimination affirmative action. This scrutiny is cold comfort for advocates of affirmative action because it is "strict in theory, but fatal in fact."[48]

Affirmative Action for Diversity

The diversity rationale for affirmative action favors race preferences because they result in the allocation of benefits to people who "look like America."[49] Furthermore, the diversity rationale suggests that diversity has more than a mere aesthetic value because people of color bring their "outlook" to the environment that affirmative action allows them to integrate.[50] In the words of Justice Powell, a black student can contribute "something" to an educational environment that a white person cannot.[51] I will call this construct "essential-diversity."

An enduring critique of essential-diversity is that it stereotypes minorities.[52] To some people, it is as ludicrous to assume that people of one race share an outlook as it is to assume that tall people or brunettes share an outlook.[53] Critics suggest that racial stereotyping by advocates of affirmative action seems oddly consistent with the racism that affirmative action would combat.[54] Considering this critique, it is ironic that essential-diversity may be the only legal justification[55] for affirmative action by entities that historically have not discriminated on the basis of race.[56]

I confess some sympathy with the traditional critique of diversity. Race is a troubling and usually inaccurate proxy for perspective.[57] There is, however, another, more persuasive way of thinking about the diversity rationale for affirmative action. This explanation, which I will call "parity-diversity," measures the fairness of resource allocation by its racial effect.[58] Thus, if the allocation of resources is grossly disparate, that allocation is prima facie unjust,[59] and it should be corrected by affirmative action unless there is a compelling explanation for the disparity. Affirmative action advocates seldom argue explicitly for parity-diversity, perhaps because of the antipathy of some toward quotas.[60] The covert rhetoric of parity-diversity can be discerned, for example, in arguments that affirmative action should be employed in higher education because without it there would be few African Americans and Latinos present in elite academic institutions.[61]

An interesting aspect of the diversity rationale for affirmative action, which distinguishes it from the past discrimination rationale, is that it critiques merit, supposedly the traditional way to allocate benefits. Proponents of the diversity rationale argue that merit criteria are unreasonably biased in favor of the white majority. These criteria might, for example, discount the importance of standardized test scores in admission to law schools, or accord substantial weight to work experience or cultural background in law school admissions. Unlike people who advocate affirmative action to address past or present discrimination, these advocates disparage traditional constructs of merit because they are inefficient or misguided: if a medical school admissions committee considers only grades and standardized test scores, it will not necessarily select the people who will become the best doctors. Later, I will employ the diversity rationale's analysis of merit to critique the criminal law's construct of demerit in the selection of individuals for punishment.

The Success of Race Preferences

Manifestations of affirmative action are commonplace in the United States.[62] African-American and Hispanic students attend virtually every prestigious academic institution in the nation, even though few of them would be admitted without explicit race preferences. Thanks to racial gerrymandering of electoral districts, the composition of the most recent Congress approached a proportional representation of African Americans.[63] Some minority-owned businesses have grown, in part, because they receive credit for their minority status when they bid for contracts.[64] If the goal of affirmative action is to advance minority participation in American education, business, and political life, it has succeeded. Affirmative action is the "but for" cause of substantial minority achievement.[65]

Have Race Preferences Harmed Minorities?

Some critics of affirmative action argue that its pervasiveness has caused successful minorities to suffer a stigma: the belief that minority achievements are the result of affirmative action, not individual merit. In response, liberals do not deny the stigma so much as they discount it. Randall Kennedy suggests, "In the end, the uncertain extent to which affirmative action diminishes the accomplishments of blacks must be balanced against the stigmatization that occurs when blacks are virtually absent from important institutions in the society."[66]

Other critics of affirmative action have warned that white backlash, actual or potential, against the beneficiaries of race preferences is a reason to terminate race preferences.[67] They express concern that the white majority will use its political power to harm minorities to the point that the costs of affirmative action exceed its benefits.[68] Like the reply to the stigma argument, supporters of affirmative action typically acknowledge the potential of white backlash to harm minorities. One proponent of affirmative action contends, however, that affirmative action is more of an excuse for the backlash than a cause of it.[69] Other advocates of affirmative action deprecate the threat of white backlash, arguing that it is not widespread or that it is to be expected from the American political process, which invariably is motivated by self-interest among special interest groups.[70]

DOES THE RATIONALE FOR AFFIRMATIVE ACTION APPLY TO THE CRIMINAL LAW?

In criminal law, as in civil law, there is tension between formal equality and white supremacy. Ostensibly color-blind criminal law will perpetuate majority black prisons as surely as ostensibly color-blind admissions policies will erase most African Americans from elite universities. Racially disproportionate allocations of criminal punishment should be as offensive to American values as are racially disproportionate allocations of resources like political representation in Congress and higher education. Thus, affirmative action in criminal law may find support among the same people who support affirmative action in civil contexts such as education and political institutions.

All three rationales for affirmative action can be applied to African-American criminal defendants.[71] In the criminal justice system, affirmative action is a justifiable remedy for the effects of past and present discrimination against black criminal defendants. While most black defendants are guilty of the crimes with which they are charged, racial hegemony is an important explanation of why and how they end up in criminal court. As we have seen in the preceding section, affirmative action attempts to redress the past and present effects of racial discrimination. The third rationale—diversity—also applies to the criminal law, under the parity-diversity theory. There is no arena of American life with more unfortunate and disparate racial consequences than criminal justice.[72]

Before I develop further my thesis, I will address an immediate concern. The reader may fear that, in advocating a class-based remedy like affirmative action for black criminal defendants, I am oversimplifying the complicated causes of criminal behavior and that I am paying insufficient homage to law-abiding black people. It is true that most African Americans do not respond to racist environments by committing crimes. That is not, however, a persuasive reason to deny affirmative action to African Americans who do respond to racist environments by committing crimes. With any class remedy, there exist some members of the group who do not require remediation. Not every woman who used a Dalkon shield became infertile. Some women did. Not every child whose mother was given thalidomide was born with deformities. Some children were. Not every African-American person is a criminal because of the lingering effects of slavery and apartheid. Some black people are.

With class-based remedies, potential beneficiaries usually have to demonstrate injury. For women harmed by Dalkon shields or thalidomide, the injuries are obvious. For black criminal defendants, the injury is less obvious but no less real: it is their criminal conduct, which must be attributed to the harm of racial discrimination. In saying there "must" be such an attribution, I draw an analogy to civil affirmative action, where the injury to blacks is their substandard performance and the harm is racial discrimination. In the civil context of affirmative action, members of a benefited group seldom have suffered the same injury. Some black people, for example, do not react to racial hegemony with substandard performances on standardized tests.[73] Yet, proponents of affirmative action acknowledge—indeed, they presume—that past or present white supremacy is the best explanation for the substandard "objective" performance of African Americans in comparison with whites and Asian Americans. Thus, race preferences attempt to mitigate the impact of race discrimination by placing the beneficiaries of affirmative action where they would be but for racial discrimination. Accordingly, if it is true that but for white supremacy many African Americans would not find themselves involved in the criminal justice system, affirmative action should play a role in keeping them out.

If, in the criminal context, antisocial conduct is the injury, we must take care to fashion compensation that does not encourage more injuries of the same kind.[74] The final section of this chapter recommends relief that should not have that effect.

I next explain why the three traditional rationales for affirmative action apply to the criminal law.

Affirmative Action for African-American Criminal Defendants as Reparation for Past Discrimination

What does America owe the black criminal?[75] The law asks exactly the opposite question and then answers it with punishment: the African-American criminal repays her debt to society by surrendering her freedom or life. The theory of why this is fair to her is grounded in retribution, or just deserts.[76] "[I]t is just to punish those who have violated the rules and caused the unfair distribution of benefits and burdens. A person who violates the rules has something others have—the benefits of the system—but by renouncing what others have assumed, the burdens of self-restraint, he has acquired an unfair advantage."[77]

In civil law, the past discrimination rationale for affirmative action recasts the traditional construct of "fair play." It suggests that because minorities have been denied the benefits of the system, they should not necessarily suffer its burdens.[78] The colloquial expression of this objective is that affirmative action "levels the playing field."[79]

To think about whether reparations for past discrimination should extend to the African-American criminal, we must explore the role of past discrimination in creating her. The relevant inquiry is not why black people commit crimes, but rather why they appear to commit so many more crimes than whites in proportionate and, in some cases, absolute terms.[80] In some sense, every person who commits a crime chooses to do so. We must therefore explore why more blacks than whites appear to choose crime.[81] If the criminal's choice is prejudiced by factors outside of her control, surely there is an argument against punishment for its own sake. If an African American's "choice" to commit crimes is the result of historical racial discrimination against blacks, then affirmative action may promote justice for black criminals much as it advances justice, for example, for less "meritorious" Hispanic applicants to go to college.

What is the relationship between the United States' wretched history of white supremacy and the present reality of prisons that teem with black people? Has the history of white supremacy caused the disproportionate incarceration of African Americans in a way that the criminal law should recognize? The consensus among scholars (and certainly among the liberals and moderates who are most likely to endorse traditional affirmative action) is that black crime is better explained by sociology than it is by either psychology or biology. For example, Norvall Morris advises that an "[a]dverse social and subcultural background is statistically *more* criminogenic than is psychosis."[82] Unsurprisingly then, virtually all of the sociological theories predict high levels of African-American criminal behavior.[83] The environmental explanation for disparate black criminality is remarkably constant, given the range of solutions to the problem.[84]

In sum, disproportionate black criminality results from something other than a disproportionate evil in black people. African-American criminality is a predictable response to the United States' historical policy of official hatred of the black race. This hatred is evidenced by slavery and by the subsequent widespread discrimination, whether de jure (mainly in the South) or de facto (in every part of the country) against black people in every sector of American life, including criminal justice, education, housing, employment, voting rights, health care, and family law.

Affirmative action acknowledges that this grotesque history is responsible for the environment of African Americans and for their substandard performance under almost every "objective" measure of achievement. When we understand that the explanation for the disproportionate frequency of black crime is environmental, we discern the connection between past discrimination and black criminality. Black criminality—like low standardized test scores, poor grades, depressed wages, and poorly capitalized businesses—is another symptom of the disease of white supremacy. It is a disease that no reasonable person would choose, if she had a choice.[85] Under the affirmative action paradigm, reparations are warranted in criminal law.

The civil law of past discrimination affirmative action demands justice for people who are rendered substandard through no fault of their own. Similarly, affirmative action cannot change the environment that causes black criminal conduct, but it can award reparations to the injured person—the African American accused. Affirmative action is a compelling theory against the punishment of African Americans as retribution or just deserts for criminal behavior that is the product of a racist environment.[86]

I should note that there is an obvious utilitarian concern with affirmative action in criminal law. There may be a social cost if black criminals are not punished, even if there is no individual or retributive argument for their punishment. But the reader should understand that, under the past discrimination rationale for affirmative action, there are social costs in any affirmative action regime. Let us be honest: all things being equal, many people, including proponents of the past discrimination rationale for affirmative action, would prefer their future brain surgeons have high grades and high MCAT scores as opposed to low grades and low scores.[87] We would prefer that our government award our tax dollars to the lowest-bidding qualified contractor, regardless of his or her skin color, not the lowest-bidding qualified minority contractor. Society incurs some limited injury when affirmative action prioritizes the ideally irrelevant category of race.

Despite their social costs, racial preferences are justified because the history of the United States has been marked by virulent white supremacy. Cost-benefit analysis reveals that the benefit of fairness to victims outweighs the societal costs of their compensation. This cost-benefit analysis does not ignore utilitarian concerns. For example, in the case of medical school applicants, minimum standards bar the admission of some minorities, regardless of the reason for their non-competitiveness. If society can be similarly protected in the criminal law context, the argument for affirmative action there gains force. To encourage readers to keep an open mind, I remind you that in the last section of this chapter, I discuss a way to constrain the social costs of affirmative action for criminal defendants.

Affirmative Action for Criminal Defendants to Correct Present Discrimination

Some people offer an alternative explanation for the high rate of incarceration of African Americans. They attribute a substantial portion of the disparity between the present rates of incarceration for blacks and whites to discrimination at the hands of lawmakers and law enforcers. There are so many African Americans in prison, the argument goes, because legislators, police, and prosecutors target them and presumably ignore or slight illegal conduct by other groups. Such discrimination may be benign, as in the case of police officers who more strictly enforce narcotics laws in minority communities, or malignant, as in the case of a hypothetical judge who sentences African Americans more severely than others who commit the same crimes. Minority communities disagree whether benign discrimination is beneficial or harmful.[88]

Regardless of the intent of actors who administer criminal justice in a racially discriminatory fashion, the racially disparate effects of that discrimination are clear, particularly in drug cases, which explain a substantial portion of the incarceration rate of blacks.[89] According to government statistics, African Americans comprise 13 percent of drug consumers, a figure roughly equivalent to their percentage of the population. Yet 33 percent of all people arrested for drug use and 74 percent of all people incarcerated for drug use are African Americans.[90]

An African American suffers racial discrimination when she is punished for conduct for which a white person would not be punished. However, she has no meaningful legal remedy for such discrimination. Selective prosecution is the theoretical cure but it is extremely difficult to demonstrate. An African American making this claim encounters the same evidentiary burdens as the Native American who, alleging employment discrimination, must prove that she was denied promotion on account of her race.[91] In both cases, the law requires a demonstration of discriminatory intent, but that, absent a smoking gun, is hard to prove. The law demands certainty before it officially brands someone a racist; it errs on the side of the alleged discriminator.[92] The practical result is that there are many cases where there is discrimination but, so far as the law is concerned, no discriminator.

In both aforementioned cases, affirmative action can come to the rescue.[93] In the employment example, race preferences ameliorate the consequences of discrimination and the lack of a suitable legal remedy by overcompensating: discrimination is rendered futile because affirmative action demands the inclusion of Native Americans in the workplace. Similarly, affirmative action could counter discrimination by actors in the criminal justice system in various ways. For example, when there is evidence, as with some drug crimes, that minorities are arrested at rates disproportionate to their actual involvement in those crimes, affirmative action might require proportionality.[94] Proportionality would require either that more whites or fewer African Americans be arrested. Alternatively, affirmative action might require identical sentences for equivalent "white" criminal conduct, such as powder cocaine use, and "black" criminal conduct, such as crack cocaine use.

There is tension between the past discrimination explanation of disproportionate black incarceration and the present discrimination rationale for affirmative action. The past discrimination argument concedes that blacks disproportionately engage in criminal conduct. The present discrimination rationale, on the other hand, assumes that blacks are selectively arrested, convicted, and incarcerated. Based on the evidence just cited, the present-day discrimination rationale offers a compelling explanation for the extraordinary number of blacks who are incarcerated for drug offenses. However, it does not explain why an extraordinary number of blacks are convicted of violent crimes. Most violent crime is intraracial. To accept the selective prosecution explanation of the high rate of black violent crime, one would have to believe that killers or rapists of white people go free, while those who harm African Americans are actively sought by the government. Given the reality of white supremacy, this seems unlikely; thus, I conclude that African Americans are disproportionately guilty of some violent crimes for the reasons stated in the preceding section.[95] Accordingly, equal opportunity affirmative action should be limited to those areas of criminal justice in which there is evidence of present discrimination against African Americans.

Affirmative Action to Achieve Diversity in Criminal Justice

There is no persuasive essentialist-diversity argument for affirmative action in criminal law. Prison, unlike Harvard College, is not intended to be a place where people contribute various viewpoints to enhance the learning environment.[96]

There is, however, a compelling parity-diversity argument. The disparate consequences of the criminal law for African Americans are striking. In civil affirmative action, the parity-diversity construct of affirmative action calls for an equal distribution of benefits. Application of its corollary in criminal law would encourage equal distribution of burdens as well. The goal would be a criminal justice system in which African Americans are a minority, as they are in the general population. Diversity affirmative action in criminal law might seek, for example, to emancipate African-American men from prison until their representation in prison falls from 50 percent to 13 percent, reflecting their true representation in society.[97]

Because punishment, particularly that of African Americans,[98] is so reified in the United States, my recommendation that it be allocated proportionally will strike some readers as strange. However, these readers should understand that its present allocation strikes many African Americans the same way. The diversity rationale for affirmative action critiques the traditional construct of demerit in the criminal context in the same way that it questions the traditional construct of merit in the civil context.

Recall the function of criminal law: to treat the immoral and dangerous. Does the law select those persons well? To believe that it does, one must also believe that more than 50 percent of the most dangerous and immoral men in this country are black.[99] One must believe that 33 percent of young black men are immoral or dangerous.[100] One must believe that African-American women, in the last few years, have become significantly less moral and more dangerous than they once were.[101]

Diversity affirmative action attributes disproportionate black criminality to the distorting influence of white supremacy on the political and legal processes by which "criminals" are named and selected for punishment. Without racial hegemony, constructs of "danger" and "immorality" would be color-blind. Immoral and dangerous persons would no longer be disproportionately located in the African-American community. Diversity affirmative action's response to white supremacy is to reconstruct the criteria by which criminals are selected to make those criteria more efficient and fair: Diversity affirmative action could improve the selection process so that it chose not only the best medical students, but also the worst criminals.[102] In criminal law, it could broaden constructs of dangerousness to include tobacco distributors and manufacturers of unsafe automobiles and airplanes. It could support the criminalization of hate speech and other forms of injury now regulated, if at all, by civil law.[103] It could make white supremacy as worthy of punishment as drugs. Perhaps diversity affirmative action could lead to a prison population that looks like America.

DOES AFFIRMATIVE ACTION EXIST IN CRIMINAL LAW?

Explicit race preferences are not present in the substantive criminal law, even though race-consciousness is. In this section, I discuss two aspects of criminal justice that help pave the way for race-based affirmative action: first, lawful race-consciousness in the administration of justice; and second, fairness preferences for some non-racial groups.

These examples of race-consciousness illustrate that the law suspends its color blindness when the opportunity cost of color blindness is inefficient law enforcement. My thesis is that to the extent the criminal law remains color-blind instead of race-conscious, the opportunity cost is an injustice for African Americans—a harm as worthy of correction as inefficient law enforcement. Examples of fairness preferences, which I will present, demonstrate how criminal law can resolve tension between formal equality and fairness by favoring members of a particular group. Thus, there is legal precedent for race preferences for the ultimate out-group in the United States—African Americans.

Race-Consciousness in the Administration of Justice

Some courts have approved the use of "racial incongruity," defined as being in a place where members of your race typically are not, as a constitutionally permissible factor for police stops. In *United States v. Weaver*,[104] for example, the Eighth Circuit supported a police officer's reliance on a racial profile of whom to stop at a Kansas City airport. The court held that blackness, in combination with factors such as nervousness, arrival from a source city for drugs, and lack of identification, is a ground for reasonable suspicion of drug dealing. The court reasoned:

[F]acts are not to be ignored simply because they may be unpleasant—and the unpleasant fact in this case is that ... young male members of black Los Angeles gangs were flooding the Kansas City area with cocaine. To that extent, then, race, when coupled with the other factors ... was a [lawful] factor in the decision to approach and ultimately detain [the black suspect]. We wish it were otherwise, but we take the facts as they are presented to us, not as we would like them to be.[105]

Race is a permissible consideration in prison administration. In fact, disciplinary segregation in prison is often cited as a paradigmatic example of the kind of race-consciousness that the Fourteenth Amendment permits.[106] In *Lee v. Washington*,[107] the Supreme Court noted that an order directing desegregation of Alabama prisons and jails should not be read as making "no allowance for the necessities of prison security and discipline."[108] Three Justices filed a concurrence

to make explicit something that is left to be gathered only by implication from the Court's opinion. This is that prison authorities have the right, acting in good faith and in particularized circumstances, to take into account racial tensions in maintaining security, discipline, and good order in prisons and jails.[109]

In *City of Richmond v. J.A. Croson*,[110] Justice Scalia's sole example of governmental color-consciousness that would survive constitutional scrutiny involved "a prison race riot, requiring temporary segregation of inmates."[111]

A third example of race-consciousness in our present criminal justice system is affirmative action preferences for minority law enforcement personnel. These preferences usually are justified by the rhetoric of past discrimination affirmative action.[112] In *Wittmer v. Peters*,[113] however, Judge Posner used a diversity analysis to endorse preferential treatment in the hiring of an African-American correctional officer at an Illinois "boot camp" for young criminals.[114] In that case, a test was given to applicants for the position of lieutenant, and a black man who ranked forty-second was appointed over white applicants who scored third, sixth, and eighth, respectively.[115] The prison administrator claimed that the appointment was necessary because 68 percent of the boot camp's inmates were black, and there were no black supervisors.[116] The black criminals were thought to be "unlikely to play the correctional game of brutal drill sergeant and brutalized recruit unless there are some blacks in authority in the camp."[117] Judge Posner affirmed the grant of summary judgment in favor of the race preference even though he acknowledged that "the Supreme Court has rejected the 'role model' argument for reverse discrimination."[118] Posner was persuaded by expert testimony that the boot camp "would not succeed in its mission of pacification and reformation with as white a staff as it would have had [absent affirmative action]."[119] He emphasized that his analysis might not apply to a regular prison, and that an argument that the security staff be racially proportionate to the inmate population would exceed "the limits of demonstrable need."[120]

Fairness Preferences in Criminal Law

There are no explicit race preferences in the criminal law. American criminal justice is putatively color-blind. Yet there are preferences for non-racial groups in the criminal law. They are better explained by political or moral constructs of justice than by legal doctrine. Below, I describe two such "fairness preferences."

Rape Shield Laws

Rules of evidence generally permit the admission of any relevant evidence when the probative value of the evidence outweighs its prejudicial effect.[121] In the typical non-rape case, the judge makes this determination; however, rape shield laws circumvent the court in favor of preferential treatment for victims of rape. Rape shield laws prevent alleged rape victims from being cross-examined about their past sexual conduct.[122] Such laws are legislatively mandated, class-based remedies designed to prevent bias against women in rape cases. The justification for these laws is not that the testimony of a rape victim under cross-examination lacks probative value, but that juries might find a sexually active woman less credible, or that certain questions could embarrass an alleged victim and possibly deter other victims from reporting similar crimes.[123] In the justice calculus, the value of fair treatment for rape victims outweighs any social utility of formal equality. Therefore, the law does not apply the same rules of cross-examination to rape victims as it does to other witnesses in criminal trials.

"Death Is Different" Jurisprudence

The Supreme Court occasionally grants preferential treatment to defendants in capital cases. For example, in *Harmelin v. Michigan*,[124] Justice Scalia wrote that the Eighth Amendment is not a judicial check on whether punishment is proportionate to the crime because that determination should be made by legislatures.[125] Justice Scalia reasoned that the concept of proportionate punishment is so amorphous that there is no way a judge could fairly determine it;[126] in reviewing a sentence, the judge would inevitably substitute her view of appropriate punishment for that of the legislature.[127] Remarkably, however, Justice Scalia would maintain the requirement of proportionality review in capital crimes because "death is different."[128] Thus, he argued for the bizarre result that proportionality review is impossible but required in death cases.[129]

"Death is different" jurisprudence is rooted in the severity of capital punishment. The result is that people guilty of the most heinous crimes sometimes receive more preferential treatment than that given to non-death eligible defendants. Death is different jurisprudence has a procedural bias reflecting extraordinary solicitude for capital defendants, although formal equality suggests that these defendants should be treated the same as others. The notion that the government should kill criminals only after an extraordinary process contradicts the value that the government should treat all accused persons the same.

These examples illustrate that although the substantive criminal law is colorblind, it favors some groups over others. It is not necessarily bound to formal equality when competing values are at stake. The time has come to ask how valuing justice for African Americans would change criminal law. If we have fairness preferences for alleged rape victims and death-eligible criminals, why not also have them for African Americans, guilty and accused?[130]

THE CONSTITUTIONAL CASE FOR AFFIRMATIVE ACTION IN CRIMINAL LAW

This chapter makes the case that justice requires affirmative action in criminal law. Would such affirmative action be constitutional? The Supreme Court's conservative majority probably would answer "no." But things change; Justices resign or die. I think the better answer is that affirmative action in criminal law would be as constitutional as other kinds of government race preferences are.

For the past discrimination rationale for affirmative action, the main legal hurdle is the strict scrutiny analysis to which, after *Adarand*, all government racial classifications seem subject. Strict scrutiny limits the breadth of affirmative action; the government entity's plan must be narrowly tailored so that it addresses exclusively the agency's past discrimination, not societal discrimination overall. This would challenge race preferences in criminal law because proponents of such affirmative action would have the burden of establishing that past discrimination in the criminal justice system explains disproportionate black criminality. Historical discrimination would not be difficult to demonstrate, but its connection to present black criminality would be. Disproportionate African-American criminality probably is more a function of discrimination in wages, employment, education, and housing than a function of discrimination in criminal justice.

For the diversity rationale of affirmative action, the strongest constitutional challenge is the prohibition against quotas. There is also a conceptual hurdle judges must surmount in applying diversity rhetoric to the unfamiliar context of crime and punishment. To allay the concerns about quotas, proportionality objectives must be expressed as goals, rather than as numerical mandates.[131]

For both the past discrimination and diversity rationales for affirmative action, racial gerrymandering cases occasion cautious optimism. To the uninitiated, the idea of racial preferences in voting seems as unusual as the idea of racial preferences in criminal law. Yet, for the former, the conceptual leap has been accomplished: race-consciousness in drawing voting districts is commonplace if controversial, and it has darkened the face of Congress and some state legislatures.[132]

The jurisprudence of legal realism also provides encouragement, over the long run, for the constitutionality of criminal law affirmative action. The Supreme Court Justices appointed by President Clinton have not exhibited the same hostility toward benign government race-consciousness that their Republican-appointed colleagues have. This is not to suggest that President Clinton's appointees to the Supreme Court will support my proposals, but at least they are not likely to create precedent, in the civil context, that will be hostile toward my proposals. As a legal realist, I believe the real battle to be waged is on the political front, and as I suggested in the introduction to this chapter, we are far from winning that battle. I note, however, some hopeful signs along the way, including awards of reparations to survivors of a particularly venomous racial attack in Rosewood, Florida,[133] and to Japanese Americans who were interned in American concentration camps during World War II.[134] When the time comes for justice for the lowest among us, we must be prepared. The following section recommends a plan.

AFFIRMATIVE ACTION FOR BLACK CRIMINAL DEFENDANTS: SIX PROPOSALS

The Proposals

1. Retribution shall not justify the punishment of any African-American criminal defendant.

2. Rehabilitation shall be the primary justification of punishment of African Americans.

3. African-American criminal defendants shall have the right to majority black juries. If convicted, they shall have the right to be sentenced by their majority black juries.

4. African Americans shall not be sentenced to death for interracial homicide.

5. Effective immediately, African Americans shall be arrested for drug possession offenses and sentenced to prison only in proportion to their involvement in those crimes, that is, they shall comprise no more than 12 percent of those arrested and 12 percent of those incarcerated.[135] African Americans whose arrest or incarceration increases the total proportion of arrested or incarcerated blacks in excess of 12 percent shall be released from custody.

6. Every jurisdiction in the United States shall maintain, within five years of enactment of this proposal, a prison population that accurately reflects the racial diversity of the jurisdiction. The percentage of African Americans in prison shall not exceed their proportion of the population of that jurisdiction by more than 2 percent.

The "Safety Net"

Implementation of each proposal shall be consistent with the utilitarian goals of criminal law. The safety benefits to society from incarceration, however, must be proved by clear and convincing evidence for African-American defendants. There shall be a rebuttable presumption that there is no social benefit to incarceration of an African American for malum prohibitum crimes.

The Theory

These proposals are premised on the reality that people have more to fear from violence than crime and that in the current regime of criminal justice, the relationship of punishment to violence is tangential when it should be direct.[136] In a country with no history of racial hegemony, this reality would be unfortunate but not necessarily unjust: legislatures, in a democracy, should enjoy the luxury of making bad law and implementing poor policy, as long as those laws are not unconstitutional. As we have seen, there is a rough consensus among those who studied the issue that the United States' historical and present inclination toward white supremacy is responsible for the disproportionate rate of black criminality.[137] The just response is criminal justice that recognizes this truth and safely compensates for it. That is the intent of my six proposals. They are not "fair" in the sense that they apply to all accused persons, but they are just in the calculus of affirmative action: if the problem is race-based, then the solution need be race-based as well.

The next section will explain, briefly, the argument for each proposal. Explication of each could, and in some cases has, consumed entire articles.[138] My purpose will be to locate these ideas within the conceptual framework of affirmative action. I predict that they will meet with the same objections as have civil race preferences, and that they would have the same success.

Proposals One and Two: The Justification of Punishment of African Americans

Proposals One and Two call for rehabilitation, not retribution, to be the justification for punishing black people.[139] These proposals are premised on the past discrimination theory of affirmative action. If the law assumes that the most compelling explanation for disproportionate black criminality is the legacy of slavery and segregation, as it does for substandard minority achievement in other arenas, it is unjust to punish the black criminal on a theory of retribution. Retribution posits, in the words of one classic text, that

it is highly desirable that criminals should be hated, that the punishments inflicted upon them should be so contrived as to give expression to that hatred, and to justify it so far as the public provision of means for expressing and gratifying a healthy natural sentiment can justify and encourage it.[140]

Whatever the just deserts of the black criminal, hate seems an excessive reaction, given the theory of fair play through which retribution constructs justice. It is, after all, hatred directed toward the black race that has contributed to her criminality in the first instance.

Accordingly, it would be much more appropriate to *help* the antisocial black criminal. Reformation is the justification of punishment that seeks to help the lawbreaker conform her conduct to the law. Although "reform as an object[ive] is no doubt very vague,"[141] it might include job training, physical and mental health care, and treatment of chemical dependencies. While such care would doubtless be beneficial to all criminals, not simply African-American ones, black criminals could assert an especial right under a theory of reparations, given the unique history of their group.

Proposal Three: Majority Black Juries with Sentencing Authority

Majority black juries for African-American criminal defendants would be in keeping with civil affirmative action's goal of correcting ongoing racial discrimination. Several scholars have documented white juror prejudice against black criminal defendants.[142] Majority black juries would prevent conviction and punishment based on this prejudice.[143]

Although less persuasive, essential-diversity, voting rights rhetoric (particularly as it concerns maximization of the minority voice) provides another rationale for majority black juries.[144] The reaction to the O.J. Simpson criminal case persuasively suggests the extent of the gulf between blacks and whites in criminal adjudications.[145] Majority black juries would allow the black defendant to be judged by his community, not unlike the way that racial gerrymandering allows the black community to elect its own representatives.[146]

The reader should not assume that majority black juries will acquit black criminals, particularly those guilty of violent crimes, merely because they are black. Although one recent study claims that black defendants are acquitted at a higher rate than white defendants, that study does not indicate the race of the jurors, nor does it purport to know the basis for the acquittals.[147] It would be surprising to learn that black jurors acquitted violent African-American criminals on ethnocentric grounds. Acquittals would not seem to serve the interests of African Americans because most violent crimes are intraracial.

My recommendation that majority black juries sentence black criminals is also premised on the present discrimination rationale for affirmative action. Several studies suggest that African-American defendants receive longer sentences than do similarly situated whites.[148] Allowing majority black juries to sentence African-American convicted criminals would help eliminate this racism. There is ample legal precedent for juror sentencing. In some states jurors recommend sentences in capital cases,[149] and in Arkansas, Kentucky, and Texas, jurors sentence defendants in some non-capital cases as well.[150]

Proposal Four: Non-Discriminatory Death Sentences

Race preferences in sentencing African Americans convicted of interracial homicides are grounded on the well-documented existence of extreme discrimination against African-American death-eligible defendants whose victims are white.[151] The Supreme Court has suggested that if race discrimination exists in the administration of criminal justice, any remedy for the discrimination would be impractical because "there is no limiting principle."[152] However, one such principle might be death.[153] As discussed, the Court has endorsed a "death is different" analysis in other contexts.[154]

The defeat of the Racial Justice Act is powerful evidence of the need for affirmative action in the administration of death penalty cases. The act, a response to *McCleskey* proposed by the Congressional Black Caucus, stated: "[N]o person shall be put to death under color of State or Federal law in the execution of a sentence that was imposed based on race."[155] The act would have allowed courts to find racial bias by having them consider, among other things, statistical evidence regarding administration of the death penalty in the relevant locale.[156] If the death-sentenced inmate established the presumption, the government would have to demonstrate a non-racial motivation for the death penalty.[157] If the government was unable to prove a non-discriminatory motive, the criminal could not be executed.[158]

The act was twice passed by the House of Representatives as part of a larger crime legislation package, and each time it was dropped from the legislation in conference committee.[159] The concern was "not about the Act's self-stated prohibition against racially motivated death sentences ... [but] [r]ather ... over the Act's implementation of that purpose and the perceived collateral effects of that implementation [in other words, that it would effectively eliminate the death penalty]."[160] In order to preserve the death penalty status quo, Congress, like the Supreme Court, chose to risk racially motivated executions.

In civil law, we have already seen that present discrimination affirmative action is the super-remedy for intractable racial discrimination.[161] It seems to work. If the super-remedy of affirmative action is ever justified to combat racial discrimination, it is surely justified in cases where the government is executing black defendants because of their race.

Proposal Five: Proportional Drug Arrests and Punishment

This proposal recognizes that affirmative action should combat present racial discrimination and promote parity in the allocation of punishment between whites and blacks. Government statistics indicate that African Americans do not disproportionately use illegal drugs, yet they comprise more than 70 percent of people incarcerated for such conduct.[162] These statistics suggest that the criminal system discriminates against black drug users. My proposal to remedy that discrimination, by imposing racially proportionate punishments on drug users, would not unduly penalize whites or blacks. After all, most white drug users are not incarcerated or otherwise punished, and the white community does not appear to suffer adverse effects as a result.

I have stated elsewhere that "[a]s far as law enforcement is concerned, what is good enough for white people is good enough for African Americans."[163] Affirmative action here would institutionalize this notion of simple justice, and presumably the white majority would embrace it. If punishment is, as Randall Kennedy has argued, a public good for the law-abiding community, my proposal will ensure that white Americans get their fair share of it.[164]

Proposal Six: Diversity in Incarceration

This proposal is justified by parity-diversity, particularly its critique of merit and, in the criminal law, demerit. The current process of selecting behaviors for criminal punishment is flawed and, worse, it is race-based; the result is the irrational and disparate selection of African Americans for government correction and control.

I do not mean to suggest that the state must abandon its role as the regulator of persons who have exhibited dangerous or immoral behaviors. Rather, I suggest that the state should regulate more efficiently the behaviors that truly threaten society. Consider the case of tobacco marketers. These people undoubtably kill;[165] in fact, they can be viewed as mass murderers or serial killers—such is the extent of the carnage resulting from tobacco. But rather than punish their antisocial conduct, the government endorses it; it even provides financial incentives for the poison makers.[166]

In another country, government subsidies of tobacco might be considered stupid but not necessarily unfair: democratic rule risks bad law. In the United States, however, white supremacy plus bad laws equal disproportionate black incarceration.[167] If a black drug dealer sold a substance with the knowledge that it would cause death, most jurisdictions would be happy to punish her. If her mens rea was less than knowledge—say she recklessly disregarded the chance that somebody would die, or she unreasonably failed to appreciate the risk imposed by her conduct—any prosecutor worth her salt could put together a good case. For the tobacco executive, however, the most that the criminal law will do is protect children from his homicidal inclination. That is more than the criminal law will do for some other public enemies: think of reckless or negligent automobile and airplane executives, air and water polluters, and the distributors of unclean food and unsafe prescription drugs.

What about drug dealers? We have already seen that the government supports those who deal tobacco. Distributors of alcohol are regulated a bit more; some states forbid stores from selling alcohol late at night, although addicts can often find respite in bars and nightclubs. On the other hand, the marketers of other substances, which are arguably less harmful than alcohol, find themselves confined in cages for years.[168] In some states, it is fashionable to cage repeat consumers and sellers of drugs for their entire lives.[169]

It is true that most of the aforementioned unpunished killers are white, and it is also true that most punished killers in the United States are African American. Most unpunished drug consumers and dealers are white, while more than 70 percent of incarcerated drug users and dealers are black.[170] The parity-diversity explanation of affirmative action relieves us of the burden to establish why this is so; instead, it moves us toward the solution that its name prescribes: proportionality.[171] Proportionality of punishment helps the criminal justice system select the real bad guys—the most dangerous and immoral. Proportionality assumes that dangerousness and immorality are not disproportionately located in the African-American community.[172]

The jurisprudence of racial realism suggests that if legal strategies to advance people of color will be implemented, they must further the interests of the white majority.[173] I expect that this would be true of my proposals as well. The United States has the highest rate of incarceration of any industrialized nation in the world.[174] I expect that implementing affirmative action in the criminal law would substantially reduce that rate of incarceration. In other words, I expect that punishment of African Americans would be "leveled down" as opposed to the punishment of whites being "leveled up." Economically and socially, the United States could not afford to imprison whites at the same rates at which it imprisons African Americans. Affirmative action promises to lower the costs of the criminal justice system because the majority of the United States prison population, 65 percent, has been incarcerated for nonviolent offenses.[175] Were some of those nonviolent offenders, particularly drug "offenders," treated outside the criminal justice system to create parity, a significant reduction in federal and state expenditures and a net increase in public safety could result.[176]

CONCLUSION

The situation, for black people, is desperate. If present trends continue, the majority of African-American men between the ages of eighteen and forty will be incarcerated by the year 2010.[177] African-American women are the fastest growing segment of the prison population.[178] In the face of these dire developments, affirmative action is a limited but proven remedy that has ameliorated racial inequities in important sectors of American society: education, employment, and democracy. Affirmative action's concept of justice should be extended to the criminal law. It is less subversive than alternatives such as race-based jury nullification[179] or revolution.[180]

It is unfortunate that race-conscious solutions sometimes engender more controversy than race-conscious problems. Affirmative action assumes, correctly, that legal and political strategies exalting color blindness are doomed to fail, or at least to fail African Americans. Our criminal courts and prisons teem with evidence of the failure thus far. At some point the criminal law's color blindness must be replaced with criminal justice. How many more black people must be punished to bring us to that day?

NOTES

Earlier versions of this chapter were presented at the Critical Race Theory Workshop, the University of Virginia School of Law Contemporary Legal Thought Lecture Series, and faculty workshops at the University of Maryland School of Law and the George Washington University Law School. I am grateful to the participants in those meetings. In addition, I thank Taunya Lovell Banks, Bob Chang, Richard Collins, Anne Coughlin, Adrienne Davis, Angela Davis, Richard Delgado, Theress Gabaldon, Dennis Greene, Lisa Ikemoto, Margaret Montoya, Jamin Raskin, Kathryn Russell, and Jonathan Siegel. Laura Fitzrandolph provided superb research assistance. This article is dedicated to Kimberly Butler, my sister, and to her newborn child, Gabriel Rene Franjou, for whom I wish a world where affirmative action in criminal law will be unnecessary.

1. NTOZAKE SHANGE, THREE PIECES 51 (1981).

2. Steven A. Holmes, *Powell Strongly Defends Use of Racial Preferences*, N.Y. TIMES, June 8, 1996, at A8.

3. In 1993, African-American men, approximately 13 percent of the male population, constituted 50.8 percent of the men in federal and state prison. This was an increase from 46.5 percent in 1980. Black and Hispanic men make up approximately three-quarters of new admissions to prisons. According to criminologist Jerome Miller, if the increased rate of incarceration of African Americans continues, by 2010, "we will have the absolute majority of all African American males between age 18 and 40 in prisons

and camps." Fox Butterfield, *More in U.S. Are in Prisons, Report Says,* N.Y. TIMES, Aug. 10, 1995, at A14. African Americans are incarcerated at a rate of more than six times that of whites—1907 per 100,000 citizens compared with 306 per 100,000 citizens for whites. *See* BUREAU OF JUSTICE STATISTICS, U.S. DEP'T OF JUSTICE, PRISONERS IN 1994, at 10 (1995).

4. As of 1991, 46 percent of women in state prison systems were African American. *See* TRACY L. SNELL, U.S. DEP'T OF JUSTICE, WOMEN IN PRISON: SURVEY OF STATE PRISON INMATES, 1991, at 2 (1994).

5. *See* MARK MAUER & TRACY HULING, THE SENTENCING PROJECT, YOUNG BLACK AMERICANS AND THE CRIMINAL JUSTICE SYSTEM: FIVE YEARS LATER 3 (1995).

6. In 1990, the average Scholastic Aptitude Test score of students from low-income families was 881 for students from white families and 692 for students from black families. See ANDREW HACKER, TWO NATIONS: BLACK AND WHITE, SEPARATE, HOSTILE, UNEQUAL 138 (1992). Despite some gains in education, *see* Shankar Vedantam, *Graduation Rates Same for Whites, Blacks,* PITT. POST-GAZETTE, Sept. 6, 1996, at A8, many states report a disparity between the academic performance of white and black students. For example, in Wisconsin, the gap in grade point averages ("GPAs") between white and black students is growing. *See* Phil Brinkman, *How to Raise Minority Achievement,* WIS. ST. J., July 18, 1996, at 1A. In Texas, in 1995, white students scored 37 percent better on the Texas Assessment of Academic Skills Test than African-American students. *See* Susan S. Richardson, *Judicial Decision Puts Minorities in Jeopardy,* AUSTIN AM. STATESMAN, July 4, 1996, at A11. In New Jersey, less than half of the 3,511 African-American students who applied to Rutgers were accepted, whereas more than two-thirds of white applicants were admitted. *See* Tia Swanson, *Admission of Black Students to State Colleges Lagging,* ASBURY PARK PRESS, June 30, 1996, at A27. Finally, in Minnesota, an overwhelming number of eighth-grade students of color failed to pass both the reading and math portions of a new state-mandated graduation exam. In Minneapolis, approximately eight out of 10 black students failed the math and reading tests while only three out of 10 white students failed both tests. *See Skills Test Failures: What They Mean in Minneapolis,* AM. POL. NETWORK, DAILY REP. CARD, June 4, 1996.

7. In 1990, the median income for white families was $36,915 and for black families it was only $21,423. *See* HACKER, *supra* note 6, at 98. The United States Glass Ceiling Commission found that 99% of senior management jobs are held by whites. In 1996, the Urban Institute reported that minority-owned firms were awarded only 57 percent of the government contracts that they would be expected to receive based on the number of such firms in business. *See* Michael A. Fletcher, *Study Says Minority Firms Underrepresented in U.S. Contracts,* WASH. POST, Oct. 31, 1996, at A3. In Richmond, Virginia, during a five-year period in the 1980s, less than 17 percent of prime contracts were awarded by the city to minorities, despite the fact that African Americans constituted half of the city's population. *See* City of Richmond v. J.A. Croson Co., 488 U.S. 469, 479 (1989).

8. There were 39 blacks in the 104th Congress (38 in the House and one in the Senate), representing approximately 7 percent of the representatives and 1 percent of the senators, despite the fact that blacks make up roughly 12 percent of the population. *See Case of Amnesia for the High Court: Justices Seem to Forget History and Reality of Race in America,* L.A. TIMES, July 2, 1995, at M4.

9. For a definition of affirmative action, see pages 375 ff.

10. For example, prior to the widespread creation of majority-minority districts, which occurred after the 1990 census, African Americans accounted for less than 5 per-

cent of the members of Congress, although they were approximately 11 percent of the voting-age population. *See* Frank R. Parker, *The Constitutionality of Racial Redistricting: A Critique of* Shaw v. Reno, 3 D.C. L. REV. 1, 2 (1995). Since the creation of the race-conscious remedy of majority-minority districts, the percentage of African Americans in Congress has gradually approached their portion of the population. *See supra* note 8.

In the contracting sphere, the Joint Center for Political and Economic Studies estimates that the greater than 300 percent expansion of black businesses from 1982 to 1992 is mainly attributable to government set-aside programs. *See* Joyce E. Allen, *The Growth and Diversification of Black Businesses*, 18 FOCUS 5–6 (1990).

Additionally, a recent study by two Michigan State University economists, Harry Holzner and David Neumark, found that affirmative action hires do just as well as or better than whites at their jobs. *See* Richard Morin, *Unconventional Wisdom: New Facts & Hot Stats from the Social Sciences: Affirming Affirmative Action Hires*, WASH. POST, Jan. 12, 1997, at C5. For example, black women hired under affirmative action programs receive higher performance ratings than white males hired in similar businesses. *See id.*

11. This is a theoretical article about justice and public policy. I concede that the legal case for many forms of affirmative action is moribund. In recent years, federal courts have severely restricted the ability of governments to employ affirmative action. *See, e.g.,* Adarand Constructors, Inc. v. Pena, 115 S. Ct. 2097 (1995); Podberesky v. Kirwan, 88 F.3d 147, 151–52 (4th Cir. 1994). In light of the re-election of President Clinton, there is a chance that affirmative action would be revived if two or three of the anti-affirmative action Justices on the Supreme Court resign or die. Chief Justice Rehnquist and Justices Scalia and Thomas consistently vote against affirmative action programs and other "benign" race preferences by the government. *See, e.g., Adarand,* 115 S. Ct. at 2098; Miller v. Johnson, 115 S. Ct. 2475, 2481–82 (1995). Justices O'Connor and Kennedy have supported, at least in theory, some government race-consciousness. *See* Shaw v. Reno, 509 U.S. 630, 643 (1993). In the United States, the aspirations of black people for justice often depend upon such fortuities. *See* Frank R. Parker, *The Damaging Consequences of the Rehnquist Court's Commitment to Color-Blindness Versus Racial Justice*, 45 AM. U. L. REV. 763, 766 (1996).

> With the critical support of the swing votes of Justices O'Connor and Kennedy, this far-right faction, made up of Chief Justice Rehnquist and Justices Scalia and Thomas, has the five votes it needs in the Court's most critical race cases to change the course of constitutional jurisprudence, reverse and undermine prior precedents, and redefine the constitutional limits on judicial and governmental remedies designed to overcome racial discrimination and promote racial equality.

Id. At any rate, this chapter is written with the hope that someone other than Justice Scalia will set the terms of the affirmative action debate.

12. Regents of the Univ. of Cal. v. Bakke, 438 U.S. 265, 407 (1978).

13. See pages 379 ff. for a discussion of sociological explanations of the relationship between discrimination and black criminality.

This article, concerned as it is with law and justice, purposely ignores the political unpopularity of affirmative action among white people. My focus is motivated in part by a frustration with recent scholarship on affirmative action that focuses almost exclusively on the efficacy of the existing programs, which to my mind are limited reforms. *See generally* Conference, *Race, Law and Justice: The Rehnquist Court and the American Dilemma*, 45 AM. U. L. REV. 567 (1996). I would prefer to discuss (at least some of the time) how far such programs should be extended, not whether they should be maintained. On a moral level, majority disfavor of affirmative action is irrelevant, even though it has material consequences. For example, 55 percent of California voters passed Proposition 209, which would outlaw all state affirmative action programs. *See* Tim Golden, *U.S. Judge Blocks Enforcing the Law over Preferences*, N.Y. TIMES, Dec. 24, 1996, at A1. If affirmative action is just, it may not be too naive to hope that its unpopularity will recede. In 1965, Martin Luther King, Jr., said, "However difficult the moment, however frustrating the hour, it will not be long, because truth crushed to the earth will rise again. ... How long? Not long ... because the arc of the moral universe is long, but it bends toward justice." David Treadwell, *Debts to Dr. King: One Man Touched So Many Lives*, L.A. TIMES, Mar. 27, 1988, at A1. On racial matters, American popular opinion changes at glacial speed, or so it seems to the victims of discrimination. (Critical race theorists, among others, have advocated judging the fairness of law by its impact on victims. *See, e.g.,* Mari J. Matsuda, *Legal Storytelling: Public Response to Racist Speech: Considering the Victim's Story*, 87 MICH. L. REV. 2320 (1989).) However, the white majority's opinion can change, as evidenced by current opposition to slavery, de jure segregation, and miscegenation laws. If and when the body politic and the Supreme Court fully realize the necessity of affirmative action in civil law, there ought to be a theory to extend the same concept of justice to the criminally accused. This chapter advances such a theory.

14. Antonia Hernandez, director of the Mexican American Legal Defense and Education Fund, has noted that affirmative action was not adequately debated at its outset and that the debate now "is being held as an afterthought." Ellis Cose, *After Affirmative Action*, NEWSWEEK, Nov. 11, 1996, at 43.

15. Of course, affirmative action also exists for non-racial groups, such as women and veterans. This article focuses exclusively on race-based affirmative action, although in my final section I consider the gender implications of one of my proposals.

16. "[O]ne way to distinguish between the civil rights laws ... and affirmative action law is to think of the former as prohibiting discrimination and the latter as permitting discrimination." ROY L. BROOKS ET AL., CIVIL RIGHTS LITIGATION: CASES AND PERSPECTIVES 1067 (1995).

17. Of course, race preferences—for white people—are perfectly American, at least from a historical preference.

18. 163 U.S. 537, 559 (1896) (Harlan, J., dissenting).

19. *Id.* at 559.

20. *See* Neil Gotanda, *A Critique of "Our Constitution Is Color-Blind,"* 44 STAN. L. REV. 1, 2–3 (1991). "A color-blind interpretation of the Constitution legitimates, and thereby maintains, the social, economic, and political advantages that whites hold over other Americans." *Id.*

21. *See* United States v. Fordice, 505 U.S. 717 (1992) (holding that states have an affirmative duty to eradicate effects of prior de jure segregation).

22. President Clinton has said in defense of affirmative action:

> It is a policy that grew out of many years of trying to navigate between two unacceptable paths. One was to say simply that we declared discrimination illegal, and that's enough. We saw that way still relegated blacks with college degrees to jobs as railroad porters, and kept women with degrees under a glass ceiling, with a lower paycheck.

Give All Americans a Chance, WASH. POST, July 20, 1995, at A12; *see also* City of Richmond v. J.A. Croson Co., 488 U.S. 469, 509 (1988) ("If the city of Richmond had evidence before it that nonminority contractors were systematically excluding minority business from subcontracting opportunities, it could take action to end the discriminatory exclusion.").

23. *See, e.g.,* Regents of the Univ. of Cal. v. Bakke, 438 U.S. 265 (1978) (affirming goal of diverse student body as compelling governmental interest in support of affirmative action in medical school admissions).

24. *See, e.g.,* John E. Morrison, *Colorblindness, Individuality, and Merit: An Analysis of the Rhetoric Against Affirmative Action,* 79 Iowa L. Rev. 313, 320–21 (1994) (stating that "America's history makes color-consciousness inevitable and gives meaning to race until society obliterates all traces of past injustices. This rhetoric often demands reparations for past injustices suffered by African Americans during the periods of slavery and segregation.") (citation omitted).

25. *See* Derrick Bell, Race, Racism and American Law § 1.13, at 39–40 (3d ed. 1992).

26. *See* W. Page Keeton et al., Prosser and Keeton on the Law of Torts, § 2, at 7, § 8, at 33–37 (5th ed. 1984).

27. Wittmer v. Peters, 87 F.3d 916, 919 (7th Cir. 1996).

28. The major exception would be people who ascribe the comparatively low achievement of African Americans to genetic inferiority (or "differences," as they would posit). *See* Richard J. Herrnstein & Charles Murray, The Bell Curve 312 (1994).

29. Regents of the Univ. of Cal. v. Bakke, 438 U.S. 265, 400–01 (1978) (Marshall, J.).

30. City of Richmond v. J.A. Croson Co., 488 U.S. 469, 552 (1989) (Marshall, J., dissenting).

31. *See* Paul Finkelman, *The Crime of Color,* 67 Tul. L. Rev. 2063, 2067–70 (1998) (positing that blackness itself constituted a crime in early America).

32. 438 U.S. 265 (1978).

33. *Id.* at 307.

34. *Id.*

35. 115 S. Ct. 2097 (1995).

36. *See* City of Richmond v. J.A. Croson Co., 488 U.S. 469, 493–94 (1989); Wygant v. Jackson Bd. of Educ., 476 U.S. 267, 274 (1986).

37. *See, e.g., Croson,* 488 U.S. at 470–74 (producing five opinions, but with a majority agreeing that strict scrutiny applies to all racial classifications challenged under the Fourteenth Amendment); *Wygant,* 476 U.S. at 267 (producing a plurality opinion and four separate concurring opinions).

38. *See Wygant,* 476 U.S. at 267–68 (plurality opinion applying strict scrutiny and finding that a race-preferential layoff provision was not narrowly tailored to achieve a compelling government interest); Fullilove v. Klutznick, 448 U.S. 448, 448–52 (1980) (plurality upholding the affirmative action program at issue).

39. Wittmer v. Peters, 87 F.3d 916, 918 (7th Cir. 1996) (holding that race was a permissible criterion in the selection of correctional officers for an Illinois "boot camp" for male criminals in which 68 percent of the criminals were African American) (citations omitted).

40. *Id.*

41. *See* pages 388 ff. This is particularly true of those affirmative action reforms justified under the past discrimination rationale.

42. See Brooks et al., *supra* note 16, at 1070.

[A] voluntary [affirmative action] program survives a Title VII [of the Civil Rights Act of 1964, which proscribes racial discrimination in employment challenges] if it is designed to mirror Title VII's purpose and does not unnecessarily trammel the interests of white males. An involuntary program is permissible under Title VII if its purpose is to remedy a Title VII violation in which the unlawful discrimination is found to be "persistent," "pervasive and egregious."

Id.

43. *See* U.S. CONST. amend. XIII (outlawing slavery); U.S. CONST. amend. XIV (guaranteeing due process and equal protection of the laws); U.S. CONST. amend. XV (guaranteeing the right to vote).

44. *See* Civil Rights Act of 1866, 42 U.S.C. § 1982 (1989); Civil Rights Act of 1870, 42 U.S.C. § 1981 (1989); Equal Employment Opportunity Act of 1972, Pub. L. No. 92-261 (codified as amended in scattered sections of 5 & 42 U.S.C.).

45. *See* HACKER, *supra* note 6, at 98; Fletcher, *supra* note 7, at A3.

46. Paul Brest & Miranda Oshige, *Affirmative Action for Whom?*, 47 STAN. L. REV. 855, 867 (1995).

47. In *City of Richmond v. J.A. Croson*, 488 U.S. 469 (1989), the Supreme Court considered a Richmond, Virginia, affirmative action program that reserved 30 percent of the city construction contracts for minorities. *See id.* at 477. Although African Americans comprised 50 percent of the population of Richmond, they had received fewer than 1 percent of such contracts in the five years before the program was implemented. *See id.* at 479–80. The Richmond plan was premised on the belief that the absence of minorities in the construction field was an effect of past discrimination. *See id.* at 480. Nevertheless, the Court held that Richmond lacked a "strong basis in evidence" that the remedial action was necessary, and that it had not been established that the absence of minorities in the construction industry was attributable to past discrimination. *See id.* at 498–500. However, in dicta, the Court suggested its analysis would be similar for present discrimination affirmative action. Justice O'Connor wrote, "It is beyond dispute that any public entity, state or federal, has a compelling interest in assuring that public dollars, drawn from the tax contributions of all citizens, do not serve to finance the evil of private prejudice." *Id.* at 492. The Court held that the Richmond plan was subject to strict scrutiny analysis under the Fourteenth Amendment. *See id.* at 493–94. In *Wygant v. Jackson Board of Education*, 476 U.S. 267 (1986), Justice O'Connor, in a concurring opinion, was more forthright about the permissible use of race preferences to prevent ongoing discrimination. She wrote that "[t]he Court is in agreement that, whatever the formulation employed, remedying past or present racial discrimination by a state actor is a sufficiently weighty state interest to warrant the remedial use of a carefully constructed affirmative action program." *Id.* at 286.

48. Adarand Constructors, Inc. v. Pena, 115 S. Ct. 2097, 2117 (1995).

49. I borrow the phrase from President Clinton, who uses it as a buzzword for people of color and white women. During the 1992 campaign, Clinton promised that if he was elected, his Cabinet and close advisers would "look like America." *See* Gwen Ifill, *Three Women Are Said to Be Candidates for Cabinet Posts*, N.Y. TIMES, Dec. 7, 1992, at A6.

50. *See* Regents of the Univ. of Cal. v. Bakke, 438 U.S. 265, 323 (1978). Justice Powell wrote:

A farm boy from Idaho can bring something to Harvard College that a Bostonian cannot offer. Similarly, a black student can usually bring something that a white person cannot offer. The quality of the educational experience of all the students in Harvard College depends in part on these differences in the background and outlook that students bring with them.

Id.

51. *See id.*

52. *See, e.g.,* Shaw v. Reno, 509 U.S. 630, 647–48 (1993); Hopwood v. Texas, 78 F.3d 932, 945 (5th Cir.), *cert. denied,* 116 S. Ct. 2581 (1996).

53. In *Shaw,* Justice O'Connor wrote:

A reapportionment plan that includes in one district individuals who belong to the same race, but who are otherwise widely separated by geographical and political boundaries, and who may have little in common with one another but the color of their skin, bears an uncomfortable resemblance to political apartheid. It reinforces the perception that members of the same racial group—regardless of their age, education, economic status, or the community in which they live—think alike, share the same political interests, and will prefer the same candidates at the polls. We have rejected such perceptions elsewhere as impermissible racial stereotypes.

509 U.S. at 647.

54. *See* Edmonson v. Leesville Concrete Co., 500 U.S. 614, 630–31 (1991). "If our society is to continue to progress as a multiracial democracy, it must recognize that the automatic invocation of race stereotypes retards that progress and causes continued hurt and injury." *Id.*

55. By "legal," I mean approved by the Supreme Court. As will be discussed in more detail below, even this justification is in jeopardy.

56. In *Regents of the University of California v. Bakke,* 438 U.S. 265 (1978). Justice Powell endorsed an admissions program at Harvard College in which membership in a racial minority group, along with other non-racial factors, was weighted favorably in admissions decisions. *See id.* at 322–24. Justice Powell believed that a university student population that "reflects the rich diversity of the United States" is valuable and impossible to achieve "without some attention to numbers." *Id.* at 323. This rationale also carried the day in *Metro Broadcasting, Inc. v. Federal Communications Commission,* 497 U.S. 547 (1990), *standard of review overruled by Adarand Constructors, Inc. v. Pena,* 115 S. Ct. 2097 (1995). In that case, the Supreme Court ruled that racial preferences by the Federal Communications Commission did not violate the Equal Protection Clause because the preferences supported the important government objective of "programming diversity." *Id.* at 569–71. In *Adarand Constructors,* the Court ruled that strict scrutiny was the appropriate standard of review for any government race classification, benign or otherwise. *See id.* at 2112–13. *Adarand* did not address whether the FCC program would have survived this heightened scrutiny.

A recent federal court of appeals decision casts doubt on the viability of diversity as a constitutionally sufficient justification for race preferences. In *Hopwood v. Texas,* 78 F.3d 932 (5th Cir.), *cert. denied,* 116 S. Ct. 2581 (1996), a divided panel of the Fifth Circuit concluded that Justice Powell's opinion in *Bakke* had never commanded the support of a majority of the Supreme Court. *See id.* at 944. The panel refused to consider essential-diversity as a compelling state interest that would justify the affirmative action program before it (the University of Texas Law School's plan involved its admissions). *See id.* at 945–46. The Supreme Court declined to review the appellate court's decision in *Hopwood,* rendering uncertain the constitutional prognosis of affirmative action for diversity. *See* Texas v. Hopwood, 116 S. Ct. 2581 (1996). At the time the Supreme Court denied certiorari, the affirmative action program had been abandoned by the University of Texas Law School. Justice Ginsburg commented, "[W]e must await a final judgment on a program genuinely in controversy." *Id.* at 2582.

57. *But see* Matsuda, *supra* note 13, at 2323–26 (positing that people of color have a unique experience because of their race).

58. *See generally id.* (advocating that the fairness of law be judged by its impact on victims).

59. *See* Paul Butler, *Racially Based Jury Nullification: Black Power in the Criminal Justice System,* 105 YALE L.J. 677, 695 n.90 (1995) (noting "precedent in … [non-criminal] law, e.g., employment discrimination law, suggesting that a racially disparate effect is either prima facie evidence of racial discrimination or otherwise indicative of a practice or policy that should be changed") (citation omitted).

60. *See* Edward W. Lempinen, *Prop. 209 Takes National Stage,* S.F. CHRON., Dec. 16, 1996, at A1 ("[P]olls say that while most people oppose quotas and set-asides, many continue to favor outreach and recruitment programs.").

61. Professor Burton Wechsler of American University Law School has stated:

> If we get rid of affirmative action, where are we going to get the doctors in the black community? … If you get rid of race-based affirmative action at American University Law School, you're not going to have any black students here. … I mentioned that to a colleague of mine who said. "Well I know where we'll get our black law students. We'll get them from Harvard." [I said w]ell, there won't be many.

Conference, *supra* note 13, at 662; *see also* Brest & Oshige, *supra* note 46, at 858 ("[A]n end to affirmative action would leave many of the nation's law schools—especially the most selective ones—with a largely white and (increasingly) East Asian student body, and with few African American, Latino, and Native American students."); Lempinen, *supra* note 60 (stating that California University officials "warned that [an anti-affirmative action proposition] could cut enrollment of blacks, Latinos and American Indians by half at the prestigious Berkeley and Los Angeles campuses").

62. Bob Dole, former senator and Republican presidential candidate, has argued that affirmative action has not benefited the poor. "Every time I drive to work in Washington, D.C., or drive down North Capitol Street, I see dozens and dozens of black men, without work. And I say to myself. 'What has this [race-conscious] law done for them?' Absolutely nothing." Blaine Harden, *Dole Woos California Voters with Support of Ballot Item; GOP Nominee Calls Affirmative Action a "Blind Alley,"* WASH. POST, Oct. 29, 1996, at A8. Of course, Dole's critique would not apply to affirmative action in criminal law, because most criminals are poor.

63. *See supra* note 8 for statistics on the 104th Congress. The 105th Congress has 37 African Americans—36 in the House and one in the Senate. *See* Charles Krauthammer, *Elections Discount Theories Challenging Racial Gerrymandering,* CHI. TRIB., Nov. 18, 1996, at N19.

64. *See* Don Lee et al., *Aftermath of Affirmative Action Ruling; Many Minorities Fear That Opportunities Will Diminish Advancement; Widespread Concern Exists That Firms That Once Stressed Affirmative Action May Ease Their Policies,* L.A. TIMES, June 14, 1995, at D1.

65. *See* ROY L. BROOKS, RETHINKING THE AMERICAN RACE PROBLEM 54 (1990) (describing studies proving effectiveness of affirmative action programs).

I feel some responsibility to "out" myself as a proud beneficiary of affirmative action. I believe that I would not have gained admission to Yale College and Harvard Law School and employment at George Washington University Law School but for affirmative action. I also believe that, in addition to granting me a privilege, each of these institutions gained in the exchange.

66. Randall Kennedy, *Persuasion and Distrust: A Comment on the Affirmative Action Debate,* 99 HARV. L. REV. 1327, 1331 (1986).

67. Justice O'Connor theorizes that race preferences "contribut[e] to an escalation of racial hostility and conflict." Metro Broadcasting, Inc. v. Federal Communications Comm'n, 497 U.S. 547, 603 (1990) (O'Connor, J., dissenting). For example, Jesse Helms capitalized on white backlash against racial preferences during his 1990 Senate re-election campaign against Harvey Gantt, an African American. Helms ran a television commercial showing the hands of a white person crumpling a rejection letter while the announcer says "and you were the best qualified. But they had to give it to a minority because of a racial quota." *See In South, It's a Divisive Race to the Finish,* CHI. TRIB., Nov. 5, 1990, at 4.

68. *See* Kennedy, *supra* note 66, at 1337–45.

69. *See* John E. Morrison, *Colorblindness, Individuality, and Merit: An Analysis of the Rhetoric Against Affirmative Action,* 79 IOWA L. REV. 313, 334–40 (1994). Racial hostility and conflict existed in the United States long before affirmative action, and as the O.J. Simpson case indicates, it exists outside the context of affirmative action. *See, e.g.,* Henry L. Gates, Jr., *Thirteen Ways of Looking at a Black Man,* NEW YORKER, Oct. 23, 1995, at 56. In response to concern about a white backlash to black jury nullification, I have noted that "if African Americans adapted their political and self-help strategies so as not to raise the possibility of white backlash, they would scarcely advance at all." Paul Butler, *The Evil of American Criminal Justice: A Reply,* 44 UCLA L. REV. 143, 155 (1996).

70. *See* Morrison, *supra* note 69, at 337.

71. I focus on African Americans because of their extreme participation in the criminal justice system compared with other groups. There is vigorous debate about which minority groups are entitled to affirmative action. *See, e.g.,* Deborah Ramirez, *Multicultural Empowerment: It's Not Just Black and White Anymore,* 47 STAN. L. REV. 957 (1995); Frank H. Wu, *Changing America: Three Arguments About Asian Americans and the Law,* 45 AM. U. L. REV. 811 (1996).

72. One in three young black men are under criminal justice supervision. *See* MAUER & HULING, *supra* note 5. In Washington, D.C., the percentage is 42 percent, *see* JEROME G. MILLER, HOBBLING A GENERATION: YOUNG AFRICAN AMERICAN MALES IN WASHINGTON, D.C.'S CRIMINAL JUSTICE SYSTEM 1 (1992), and in Baltimore, Maryland, it is 56 percent, *see* NATIONAL CTR. ON INSTS. AND ALTERNATIVES, HOBBLING A GENERATION: YOUNG AFRICAN AMERICAN MALES IN THE CRIMINAL JUSTICE SYSTEM OF AMERICA'S CITIES: BALTIMORE, MARYLAND 1 (1992). In California, nearly two-thirds of all black men are arrested between the ages of 18 and 30. *See* Robert Tillman, *The Size of the "Criminal Population": The Prevalence and Incidence of Adult Arrest,* 25 CRIMINOLOGY 561, 576 (1987).

73. *See* HERRNSTEIN & MURRAY, *supra* note 28, at 272–76.

74. Of course, some observers believe that this is exactly what the present criminal justice system accomplishes. Jesse Jackson, in an address to the 1992 Democratic National Convention, stated that "jail is a step up" for many black inner-city youths. *See* Fox Butterfield, *Are American Jails Becoming Shelters from the Storm,* N.Y. TIMES, July 19, 1992, at A4. Jackson said, "Once they are jailed, they are no longer homeless. Once they are jailed, they have balanced meals. Once they are jailed, they will no longer be hit by drive-by shootings." *Id.; see also* Robert Blecker, *Haven or Hell? Inside Lorton Central Prison:*

Experiences of Punishment Justified, 42 STAN L. REV. 1149, 1244–48 (1990) (advocating a humane prison environment and criminal justice system to discourage recidivism).

75. Justice Scalia has written: "[U]nder our Constitution there can be no such thing as either a creditor or a debtor race. . . . In the eyes of the government, we are just one race here. It is American." Adarand Constructors, Inc. v. Pena, 115 S. Ct. 2097, 2118–19 (1995) (Scalia, J., concurring).

76. Retribution is the only theory of punishment that focuses on the criminal defendant's individual blameworthiness. The other major justifications of punishment—deterrence, isolation, and rehabilitation—are primarily utilitarian.

77. HERBERT MORRIS, ON GUILT AND INNOCENCE 34 (1976).

78. For example, in the traditional sense of fair play, preferences for Hispanics in college admissions ordinarily would be unjust if Hispanics were just like whites in all respects relevant to qualifying for admission. However, proponents of past discrimination affirmative action presume that they are not, and that this disparity is not the fault of Hispanics. Accordingly, it is unfair to deny them admission using criteria that favor whites. Race preferences give the Hispanic candidate a well-deserved headstart because she started the race with a broken leg.

79. Leveling the playing field for black criminals will not prevent crime. For two reasons, however, this fact does not defeat the justice of reparations affirmative action for African-American criminals. First, retributive punishment is justified by moral blameworthiness, not the utilitarian goal of crime prevention. Second, racial preferences in the civil law also are not intended to correct directly the environmental factors that cause substandard minority performance; indeed, under the past discrimination theory, this would be impossible because one cannot reverse history. Rather, affirmative action tries to compensate for a discriminatory environment by putting minorities where they would be had the ugly past never occurred. There is usually some hope that, over time, the compensation will improve the inferior environment of minorities (at least to the extent of making it equal to the white majority's environment) so that, one day, racial preferences no longer will be required.

80. This is not the case with drug possession offenses. *See* pages 383 ff.

81. This focus will free us of the intractable issue in criminal law of individual will versus social determinism writ large; we will not have to solve that issue but rather, and more simply, understand how race matters in the equation.

82. Norval Morris, *Psychiatry and the Dangerous Criminal,* 41 S. CAL. L. REV. 514, 520 (1968); *see also* MARVIN D. FREE, AFRICAN AMERICANS AND THE CRIMINAL JUSTICE SYSTEM 43–64 (1996). There are, of course, some biological theories, *see id.* at 64–68, but the evidence is not persuasive. While biological theories also exist to explain substandard minority achievement, affirmative action assumes, correctly I believe, that these theories are not the best explanation.

83. *See* FREE, *supra* note 82, at 45. "Three strain theories frequently used to explain crime are anomie theory, reaction-formation theory, and differential opportunity theory. Each intimates that relatively powerless groups, such as African Americans and other minorities, should be more likely to engage in crime than more favorably situated groups." *Id.*

84. Michael Tonry describes the consensus:

[C]rime by young disadvantaged black men does not result primarily from their individual moral failures but from their misfortune of being born in places and times and under circumstances that make crime, drug use, and gang membership look like reasonable choices from a narrow range of not very attractive options.

There is no other defensible explanation for why crime, delinquency, and drug use are so extraordinarily more prevalent among disadvantaged minority youth than among other youth. Few outside the lunatic fringes of American society believe or are prepared to argue that genetic or biological factors explain disproportionate black offending. Some conservatives apparently still subscribe to "culture of poverty" explanations of black disadvantage, but because no one doubts that culture in the shorter or longer term is shaped by environmental conditions, this merely changes the contextual description of the forces that shape disadvantaged young men's choices.

MICHAEL TONRY, MALIGN NEGLECT—RACE, CRIME, AND PUNISHMENT IN AMERICA 134 (1995).

85. "Choice" is a loaded word in the criminal context. It is true, in some absolute sense, that the criminal makes a choice to disobey the law; my argument is that when the choice is influenced by race, retributive justice is an inappropriate social response. The exhortation "obey the law" should not end the legal and moral response to the black criminal any more than "study harder" should end the response to the minority college applicant with lower standardized test scores.

86. But should the criminal law recognize environment as a cause of antisocial conduct? For help, we turn to the Model Penal Code—the most influential modern statement of criminal justice—and extrapolate from its teachings on the doctrine of causation. The Model Penal Code's answer is short and sweet: a factor causes a result if it is fair to say that it does. See MODEL PENAL CODE § 2.03(2)b, (3)(b), and commentary (1985). I describe my interpretation here as an "extrapolation" because the Code's framers probably intended its construct of causation to be limited to actus reus problems of causation, for example, if Lakeisha commits suicide to avoid being assaulted by Bob, is it fair to punish Bob for "causing" Lakeisha's death? Professor Joshua Dressler notes, however, that "perhaps the broadest non-utilitarian principle of excuse law states that no person should be blamed for conduct if it was caused by a force over which she has no control." JOSHUA DRESSLER, UNDERSTANDING CRIMINAL LAW § 17.03, at 183–186 (1987) (citing Joshua Dressler, *Professor Delgado's "Brainwashing" Defense: Courting a Determinist Legal System*, 63 MINN. L. REV. 335, 359–60 (1979)). Dressler observes that the principle is "plausible on its face and represents the views of some scholars and courts," but is not generally practiced perhaps because acceptance "would threaten to lead society down 'the cul-de-sac of . . . determinism,' whereby nobody would be blamed or punished for her wrongful acts." *Id.* My thesis assumes that race is the stopgap to the slippery slope problem. Any race-based affirmative action regime implicitly exalts racial justice when it does not address other forms of injustice (e.g., class); this does not necessarily suggest a disregard of non-racial oppression, but rather a recognition that a line needs to be drawn somewhere, and that race (and sometimes gender) is a good place to draw it. The Model Penal Code recognizes that, in the law, causation analysis is not scientific, for every result has many causes: I teach criminal law at George Washington University because the dean asked me to, and because there was a slave trade in Africa, and because I used to be a prosecutor, and because, many years ago, my parents had sex one night in April. The most the law can do, according to the Code, is invite the jury to *select* a cause in order to assess criminal responsibility; the jury should be guided by "common sense and fairness." *Id.* § 14.04, at 169–70.

87. *See* Regents of the Univ. of Cal. v. Bakke, 438 U.S. 265, 277 n.7 (1978) (comparing Alan Bakke's MCAT scores with those of regular and special admittees at UC Davis Medical School).

88. For an argument that minority communities are better off with more law enforcement than are white communities, see Randall Kennedy. *The State, Criminal Law, and Racial Discrimination: A Comment,* 107 HARV. L. REV. 1255 (1994). For a contrary argument, see Butler, *supra* note 69.

89. In 1992, 58 percent of federal prisoners were drug offenders. *See* TONRY, *supra* note 84, at 81–82.

90. *See* Pierre Thomas, *One in Three Young Black Men in Justice System: Criminal Sentencing Policies Cited in Study,* WASH. POST, Oct. 5, 1995, at A1 (describing study). One reason for the racial discrepancy in narcotics punishment is the severe penalties for crack, a form of cocaine used mainly by blacks. *See id.* In a federal prosecution, defendants receive the same punishment for possession of five grams of crack as they do for possession of 500 grams of powder cocaine, the form of the drug favored by whites. *See id.* Many state laws also punish crack cocaine offenders more severely than powdered cocaine offenders although, chemically, the two forms of the drug are virtually identical. There is controversy about whether crack cocaine is objectively "worse" (e.g., more addictive or more likely to induce violent behavior) than powder cocaine. Some critics argue that the severe punishment for crack cocaine offenses harms African Americans, particularly when the costs to the black community of having so many of its citizens locked up are considered. To the argument that a community is better off with its lawbreakers in prison, they respond that the white community does not appear to experience significant social disorder when most of its drug offenders are not imprisoned.

Michael Tonry has accused politicians of "malign neglect" in waging a war on drugs that had the foreseeable result that blacks "have been arrested, prosecuted, convicted, and imprisoned at increasing rates since [the inception of the war], and grossly out of proportion to their numbers in the general population or among drug users." *See* TONRY, *supra* note 84, at 105.

91. To establish a selective prosecution claim, the plaintiff must show that the "federal prosecutorial policy had a discriminatory effect and that it was motivated by a discriminatory purpose. To establish a discriminatory effect in a race case, the claimant must show that similarly situated individuals of different race were not prosecuted." United States v. Armstrong, 116 S. Ct. 1480, 1487 (1996) (citations omitted). To prove discrimination in employment pursuant to Title VII of the Civil Rights Act of 1964, the injured party usually must show that she is a member of a suspect class and that she was treated differently because of her membership in that class. The problem in both situations is that the discretion vested in the decisionmakers makes it relatively easy to disguise a racist motive, or to cast it in non-racial terms. In the case of selective prosecution, *Armstrong* compounds the problem by severely limiting discovery by persons who allege selective prosecution. *See id.* at 1485. For employment discrimination, the Civil Rights Act of 1991 permits a plaintiff to establish a prima facie case of disparate impact by showing that a race neutral employment practice has a disproportionately negative effect on a protected class. *See* BROOKS ET AL., *supra* note 16, at 462; *see also* Shaw v. Reno, 113 S. Ct. 2816 (1993).

92. In part, the difficulty of proof is attributable to aversive racism, of which the discriminator may not even be aware. *See* Charles R. Lawrence III, *The Id, the Ego, and Equal Protection: Reckoning with Unconscious Racism* 38 STAN. L. REV. 317, 321–22 (1987).

93. That not all African Americans are troubled by disparate enforcement of criminal laws is not evidence that the problem deserves no remedy. Some African Americans, for example, Ward Connerly, author of California's anti-affirmative action Proposition

209, and Justice Clarence Thomas, oppose racial preferences. African-American disunity on civil affirmative action is not proof that racial preferences are unjust; rather the disagreement evidences that the black "community" is not monolithic.

94. In the criminal law context, equal opportunity affirmative action would be premised on the idea that punishment targeted at African Americans is undesirable. The contentiousness of this proposition demonstrates the stigma of criminality that blacks suffer, and responds to the concern that race preferences in criminal justice would stigmatize innocent African Americans. Imagine the argument that, for conduct in which members of all ethnic groups engage, Jewish Americans ought to be selectively imprisoned for the good of their own community. I think we would correctly call such a policy anti-Semitic. But with regard to punishment for African Americans, racism seems different than discrimination.

With or without affirmative action, African Americans face a stigma of criminality. That is the meaning of the women who cross to the other side of the street when I walk behind them. In both the civil and criminal contexts, race preferences do not *eliminate* the stigma, but they do *recast* it—from an assumption of demerit to a doubt of merit. Without affirmative action, the stigma is confirmed by the relative dearth of blacks among the pool of those considered objectively meritorious (measured as "qualified," in the civil context, or "law-abiding," in the criminal context). With affirmative action, some blacks have a seat at the table, but they are stigmatized as undeserving—belonging at a community college instead of Harvard or in prison instead of on the street. The political necessity of having to choose a stigma is unfortunate, but I suspect many African Americans would select the stigma of affirmative action—especially if it is the price of the ticket for the advancement of their people.

95. *See* pages 381 ff.

96. *But see* Wittmer v. Peters, 87 F.3d 916 (7th Cir. 1996) (applying essential-diversity rhetoric to uphold an affirmative action program at a prison boot camp) (discussed further pages 385 ff.

97. In 1994, for the first time in American history, there were more African American men in prison than white men. *See Blacks Are Majority in U.S. Prisons: Number of Inmates at All-Time High,* JET, Dec. 18, 1995, at 59.

98. *See* Finkelman, *supra* note 31, at 2063.

99. *See supra* note 3 and accompanying text.

100. *See supra* note 90 and accompanying text.

101. A 1995 study by the Sentencing Project reported that the number of African American women under the supervision of the criminal justice system rose 78 percent between 1989 and 1994. *See* David Holstrom, *Why Young African-American Men Fill U.S. Jails,* CHRISTIAN SCI. MONITOR, Oct. 6, 1995, at 12.

102. Diversity affirmative action is consequentialist; it does not address the root causes of African-American criminal conduct. Acknowledging that truth does not so much defeat the theory as connect it to other types of affirmative action. In the civil law context as well, racial preferences are limited reforms that treat symptoms but not the actual disease. While minorities anxiously await the day when a cure is found, symptomatic relief is preferable to none at all.

103. *See* Matsuda, *supra* note 18 (proposing that hate speech be criminalized).

104. 966 F.2d 391 (8th Cir. 1992).

105. *Id.* at 394 n.2. *Weaver* represents the traditional view on this issue. A few courts, however, have taken the position that suspicion on grounds of racial incongruity is "in-

vidious" discrimination. *See, e.g.,* City of St. Paul v. Uber, 450 N.W.2d 623, 628 (Minn. Ct. App. 1990).

106. *See, e.g.,* Cruz v. Beto, 405 U.S. 319, 321 (1972); Lee v. Washington, 390 U.S. 333, 334 (1967); Stewart v. Rhodes, 478 F. Supp 1185, 1189 (S.D. Ohio 1979).

107. 390 U.S. 333 (1967).

108. *Id.* at 334.

109. *Id.* (Black, J., Harlan, J., and Stewart, J., concurring).

110. 488 U.S. 469 (1989).

111. *Id.* at 521 (Scalia, J., concurring).

112. *See, e.g.,* Barhold v. Rodriguez, 863 F.2d 233 (2d Cir. 1988); Detroit Police Officers' Ass'n v. Young, 608 F.2d 671 (6th Cir. 1979); Minnick v. California Dep't of Corrections, 95 Cal. App. 3d 506 (1979).

113. 87 F.3d 916 (7th Cir. 1996).

114. *See id.*

115. *See id.* at 917.

116. *See id.*

117. *Id.* at 920.

118. *Id.* at 919.

119. *Id.* at 920.

120. *Id.*

121. *See, e.g.,* FED. R. EVID. 403.

122. *See, e.g.,* FED. R. EVID. 412.

123. *See* SANDFORD H. KADISH & STEPHEN J. SCHULHOFER, CRIMINAL LAW AND ITS PROCESSES 373–74 (6th ed. 1995).

124. 501 U.S. 957 (1991).

125. *See id.* at 975–76.

126. *See id.* at 985–86.

127. *See id.* at 988–89.

128. *Id.* at 994 (citing Turner v. Murray, 476 U.S. 28, 36–37 (1986); Eddings v. Oklahoma, 455 U.S. 104 (1982); Beck v. Alabama, 447 U.S. 625 (1980)).

129. *See* Richard A. Rosen, *Felony Murder and the Eighth Amendment Jurisprudence of Death,* 31 B.C. L. REV. 1103, 1146–63 (1990).

130. Other legal scholars have recommended fairness preferences in the criminal justice system. For a thoughtful proposal that courts consider race when judging the constitutionality of police interactions with African Americans, see Tracey Maclin, *Black and Blue Encounters—Some Preliminary Thoughts About Fourth Amendment Seizures: Should Race Matter,* 26 VAL. U. L. REV. 243 (1991). Professor Maclin explicitly rejected conceptualizing his proposal as affirmative action. *See id.* at 272. He argued that race consciousness by courts in reviewing police stops is required by the Fourth Amendment's requirement that searches be reasonable. *See id.* at 250. Professor Richard Delgado, in an article that anticipated the "black rage" defense, considered whether the law should excuse conduct precipitated by a deprived environment. *See* Richard Delgado, *"Rotten Social Background": Should the Criminal Law Recognize a Defense of Severe Environmental Deprivation?,* 3 LAW & INEQ. J. 9, 54–79 (1985). Professor Charles Ogletree has suggested that "to help remedy the pervasive racial discrimination in our criminal justice system, judges should be given discretion to take into account an offender's race as a mitigating factor." Charles J. Ogletree, Jr., *The Death of Discretion? Reflections on the Federal Sentencing Guidelines,* 101 HARV. L. REV. 1938, 1960 (1988). Professor Regina

Austin has called for a "politics of identification" that would "make the legal system more sensitive to the social connection that links 'the community' and its lawbreakers and affects black assessments of black criminality." Regina Austin, *"The Black Community,"* *Its Lawbreakers, and a Politics of Identification* 65 S. CAL. L. REV. 1769, 1815 (1992).

131. *Cf.* Regents of the Univ. of Cal. v. Bakke, 438 U.S. 265, 315–19 (1978) (Powell, J.) (concluding that a public university's medical school may not use quotas to create ethnic diversity in the student body, but rather may use race as a "plus" when making an admissions decision).

132. What is the basis for affirmative action in democracy? The most persuasive explanation probably is not the past discrimination rationale, given the requirement that relief must be narrowly tailored. In *United Jewish Organizations v. Carey*, 430 U.S. 144 (1977), the Court stated that "the permissible use of racial criteria is not confined to eliminating the effects of past discrimination in districting or apportionment." *Id.* at 161. Subsequent cases, including *Shaw v. Reno*, 509 U.S. 630 (1993), and *Miller v. Johnson*, 115 S. Ct. 2475 (1995), signal a greater reluctance by the Court to embrace racially gerrymandered districts, but the Court has never ruled that such districts are per se unconstitutional. In both *Shaw* and *Miller*, the race preferences were defended more on the ground that they enhanced African American voting strength than that they were remediation for poll taxes and grandfather clauses. In *Shaw*, Justice O'Connor cited *Carey* for the proposition that it is acceptable to create districts that will "afford fair representation" to minority groups whose members "are sufficiently numerous." *Shaw*, 509 U.S. at 651 (citing *Carey*, 430 U.S. at 168). Although many states have a wretched history of denying blacks the franchise, none still do so and, at any rate, remedying that problem is not the popular justification for racial gerrymandering. Rather, the wisdom of grouping African Americans together for voting purposes is that it enhances their voting strength; the African-American voice is allowed to be heard. This sounds like essential-diversity but, as we have seen, essential-diversity sometimes provides the legal cover for her outlaw sister—parity-diversity. *See* pages 375 ff.

Think about the evidence usually set forth to establish the need for majority-minority districts. It shows the dearth of minority elected officials in districts that have significant minority populations. The evidence of the success of race preferences is the increase in the number of black elected officials. This is the rhetoric of parity-diversity, and it seems to command the covert support of several Supreme Court Justices. It is significant that the racial gerrymandering cases do not emphasize a connection between past discrimination at the ballot box and the present submergence of the minority voice; as a practical matter, the connection seems only tenuous, like the connection between past discrimination in criminal law and black criminality. But despite the danger that the attenuation poses to surviving strict scrutiny analysis, the Supreme Court has permitted color-consciousness in the service of achieving a more representative democracy. I suggest that the same theory could be employed in the criminal law.

133. *See* Adam Yeomans, *Florida Pays Survivors of a 1923 Racist Attack*, L.A. TIMES, Feb. 12, 1995, at A14.

134. *See Bush Signs Japanese-American Reparations Guarantee*, L.A. TIMES, Nov. 22, 1989, at A12 (describing congressional authorization of $20,000 per survivor for a total of $1.2 billion).

135. According to the 1990 Census, the total population of the United States was 248,709,873. *See* BUREAU OF THE CENSUS, U.S. DEP'T OF COMMERCE, 1990 CENSUS OF POPULATION, SOCIAL AND ECONOMIC CHARACTERISTICS 4 (1993). Of the total population, 29,930,524

were African American. *See id.; see also* HACKER, *supra* note 6, at 15 (noting that if accounting for an undercount, African Americans make up 12.5 percent of the population). The "twelve percent" solution is one that applies to the nation as a whole. In individual jurisdictions where African Americans constitute a larger or smaller share of the population, the number would be adjusted accordingly.

136. *See* THE REAL WAR ON CRIME: THE REPORT OF THE NATIONAL CRIMINAL JUSTICE COMMISSION 9 (Steven R. Donzinger ed., 1996) [hereinafter THE REAL WAR ON CRIME].

> The vast majority of crime in America is not violent. One in ten arrests in the United States is for a violent crime. Only 3 in 100 arrests in the United States are for a violent crime resulting in injury. When people think of locking up criminals, they usually have an image in mind of a violent offender—a murderer or a rapist. But ... the vast majority of people filling ... prisons are nonviolent property and drug offenders.

Id.

137. *See* pages 379 ff.

138. *See, e.g.,* Angela J. Davis, *Benign Neglect of Racism in the Criminal Justice System,* 94 MICH. L. REV. 1660 (1996) (addressing the use of arrest statistics in analyzing racial bias in the criminal justice system); Note, *The Case for Black Juries,* 79 YALE L.J. 531 (1970) (advocating the use of majority black juries).

139. Jeremy Bentham made a similar but non-race-based argument that punishment should not be inflicted in the following circumstances:

> 1. Where it is groundless: where there is no mischief for it to prevent; the act not being mischievous upon the whole. 2. Where it must be inefficacious: where it cannot act so as to prevent the mischief. 3. Where it is unprofitable; or too expensive: where the mischief it would produce would be greater than what it prevented. 4. Where it is needless: where the mischief may be prevented, or case of itself, without it: that is, at a cheaper rate.

Jeremy Bentham, *An Introduction to the Principles of Morals and Legislation, in* THE UTILITARIANS 162, 166 (Jeremy Bentham & John Stuart Mill eds., 1961). My affirmative action proposal would apply this criteria to African Americans, with the additional requirement that the utilitarian benefits of punishment be proved, to the jury, by clear and convincing evidence.

140. JAMES FITZJAMES STEPHEN, A HISTORY OF THE CRIMINAL LAW OF ENGLAND 81–82 (1883).

141. H.L.A. HART, PUNISHMENT AND RESPONSIBILITY 26 (1968).

142. *See, e.g.,* Sheri Lynn Johnson, *Black Innocence and the White Jury,* 83 MICH. L. REV. 1611 (1985). Professor Johnson's seminal article surveys empirical evidence regarding racial discrimination by juries in determining guilt and in sentencing. After examining trial data and mock jury studies, she concluded that racial bias is present in both, although she noted that the evidence of discrimination in guilt determination is more consistent. *See id.* at 1618–25, 1636–38. To counter or eradicate this discrimination, Professor Johnson proposes a "right to a jury including racially similar jurors." *Id.* at 1695. This proposal would require that at least three jurors per panel be "racially similar" to the defendant. *See id.* at 1698–99; *see also* Nancy L. King, *Post-Conviction Reviews of Jury Discrimination: Measuring the Effects of Juror Race on Jury Decisions,* 92 MICH. L. REV. 63 (1993) (supporting Professor Johnson's conclusion that "jurors will tend to convict other-race defendants under circumstances in which they would acquit same-race defendants").

143. The Supreme Court has suggested on numerous occasions that no accused person has a right to have members of a particular race on her jury. *See* Batson v. Kentucky, 476 U.S. 79, 85 (1986) (citing Strauder v. West Virginia, 100 U.S. 303, 305 (1880)); Hernandez v. Texas, 347 U.S. 475 (1954).

144. Redistricting plans created by the Department of Justice during the Bush administration had the "intended effect of maximizing the election of black candidates." Kevin Sack, *Victory of 5 Redistricted Blacks Recasts Gerrymandering Dispute*, N.Y. TIMES, Nov. 22, 1996, at A1; *see also* Joan Biskupic, *Justices Revisit Issue of Minority Voting Districts*, WASH. POST, Dec. 10, 1996, at A4.

145. *See* Gates, *supra* note 69.

146. Race may be used as a factor when drawing district lines as long as it is not the predominant factor. *See* Miller v. Johnson, 115 S. Ct. 2475, 2488 (1995); *see also* Shaw v. Reno, 113 S. Ct. 2816, 2823–24 (holding that racially gerrymandered districts are not per se unlawful but rather must be subjected to strict scrutiny).

147. This study is discussed in Robert Lerner, *Acquittal Rates by Race for State Felonies*, in RACE AND THE CRIMINAL JUSTICE SYSTEM: HOW RACE AFFECTS JURY TRIALS 85 (Gerald A. Reynolds ed., 1996). For an excellent critique of Lerner's methods, *see* Roger Parloff, *Speaking of Junk Science*, AM. LAW., Jan.-Feb. 1997, at 5–7.

148. In his fine book *African Americans and the Criminal Justice System*, Marvin Free examines numerous studies on racial bias in sentencing decisions. *See* FREE, *supra* note 82, at 94–103. He observes ambiguity in the research on race and sentencing. *See id.* at 94. Some studies indicate that black defendants face race discrimination in sentencing. *See id.* at 96–103. Other studies indicate that blacks do not face discrimination. *See id.* Free notes that newer studies have found more evidence of "widespread racial bias in sentencing than was recognized in previous studies." *Id.* at 95. Free observes that courts at sentencing make two decisions: whether to incarcerate and the length of any incarceration. *See id.* at 96. In light of these two distinct decisions by judge or jury, Free divides his analysis into two parts. *See id.* On balance, Free's examination of empirical evidence showed that juries discriminated when deciding whether to incarcerate. *See id.* at 98, 100. He notes, however, that the racial disparities varied by jurisdiction, type of offense, and context. *See id.* Equal opportunity affirmative action requires a finding of discrimination by the institution that grants the race preference. Accordingly, such a finding would be necessary before this proposal could be instituted in a jurisdiction.

With regard to discrimination in sentence length, Free was unable to draw conclusions from the existing research. *See id.* at 103. Some studies showed disparities, some showed disparities of little statistical significance, and others found no direct link between race and sentence severity. *See id.* at 101. He cautioned, however, that "failure to find evidence of racial discrimination at this stage of the criminal justice system does not preclude the possibility that discriminatory factors were operative earlier in the proceeding." *Id.* at 103.

In contrast, Professor Nancy King believes that juror race plays a larger role in sentencing decisions than it does in decisions about guilt or innocence. *See* King, *supra* note 142, at 96 n.126. She notes, however, that the role race plays may depend on the type of sentencing a jury performs. *See id.* at 96. Racial bias increases, she found, when choosing between a life sentence and a death sentence and decreases when jurors are to choose a term of years of probation. *See id.* at 96–97.

149. *See, e.g.,* CAL. PENAL CODE § 190.3 (West 1988); FLA. STAT. ANN. § 921.141 (West 1988); TENN. CODE ANN. § 39-13-204 (1991).

150. *See* King, *supra* note 142, at 122.

151. For example, in *McCleskey v. Kemp,* 481 U.S. 279 (1987), the Court considered a statistical study by Professors David C. Baldus, Charles Pulaski, and George Woodworth (the Baldus study), which suggested that the death penalty was assessed in 22 percent of the cases involving black defendants and white victims, but in only 8 percent of cases involving white defendants and white victims. *Id.* at 286.

152. *Id.* at 318.

153. The Court expressly rejected this argument in *McCleskey,* but its analysis was limited to McCleskey's claims of violations of his Eighth and Fourteenth Amendment rights. *Id.* My thesis does not argue that race preferences for black criminals are required by the Constitution.

154. *See* pages 385 ff.

155. H.R. 4017, 103d Cong. (1994).

156. *See id.*

157. *See id.*

158. *See id.*

159. *See* Don Edwards & John Conyers, Jr., *The Racial Justice Act—A Simple Matter of Justice,* 20 U. DAYTON L. REV. 699, 700–01 (1995).

160. Symposium, *Violent Crime Control and Law Enforcement Act of 1994,* 20 U. DAYTON L. REV. 557, 653 (1995).

161. *See* pages 375 ff.

162. *See* MAUER & HULING, *supra* note 5, at 13 tbl. 6.

163. Butler, *supra* note 69, at 154.

164. *See* Kennedy, *supra* note 88. Of course, affirmative action might result in decreased enforcement of drug laws in the African-American community as opposed to increased enforcement in the white community. As I suggest *infra* text accompanying notes 173–76, I would endorse this result. To accomplish equal opportunity in the short term, some guilty African-American drug offenders might have to be emancipated from criminal justice control. If this seems perverse, we should recall other doctrinal elements of the criminal law that, at times, allow the guilty to go free. These include the burden of proof beyond a reasonable doubt, the exclusionary rule, and jury nullification. Each of these doctrines tolerates non-punishment of the guilty in the service of a higher ideal of justice.

165. Tobacco smoking kills between 400,000 and 500,000 people every year. *See* Janny Scott, *Study Links Ads, Coverage of Smoking Hazards,* L.A. TIMES, Jan. 30, 1992, at A27; *see also* Kurt L. Schmoke, *An Argument in Favor of Decriminalization,* 18 HOFSTRA L. REV. 501 (1990) ("In 1985 alone, approximately 390,000 people died from tobacco related diseases.").

166. *See* Robert Greene, *Government to Continue to Support Tobacco,* FT. LAUDERDALE SENTINEL, Sept. 8, 1996, at 8A.

167. For an excellent discussion of the racial construction of crime, see Dorothy E. Roberts, *Crime, Race, and Reproduction,* 67 TUL. L. REV. 1945, 1954–61 (1993). "Race is built into the normative foundation of the criminal law. Race becomes part of society's determination of which conduct to define as criminal." *Id.* at 1954.

168. In California, for example, people convicted of possession of marijuana with the intent to distribute for sale are jailed for two to five years. *See* CAL. HEALTH & SAFETY CODE §§ 11359, 11360(a) (West 1991 & Supp. 1997).

169. For example, California's Three Strikes Law considers marijuana possession and distribution a felony that counts toward an offender's three strikes. *See* CAL. PENAL CODE § 1170.12 (West Supp. 1997). This broadly written law covers more than 500 felonies, including petty theft and drug possession. The law has resulted in the jailing of substantial numbers of nonviolent offenders. According to a study by the Campaign for Effective Crime Policy, 85 percent of those sentenced under the Three Strikes Law were involved in nonviolent crimes. See Angie Cannon, *3-Strikes Laws Swing and Miss, Survey Indicates,* DENV. POST, Sept. 10, 1996, at A1. As of 1996, 192 people had been sentenced for second and third strikes for marijuana possession, compared with 40 for murder, 25 for rape, and 24 for kidnapping. *See id.*

170. *See* MAUER & HULING, *supra* note 5, at 13 tbl. 6.

171. I hope that parity in drug cases will not lead to the criminalization of tobacco and the return of prohibition. The wiser diversity policy would be to "level down" the criminal justice interest in other drugs, thereby treating those drugs more like alcohol and tobacco. For persuasive arguments in favor of regulating most drug problems through public health means, as opposed to punishment, see Schmoke, *supra* note 165, and Randy E. Barnett, *Bad Trip: Drug Prohibition and the Weakness of Public Policy,* 103 YALE L.J. 2593 (1994). For a discussion of the potential effect of drug prohibition on the African American community, see Butler, *supra* note 69, at 152–55.

172. Who else, other than African Americans, should receive parity in criminal justice? Earlier I observed that race-based affirmative action resolves, or avoids, the slippery slope problem by prioritizing racial justice over other forms of discrimination. There is, however, a group that experiences even more disparity in criminal justice than African Americans: men. As of 1994, 4,367,500 men, but only 762,200 women were under correctional supervision in the United States. *See* BUREAU OF JUSTICE STATISTICS, U.S. DEP'T OF JUSTICE, 1995 SOURCEBOOK OF CRIMINAL JUSTICE STATISTICS 540 tbl. 6.2 (1996). This raises an important issue: should women be proportionately incarcerated, that is, should women comprise 50 percent of those in prison? Once again, the answer might depend upon the reason for the disparity. Is it possible that men are more dangerous or immoral, for reasons that are deserving of punishment? The gender answer is less clear than the race answer; some posit that women, as a group, are less dangerous than men, as a group, for reasons owing to biology. See Scott LaFee, *Is Violent Behavior Rooted in Social Conditions or Biochemistry? An Evil Examined,* SAN DIEGO UNION-TRIB., Nov. 13, 1996, at E1. I understand that biology is as irreversible as past discrimination, but that is where I would draw the line at determinism as an excuse. I would punish men even if the gender disparity in their criminality stems from biology. I have no doubt that my reasons will strike some as being arbitrary. For a critique of biological theories of crime, as well as an analysis of how those theories are racialized, see Roberts, *supra* note 167, at 1965–68. I also understand that one could use the diversity critique of demerit to argue that women's violence and immorality are insufficiently measured by the criminal law. It is a thorny problem that, I am happy to say, need not be resolved in this chapter. In civil affirmative action, the same problem arises in understanding how gender diversity should be measured in, for example, an engineering school or a military institution. For

a sensitive analysis of the intersection of race and gender subordination in criminalizing conduct by African-American women, see generally *id.*

173. *See* Derrick A. Bell, Jr., Brown v. Board of Education, and *The Interest-Convergence Dilemma*, 93 HARV. L. REV. 518 (1980).

174. *See* THE REAL WAR ON CRIME, *supra* note 136, at 33 ("The population of Americans incarcerated on any given day would qualify as the sixth-largest city in the country and is equal to the total combined populations of Seattle, Cleveland, and Denver.").

175. *Id.* at 17.

176. Prison "care" is notoriously expensive, averaging approximately $22,000 per prisoner for each year of incarceration. *See id.* at 21. "Three strikes" laws, which demand life imprisonment for many nonviolent drug offenders, raise these costs even higher because the costs of incarceration increase as inmates age. The government spends approximately $69,000 per year per prisoner for inmates over the age of 55. *See id.* There are obvious opportunity costs associated with spending so much money on punishment. California, for example, in 1994 allocated more of its state budget to prisons than to higher education. *See id.* at 48.

An empirical analysis by the Rand Corporation found that early intervention programs targeting the children of poor, single mothers prevented more crime, per dollar spent, than three strikes laws. *See* Carla River, *Study Finds Aid Outdoes "3 Strikes" in Crime Fight Prevention: Rand Corp. Says Cash Graduation Incentives and Parent Training Are More Cost-Effective*, L.A. TIMES, June 20, 1996, at A3. The estimate of the deterrent value of these programs was based on long-range projections of those likely to commit crime. *See id.* Successful early intervention programs included parental training and family counseling, but the most effective was a program that provided financial incentives (cash and scholarships) for potential high school dropouts to stay in school. *See id.* It was estimated that this program would, if adopted statewide, prevent 258 serious crimes per $1 million spent, as opposed to the 60 serious crimes three strikes laws prevent for the same amount of money. *See id.*

177. *See supra* note 3.

178. *See supra* note 101.

179. *See generally* Butler, *supra* note 59.

180. *See* Paul Butler, *O.J. Reckoning: Rage for a New Justice,* WASH. POST, Oct. 8, 1995, at C1 ("[I]f [the white majority] keep[s] locking [African Americans] up soon and very soon [African Americans] will go the direction of all the oppressed. You can put your tanks in the city square and [African Americans] will walk right up because [they will] have nothing left to lose.").

16

At a Crossroad: Affirmative Action and Criminology

Wilson R. Palacios, Chinita Heard, and Dorothy L. Taylor

INTRODUCTION

The current social and political climate in society is rather alarming regarding social justice programs. There is a social tenor being webbed throughout this country that has conservatives feeling vindicated, liberals feeling abandoned, and the rest of us feeling confused and apathetic in our ability to affect social change. Boxil (1994, 1) added, "Black people have marked with deepening apprehension the development of a certain trend in the nation's racial policies." However all people of color are attempting to understand the professional and personal implications stemming from the latest assaults on social justice programs such as affirmative action.

While social justice programs have targeted a variety of areas (e.g., education, employment, the political structure, housing, and voting rights), none has engendered more passion and controversy than affirmative action (see Abram 1991; Chavez 1997; Glazer 1991; Hudson 1995; Nisbet 1991; Spickard 1991; Staples 1995). Many critics of affirmative action believe that society has changed so that it is more tolerant of racial and ethnic minorities. However, Staples (1995, 6) suggested, "The notion of a color blind society, with no need for affirmative action, is a fantasy at this point. Race is the most divisive variable extant in the U.S." Moreover, Hudson (1995, 16) added, "Affirmative action is quintessentially a question of race, rights and justice in a nation long and deeply divided by color prejudice."

The opponents of affirmative action equate diversity in the workplace with a change in people's attitudes and belief systems when it comes to people of color and gender. Such a stance merely examines the issues from a "quota" perspective, which is an inaccurate context in which to examine affirmative action, one that nullifies open debate concerning issues that are relevant to affirmative action's effectiveness as a social justice program (see Braun 1995). According to Braun (1995, 7), "The truth is that affirmative action has helped every American, not just women and minorities. It is about ending preferential treatment when it comes to race/ethnicity and gender in the areas of employment, housing, and education. It is about opening up our social and economic institutions so that it works for all, and not just for one group." Furthermore, it is about access to professional social networks for individuals who work in these institutions (e.g., academe, public and private schools/colleges/universities, private industry, medicine, law, and the criminal justice system). If such access is denied, social isolation both professionally and personally is yet another form of de jure segregation (see Berg and Bing 1990; Heard and Bing 1993; Patterson 1998).

AFFIRMATIVE ACTION: GOING BEYOND THE HEADCOUNT

Despite over twenty years of affirmative action or, as some would argue, a "quota" American legacies continue, including but not limited to the following (Massey and Denton 1993; Mfume 1997; Orlans 1992; West 1997; Wilson 1999, 96):

1. inadequate childcare
2. unaffordable health care
3. underemployment
4. overcrowded public schools and unqualified teachers
5. a steady growth in the number of census tracts classified as ghetto poverty areas
6. a decline of minority-owned small businesses
7. minority underrepresentation both as students and as faculty throughout all levels of higher education
8. institutional cultural racism
9. residential segregation

These destructive structural arrangements (Wilson 1996) and racist ideology have produced different experiential realities (Hamilton 1992) between and among all racial and ethnic groups (see Blauner 1989; Thernstrom and Thernstrom 1998, 1997). These hardened realities have created an atmosphere of alienation and great misgivings about any attempts to correct any of these social/human injustices. For example, Massey and Denton (1993, 235) argued, "By tolerating the persistent and systematic disenfranchisement of blacks from housing markets, we send a clear signal to one group that hard work, individual enterprise, sacrifice, and aspirations don't matter; what determines one's life chances is the color of one's skin." This signal is also carried over into the employment and educational system.

Despite these lived experiences, critics of affirmative action truly believe the playing field has finally been leveled. However, in a survey of African-American faculty working in criminology and criminal justice programs throughout the country, 42 percent reported feeling isolated from the academic community (Heard and Bing 1993). A recent article in *USA Today* (Mauro 1998), noted about 85 percent of minority women lawyers left their firms before their seventh year of practice due to professional isolation, compared to 74 percent of their white counterparts. Mauro (1998, 2) added, "Although, nationwide, minority representation among law students has doubled in the last dozen years to 20%, officials at the American Bar Association fear that number will go down as affirmative action programs are scrapped at the state-run law schools."

Affirmative action does not operate in a vacuum. People of color bring to the professional table different lived experiences as compared to their white counterparts, which may affect their professional trajectory. Being admitted or hired is only the first step; compared to the process involved, it may be easier than most care to realize, especially for pundits of affirmative action. For instance, in addition to feeling alienated people of color must also contend with deficient "sponsorship" and "orientation" (see Berg and Bing 1990). Each item refers to one's ability to access and successfully maneuver formal and informal social networks, such as pre– and post–graduate school mentoring, professional organizations, pedigree of university attended, senior-level job opportunities (above assistant professor level), major professors, negotiating skills, funding resources, and consultation opportunities (Young and Sulton 1991). Such networks have been traditionally exclusive of people of color (see Heard and Bing 1993; Young and Sulton 1991). Heard and Bing (1993) highlight the urgency of going beyond "token" measures and revamping the academic and professional community to one that is inclusive of and for people of color.

WHERE'S THE MINORITY TAKEOVER IN HIGHER EDUCATION?

Despite all the claims of "success" by opponents of affirmative action in admitting students of color, the academic and professional (i.e., law and medical school) community has been experiencing a severe shortfall. For example, during 1992–1993 only 5 percent and 4 percent of law (LLB or juris doctorate) degrees conferred went to African Americans and Hispanics, while 85 percent were awarded to whites (NCES 1995). Moreover, 3 percent of judges at all levels are African Americans, and Hispanics and Asian Americans represent only about 2 percent of law school faculty (Mauro 1998). A 1998 survey found only 2 percent of African Americans and 3 percent of Hispanics earned a doctorate in either law or legal studies (NCES 1998). Furthermore, while 20 percent of law school graduates are now persons of color attending schools ranked within the top ten, less than 2 percent of the clerks ever employed by the sitting Justices were African American, and only 1 percent were Hispanic (Wu 1999). Gaitan (1999, 3) suggests, "While 25% of Americans are ethnic minorities, the legal profession remains a

predominately white profession—approximately 93% of lawyers in this country are white."

An American Bar Association telephone survey of 1,002 lawyers found despite practicing a common law, African-American lawyers and white lawyers see
matters very differently when race is involved (ABA 1999). For instance, about
70 percent of black lawyers believe the amount of racial bias in the justice system is equal to that found in society while 46 percent of white lawyers believe
it to be less (ABA 1999). About 67 percent of African-American lawyers compared to 15 percent of white lawyers have witnessed examples of racial bias in
the justice system within the past three years (ABA 1999). Carter (1999, 2) adds,
"The results show often conflicting perceptions for African-American and white
lawyers, both on issues tearing at the heart of the profession and in the routine,
nuts-and-bolts workings of the justice system."

Between 1994 and 1995, about 19 percent of first-professional degrees (J.D.
or M.D.) were conferred on minority students, while 78 percent were conferred
on white students (NCES 1998). According to the National Center for Education
Statistics (1995, 208) in the fall of 1993 people of color comprised 23 percent of
the total undergraduate and graduate college enrollment while whites comprised
about 77 percent. This trend remained unchanged according to a 1998 survey,
which found students of color representing about 23 percent of individuals with
four or more years of college and whites about 86 percent (NCES 1998).

Furthermore, for men, 73 percent of whites, 6 percent of African Americans,
and 4 percent of Hispanics earned a master's degree between 1995 and 1996
(NCES 1998). For women, 70 percent of whites, 5 percent of African Americans,
and 3 percent of Hispanics earned a master's degree for the same time period
(NCES 1998). A recent survey by the U.S. Department of Education found of
the total doctorates earned between 1995 and 1996, 65 percent were earned by
whites, 4 percent were earned by African Americans, and 3 percent by Hispanics (NCES 1998). A 1996 employment survey in psychology found women and
people of color accounted for respectively 44 percent and about 9 percent of
Ph.D.s in the workforce (APA 1999).

In 1997 the *Chronicle of Higher Education* conducted a general survey of
earned doctorates. There were 52 percent men and 46 percent women with doctorates in the social sciences (*Chronicle* 1999). Of this group, 80 percent were
white, about 5 percent were African American, about 4 percent were Hispanic,
6 percent were Asian, and less than 1 percent American Indian (*Chronicle* 1999).
In addition, a 1998 survey of recent Ph.D. graduates in sociology found about
67 percent of non-academics and about 49 percent of academics relying on informal networks (i.e., colleagues and friends) as an employment strategy (Spalter-
Roth, Thomas, and Sutter 1999). For academics, about 48 percent relied on their
faculty advisors as a source for job opportunities (Spalter-Roth et al. 1999).

The fact remains that in higher education, the degree one receives along with
"sponsored mobility" (also known as the Old Boy network, see Wu 1999) impacts one's professional trajectory (see Heard and Bing 1993; Mikelson and

Oliver 1991; Spalter-Roth, Levine, and Sutter, 1999). For instance, according to an American Sociological Association report, *The Pipeline for Faculty of Color in Sociology*, there were 75 percent whites and 25 percent people of color working as an instructor/lecturer in Ph.D.-granting departments (Spalter-Roth, Levine, and Sutter 1999). At the assistant level, there were about 72 percent white professors and 28 percent professors of color (Spalter-Roth et al. 1999). However at the senior levels (i.e., associate and full professor), white professors accounted for 86 percent and 91 percent, while professors of color accounted for only 14 percent and 9 percent of such senior positions (Spalter-Roth et al. 1999).

A survey of instructional faculty at the University of South Florida found 40 percent whites and 4 percent people of color working at the instructor/lecturer level (USF 1999). At the assistant level, there were about 47 percent white professors, 3 percent Hispanic professors, and 4 percent African-American professors (USF 1999). At the senior levels (i.e., tenured associate and full professor), white professors accounted for 66 percent and 82 percent, while African-American professors accounted for 5 percent and 2 percent, and Hispanic professors accounted for 2 percent for both tenured associate and professor positions (USF 1999).

According to Spalter-Roth, Levine, and Sutter (1999, 4) this overrepresentation of white professors in the top rung of the academic ladder may be due to one or both of the following processes: disproportionate rates of promotion of whites and/or hold-over effects from the substantial cohort of white professors that was hired in the 1960s and 1970s, making it through the ranks before affirmative action altered hiring practices. The former represents discriminatory promotion practices and/or inadequate mentoring of young researchers after graduate school, while the latter merely reflects a cohort effect, which may correct itself as older white Ph.D.s retire (Spalter-Roth et al. 1999).

Minority Voices Silenced in the Classroom

Critics of affirmative action (see Chavez 1997; Loury 1998; Mansfield 1991; Murray 1984; Nisbet 1991; Raspberry 1991) have provided the catalyst for recent crusades against affirmative action in such states as California, Washington, Michigan, Texas, Georgia, Maryland, Louisiana, Mississippi, and Florida (see Gaitan 1999; Healy 1997; Lederman 1997; Loury 1998; Selingo 1999; Taylor and Liss 1992). What is currently going on in these states is a deliberate dismantling of the little progress achieved in higher education (see Gaitan 1999). The messengers of this abolitionists' movement (Loury 1998) have ingeniously shrouded their attacks under the guise of "equal protection" (Gaitan 1999). Legislative amendments such as Washington's Initiative 200, California's Proposition 209, and Florida's Civil Rights Initiative are attempts to destroy any honest commitment to minority representation in the classroom, for students and faculty. According to Paterson and Sellstrom (1999, 2), "After the Regents of the University of California eliminated affirmative action in student admissions, the number of students of color admitted to the university declined sharply. In September 1998, the freshman class at UC Berkeley enrolled 50% fewer students of color compared to the prior year."

Supporters of such legislative tactics are leading the anti-affirmative action charge under the ideology of individualism, egalitarianism, constitutionalism, political freedom, and equality before the law (Hamilton 1992). In addition, affirmative action pundits argue that discrimination is no longer to be viewed as a serious problem in this nation (Taylor and Liss 1992). Taylor and Liss (1992, 31) add, "Such critics claim that it is time to wipe the slate clean, to assume, in an extension of Lyndon Johnson's vivid imagery, that everyone who is now at the starting line is unburdened by any chains and has an equal chance." However, Berry (1997, 307) contends, "An African-American is discriminated against not because his name is James but because he is an African-American. A woman is discriminated against not because her name is Judy or Jane but because she is a woman." Loury (1998, 42) adds, "In the brave new dispensation, color is supposed to be irrelevant, yet everywhere we look in America, people are attending assiduously to race."

A review of experiences and challenges of racial minorities in and outside of the classroom provides an amount of overwhelming evidence against the myth of a color-blind society. For instance, within a two-year period, the National Institute against Prejudice and Violence documented at least 200 reports of campus ethnic racial violence. In addition to reports of physical and verbal harassment of Jews and homosexuals, African Americans at predominately white university campuses encountered the most harassment (Hacker 1992). According to a 1997 crime report focusing on bias motivated crime, such criminal events occurring on school and college campuses accounted for 11 percent of the total incidents reported to law enforcement agencies (UCR 1997). Overall, 39 percent of single-bias incidents were characterized as anti-black, 79 percent were anti-Jewish, 59 percent were anti-Hispanic, and 69 percent were anti–male homosexual (UCR 1997). These sobering statistics offer evidence that color consciousness (Dyson 1996) and not color blindness still is part of the American psyche.

In the classroom, racial insensitivity can affect the college dropout rate and what career track students of color elect as their course of study. Bing, Heard, and Gilbert (1995, 136) found that 50 percent of African-American students and only 9 percent of white students agreed that professors were insensitive to issues regarding race. Also, Feagin (1992) found that the quality of feedback related to academic performance, along with insensitivity toward research on racial, gender, and ethnic issues, may negatively affect minority students to the point that they eventually drop out of college. In addition, an increased attrition rate for students of color may also affect the racial/ethnic composition of certain professions (such as criminology and criminal justice), as previously discussed (see also Strosnider 1997).

Minority Voices Silenced Outside the Classroom

The siege of affirmative action programs is also evident in the courtroom. Since the 1990s, the judicial arena has been anything but friendly for those seeking redress for discriminatory practices based on one's racial and/or ethnic status. The exception to this has been for those who have claimed instances of "reverse discrimination" (Healy 1997; Pachon 1997). The Supreme Court has proceeded to scrutinize all affirmative action measures according to the same standard as invidious discrimination (Jones 1997). The judicial redress once found in the Supreme Court cases of *Bakke* and *Weber* were now being reformulated and judged according to the constitutional standard of "strict scrutiny" (see Jaschik 1995).

Court cases such as *Adarand Constructors, Inc. v. Pena, Richmond v. J.A. Croson Co., Hopewood v. Texas,* and *United States v. Paradise* represent this new constitutional standard of strict scrutiny (Jones 1997). As a result, Jones (1997, 148) stated, "Conservatives hailed the Supreme Court's decisions as the end of affirmative action and other social experiments." Although careful examination of the Court's decisions in such cases reveal that while it became difficult to institute programs to correct for past social and economic inequities, the Court also refused to end such social justice programs (Jones 1997).

The outcome of this Court's tenure has been to redirect the issue of affirmative action into the lower courts and to focus on how the law is applied in carrying out such initiatives. It has also assisted in fueling the debate between those who are calling for the preservation, if not an improvement, of affirmative action (Harris 1997; West 1997) and those who truly believe that we live collectively in a color-blind society (see Chavez 1997).

The impact of the *Hopewood* ruling, forcing the elimination of race as a factor in admissions policies, is expected to have negative consequences in Texas, Louisiana, Michigan, and Mississippi. While the Fifth Circuit U.S. Court of Appeals ruling is expected to reduce minority enrollment in undergraduate programs, a significant decline in minority admissions is expected to occur in graduate programs, including law and medicine (Strosnider 1997). The reality here is that the massive invasion of "unqualified" minority students, which critics of affirmative action have asserted in the past, has never happened. Affirmative action opponents, such as Linda Chavez, claim that universities have become saturated with unprepared and underqualified minority students and faculty—a form of reverse discrimination (Pachon 1997). However, the statistics presented herein have indicated otherwise. While an assessment of the long-term consequences of the most recent anti-affirmative action campaign would be premature at this juncture, an immediate impact may be an end to ethnic and cultural diversity both in and outside of the classroom. This represents a dilemma for those involved in teaching and mentoring the next generation of scholars in such fields as criminology and criminal justice.

AFFIRMATIVE ACTION AND THE STUDY OF CRIME

Despite over twenty years of affirmative action, people of color are without a doubt severely underrepresented in higher education and in certain types of professions. They are, however, overrepresented in the criminal justice system. According to the American Bar Association, on any given day, an estimated one in three African-American men between the ages of 20 and 29 is in prison, on probation, or on parole (ABA 1995). A Bureau of Justice Statistics report estimated 7 percent of African-American males in their twenties and thirties were in prison in 1997 (Beck and Mumola 1999, 10).

Between 1989 and 1994 there was a 78 percent increase in the number of African-American women under correctional supervision (ABA 1995). Black non-Hispanic females were more than twice as likely as Hispanic females and eight times more likely than white non-Hispanic females to be in prison in 1997 (Beck and Mumola 1999, 11). Moreover, while just under 10 percent of African Americans are represented in higher education, they do account for about 49 percent of prisoners under state or federal jurisdiction in 1997 (see Beck and Mumola 1999; Walker, Spohn, and DeLone 2000). Marshall (1997) suggested that the United States, a country that already has a high incarceration rate— 1,302,019 men and women at yearend 1998 (Beck and Mumola 1999)—relative to other industrialized nations, locks up African-American men at a rate six times that of white men (see also Tonry 1995).

There are numerous positions as to why minorities are overrepresented in the legal system (for a review see Walker, Spohn, and DeLone 2000). While a comprehensive review of each argument is beyond the scope of this chapter some advance the idea that such overrepresentation reflects contextual rather than systematic discrimination (Walker, Spohn, and DeLone 2000). Walker, Spohn, and DeLone (2000, 16) define contextual discrimination as "discrimination found in particular contexts or circumstances—e.g., certain regions, particular crimes, certain victim-offender relationships." But the contextualization of crime and criminals goes far beyond what the authors describe. In order to understand the legal system, one must examine such disparities as an outcome of race/ethnicity, gender, social class, and specific social, economical, and political arrangements intersecting before the legal system (for a succinct review of these issues see Arrigo 1996; Bridges and Beretta 1994; Daly 1994; Hagan and McCarthy 1994; Hawkins 1994; Manning 1994; Spohn 1994).

In addition to correctional facilities, other areas of both the adult and juvenile justice system represent the effects of racial and ethnic disparities and the racialization of justice in America (see Bailey 1996; Bohm 1991; Chiricos 1996; Clark 1991; Nelson 1991; Patterson and Patterson 1996; Smith, Graham, and Adams 1991; Tollett and Close 1991; Walker, Spohn, and DeLone 2000). These areas include the following:

- probation
- sentencing

- death penalty
- the adjudication process
- pretrial process
- policing practices and behavior

While significant improvements have been made in safeguarding the procedural rights of people of color in each of these six areas, minorities find themselves coming to terms with the burden that racial and ethnic stereotypes and prejudices often influence where in the system they fall (Walker, Spohn, and DeLone 2000). Walker, Spohn, and DeLone (2000, 290) add, "Although reforms have made systematic racial discrimination unlikely, the American criminal justice system has never been, and is not now, color-blind."

AFFIRMATIVE ACTION AND MINORITIES AS CRIMINAL JUSTICE PROFESSIONALS

Just as critics of affirmative action are quick to conclude a minority "over-representation" in higher education, the same kind of misinformation is seen in examining the progress of people of color as criminal justice professionals. For instance, a 1999 report by the Bureau of Justice Statistics suggests that racial and ethnic minorities comprised 19 percent of full-time sworn officers in sheriffs' departments (BJS 1999). Black and Hispanic sheriff's deputies accounted for about 11 percent and 6 percent of these full-time sworn officers (BJS 1999). Cities such as Atlanta and Detroit have a significant presence of black police officers (Marshall 1997). However, examining minority representation in law enforcement strictly with aggregated data is misleading.

The fact is that law enforcement agencies are mandated, for accreditation purposes, to contain a minority workforce comparable to the service community (as cited in Walker, Spohn, and DeLone 2000). A better measure of minority representation would be the Equal Employment Opportunity (EEO) index (Walker et al. 2000). Tested against such an index, only a few police departments (e.g., Los Angeles, Washington, D.C., and Detroit) have minority police officers comparable to their numbers in the general population (Marshall 1997). Other cities, such as New York City, have failed to meet this accreditation standard in the past (as cited in Walker et al. 2000). Similar trends are noted for other branches of the criminal justice system.

Modest increases in the hiring of minority personnel in such areas as corrections and the judiciary (see Walker et al. 2000) have been exactly that—modest. Moreover, what little advancement has been made has come about because of federal mandates and initiatives such as affirmative action. Furthermore, the increases have not been so significant for minority police officers in management or supervisory positions in law enforcement or corrections (Walker et al. 2000).

While an increase in minority personnel is no guarantee of eliminating the inherent disparities of the criminal justice system, it has changed the professional subculture. More and more police officers are breaking with the peer culture and questioning the morality and legality of such practices as pretextual car stops (e.g., "driving while black or brown"), use of excessive force, "zero tolerance" policing, and the use of racial profiling (Cole 1999). However, all of this stands to change as the flurry of anti–affirmative action rhetoric threatens to silence this minority voice.

DISCUSSION AND CONCLUSION

The social sciences, specifically criminology, are at a crossroad. Recent attacks on affirmative action threaten the discipline. The anti–affirmative action movement will change the sociodemographic profile of students majoring in the discipline. It will influence pedagogy as it is practiced and communicated in classrooms throughout public and private universities. It will also affect specific areas of research and subsequent funding of such topics as the following:

women substance users and their children

minority drug use and the community

environmental crime and minority communities

ethnicity and crime

"machismo" and violent behavior patterns

domestic violence in the minority community

minorities as criminal justice professionals

In the end, criminological discourse in the classrooms, at professional conferences, in professional periodicals, and in the private sector will reflect and be judged according to one standard. This is simply unconscionable, given the subject matter and what is at stake.

Contemporary criminologists have only begun to recognize the importance of critically examining the manner in which race, class, and gender influence one's motivations, opportunities, and resiliency towards crime (Lynch 1996). The study of crime and criminals is unquestionably a study of the contextualization of race, ethnicity, gender, and class. Moreover, "new" criminologists have the responsibility of examining the manner in which race, gender, and class simultaneously interact with who is officially processed in the criminal justice system and how (see Barak 1996; Danner 1996; Goodley 1996; Granovetter 1985; Lynch 1996; Welch 1999). If criminology and criminal justice, as a discipline, has become theoretically stagnated, as some claim it has (see Lynch 1996), then our only hope lies in the professional pipeline. However, anti–affirmative action legislation presents a formidable challenge to a balanced study of crime and criminals.

REFERENCES

Abram, Morris. (1991). Fair Shakers and Social Engineers. In Russel Nieli (Ed.), *Racial Preference and Racial Justice*. (Pp. 29–44). Washington, DC: Ethics and Public Policy Center.

American Bar Association. (1999). Divided Justice: Differing Opinions. Retrieved November 18, 1999. <http://www.abanet.org/journal/feb99/02rlede. html>.

———. (1995). Facts about the American Criminal Justice System. *American Bar Association*. October 1995. Retrieved on November 18, 1999. <http://www.abanet.org /media/mar97/cj4.html>.

American Psychological Association. (1999). *Demographic Shifts in Psychology*. Retrieved November 14, 1999. <http://research.apa.org/gen1.html>.

Arrigo, Bruce. (1996). Postmodern Criminology on Race, Class, and Gender. In Martin D. Schwartz and Dragan Milovanovic (Eds.), *Race, Gender, and Class in Criminology*. (Pp. 73–90). New York: Garland Publishing.

Bailey, Frankie. (1996). The "Tangle of Pathology" and the Lower-Class African-American Family: Historical and Social Sciences Perspectives. In Michael J. Lynch and E. Britt Patterson (Eds.), *Justice with Prejudice: Race and Criminal Justice in America*. (Pp. 49–71). Albany, NY: Harrow and Heston.

Barak, Gregg. (1996). Mass-mediated Regimes of Truth: Race, Gender, and Class in Crime "News" Thematics. In Martin D. Schwartz and Dragan Milovanovic (Eds.), *Race, Gender, and Class in Criminology*. (Pp. 105–124). New York: Garland Publishing.

Beck, Allen, and Christopher Mumola. (1999). Prisoners in 1998. *Bureau of Justice Statistics Bulletin*. Washington, DC: U.S. Department of Justice, Office of Justice Programs.

Berg, B., and Robert Bing. (1990). Mentoring Members of Minorities: Sponsorship and the Gift. *Journal of Criminal Justice Education*. 1(2): 153–165.

Berry, Mary. (1997). Affirmative Action: Why We Need It, Why It Is under Attack. In George E. Curry (Ed.), *The Affirmative Action Debate*. (Pp. 299–313). Reading, MA: Addison-Wesley Publishing Company.

Bing, Robert, Chinita Heard, and Evelyn Gilbert. (1995). The Experiences of African-Americans and Whites in Criminal Justice Education: Do Race and Gender Differences Exist? *Journal of Criminal Justice Education*. 6(1): 123-145.

Blauner, Bob. (1989). *Black Lives, White Lives: Three Decades of Race Relations in America*. Berkeley: University of California Press.

Bohm, Robert. (1991). Race and the Death Penalty in the United States. In Michael J. Lynch and E. Britt Patterson (Eds.), *Race and Criminal Justice*. (Pp. 71–85). Albany, NY: Harrow and Heston.

Boxil, Bernard. (1994). *Blacks and Social Justice*, rev. ed. Lanham, MD: Rowman and Littlefield.

Bridges, George S., and Gina Beretta. (1994). Gender, Race, and Social Control: Toward an Understanding of Sex Disparities in Imprisonment. In George S. Bridges and Martha A. Myers (Eds.), *Inequality, Crime, and Social Control*. (Pp. 158–175). Boulder, CO: Westview Press.

Bruan, Carol M. (1995). Affirmative Action and the Glass Ceiling. *The Black Scholar*. 25(3): 7–15.

Bureau of Justice Statistics. (1999). *Sheriffs' Department, 1997*. October. Washington, DC: U.S. Department of Justice, Office of Justice Programs.

Carter, Terry. (1999). White and Black Lawyers May Practice the Same Law, but They Have Decidedly Different View of How the System Works. Retrieved November 18, 1999 <http://www.abanet.org/journal/feb99/o2rlede.html>.

Chavez, Linda. (1997). Promoting Racial Harmony. In George E. Curry (Ed.), *The Affirmative Action Debate*. (Pp. 314–325). Reading, MA: Addison-Wesley Publishing Company.

Chiricos, Theodore. (1996). Moral Panic as Ideology: Drugs, Violence, Race and Punishment in America. In Michael J. Lynch and E. Britt Patterson (Eds.), *Justice with Prejudice: Race and Criminal Justice in America*. (Pp. 19–48). Albany, NY: Harrow and Heston.

Chronicle of Higher Education. (1999). Facts and Figures. Survey of earned doctorates. Retrieved November 17, 1999. <http://chronicle.com/weekly/v45/i18/recipients.htm>.

Clark, David. (1991). Ethnic Bias in a Correctional Setting: The Mariel Cubans. In Michael J. Lynch and E. Britt Patterson (Eds.), *Race and Criminal Justice*. (Pp. 113–125). Albany, NY: Harrow and Heston.

Cole, David. (1999). Race, Policing, and the Future of the Criminal Law. Retrieved on November 18, 1999. <http://www.abanet.org/irr/summer1999humanrights/cole.html>.

Daly, Kathleen. (1994). Gender and Punishment Disparity. In George S. Bridges and Martha A. Myers (Eds.), *Inequality, Crime, and Social Control*. (Pp. 117–133). Boulder, CO: Westview Press.

Danner, Mona. (1996). Gender Inequality and Criminalization: A Socialist Feminist Perspective on the Legal Social Control of Women. In Martin D. Schwartz and Dragan Milovanovic (Eds.), *Race, Gender, and Class in Criminology*. (Pp. 29–48). New York: Garland Publishing.

Dyson, Michael. (1996). *Race Rules: Navigating the Color Line*. New York: Vintage Books.

Feagin, J. (1992). The Continuing Significance of Racism: Discrimination against Black Students in White Colleges. *Journal of Black Studies*. 22: 546–578.

Gaitan, Jose. (1999). Letter from the Chair, American Bar Association Commission on Opportunities for Minorities in the Profession. November.

Glazer, Nathan. (1991). Racial Quotas. In Russel Nieli (Ed.), *Racial Preference and Racial Justice*. (Pp. 3–28). Washington, DC: Ethics and Public Policy Center.

Goodey, Jo. (1996). Adolescence and the Socialization of Gendered Fear. In Martin D. Schwartz and Dragan Milovanovic (Eds.), *Race, Gender, and Class in Criminology*. (Pp. 267–292). New York: Garland Publishing.

Granovetter, Mark. (1985). Economic action and social structure: The problem of embeddedness. *American Journal of Sociology*. 91(3): 481–510.

Hacker, Andrew. (1992). *Two Nations: Black and White, Separate, Hostile, and Unequal*. New York: Ballantine Books.

Hagan, John, and Bill McCarthy. (1994). Double Jeopardy: The Abuse and Punishment of Homeless Youth. In George S. Bridges and Martha A. Myers (Eds.), *Inequality, Crime, and Social Control*. (Pp. 195–214). Boulder, CO: Westview Press.

Hamilton, Charles. (1992). Affirmative Action and the Clash of Experiential Realities. *Annals of the American Academy of Political and Social Sciences*. Newbury Park, CA: Sage Publications, pp. 10–18.

Harris, Louis. (1997). The Future of Affirmative Action. In George E. Curry (Ed.), *The Affirmative Action Debate*. (Pp. 326–336). Reading, MA: Addison-Wesley Publishing Company.

Hawkins, Darnell. (1994). Ethnicity: The Forgotten Dimension of American Social Control. In George S. Bridges and Martha A. Myers (Eds.), *Inequality, Crime, and Social Control*. (Pp. 99–116). Boulder, CO: Westview Press.

Healy, Patrick. (1997). Lawsuit Attacks Race-Based Policies in University System of Georgia. *Chronicle of Higher Education*, March 1997. Retrieved December 6, 1999. <http://chronicle.com/che-data/articles.dir/art-43.dir/issue-27.dir/27a02501.htm>.

Heard, Chinita, and Robert Bing, III. (1993). African-American Faculty and Students on Predominantly White University Campuses. *Journal of Criminal Justice Education*. 4(1) (Spring): 1–13.

Hudson, Blain, J. (1995). Simple Justice: Affirmative Action and American Racism in Historical Perspective. *The Black Scholar*. 25(3): 16–22.

Jaschik, Scott. (1995). Supreme Court Deals Another Blow to Affirmative Action. *Chronicle of Higher Education*. June 1995. Retrieved on December 6, 1999. <http://chronicle.com/che-data/articles.dir/art-41.dir/issue-41.dir/41a02101.htm>.

Jones, Elaine. (1997). Race and the Supreme Court's 1994–95 Term. In George E. Curry (Ed.), *The Affirmative Action Debate*. (Pp. 146–156). Reading, MA: Addison-Wesley Publishing Company.

Lederman, Douglas. (1997). Lawsuit Challenges Affirmative Action at University of Washington. *Chronicle of Higher Education*. March 1997. Retrieved on December 6, 1999. <http://chronicle.com/che-data/articles.dir/art-43.dir/issue27/27a02702.htm>.

Loury, Glenn. (1998). An American Tragedy: The Legacy of Slavery Lingers in Our Cities' Ghettos. *Brookings Review*. 16(2): 38–42.

Lynch, Michael. (1996). Class, Race, and Gender in Criminology: Structured Choices and the Life Course. In Martin D. Schwartz and Dragan Milovanovic (Eds.), *Race, Gender, and Class in Criminology*. (Pp. 3–28). New York: Garland Publishing.

Manning, Peter. (1994). The Police: Symbolic Capital, Class, and Control. In George S. Bridges and Martha A. Myers (Eds.), *Inequality, Crime, and Social Control*. (Pp. 80–98). Boulder, CO: Westview Press.

Mansfield, Harvey. (1991). The Underhandedness of Affirmative Action. In Russel Nieli (Ed.), *Racial Preference and Racial Justice: The New Affirmative Action Controversy*. (Pp. 127–140). Washington, DC: Ethics and Public Policy Center.

Marshall, Ineke. (1997). *Minorities, Migrants, and Crime: Diversity and Similarity across Europe and the United States*. Thousand Oaks, CA: Sage Publications.

Massey, Douglas, and Nancy Denton. (1993). *American Apartheid: Segregation and the Making of the Underclass*. Cambridge, MA: Harvard University Press.

Mauro, Tony. (1998, August 5). Minorities Not Reaching Top Legal Levels. *USA Today*, pp. 1–2.

Mfume, Kweisi. (1997). Why America Needs Set-aside Programs. In George E. Curry (Ed.), *The Affirmative Action Debate*. (Pp. 121–129). Reading, MA: Addison-Wesley Publishing Company.

Mikelson, Roslyn, and Melvin Oliver. (1991). Making the Short List: Black Candidates and the Recruitment Process. (Pp. 149–166). In P.G. Altbach and K. Lomotey

(Eds.), *The Racial Crisis in American Higher Education*. Albany: State University of New York Press.

Murray, Charles. (1984). *Losing Ground: American Social Policy 1950–1980*. New York: Basic Books.

National Center for Education Statistics. (1998). *Postsecondary Education 1998*. Washington, DC: Office of Educational Research and Improvement. U.S. Department of Education.

————. (1995). *Digest of Education Statistics 1995*. Washington, DC: Office of Educational Research and Improvement. U.S. Department of Education.

Nelson, James. (1991). Disparity in the Incarceration of Minorities in New York State. In Michael J. Lynch and E. Britt Patterson (Eds.), *Race and Criminal Justice*. (Pp. 145–160). Albany, NY: Harrow and Heston.

Nisbet, Lee. (1991). Affirmative Action: A Liberal Program? In Russel Nieli (Ed.), *Racial Preference and Racial Justice*. (Pp. 11–116). Washington, DC: Ethics and Public Policy Center.

Orlans, Harold. (1992). Affirmative Action in Higher Education. *Annals of the Academy of Political and Social Sciences*. Newbury Park, CA: Sage Publications, 144–158.

Pachon, Harry. (1997). Invisible Latinos: Excluded from Discussions of Inclusion. In George E. Curry (Ed.), *The Affirmative Action Debate*. (Pp. 184–190). Reading, MA: Addison-Wesley Publishing Company.

Paterson, Eva, and Oren Sellstrom. (1999). Equal Opportunity in a Post-Proposition 209 World. Retrieved November 18, 1999. <http://www.abanet.org/irr/summer1999humanrights/paterson.html>.

Patterson, E. Britt, and Laura Davidson Patterson. (1996). Vice and Social Control: Predispositional Detention and the Juvenile Drug Offender. In Michael J. Lynch and E. Britt Patterson (Eds.), *Justice with Prejudice: Race and Criminal Justice in America*. (Pp. 104–120). Albany, NY: Harrow and Heston.

Patterson, Orlando. (1998). Affirmative Action: Opening Up Workplace Networks to Afro-Americans. *Brookings Review*. 16(2) (Spring): 17–23.

Raspberry, William. (1991). Affirmative Action That Hurts Blacks. In Russell Nieli (Ed.), *Racial Preference and Racial Justice: The New Affirmative Action Controversy*. (Pp. 429–434). Washington, DC: Ethics and Public Policy Center.

Selingo, Jeffrey. (1999). A Quiet End to the Use of Race in College Admissions in Florida. *Chronicle of Higher Education*, December 1999. Retrieved on December 6, 1999. <http://chronicle.com/search97cigi/s97>.

Smith, Douglas, Nanette Graham, and Bonney Adams. (1991). Minorities and the Police: Attitudinal and Behavioral Questions. In Michael J. Lynch and E. Britt Patterson (Eds.), *Race and Criminal Justice*. (Pp. 22–35). Albany, NY: Harrow and Heston.

Spalter-Roth, Roberta, Felice Levine, and Andrew Sutter. (1999). The Pipeline for Faculty of Color in Sociology. *American Sociological Association Research Program on the Discipline and Profession. Research in Brief*. Washington, DC.

Spalter-Roth, Roberta, Jan Thomas, and Andrew Sutter. (1999). New Doctorates in Sociology: Professions Inside and Outside of the Academy. July. *American Sociological Association Research Program on the Discipline and Profession. Research in Brief*. Washington, DC.

Spickard, Paul. (1991). Why I Believe in Affirmative Action. In Russel Nieli (Ed.), *Racial Preference and Racial Justice*. (Pp. 105–110). Washington, DC: Ethics and Public Policy Center.

Spohn, Cassia. (1994). Crime and the Social Control of Blacks: Offender/Victim Race and the Sentencing of Violent Offenders. In George S. Bridges and Martha A. Myers (Eds.), *Inequality, Crime, and Social Control*. (Pp. 249–268). Boulder, CO: Westview Press.

Staples, Robert. (1995). Black Deprivation, White Privilege: The Assault on Affirmative Action. *The Black Scholar*. 25(3): 2–6.

Strosnider, Kim. (1997). Minority Enrollment Would Drop Without Preferences. *Chronicle of Higher Education*, January 1997. Retrieved on December 6, 1999. <http://chronicle.com/che-data/articles.dir/art-43.dir/issue-21.dir/21a02801 .htm>.

Taylor, William, and Susan Liss. (1992). "Affirmative Action in the 1990s: Staying the Course." *Annals of the American Academy of Political and Social Sciences*. Newbury Park, CA: Sage Publications, 30–37.

Thernstrom, Abigail, and Stephan Thernstrom. (1998). Black Progress: How Far We've Come—and How Far We Have to Go. *Brookings Review*. 16(2) (Spring): 12–16.

———. (1997). *America in Black and White: One Nation, Indivisible*. New York: Simon & Schuster.

Tollett, Ted, and Billy R. Close. (1991). The Over-representation of Blacks in Florida's Juvenile Justice System. In Michael J. Lynch and E. Britt Patterson (Eds.), *Race and Criminal Justice*. (Pp. 86–99). Albany, NY: Harrow and Heston.

Tonry, Michael. (1995). *Malign Neglect: Race, Crime, and Punishment in America*. New York: Oxford University Press.

Uniform Crime Reports. (1997). Hate Crime Statistics 1997. Clarksburg, VA: U.S. Department of Justice, Federal Bureau of Investigations.

University of South Florida. (1999). Instructional faculty survey. *University of South Florida Fact Book, 1998–1999*. Retrieved December 4, 1999. <http://usfweb .usf.edu/usfirp/fb99/p135.htm>.

Walker, Samuel, Cassia Spohn, and Miriam DeLone. (2000). *Race, Ethnicity, and Crime in America: The Color of Justice*, 2nd ed. Belmont, CA: Wadsworth Publishing.

Welch, Michael. (1999). *Punishment in America: Social Control and the Ironies of Imprisonment*. Thousand Oaks, CA: Sage Publications.

West, Cornel. (1997). Affirmative Action in Context. In George E. Curry (Ed.), *The Affirmative Action Debate*. (Pp. 31–38). Reading, MA: Addison-Wesley Publishing Company.

Wilson, William J. (1999). *The Bridge over the Racial Divide: Rising Inequality and Coalition Politics*. Berkeley: University of California Press.

———. (1996). *When Work Disappears: The World of the New Urban Poor*. New York: Vintage Books.

Wu, Frank. (1999). Diversity and Justice at the Supreme Court. American Bar Association Commission on Opportunities for Minorities in the Profession. November. 2–4.

Young, Vernetta, and Anne Sulton. (1991). Excluded: The Current Status of African-American Scholars in the Field of Criminology and Criminal Justice. *Journal of Research in Crime and Delinquency*. 28(1) (February): 101–116.

17

On the Horns of a Dilemma: Criminal Wrongs, Civil Rights, and the Administration of Justice in African-American Communities

Darnell F. Hawkins

> Neither slavery nor involuntary servitude, *except as a punishment for crime whereof the party shall have been duly convicted*, shall exist within the United States, or any place subject to their jurisdiction. (Constitution of the United States, Amendment XII, Section 1, 1865) (emphasis added)

As American society enters the twenty-first century, the nation's legacy of racial, ethnic, and socioeconomic inequality continues to be reflected in crime and punishment, and in ways not strikingly different from centuries past. Consider the following interrelated facts and observations:

- The size of the prison population in the United States has reached unprecedented levels, having grown nearly 500 percent from 1972 to 1998. This rate of increase exceeded by a wide margin the growth in the nation's crime rate during the period. Between 1985 and 1995 federal and state governments opened a new prison each week to cope with the flood of new prisoners (Mauer 1999, 1).

- Between 1980 and 1996, state and federal incarceration rates (per 100,000 citizens) grew by over 200 percent. During this 17-year period, incarceration rates for African Americans rose by 184 percent; for Latinos, 235 percent; and for non-Hispanic whites, 164 percent. The dominant factor driving that growth was drug offending, which grew by ten times (Blumstein and Beck 1999, 17).

- On June 30, 1999, 1,860,520 persons were confined in state or federal prisons or in local jails. An estimated 11 percent of the nation's black males, 4 percent of Hispanic males, and 1.5 percent of white males in their twenties and early thirties were in prison or jail on that date (U. S. Department of Justice 2000, 1–2).

- During the early 1980s, the nation witnessed the entry of a smokable form of cocaine, "crack," into drug markets in the nation's largest cities. By the mid-1980s, state legislatures revised existing laws or passed new laws aimed at imposing greater penalties on those trafficking in cocaine. Purportedly guided by the belief that crack was more addictive and posed greater threats to the public than cocaine powder, this newer form of the drug became the target of the most severe penalties. Federal legislation passed as part of the Anti-Drug Abuse Act of 1988 imposed a five-year minimum sentence for possessing or selling five grams of crack. To receive the same five-year sentence, a person would have to possess 500 grams of powdered cocaine. Members of the Black Congressional Caucus supported the passage of the legislation, but later came to oppose it.

- During the decade spanning the mid-1980s to the mid-1990s, the nation witnessed a dramatic increase in rates of firearm-related lethal and non-lethal violence among African-American and Latino youths living in the nation's largest cities. The homicide victimization rate for 15- to 19-year-old African-American males increased from 37.4 per 100,000 youths in 1985 to 105.3 per 100,000 in 1990. The rate for white males in this age range increased from 18.4 to 26.5 during this period (Fingerhut 1993, 9).

- Alarmed by increased youthful violence, which was associated with gangs and the proliferation of "open air" crack drug markets, many grass roots organizations in African-American urban communities initiated efforts during the 1980s and 1990s to tackle these problems. Nationwide, these organizations supported the passage of ordinances requiring curfews for youths and various anti-gang measures. In Chicago, black community groups and aldermen threw their support behind a controversial anti-loitering ordinance that targeted suspected gang members. When the constitutionality of that 1992 ordinance was challenged by various groups in an appeal that was heard eventually by the U.S. Supreme Court, several Chicago community groups submitted a brief in support of the ordinance (Meares 1998; Meares and Kahan 1998).

- A September 2000 newscast on a local television station in Chicago reported that an organization representing residents of Englewood, an economically depressed black neighborhood on the south side of the city, had thrown its support behind an effort to install video cameras on utility poles in the community. These would be used to monitor activities in areas with the highest crime rates. The plan was also said to be supported by the alderman for the area, an African American, and by the local branch of the American Civil Liberties Union.

- During an era in which African Americans achieved unprecedented access to the American political and socioeconomic mainstream and the nation at large prospered, the decades of the 1980s and 1990s also witnessed disturbing acts of racial intolerance, hoaxes and macroaggression (Russell 1998). The 1990s alone saw several instances of deadly, racially motivated attacks on African Americans, Asian Americans, Latinos, and Jews. During the same period charges of racial bias and profiling, as evidenced by police use of deadly force and decisions to stop and detain citizens, prompted a lively debate within the legal profession and the wider public (Miller 1996; Kennedy 1997; Cole 1999).

The major argument presented in this chapter is that these disturbing developments and trends mark the contours of a significant race-crime-punishment dilemma that confronts all of American society, but particularly African-American communities and those who seek solutions to the problems they face. I suggest that this dilemma derives from two currents evident in contemporary thinking about race in the United States: (1) a lack of consensus regarding the causes of persisting racial inequality and what can be done to reduce it and (2) an ideological and public policy impasse linked to contradictions inherent in evidence of both progress and retrogression in the social standing of persons of African ancestry in the United States during the last several decades. I explore this dilemma using analytic constructs derived from the sociology of knowledge, critical race theory, and discourse analysis—perspectives not fully or widely used in traditional criminological research. I examine how the ideological currents described herein are manifested in the ways that the American public and social scientists who study crime and punishment perceive, explain, and respond to the noteworthy contemporary trends and developments in the administration of justice just outlined.[1]

EXPLAINING AND FIXING RACIAL INEQUALITY IN AMERICAN SOCIETY: THE DRIFT TOWARD THE IDEOLOGY OF MERITOCRACY

For most observers, one of the puzzling aspects of the racial inequality evident in recent crime and punishment statistics is the "best of times/worst of times" portrait of American society that the data seem to draw. The pronounced racial polarization in the administration of justice comes after several decades of quite dramatic improvement in the overall socioeconomic and political status of African Americans. It follows a period of what appears to have been significant progress in race relations for the nation and also a period of enormous innovation and transformation within the justice system. Begun in earlier decades, the 1980s and 1990s marked the culmination of the enactment of many constitutionally mandated procedural safeguards designed to protect the rights of criminal suspects of all races and to prevent some of the blatant race-linked miscarriages of justice seen previously (Kennedy 1997, 2001; Hawkins 2001; Hawkins and Herring 2000).

Given the high hopes for social change and racial harmony that existed among much of the American public during the 1950s and 1960s, these societal trends and developments were expected to have a positive impact on the level of racial disparity in crime and punishment in the nation. Also contributing to such rising expectations were race-linked governmental initiatives such as Lyndon Johnson's War on Poverty and various attempts during the same period and later to use expanded welfare benefits to provide safety nets for the economically disadvantaged. Together, these reforms were expected to reduce black-white crime and the punishment gap through their ameliorative effects on the "propensity" or "necessity" for criminal involvement among blacks and on the likelihood of racial discrimination by whites. The fact that such expectations appear to be largely unfulfilled at the turn of the twenty-first century constitutes one horn of the dilemma now facing American society. Confronting the nation is the irony and seeming inconsistency of a large and growing racial disparity in the administration of justice amid evidence of black socioeconomic progress and reductions in many of the more blatant forms of interracial conflict that have historically characterized American race and ethnic relations. A similar paradox of stagnation or growing inequality alongside perceptions and evidence of progress has been noted in debates surrounding racial disparity in other dimensions of American social and economic life, such as educational attainment, labor-force participation and earnings, family structure, home ownership, and health (Jaynes and Williams 1989; Jackson 2000; Smelser, Wilson, and Mitchell 2001).

Cognizant of the largely successful eradication of major statutory and common law embodiments of de jure segregation and discrimination in the United States during the 1950s and 1960s, both the American public and academic analysts have subsequently grappled with the task of attempting to explain the continuing, often extreme racial disparity in various economic and sociodemographic indices of the nation's social well-being. Of the numerous public policy debates and social science research initiatives related to race matters that have been launched in the United States since the 1960s, most have been concerned in various ways with this problem of accounting for inequality between the races in a post–legal apartheid society.

Indeed, parts of this debate arose even as the nation was in the midst of the first of many legal reforms that would dramatically alter American society. For example, within a year of the passage of the 1964 Civil Rights Act, Daniel Patrick Moynihan, one of the architects of Lyndon Johnson's War on Poverty, used the *Moynihan Report* (1965) to address questions of racial inequality and public policy in a post–civil rights era. His report on black family life set the stage for a continuing, hotly contested sociopolitical and ideological debate, one that has increasingly come to be characterized by a questioning of the *causal* link between racism and *persisting* racial inequality in the United States. The report, like many subsequent studies of socioeconomic and racial inequality, acknowledged the existence of racism; but its discussion of the impact of such bigotry on the well-being of black Americans tended to emphasize the past. Critics noted that although Moynihan made much of the effects of the legacy of slavery and Jim Crow on black family life, one of the major shortcomings of the document was its failure to document how *contemporary, non-legally sanctioned forms of racism* affected the black family. Thus, it appears that just one year after its passage, the civil rights legislation of 1964 was seen by Moynihan and many policy makers as having corrected the worst aspects of the nation's racist past. On the other hand, even his most ardent critics accepted Moynihan's underlying message—the need to identify the *causes* of persisting racial inequality in the United States.[2]

Beginning with the *Moynihan Report* and reaching a kind of crescendo during the decades of the 1980s and 1990s, attempts to explain American racial inequality have been characterized by a noticeable ideological drift or shift. There has been a movement away from an emphasis on racial bigotry and discrimination as reasons for inequality and toward explanations grounded in the belief that the reforms of the last several decades have resulted in, or brought the nation close to, a truly colorblind meritocracy. That drift is evident in both scholarly research and in public beliefs and perceptions. Public opinion surveys conducted during the last three decades have revealed increased acceptance among the American public, especially whites, of the belief that at this point in the nation's history, racial disparity in social outcomes and inequality in all spheres of American life can be attributed less to systemic bigotry and racism than to the intricate workings of a presumably egalitarian and meritocratic society (Bobo 1988, 2001; Bobo and Smith 1998; Hacker 1992; Bonilla-Silva 1997; Hochschild 1995).[3]

The positive reception given by many to the title and presumed message of William Julius Wilson's 1978 book, *The Declining Significance of Race*, was indicative of the nation's embrace of the ideology of meritocracy and colorblindness in the immediate post–civil rights era. However, the often-heated discourse that followed its publication gave evidence of the strong emotions associated with the debate among both defenders and detractors of the idea symbolized by the title. Further, it revealed that belief in the idea that race is a less critical determinant of one's life chances in a post–civil rights era is shared by both politically liberal and conservative Americans, including many African Americans. The public notice given to the work of African-American political conservatives in the 1970s and 1980s and to the recent book by John McWhorter (2000) also symbolizes the search among white and nonwhite Americans for revised interpretations of the causes of black social and economic disadvantage that deemphasize the role of racism.[4]

Thinking about Race, Crime, and Punishment: The Appeal of "Just Deserts"

Quite clearly, to the extent that it can be shown to exist, the widespread acceptance of more meritocratic and egalitarian views of the causes of racial inequality has profound implications for how Americans interpret and explain the facts and observations with which this chapter began. Beliefs about crime and punishment, like views of other social outcomes, have been greatly affected by the altered perceptual and public opinion landscape that has emerged since the 1960s.[5] I contend that scholarly discourse on the subject of crime and punishment at the turn of the twenty-first century reflects a growing lack of consensus about the causes of the persistent and widening racial gap seen over time in the nation's justice system. Just as recent public opinion surveys have shown a questioning of the role of racial animus and a drift toward egalitarian, meritocracy-based explanations for racial disparity in other spheres, such perceptions are also increasingly evident in scholarly criminological thought and in the public's views of crime and punishment.

At the center of this shift in thinking about race and crime is the longstanding query as to whether the disproportionate presence of African Americans within the nation's justice system is *primarily* a reflection of racial differences in rates of involvement in crime or *primarily* a function of prejudice and bias in the administration of justice. In the remainder of this chapter I attempt to show how in response to this query contemporary academic discourse and public and political discourse on race, crime, and punishment in the United States show clear evidence of the kind of post-1960s ideological drift earlier described.[6] The belief expressed in many recent opinion polls that American society can now be characterized as a "level playing field" and colorblind have their counterparts in thinking about race and crime. These concepts allude to, of course, a belief in the equality of opportunity. When applied to crime and punishment, the belief becomes one of "just deserts." This is the idea that while racially disproportionate rates of punishment are undesirable in many respects, they are an understandable and logical consequence of racially disparate rates of criminal offending. The most extreme proponents of this view appear to accept the view that disparate rates of offending explain *all* of the racial difference observed in rates of criminal punishment. I suggest that both the promulgation and increasing acceptance of a "just deserts" point of view is one dimension of the much broader change in American public and scholarly perceptions described in this chapter. Recently Sampson and Wilson (1995) questioned the usefulness of an either/or approach that pits racial discrimination against differential offending in discussions of racial disparity within the criminal justice system. I have made similar observations in earlier work. The fact remains, however, that this explanatory dichotomy has been and remains an integral part of public and scholarly discourse about race and crime.

Pre-1960s Discourse on Race and Crime

The emergence of a "just deserts" versus "racial discrimination" debate within the study of crime and justice and attempts at its resolution predates by many decades the era of the modern Civil Rights Movement.[7] Concern for the problem can be found in the work of early criminologists such as W. E. B. Du Bois at the turn of the twentieth century and Thorsten Sellin during the 1920s and 1930s (Hawkins 1995). Each noted that the sizeable difference between the reported crime rates of African Americans and whites could not be attributed *entirely* to bias in the administration of justice. Each noted the fact that *actual* criminal involvement among blacks was probably higher than that found among whites and sought to explain the sources of that difference. Writing as they were during a time when American race relations and the plight of African Americans clearly reflected the nation's legacy of slavery and its oppressive aftermath, both Du Bois and Sellin also paid considerable attention to the contribution of racial discrimination to the disproportionate presence of African Americans within the nation's criminal justice system. Each was careful to note that *official* measures of criminal involvement were biased and overstated the *real* crime rate of African Americans. Except among social Darwinists of the period, the notion of racial disparity in crime as largely or entirely a manifestation of the workings of an egalitarian society was an alien concept for many obvious reasons. The blatant bias evident in the administration of justice during this period argued forcefully against any mainstream academic or public acceptance of the belief that black-white disparity in criminal justice system outcomes was *entirely* a matter of "just deserts."

For example, the numerous, often widely publicized instances of racial bias in the administration of justice occurring in the half-century from the 1910s up to the mid-1960s made many among the American public aware for the first time of the plight of African Americans living in the South and the injustice of the southern justice system. Lynchings of the period were routinely reported in black-owned and also many mainstream newspapers. The widely cited case involving accusations of interracial rape that occurred in 1931 near Scottsboro, Alabama, led to public outcry and resulted in the path-breaking U.S. Supreme Court decision, *Powell v. Alabama* in 1932. That decision and other less publicized court decisions of the 1910s through 1940s became the pillars of the judicial reforms that came to constitute a "due process revolution" in American laws of criminal procedure (Kennedy 1997, 94–106). The fact that many of the most influential court decisions of this period and later were initiated by the National Association for the Advancement of Colored People and involved black or Latino defendants (e.g., *Miranda v. Arizona* 1966) was cited by many observers as evidence of the existence of racial bias in the American justice system. At the same time, such decisions were also seen as proof of the sincerity and success of efforts by American society to eradicate racism and to prevent the racial injustice the cases exposed. Thus, the nation's "due process revolution" came to be seen as a critical and inextricable component of the struggle for racial justice and civil rights. But the path toward the legal and social reform that these cases were said to represent was hardly a linear one.

Meritocracy Meets Law and Order: Crime and Punishment in the 1970s–1990s

At the same time that the 1960s came to be associated with legal reforms that symbolized progress in American race relations, the decade also gave rise to events which highlighted racial inequality both within and outside the criminal justice system. The urban riots of 1965–1968, coupled with a gradual rise during the period in rates of serious crime in the United States, especially in the urban North, had a profound impact on both race relations and explanations for racial inequity in crime and punishment over the next decades. These urban riots and an emerging "crime wave" provided both support for and challenges to the drift toward "just deserts" and procedural fairness and equality found in public and scholarly discourse about race, crime, and punishment. Both the disturbances and the upward trend in crime rates tended to highlight racial differences in crime and punishment. Partly in response to these developments, the early 1970s saw the emergence of criminological studies responding specifically to questions regarding the causes of the black-white gap in crime and punishment.

Marvin Wolfgang and Bernard Cohen, authors of a perceptive monograph written at the beginning of this period, *Crime and Race: Conceptions and Misconceptions* (1970), provided glimpses of both traditional and then emerging views of the relationship among race, crime, and the administration of justice. Like Du Bois and Sellin before them, Wolfgang and Cohen struggled with the perennial query regarding how much of the disproportionate presence of African Americans within the justice system could be attributed to *real* differences between the races in criminal conduct, as opposed to selective enforcement of the laws. While acknowledging the higher than average rates of crime among African Americans, the authors also noted the problems that stem from racially biased policing, a much debated concern in the years following the 1967 and 1968 urban riots. Their study also visited the popular discourse of the period concerning the increasing importance of previously underemphasized forms of institutional racism, made more salient in the wake of civil rights reforms that made illegal earlier, more blatant de jure modes of discrimination.

Although the Wolfgang and Cohen investigation itself was clearly not a study that marked a sharp break with the past or with liberal, mainstream criminological views of the "causes" of racial inequality in the administration of justice, it appeared at the beginning of a decade during which such a break would become more obvious in the literature. As some indication of things to come, the writing of Wolfgang and Cohen's monograph was prompted by the authors' concern for the factual and perceptual distortions created by media accounts and political rhetoric that emerged in response to the urban riots of the period. During this period, the media and some political leaders frequently used accounts of such disturbances as an occasion to portray blacks as being non–law abiding, dangerous, violent, and prone to criminal involvement. These are depictions of race and crime that were explicitly challenged by the authors. The need for such a rebuttal reflected the fact that during the years following the urban riots of 1965–68, "crime" and criminality in America became terms largely synonymous with black residents of inner-city ghettoes, and appeals for law and order took on a decidedly "racialist" character (e.g., see Feld 1999 for a discussion of how such racialized perceptions affected the administration of juvenile justice during this same period).

Despite partisan political rhetoric, which has suggested otherwise, the fixation on race and crime and the candid support for race-linked public policies and laws during this period and later were not limited to conservative Republicans. It is true that Republicans, having little expectation of winning a sizeable black vote, did make race baiting something of a cottage industry in presidential elections of the period of the late 1960s and beyond. On the other hand, many Democratic political candidates at the state and local levels used very similar tactics and appeals to prejudice. These efforts among Democrats to link blacks and crime were not limited to the South, where such strategies were commonplace in the form of the Dixiecrat tradition. Many Democratic political leaders within urban centers of the North and West that had experienced the urban unrest of the period also sought to highlight racial differences in criminal conduct. Further, both Democrats and Republicans have supported many of the more hard-line crime control measures passed by local, state, and federal governments over the last three decades.

All of these developments left their marks on the ideological drift described in this chapter. Consistent with the observation that all science reflects the values and sociopolitical conditions of the society from which it emerges, mainstream criminological researchers of the period became enmeshed, both knowingly and unknowingly, in debates surrounding the convergence of a dual set of mutually reinforcing ideological forces. The first was the aforementioned post-1964 "drift" by the American public and academics away from the belief that racism in the administration of justice plays a *significant* role in explaining racial disparity in rates of criminal punishment. The second was symbolized by a deepening of the nation's *moral panic*, a label given to the seeming hysteria that characterized public opinion and American politics on the subject of crime and punishment in the late 1960s and 1970s. Purportedly emerging in response to rising crime rates, such panic was associated with the advocacy among the nation's political leaders of "law and order" policies and harsher punishment for all criminals, but most notably for urban blacks whose rates of criminal involvement were seen as particularly serious and disproportionate. If the former instance of ideological change represented a more or less benign belief in "progress" toward solving the nation's race relations problem, the latter reflected a revival at the level of national and cross-regional politics of some of the more sinister views of black criminality that were popular in the South during the periods of Reconstruction and Jim Crow.

As an enterprise characterized by some degree of liberalism and a professed commitment to scientific empiricism, mainstream criminology of the period successfully resisted some of the more extremist reactions to black crime and criminality found among politicians and many in the public. Some would argue that it acted as a bulwark against the widespread acceptance of the kind of retrogressive thinking about race and crime that made its way into public discourse and American politics, especially during the decade of the 1970s. At the same time, mainstream criminology was quite receptive to the ideological drift toward revised views of the causes of racial inequality that the civil rights revolution had spawned. By the late 1970s and early 1980s, writing about race and crime in mainstream criminology showed substantial evidence of such revisionist thinking.[8]

Perhaps the most notable of the criminological investigations that informed the new discourse on race, crime, and justice were several journal articles written by Michael Hindelang, with the most widely cited of these appearing in the *American Sociological Review*. Hindelang's (1978, 1981) work was a methodologically oriented investigation of the extent of differences in the reporting of crime using arrest statistics (Uniform Crime Reports) as compared to victimization statistics provided in the then recently inaugurated National Crime Survey (NCS). The Uniform Crime Reports (UCR), a source of national arrest data compiled by the Federal Bureau of Investigation, had been used by crime analysts for several decades but was often said to provide a biased measure of *real* crime. The National Crime Survey was said to provide more accurate counts and estimates of actual criminal behavior. As a means of showing the utility and substantive importance of comparing and contrasting findings from these competing sources of crime data, Hindelang analyzed differences in rates of criminal offending using arrest data and crime victimization reports for common law crimes such as assault, robbery, burglary, larceny-theft, and the like.

At issue in the illustrative exercises used in both journal articles was the question of to what extent the sociodemographic profile (gender, age, race, etc.) of criminal offenders seen in the UCR diverged from that seen in the National Crime Survey. In both investigations, he concluded that sociodemographic attributes of offenders, including their race, observed in arrest statistics very closely approximated attributes observed in the national victimization survey. The fact that arrest and victimization data produced quite similar estimates of the size of the racial gap in offending was said, particularly by later researchers, to suggest that racial bias in law enforcement and crime detection could not account for the size of the racial disparity seen in the UCR. That is, African Americans were shown to have substantially higher rates of *actual* or *real* criminal involvement, as measured by reports of victimization—reports that could not be said to be affected by racially biased law enforcement.[9]

Having accepted Hindelang's seeming rejection of the idea of racial bias as a significant determinant of the disproportionate entry (via arrest) of African Americans into the criminal justice system, mainstream criminologists next turned their attention to analyses of race effects at other stages of the system.[10] Representative of these studies was Blumstein's (1982) contrast of the level of racial disproportionality in rates of arrest versus the racial disparity seen in rates of imprisonment. His study was conducted partly in response to charges levied during the late 1970s that the very large racial imbalance seen in rates of imprisonment resulted primarily from racial discrimination (e.g., see Christianson 1981). Blumstein's finding that high arrest rates among blacks accounted for *most* of the racial disproportionality in the nation's prison population added impetus to the meritocratic, "just deserts" drift in thinking about race, crime, and punishment. The tendency of later researchers to cite the study as evidence of an absence of racial discrimination occurred despite Blumstein's acknowledgment of the possibility that post-arrest bias in the administration of justice might be a contributing factor in some of the unexplained variance he observed. Nevertheless, Blumstein's own finding that only 20 percent of the difference in race-specific rates of imprisonment remained unexplained by racial differences in arrests led many later analysts to focus on the high (80%) rate of congruence between race-specific arrest and imprisonment data, ignoring his speculation about persisting bias. Because of his overall findings that racial differences in rates of imprisonment largely "track" rates of criminal involvement as reported in official crime data for arrests, his study has been subsequently cited as evidence of minimal racial bias in the transition from arrest to imprisonment. Indeed, in a 1993 revisit to the same issue using more recent data, Blumstein appeared to acknowledge that some readers of his earlier work used it to conclude that there is no racial discrimination in the criminal justice system (1993, 759).

By 1987 the drift within mainstream American criminology toward more meritocratic views of American society and "just deserts" conceptions of the relationship among crime, punishment, and race appears to have reached a high-water mark with the publication of William Wilbanks' *The Myth of a Racist Criminal Justice System*. The book became the object of considerable notice and debate among academic criminologists, the media, and the wider public. Although his views were assailed by many minority and critical criminologists (e.g., see Georges-Abeyie 1990, 11; MacLean and Milovanovic 1990), Wilbanks' professed emphasis on the importance of "facts," "research findings," and "methodological rigor" appealed to many mainstream criminologists. In addition, his conclusions resonated with many of the views on crime and punishment held by much of the American public in the aftermath of two decades of media- and politics-driven *moral panic* and law-and-order politics that tended to highlight the crime of urban African Americans.

While acknowledging the presence of racist individuals in positions of power within the nation's criminal justice system (1987, 5–6), Wilbanks argued that the belief in widespread, systematic discrimination against blacks is a myth. He did not deny the existence of institutionalized and officially sanctioned discrimination against African Americans during the past, but tended to view such bias in the administration of justice as part of a bygone era (1987, 8). Although the book was criticized by some mainstream criminologists for taking a more absolutist stance toward the interpretation of available data than is warranted, for many, the book served to support and extend the findings of earlier work that had suggested that racial differences in criminal offending likely explain most, if not all, of the racial disparity seen within the justice system. Indeed, many of the conclusions reached by Hindelang, Blumstein, and Wilbanks have been supported in numerous follow-up investigations; their view that high crime rates among African Americans drive *most* of the racial disparity seen within the criminal justice system was a stance also taken by the National Research Council in its 1989 review of the status of black Americans (Jaynes and Williams 1989, chapter 7). The value of such studies probably lies in the renewed attention they brought to the social conditions that produce high rates of crime within minority communities.

It is my contention, however, that the shift in viewpoint, of which these studies are a part, has also produced other, somewhat more covert and potentially more unsettling ideological twists and turns. For example, during the earliest decades of the period that encompasses the trends observed in this chapter, various supporters of what I have labeled an emerging "just deserts" position were quite adamant in their insistence that racial discrimination *within the larger society* played a decisive etiological role in producing the socioeconomic conditions that led to comparatively higher rates of criminal offending among African Americans and, therefore, their greater presence within the criminal justice system. That is, although they seemed to downplay the role of racial bias in severely "inflating" the numbers of African Americans who were unfairly arrested or who unjustly traversed the justice system from beginning to end, the potential role of racism in producing higher rates of *actual* criminal behavior among blacks was acknowledged. Indeed, this likelihood is explicitly noted by Hindelang (1978) in his concluding observations and by Wilbanks in the introduction to his book (1987, 7). During the beginning of the period spanning these studies, public opinion polls suggested that many within the larger public still held to the belief that racism in American society negatively affected the life chances of African Americans, resulting in the kinds of social conditions conducive of criminal conduct.

On the other hand, considerable evidence suggests that over the last two decades, there has been a gradual rejection within mainstream American society of even this basic premise, that is, the idea that racial discrimination plays a major role in affecting the life chances of African Americans, including their risk of criminal offending (e.g., see Hacker 1992; Hochschild 1995; Herring 1997; Bobo and Smith 1998; Hochschild and Rogers 2000; Bobo 2001). Perhaps the most public display of this rejection has been the attack on affirmative action guidelines and policies. In a full embrace of supposed meritocratic ideals, white Americans and members of some racial minorities as well increasingly have rejected the premise that the higher rates of poverty, family disruption, and joblessness found among African Americans can be attributed to the effects of discrimination. By extension, racial discrimination has been rejected as a cause of the disproportionately high rates of crime found within African-American communities. While *The Bell Curve: Intelligence and Class Structure in American Life* (Herrnstein and Murray 1994) represents one of the more extremist statements of this position, it has found adherents in many quarters, including those who study crime and justice. See Regulus (1995), and Miller (1996) and Hawkins (1990, 1995) for critiques of these views within the study of crime and justice.[11]

This increasingly multifaceted drift toward a belief in the limited importance of racial discrimination in modern American society has profound implications for how the social facts with which I began this chapter are "interpreted" by criminologists and the American public. I will return to delineate some of those implications later, but first, let us explore another of the horns of the dilemma which those social facts bring to the fore.

Opposing Viewpoints and Critical Criminological Perspectives

The views of crime and punishment I have described to this point obviously do not represent the totality of thinking about crime and justice matters in the United States during the last several decades. There have been many dissident voices. Yet, to the extent that the beliefs about race, crime, and punishment I describe represent the *mainstream* of American public and criminological thought on this topic, that ideological shift in direction has greatly affected law, public policy, and public discourse surrounding the topic. Much evidence suggests that these ideological positions have indeed become widely held and mainstream perceptions and beliefs.

In considering dissident voices, one obvious question is what role has been played by the work of "critical," "radical," and "minority group" criminologists in shaping discourse and public policy. After all, as is the case for mainstream analysts, the study of race differences has been central to the research and pedagogy of these non-mainstream observers of the crime and justice scene in the United States during the last several decades. It is also true that the decades of the 1970s through the 1990s marked the emergence of several anti-mainstream currents within American and Western European social thought and the entry of the first significantly large group of African Americans and other minorities into the criminological and other social science professions. Even a cursory reading of criminological literature during the 1970s reveals a very strong current of thought that goes counter to the drift toward meritocratic and "just deserts" ideals. Contributors to this critical literature include social theorists with a bent toward criminology such as Alvin Gouldner and Eric Fromm. They also include adherents to the "conflict" perspective within criminology such as Richard Quinney, Austin Turk, and William Chambliss in the United States and Ian Taylor, Paul Walton, and Jock Young in Great Britain. All offered much to contest and challenge mainstream criminological views. Like Du Bois and Sellin before them, critical and minority criminologists rejected the notion that the sizeable racial gap seen in rates of arrest, prosecution, and sentencing in the United States could be attributed primarily to differences in rates of offending.

Many of the most insightful of these perspectives appeared in the form of theoretical treatises that appeared in the late 1960s and early 1970s. Indeed, for much of the decade of the 1970s it appeared that critical criminological perspectives typically found at the periphery of mainstream American criminology were making some headway in countering some of the "just deserts" notions of the sources of racial inequality that had begun to emerge. Indeed, by the end of

the decade it appeared that critical views were finding their way into those out-
lets within the criminological mainstream that specialized in publication of
quantitative analyses. The empirical literature during this period was marked
by the publication of numerous articles that used quantitative data and often
multivariate analytic methods to "test" various propositions derived from conflict, critical, and radical perspectives. Despite the seeming potential of these
quantitative analyses to offer an epistemological and pedagogical counterpoint
to the meritocracy-based arguments that by then had begun to guide recent
mainstream criminology, it is my contention that critical criminological perspectives have failed to do so. A full examination of the basis for this assertion
is beyond the scope of the present chapter, but several points can be made.

First, there is some evidence that some portion of the literature generated during the 1970s and 1980s that purported to empirically assess conflict and class-
based theories of crime and justice was produced by researchers whose personal
views were often antithetical to ideas presented in those theories. While many
of these studies were guided by objectivity and sound principles of scientific
analysis, others seemed to reflect the work of analysts who were motivated
largely by the desire to use their research as an opportunity to "trash" what
they perceived as unsubstantiated, untested pronouncements found in conflict,
critical, and class-based theories. In addition, even for the most well-intentioned
and unbiased researchers, the operationalization, for the purposes of testing, of
many of the theories embodying critical views of race, crime, and justice posed
many challenges. As in other areas of research, such attempts often resulted in
misspecified models or, in the instance of conflict theory testing, grossly over-
simplified versions of the theories at hand (Hawkins 1987). In response to such
developments, many conflict criminologists came to view much of the quantitative work of the period as a kind of "mindless empiricism," which was ultimately at odds with their own, more critical views of group differences in crime
and punishment.

Therefore, in retrospect, many of the findings regarding race effects in the administration of justice in the United States during the 1970s and early 1980s
have a decided ideological dimension, and one that is potentially reflected in the
temporal sequencing of findings. For example, in an important, thorough review
of studies of race and sentencing, Hagan and Bumiller (1983) noted patterns
seemingly consistent with the notions of ideological drift at issue in this chapter. They found that studies on the effect of race on sentencing decisions conducted after 1968 produce findings quite inconsistent with findings from earlier
decades, with studies conducted before 1968 being more likely to report evidence
of racial discrimination. Do such findings reveal a reduction in actual racial discrimination in sentencing since 1968? Hagan and Bumiller report that some of
the difference in findings across the years can be attributed to methodological
concerns, that is, differences can be explained by the presence or absence in studies of relevant controls such as offense and criminal record. The more recent
studies were often more methodologically sophisticated. Important for the pres-

ent discussion, the authors reported that for post-1968 studies, there was a 50-50 split in the percentages of studies reporting a finding of racial discrimination versus no discrimination.

Using such inconclusive data and other similarly conflicting data culled from other sources, William Wilbanks (1987) would attempt to make a convincing argument that the criminal justice system is *not* racist. Even for more cautious, skeptical, and historically informed analysts of crime and justice, such data lead to questions as to whether racial discrimination was less prevalent in the administration of justice in earlier years than it was several decades later. The even "split" in the proportion of studies reporting racial discrimination may well reflect the real world of crime and the administration of justice in post-1968 America. It may also reflect the selective targeting of conflict views of race and justice. Whatever its origins, the findings do little to resolve the ideological impasse with which this chapter is concerned. Indeed, the data seem to support equally the claims made by both "just deserts" and critical crime analysts. The large percentage of studies reporting some evidence of discrimination would appear to lend credence to the arguments of many critical analysts during the 1980s that racism in the administration of justice was not a thing of the past. On the other hand, a drop in the proportion of findings of discrimination when comparing the pre- and post-1968 periods would seem to suggest evidence of societal "progress."

The inability of critical theory and research to impact the drift toward meritocracy-based notions of "just deserts" within criminology has also been impeded by divisions of labor among those who study race, crime, and justice in the United States. Most critical analysts tend to pay little, if any, attention to the question of what factors contribute to the *etiology* of individual acts of criminal behavior. This tendency is mirrored by the failure of many of those who study crime rates and offenders to examine the administration of justice. These failures result from a mix of ideological and disciplinary orientations and the realities of the limitations of data collection, sampling, and research design.

Built into most critical perspectives on crime and justice is an implicit acknowledgment that poverty, disadvantage, and racial and class oppression play a determining role in creating the social conditions that may lead to criminal involvement on the part of oppressed individuals. Thus, there is within this tradition an epistemological basis for research on the individual offender, and most critical or conflict analysts appear to accept the fact that racial and other social groupings differ in their *actual* rates of criminal offending. On the other hand, most conflict or radical criminological researchers who choose to conduct empirical analyses have preferred to trace the etiological roots of racial and class differences in criminal involvement largely to the problem of biased patterns of law making, law enforcement, and criminal punishment. Hence, most of the post-1970 testing of conflict theory referred to earlier involved an examination of race effects *in the administration of justice*. The Marxian concern for the "misery" and plight of the oppressed is acknowledged but not subjected to quantitative analysis.

At the same time that critical and conflict analysts have failed to ponder fully the question of what explains "individual" differences in criminal conduct, those criminologists and behavioral scientists who conduct such studies seldom collect data that might allow them to examine the potential for bias in the administration of justice. Often such investigations are replete with reminders from researchers that their etiological analyses do not take into account all of the factors that might account for the extreme racial and ethnic disparity that is often seen in criminal justice data. Particularly during earlier decades, many analysts of crime rates and individual offending explicitly acknowledged the possibility that bias on the part of decision makers may explain part of the racial disparity they observed. For most researchers, these claims consist primarily of conjecture, given the lack of data needed to empirically assess their validity.

The failure or inability of researchers in both traditions to probe those other dimensions of the research landscape to which they allude does much to foster the dilemma that is the subject of this chapter. At the worst, research in each tradition may falsely convey the idea that the unexamined and unexplained variance in racial disparity is of little significance. This is likely to be the conclusion drawn when empirical analyses designed to explain rates or determinants of individual offending are accompanied by such contemporary descriptive labels as "at risk," "high risk," "underclass," "inner city," and the like. In addition, studies that highlight "racial profiling," "over-policing," "bias," and the like while failing to acknowledge group differences in behavior may pose similar problems.[12]

Despite the seeming failure of critical, radical, and minority perspectives to significantly alter the drift toward the meritocratic, "just deserts" tendencies seen in contemporary American society and criminology, it is their continued presence and salience that contribute to the workings of the dilemma this chapter has sought to describe. Contemporary events and public policies, such as the War on Drugs, racial profiling, the imposition of the death penalty, the killing of citizens by the police, the disparity in sentencing guidelines for powder versus crack cocaine, and even the widening racial gap seen in rates of imprisonment, seem to cry out for alternatives to notions of "just deserts" and a "level playing field." Far from having lost their relevance at the turn of the twenty-first century, the accuracy of the basic arguments and tenets of conflict and critical criminologists appear to be confirmed with each day's newspaper headlines.

AFRICAN AMERICANS, CRIME, AND JUSTICE AT THE TURN OF THE CENTURY: THE SEARCH FOR SOLUTIONS

Most of the examples of racial discord and disparity with which I began this chapter span the period from the mid-1970s to the mid-1990s, a period of major social change in the United States. This was a time when the nation not only reaped the benefits of unprecedented "revolutions" in civil rights and due process, but also witnessed a dramatic rise in rates of violence and other crime, most notably in urban and minority communities. As this chapter has attempted to show, both of these sets of events—rising crime and racial reform—had profound effects on thinking about racial differences in rates of crime and punishment. The ideological drift that has been evident has not been limited to white Americans. A shift in attitudes toward crime and punishment can be observed among African Americans, whose historic disadvantage as crime *victims*, as opposed to criminal offenders, has frequently been underemphasized or ignored (Jaynes and Williams 1987, 464–72). Particularly during the 1970s and 1980s, when drive-by shootings, gang warfare, and open-air drug markets became commonplace in some disadvantaged urban neighborhoods, much of the public outcry came from within the affected communities themselves. Campaigns designed to stem the loss of young lives and protect citizens from errant gunfire were largely grassroots efforts arising from the most severely impacted neighborhoods. Further, although national crime rates have since turned downward from their peaks of the early 1990s, the nation's poor, urban minority communities remain areas of high rates of offending and victimization (Sampson and Wilson 1995; McCord 1997; Meares 1998); racially differentiated patterns of law enforcement associated with the War on Drugs remain a symbol of persisting racial inequality and a flashpoint for discontent and racial unrest (Miller 1996; Cole 1999; Russell 1998; Kennedy 1997, 2001; Hawkins 2001).

These observations remind us that discussions about crime and punishment are ultimately much more than excursions into the particulars of rhetoric and discourse. Crime and the societal response to it are ground-level phenomena that affect real people and the communities in which they live. Hence, an integral and inextricable part of the debate over the causes of persisting racial disparity in crime and punishment in the United States has been the question of what can be done to reduce it. The desire to reduce the level of such inequality in the United States is a professed goal of both liberal and conservative politicians and of most analysts of the nation's crime problem. But the attempt to translate perceived causes of racial differences in crime and punishment into practical, ground-level solutions and public policies is not only an inherently difficult task; it is further complicated by the considerable discord that now pervades discussions of race, crime, and justice. I conclude with a brief discussion of this aspect of the dilemma described in this chapter.

Although the race-crime nexus remains a perennially American problem, it has been my contention in this chapter that to a much greater extent than it has been in the past, the current debate over race and crime has revealed an American dilemma of rather recent vintage. This is a dilemma that bears some resemblance to the race relations quandary described many decades ago by Myrdal (1944), but it also carries the imprint of the enormous social change that the nation has experienced since that work appeared. While debates about race and crime in the United States today closely resemble those of earlier decades, the way that we think about such matters has been transformed in many respects.

The question of what we can do to reduce racial inequality in crime and justice in the United States at the turn of a new century further highlights the contours of this new dilemma. This chapter has probed an ideological shift in the way that American society has come to think about the *causes* of racial inequality in crime and punishment. A similar shift can be seen in thinking about *public policies* and *legal remedies* aimed at addressing the race-crime problem.

In a particularly insightful recent essay on race and crime matters, Sampson and Wilson (1995, 37) write:

> Overall, the evidence is clear that African-Americans face dismal and worsening odds when it comes to crime in the streets and the risk of incarceration. . . . Despite this evidence the discussion of race and crime is mired in an unproductive mix of controversy and silence. At the same time that articles on age and gender abound, criminologists are loath to speak openly on race and crime for fear of being misunderstood or labeled racist.

While their observations may not apply to the vast body of criminological research conducted over the course of the last century (see Hawkins 1995), these are valid and largely accurate observations regarding the way that contemporary criminologists have responded to the topic. However, to suggest as they do that the fear of being labeled a racist explains such reluctance tells only part of the story and may indeed oversimplify a much more complex phenomenon.

Since the turn of the twentieth century, "liberal" American criminologists who study race and crime have been forced to respond to what are now labeled "essentialist" views of race. These views hold that there are innate differences between those human groupings labeled as "races" and that differences in behavior arise from that racial difference. From their critiques of the social Darwinist views of the past to the sociobiological notions that exist today, liberal, mainstream criminologists have welcomed the opportunity to attempt to rebut such notions. In many ways modern criminological theory is a product of the growth and development of those early attempts at rebuttal of essentialist views of racial *and ethnic* differences in rates of criminal involvement. Far from fearing the discussion of race and crime, prior to the 1970s many liberal mainstream criminologists sought the opportunity to set the record straight on such matters (Hawkins 1995).

Fast forward to the 1980s and 1990s, the period about which Sampson and Wilson were largely concerned, and a different epistemological climate does indeed exist. Consistent with the arguments put forth in this chapter, it is my contention that such inattentiveness to race and crime among criminologists today partly reflects the reluctance of contemporary researchers to enter into what has become in recent years an even more hotly contested and ideological arena than that which existed in earlier decades. This is an arena in which the moral and intellectual certitude that once guided liberal thinking about race and crime has been challenged. This challenge has come not from breakthroughs in "reactionary" thought or a triumph of conservative social policy, but has seemingly resulted from the achievement of some of the very goals for which liberals have long struggled. Having made significant breakthroughs of the kind long sought after by liberal analysts of race and crime, it is not completely surprising that many contemporary researchers, particularly those of a liberal bent, may be somewhat reluctant to join discussions aimed largely at explaining the *persistence* of racial inequality in crime and punishment and what can be done to solve the problem. On the other hand, it is hardly accurate to say that contemporary researchers ignore racial differences in rates of crime and punishment. The use of "race" as a variable in statistical analyses and attempts to examine "race effects" are an even more ubiquitous part of criminological research today than during the recent past. Equally ubiquitous is the detailed reporting of racial differences in crime and punishment seen in various government documents.

Consistent with the description of the dilemma set forth in this chapter, I suspect that for most criminologists writing and conducting research in an era that can be described as post–civil rights law, post–War on Poverty, and post–criminal justice system reform, the reluctance to discuss race and crime may stem from the fear of being perceived as having nothing meaningful or insightful to say about the causes of persisting racial inequality. Such fears may be heightened further by the fact that, much more so than during the past, discussions of race and crime are less "academic" and are instead almost immediately linked directly to ongoing discussions of social policy. Given the seemingly increasing complexity of the race-crime nexus, discussions of race and crime may engender apprehension among social scientists precisely because there are no easy solutions or fixes. In an American society that has moved decidedly toward more punitive stances toward punishment for crime, toward scholarly and public pronouncements that tend to discount the existence of racial discrimination, even the most well-intentioned discussions of the race-crime nexus can be distorted and used to buttress policies far removed from those envisioned by many of the researchers who choose to study this problem.

The failure of the imagination that characterizes the work of many well-meaning criminologists and other social scientists when they ponder the question of what can be done to reduce racial inequality may also stem from the view that, as a society, we have already "tried" or successfully enacted most of the reforms thought to be needed to solve the race-crime problem. Indeed, in many of the numerous public discussions of race and crime in which I have participated in the last decade and more, one frequently encounters a profound sense of pessimism that anything *new or innovative* can be done to significantly reduce racial inequality. This sentiment is particularly evident among those researchers old enough to remember the civil rights struggles and the War on Poverty of the 1960s and the enactment of due process and sentencing reform laws of the next decade. Indeed, the very persistence of the "race problem" in criminal justice is used by some to argue that such reforms of the past were incapable of addressing the "root" causes of racial differences.

While most of the discussion in this chapter has pitted what some may consider to be traditional "liberal" and "conservative" takes on the relationship

among race, crime, and punishment in the United States, the dilemma I describe
has also resulted in a lack of agreement within the ranks of liberal activists, scholars, and interpreters of crime and justice trends in the United States. It has also
exposed and exacerbated frequently ignored ideological and class divides among
African Americans. These divides, both inside and outside the African-American
community, have obvious implications for efforts to devise and reform laws and
criminal justice policies aimed at reducing the level of racial inequality. Given
the race-crime dilemma that confronts American society, there has been a tendency in the media and in some academic writings to depict disagreements
among liberals and between segments of the black community in ways not unlike those traditionally used to contrast liberal and conservative views of crime
and criminal justice. The divides have been sometimes described simplistically
as pitting those who stress the importance of guarding the rights of criminal offenders against those who seek to protect and safeguard the rights of victims of
crime in black communities. Some of that labeling has surfaced within the ranks
of liberal and black analysts of crime and justice.

For example, in the writings on the subject, legal scholars such as Kennedy
(1997, 7–12), Meares (1998), and Meares and Kahan (1998) have attempted to
distinguish themselves from other critical analysts of race, crime, and justice
(e.g., Butler 1995) by stressing the importance of protecting the black community from crime. As I have noted, genuine concern for the black crime victim
had been missing from most of the earlier discourse on race, crime, and justice
in the United States. To their credit, both Kennedy and Meares have achieved
some success in extending the umbrella and mantra of the larger victim-rights
movement, which has gained much political ground during the last several decades, to include poor, urban African Americans, who constitute the nation's
largest demographic grouping of crime victims. My own work on homicide
among African Americans has been designed to achieve similar objectives
through arguments regarding the historical devaluation of black life in the
United States (Hawkins 1986).

Both the scholarly work that has highlighted the plight of black crime victims
and grassroots efforts at crime control within the black community have shown
that attitudes and opinions toward crime and support for crime prevention policies within the African-American community are quite varied and increasingly
more complex. It has further shown that the risk and likelihood of criminal victimization *within* the black population varies substantially and that this likelihood greatly affects the level of support for various crime control measures
(Meares 1998). Further, persons residing in many poor, urban African-American
communities favor some crime control measures not strikingly different from
those now widely advocated by white, more affluent suburbanites. Such findings lend support to Wilson's (1978) observations regarding the significance of
class divisions within African-American communities and Anderson's (1990,
1998, 1999) finding of notable class-like divisions within lower-income black
communities. Some of these within-race differences appear to be directly linked

to the likelihood of criminal involvement and support for anti-crime measures. But, in a society that increasingly views black offenders as no longer (or much less so than during the past) the "victims" of the criminal justice system itself, the new focus on black crime victims may have come at a price. That price may be the further erosion of already waning scholarly and public support for programs and policies designed to reduce racial disproportionality within the justice system and protect the rights of black and other criminal defendants.

Consider, for example, observations made by Randall Kennedy in an exchange with David Cole, a colleague of Kennedy's and a staunch advocate of the view that racial discrimination is an endemic feature of the administration of justice in the United States today (Cole 1999). In a widely noted debate with Cole, Kennedy is reported to have said:

Police brutality is of course a terrible thing ... but blacks at every income level are also more likely to be murdered, raped, burgled, assaulted. ... If you put the question of black victimization at the center, protecting minority communities from crime may mean putting more minority criminals in jail. (Press 2000, 48)

Kennedy has been described by some observers as a somewhat more conservative commentator on the subject of race, crime, and justice than a fellow law professor, Paul Butler, who advocates among other things "jury nullification" as a means of addressing the problem of racial bias within the justice system. On the other hand, Kennedy has been a strong opponent of racial profiling of motorists and other crime suspects and of prosecutorial exclusion of blacks from juries in criminal trials. Nevertheless, in a society that savors sound bites, his comments provide fodder for those politicians who advocate some of the reckless social policies and laws that have resulted in the current confinement in the nation's prisons of more than two million Americans, half of whom are African Americans. It is worth noting in this regard that many of the black urban community leaders who called for more aggressive policing in the early 1990s are now forced to respond to charges from their communities of police brutality and use of deadly force, racial profiling and targeting, and the like. There are some indications that views such as those held by Kennedy and Meares, like those of William Julius Wilson in years past, have been used to support policies quite at odds with the themes and concerns found within the authors' larger bodies of work. The fact that these researchers are African Americans also becomes a factor in the use and misuse of their work.

The grim crime and justice statistics presented at the start of this chapter graphically remind us that much remains to be done to remedy the plight of African Americans and reduce racial inequality. While most contemporary observers, including those whose views are frequently contrasted, would likely agree that African-American communities must be protected from the racism-produced social forces that lead to conditions that cause disproportionate involvement in *real* crime, they must also be protected from racist attitudes, laws, and social policies (overt or hidden) that treat being young, black, male, and poor as *the* crime. This goal will not be accomplished easily in a society that has historically denied the importance of social class in determining life chances and often ignores the significance of the deeply entrenched class divisions that permeate American society. It will be even more difficult in a society where our very success at enacting some of the legal and social reforms needed to provide protections against racism and reduce inequality have led to the mistaken belief that racial bias no longer exists or that all possible remedies have already been tried.[13]

NOTES

1. An issue not fully explored in this chapter is the question of whether the present analysis illustrates an instance in which academic criminologists merely respond to a larger societal ideological shift/drift or whether their research has played a pivotal role in "causing" or escalating the changes described. Clearly, the drift in perceptions described herein represents changes that extend far beyond academia and criminology; as such, the illustrative criminological studies I cite may be seen as responding to and reflecting those altered perceptions. On the other hand, I believe that academically oriented work on crime and justice in the United States has had and continues to have a significant impact on public perceptions, law, and social policy. This is so despite the claims of many criminologists that their work is seldom acknowledged by policy makers.

2. The *Moynihan Report* represents a neoconservative critique of traditional liberal thinking about race and inequality. The debate that the work precipitated has become a major area of contention within liberal circles.

3. These researchers have used such labels as "colorblindness," "level playing field," "evenhandedness," and similar terms to characterize contemporary public beliefs about the role of race in shaping life chances and socioeconomic outcomes in the United States.

4. I do not mean to imply that the belief in the existence of a meritocracy, notions of just deserts, and the tendency to attribute criminality to the weaknesses and foibles of *individuals* were ever absent from either public or scholarly discourse in the United States. Indeed, as many have noted, these beliefs are an integral part of what has been labeled the "American creed." I acknowledge further the historical persistence of social Darwinism in discourse regarding crime and the administration of justice. I do contend, however, that the acceptability of biological determinist views and societal adherence to other ideals purported to be part of the American creed have waxed and waned over time, with much of the change being attributed to the nature and strength of challenges to the accuracy and salience of such beliefs at any given time. For instance, while extreme levels of racial and socioeconomic inequality can be used to support the "survival of the fittest" tenets of social Darwinism, such inequality may appear inconsistent with the claims of "equal opportunity" and a "level playing field" that undergird the notion of a meritocracy. Given this paradox, it is my contention that racial inequality posed a greater threat to the idea of an American meritocracy during the earliest decades of the twentieth century than during the years that followed the legal reforms of the 1960s. The "drift" I describe represents in large part a change in the "liberal" discourse about race, race relations, and criminal justice. Like all large-scale ideological change, that discourse now finds adherents among Americans of all races.

5. The *Moynihan Report* was not silent on the question of the causes of racial disparity in crime and punishment. Moynihan argued that high rates of delinquency among black youth, particularly males, could be attributed to the absence of fathers in the home. This is, of course, a theme that has become part of much subsequent research on delinquency among criminologists and other social and behavioral scientists.

6. The "drift" I describe herein and its consequences have been noted by many observers of contemporary race relations. For example, Gilroy (1990) charted the transformation of ideologies of race and racism in post-1960s Britain and notes many parallels to the American scene. Important for the present discussion, he shows how earlier notions of biological determinism have been supplanted by newer forms of cultural nationalism that achieve many of the same separatist objectives. Apple (1988) examined changing perceptions of racial inequality in educational attainment in post–World War II Britain and the United States and attributes many of the trends I describe in this chapter to the rise of right-wing politics. He also notes the extent to which discourse about crime and justice also marked the boundaries of this ideological change in American and British politics. Bonilla-Silva and Lewis (1999) have labeled current thinking about race in the United States "the new racism," suggesting that such discourse simply serves to justify extant patterns of racial privilege. My own depiction of the shift in public opinion and scholarly discourse in this chapter recognizes its link to racial hegemony and the contradictions that arise from efforts to justify and maintain it. On the other hand, I tend to deemphasize somewhat the willfulness, intentionality, and racial animus underlying the ideological shift I describe, since I believe that the change also reflects many attributions that arise from non-conscious processes and seemingly plausible assumptions shared by many in the public from varying racial and social-class statuses.

7. Here the term "just deserts" is used as a group-level attribute rather than an individual-level one. Its conventional use as a description of the extent to which punishment is deserved on the basis of an *individual's* conduct is extended to describe the extent to which racial disparity arises from *group* differences in criminal involvement in crime versus disproportionate targeting of members of that group by law enforcement or differential post-arrest system processing.

8. The criminological studies I have chosen to discuss are cited solely as *exemplars* of movement over the last three decades within criminological research toward the belief that overt racial discrimination *within the administration of justice* accounts for little of the racial difference we currently observe. Many other studies could also have been cited in support of this belief, but such documentation is beyond the scope of the present chapter. I do not contend, as later discussion will illustrate, that the conclusions reached by researchers who have taken such positions are entirely without basis or merit. Indeed, it is the plausibility and seeming soundness of the conclusions reached by these researchers in a post–civil rights era that contribute to the race-crime-punishment dilemma I describe in this chapter.

9. As noted, this finding does not differ from conclusions reached many decades earlier by researchers such as Du Bois and Sellin. Nevertheless, the Hindelang finding resulted from the utilization of more complete *national* crime statistics (the UCR and the NCS) than were available to Du Bois and Sellin. Both wrote before the 1930s advent of the UCR. The use of such data made Hindelang's work more credible and added a mantle of scientific empiricism that the other authors could not claim. But, in line with the discussion in this chapter, his finding was also more credible because it was consistent with the revised perceptions of a post–civil rights era.

10. One measure of the acceptance of Hindelang's work is the extent to which it was subsequently cited by other researchers. My reading of the literature suggests that it is very widely cited and is frequently used to illustrate both the close fit between the UCR and the NCS and the idea that bias likely plays only a minor role in explaining racial differences in justice-system involvement.

11. Numerous criminologists have argued that racism in the larger society is itself criminogenic or that it produces criminogenic social conditions which make African Americans more prone to criminal involvement. Nevertheless, by the end of the 1990s, even that article of faith (in the effects of racism) appears to have been much less widely accepted than in earlier decades. It was replaced by much more skepticism regarding the belief that racism had a direct effect on criminal involvement and by much unwillingness to attribute high rates of black impoverishment, single-parent families, and the like to the behaviors of whites.

12. It is not my contention that group differences in actual criminal involvement do not account for a substantial portion of the racial disparity seen in arrests, convictions, and imprisonment in the United States today. Substantial evidence shows this to be the case. On the other hand, the question of precisely how much of the disparity can be attributed to overt and subtle forms of bias and discrimination, either individual or institutional, is largely unanswered. Further, even if one accepts the idea that *real* crime rates are higher among African Americans than among whites, it is equally clear that for a number of crime categories, various components of the administration of justice are "where the action is." These include assorted "victimless" and "public order" crimes (e.g., drugs, prostitution, loitering, vagrancy, gambling, disorderly conduct, nuisance) for which there is less than universal agreement regarding the danger they pose to society and whose detection and enforcement depend largely on the activities and perceptions of the police. In most African-American communities, the public policy and legal dilemmas surrounding crime and justice center as much around the "actions" of the police and other agents of the criminal justice system as around the victimization that results from alarmingly high rates of interpersonal violence and property crime.

13. At the time of this writing, a (2001) report from the Department of Justice concluded that there is no evidence of racial bias or discrimination in the administration of the death penalty by the federal government. The report coincided with the resumption of federal executions after a rather lengthy hiatus.

REFERENCES

Anderson, Elijah E. 1990. *Streetwise: Race, Class, and Change in an Urban Community.* Chicago: University of Chicago Press.

Anderson, Elijah E. 1998. "The Social Ecology of Youth Violence." Pp. 65–104 in M. Tonry and M.H. Moore (Eds.), *Youth Violence.* Special issue of *Crime and Justice: A Review of Research*, vol. 24. Chicago: University of Chicago Press.

Anderson, Elijah E. 1999. *Code of the Street.* Philadelphia: W.W. Norton and Company.

Apple, Michael W. 1988. "Redefining Equality: Authoritarian Populism and the Conservative Restoration." *Teachers College Record* 90 (Winter): 167–184.

Blumstein, Alfred. 1982. "On the Racial Disproportionality of the United States' Prison Populations." *Journal of Criminal Law and Criminology* 73: 1259–81.

Blumstein, Alfred. 1993. "Racial Disproportionality of U.S. Prison Populations Revisited." *University of Colorado Law Review* 64: 743–760.

Blumstein, Alfred, and Allen J. Beck. 1999. "Population Growth in U.S. Prisons, 1980–1996." Pp. 17–61 in Michael Tonry and Joan Petersilia (Eds.), *Prisons*. Special issue of *Crime and Justice: A Review of Research*, vol. 6. Chicago: University of Chicago Press.

Bobo, Lawrence. 1988. "Group Conflict, Prejudice, and the Paradox of Contemporary Racial Attitudes." Pp. 85–114 in P. Katz and D. Taylor (Eds.), *Eliminating Racism: Profiles in Controversy*. New York: Plenum.

Bobo, Lawrence. 2001. "Racial Attitudes and Relations at the Close of the Twentieth Century." Pp. 264–301 in N.J. Smelser, W.J. Wilson and F. Mitchell (Eds.), *America Becoming: Racial Trends and Their Consequences*, vol. 1. Washington, DC: National Academy Press.

Bobo, Lawrence, and R. Smith. 1998. "From Jim Crow Racism to Laissez Faire Racism: The Transformation of Racial Attitudes." Pp. 182–220 in W. Katkin, N. Landsman, and A. Tyree (Eds.), *Beyond Pluralism: Essays on the Conception of Groups and Group Identities in America*. Urbana: University of Illinois Press.

Bonilla-Silva, Eduardo. 1997. "Rethinking Racism: Toward a Structural Interpretation." *American Sociological Review* 62: 465–480.

Bonilla-Silva, Eduardo, and Amanda Lewis. 1999. "The New Racism: Racial Structure in the United States, 1960s–1990s." Pp. 55–101 in Paul Wong (Ed.), *Race, Ethnicity, and Nationality in the United States*. Boulder, CO: Westview.

Butler, Paul. 1995. "Racially Based Jury Nullification: Black Power in the Criminal Justice System." *Yale Law Journal* (December) 105: 677–725.

Christianson, Scott. 1981. "Our Black Prisons." *Crime and Delinquency* 27: 364–375.

Cole, David. 1999. *No Equal Justice: Race and Class in the American Criminal Justice System*. New York: New Press.

Feld, Barry C. 1999. *Bad Kids: Race and the Transformation of the Juvenile Court*. New York: Oxford University Press.

Fingerhut, Lois. 1993. "Firearm Mortality among Children, Youth, and Young Adults 1–34 Years of Age: Trends and Current Status: United States, 1985–90." *Advance Data from Vital and Health Statistics, No. 231*. Hyattsville, MD: National Center for Health Statistics.

Georges-Abeyie, Daniel. 1990. "The Myth of a Racist Criminal Justice System?" Pp. 11–14 in B. MacLean and D. Milovanovic (Eds.), *Racism, Empiricism and Criminal Justice*. Richmond, B.C. (Canada): The Collective Press.

Gilroy, Paul. 1990. "One Nation under a Groove: The Cultural Politics of 'Race' and Racism in Britain." Pp. 263–281 in David Theo Goldberg (Ed.), *Anatomy of Racism*. Minneapolis: University of Minnesota Press.

Hacker, Andrew. 1992. *Two Nations: Black and White, Separate, Hostile, Unequal*. New York: Scribners.

Hagan, John, and Kristin Bumiller. 1983. "Making Sense of Sentencing: A Review and Critique of Sentencing Research." Pp. 1–54, in A. Blumstein, J. Cohen, S.E. Martin, and M.H. Tonry (Eds.), *Research on Sentencing: The Search for Reform*. Washington, DC: National Academy Press.

Hawkins, Darnell F. 1986. *Homicide Among Black Americans*. Lanham, MD: University Press of America.

Hawkins, Darnell F. 1987. "Beyond Anomalies: Rethinking the Conflict Perspective on Race and Criminal Punishment." *Social Forces* 65: 719–45.

Hawkins, Darnell F. 1990. "Explaining the Black Homicide Rate." *Journal of Interpersonal Violence* 5 (June): 151–163.

Hawkins, Darnell F. 2001. "Commentary on Randall Kennedy's Overview of the Justice System." Pp. 32–51 in N.J. Smelser, W.J. Wilson, and F. Mitchell (Eds.), *America Becoming: Racial Trends and Their Consequences*, vol. 2. Washington, DC: National Academy Press.

Hawkins, Darnell F. (Ed.). 1995. "Ethnicity, Race, and Crime: A Review of Selected Studies." Pp. 11–45 in D.F. Hawkins (Ed.), *Ethnicity, Race, and Crime: Perspectives across Time and Place*. Albany: State University of New York Press.

Hawkins, Darnell F., and Cedric Herring. 2000. "Race, Crime and Punishment: Old Controversies and New Challenges." Pp. 240–275 in J.S. Jackson (Ed.), *New Directions: African Americans in a Diversifying Nation*. Washington, DC: National Policy Association.

Herring, Cedric (Ed.). 1997. *African Americans and the Public Agenda: The Paradoxes of Public Policy*. Thousand Oaks, CA: Sage.

Herrnstein, Richard, and Charles Murray. 1994. *The Bell Curve: Intelligence and Class Structure in American Life*. New York: Free Press.

Hindelang, Michael J. 1978. "Race and Involvement in Common Law Personal Crimes." *American Sociological Review* 46: 93–109.

Hindelang, Michael J. 1981. "Variation in Sex-Race-Age-Specific Incidence Rates of Offending." *American Sociological Review* 46: 461–474.

Hochschild, Jennifer L. 1995. *Facing Up to the American Dream: Race, Class, and the Soul of the Nation*. Princeton: Princeton University Press.

Hochschild, Jennifer L., and Reuel R. Rogers. 2000. "Race Relations in a Diversifying Nation." Pp. 45–85 in James S. Jackson (Ed.), *New Directions: African Americans in a Diversifying Nation*. Washington, DC: National Policy Association.

Jackson, James S. (Ed.). 2000. *New Directions: African Americans in a Diversifying Nation*. Washington, DC: National Policy Association.

Jaynes, Gerald D., and Robin M. Williams (Eds.). 1989. *A Common Destiny: Blacks and American Society*. Washington, DC: National Academy Press.

Kennedy, Randall. 1997. *Race, Crime and the Law*. New York: Pantheon Books.

Kennedy, Randall. 2001. "Racial Trends in the Administration of Justice." Pp. 1–20 in N.J. Smelser, W.J. Wilson, and F. Mitchell (Eds.), *America Becoming: Racial Trends and Their Consequences*, vol. 2. Washington, DC: National Academy Press.

MacLean, Brian, and Dragan Milovanovic. 1990. *Racism, Empiricism and Criminal Justice*. Richmond, B.C. (Canada): The Collective Press.

Mauer, Marc. 1999. *Race to Incarcerate*. New York: W. W. Norton and Company.

McCord, Joan (Ed.). 1997. *Violence and Childhood in the Inner City*. New York: Cambridge University Press.

McWhorter, John. 2000. *Losing the Race: Self-Sabotage in Black America*. New York: Free Press.

Meares, Tracey L. 1998. "Place and Crime." *Chicago Kent Law Review* 73: 669–705.

Meares, Tracey, and Dan M. Kahan. 1998. "Law and (Norms of) Order in the Inner City." *Law and Society Review* 32: 805–838.

Miller, Jerome. 1996. *Search and Destroy: African-American Males in the Criminal Justice System*. Cambridge: Cambridge University Press.

Moynihan, Daniel P. 1965. *The Negro Family: The Case for National Action*. Office of Policy Planning and Research, United States Department of Labor, March. Washington, DC: U.S. Government Printing Office.

Myrdal, Gunnar. 1944. *An American Dilemma*. New York: Harper and Brothers.

Press, Eyal. 2000. "Does the Law Focus Too Much on Black Suspects—Or Too Little on Black Victims?: Two Scholars Square Off." *Lingua Franca* 47(October): 47–58.

Regulus, Thomas A. 1995. "Race, Class, and Sociobiological Perspectives on Crime." Pp. 46–65 in D.F. Hawkins (Ed.), *Race, Ethnicity, and Crime: Perspectives across Time and Place*. Albany: State University of New York Press.

Russell, Katheryn K. 1998. *The Color of Crime: Racial Hoaxes, White Fear, Black Protectionism, Police Harassment, and Other Macroaggressions*. New York: New York University Press.

Sampson, Robert J., and William Julius Wilson. 1995. "Toward a Theory of Race, Crime, and Urban Inequality." Pp. 37–54 in J. Hagan and R.D. Peterson (Eds.), *Crime and Inequality*. Stanford, CA: Stanford University Press.

Smelser, Neil, William J. Wilson, and Faith Mitchell (Eds.). 2001. *America Becoming: Racial Trends and Their Consequences*, vols. 1 and 2. Washington, DC: National Academy Press.

U.S. Department of Justice. 2000. *Prison and Jail Inmates at Midyear 1999*. Office of Justice Programs, Bureau of Justice Statistics, Publication Number # NCJ 181643. Washington, DC: U.S. Government Printing Office.

U.S. Department of Justice. 2001. *The Federal Death Penalty System: Supplementary Data Analysis and Revised Protocols for Capital Case Review*, Washington, DC, June 6. http://www.usdoj.gov/dag/pubdoc/deathpenaltystudy/htm.

Wilbanks, William. 1987. *The Myth of a Racist Criminal Justice System*. Monterey, CA: Brooks/Cole.

Wilson, William J. 1978. *The Declining Significance of Race: Blacks and Changing American Institutions*. Chicago: University of Chicago Press.

Wolfgang, Marvin, and Bernard Cohen. 1970. *Crime and Race: Conceptions and Misconceptions*. New York: Institute of Human Relations Press.

Name Index

Subject Index

Affirmative action, 329; in criminal law and legal professions, xvii, xviii, 329, 373–429

African Americans, xi, xii, xiii, xvi, xviii, 10, 24, 34, 36, 69, 100, 171 n.288, 180, 286 nn.45 ,47, 409–10 n.135, 432, 437; and affirmative action, 373–429; and arrests/sentencing for drug offenses, 12–13, 121, 197–232, 267 n.22, 342 n.10, 390, 393, 409 n.135; attitudes toward drug law enforcement among, 271–83; and criminal involvement, 38, 39, 68, 70, 77, 79–80, 82, 87, 100, 339, 382, 397 n.11, 403–04 nn.73–75, 404–05 n.84; drug use among, 297–99, 342 n.10; and family structure, 5, 9, 11–23; fear of, 173, 190; and gangs, 120, 121, 139, 156 nn.113–14, 156–57 nn.120–21, 159 n.107, 173–76, 182, 183, 187, 190, 192–93; and higher education, 89 n.8, 417–23; on juries, 330, 391–92, 410–11 nn.142–43; and police stops/surveillance, 172 n.291, 233–50, 300–02, 327, 329, 332–40, 342 n.9; rates of imprisonment among,

6, 29, 30, 31,61, 99, 192, 269–70, 325, 326, 342 n.10, 373, 381, 383, 393–95, 395–96 nn.3–5, 448

Age-Crime Curve, 44, 68, 79, 81, 89 n.13

American Indians, 182, 315; and higher education, 418. *See also* Native Americans

Arizona: anti-gang initiatives in, 173–196; Department of Juvenile Corrections, 175, 177, 185–86, 191, 193

Asians/Asian-Americans, 171 n.288, 380, 402 n.61, 432; and gangs, 120, 123, 126, 132, 135, 146 n.37, 155 n.110, 156 nn.113–14, 158 n.139, 161 n.165, 168 n.236; and higher education, 417

Blacks. *See* African Americans

Buddhism: and conceptions of justice, 362–63, 366

California, 325, 402 n.72, 413 nn.168–69, 419–20; gang databases in, 109–172; juvenile justice practices in, 96–98; three-strikes laws in, 56, 57, 60–62, 64

About the Editors and Contributors

SIMON ADETONA AKINDES is an assistant professor of Instructional Technology in the Teacher Education Department at the University of Wisconsin-Parkside. He previously taught at Cleveland State University and at Ohio University, where he earned his doctorate in education (instructional technology.) He has published numerous articles that focus on his main interests: the cultural studies of technology, computers in education, and popular music in West Africa. Dr. Akindes also taught English, French, and Spanish in Benin and Ivory Coast where he published language-related educational books.

PAUL BUTLER is a professor of law at George Washington University. He is a graduate of Yale College and Harvard Law School and was a prosecutor with the United States Department of Justice. He teaches and writes in the areas of criminal law and race relations law. His articles have been published in the academic and popular press, including the *Yale Law Journal*, the *Harvard Law Review*, the *Washington Post*, and the *Los Angeles Times*. He is a frequent commentator on legal issues for CNN, National Public Radio, and Fox News.

WILLIAM J. CHAMBLISS is a professor of sociology at George Washington University. He has been studying crime and the sociology of law since the 1960s and has authored over fifteen books in these fields. In 1999 he was awarded an honorary doctorate of laws from the University of Guelph in recognition of his research and writing. He also has received numerous awards from the American Sociological Association and the American Society of Criminology. He is past president of the American Society of Criminology and the Society for the Study of Social Problems. His research and teaching have taken him to Nigeria, England, Thailand, Sweden, Norway and Zambia, where he was a Fullbright Fellow in 1989–1990. His most recent work, *Power, Politics, and Crime,* is an analysis of the politics underlying current criminal justice policies in the United States. Currently he is working on a book on piracy and smuggling.

TODD R. CLEAR is Distinguished Professor, John Jay College of Criminal Justice, City University of New York. In 1978, he received his Ph.D. in criminal justice from the University at Albany. Clear has published extensively on topics of correctional policy and justice system reform. His most recent books are *The Offender in the Community*, published by Wadsworth, *The Community Justice Ideal*, by Westview, and *Harm in American Penology*, published by SUNY Press. He is currently involved in studies of religion and crime, the criminological implications of "place," and the concept of "community justice."

ANGELA J. DAVIS is a professor of law at the American University, Washington College of Law, where she teaches criminal law, criminal procedure, and a seminar on race, crime, and politics. Professor Davis has been a visiting professor at George Washington University Law School and has served on the adjunct faculty at George Washington, Georgetown, and Harvard Law Schools. Davis's publications include articles on racism in the criminal justice system and prosecutorial discretion. She is a former director of the Public Defender Service for the District of Columbia and serves on the Board of Trustees of the Southern Center for Human Rights.

DAVID F. GREENBERG received his Ph.D. in physics from the University of Chicago and is a professor of sociology at New York University. Over the years the focus of his research has shifted from theoretical high-energy physics to crime, law, deviance, human sexuality, mathematical modeling, statistical methodology, and ancient Near East studies. He worked in civil rights campaigns in South Carolina and Chicago and was active in CORE (Congress of Racial Equality), the Student Mobilization Committee to End the War in Vietnam, and the Pittsburgh Resistance. He was a founding member of CADRE (Chicago Area Draft Resistors), Chicago Connections (a prisoner support group), the New American Movement, and Democratic Socialists of America.

DARNELL F. HAWKINS is Professor of African-American Studies, Sociology and Criminal Justice at the University of Illinois at Chicago. Professor Hawkins received a Ph.D. in sociology from the University of Michigan in 1976 and a J.D. from the Law School of the University of North Carolina at Chapel Hill in 1981. He teaches and conducts research in criminology, sociology of law, and race and ethnic relations He is the editor of *Homicide Among Black Americans* (University Press of America, 1986); *Ethnicity, Race and Crime: Perspectives across Time and Place* (State University of New York Press, 1995); and *Violent Crimes; Assessing Race and Ethnic Differences* (Cambridge University Press, forthcoming).

CHINITA HEARD is Director of Harte Honors College and Assistant Vice President for Academic Affairs at Stillman College in Tuscaloosa, Alabama. Previous positions include professorships at Indiana University in Fort Wayne and the University of Texas at Arlington, where she was the recipient of the Gertrude

Golladay Memorial Award for Outstanding Teaching. She is a member of the Academy of Criminal Justice Sciences and the 1999 recipient of the Minorities and Women Section Leadership Award. Also, she is a member of the American Society of Criminology where she served as the first elected chair of the Division on People of Color and Crime. Currently, she serves on the Editorial Board of the journal *Criminology*. She holds a Ph.D. in criminology from Florida State University and is an Alumnae of Distinction from Alabama State University. She holds certifications in Peers Making Peace, as well as Christian Marriage and Family Therapy. Her research interests include higher education issues, youth development, prevention and intervention issues, program development and evaluation, and faith-based issues.

NOLAN E. JONES joined the National Governors' Association (NGA) in July 1978. Currently, he serves as director for the Human Resources Committee, which covers issues relating to welfare/workforce reform, health care reform, and education issues. His specialty is criminal justice and public safety. In addition, Dr. Jones has served as a member of the Federal Emergency Management Agency (FEMA) "Study Advisory Group" to assess the capabilities and resources needed by the nation's emergency management system, the National Crime Prevention Council, and the Hilton Foundation–sponsored National Advisory Committee on family violence. From 1990 to 1992, Dr. Jones served on the Council of the American Political Science Association.

RICHARD P. KRECKER, JR., is an attorney who has represented juveniles since 1988. He holds a J.D. from Arizona State University (1986). He received his B.A. in political science from the University of California at San Diego (1981). He pursued graduate studies in the Division of Educational Leadership and Policy Studies and has published research on education finance and policy. He currently practices exclusively in the areas of juvenile delinquency and dependency law.

BARRY A. KRISBERG has been the president of the National Council on Crime and Delinquency (NCCD) since 1983. He is known nationally for his research and expertise on juvenile justice issues and is called upon as a resource for professionals and the media. Dr. Krisberg received his master's degree in criminology and a doctorate in sociology, both from the University of Pennsylvania. His memberships include the National Association of Juvenile Correctional Administrators, and the Association of Criminal Justice Researchers. In 1993 he was the recipient of the August Vollmer Award, the American Society of Criminology's most prestigious award. Dr. Krisberg has several books and articles to his credit including *Crime and Privilege; The Children of Ishmael: Critical Perspectives on Juvenile Justice* with James Austin; *Juvenile Justice: Improving the Quality of Care; Reinventing Juvenile Justice* with James Austin; and *A Sourcebook: Serious, Violent, and Chronic Juvenile Offenders* with James C. Howell, J. David Hawkins, and John J. Wilson.

STACEY LEYTON is a 1998 graduate of Stanford Law School. After graduating, she served as a law clerk for Judge Stephen Reinhardt of the United States Court of Appeals for the Ninth Circuit (1998–1999), Judge Susan Illston of the United States District Court of the Northern District of California (1999–2000), and Judge Stephen Breyer of the U.S. Supreme Court (October 2000 Term). She is now an associate at Altshuler, Berzon, Nussbaum, Rubin, and Demain, a small San Francisco litigation firm that specializes in labor and employment, environmental, constitutional, campaign and election, and civil rights law.

JAMES P. LYNCH received his Ph.D. in sociology from the University of Chicago in 1983. Before joining the American University faculty, he was with the Office for Improvements in the Administration of Justice (OIAJ) in the United States Department of Justice and a research associate at the Bureau of Social Science Research (BSSR). Professor Lynch specializes in crime statistics, victim survey methodology, opportunity models of victimization risk, and theories of the role of punishment in social control. He teaches primarily the quantitative methods sequence in the Department of Justice, Law and Society, but he has also taught courses on comparative justice systems and on immigration policy and crime control. Since coming to American University, Professor Lynch has published one book, *Understanding Crime Incidence Statistics* (with Albert D. Biderman), two monographs, and over fifty articles, book chapters, and reports. He has received grants from the National Institute of Justice (NIJ), the American Statistical Association (ASA), the Robert Wood Johnson Foundation and the National Science Foundation (NSF), as well as a fellowship from the Bureau of Justice Statistics (BJS). He has served on numerous committees in the American Society of Criminology and as chair of the American Statistical Association's Committee on Law and Justice Statistics. Professor Lynch is currently on the editorial boards of *Criminology* and the *Journal of Quantitative Criminology*. He is working on a series of papers examining the effects of imprisonment on less coercive institutions of social control, including families and communities.

TRACEY L. MEARES is a professor of law and director of the Center for Studies in Criminal Justice at the University of Chicago Law School. She is jointly appointed as a research fellow at the American Bar Foundation. Meares received her J.D. from the University of Chicago Law School after receiving her B.S. in general engineering from the University of Illinois at Urbana-Champaign. Meares's teaching and research interests center on criminal procedure and criminal law policy, with a particular emphasis on empirical investigation of these subjects. In addition to her appointments at the University of Chicago and the American Bar Foundation, she is a faculty member of the University of Chicago Center for the Study of Race, Politics, and Culture and of the executive committee for the Northwestern/University of Chicago Joint Center for Poverty Research.

SAMUEL L. MYERS, JR., is Roy Wilkins Professor of Human Relations and Social Justice at the Hubert H. Humphrey Institute of Public Affairs at the University of Minnesota, where he specializes in research on race and public policy. He is co-editor with Margaret Simms of *The Economics of Race and Crime* (Transaction Press, 1988); co-author with William Darity of *Persistent Disparity: Race and Economic Inequality in the U.S. since 1945* (Edward Elgar Publishing, 1998); co-author with Caroline Sotello Viernes Turner of *Faculty of Color in Academe: Bittersweet Success* (Allyn & Bacon, 2000); and co-author with William Darity, William Sabol, and Emmett Carson of *The Black Underclass: Critical Essays on Race and Unwantedness* (Garland Press, 1994). Myers is a graduate of Morgan State University and received his Ph.D. in economics from Massachusetts Institute of Technology.

WILSON R. PALACIOS is an assistant professor in the Department of Criminology at the University of South Florida (Tampa). He holds a Ph.D. from the University of Miami, Department of Sociology. His research interests include drug cultures, qualitative research methods and analysis, and epidemiology of substance use and misuse.

LLAD PHILLIPS has been a faculty member at the University of California, Santa Barbara, since 1967. Dr. Phillips attended UC Berkeley and earned bachelor degrees in chemistry and economics. His Ph.D. in economics was conferred at Harvard University. Prior to joining the UC faculty, he worked as a nuclear chemist and as an economist for the U.S. Bureau of Labor Statistics. At UCSB, Professor Phillips served as Chair of the Economics Department from 1979–1984 and as Acting Provost of the College of Letters and Science from 1991–1994. Professor Phillips' major fields of specialization are labor economics, the economics of criminal justice, and applied econometrics. Over the years, he has studied economic crimes, the economics of crime control, police effectiveness, crime deterrence, drug abuse, and prison costs; and he has evaluated the inefficiencies of the criminal justice system. He is the author of several books, and he has approximately 100 published research articles. His most recent article, "The Impact of Income and Family Structure on Delinquency," with William Comanor, was published in the *Journal of Applied Economics*, November 2002.

RICHARD QUINNEY is the author of *The Social Reality of Crime* (Little, Brown, 1970), *Critique of Legal Order: Crime Control in Capitalist Society* (Little, Brown, 1973) and *Class, State, and Crime: On the Theory and Practice of Criminal Justice* (McKay, 1977). His autobiographical writings are contained in *Journey to a Far Place: Autobiographical Reflections* (Temple University Press, 1991), *For the Time Being: Ethnography of Everyday Life* (State University of New York Press, 1998), and *Borderland: A Midwest Journal* (University of Wisconsin Press, 2001). He has been a Fullbright lecturer in

Ireland, and he received the Edwin H. Sutherland award for his work on criminological theory. He is a professor emeritus of sociology at Northern Illinois University.

DINA R. ROSE is Director of Research at the Women's Prison Association. She has a B.S. in journalism from Boston University and an M.A. and a Ph.D. in sociology from Duke University. Her research interests include the impact of crime and criminal justice on communities, the concept of parochial social control and social networks, and policy considerations of women and families in criminal justice. She has published papers in *Criminology, Crime and Delinquency,* and *Social Forum,* as well as other journals.

LEE E. ROSS is an associate professor of criminal justice at the University of Wisconsin–Parkside, where he serves as Chair of the Criminal Justice Department. A graduate of Rutgers University, his research interests span a variety of areas, from his seminal work on religion and social control theory to more recent publications on African-American interests in law enforcement. As editor of *African-American Criminologists: 1970–1996, An Annotated Bibliography,* his scholarship can be found in a variety of academic journals including *Justice Quarterly, Journal of Criminal Justice, Journal of Crime and Justice, The Justice Professional, Sociological Focus, Sociological Spectrum,* and *Corrections Today.* Prior to becoming a professor, Dr. Ross spent seven years as an officer in the U.S. Customs Service. Currently, he directs an internship program and is the recipient of various awards for teaching excellence, including the Wisconsin Teaching Fellow and his recent selection as a Wisconsin Teaching Scholar.

WILLIAM J. SABOL is a senior research associate at the Center on Urban Poverty and Social Change at Case Western Reserve University, where he is the center's associate director for community analysis. His research encompasses a variety of issues related to the criminal justice system and the communities that these systems are intended to serve. Prior to going to Case Western, he directed research projects on sentencing policy at the Urban Institute's Program on Law and Behavior. There, he was the director of the Federal Justice Statistics Resource Center where, among other things, he designed and maintained a statistical reporting system on federal criminal prosecutions for the Bureau of Justice Statistics. Dr. Sabol received his Ph.D. in public policy from the University of Pittsburgh in 1988.

JEFFREY W. SPEARS is an assistant professor of criminal justice in the Department of Sociology and Criminal Justice at the University of North Carolina at Wilmington. His research has appeared in *Justice Quarterly, Journal of Crime and Justice, Women and Criminal Justice,* and *American Journal of Criminal Justice.* His current research interests include sentencing and prosecutorial decision making.

CASSIA C. SPOHN is a professor of criminal justice at the University of Nebraska at Omaha, where she holds a Kayser Professorship. She is the co-author of two books: *The Color of Justice: Race, Ethnicity, and Crime in America* (with Sam Walker and Miriam DeLone) and *Rape Law Reform: A Grassroots Movement and Its Impact* (with Julie Horney). She has published a number of articles examining prosecutors' charging decisions in sexual assault cases and exploring the effect of race/ethnicity on charging and sentencing decisions. Her current research interests include the effect of race and gender on court processing decisions, victim characteristics and case outcomes in sexual assault cases, judicial decision making, sentencing of drug offenders, and the deterrent effect of imprisonment. In 1999 she was awarded the University of Nebraska Outstanding Research and Creative Activity Award.

RANDOLPH N. STONE has served since 1991 as Clinical Professor of Law at the University of Chicago's Edwin F. Mandel Legal Aid Clinic where he helped create the Criminal and Juvenile Justice Project, a program that provides law and social work students with the supervised opportunity to defend children accused of criminal and delinquent behavior. Professor Stone was the first African-American to hold the position of Public Defender of Cook County, Illinois. He is a past Chair of the American Bar Association's Criminal Justice Section and currently serves on the Illinois Supreme Court's Board of Admissions to the Bar. Professor Stone, a graduate of the University of Wisconsin Law School, writes and teaches criminal and juvenile law and justice, clinical legal education, legal ethics, evidence, and trial advocacy.

DOROTHY L. TAYLOR received her Ph.D. at Florida State University. She is an associate professor of sociology at the University of Miami; coordinator of the Criminology Internship Program; and program faculty member in Caribbean, African, and African-American Studies. Her interests are in criminology, delinquency theories, minorities and criminality, and internships. Dr. Taylor is involved with a number of national and local professional organizations, including the Academy of Criminal Justice Sciences, American Society of Criminology, and the Community Relations Board of Dade County. Her current publications include *The Positive Influence of Bonding in Female-Headed African American Families* and *Jumpstarting Your Career: An Internship Guide for Criminal Justice*. Her numerous articles have appeared in such journals as the *Journal of Criminal Justice Education*, the *Journal of Black Psychology*, *Law and Human Behavior*, *Juvenile and Family Court Journal*, and the *Journal of Applied Social Psychology*.

HAROLD L. VOTEY, JR., is a professor emeritus of economics at the University of California, Santa Barbara, where he directed the Community and Organization Research Institute for twenty-two years. His research into economic explanations for crime generation and control began in 1968, much of it in partnership with Llad Phillips, a colleague at UCSB. That research has not been limited to the U.S. crime scene but has also involved research conducted in London at the London School of Economics, at Norway's Transportekonomisk Institutt, and Sweden's National Council for Crime Prevention. Much of his research has focused on the design and testing of models of criminal behavior of youth in which causal factors, investment in human capital, family influences, and the forces of deterrence and incapacitation could be taken into account. Dr. Votey received his Ph.D. in economics from the University of California, Berkeley, in 1968.

MARJORIE S. ZATZ is a professor of justice studies and Associate Dean of the Graduate College at Arizona State University. She holds a Ph.D. in sociology with a minor in Latin American studies from Indiana University (1982). Professor Zatz has written extensively on criminal justice issues in the United States and Latin America. Her most recent book, co-edited with Coramae Richey Mann, is *Images of Color, Images of Crime* (Roxbury Publishing Company, 2002). She has also published over thirty scholarly articles and book chapters. Professor Zatz was a member of the National Criminal Justice Commission from 1994 to 1996. She is the recipient of the 1997 Herbert Block Award of the American Society of Criminology and the 2000 W. E. B. Du Bois Award from the Western Society of Criminology.

DATE DUE

77 053

DEC 16 2010

GAYLORD

PRINTED IN U.S.A.